Just Practice

A Social Justice Approach to Social Work

Second Edition

Janet L. Finn, Ph.D.
Professor
School of Social Work
University of Montana

and

Maxine Jacobson, Ph.D.
Associate Professor
School of Social Work
University of Montana

Exclusive marketing and distributor rights for
U.K., Eire, and Continental Europe held by:

Gazelle Book Services Limited
Falcon House
Queen Square
Lancaster
LA1 1RN
U.K.

eddie bowers publishing co., inc.
P. O. Box 130
Peosta, Iowa 52068-0130 USA

www.eddiebowerspublishing.com

ISBN 978-1-57879-072-2

Copyright © 2008, by *eddie bowers publishing co., inc.*

Printed in the United States of America

*In memory of my father, Tom Finn, and in gratitude
to the many women and men, young and old, in Chile and
the U.S. who have taught me so much about the meaning
and power of social justice work.*

*To my cousins Gilbert and Lillian Garber (Gillian)
who taught me the meaning of family and helped me
to appreciate the importance of history.
L'shalom v'da'at..*

Contents

Chapter 1

Introduction   1

Chapter 2

Imagining Social Work and Social Justice   13

Chapter 3
Looking Back
63

Chapter 4
Values, Ethics, and Visions   **109**

Chapter 5
Just Thinking: Theoretical Perspectives
on Social Justice-Oriented Practice　　163

Chapter 6
Just Get Started: Engagement   211

Chapter 7
Just Understanding: Teaching-Learning   265

Chapter 8
Action and Accompaniment

313

Chapter 9
Evaluating, Reflecting On, and Celebrating Our Efforts   377

Chapter 10

Just Futures: Social Justice-Oriented Practice in the 21ˢᵗ Century   413

Appendix A
United Nations Universal Declaration of Human Rights

Appendix B
Social Justice Film Suggestions

Bibliography

List of Credits and Permissions

Index

Reflections and Actions

Chapter 8

Chapter 9

Chapter 10

List of Figures

Acknowledgments

Just Practice has been shaped by many people and experiences. The references and bibliography offer only one perspective on the thinking that has influenced this book. *Just Practice* is also the product of ongoing reflection, action, and dialogue with students, community members, "clients," colleagues, and friends. We would like to thank students in the School of Social Work at The University of Montana who have engaged in the theory and practice of social justice work and who have used, developed, and critiqued the action/reflection moments used in the text. Their critiques and suggestions have been invaluable in shaping the second edition of *Just Practice*. The book has been significantly revised and developed over the past 4 years of classroom dialogue and engagement. While we have maintained the Just Practice Framework, we have considerably expanded discussion of the challenges and possibilities of social justice work in diverse arenas of practice. We are grateful to the many students who shared their reflections, engaged in individual and collective action, invented new possibilities of linking theory and practice, and minced no words in telling us when a learning exercise was going nowhere. Their voices and insights have contributed to a more richly textured book.

We also express our gratitude to colleagues Jennifer Stucker, Eastern Washington University; Lynn Nybell, Eastern Michigan University; Linwood Cousins, Longwood University; Rosemary Barbera, Monmouth University; and Sadye Logan, University of South Carolina-Columbia for their thoughtful conversations, critiques, and reviews that have strengthened *Just Practice*. We give special thanks to our social work colleagues at The University of Montana with whom we have been engaged in the grand adventure of developing a new MSW program, which has embraced *Just Practice* as the foundation practice text. It is exciting to be part of a learning organization where new thinking can be tested and new directions for thought and practice explored.

Our thinking and practice have been challenged and transformed through ongoing relationships and conversations with mentors and friends. We thank Norm and Connie Waterman, whose long-term commitment to just practice made a difference in state-based social services in Montana; Sherry Ortner, who led us to the possibilities of practice theory; Rosemary Sarri, whose indefatigable dedication to social justice has influenced two generations of social work practitioners, educators, policy makers, and researchers; Michael Reisch, whose important work on the history, politics, and future of social work has helped shape the framework of *Just Practice* and continues to challenge and inspire; Paul Miller for his important contributions to social justice work in Montana; Ovadia Vargas, Claudina Nuñez, Gloria Rodríguez, and Bruni Rodríguez for lessons in social justice from a Chilean perspective; Ryan Tolleson Knee, who has been a leader, supporter, friend, risk taker, and grounding force through the development of the MSW program and the development of *Just Practice*; Scott Nicholson for his inspiration regarding the border-crossing potential of social work; Bob Oaks and Molly Moody of the North Missoula Community Development Corporation for being role models, mentors, and collaborators in actualizing the concepts and principles of *Just Practice* at the community level; the Finding Solutions to Food Insecurity steering committee for challenging and disrupting our notions about race, class, and ability and accompanying us on this journey to translate academic knowledge into a working theory of social justice-oriented practice; and the many other women and men who live *Just Practice* everyday through their actions and commitment and who have shared their stories and insights with us over the years.

We deeply appreciate the participation of students, alumni, community practitioners, and colleagues around the country who shared essays and exercises with us for inclusion in this volume. Thanks to Carol Hand, Rosemary Barbera, Cindy Hunter, Nancy McCourt, Chuck Wayland, Bonnie Buckingham, Eric Diamond, and Annie Kaylor for their wonderful contributions that truly expanded the dialogue and the teaching-learning possibilities of *Just Practice*. We look forward to broadening the conversation through the second edition. We offer our deepest heartfelt thanks to Patsy Clark and Kate Pruitt, smart, talented, committed women who have been with us every step of the way as the second edition of *Just Practice* took shape. Their research skills, critical thinking, great humor, creative insights, and good company have kept us going over the past year.

Preface

Social work in the 21st century faces profound challenges. While advances in information and communication technologies have shrunk distances of time and space, the expansion of the global market has contributed to a widening gap between rich and poor. We are experiencing both global aging and increasing rates of child poverty. The displacement and migration of human populations in response to war, economic dislocation, and environmental disasters pose challenges to states and nations and notions of social welfare. Nearly 60 years have passed since the signing of the Universal Declaration of Human Rights, yet violations of those rights continue worldwide.

When we wrote the first edition of *Just Practice*, the United States had not yet declared war on Iraq. In the last 3 years our sensibilities have been assaulted by the military scandal in Abu Ghraib, the contradictions of a "freedom-fighting" crusade where talk of democracy is just plain talk, and where soldiers and civilians continue to die everyday for a cause whose logic no one has clearly ever understood. "Terrorism" has become a subject of everyday conversation as the United States has confronted its vulnerability in the world. Even objects as innocuous as nail clippers, water bottles, and tweezers are viewed as potential weapons of mass destruction today.

We have witnessed another problematic election in the United States, a war whose initial justification had been proven false, and explosive crises in the Middle East. The world was transfixed with shame and disbelief as the ugly underbelly of U.S. racism was exposed for all to see in the aftermath of Hurricane Katrina. On the U.S. domestic front, the state-based social safety net continues to erode as welfare responsibilities devolve to local communities and charities and systems of care and control are increasingly privatized. Political leaders espouse family values at the same time that increasing numbers of children are placed in out-of-home care. Social work in the 21st century calls for new ways of thinking and acting in order to address these challenges and realize our professional commitment to social justice. *Just Practice* responds in a critical and integrated way to these concerns and offers new possibilities for theory and practice.

Just Practice introduces a new framework for social work that builds upon five key themes: *meaning, context, power, history,* and *possibility*. How do we give meaning to the experiences and conditions that shape our lives? What are the contexts in which those experiences and conditions occur? How do structures and relations of power shape people's lives and the practice of social work? How might a historical perspective help us grasp the ways in which struggles over meaning and power have played out, and better appreciate the human consequences of those struggles? We argue here that meaning, power, and history are key components to understanding the "person-in-context." It is from that culturally, politically, and historically located vantage point that we appreciate constraints and imagine possibilities for justice-oriented practice. *Just Practice* prepares social workers to engage in new forms of collaborative assessment, planning, intervention, and institution building that 21st century practice demands.

Just Practice is based on a pedagogy of popular education that envisions knowledge development as a collaborative teaching-learning process. We argue that a participatory process, grounded in dialogue and critically attuned to questions of power and inequality, is fundamental to social justice work. The text is designed to facilitate participatory learning in the classroom and to prepare students for participatory approaches to *engagement, teaching/learning, action, accompaniment, evaluation, reflection,* and *celebration,* the seven core processes of the Just Practice Framework. Linkages among practice, research, and policy are integrated throughout the text. We pay particular attention to the diversity of social work practice and to the possibilities of transforming spaces of inequality, oppression, and marginality into spaces of hope, places of connection, and bases for action.

Just Practice is written with an audience of students in U.S. schools of social work in mind. However, we believe that meaningful engagement with questions of social justice demands a global perspective. We draw on the history of social justice in U.S. social work and beyond U.S. borders to expand our thinking. In this age of transnational movements of people, power, and information, social work practice needs to embrace a commitment to social justice that crosses national, geographic, cultural, and disciplinary boundaries. *Just Practice* provides possibilities and tools for thinking globally even when we are engaged in the most micro and local levels of practice.

Just Practice is the product of a decade-long process of collaboration, dialogue, and reflection on our own experiences as social work practitioners, researchers, and educators. It reflects our ongoing efforts to grapple with the tensions and contradictions of the profession and our place within it. We are both U.S.-born white women with ties to working-class communities and rural places. Both of us have lengthy histories of employment in human services (child welfare, juvenile justice, chemical dependency treatment, sexual abuse investigation and treatment, and foster care). We both decided at particular points in our careers to leave direct social work practice and pursue doctoral education. We needed to reflect on our practice, challenge the limits of our understanding, and explore alternative theoretical and practice possibilities. As our paths crossed through these journeys, we began to talk and work together. Through our many conversations, a vision of *Just Practice* took shape. With the help of students and colleagues, we translated that vision into words. We look forward to expanding the vision in dialogue with our readers.

Plan of the Text and Overview of the Chapters

Just Practice presents an innovative and needed intervention in theory and skills for social work practice. Its central theme, a social justice-oriented approach to social work, reflects the mandates of the Council on Social Work Education to better integrate themes of social justice and diversity, concerns of marginalized and vulnerable populations, human rights, and social science knowledge into the theory and practice of social work. *Just Practice* responds in a critical and integrated way to each of these concerns. It provides a new framework for social work that articulates the linkage of epistemology, theory, values, and skills of practice.

Just Practice is divided into 10 chapters in which the five key themes of meaning, context, power, history, and possibility and the seven core processes of engagement, teaching-learning, action, accompaniment, evaluation, critical reflection, and celebration are developed. The text itself is designed to be interactive and to provide a model for integrating theory and practice. Each chapter contains numerous action and reflection exercises in which substantive material is accompanied by hands-on opportunities for individual or group action, skill development, and critical reflection. Each chapter also contains a variety of food for thought, from quotes and guidelines for practice to suggestions for websites and other resources. At the end of each chapter is a story, a case study, and resources, or a set of examples that exemplify the integration of social work and social justice, or provide an opportunity for synthesizing material presented in the chapter. These are designed to engage readers as partners in dialogue in the teaching-learning process, develop critical thinking skills, and promote practice competence. Discussion questions, suggested readings, and resources are included at the end of each chapter to stimulate further critical inquiry.

Chapter 1 introduces readers to the story of social work. We provide an overview of the "official" story, highlighting key themes, people, and moments in the emergence of the social work profession in the United States. We provide a rationale for telling a different story, one that brings to light the often hidden and marginalized efforts of past and present advocates for and practitioners of "social justice work." In so doing we open the door to exploring and appreciating a rich legacy that continues to inform and inspire 21st century social work practice.

Chapter 2 begins the process of imagining social work within a social justice context and examining the challenges and possibilities this poses for the social work profession. Readers are introduced to ways of conceptualizing social work and social justice, the linkage between them, and the implications for practice. International meanings of social work are presented that further explore the cultural, historical, and political context of practice. The five key concepts of the Just Practice Framework—meaning, context, power, history, and possibility—are introduced, developed, and illustrated through exercises and examples.

Chapter 3 examines the practices, actors, institutions, and contexts involved in the emergence of social work as a profession. The chapter examines the significance of history and a historical perspective on social work practice. It expands on and challenges the story of social work presented in the here. Readers are invited to explore the silences, shifts, and omissions in the history of social work and to consider the implications for contemporary social work. Special attention is paid to the contributions of advocates and activists whose histories have been largely ignored or erased from the social work canon. The chapter foregrounds the economic and political contexts that shaped the profession and practice of social work in the 20th century. Readers are presented with a long view of social work history and the tensions therein. The chapter highlights the Rank and File movement, the Great Depression, and McCarthyism as aspects of historical knowledge that are essential to understanding the course of contemporary social work practice.

Chapter 4 examines the concept of values, the practice of valuing, and the relationship of values to social work practice. Readers are introduced to the core values of the profession as articulated by the NASW Code of Ethics. We explore values and ethics in context, look at the historical evolution of the Code of Ethics, and examine alternative conceptualizations of social work ethics and frameworks for ethical decision making. A comparison of ethical principles developed in diverse national and international contexts illustrates the interplay of politics, history, and values. The discussion moves from a broad perspective on values and valuing to the personal level and engages the reader in the work of self-assessment regarding personal and professional values. The chapter presents The Universal Declaration of Human Rights as a foundation for ethical practice and introduces the concept of an "ethics of participation" as a starting point for social justice work.

Chapter 5 addresses the concept of theory and the practice of theorizing. We challenge perspectives that confine theory to the world of "experts." Instead, we explore theorizing as part of our human capacity and concern for "making sense" of the world and our experience in it. Examples are used to illustrate a step-wise process of theory development and the need to be informed makers and users of theory. The relationship of theory to the standpoint and values of the theorist is examined. The chapter reviews the dominant theories shaping contemporary social work practice and critiques each approach in terms of its strengths and limitations. We introduce a range of critical social theory, including feminist, critical race, and practice theories, and consider their implications for social justice work. The core processes of the Just Practice Framework—engagement, teaching-learning, action, accompaniment, critical reflection, evaluation, and celebration—are presented and defined. We conclude the chapter with a matrix of queries that link the core processes to the five key concepts of *Just Practice*.

Chapter 6 develops the skills, activities, and issues involved in the process of engagement. Readers are encouraged to explore the meaning of engagement as both a process and a commitment. Engagement provides the entrée to social justice work in community, organizational, and interpersonal contexts. We examine the centrality of relationship to social justice work. We develop the concept of anticipatory empathy as a time for self-reflection and preparation for engagement with the context of and participants in the change process. We explore a range of listening and communication skills central to the process of engagement. These include observation; attending to issues concerning trust, power, and difference; exploring meanings and interpretations; and respecting resistance. We pay particular attention to engaging groups, given the importance of collaboration in social justice work.

Chapter 7 introduces and defines the core process of teaching-learning and the importance of teamwork for justice-oriented social work practice. Readers are introduced to the processes of mutual aid that contribute to effective teamwork. We reframe the assessment process as one of co-learning and examine issues of power and positionality in the teaching-learning process. The chapter provides guides and tools for systematic inquiry into communities and a community-context of practice. We present several traditional and alternative methods for teaching and learning about people in familial, communal, and historical contexts. We create opportunities for readers to reflect on their cultural meaning systems and learn through difference.

Chapter 8 introduces and defines the core concepts of action and accompaniment. Readers explore the thinking and skills of action and are introduced to the roles of social justice work. We develop strategies for participatory planning and decision making and for animating and activating the change process. Readers are introduced to skills and strategies for negotiating difference, addressing anger, building coalitions, and engaging in policy practice. We consider the possibilities of popular education for engaging people in the daily issues that affect their lives. The thinking and skills of accompaniment are explored as well as the learning potential inherent in the accompaniment process.

Chapter 9 presents the final three core processes of evaluation, critical reflection, and celebration. We explore diverse approaches to and assumptions about evaluation and questions of its reliability and validity. We discuss the role of the researcher as *briocoleur* and consider the possibilities of participatory approaches to evaluation that include the voices of people in the issues that concern their lives. Several examples of participatory research illustrate the wisdom of citizen involvement in the formation, planning, and implementation of community projects. The chapter looks at why evaluation is important, what processes and players should be assessed, and how to go about conducting evaluations. Various methods of participatory evaluation are described, providing a wide array of options for evaluation design and the dissemination of results. Cautions, considerations, and challenges of the work are discussed. We address the process of critical reflection, explore its linkage to social justice work, and consider ways to develop reflective capacity. The core process of celebration is presented and developed as an integral component of justice-oriented practice. We introduce readers to a variety of ways in which to think about and celebrate the joy and beauty of the work.

Chapter 10 begins by looking at predictions concerning the future of social work and ways in which social workers can prepare themselves to address these concerns. Readers revisit the Just Practice Framework and are asked to consider its usefulness as a flexible structure to address the fundamental issues that shape contemporary social work practice. Finally, 16 principles of social justice work synthesized from the Just Practice approach are presented and discussed.

Introduction

Social work as we know it today was born of a sense of responsibility to society. So ran the report of the Committee on Education for Social Work at a recent National Conference of Charities. But that statement does not bring us very far on the road to knowing what social work really is. Is it charity? Is it social reform? Is it professional doing good and earning one's living by it? Is it doing for people what they cannot do for themselves? Is it "an effort to perfect social relationships?" If you applied for membership in a Social Workers' Club and gave any or all of these qualifications, would you be accepted? Nobody knows.
Arthur James Todd (1920), The Scientific Spirit and Social Work[1]

AN INVITATION AND CHALLENGE TO OUR READERS

Welcome to the complex and dynamic terrain of social work. Some of you will be reading this book because you are planning to pursue a career in social work. Perhaps your image of the field is still fuzzy, waiting to be developed in the coming weeks and months. Others may encounter this book after years of experience in the social work profession. Perhaps your own life and work experiences, political commitments, or concerns about people's everyday struggles for survival, rights, and dignity have brought you to these pages. You may have a clear image of social work practice in mind. Depending on your experience, it may be an image you wish to emulate, or it may be one you wish to change.

We invite you to accompany us on this journey into social work and social justice. This is not a guided tour where the reader is the passive recipient of the guides' wisdom. Rather, this is a journey that we take together, teaching, learning, and creating knowledge as we go. *Just Practice* is a different kind of book. It is not a collection of "facts" about the practice of social work. It does not offer much in terms of cookbook "solutions" to various human problems. *Just Practice* is a foundation and starting point for ongoing dialogue and critical inquiry, which, in turn, can serve as a base for your own critical and creative practice of social work.

We invite you to be more than a reader of the text. We challenge you to be an active participant in crafting the possibilities for bridging social work and social justice. We pose more questions than answers. We offer learnings from our experience and that of others, and we invite you to do the same. We challenge our readers and ourselves to walk the talk of social justice in our daily practice of social work.

So, unbuckle your seatbelts and prepare for the journey. Social justice–oriented social work practice is neither spectator sport nor sedentary activity.

WHY JUST PRACTICE?

Many textbooks have been written about the practice of social work. Why do we need another one? What does *Just Practice* offer that is different from the books that have come before it? *Just Practice* puts social work's expressed commitment to social justice at center stage. We offer a framework for thinking about and practicing social work that embraces and engages with the visions, hopes, and challenges of building and living in a just world. It is one thing to say that social workers are "against" injustice or "for" social justice. It is another to translate that claim into an integrated model for practice. As Michael Reisch (2005, p. 157) argues, "Critical social work can still serve as a conceptual framework or vehicle that will contribute to efforts to resist contemporary political-economic developments such as globlisation." We offer the *Just Practice* framework as a guide to critical social work that integrates politics and practice, translates the concept of social justice into concrete action, and honors the complex multicultural terrain of the 21st century (see Reisch, 2005, pp. 170–171).

We draw knowledge and inspiration from many committed social work practitioners, scholars, and activists who have come before us. We explore the contradictions in the field of social work where the rhetoric of social justice has often been inconsistent with practices of containment and control (Abramovitz, 1998; Specht & Courtney, 1994; Withorn, 1984). We seek insight from those who have lived the consequences of unjust social arrangements and from those who have posed challenges to injustice only to find their voices silenced and their contributions neglected in the history of social work practice (see Reisch & Andrews, 2001). We draw inspiration from social workers actively engaged with the personal and political dilemmas of linking a commitment to social justice to their everyday practices in social welfare institutions and to the challenges of globalization (Ferguson, Lavalette, & Whitmore, 2005; Midgley, 1997). They have pushed us to challenge our own certainties about the world and to open ourselves to transformative possibilities. We grapple with the tensions and contradictions that have shaped the history of the social work profession, and we challenge readers to do the same. The writing and reading of textbooks are not only intellectual exercises, they are also forms of political practice. What stories are told and which ones are omitted? How are the stories told interpreted and put to use? We invite you to question, talk back, and challenge us throughout this journey.

Just Practice is interactive in design, structured to engage readers in an action-reflection dialogue about the challenges and possibilities of what we term "social justice work." *Just Practice* examines the interplay of social work and social justice in historical and cross-national contexts, explores shifts in the profession's orientation and value base over time, and compares diverse approaches to social work across a range of social and political contexts. This examination sets the stage for exploring the processes and developing the skills of justice-oriented social work. We offer readers a model for and examples of "engaged practice," where people struggle with everyday contradictions and restrictions in ways that reflect a vision of social justice and the hope that "another world is possible" (Ferguson, Lavalette, & Whitmore, 2005, p. 4).

Just Practice is informed by contemporary directions in social and cultural theory (e.g., feminist, social constructionist, post-colonialist, practice, and critical political economy and race theories), which attend to questions of meaning, context, power, history, and possibility in understanding and shaping processes of individual and social change. We address the power of current neoliberal ideologies regarding social welfare and citizenship, market-based approaches to social work, and their consequences in the everyday lives of poor and vulnerable populations. We encourage readers to examine the social construction of human problems and their solutions and the ways in which the language and labels of helping professions map onto practices of caring, containment, and control. Questions of gender, class, race, and sexual identity are explored not as "issues" of "populations at risk" but as key axes around which practices of and beliefs about inequality and difference are structured, reinforced, and contested. We challenge readers to examine the classism, heterosexism, and racism embedded in social life, and in social work itself, before turning attention to "target populations." We argue that ongoing critical questioning of one's own certainties is a central component of social justice work, and we create opportunities for self-reflection throughout the text. Likewise, readers are asked to explore alternative ways of thinking and acting in the world that are informed by these diverse perspectives.

A STORY OF SOCIAL WORK PRACTICE

What Is Social Work and How Do We Tell Its Story?

There are many ways to tell the story of social work practice. Some stories offer a chronology of social work's emergence as a profession. Others have analyzed social work's preoccupation with profession-building activities, arguing that it has strayed from its commitment to the poor and concern for social justice in the process (Specht & Courtney, 1994; Wenocur & Reisch, 1989). Some recount the tensions and debates that shape the field, with particular attention to social work's vacillation between providing social service and promoting social change (Abramovitz, 1998; Withorn, 1984). Some describe the diverse arenas in which social workers practice, such as child welfare, mental health, and gerontology, and the knowledge base and skills needed for each. Most U.S. texts refer only to domestic influences on social work thought and practice. A few seek to illuminate the contributions of both insiders and outsiders who challenge the profession's priorities, practices, and its very reason to be. Each account offers a partial view, shaped by the beliefs, values, and perspective of the narrator.

We have made the claim that *Just Practice* tells a different sort of story about the practice of social work. You may be asking, "Different from what?" As an entry point to the Just Practice approach, let us tell one story of social work practice. We draw from a range of historical and contemporary social work literature in telling a story of the emergence of the practice of social work in the United States and its evolution over the course of the 20th century. This story provides readers with a common frame of reference, a rough sketch of the profession, if you will. In Chapter 3 we return to the history of social work and offer different ways of telling the story. We invite you to return to this sketch as you make your way through the text. What would you erase?

What would you elaborate? What would you challenge? How would you write the story of social work practice to mark the starting point of a journey into social justice work?

According to the *Social Work Dictionary* (Barker, 2003), social work constitutes "the professional activity of helping individuals, families, groups, or communities to enhance or restore their capacity for social functioning and for creating societal conditions favorable to that goal" (p. 408). Karla Krogsrud Miley, Michael O'Melia, and Brenda DuBois (2007, p. 8) describe social work as a "profession that supports individuals, groups, and communities in a changing society and creates social conditions favorable to the well-being of people and society." These statements encompass a dual focus on individual needs and social conditions that has long been a source of both tension and possibility in the profession. Further, given the breadth and generality of these definitions of professional social work practice, it seems that contemporary social workers, like their foremothers and forefathers, still struggle to define what they do. It seems as if social workers face an ongoing quandary as the opening quotation to this introduction suggests: Am I in the social work club? Is it a club I want to belong to? Let's take a look at the formation of the club and the struggles over what constitutes membership.

How Social Work Came to Be

The practice of social work in the United States emerged alongside and in response to the contradictions and crises of late 19th and early 20th century industrial capitalism. Industrialization, immigration, and urbanization challenged the social order of things. Widespread poverty, the growth of urban slums, and the challenges of "assimilating" culturally different groups posed social, economic, and political problems for the young nation. Two fundamentally different modes of intervention, the Charity Organization Societies and the Settlement House Movement, emerged in response to these conditions. The Charity Organization Societies saw social problems as the result of individual deficits, such as lack of moral character, training, discipline, or personal capacity. They sought to intervene through "scientific philanthropy," that is, a systematic and painstaking effort to identify personal shortcomings and provide proper support and guidance. The Settlement House Movement, in contrast, focused on the social environment and lack of understanding that contributed to poverty and personal strife. They sought change through education and social action. Thus, the emergent forms of social work practice were in tension with one another from the start, with one emphasizing person-changing interventions and the other focusing on the need to change social conditions (this history is explored in depth in Chapter 3). Both, however, were experiments in human betterment that sought a systematic, scientific approach to their work, variably influenced by the emerging disciplines of psychology, sociology, and psychiatry. These organizations also became vehicles for the entry of women into the newly forming helping professions and into social welfare policy arenas.

The Professionalization of Social Work

Social work was initially conceived as a philanthropic effort and staffed by volunteers (*Encyclopedia of Social Welfare History*, 2006). By the turn of the 20th century, however, social workers were staking claims to their body of knowledge and

CHECK IT OUT ON THE WEB!

For an insightful and interactive account of Social Work History, visit the Social Work History Station online at http://www.idbsu.edu/socwork/dhuff/history/central/core.htm. This wonderful resource was developed by Professor Dan Huff, School of Social Work, Boise State University, Boise, Idaho as a Council on Social Work Education Millenium Project. The station includes a comprehensive history of early social work, photo gallery, biographies, and a number of off-site virtual excursions. Take a moment to step back in time. Hear Jane Addams speak. Learn about social work responses to the Depression. Listen to the songs of Woody Guthrie or to the words of Franklin D. Roosevelt's first address to the nation.

systematizing their methods of diagnosis and technologies of intervention. Schools of philanthropy, established initially in New York and Chicago, offered training in a scientific approach to social problems. Social workers learned to conduct research, analyze social policy, manage organizations, and deliver services. Specialized arenas of practice in medical, psychiatric, and school social work began to emerge, and practitioners began to define themselves as professionals.

Throughout the early 1900s, social work practitioners were working hard to build the new profession. They were forming organizations, staking claims to a base of knowledge and skills, and expanding programs of professional study (Huff, 2006). Despite these efforts, the professional status of social work practice remained in doubt. In a 1915 speech to the National Conference on Charities and Corrections, Dr. Abraham Flexner posed the question, "Is social work a profession?" His answer cast doubt on social work's professional status, given its propensity for low-paid, altruistic practice. He claimed that social work lacked both a systematic body of knowledge and theory and societal sanction to act in a particular sphere, characteristics he saw as fundamental to a profession (NASW, 1977, p. 485; Specht & Courtney, 1994, p. 87). Flexner's pessimistic view fueled efforts to establish social work's credibility as a profession.

In response, social workers shifted their energies further toward person-changing approaches and the expanding array of tests, measurements, and technologies that informed those approaches. The work of Sigmund Freud, the father of psychiatry, was influential in shaping thought about psychodynamic processes and furthering the individual treatment approach. Social casework, modeled after the medical approach to diagnosis and treatment, became the hallmark of the social work profession. Mary Richmond's classic text *Social Diagnosis* (1917) became the foundation for social casework. Importantly, Richmond embraced the scientific approach to investigation and diagnosis and advocated for attention to the social context of individual experience. Richmond saw the need to appreciate a person's history in order to get to the root cause of the problem. She envisioned social diagnosis as an interpretive as well as investigative process. Her work contributed to an understanding of the "person-in-environment" perspective, which continues to be a fundamental premise in social work practice.

The budding profession was moving away from collaborative, community-based work to a more individualized approach. Social workers were coming together to form organizations that reflected and promoted professional status. The National Conference of Social Workers, emerging from its predecessor, the National Conference on Charities and Corrections, was founded in 1917. In that same year the National Social Workers' Exchange, which sought to promote the employment and working conditions of social workers, was formed. In 1921 the group changed its name to the American Association of Social Workers (Huff, 2006).

Following World War I, social work embraced a psychoanalytic approach. Throughout the 1920s, social workers sought to legitimize their practice through close affiliation with psychiatry and medicine. Psychoanalytic casework became a predominant mode of practice as social workers crafted specializations in mental health and in psychiatric and medical social work. Social workers claimed social casework as the purpose and method of social work practice. The casework approach placed emphasis on individual experience, the worker-client relationship, and helping the client properly adjust to prevailing social standards (Johnson &

Yanca, 2007, p. 21). In 1929 Porter Lee, the president of the National Conference on Social Work and dean of the New York School of Philanthropy, proclaimed that social work was no longer about cause (social activism) but about function (service) (Lee, 1930). Specht and Courtney write:

> Porter Lee… announced the end of social work as a social movement. The "service," he said (by which he meant the function of professional social work), would henceforth have top priority. The "movement" (by which he meant the cause of social reform and betterment) would have to take a back seat. (1994, p. 88)

These factors combined to enhance social work's status and credibility as a profession and to simultaneously move the developing profession away from work with the poor.

Social Work and the Public Welfare Domain

During the 1920s social workers were also expanding their professional influence and practice base into the public sector. Some brought their experiences as reformers honed in the Settlement House Movement to bear in the administration of new public institutions. For example, Julia Lathrop became the first director the Children's Bureau, and Florence Kelly headed the Consumers' League. Both women had been residents of Chicago's Hull House, the premier Settlement House founded by pioneer social worker Jane Addams in 1889. Harry Hopkins, a former resident of New York's Henry Street Settlement, became the New York State public welfare administrator under then-Governor Franklin Roosevelt.

The Great Depression fundamentally challenged the ways in which both social work and the general public thought about poverty. Given the widespread misery, notions of poverty as personal failure did not hold up. Some social workers began to turn away from individualist practice models in favor of reform. Some assumed leadership roles in crafting new public welfare policies and programs in response to broad-based needs. As Governor, Franklin Roosevelt, with the support of social workers such as Harry Hopkins and his state labor secretary Frances Perkins, began to implement relief efforts in New York, which became models for efforts around the country. As President, Roosevelt drew on the knowledge and skills of social workers in shaping the New Deal relief programs and the social insurance program that followed. Perkins and Hopkins played key roles in drafting the 1935 Social Security Act, which Huff terms the "most important single piece of legislation in the 20th century" (Chap. 5-5). According to Huff (2006), these efforts served to enhance public opinion of the social work profession.[2]

The Professional Domain and Debates

By the 1930s schools of social work were expanding, and professional organizations were well established. The American Association of Social Workers had established educational criteria for membership in the social work profession by the early 1930s. With the passage of New Deal social legislation, social workers expanded their professional domain into planning, management, and service delivery in public bureaucracies as well as in private charities. While there was a revitalized interest in group and community work, an individualist ideology continued to dominate practice. However, within the practice of social casework itself, differing perspectives emerged. Proponents of the Freudian-influenced "diagnostic" approach, which had dominated practice thinking for two decades, were being challenged by the rise of the functional approach to social work practice.

The Functional School, developed at the University of Pennsylvania in the 1930s, rejected Freudian determinism. Influenced by the work of psychologist Otto Rank, advocates of the functional approach embraced a more optimistic and growth-oriented view of human nature. The functional approach was characterized by a view of clients as self-determining and of the social work relationship as a helping process that releases the client's power for choice (NASW 1977, p. 1554). Functionalists promoted a worker-client relationship grounded in mutuality (Reisch, 2005). They differentiated helping from "treatment," emphasized the role and responsibilities of the social worker, and argued that the practice of social work is a helping process that involves giving focus, direction, and content in the context of relationship (Johnson & Yanca, 2007, pp. 22, 458). According to proponents of the functional approach, the purpose of social work is

> …the release of human power in individuals, groups, and communities for personal fulfillment and social good and the release of social power for the creation of the kind of society, social policy, and social institutions that make self-realization most possible for all men. (NASW,1977, p. 1281)

The functionalists emphasized the importance of process, respect for human dignity, and concern that every individual have the chance to reach his or her potential. Their position challenged and helped advance thought and practice of the diagnostic school.

One of the foremost thinkers of the diagnostic school was Gordon Hamilton. As a casework practitioner and educator, she was an influential voice in social casework theory. Hamilton recognized Freud's contributions to casework and the power of psychodynamic processes. At the same time, she argued for social workers to retain a commitment to poor families and to the ways in which social and economic factors contribute to personal distress (NASW, 1977, p. 518). Hamilton was a strong advocate for linking social casework, social welfare policy, and social action. She redefined "diagnosis" as a "working hypothesis" for understanding the person with the problem as well as the problem itself (Johnson & Yanca, 2007, p. 22). Her diagnostic approach was contextualized and interpretive; she called for appreciation of both the objective situation and the client's subjective interpretation of the situation (Johnson & Yanca, 2007). She describes the helping process as the interplay of study, diagnosis, and treatment. Her 1940 book *Theory and Practice of Social Casework* became a definitive text in articulating the diagnostic approach. The philosophical and theoretical differences between the diagnostic and functionalist schools of social casework were the source of ongoing debate throughout the 1940s. Strains of that debate still continue to influence theory and practice.

During this era, social group work and community organization became more broadly recognized as methods of social work practice. Some group workers adhered to the functionalist school and others to the diagnostic school. For example, Hamilton recognized the importance of group theory and process in understanding the dynamics of family. Social workers engaged in the development of theories and methods of group work as a means of effecting individual and interpersonal change. With the growth of human service bureaucracies, the 1940s also saw a growing interest in community organization to tackle larger scale or "macro" issues. The field and practice of social planning became a more recognized component of social work practice (Johnson & Yanca, 2007, pp. 22–24). The social work profession came to identify itself in terms of three key aspects of practice—casework, group work, and community organization—and to prepare practitioners with expertise in a particular field. However, the bulk of practice efforts continued to be directed toward person-changing interventions. Social workers continued to build and expand professional organizations throughout the 1950s. The Council on Social Work Education (CSWE) was founded in 1952 from the merger of two predecessor organizations. In 1955, seven professional groups came together to form the National Association of Social Workers (NASW). CSWE and NASW are the predominant social work professional organizations in the United States today.

Steps Toward Synthesis and a Generalist Approach

By the 1950s, social workers were expanding their professional influence into the fields of health and mental health. They were also seeking a synthesis between the diagnostic and functional approaches to practice. They explored the underpinnings of the social worker–client relationship and the principles, such as acceptance, individualization, promotion of client self-determination, and confidentiality, that would promote growth and change (Biestek, 1957). Their work in articulating principles of social work practice continues to guide the profession today. In 1957, Helen Harris Perlman proposed a new conceptualization of social casework that brought together the functional and diagnostic approaches. She articulated casework as a problem-solving process that reframed "diagnosis" as a broader process of assessment and incorporated the functionalists' assumptions about the potential for human growth and competence. Her more encompassing approach had implications not only for social casework; it also provided a theoretical link among the multiple approaches to social work practice from casework to group work and community organization (Johnson & Yanca, 2007, p. 24; Perlman, 1957).

Social workers were influenced by developments in sociology, psychology, and communication theory in the post-war years. They began to articulate the practice of social work in terms of five central concepts—assessment, person-in-situation, process, relationship, and intervention (Johnson & Yanca, 2007, p. 27). By 1970, social work practice was conceptualized as a problem-solving process that could be applied at multiple levels, from the individual to the group, organization, and community. Some practitioners challenged the division of social work in terms of casework, group work, and community organization and called for a unified approach to practice that addressed social work's dual focus on individual functioning and social conditions (Bartlett, 1970). In 1973, Allen Pincus and Anne Minahan published *Social Work Practice: Model and Method*, which incorporated a systems perspective and put forth a model of social work as a process of planned change (See Chapter 5 for further discussion of systems theory and its contributions to social work theory and practice). Their work provided a foundation for what has come to be known and widely accepted as a "generalist" approach to social work practice.

Over the past 30 years, social workers have developed and laid claim to a generalist approach as the foundation for social work practice. The generalist approach is, in many ways, an attempt to weave together various threads of influence on the profession. The generalist approach addresses the importance of the interplay of persons and larger systems in the process of assessment and intervention. It recognizes the centrality of relationships in the helping process and sees the process of change as patterned, sequential, and unfolding over time. Miley, O'Melia, and DuBois (2007) state that generalist social work:

> Provides an integrated and multileveled approach for meeting the purposes of social work. Generalist practitioners acknowledge the interplay of personal and collective issues, prompting them to work with a variety of human systems—societies, communities, neighborhoods, complex organizations, formal groups, families, and individuals—to create changes which maximize human system functioning. (p. 10)

The generalist perspective that encompasses individual concerns and social conditions is often highlighted as a unique and defining feature of social work practice. However, as Landon (1999) notes, there is no agreed-upon definition of generalist practice among social workers. In many ways this late 20th century meeting of the social work minds harkens back to the conundrum of social work expressed 80 years earlier.

Late 20th Century Opportunities and Challenges

The Kennedy Administration of the 1960s saw further expansion of social work in the areas of mental health, public welfare, and social action. At the same time, the social change orientation of the 1960s, from the civil rights movement to the women's movement, antiwar movement, and the war on poverty, challenged the dominant assumptions about the nature and place of professionalism in social work practice. While President Johnson's Great Society promoted grassroots community action, NASW promoted regulation and licensing of social workers as a "consumer protection measure" (Encyclopedia of Social Welfare History of North America, 2006, p. 4). Social work education expanded in the 1970s as the profession retreated once again from social action to individual treatment. However, the challenges of the 1960s left their mark on social work as the profession began to seriously contemplate what it meant to engage in practice that was inclusive and culturally sensitive.

Since the early 1970s social work education programs have been mandated by CSWE to include content on diversity. Social workers faced the challenge of increasing cultural pluralism in the United States and needed to rethink professional knowledge and skills to meet this challenge (Winkelman, 1999). Wynetta Devore and Elfriede Schlesinger's foundational text, *Ethnic-Sensitive Social Work Practice* (1981), articulated this challenge and began to map out ways to "adapt social work practice skills to specific ethnic realities" (Winkelman, 1999, p. 4). In the ensuing 25 years social work educators and practitioners have developed approaches and debated issues regarding culturally sensitive and competent approaches to practice, with many championing strengths-based and empowerment approaches (these approaches are addressed in Chapter 5). More recently social workers have been called upon to engage in evidence-based practice, an approach that asserts the importance of linking specific intervention strategies to empirical research of their effectiveness (Cournoyer, 2004; Dewees, 2006, p. I-6). The Council on Social Work Education, along with many social work practitioners, has wholeheartedly embraced this approach. However, some members of the profession have been wary about what gets evaluated and how and what aspects of the change process may be marginalized in the search for "evidence" (Dworkin, 2005). During this same time, the state-based regulation and licensing of social workers has expanded. Many professional social workers shifted to private practice as public funding for social services deteriorated in the last two decades of the 20th century. As the *Encyclopedia of Social Welfare History in North America* concludes: "In spite of its growth, Congress and the administration ignored the social work profession in 1996 as they reformed the federal-state public assistance program by imposing work requirements and time limits. By the end of the twentieth century, social work in the United States was secure, but uncertain about its mission and it relationship to the welfare state" (2006, p. 5).

For over a century, social work practice has struggled to negotiate the tensions of what has been constructed as a dual mission—responding to individual human needs and to the social conditions that contribute to those needs. At the same time, social workers have been concerned with establishing themselves as a legitimate profession with the authority, sanction, and expertise to claim a portion of the helping profession turf. The efforts of professionalization have often worked at cross-purposes to the values of social justice, with social workers distancing themselves from rather than engaging with broader struggles for social, political, and economic justice. At present it seems that person-changing interventions continue to dominate the profession, despite expressed professional values of social justice. Stanley Witkin (1998) wrote of this trend nearly 10 years ago and challenged social workers to ask why this is so. It is a question we must continue to grapple with today.

TELLING A DIFFERENT STORY

So, what is the moral to this story of social work practice? We contend that the moral of the story lies in both what the story tells and what it omits. This story of social work practice highlights (and critiques) key aspects of the "official story," the one passed down from teacher to student in many social work texts. It is a story that gives largely a "view from above"—social work practice as seen by the makers of theory and method and the builders of the profession. It highlights a few key figures and their contributions. It is a story of social workers talking to and past other social workers as they try to build, strengthen, and legitimize a profession of helping. It is a story that leaves out much of the political, historical, and cultural context of social work practice. It is a story that silences many voices of critics inside and outside of the profession who have challenged the direction of practice and posed alternatives. It is a story devoid of the politics of practice, and of the political consequences for those who engaged in radical forms of practice and made claims for social justice (Reisch, 2005; Reisch & Andrews, 2001). And it is a story with no "view from below," that is, from the perspectives of those affected by adverse social conditions. We argue that by passing down this story from teacher to student, we reproduce and promote a partial view of social work, one that emphasizes person-changing interventions and adaptation to social conditions.

Just Practice tells a different sort of story, one that looks both to and beyond the leading men and women in building the profession. It is in part a reclamation project, recovering the histories, stories, collective memories, and sense of urgency and possibility that sparked the imagination and fueled the commitment of those engaged in social justice work. We argue that justice-oriented social work practice is informed by critical dialogue with both noted molders and shapers of the profession and with those whose stories have been silenced and excluded from the official history. We need to ask what is at stake in the telling of a story. How might a different sort of story inform a different sort of vision for social work practice in the present and future? *Just Practice* tells a story of the meanings, contexts, histories, power, and possibilities of social work and its awkward embrace of social justice. The *Just Practice* story informs a new way of imagining and practicing what we call "social justice work." We hope you find the journey into social justice work informing and inspiring. We look forward to learning where the journey takes you.

End Notes

[1]Todd, A. J. (1920). The scientific spirit and social work. NY: MacMillan.

[2]See Huff for a discussion of the uneven benefits of the New Deal programs. Women and people of color were not equal participants with white men in the New Deal programs.

2

Imagining Social Work and Social Justice

> *Social justice is the end that social work seeks, and social justice is the chance for peace.*
>
> Ramsey Clark (1988)[1]

CHAPTER OVERVIEW

In Chapter 2 we locate social work within a social justice context. We introduce the idea of "social justice work" and its importance for rethinking social work practice. We examine broadly accepted contemporary definitions of social work in the United States and in an international context, and we ask you to think about the implications of these diverse meanings for social work practice. This sets the stage for locating concepts of social work in cultural, political, and historical contexts. Likewise, we discuss meanings of social justice and pose the following questions:

- What is the relationship between social work and social justice?
- What are the common goals?
- How do their definitions shape the form, content, and context of social work practice?
- How are both social work and social justice tied to questions of difference, inequality, and oppression?
- How do we engage in social justice work in our everyday practice of social work?

We introduce the Just Practice Framework and its five key concepts - meaning, context, power, history, and possibility. The Just Practice Framework will provide the foundation for integrating theory and practice. Key concepts are developed and illustrated through examples and reflection and action exercises. They push us to explore taken-for-granted assumptions about reality - those ideas, principles, and patterns of perception, behavior, and social relating we accept without question. As learners, this moves us beyond the bounds of familiar and comfortable contexts to challenge old beliefs and ways of thinking. We consider the power of language and image in shaping understandings of social problems and social work. We explore concepts of social work as a critical and transformational practice, consider the social work profession itself as a site of struggle, and seek to open up challenges and possibilities of that struggle (Adams, Dominelli, & Payne, 2005; Allan, Pease, & Briskman, 2003; Ferguson, Lavalette, & Whitmore, 2005) .

JUST PRACTICE FRAMEWORK

Five Key Concepts:
1 - meaning
2 - context
3 - power
4 - history
5 - possibility

SOCIAL JUSTICE WORK

The Idea of Social Work

Each of us has an idea or an image of social work that we carry around in our heads. For some of us this image comes from our experiences as paid or volunteer workers in a state-based agency or community service organization. Others of us may have known social work from the other side, as a "consumer" of services, perhaps as a child in the foster care system, a shelter resident, or a single parent trying to survive on "Temporary Assistance to Needy Families (TANF)"[2] Some of us may have little or no experience with the practicalities of social work. Perhaps we have taken a course or two, or we have known social work mainly through its representations in the media where social workers seem to be stereotyped as child-snatching villains or heroes. Nonetheless, we have an impression, a mental image if you will, of social work and what we envision ourselves doing as social workers. Accordingly, each of us has an idea or an image of social justice. For some of us, social justice relates to notions of equality, tolerance, and human rights. Others of us know social justice through its absence, for example, through personal experiences of injustice, degradation, exclusion, and violence.

REFLECTION:　Meanings of Social Work and Social Justice

Take a minute to consider what social work and social justice mean to you. Most of us take these constructs for granted. We assume we know their meaning. At the same time, we believe others hold these same meanings. What is social work? What is social justice? Now think of the relationship between the two. Might some meanings of social work and the ways in which it is practiced neglect considerations of social justice? What images come to mind? Or might these meanings be inextricably linked, making it difficult to tell them apart? What examples of social work practice illustrate the interrelationship of social work and social justice?

Linking Social Work and Social Justice

The reflection exercise above asks you to think about the meanings of social work and social justice, to explore their relationship, and to make concrete applications to the world of practice. Our bias is that social work should have a middle name - social "justice" work. Thinking about social work as social justice work accomplishes several important goals:

◆　Social justice work highlights that which is unique to social work among the helping professions (Wakefield, 1988a, 1988b). Few other professions have identified challenging social injustice as their primary mission (NASW, 1996).

♦ Social justice work implies that we take seriously the social justice principles of our profession and use these to guide and evaluate our work and ourselves as social workers. In subsequent chapters, we will introduce you to early justice-oriented social workers such as Jane Addams and Bertha Capen Reynolds, who have already paved the way.

♦ Social justice work reminds us of the need for a global perspective on social work as the forces of global capitalism and practices of free-market neoliberalism leave their mark on our own and distant economies, creating greater gaps between the rich and the poor and transgressing the boundaries of nations and national sovereignty (Ferguson, Lavalette, & Whitmore, 2005; Finn, 2005; Harris, 2005; Keigher & Lowery, 1998; Korten, 2001; Ramanathan & Link, 1999).

Some might say that giving social work "justice" as a middle name is hardly necessary. After all, social justice is a core part of the profession's values. For more than a century social workers have dedicated themselves to improving life conditions for vulnerable and marginalized individuals and groups and advocating for social policies. Social workers have been champions of civil rights and activists for human rights. As Lena Dominelli asserts, "promoting social justice and human development in an unequal world provides the *raison d'etre* of social work practice (2002, p. 4)." However, Dominelli and others have also pointed to social work's long history of implication in systems of containment, control, and paternalism, arguing persuasively that social work is not a chaste profession in terms of perpetuating injustices (Dominelli, 2002; Margolin, 1998; Withorn, 1984). Bob Sapey (2003), writing from the perspective of disability advocacy, contends that, for many "consumers" of service, the notion of "anti-oppressive social work," or social justice work, is an oxymoron, given the ways in which the profession has historically viewed the "client" through a top-down lens that imposes a demeaning status. Thus we cannot assume that by doing social work we are engaged in social justice work. The everyday struggle for social justice demands ongoing vigilance, resistance, and courage.

> *How far have we progressed? The test of our progress is not whether we add more to the abundance of those who have much; it is whether we provide enough for those who have too little.*
>
> - President Franklin D. Roosevelt, second inaugural address, 1937

The Challenge of Social Justice Work

We do not need to look far to see that much injustice persists in the world. The Universal Declaration of Human Rights is nearly 60 years old, yet violations of human rights and struggles to recognize and realize these rights continue on many fronts. Those struggles force us to ask, what conditions of humanity are necessary

REFLECTION: State of Human Development

In 1990, the United Nations began issuing an annual Human Development Report, documenting the global state of human well-being. The report provides a ranking of countries according to the "Human Development Index" - a composite score that incorporates life expectancy at birth; adult literacy rate; school enrollments; and Gross Domestic Product per capita. In 2005 Norway ranked first among 177 countries, Niger ranked last, and Paraguay in the middle. The United States ranked tenth on the list. The report also highlights the unequal state of human development globally.

Massive poverty and obscene inequality are such terrible scourges of our times - times in which the world boasts breathtaking advances in science, technology, industry and wealth accumulation - that they have to rank alongside slavery and apartheid as social evils.

- Nelson Mandela, 2005

Consider some of these facts:

♦ The global gulf between rich and poor has grown. The richest 1% has as much income as the poorest 57%.

♦ More than 1 billion people survive in abject poverty, living on under $1 a day. 40% of the world - 2.5. billion people live on less than $2 a day.

♦ In 2003 the AIDS pandemic claimed 3 million lives and left another 5 million infected.

♦ One-fifth of humanity lives in countries where many people spend $2 dollars a day on a cappuccino. Another fifth of humanity survives on less than $1 a day and lives in countries where children die for want of a simple anti-mosquito bed net.

♦ Someone living in Zambia in 2005 has less chance of reaching age 30 than someone born in England in 1849.

♦ The world's richest 500 individuals have a combined income greater than that of the poorest 416 million.

♦ There are still 800 million people in the world lacking in basic literacy skills. Two-thirds are women.

♦ More than 10 million children die before their fifth birthday each year. Sub-Saharan Africa's share of child mortality is growing. The region accounts for 20% of births but 44% of deaths.

♦ More than 80 million people, including one in three pre-school children, suffer from malnutrition.

♦ More than 1 billion people lack access to safe water and 2.6 billion lack access to improved sanitation.

♦ Some 38 million people are now infected with HIV - 25 million of them in Sub-Saharan Africa. In 1980 child death rates in Sub-Saharan Africa were 13 times higher than in rich countries. They are now 29 times higher.

♦ The risk of dying from pregnancy-related causes ranges from 1 in 18 in Nigeria to 1 in 8,700 in Canada.

Source: Human Development Report, 2005, pp. 3 - 32

for people to claim the most basic of human rights—the right to have rights (Arendt, 1973, p. 296, cited in Jelin, 1996, p. 104)? Struggles for women's rights continue around the world in the face of persistent gender inequality and violence. The Convention on the Rights of the Child was adopted by the United Nations in 1989, but children throughout the world continue to be viewed as less than full humans and are exploited in families, factories, sex trades, and armed conflict (Chin, 2003; Healy, 2001; Nordstrom, 1999). Amnesty International and Human Rights Watch have taken the United States to task for having the world's highest incarceration rate, further marked by the disproportionate imprisonment of people of color, the systematic sexual abuse of women prisoners, and the growing over-representation of people diagnosed with serious mental illness being held in jails and prisons around the country (Human Rights Watch, 2006). The rights associated with citizenship and "home" are denied to 23 million refugees displaced from their homelands by war and its social, political, and economic devastation (Lyons, 1999, p. 110). How can we speak of universal human rights when more than 1 billion people earn less than one dollar per day, when 800 million adults are illiterate, and when more than 1 billion people lack access to safe water (United Nations Development Programme, 2005)? These are some of the challenging questions we face when we take social justice work seriously.

TAKING A GLOBAL PERSPECTIVE

Confronting Inequality and Interdependence

Ideological precepts written into the U.S. Constitution over 200 years ago speak of "equality and justice for all." These same precepts continue to feed the fires of revolutionary claims and movements around the world. Yet as Figure 2.1 indicates, the contemporary world is characterized by brutal inequalities of wealth and poverty. As this topsy-turvy image suggests, it is an unstable world with no solid foundation. We argue that the foundation must be built from the bottom up with the help of social justice work. We believe that meaningful engagement with questions of social justice demands a global perspective. We will be reflecting on the history of social justice in U.S. social work, and we will draw from knowledge and practice beyond U.S. borders to challenge and expand our thinking. In this age of transnational movements of people, power, and information, we need an approach to social justice work that crosses national, geographic, cultural, organizational, and professional boundaries and expands our thinking along the way. We need an approach that is transformational, one that "meets the objective of promoting well-being by changing current configurations of inequality and diswelfare that prevent people from realizing their full potential as self-determining agents" (Adams, Dominelli, & Payne, 2005, p. 2).

We find inspiration in the work of international social workers and social welfare organizations for framing a global understanding of social work. For example, the International Federation of Social Workers (IFSW), in trying to develop a global definition of social work, has identified three concepts that are key to justice-oriented social work: *peace, environment,* and *citizenship* (IFSW, 1997).

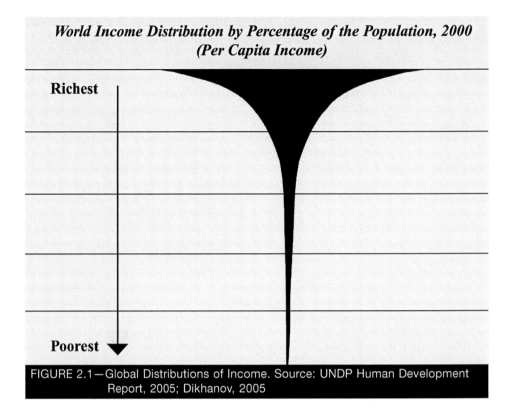

World Income Distribution by Percentage of the Population, 2000 (Per Capita Income)

Richest

Poorest

FIGURE 2.1—Global Distributions of Income. Source: UNDP Human Development Report, 2005; Dikhanov, 2005

Oxfam, a nongovernmental international aid organization, argues that we have to attend to the basic rights of subsistence and security before we can address other human rights (Lyons, 1999, p. 9). Karen Lyons, a social work educator at the University of East London, argues that if we are to think of social work and social justice on a global scale for the 21st century, we need to think about poverty, migration, disasters, and their global effects (1999, p. 14). Lynne Healy argues the need to pay simultaneous attention to global interdependence and social exclusion, or the forces of social and economic marginalization that deny whole populations the right to participate in opportunities available in society (2001, p. 101). Jim Ife and Elizabeth Reichert contend that it is imperative for social work to embrace and operate from a human rights perspective (Ife, 2001; Reichert, 2003). Further, the daily headlines across the globe inform us of the ongoing ravages of war and the human and environmental consequences of earthquakes, tsunamis, hurricanes, and other natural and human-made disasters. Clearly, these challenging issues are interrelated, and we will return to them to explore patterns that connect throughout the book.

Challenging Our Thinking

The challenge of social justice work calls for challenging ways of thinking. That is, we have to challenge ways we have been taught to think and critically engage with perspectives that disrupt our certainties about the world, our assumptions about what is "right," "true," and "good." Our (the authors') own perspectives have been shaped by diverse influences ranging from African American and Italian social theorists and activists (W.E.B. Dubois and Antonio Gramsci) to French philosophers (Michel Foucault), Brazilian and U.S. popular educators (Paulo Freire and Myles Horton), "first" and "third" world feminists (bell hooks, Patricia Hill

Collins, Chandra Talpade Mohanty), critical social and cultural theorists in Europe and North America (Pierre Bourdieu, Henry Giroux, David Harvey, Sherry Ortner, Dorothy Smith, Iris Marion Young) and indigenous scholar-activists (Linda Tuhiwai Smith). We include a selected bibliography of these works at the end of this chapter.

There are common threads among these diverse influences on our thinking. They have challenged us to examine the social construction of reality, that is, the ways we as human beings use our cultural capacities to give meaning to social experience. They pose questions about the relations of power, domination, and inequality that shape the way knowledge of the world is produced and whose view counts. Moreover, they call on us not only to question the order of things in the world but also to be active participants in social transformation toward a just world. To understand social justice work and to engage in justice-oriented practice, we must first think critically about its component parts by looking at meanings of social work and social justice.

MEANINGS OF SOCIAL WORK

Struggles Over Definition

Perhaps there are as many meanings of social work as there are social workers. When adding movement across time and place to the mix, the meaning of social work becomes a kaleidoscope of interpretations. As noted in Chapter 1, there have been struggles for control of social work's definition and direction since its inception. Partially, this struggle is attributable to what some believe is social work's dualistic nature and location, wedged between addressing individual need and engaging in broad-scale societal change (Abramovitz, 1998). A justice-oriented definition of social work challenges the boundaries between the individual and the social. Instead, it considers how society and the individual are mutually constituting—we individually and collectively make our social world and, in turn, through our participation in society and its institutions, systems, beliefs, and patterns of practice, we both shape ourselves and are shaped as social beings (Berger & Luckman, 1966). The progressive U.S. social worker, educator and activist Bertha Capen Reynolds (1942) called this "seeing it whole." Historically, forces both within and outside social work have influenced its dominant definition. In Chapter 3 we follow the course of these tensions and strains as we explore the history of social work in the United States.

First, we start with some commonly held contemporary definitions of social work in the United States and then move to alternative and international definitions. We ask you to consider this question: How is it that a profession that calls itself by one name—social work—can have such diverse meanings and interpretations? Also, think about the different contexts that shape these meanings, and how these translate into different ways of conceptualizing social work practice. How do countries with different dominant value systems from that of the United States practice social work? How do these practices differ from our own? Do practitioners in other national and political contexts understand the meaning of social justice differently than we do in the United States? How do you explain this difference?

Official Meanings

Professions have formalized organizations that oversee their functioning, determine standards, and monitor practice. The Council on Social Work Education (CSWE), for example, is the accrediting body for schools of social work education in the United States. CSWE's primary role is to ensure the consistency of knowledge, values, and skills disseminated through social work education. According to CSWE:

> Social work practice promotes human well-being by strengthening opportunities, resources, and capacities of people in their environments by creating policies and services to correct conditions that limit human rights and the quality of life. The social work profession works to eliminate poverty, discrimination, and oppression. Guided by a person-in-environment perspective and respect for human diversity, the profession works to effect social and economic justice worldwide. (CSWE, 2001, rev. 2004, p. 2)

The profession of social work is based on the values of service, social and economic justice, dignity and worth of the person, importance of human relationships, and integrity and competence in practice. With these values as defining principles, the purposes of social work are:

- To enhance human well-being and alleviate poverty, oppression, and other forms of social injustice.
- To enhance the social functioning and interactions of individuals, families, groups, organizations, and communities by involving them in accomplishing goals, developing resources, and preventing and alleviating distress.
- To formulate and implement social policies, services, and programs that meet basic human needs and support the development of human capacities.
- To pursue policies, services, and resources through advocacy and social or political actions that promote social and economic justice.
- To develop and use research, knowledge, and skills that advance social work practice.
- To develop and apply practice in the context of diverse cultures. (CSWE, 2001, rev. 2004, Section 1.0, p. 4)

The National Association of Social Workers (NASW) is the largest organization of professional social workers in the United States. It works to enhance the professional growth and development of its members, both bachelor of social work (BSW) and master of social work (MSW) practitioners. NASW also helps to create and maintain professional standards and to advance social policies. The Preamble to the NASW Code of Ethics contains the following definition of social work:

> The primary mission of the social work profession is to enhance human well-being and help meet the basic human needs of all people, with particular attention to the needs and empowerment of people who are vulner-

able, oppressed, and living in poverty. A historic and defining feature of social work is the profession's focus on individual well-being in a social context and the well-being of society. Fundamental to social work is attention to the environmental forces that create, contribute to, and address problems in living. (NASW, 1999, p. 1)

The *Social Work Dictionary,* published by NASW (Barker, 2003), defines social work as:

♦ The applied science of helping people achieve an effective level of psychosocial functioning and effecting societal changes to enhance the well-being of people.

♦ According to NASW, "Social Work is the professional activity of helping individuals, groups, or communities enhance or restore their capacity for social functioning and creating conditions favorable to this goal." (Barker, p. 408)

What do the CSWE and the NASW definitions of social work mean to you? Where do you see common ground and differences? How do these definitions compare with your own definition of social work? Like other definitions of a profession, these embody the value systems of their creators. CSWE and NASW have the power to officially sanction not only how we define social work but also how we outline the parameters of its practice and articulate the values believed to be central to the work. This official sanction refers not only to words and to the language we use to describe what we do but also to the actions we take that exemplify our practice. These definitions are also evolving, responding to pressures from constituents and social conditions. For example, prior to the recent revision of its *Educational Policy and Accreditation Standards,* CSWE did not specifically charge social workers with the responsibility to respond to conditions that limit human rights. In addition, human rights are not discussed further in the policy document, suggesting a lack of clarity regarding *how* to bring them to bear in social work education and practice. Throughout this journey we ask that you return to these definitions from time to time and reflect on the challenges and possibilities of translating words to action.

CSWE and NASW are powerful meaning-makers in defining the nature of social work in the United States. More often than not, social work texts include these definitions of social work in their introductory chapters (for example, see Boyle, Hull, Mather, Smith, & Farley, 2006; Miley, O'Melia, & DuBois, 2007); Sheafor, Horejsi, & Horejsi, 2006). Although these are certainly the most dominant definitions, they are not the only ones. Next, we will look at some alternative meanings, those that challenge and go beyond the dominant definitions. These meanings of social work speak directly of its inescapable political nature and ask us to consider issues of power as they concern social workers' relationships to those with whom they work. As you read the following definitions, write down what you think might be factors that shape different meanings of social work and definitions of the helping relationship.

What meanings are communicated by the CSWE and the NASW in their definitions of social work? How might these meanings guide practice? For example, think of yourself working with children and families or in a health care or community center. Given these definitions, how might you relate to the people, the neighborhoods, and the communities with whom you work? Would your relationships be top-down, bottom-up, or side-by-side? How would you work to promote, restore, maintain, and enhance human functioning? What actions would you take to correct conditions that limit human rights and quality of life? Where would you turn to gain an understanding of human rights? Now let's shift our vision from "inside" the profession and look at meanings of social work from the "outside," through the eyes of those whom social work is meant to serve. For example, imagine yourself to be:

♦ a homeless person turned away from a full shelter for the third night in a row;

♦ a 9-year-old child in a receiving home awaiting temporary placement in a foster home;

♦ a school principal making a referral of child neglect to the local child protection services office;

♦ an undocumented resident of the United States whose young child, born in the United States, is in need of emergency health care;

♦ a TANF (Temporary Assistance for Needy Families) recipient whose monthly benefit has been reduced for failure to provide proper documentation of a part-time day care arrangement.

How would you define social work through these eyes? As you look at the meaning of social work from an outsider point of view, does this change your conceptions of social work? What concrete actions and results would demonstrate to you that the social work profession is realizing its stated purpose?

Other Meanings to Consider

Social Work as a Transformative Process

Paulo Freire (1974, 1990), a Brazilian educator, argues that social work is a transformative process in which both social conditions and participants, including the social worker, are changed in the pursuit of a just world. Freire is noted for his contributions to popular education, a social-change strategy wherein people affected by oppressive social conditions come together to reflect on their circumstances, become critically conscious of the root causes of their suffering, and take liberating action. (We address popular education further in Chapters 6 and 7.) Freire taught literacy to Brazilian peasants through group discussion that prompted critical reflection on their life conditions. Weiler (1988) writes that Freire:

> . . . is committed to a belief in the power of individuals to come to a critical consciousness of their own being in the world. Central to his pedagogical work is the understanding that both teachers and students are agents, both engaged in the process of constructing and reconstructing meaning. (p. 17)

In Freire's view, social work involves critical curiosity and a life-long, committed search for one's own competence; congruence between words and actions; tolerance; the ability to exercise "impatient patience"; and a grasp of what is historically possible. Similarly, Stanley Witkin (1998, p. 486) asks us to consider social work as contextually relevant inquiry and activity focused on individual and social transformation that promotes human rights, social justice, and human dignity. Robert Adams, Lena Dominelli, and Malcolm Payne (2005) frame social work as a transformational, reflexive, and critical practice with individuals, communities, families, and groups that enhances social solidarity, deepens social interaction, and reduces inequality. They argue that transformation does not mean revolution. It is about continuity as well as change. It is a creative process that moves beyond technique, procedures, and managerialism; it engages with the structures of people's lives (pp. 12-4). They state,

> Ultimately, we may achieve transformation of the service user's situation, the setting for practice, the policy context, and, not least, ourselves. In transforming ourselves, we enhance our capacities for self-awareness, self-evaluation, and self-actualization or personal and professional fulfillment. (p. 14)

These depictions highlight the transformation of both social conditions and ourselves in the process.

Social Work as a Political Process

A number of writers have argued that social work practice is fundamentally a political activity. According to Norman Goroff, those who attribute human problems to personal deficits are assuming a conservative stance that supports the status quo (1983, p. 134, cited in Reisch, 2005). David Gil (1998, pp. 104-108), along with other scholars of social work (Barber, 1995; Fisher, 1995; Reisch, 1997, 1998b), affirms the undeniably political nature of social work and its value system. He believes social work should confront the root causes of social problems by moving beyond mere technical skills. Like Freire, Gil asserts that social work must promote critical consciousness, that is, an acute awareness of the interconnected nature of individuals, families, and communities, and a society's political, economic, and social arrangements. To achieve these ends, Gil contends that social workers must strive to understand their own and others' oppression (and privilege) and consider alternative possibilities for human relations. He, too, argues that there is need for fundamental social change. Dennis Saleebey concurs with Gil as he asserts, "practice that is guided by social and economic justice requires methods that explicitly deal with power and power relationships" (2006, p. 95). Similarly, Adams, Dominelli, and Payne (2005) call on social workers to "connect our interpersonal actions with our political objectives" (p. 2). They contend that our behavior as practitioners "is a social and political statement about how we think social relationships should move forward" and how we confront barriers to social justice (p. 3).

Social Work as Critical Practice

In a similar vein, advocates of *critical social work* argue that the central purpose of social work is social change to redress social inequality. They examine class, race, gender, and other forms of social inequality and their effects on the marginalization and oppression of individuals and groups. They, too, pay particular attention to the structural arrangements of society that contribute to individual pain (Allan, Pease, & Briskman, 2003). These ideas about social work resonate with Bertha Capen Reynolds' (1934, 1942, 1963) contributions to the profession. Reynolds was a social worker and social work educator in the United States whose life and work modeled a commitment to progressive, justice-oriented social work. Reynolds' work bridged the individual and the social. Like many social workers of her time, she was trained in psychoanalytic techniques, but she never lost sight of the contextual nature of individual problems. Reynolds set forth "five simple principles" she believed necessary to the practice of social work:

1. Social work exists to serve people in need. If it serves other classes, it becomes too dishonest.
2. Social work exists to help people help themselves. . . we should not be alarmed when they do so by organized means, such as client or tenant or labor groups.
3. The underlying nature of social work is that it operates by communication, listening, and sharing experience.
4. Social work has to find its place among other social movements for human betterment.
5. Social workers as citizens cannot consider themselves superior to their clients as if they do not have the same problems (Reynolds, 1963, pp. 173-175).

GET INVOLVED!

Visit the Social Welfare Action Alliance online and learn how you can help build a progressive force for social change.
http://socialwelfare-actionalliance.org

Reynolds' understanding of social work continues to inspire individuals interested in social change as attested to by the progressive social work organization founded in her name, formerly the Bertha Capen Reynolds Society, now the Social Welfare Action Alliance.

Michael Reisch has explored the history of radical social work in the United States and argued for the recognition of social work as a political process (Reisch, 1998b, 2005; Reisch & Andrews, 2001). He examines the historic and contemporary understandings and possibilities of *critical* social work and its potential to resist the political and economic inequalities resulting from 21st century globalization. Reisch (2005) states,

Critical social work challenges conventional assumptions about poverty, race, and gender, and the basic functions of a market-driven political-economic system. In addition, critical social work heightens awareness of the historical and contemporary relationship between social justice and social struggle. (p. 157)

Conceptualizations of social work as a critical, political, and transformational process are central to our understanding of social justice work. Throughout the text we draw on the insights of critical thinkers and practitioners in both challenging the bounds and expanding the possibilities of practice.

International Meanings of Social Work

International Federation of Social Workers' Definition

Much can be learned about social work when we step outside U.S. soil and learn about its meaning on different social, political, and cultural terrain. Professional organizations other than CSWE and NASW have set forth definitions of social work. For example, the International Federation of Social Workers (IFSW) is a global organization founded on the principles of social justice, human rights, and social development. IFSW strives to achieve these aims through the development of international cooperation between social workers and their professional organizations. In 2000, IFSW developed a new definition of social work, replacing a definition adopted in 1982 and reflecting the organization's effort to address the evolving nature of social work. In 2001, IFSW joined with another major international social work body, the International Association of Schools of Social Work (IASSW), in agreement on the following as a common definition of social work:

> The social work profession promotes social change, problem solving in human relationships and the empowerment and liberation of people to enhance well-being. Utilising theories of human behaviour and social systems, social work intervenes at the points where people interact with their environment. Principles of human rights and social justice are fundamental to social work.[3]

It is important to note that the IFSW/IASSW definition specifically addresses human rights and liberation as foundational to social work. How does this compare with the definitions put forth by NASW and CSWE?

Global Interdependence

In keeping with international concerns and connections, other social workers continue to forge new definitions of social work that capture global concerns and ideals. For example, Rosemary Link, Chathapuram Ramanathan, and Yvonne Asamoah (1999) contend that a global approach to social work must view the world as a system of interdependent parts, account for the structures that shape human interactions, and challenge culture-bound assumptions about human behavior. For instance, they point out the culture-bound nature of concepts such as "independence," "self-esteem," and "motivation" that have been predicated on particular modern Western concepts of personhood and the self. They call on social workers to reach for constructs that can relate to differing cultural contexts "such as interdependence of self (with family, village, and community life), social well-being, empowerment, resilience, reverence for nature, artistic expression, and peace" (p. 30). Similarly, Lynne Healy (2001) situates social work internationally as a force for human global change and development. She argues that the concepts of human rights, multiculturalism, social exclusion/inclusion, security, and sustainability are central to social work in a global context (pp. 266-267).

Defining Social Work in Diverse National Contexts

We have chosen the snapshots below to illustrate the meaning of social work in diverse national contexts. We hope these will spark your interest to investigate other countries on your own. Here are some clues about social work. See if you can guess the country. (Answers in endnotes for this chapter.)

◆ Social work in this country bears some resemblance to social work in the United States because these countries share a common border. Social work started here at approximately the same time as it did in the United States. This country exported practice methods and philosophies from the United States and Great Britain. In fact, the country's longest serving prime minister was employed at Hull House in Chicago as a caseworker when it was under Jane Addams' leadership. In part, this explains the commonality of social services and policies adopted in this country during the 1940s when compared to the United States (e.g., income security programs, minimum wage legislation, old age security, family allowances, and unemployment insurance). There are also some startling differences. For example, this country created a universal medical care program and a comprehensive and integrated social assistance program in the 1960s (Hopmeyer, Kimberly, & Hawkins, 1995). What factors might account for the different meanings of social work in this country compared to the United States?

◆ As part of this country's historic ideology, for hundreds of years a good society was a society where the masters at different levels were just and took good care of their subordinates (Frick, 1995). Beginning in the 1930s, this country evolved from the concept of the state as the benevolent caretaker toward a new ideology based on solidarity, democracy, equality, and brotherhood. "Individual rights as citizens were stressed together with the belief in collective solutions to social problems and a preparedness to use the state as an instrument for such solutions" (Frick, 1995, p. 146). What is the meaning of social work in a country that bridges individual rights and collective solutions?

◆ Social work was initiated in this country by an American missionary who set up an organization based on the Settlement House model in 1926. With funding from a wealthy industrialist of the country, the first school of social work was started in 1936. It focused on urban problems and the needs of the rural immigrant workforce coming to the city for factory work. A second school, heavily supported by the YWCA, was established in 1946, and U.S. influence permeated in the training and practice of social workers for many years. At the same time, however, social work was also being shaped by this country's struggle for independence and its embrace of "modernization and development" in the post-World War II era. In contrast to its U.S. counterpart, social work in this country came to be seen and practiced as a form of social development. (Healy 2001, pp. 23-24; Kuruvilla, 2005, pp. 41-54).

◆ During the Allied occupation of this country after World War II, social work and a system of social welfare were introduced based on models developed in the United States. This is a good example of a powerful meaning-maker spreading its ideas of social work to another country. While it may be efficient to buy something ready-made, often a good fit to new surroundings is sacrificed in the process. However, in this country's case there was no other choice. With conquest and domination came the power to impose meanings on a culture and its people. Old meanings were replaced with new ones and in the process, the importance of cultural congruence was ignored. While this country continues to forge an indigenous system of social welfare, social casework is still the dominant model of practice. A continued reliance on imported theories and models of practice has impeded social work's capacity to respond to changing demographic, social, and economic conditions (Healy, 2001; Matsubara, 1992; Okamoto & Kuroki, 1997).

♦ This was the first country in South America where social work emerged, beginning in 1925. Influenced initially by European models of practice, the profession underwent a transformation during the 1960s. The theories of Paulo Freire, the noted Brazilian popular educator mentioned earlier, who was living in exile in this country, had a transformative influence on both the practice and the teaching of social work. Consciousness-raising and rethinking the power dynamics inherent in the social worker/client relationship became points of reflection that changed the nature of practice. Social workers in this country contested the individualistic, apolitical emphasis of social work in other countries, and critiqued models imported from the U.S. as imperialistic. However, 17 years of military dictatorship (1973-1990), accompanied by a transformation of the economy to a model of free market neoliberalism and repression of social movements and academic freedom, severely affected social work education and practice. While some social work practitioners and educators continue to embrace a critical approach to practice, others have retreated to individualistic, person-changing approaches (Finn, 2005; Jimenez & Aylwin, 1992).[4]

MEANINGS OF SOCIAL JUSTICE

Understanding Social Justice in Context

Notions of justice have been debated since the days of Socrates, Plato, and Aristotle. Like social work, the meaning of social justice is contextually bound and historically driven. The ideas we have about social justice in U.S. social work are largely derived from Western philosophy and political theory and Judeo-Christian religious tradition. The *Social Work Dictionary* defines social justice as "an ideal condition in which all members of a society have the same rights, protection, opportunities, obligations and social benefits. Implicit in this concept is the notion that historical inequalities should be acknowledged and remedied through specific measures. A key social work value, social justice entails advocacy to confront discrimination, oppression, and institutional inequities" (Barker, 2003, p. 405). Our conceptions of justice are generally abstract ideals that overlap with our beliefs about what is right, good, desirable, and moral (Horejsi, 1999). Notions of social justice generally embrace values such as the equal worth of all citizens, their equal right to meet their basic needs, the need to spread opportunity and life chances as widely as possible, and finally, the requirement that we reduce and where possible, eliminate unjustified inequalities.

Some students of social justice consider its meaning in terms of the tensions between individual liberty and common social good, arguing that social justice is promoted to the degree that we can promote positive, individual freedom. Others argue that social justice reflects a concept of fairness in the assignment of fundamental rights and duties, economic opportunities, and social conditions (Miller, 1976, p. 22, cited in Reisch, 1998a). In their 1986 pastoral letter, the U.S. Catholic Bishops' Conference outlined three concepts of social justice[5]:

1 **Commutative Justice** - calls for fundamental fairness in all agreements and exchanges between individuals or private social groups.

2 **Distributive Justice** - requires that the allocation of income, wealth, and power in society be evaluated in light of its effects on people whose basic material needs are unmet.

3 **Social Justice** - implies that people have an obligation to be active and productive participants in the life of society and that society has a duty to enable them to participate in this way. The meaning of social justice also includes a duty to organize economic and social institutions so that people can contribute to society in ways that respect their freedom and the dignity of their labor (U.S. Catholic Bishops, 1986).

A number of social workers and social theorists concerned about questions of social justice have turned to the work of philosopher John Rawls (1995) and his theory of justice. For example, Wakefield (1988a) argues that Rawls' notion of distributive justice is the organizing value of social work. Rawls (1995) asks, what would be the characteristics of a just society in which basic human needs are met, unnecessary stress is reduced, the competence of each person is maximized, and threats to well-being are minimized? For Rawls, distributive justice denotes "the value of each person getting a fair share of the benefits and burdens resulting from social cooperation" both in terms of material goods and services and also in terms of nonmaterial social goods, such as opportunity and power (Wakefield, 1988a, p. 193).[6] Rawls tries to imagine whether a small group of people, unmotivated by selfish interests, could reach consensus regarding the characteristics of a just society. In his book *A Theory of Justice* (1995), Rawls imagines such a small group, selected at random, sitting around a table. He places an important limit on this vision: No one at the table knows whether he or she is rich or poor; black, brown, or white; young or old. He assumes that, without knowledge of their own immediate identities, they will not be motivated by selfish considerations. Rawls concludes that the group will arrive at two basic principles:

 Justice as Fairness: "According to this principle, each person has an equal right to the most extensive basic liberty compatible with a similar liberty for others" (Albee, 1986, p. 897).

Just Arrangements: "Social and economic inequalities are arranged so that they are both to the greatest benefit of the least advantaged and attached to offices and positions open to all under conditions of fair and equal opportunity" (Albee, 1986, p. 897).

From this perspective, society must make every attempt to redress all those social and economic inequalities that have led to disadvantage in order to provide real equality of opportunity. This demands a redistribution of power; the rejection of racism, sexism, colonialism, and exploitation; and the search for ways to redistribute social power toward the end of social justice (Albee, 1986, p. 897).

Social Workers Conceptualize Social Justice

Reisch (1998a) draws on Rawls' principle of "redress," that is, to compensate for inequalities and to shift the balance of contingencies in the direction of equality, in articulating the relationship of social work and social justice. He argues that a social justice framework for social work and social welfare policy would "hold the most vulnerable populations harmless in the distribution of societal resources, particularly when those resources are finite. Unequal distribution of resources would be justified only if it served to advance the least advantaged groups in the community" (Rawls, 1995; Reisch, 1998a, p. 20). The concept of distributive justice is central to a number of discussions of social justice and social work. For example, in her social work practice text, Marty Dewees (2006) states that social justice concerns the means by which societies allocate their resources, which consist of material goods and social benefits, rights, and protections. Dorothy Van Soest and Betty Garcia (2003, p. 44) write, "Our conception of social justice is premised on the concept of distributive justice, which emphasizes society's accountability to the individual. What principles guide the distributions of goods and resources?" Van Soest and Garcia address five perspectives on distributive justice that help us grasp the complexity of the concept and critically examine our own thinking. Three of these perspectives—utilitarian, libertarian, and egalitarian—are prescriptive in nature, speaking to a view of what social justice should be. Another, the racial contract perspective, offers a description of the current state of society and the unequal system of privilege and racism therein. A fifth view, the human rights perspective, makes human rights central to the discussion of social justice (p. 45). Van Soest and Garcia's overview of these five perspectives is summarized in Figure 2.2.[7]

Dennis Saleebey (1990, p. 37), a pioneer in the development of a strengths perspective, has also explored the meaning of social justice for social work. He contends that the following conditions must be met to achieve social justice:

1. Social resources are distributed on the principle of need with the clear understanding that such resources underlie the development of personal resources, with the proviso that entitlement to such resources is one of the gifts of citizenship.

2. Opportunity for personal and social development are open to all with the understanding that those who have been unfairly hampered through no fault of their own will be appropriately compensated.

Five Perspectives on Distributive Justice

	Utilitarian	Justice is arrived at by weighing relative harms and benefits and determining what maximizes greatest good for greatest number.
	Libertarian	Distribution of goods and resources occurs by natural and social lottery and is inherently uneven. Justice entails ensuring the widest possible latitude of freedom from coercion regarding what people accumulate and how they dispose of it.
	Egalitarian	Every member of society should be guaranteed the same rights, opportunities, and access to goods and resources. Redistribution of resources is a moral obligation to ensure that unmet needs are redressed.
	Racial Contract	Addresses the current state of society, rather than the way things "should" be. Argues that the notion of the "social contract" as the basis of Western democratic society is a myth. The contract did not extend beyond white society. Thus white privilege was a constitutive part of the "social contract" and must be dismantled in the struggle for social justice.
	Human Rights	Social justice encompasses meeting basic human needs; equitable distribution of resources; and recognition of the inalienable rights of all persons, without discrimination.

FIGURE 2.2

3. The establishment, at all levels of a society, of agendas and policies that have human development and the enriching of human experience as their essential goal and are understood to take precedence over other agendas and policies, is essential.

4. The arbitrary exercise of social and political power is forsaken.

5. Oppression as a means for establishing priorities, for developing social and natural resources and distributing them, and resolving social problems is forsworn.

How does this fit with your understanding of social work and social justice? Where do you find these principles honored in social work practice? Where do you find them violated? How should you as a social justice worker respond to that violation?

Summary

These important efforts to conceptualize the meaning of social justice and its relation to social work help us begin to map the challenging territory ahead. Even as these writers spell out principles of social justice, they reveal how complex the concept becomes as we try to translate it into policies and practices. And if we look closely at these brief discussions above, we see that they, too, are filled with certainties grounded in particular worldviews that value particular understandings of individual personhood, rights, equality, and fairness. However, as Lyons (1999) reminds us, these certainties may not fit with other culturally grounded conceptualizations of social relations or selfhood. How do notions of cultural rights, which are of critical importance to indigenous people, fit into these depictions of social justice? How should group or collective rights be recognized and addressed?

Similarly, there are particular understandings of resources, development, and compensation assumed in discussion of rights and justice that also may hold very different meanings to different groups. For example, the notion of monetary compensation for harm done to people or a group is a very historically, culturally, and socially particular idea. For many people, it is inconceivable, even offensive, to negotiate a material compensation for personal or social harm. These conceptualizations of justice also speak to broad societal responsibilities. These responsibilities cannot be readily confined to the concerns and obligations of particular states or nations. These are issues that cross borders. If we limit our focus on the situation of justice within a given state, we miss the questions of fundamental inequalities among states and the transnational policies and practices that maintain and justify them. Can one make meaningful claims for social justice in the United States if those claims are premised on the exploitation of people outside U.S. borders? As Lyons (1999) notes, citizenship as it is conceptualized and practiced at the national level is inherently exclusionary when we consider the differences in power and access to resources among states. If we take the principles of distributive justice, social justice, and environmental sustainability seriously then we have to develop an international or transnational perspective on what we mean by the obligations of citizenship. This is a big challenge, and one that we will keep with us as we build our road to social justice by walking it.

Thus far, we have been probing the multiple meanings of social work and social justice and the dynamic relationship between them. We have encountered differing perspectives about the nature of the profession, the meaning and power of social justice therein, and the implications for practice. In order to effectively engage with these diverse meanings and explore the interplay of social work and social justice, we need to examine questions of difference and the relationship of difference to forms and practices of inequality and oppression.

Reflection on Distributive Justice

Return to the quote by Franklin Roosevelt on p. 15. What perspective on distributive justice seems to inform the message from his second inaugural address? How did that perspective influence the direction of social welfare policy under Roosevelt?

THINKING ABOUT DIFFERENCE, OPPRESSION, AND DOMINATION

Beyond Diversity

The practice of social justice work and the complexities inherent in meanings of social justice call on us to examine questions of difference, oppression, and domination. We will do so throughout the book, and we encourage all of us to do so in our everyday lives. It is not enough to talk about and celebrate human diversity. We need to go further and challenge ourselves to address the historical, political, and cultural processes through which differences and our ideas about difference are produced (Dirks, Eley, & Ortner, 1994; Hill Collins, 1990; Van Soest & Garcia, 2003). As Beth Glover Reed and colleagues (Reed, Newman, Suarez, & Lewis, 1997, p. 46) argue, "recognizing and building on people's differences is important and necessary, but not sufficient for a practice that has social justice as a primary goal." For social justice work, "both *difference* and *dominance* dimensions must be recognized and addressed. Developing and using individual and collective critical consciousness are primary tools for understanding differences, recognizing injustice, and beginning to envision a more just society" (Reed et al., 1997, p. 46). We have to look not only at differences, but also at the ways in which differences are produced and their relationship to the production and justification of inequality. We are challenged to recognize and respect difference at the same time that we question how certain differences are given meaning and value. We need to work collectively to understand and challenge connections among forms of difference, relations of power, and practices of devaluation.

Difference

Let's think for a moment about the concept of difference. How do we categorize human difference? What are the "differences that make a difference," so to speak? What meanings do we give to particular forms of difference in particular contexts? What meanings do we give to the categories through which social differences are named and marked? How do we construct images of and assumptions about the "other"—a person or group different from ourselves? Too often, the marking of difference also involves a devaluing of difference, as we have witnessed historically and continue to see today, for example, in the social construction of race, gender, or sexual orientation. Author H.G. Wells (1911) presents a classic example of difference and devaluation in his short story, "The Country of the Blind." Nuñez, an explorer and the story's protagonist, falls into an isolated mountain valley and is rescued by the valley's curious inhabitants. Once Nuñez realizes that all of the residents are blind and have no conception of "sight," he muses, "in the country of the blind the one-eyed man is king." He assumes that, by virtue of his sight, he is superior to the valley's residents. The residents, in turn, find Nuñez unable to respond to the most basic rhythms and rules of their society. They see him as slow and childlike, and they interpret his nonsensical ramblings about this thing called "sight" as another sign of his unsound mind (Wells, 1911). Wells skillfully illustrates the ways in which our constructions and (mis)understandings of difference are linked to assumptions about worth, superiority, and inferiority, and ways in which they inform relations of domination and subordination.

In our social work practice we are called upon to be constantly vigilant of the ways in which ahistorical understandings of diversity—or calls for appreciating the "sameness" of our underlying humanity—may blind us from recognizing the ways in which unjust structural arrangements and histories of exclusion and oppression shape the meaning and power of difference. In writing about the shortcomings of traditional social work models in the Australasian and Pacific region, Ingrid Burkett and Catherine McDonald argue that these models "have a tendency to blind practitioners to the particularities of, for example, Australia's colonial past in which racism and intolerance for difference figure highly" (2005, p. 181). They continue, "While political rhetoric celebrates Australian multiculturalism, the reality has been the containment of diversity that continues to exoticize the Other and promote erroneous ideas of the existence of fixed separate cultures (Bhabba in Harrison, 2003) rather than encourage ongoing engagement with difference" (2005, p. 181). In other words, Burkett and McDonald argue that surface rhetoric of diversity may constrict rather than expand honest exploration of difference. Might their critique be relevant for social work practice in the United States as well? We will revisit these themes as we elaborate the foundations and possibilities of social justice work in the following chapters.

REFLECTION: **Meanings of "Race" and the Making of Difference**

One of the most powerful social categories for making and marking human difference is that of "race." As social scientists have acknowledged, "race" is a social, not biological, concept. It is a complex social construction with profound human consequences. Read the American Anthropological Association's statement on race that follows and consider the following questions: Does this discussion of "race" inform or challenge your thinking? How so? Why is history important in understanding the concept of "race?" What questions does this raise about other categories of difference and the social meanings given to forms of human diversity? Where else do we see human difference constructed in terms of "rigid hierarchies of socially exclusive categories?" Is it possible to think of human difference outside of hierarchies and categories? How might a critical examination of the concept of "race" inform social justice work?

The following statement was adopted by the Executive Board of the American Anthropological Association in May 1998, based on a draft prepared by a committee of representative anthropologists. The Association believes that this statement represents the thinking and scholarly positions of most anthropologists.

> In the United States both scholars and the general public have been conditioned to viewing human races as natural and separate divisions within the human species based on visible physical differences. With the vast expansion of scientific knowledge in this century, however, it has become clear that human populations are not unambiguous, clearly demarcated, biologically distinct groups. Evidence from the analysis of genetics (e.g., DNA) indicates that most physical variation, about 94%, lies within so-called racial groups. Conventional geographic "racial" groupings differ from one another only in about 6% of their genes. This means that there is greater variation within "racial" groups than between them. In neighboring populations there is much overlapping of genes and their phenotypic (physical) expressions. Throughout history whenever different groups have come into contact, they have interbred. The continued sharing of genetic materials has maintained all of humankind as a single species.

> Physical variations in any given trait tend to occur gradually rather than abruptly over geographic areas. And because physical traits are inherited independently of one another, knowing the range of one trait does not predict the presence of others. For example, skin color varies largely from light in temperate areas in the north to dark in tropical areas in the south; its intensity is not related to nose shape or hair texture. Dark skin may be associated with frizzy or kinky hair or curly or wavy or straight hair, all of

which are found among different indigenous peoples in tropical regions. These facts render any attempt to establish lines of division among biological populations both arbitrary and subjective.

Historical research has shown that the idea of "race" has always carried more meanings than mere physical differences; indeed, physical variations in the human species have no meaning except the social ones that humans put on them. Today scholars in many fields argue that "race" as it is understood in the United States of America was a social mechanism invented during the 18th century to refer to those populations brought together in colonial America: the English and other European settlers, the conquered Indian peoples, and those peoples of Africa brought to provide slave labor.

From its inception, the modern concept of "race" was modeled after an ancient theorem of the Great Chain of Being, which posited natural categories on a hierarchy established by God or nature. Thus "race" was a mode of classification linked specifically to peoples in the colonial situation. It subsumed a growing ideology of inequality devised to rationalize European attitudes and treatment of the conquered and enslaved peoples. Proponents of slavery in particular during the 19th century used "race" to justify the retention of slavery. The ideology magnified the differences among Europeans, Africans, and Indians, established a rigid hierarchy of socially exclusive categories, underscored and bolstered unequal rank and status differences, and provided the rationalization that the inequality was natural or God-given. The different physical traits of African-Americans and Indians became markers or symbols of their status differences.

As they were constructing US society, leaders among European-Americans fabricated the cultural/behavioral characteristics associated with each "race." Linking superior traits with Europeans and negative and inferior ones to blacks and Indians. Numerous arbitrary and fictitious beliefs about the different peoples were institutionalized and deeply embedded in American thought.

Early in the 19th century the growing fields of science began to reflect the public consciousness about human differences. Differences among the "racial" categories were projected to their greatest extreme when the argument was posed that Africans, Indians, and Europeans were separate species, with Africans the least human and closer taxonomically to apes.

Ultimately "race" as an ideology about human differences was subsequently spread to other areas of the world. It became a strategy for dividing, ranking, and controlling colonized people used by colonial powers everywhere. But it was not limited to the colonial situation. In the latter part of the 19th century it was employed by Europeans to rank one another and to justify social, economic, and political inequalities among their peoples. During World War II, the Nazis under Adolf Hitler enjoined the expanded ideology of "race" and "racial" differences and took them to a logical end: the exterminations of 11 million people of "inferior races" (e.g. Jews, Gypsies, Africans, homosexuals, and so forth) and other unspeakable brutalities of the Holocaust.

"Race" thus evolved as a world view, a body of prejudgments about human differences and group behavior. Racial beliefs constitute myths about the diversity in the human species and about the abilities and behavior of people homogenized into "racial" categories. The myths fused behavior and physical features together in the public mind, impeding our comprehension of both biological variations and cultural behavior, implying that both are genetically determined. Racial myths bear no relationship to the reality of human capabilities or behavior. Scientists today find that reliance on such folk beliefs about human differences in research has led to countless errors.

At the end of the 20th century, we now understand that human cultural behavior is learned, conditioned into infants beginning at birth, and always subject to modification. No human is born with built-in culture or language. Our temperaments, dispositions, and personalities, regardless of genetic propensities, are developed within sets of meanings and values that we call "culture." Studies of infant and early childhood learning and behavior attest to the reality of our cultures in forming who we are.

It is a basic tenet of anthropological knowledge that all normal human beings have the capacity to learn any cultural behavior. The American experiences with immigrants from hundreds of different language and cultural backgrounds who have acquired some version of American culture traits and behavior is the clearest evidence of this fact. Moreover, people of all physical variations have learned different cultural behaviors and continue to do so as modern transportation moves millions of immigrants around the world.

How people have been accepted and treated within the context of a given society or culture has a direct impact on how they perform in that society. The "racial" world view was invented to assign some groups to perpetual low status, while others were permitted access to privilege, power, and wealth. The tragedy in the United States has been that the policies and practices stemming from this world view succeeded all too well in constructing unequal populations among Europeans, native Americans, and peoples of African descent. Given what we know about the capacity of normal humans to achieve and function within any culture, we concluded that present-day inequalities between so-called "racial" groups are not consequences of their biological inheritance but products of historical and contemporary social, economic, educational, and political circumstances.

- American Anthropological Association, Washington, DC, 1998.

The Concept of Positionality

We construct human difference in terms of cultural practices, gender, racial/ethnic identification, social class, citizenship, sexual orientation, and other forms of identification. Our "*positionality*," or location in the social world, is shaped in terms of these multiple identifications. Our positionality configures the angle from which we gain our partial view of the world. For some, that is a position of relative privilege and for others, a position of subordination and oppression. As Bertha Capen Reynolds reminds us, it is the mission of social justice workers to align themselves with those who have experienced the world from positions of oppression and work to challenge the language, practices, and conditions that reproduce and justify inequality and oppression. To do so we must recognize and learn from our own positionality, consider how we see and experience the world from our positioning in it, and open ourselves to learning about the world from the perspectives of those differently positioned. As Reed et al. (1997) contend:

> Although some people suffer a great deal more than others, positionality implies that each and every one of us, in our varied positions and identities as privileged and oppressed, are both implicated in and negatively affected by racism, sexism, heterosexism, homophobia, classism, and other oppressive dynamics. The recognition of positionality, and of one's partial and distorted knowledge, is crucial for individuals of both dominant and subordinate groups, or we all contribute to perpetuating oppression. (p. 59)

Positionality is an unfamiliar word in our vocabulary. We hope you will find it to be a useful concept in thinking about the ways in which our understanding and worldviews are shaped by our various locations in the social world. In the following side bar, Carol Hand, a professor of social work at The University of Wisconsin-Oshkosh, shares a story and assignment that she uses in helping students engage with the concept of positionality.

The Paradox of "Difference" and the Importance of Self–Awareness
By Carol A. Hand

Introduction

As an *Ojibwe* educator and practitioner, I know that the significance of difference is an ever-present challenge. Differences are more than skin deep and have profound consequences for our ability to understand others, and hence to be of service to those who need assistance. Yet to emphasize difference without recognizing the shared humanity that unites us can reify divisions and socially constructed power differentials. Two stories illustrate this paradox.

The *Parable of the Nile* describes the danger of ignoring the significance of difference. Briefly, the story tells of a monkey that was swept into the raging Nile by torrential rains. Just as the monkey reached the end of its endurance, it spied a branch hanging over the water and was able to pull itself from the river and was thus saved from drowning. Wishing to spare another from death, the monkey reached down into the turbulent water to save a fish that was struggling against the current, and lifted the fish into the air. The monkey was baffled by the fish's lack of gratitude. To take this parable to its logical conclusion, we should refrain from any actions that are intended to help others who are different.

An image shared by Joel Goldsmith (1961) provides another way of looking at difference. If one imagines looking at the earth from the moon, one sees distinct land masses, continents and islands that are separated by vast expanses of water. Each is alone and appears distinct. If one looks deep enough, below the surface of the water, one finds that they are in reality connected. From this vantage point or worldview, the monkey's actions make perfect sense. These two perspectives, or "positions," illustrate the paradox of making sense of "difference" in a way that promotes understanding and life-affirming action.

One first step for reconciling these two perspectives is cultivating critical self-awareness. Understanding how one makes sense of the world, how one has been socialized to see oneself and others who are "different," and the values that underlie the meaning of differences, are crucial dimensions to explore on an ongoing basis. In an effort to explore how to promote critical self-reflection for social work graduate students, I designed an exercise to encourage students to begin to develop an understanding of their "positionality" and its effect on relations with clients, peers, and people in positions of authority. The class assignment, named a *positionality montage*, is required for the Human Behavior in the Social Environment Class (HBSE II: Difference, Diversity, and Oppression) during the second semester of the foundation year. The assignment, described below, has had a profound effect on many MSW students.

Positionality Montage Description

An important course objective is to encourage class members to reflect critically on their own "positionality," and how it affects their worldview and values, influences understanding of difference, and shapes interaction with others. This assignment is designed to focus on understanding self in relation to history, meaning, context, and power as a foundation for self-aware professional practice.

So why is the assignment called a montage? According to *Webster's Dictionary*, montage is the "art or process of making a composite picture by bringing together into a single composition a number of different pictures and arranging these ... so that they form a blended whole while remaining distinct" (1984, p. 922). Positionality reflects many dimensions. For the purposes of this class, the dimensions include:

1. race/skin color/ethnicity/nationality/first language,
2. gender,
3. socioeconomic class,
4. age,
5. sexual orientation,
6. religion/spiritual belief system, and
7. ability/disability.

This assignment is designed to encourage critical self-reflection by exploring each of these dimensions, to gain an understanding of what each of these dimensions means personally, how these meanings developed, how your life has been shaped by larger social interpretations of these dimensions singularly or in combination, and how these meanings affect your stance toward difference. Or more clearly stated, the purpose is to answer the questions "Who am I?" and "How does this affect how I relate to others who are different?" These are complex questions, and the answers are ever-changing. In order to make the task more doable, the assignment has four components. The first is a brief description of six categories. The second component is a more in-depth discussion of the remaining dimension. The choice of which category to focus on in more depth should be based on what you feel has been the most important influence on your personal and/or professional development, or that dimension that has been the most "invisible," and thus perhaps the most taken for granted. The third component is to describe or synthesize how these seven dimensions interlock, providing a specific example that illustrates the effect in your work with those in authority, peers, and clients. The final component is a brief description of any new insights and implications for future practice.

You are encouraged to be creative with this assignment. You can interweave photographs, a family tree, documents or stories from ancestors, family celebrations, or rituals based on cultural/ethnic roots, songs, videos, and so forth.

Final Thoughts

Critical self-awareness is an essential foundation for effective social justice work. Before one can "shift center" as Andersen and Collins recommend, one must be aware of one's center. Yet, critical self-awareness is but one of many steps in the complex, life-long process of understanding and embracing diversity. Relating to diversity is a multidimensional endeavor that involves not only seeing one's position at present, but also reflecting on one's experiences within the contexts of personal and world history, power differentials, and socially constructed meanings of difference. It requires understanding one's privileges and oppression. And it requires the courage to make mistakes and to look foolish and the grace to face conflict as one takes the initiative to be a bridge. It is my belief that we can find common ground based on honoring the richness of others' experiences and perspectives.

References:

Andersen, M. L. & Collins, P. H. (2004). *Race, class, and gender: An anthology* (5th ed.)
     Belmont, CA: Thompson Wadsworth.

Goldsmith, J. (1961). *The thunder of silence.* New York: Harper & Row, Publishers.
     Webster's encyclopedic unabridged dictionary of the English language (1984). New
     York: Gramercy Books.

Carol A. Hand, a member of the *Sokaogon* Band of the *Ojibwe* Tribe, is an Associate Professor at The University of Wisconsin-Oshkosh. She developed the exercise at The University of Montana.

Discrimination

A critical understanding of difference requires a clear grasp of *discrimination.* As Van Soest and Garcia (2003) describe:

> Discrimination represents an action intended to have a "differential and/or harmful effect on members" of a group (Pincus, 2000, p. 31). It has been characterized as responses that create distance, separation, exclusion, and devaluation (Lott, 2002). Pincus (2000) suggests that individual and institutional discrimination represent behavioral and policy actions that are intended to have a harmful effect, whereas structural discrimination refers to policies and behaviors that may be neutral in intent yet have negative, harmful consequences on target groups. When discrimination is buttressed by social power it represents racism and oppression. When not backed by social power, biased behaviors represent individual discriminatory actions. (p. 33)

> ### Food for Thought: Four Components of Discrimination
> ### (Link and Phelan, 2001)
>
> 1. Distinguishing between and labeling human differences
> 3. Linking the labeled persons to undesirable characteristics
> 4. Separating "them" (the labeled persons) from "us"
> 5. Culminating in status loss and discrimination that lead to unequal outcomes or life chances.
>
> What are some examples of these components of discrimination from contexts of social work practice? What are some examples of unequal outcomes or life chances? What are some ways to challenge discriminatory practices?

Oppression

Oppression may be defined as the unjust use of power and authority by one group over another. It may entail the denial of access to resources, silencing of voice, or direct physical violence, and it denigrates the humanity of oppressor and oppressed. Van Soest and Garcia (2003, p. 35) argue that there are common elements in all forms of oppression. These include:

◆ Oppression bestows power and advantage on certain people who are regarded as the "norm" against whom others are judged (e.g., white, male, heterosexual).

◆ Oppressions are maintained by ideologies of superiority or inferiority and by threat (and reality) of both individual and institutional forms of violence.

◆ Oppressions are institutionalized in societal norms, laws, policies, and practices.

◆ Oppression works to maintain the invisibility of those oppressed.

As Van Soest and Garcia (2003, p. 32) describe, racism is one form of oppression that is deeply entrenched in the United States. Racism as defined by Bulhan (1985, p.13, cited in Van Soest & Garcia, p. 32) is the "generalization, institutionalization, and assignment of values to real or imaginary differences between people in order to justify a state of privilege, aggression, and/or violence." Racism works through the complex interplay of psychological, sociopolitical, economic, interpersonal, and institutional processes. Van Soest and Garcia argue that a critical awareness of racism is the foundation for learning about experiences of oppression, given the primacy of racism in American life (p. 33).

Five Faces of Oppression

Feminist philosopher Iris Marion Young identifies "five faces of oppression" to distinguish among various ways in which oppression is manifest in people's everyday experience. Where do you see examples of these forms of oppression in your community? What are some ways in which you could interrupt and challenge these forms of oppression?

Exploitation: Steady process of the transfer of the results of the labor of one group to benefit another group. Denial of the social and economic value of one's paid and unpaid labor. Examples include unsafe working conditions, unfair wages, and the failure to recognize the labors of whole sectors of a society, such as women's work as caregivers.

Marginalization: Creation of "second-class citizens" by means of the social, political, and economic exclusion of people from full participation in society, who are often subjected to severe material deprivation as a result.

Powerlessness: Denial of access to resources and of the right to participate in the decisions that affect one's life. Lack of power or authority even in a mediated sense to have a meaningful voice in decisions.

Cultural Imperialism: Imposition of dominant group's meaning system and worldview onto another group such that the other group's meaning systems are rendered invisible and "other," thus marking the other group as different and deviant.

Violence: Systematic violation, both physical and structural, leveled against members of oppressed groups. Unprovoked attacks, threats, reigns of terror, humiliation, often accompanied by a high degree of tolerance or indifference on the part of the dominant society.

Adapted from Iris Marion Young (1990), *Justice and the Politics of Difference.*
Princeton: Princeton University Press.

Domination

Patricia Hill Collins (1990), writing from her positioning as a black feminist woman, argues that we cannot think of difference, oppression, and domination in "additive" terms. Instead, she challenges us to critically examine interlocking systems of oppression, such as those of racism, classism, and sexism, their systematic silencing of "other" voices and ways of knowing the world, and their power in determining and (de)valuing difference. She writes,

> Additive models of oppression are firmly rooted in the either/or dichotomies of Eurocentric, masculinist thought. One must either be Black or white in such thought systems—persons of ambiguous racial and ethnic identity constantly battle with questions such as, "What are you, anyway?" This emphasis on quantification and categorization occurs in conjunction with the belief that either/or categories must be ranked . . . Replacing additive models of op-

pression with interlocking ones creates possibilities for new paradigms. The significance of seeing race, class, and gender as interlocking systems of oppression is that such an approach fosters a paradigmatic shift of thinking inclusively about other oppressions, such as age, sexual orientation, religion, and ethnicity. (p. 224)

Hill Collins asks us to think in terms of *matrices* of domination. She further states,

> In addition to being structured along axes such as race, gender, and social class, the matrix of domination is structured on several levels. People experience and resist oppression on three levels: the level of personal biography; the group or community level of the cultural context created by race, class, and gender; and the systemic level of social institutions. Black feminist thought emphasizes all three levels as sites of domination and as potential sites of resistance. (p. 227)

Hill Collins challenges us to recognize the critical perspectives of those who have experienced the world from positions of oppression and to engage in critical dialogue and action to challenge and change relations of power and domination that reproduce social injustice. Similarly, Van Soest and Garcia (2003, p. 37) note that, given the complexity of our positionalities, we may simultaneously be targets of oppression and bearers of privilege. As social justice workers it is important to be mindful of the ways these forces converge in our own lived experience and be open to learning about the experiences of others. In order to meaningfully engage in social justice work, we must start by both honoring difference and critically examining its production. We need to recognize our own positionalities in the social world and the fact that our worldviews are always partial and open to change. We have to "learn how to learn" about other people, groups, and their experiences (Reed et al, 1997, p. 66). We turn now to an overview of the Just Practice Framework, which will be our guide to that process.

The Social Justice Scrapbook

Each class member brings to class newspaper and magazine articles that illustrate value dilemmas and social justice challenges. Take time as a class each week to review and discuss one another's contributions to the scrapbook. As a class, build a collective archive of social justice over the course of the semester. One member of the class could take on the job of archivist, or the class as a whole might revisit the collection at the end of the term and decide how to organize and present the material gathered. Another option is to take time outside of class to review the scrapbook and reflect on the issues raised. How are concepts and practices of difference, oppression, and domination revealed? What "isms" play out in these accounts? How are they being challenged? What "isms" have you internalized? Where do you find your views and values most challenged? How would you address the challenge?

A
C
T
I
O
N

JUST PRACTICE FRAMEWORK: MEANING, CONTEXT, POWER, HISTORY, AND POSSIBILITY

As we mentioned in the introduction, the Just Practice Framework emerged from our own practice, reflection, and long-term dialogue regarding the meaning of social justice work and the challenges of linking thought and action. The process of integrating social work and social justice to build a coherent understanding of social justice work revolves around five key concepts and their interconnections: *meaning, context, power, history,* and *possibility.* These key concepts are the foundation of the Just Practice Framework. This framework brings together a set of interrelated concepts that help to explain social justice work and guide the development and implementation of Just Practice principles and skills.

Take a minute to consider the following questions: How do we give *meaning* to the experiences and conditions that shape our lives? What are the *contexts* in which those experiences and conditions occur? Who has the *power* to have their interpretations of those experiences and conditions valued as "true?" How might *history* and a historical perspective provide us with additional contextual clues and help us grasp the ways in which struggles over meaning and power have played out and better appreciate the human consequences of those struggles? And how do we claim a sense of *possibility* as an impetus for just practice? We will expand on these key concepts through this book. We begin with a brief introduction of each concept in this chapter to provide a foundation for future reflection.

Meaning

Meaning is often defined as the purpose or significance of something. All human beings are meaning-makers. We make sense of the world and our experiences in it through the personal lenses of culture, race, place, gender, class, and sexual orientation. We come to new experiences with a history that influences our ways of making sense of our circumstances. Sometimes we share meaning with others based on commonalities of social experience and life circumstances. Often, however, we differ from others in how we come to understand ourselves, others, and the events and circumstances surrounding our lives. Think for a moment about the partiality of our knowledge, the difficulty we have in fully understanding another person's experience or what sense this person makes of happenings and circumstances. For this very reason, in social work practice it is essential that we attempt to understand how others make sense of their world and the commonalities, tensions, and contradictions this creates as we compare their meanings with our own. At the same time we need to stay mindful of the partiality of our own understanding. Just Practice means grappling with the ways in which we individually and collectively make sense of our worlds. Meanings can constrain us, keep us stuck, or create new possibilities for ourselves and the people with whom we work.

Searching for meaning requires reflexivity. This is the act of reflection, a process of self-reference and examination. It is a foundational skill upon which to build the knowledge base and skills of just practice. Although it may not appear to be the case, reflection takes practice. It requires going beyond surface content to contemplate meanings, to submerge oneself in thoughtful reverie, to question taken-for-granted assumptions about reality, to consider the significance of situations and circumstances, and to share these thoughts with others through critical dialogue and critical question posing. Critical dialogue "is the encounter between men [sic], mediated by the world, in order to name the world" (Freire, 1974, p. 76). It is a process of engagement with others to develop, recreate, challenge, and affirm meaning. Critical question-posing differs from ordinary question-posing. Critical questioning asks learners to make connections among seemingly disparate issues or events or to discover the underlying themes that resonate or have a pervasive influence for an individual, group, organization, or community.

REFLECTION: Meaning

Take a moment to think about the word "welfare." What images do you associate with the word? Would you describe those images as generally positive or generally negative? How do they compare to the images you associate with "well-being?" Political debates regarding "welfare reform" over the past 25 years have served to vilify both the concept of "welfare" and those who receive certain forms of public support. Poor, single mothers, especially women of color, have been held responsible for a host of social ills. Their status as "welfare recipients" has become a source of condemnation. How has the meaning of "welfare" shifted over time? What would a social welfare policy look like that embraced an understanding of welfare as "a state of health, prosperity, happiness, and well-being?"

Context

Context is the second key concept. Context is the background and set of circumstances and conditions that surround and influence particular events and situations. Social work's legacy, and what distinguishes it from other helping professions, is its fundamental view of individuals, groups, organizations, and communities within a larger framework of interactions. These considerations include cultural beliefs and assumptions about reality and social, political, and economic relationships. Context shapes meaning and helps us make sense of people, events, and circumstances. We know this only too well when we take something (person or life event) out of context and attempt to understand it devoid of its surrounding. If we ignore context, our interpretation of a situation is myopic. We see only that which fits on the slide but nothing beyond the microscope. We miss the intricate connections, patterns, and dynamic relationships. In sum, context shapes what is seen as possible or not possible (Locke, Garrison, & Winship, 1998, p. 14).

We often think of social work practice in terms of interpersonal, organizational, community, and sociopolitical contexts. While for analytic purposes we may focus on one at a time, our practice plays out in these multiple and mutually influencing contexts. Consider for a moment the context of agency-based social work practice. Social workers work in organizations situated in communities and neighborhoods. The characteristics of communities and neighborhoods differ. Some have an abundance of resources and helping networks and others have to make do with little but their own ingenuity. Communities and organizations have distinct cultures that include spoken and unspoken rules and established patterns of commonly shared values and beliefs. Organizations, for example, are generally funded by state, federal, or private sources, each of which mandates funding allocations, types of services, who can be served, and the rules and regulations for receiving services. As we expand our contextual horizons, we discover that state and federal policies are linked to services, and these also are embedded with assumptions about what constitutes a social problem and how it should be addressed. Policies are, in effect, cultural snapshots framed by particular assumptions and philosophies of what is true, right, and good. Think for a moment about how these various contexts influence and shape both the worker and the work.

| *REFLECTION:* | **Rural Context of Practice** |

Imagine yourself in western rural America. You are a child protective service worker working in a two-person agency. The town you practice in has a population of barely 2,000 inhabitants, and the locals are quick to say there are more cattle than people. The nearest metropolis is a full day's drive away. The community has few social service resources and those that exist are staffed much like your own agency, mostly solo operations that are understaffed and overworked. Although policies that govern your work are decided in the legislative chambers hundreds of miles down the road, they shape your daily existence from the supplies you are allocated to the procedures that structure your work. This ranching community takes pride in its rugged individualism. Families survive and thrive by sheer grit and stubborn determination during long winters when the wind-chill factor can reach 60 degrees below zero. Take a few minutes to think about the various ways in which your child protection work might be affected in this situation by context. What comes to mind?

Power

Power is the third key concept. Numerous scholars have investigated its meaning and proposed interpretations ranging from the abstract to the practical. Generally, the idea of power embodies purpose or intent. Dennis Wrong (1995, p. 2) defines power as the "capacity of some persons to produce intended and foreseen effects on others." Some have viewed power from a standpoint of exclusion, domination, and repression. However, Homan (2004, p. 43) argues that, "Power is not to be confused with dominance. Power is based on the ability to provoke a response. Power can be used to dominate, to collaborate, or to educate." Power can be manipulative but it does not have to be. Michel Foucault (1979) describes power as follows:

> What gives power its hold, what makes it accepted, is quite simply the fact that it does not simply weigh like a force that says no, but that it runs through, and it produces things, it induces pleasure, it forms knowledge, it produces discourse; it must be considered as a productive network which runs through the entire social body much more than as a negative instance whose function is repression. (p. 36)

There are many ways to conceptualize power. French sociologist Pierre Bourdieu (1984) writes about the importance of symbolic power. He describes symbolic power as the power to impose the principles of the construction of reality on others. He argues that this is a key aspect of political power. Others have pointed to the power of language and rhetoric, the power of emotion, and the power of collective memory as sources for resistance and motive forces for action on the part of people in less powerful positions (Freire, 1990; Gramsci, 1987, Kelly & Sewell, 1988; Tonn, 1996). Through a workshop they conducted in Tapalehui, Mexico, Janet Townsend and her colleagues learned that poor, rural Mexican women had something to say about power (Townsend, Zapata, Rowlands, Alberti & Mercado, 1999). The women, activists in grassroots organizations, joined academic women to discuss women's power, roads to activism, and possibilities for transformative social practice. Drawing from the women's on-the-ground experience, the authors identified four forms of power: (1) power over, (2) power from within, (3) power with, and (4) power to do. They describe *power over* as institutional and personal forms and practices of oppression that often serve as poor women's first reference point in discussion of empowerment. As women get out of their houses and come together to share their struggles and hopes with other women, they begin to discover the *power from within*. They discover *power with* others as they organize to address the conditions that affect their lives. They articulate the *power to do* in concrete, material terms, such as making money, designing projects, and getting funding. Through close attention to accounts of lived experience, the authors are able to present a nuanced view of the ways in which poor rural women give meaning to and negotiate the relations of power that affect their lives.

Four Forms of Power
(1) power over
(2) power from within
(3) power with
(4) power to do

What meaning does power have for you? Who or what has the power to affect your own or another's behavior? How is power created, produced, and legitimized, and what are the varied ways in which it can be used? How might power influence the nature of the relationships you form in social work practice with those with whom you work and those for whom you work?

Meanings of Power

As a class, take turns bringing in images of what power means to you. The images may be of your own creation, photos or texts from magazines, a collage, and so forth. Describe these images in class, place them in a container with other classmates' contributions, and pass the container on to a classmate. The classmate has the responsibility of carrying the container home, adding his or her own image, and bringing the image and container back to the next class meeting. At the end of the term, as a class, engage in a collective decision-making process regarding what you wish to do with the images. For example, you could design a collage incorporating all of the images and hang it in a public place where it may evoke further dialogue. The exercise creates an opportunity to reflect on both individual and collective representations of power. It demands responsibility on the part of the participants, and it opens discussion regarding many forms of power.

Take a moment to think about how these understandings of power might translate into your work as a social worker. What does power mean to the social worker? Is it about control or being in charge? Does it connote expert knowledge or knowing what is right for others? To what forms and sources of power might you have access as a social worker? What sorts of cautions and challenges does power evoke in practice? Can you think of examples from social work that illustrate Townsend et al.'s notions of power over, power from within, power with, and power to do?

A
C
T
I
O
N

History

History is the fourth key concept. The dictionary defines history as "a chronological record of significant events, as of the life or development of a people or institution, often including an explanation of or commentary on those events" (American Heritage Dictionary, 2000). Jenkins (1995, pp. 20-21) describes history as being composed of individual discrete facts that paint a "picture of the past" made up of the impressions of the historian. History is also defined as a story or a tale, hinting that it might fall somewhat short on truth value. This latter definition gets at the socially constructed, mutually constituted nature of knowledge (Gergen, 1999), which suggests that to understand history, it is important to know the storyteller. Clearly these definitions indicate that history is much more than an objective reporting of the facts.

Howard Zinn (1995, pp. 7-9) illustrates well the inescapable ideological presence of the historian in *A People's History of the United States*. For example, he recounts the European invasion of the Indian settlements in the Americas and the heroizing of Christopher Columbus in the stories of history read by school children. Forgotten in most historical reports is an alternative story of America's discovery, one less inclined to see the genocide of Indian people and their culture as a reasonable price to pay for progress (p. 9). Zinn (1995) suggests that the closest we can come to objectively reporting the past is to consider all the various subjectivities in a situation. These subjectivities include the opinions, beliefs, and perceptions of the historian. Carr (1961) also reminds us of the importance of the historian and the historian's social and historical background when he tells us, ". . . the facts of history never come to us 'pure,' since they do not and cannot exist in a pure form; they are always refracted through the mind of the recorder" (p. 16). Innumerable factors affect perceptions. These include gender, race, class, religion, sexual orientation, and political ideology, to name a few. Whereas the historian may be able to accurately report chronology, that is when a specific event occurred, where it occurred, and the players involved, the event is storied through the layered nuance of the historian's perspective. History, then, is at best a partial perspective.

Paulo Freire (1990, p. 9) adds yet another dimension to the meaning of history and understands it as a critical factor in shaping the work of justice-oriented social workers. He envisions ordinary people as active players in its creation. Freire contends that we are historical beings, meaning that, unlike animals, we are conscious of time and our location in time. History is a human creation and we are continually making history and being shaped by history:

> As I perceive history, it is not something that happens necessarily, but something that will be made, can be made, that one can make or refrain from making. I recognize, therefore, the importance of the role of the subjective in the process of making history or of being made by history. And this, then, gives me a critical optimism that has nothing to do with history marching on without men, without women, that considers history outside. No, history is not this. History is made by us, and as we make it, we are made and remade by it. (Freire, 1974, pp. 3-4)

Freire's understanding of history resonates with that of the members of the Kensington Welfare Rights Union, a Philadelphia-based poor people's organization dedicated to ending poverty and championing economic human rights. They state, "We are readers of history. Especially for leaders and organizers from the ranks of the poor, reading and interpreting history is a matter of survival" (Baptist & Bricker-Jenkins, 2002, p. 197). This idea that we are all makers of history opens up spaces of possibility and hope as people engage with life to create history and be created by history. With these definitions in mind, let us consider why history is important to our work as social workers. The following sidebar offers an opportunity to reflect on why history matters.

REFLECTION :   **Connecting with History**

Take a moment to think about the life experiences that have shaped your decision to become a social worker. Share your story with fellow students in pairs or in small groups. When did you decide to become a social worker? What social, political, economic, familial, or cultural circumstances, situations, or events shaped your decision? What other careers had you considered? What made you change your mind? Or perhaps you are still undecided about your career goal. As you share your story with other classmates, do you discover similar influences that affected your decisions to become social workers? What do you notice about the histories of other students that differ from your own? How might history influence the way in which social work is practiced? Now take a moment to think of an important historical event occurring at the time of your birth, or during your formative years, for example, threat of nuclear war, the fall of the Berlin Wall, the Vietnam War, the "first" Gulf War, President Kennedy's assassination, the Challenger explosion, the passage of *Roe v. Wade*, or the September 11th attack on the World Trade Center. What historical events stand out, and how have they affected your way of perceiving or acting in the world? How might a historical perspective be helpful to your work as a social worker? Take a moment to write down a few reasons and discuss them with others.

Possibility

Possibility is the fifth key concept. This concept asks us to consider what is historically possible and to move beyond the past and the present to contemplate alternatives for the future. A sense of possibility enables us to look at what has been done, what can be done, and what can exist. It engages us in reflection, and helps us formulate a vision of something different. It is a way to get unstuck from deterministic, fatalistic thinking of "that which has been will always be." As historian E. P. Thompson reminds us, it is possible for people to make something of themselves other than what history has made of them (Thompson, 1966).

Possibility challenges us to think differently about practices, people, and programs. It draws attention to human *agency*, or the capacity to act in the world as intentional, meaning-making beings, whose actions are shaped and constrained, but never fully determined by life circumstances. Australian social work educators Anthony Kelly and Sandra Sewell (1988) write about "a trialectic logic," or a logic of possibility, as a key part of community building. They write: "The task of a trialectic logic is to grasp a sense of wholeness which emerges from at least three sets of possible relationships among factors. . . it is out of the context of their interdependent relationships that new insights into social realities can emerge, and hence new ways to solve problems" (pp. 22-23). As we expand our possibilities for thinking, we may change the way a problem is perceived and envision new possibilities for action. Kelly and Sewell exemplify the logic of possibility with the title of their book, *With Head, Heart and Hand*. They write,

> Knowing, feeling and doing describe three human capacities, each one important in itself. No one of these, by itself and without addition of the other two is enough. Even taken in pairs, no two are sufficient without the third:
>
> ◆ **head and hand** (without **heart)** is a familiar combination in public life—the politician or public administrator whose feelings are blocked, or considered irrelevant;
>
> ◆ **heart and hand** (without **head**) leads to impulsive and undisciplined action;
>
> ◆ **head and heart** (without **hand)** leaves us stuck with knowledge and good intentions, but with no action direction to pursue.
>
> To bring all three together, in a piece of work or in a relationship or to an understanding of our context, is to expand a social reality to at least three factors. **Head, heart** and **hand** points to a quality of wholeness—even if an attempt at wholeness—in life and work. (pp. 23-24)

It is this spirit of hope and sense of possibility that we wish to infuse in the thinking and practice of social justice work. Throughout the text we will share the stories of courage and inspiration from people who have confronted contradictions and worked to transform oppressive life circumstances into spaces of hope, places of possibility, and bases for critical and creative action.

REFLECTION :   **Probing the Possibilities**

Take a close look at this figure. How many squares do you see? Now get together with a classmate. Compare numbers and the ways you counted the squares. Working together, can you expand the possibilities and find more squares? What are some other concrete examples of expanding the possibilities once you are able to see things from another perspective?

Putting It All Together

Meaning, context, power, history, and possibility and the ways in which they inter-relate provide a framework for critical analysis (see Figure 2.3). They provoke us to question our assumptions about reality and make us look at how certain assumptions gain currency at certain moments in time. As a foundation for social justice-oriented social work practice these key concepts invite us to question received truths. We use them as a point of departure and a framework for reflection. How are certain ideas accepted as true? How have those ideas changed over time? What evidence is brought to bear to support their truth claims? What goes without saying in our assumptions and actions? How do rather arbitrary ideas about what constitute "correct" social relationships and behaviors, values, and concepts come to be seen as "natural" and "true"?

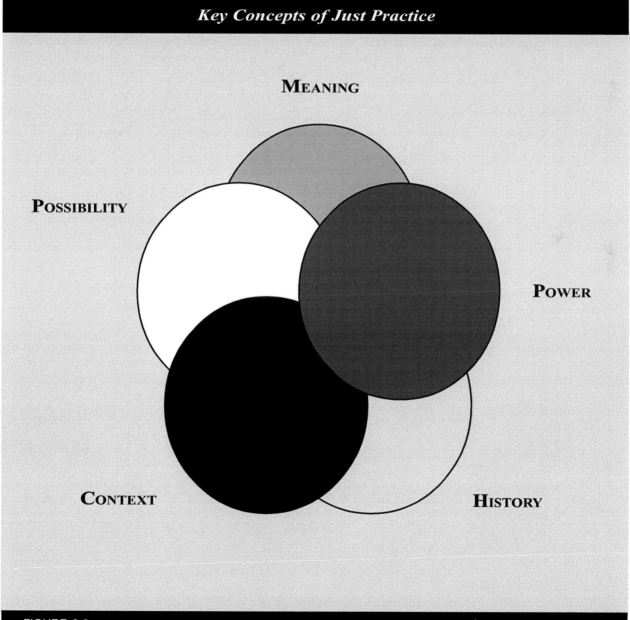

Key Concepts of Just Practice

MEANING

POSSIBILITY

POWER

CONTEXT

HISTORY

FIGURE 2.3

Think for a moment about some of the arbitrary concepts that shape the way we think and act in the world. For example, concepts of time and money, the side of the road on which one drives, or the people one considers to be family. Over time, these arbitrary and variable concepts have become structured, institutionalized, and rule-bound in differing sociocultural contexts. They have become infused with meaning. We have been learning about and absorbing those meanings just like the air we breathe since infancy. We have learned some of these rules so well that they seem natural, given, and absolutely true. They are so much a part of our experience that they go without saying. If we encounter someone who lives by a different set of rules, our response is often to think that her rules are wrong while ours are right. In other words, the deep meanings of these taken-for-granted certainties have become intertwined with our power of judgment and our valuing of good and bad or right and wrong.

Social justice work challenges us to examine the social construction of reality, that is, the ways we use our cultural capacities to give *meaning* to social experience. It guides us to look at the *context* of social problems and question the relations of *power*, domination, and inequality that shape the way knowledge of the world is produced and whose view counts. It forces us to recognize the importance of *history* and a historical perspective to provide a window into how definitions of social problems and the structuring and shaping of institutions and individuals are time-specific and contextually embedded. Finally, social justice work opens up the *possibility* for new ways of looking at and thinking about programs, policies, and practices, and to envision the people with whom we work and ourselves as active participants in social transformation toward a just world.

REFLECTION :   The Five Key Concepts

Take a minute to reflect on something that is very meaningful to you. Perhaps it is a photo or letter that brings to mind a special person or event. Maybe it is a small daily ritual practiced with people you love, such as kissing your children goodnight. Or it might be a family or religious celebration in which you participate or a routine that is practically a part of who you are. Think about the meaning you give to and take from this object or action. How has that meaning been shaped? What are the contexts or the events and circumstances surrounding this object or action? Have these changed over time? Imagine the loss of this meaningful part of your life. Who or what might have the power to take it from you? How might you respond? These are questions about meaning, context, power, history, and possibility. We ask that you hold on to the images from this exercise as one way of staying personally connected to the key concepts of social justice work.

THE CRAZY QUILT OF JUST PRACTICE

University of Montana MSW alumna Annie Kaylor wrote the following reflection essay after reading Chapter 2 and being introduced to the five themes of Just Practice during her first semester in graduate school.

My great-grandmother held a crazy quilt and told a story of my family by pointing to each piece of fabric and explaining where each piece came from. A crazy quilt is created by small sections of scrap fabric and old clothing that are pieced together to create a beautiful quilt. One piece of the quilt was from her mother's apron, parts of a worn baby blanket, and a section of her father's work shirt. Each small piece told a story that became part of a large story of my family. Such are the concepts of meaning, context, power, and history that come together to create unique "quilts" of our lives to explain our story and where we dream of being in the future.

Just Practice describes the five key concepts of social work in separate sections, but after reading and contemplating the text it is apparent that the concepts overlap and work together. The cover of our textbook [1ˢᵗ Edition] shows the key concepts of social work as puzzle pieces that fit together. I propose that the five key concepts are more like pieces in a crazy quilt; a quilt is not as rigid as a puzzle and is freer flowing. A quilt can wrap around a person to show, "This is who I am and where I come from." I think back to our first day of orientation several weeks ago when we all came together for the first time. We each in a sense wore our "quilts" around us to show others our story and how we came to be at the orientation.

The first key concept listed in the text is meaning. The text states that one needs to have self-reflection and examination to search for meaning. I pose an additional need for a person to move outside one's comfort zone and really challenge oneself and face adversity. A person should live in and be exposed to poverty and oppression firsthand in order to be able to fully relate to others in those situations. Actually living the experience will assist an individual to develop critical questions and more feasible solutions to the social problems in our society. In addition, a person experiences immense personal growth when faced with adversity. During my 2 years in the volunteer service, I lived in poverty, faced oppression, and experienced discrimination. These experiences added to my "quilt" and help me to understand the struggles my clients face.

The concept of context helps one to understand the social, political, economic, and cultural aspects of where a person comes from. The text states that policies are cultural snapshots. This statement rings true with Child and Family Services' (CFS) policy that emphasizes prioritizing the placement of children with relatives. This allows the children to be reared in their culture and ensures their family's values and traditions are passed on to the next generation. In a recent experience, CFS policy directed me to go against the recommendations of multiple professionals on a treatment team by placing the children with relatives who were not as skilled as other therapeutic foster family options. The State of Montana recognizes the importance of family preservation and this is apparent in policy at CFS.

The key concept of power has many different definitions and may be interpreted in a positive or negative manner. I have a very broad scope of power in my life. In my position as a case manager at CFS, I have the power to remove children from abusive situations. I also have the power to work with birth parents and empower them to seek change in their lives to be reunited with their children. I chose to use my power in my position to "empower" my clients by using a family-focused and strengths-based approach. In my lifetime, I have witnessed an individual having power over another person in a domestic violence dispute, an individual having power from within to overcome an addiction to alcohol, power with to organize community members to protest violence, and an individual with the power to do what is necessary by completing a treatment plan and being reunited with her children.

The text states that history paints a "picture of the past." In my mind, a person's whole "quilt" speaks of her history. The "quilt" tells of the context from which a person comes, the meaning she has found in life and the power struggles she has faced. We as social workers need to understand a client's history or "quilt." I have worked with many clients who shared with me their life stories of growing up in dysfunctional families or being in foster care themselves. One cannot practice good social work without knowing the possible generations of family problems that have influenced the individual. One needs to look to the root of the problem to be able to successfully work with a client. We must know a client's history to empower the person to make changes and move forward.

The fifth concept of possibility asks us to look beyond the past and present to what the future may hold. Possibility is interconnected with meaning, context, power, and history because one must know where she comes from and who she is to be able to move forward and plan for the future. When we engage clients in working on treatment plans, we are looking at the root of the problems but also to the future by planning for reunification and success of the parents. Possibility is the part of the "quilt" that one may picture in his mind and plan for but is not actually sewn to his "quilt" yet because he has not yet lived the experience.

Meaning, context, power, history, and possibility: Five basic words, yet they mean so much to the profession of social work. In my interpretation, these key concepts come together to form a figurative "quilt" of each person's life. The experiences and life histories of individuals are pieced together in a "quilt" to tell a story. Everyone has a "quilt" to share, and we cannot practice just social work without seeing and understanding another person's "quilt."

CHAPTER SUMMARY

In this chapter we have examined the meanings of social work and social justice and the relationship between them. We have attempted to expand our thinking on the meaning of social work by looking beyond U.S. borders. We have argued that social justice work demands that we take questions of difference, inequality, and oppression seriously. In so doing, we are challenged to probe the ways in which differences are produced and how they map on to values. We have introduced five key concepts that constitute the Just Practice Framework, and we have offered opportunities for both action and reflection. We close this chapter with a powerful essay by John Brown Childs that provides an opportunity to reflect on the themes of meaning, context, power, history, and possibility. In Chapter 3 we turn to questions of history.

**Teaching–Learning Resource:
Reflections on the Themes of Meaning, Context,
Power, History, and Possibility**

The following essay poignantly addresses the themes of meaning, context, power, history, and possibility that are at the heart of social justice work. Take a moment to read and reflect on John Brown Childs' story. What feelings does the story evoke? How does he challenge dominant views of "race" and "difference"? What lessons for social justice work can be learned?[8]

Red Clay, Blue Hills: In Honor of My Ancestors
by John Brown Childs

> In every place visited among the Sakalava we found events and names recalled by tradition still living in memory… we have heard the Sakalava invoke these names in all important activities of their social life and recall with pride these events…
>
> > Charles Guillain (1845), cited in Raymond K. Kent, *Early Kingdoms in Madagascar, 1500-1700*

I must speak about my ancestors. It is from them that I have received the desire to contribute to the best of my ability to what I hope is constructive cooperation leading to justice, equality, and peace in the world. I owe it to them to make these comments. What I say in these pages flows from two great currents, the African and the Native American, whose conflux runs through my family and infuses my spirit today. In the 1990s, when I went to visit my family in Marion, Alabama, my cousin Arthur Childs, who had served as a lieutenant in World War II in Burma, and who was the family storyteller, took me immediately to the cemetery, where in the midst of red clay dust he told me the histories of those who had passed on.

The African-Malayo grandmother of my grandmother of my grandmother of my grandmother, known as The Princess to her captors, was born in Madagascar, an island peopled by populations from the Pacific and Africa. In 1749, the Princess was a member of a Madagascan delegation on board a French ship bound for France, where she apparently was to go to convent school. Their ship was captured by English privateers. All the Madagascans on board were captured and sold into slavery in the English colonies. My ancestress found herself in chains, being sold as property to a Thomas Burke, a leading figure in North Carolina government, to be given as a wedding present for his new wife at a wedding ceremony in Norfolk, Virginia (Bond, 1972, 22). The story handed down within both the Burke family and my relations is that when "the Princess was brought first to the Virginia plantation where she began her career as a slave, the other enslaved Africans acknowledged her royal origin and gave her the respect due to one of her background" (Bond, 1972, 23).

The descendants of the Princess established their families in the red clay country of Marion, where they (as property of whites) had been transferred through the infamous network of the slave trade. Marion, in Perry County, Alabama, has for a long time been a dynamic wellspring in southern African-American life. Marion is where my father's forebears, Stephen Childs and family, created the Childs Bakers and Confectioners, Growers, and Shippers store on Main Street. This store was an economic bulwark of the African American community there. My father, born in the heart of what had been the slave-holding region of the southern United States, was named after John Brown, the revolutionary fighter who gave his life in the battle against slavery.

Marion is where James Childs and nine other African-Americans, newly liberated from slavery after the Civil War, established the first African American school, The Lincoln Normal School, in the late 1860's...

The school's teachers were housed in a building that had been taken away from the Ku Klux Klan, whose aim was to keep people of African descent in subordination and indignity...

Lincoln Normal School went on to become an influential African-American educational institution. Dr. Horace Mann Bond noted the broad community significance of the Perry Country Lincoln Normal School in his study of Black American Scholars, which analyzes the roots of southern African-Americans holding Ph.Ds after the Civil War...

Among my relatives influenced by Lincoln Normal was William Hastie, a civil rights legal advocate and the first African-American federal circuit court of appeals judge, as well as an important participant in President Franklin Delano Roosevelt's "Black Cabinet." In 1943 Hastie resigned a government position as assistant to the U.S. Secretary of War to protest over racial segregation of the African-Americans in the U.S. military.

My Childs family relations, along with other African Americans in Marion, worked in the midst of Ku Klux Klan country, to create Lincoln Normal School as a sustaining community in the midst of a dangerous, often lethal environment of racial oppression. They sought to use their roots in the rural and small-town Deep South as a basis for construction of a bastion of justice and dignity.

I was born in 1942 in the Roxbury ghetto of Boston, Massachusetts. As a small child I lived in a housing project called Bataan Court. My birthplace is only a few miles north of a state recreational park; there, in the Blue Hills is a body of water called by its Native American name *Punkapoag*, which means "the Place of the Fresh Water Pond." Punkapoag is where some of my mother's Native-American ancestors once lived. My relations were members of the Algonkian confederacy known as the Massachusetts—or to be more precise, *Massachuseuck*, which means "The Place of the Big Hills." The Massachusetts nation, like many Native American nations, was an egalitarian confederacy comprising several communities such as the Punkapoag, the Nipmuck, and Neponset, and the Wesaguset.[1]

Closely related neighbors of the Wampanoag ("The People of the Dawn"), who, as with the Nipmuck ("The People of the Fresh Water Place") today are vibrant communities in Massachusetts, these ancestors of mine encountered Europeans under the command of Giovanni de Verrazano in 1524. Verrazano described the Massachusett as a "most beautiful" people who were "sweet and gentle, very like the manner of the ancients." They were, he observed, expert sailors who can "go to sea without any danger" in boats made "with admirable skill" (Brasser, 1978, p. 78). Almost one hundred years later, in 1614, Captain John Smith, while "visiting" the Massachusett, described their land as " the paradice [sic] of all these parts" (Salwen, 1978, p. 170). This paradise was soon decimated by the wave of epidemics that ravaged much of new England as larger ships carrying more Europeans brought diseases such as smallpox, to which native peoples had no immunity…

The Massachusetts people were particularly hard hit this way. Their population plummeted from an estimated thirty thousand to a few hundred by the mid 1650s. By that time, the surviving members of those nations that had been undermined were forcibly concentrated into small villages called "Praying Towns" where they were supposed to adapt to and adopt Christianity. One of these towns was Punkapoag, originally the main home of the Massachusetts, but later turned into a mix of concentration camp/ refugee center…

Many of the Praying Town inhabitants, the so-called Praying Indians, although they provided men to serve in colonial militias (against the French) were attacked, dispersed and killed. For those who survived, and for their descendants, such atrocities clearly drew the final bloody message that their ancient homelands were no longer the richly textured environments of deeply rooted free-life, but had to a large degree become the places of tears. Many Narragansett, Pequod, Mohegan, Massachusett, and other natives were now exiles "in the land of the free" (Lyons, 1992). As a coherent cultural entity, the Punkapoag community of the Massachusett confederacy, with it members forced into exile and finding intermarriage with other peoples the only means of survival, ceased to exist as a social whole.

Responding to the long decades of cultural erosion and terrorism directed against them, a gathering of Christian native peoples, including some of my ancestors, under the leadership of Rev. Samson Occom—a Mohegan man and a Presbyterian minister who had struggled against great odds to attain his "calling"—sought and were generously given land by the Oneida nation in what in now New York State. It was there, in a 1774 ceremony, that they were adopted as "the younger brothers and sisters" of the Oneida.

My Native American ancestors, whose family name had become Burr, intermarried with the Oneida. Eventually, in the early 1800s, they moved back to their ancestral homeland of Massachusetts (see Doughton, 1998). Eli and Saloma Burr, my great, great, great grandfather and grandmother, settled in the western part of Massachusetts near Springfield. Eli and Saloma, and their children Vianna, Fidelia, Alonzo, and Albert, are listed in the 1868 Massachusetts State "Indian" census as Oneida people. Eli's grandfather has been an "Oneida chief" according to these state records. Eli and Saloma's children married African-Americans, including Zebadee Carl Talbott, a sharpshooter and "one of the best pistol shots in the country" according to a *Springfield Republican* report. One of the grandchildren, James Burr, became well known as an African-American inventor.

A 1915 obituary in the Massachusetts *Springfield Republican* newspaper noting the death of one of their grandsons, John Burr, contains information that could have only come from the Burrs, namely, that his ancestors were originally from "Ponkapog," Massachusetts, and that they had been adopted by the Oneida in the 1700s. So, well over 100 years after their ancestors had left New England for the Oneida sanctuary of Brothertown, the Burrs still carried the memories both of their Massachusetts origins and of the importance of their adoptive Oneida homeland.

From these currents of Massachusueck/Brothertown-Oneida and Africa came my mother Dorothy Pettyjohn, who was born in Amherst, Massachusetts. She became a teacher who, as a young woman, went to "Cotton Valley" in Alabama of the 1930s to teach in a school for impoverished rural African-American children not far from Marion and its Lincoln Normal School. It was there that she met and married my father. So, the waves of oppression, crashing over many peoples, driven from their land, forged many of them into complex syntheses of memory and belonging that link African and Native America for me.

In 1835, Alexis de Tocqueville's soon to be famous, vast overview of the young United States, entitled, *Democracy in America*, was published. Among his otherwise astute descriptions based on his travels in "America," Tocqueville inaccurately pictures what he calls "the three races of the United States." These are, he says, "the white or European, the Negro, and the Indian" which he claims are always distinctly separate populations. Concerning "the Negro" and "the Indian" he writes that these "two unhappy races have nothing in common, neither birth, nor features, nor language, nor habits" (1954, p. 343; for an epic depiction of the cross-currents created by oppression in the Americas, see Galeano, 1985).

If this assertion by Tocqueville were true, then I could not exist, given my African and Native American currents that have flowed together for more than two hundred years. My family relations cannot be compartmentalized into these rigid sealed-off categories such as those suggested by Tocqueville. Nor can the depths of their courage be plumbed by his superficial description of the "unhappy races," no matter how terrible their tribulations as they have flowed through so many valleys of oppression. Today I recognize that from Punkapoag in Massachusetts, and Brothertown in New York State, to Lincoln Normal School in Alabama, my relations were among those establishing roots in what they hoped would be sustaining communities that could buffer people against the forces of hatred while offering solid ground for justice and dignity. I know that my connection to my ancestors is not only genealogical, as important as that is. My connection to them is also that of the spirit. I have for many years worked alongside those trying to create places of freedom from injustice. I continue to do so today. I now understand, after years of my own internal development, with guidance from elders and friends, that this work of mine is propelled by those currents flowing from the springing hopes of my ancestors.

I do not feel like one of those "crossing border hybrids," now so much discussed by scholars who examine post-modernity. Nor does the older Latin American term "Zambo" for "half Black/ half Indian," describe how I know myself. It is not in such a divided fashion that I recognize my existence. To the contrary, in the language of my Algonkian ancestors, *Noteshem*—I am a man—who stands at *newishewannock*, "the place between two strong currents." Without these two distinct streams there can be no such "in-between place" to be named as such. But, at the same time, this place is real and complete unto itself. In the same way, I emerge a full man, not a simple bifurcated halfling, from the two strong currents of Africa and native America. It is this *newishewannock* that marks the place of my spirit, and that propels me today.

---

[9] Such confederacies were fluid, and their composition could change over time.

References:

Bond, Horace Mann. *Black American Scholars: A Study of their Origins.* 1972, Detroit, Mich: Balamp.

Brasser, T.J. "Early Indian-European contacts," In *Handbook of North American Indians*, 1978, ed. Bruce Trigger, et al. Washington D.C., Smithsonian Press.

Doughton, Thomas, L. "Unseen Neighbors: Native Americans of Central Massachusetts: A People Who had 'Vanished.'" In *After King Philip's War: Presence and Persistence in Indian New England*, 1998, ed. Colin G. Calloway. Hanover, N.H.: University Presses of New England.

Galeano, Eduardo. *Memory of Fire* (3 volumes), 1985. New York: Pantheon.

Kent, Raymond K. *Early Kingdoms in Madagascar, 1500-1700,* New York: Holt, Rinehart and Winston.

Lyons, Oren. "The American Indian in the Past." In *Exiled in the Land of the Free: Democracy, Indian Nations, and the U.S. Constitution,* 1992, ed. Oren Lyons et al. Santa Fe: Clear Light.

Salwen, Bert. "Indians of Southern New England and Long Island, Early Period." In *Handbook of North American Indians*, 1978, ed. Bruce Trigger et al. Washington, D.C.: Smithsonian Institution.

Tocqueville Alexis de. *Democracy in America.* 1960, New York: Vintage.

Questions for Discussion

1. What insight can be gained from an understanding of social work beyond U.S. borders?

2. What are some social justice issues affecting residents of your community? What understandings of social justice stem from these issues?

3. In what ways have you experienced the valuing and devaluing of difference?

4. What challenges does the Universal Declaration of Human Rights (UDHR) (Appendix A) pose for social work? What are some ways in which you would incorporate UDHR principles into your practice of social justice work?

5. How do you make sense of the key concepts of meaning, context, power, history, and possibility through your reading of John Brown Childs' story of "Red Clay, Blue Hills: In Honor of My Ancestors"?

Suggested Readings

DuBois, W.E.B. (1989). *The souls of black folks.* New York: Bantam.(Originally published in 1903)

Foucault, M. (1980). *Power/knowledge: Selected interviews and other writings, 1972-1980.* (Ed. and Trans. C. Gordon). New York: Pantheon.

Freire, P. (1974). *Pedagogy of the oppressed.* New York: Seabury Press/Continuum.

Giddens, A. (1979). *Central problems in social theory: Action, structure, and contradiction in social analysis.* Berkeley: University of California Press.

Giroux, H. (1981). *Ideology, culture & the process of schooling.* Philadelphia: Temple University Press.

Gramsci, A. (1971). *Selections from the prison notebooks.* New York: International.

Hill Collins, P. (1990). *Black feminist thought: Knowledge, consciousness, and the politics of empowerment.* Boston: Unwin Hyman.

hooks, b. (1994). *Feminist theory from margin to center.* Boston: South End Press.

Horton, M. (with Judith Kohl and Herbert Kohl). (1998). *The long haul: An autobiography.* New York: Teachers College Press.

Mohanty, C. (1991). Under western eyes: Feminist scholarship and colonialist discourses. In C. Mohanty, A. Russo, & L. Torres (Eds.), *Third world women and the politics of feminism* (pp. 51-80). Bloomington, IN: Indiana University Press.

Ortner, S. (1989). *High religion: A cultural and political history of Sherpa Buddhism.* Princeton: Princeton University Press.

Smith, D. (1987). *The everyday world as problematic.* Toronto: University of Toronto Press.

Smith, L. Tuhiwai (1999). *Decolonizing methodologies: Research and indigenous peoples.* London: Zed Books.

Young, I. M. (1990). *Justice and the politics of difference.* Princeton: Princeton University Press.

End Notes

[1] From Ramsey Clark (1988) Social justice and issues of human rights in the international context. In D. S. Sanders & J. Fischer (Eds.), *Visions for the future: Social work and the Pacific Asian perspective* (pp. 3-10). Honolulu: University of Hawaii Press.

[2] TANF is the title of the time-limited public assistance program that replaced Aid to Families with Dependent Children (AFDC) as a result of the 1996 welfare reform in the U.S. TANF is not an entitlement program. The program entails work requirements and places a cap on benefit eligibility.

[3] According to the IFSW website (www.ifsw.org): "This international definition of the social work profession replaces the IFSW definition adopted in 1982. It is understood that social work in the 21st century is dynamic and evolving, and therefore no definition should be regarded as exhaustive." The definition was adopted by the General Meeting of the International Federation of Social Workers, Montreal, Canada, July, 2000.

[4] Key for countries: Canada, Sweden, India, Japan, and Chile.

[5] These points are drawn from U.S. Catholic Bishops (1986). *Economic justice for all: Pastoral letter on Catholic social teaching and the U.S. economy.* The excerpts quoted here correspond to points 69, 70, 71, and 72 in the Pastoral Letter.

[6] For a more thorough discussion of Rawls' concept of distributive justice and its relation to social work see Jerome Carl Wakefield's important articles "Psychotherapy, Distributive Justice, and Social Work," Parts I and II, *Social Service Review*, 62(2/3), 1988.

[7] This table is based on Van Soest and Garcia's discussion in *Diversity Education for Social Justice* (2003, pp. 44-50).

[8] Permission to reprint this essay courtesy of John Brown Childs.

3

Looking Back

We do need to learn history, the kind that does not put its main emphasis on knowing presidents and statutes and Supreme Court decisions, but inspires a new generation to resist the madness of governments trying to carve the world and our minds into their spheres of influence.

Howard Zinn, (1990), *The Use and Abuse of History*[1]

You can't cut off the top of a tree and stick it in the ground somewhere and expect it to grow—you have to know the roots.

Myles Horton (1998), *The Long Haul*[2]

CHAPTER OVERVIEW

In Chapter 3 we examine the practices, actors, institutions, and contexts in the emergence of social work as a profession. We claim a historical perspective for social justice work and illustrate how this perspective helps us become critical actors in our profession. We explore the development of social work alongside industrial capitalism and consider the significant tensions, struggles, and contradictions that shifts in the political economy created for social work. We invite readers to explore the silences, shifts, and omissions in the history of social work practice. We organize our representation of social work's history thematically in order to highlight important dimensions that help us understand social work today. We call attention to the contributions of advocates and activists whose histories have been largely ignored or erased from the social work canon. Our examples highlight people both inside and outside the boundaries of social work whose work reflects social justice-oriented practice. We link social work's history to struggles for human rights, peace, and citizenship, and we explore marginalized or long-forgotten models and strategies of practice.

CLAIMING A HISTORICAL PERSPECTIVE FOR SOCIAL WORK

Why Does History Matter?

Why look back? Why scrutinize our personal or familial history, revisit yesterday's trials and triumphs of the social work profession, or map out the evolution of a social problem and its ever-changing political, economic, and cultural context? What can history teach us about today? And what lessons can it offer to guide us to a just tomorrow? In this section, we present some reasons why a historical perspective is important to justice-oriented social work practice. We invite you to expand on our list.

History Serves as a Warning Device

History compels us to scrutinize the present. Discovering our biases today is easier if we seek to critique the past (Zinn, 1970). When we look back we can more clearly see the whole of a situation and its mitigating factors. Here the old saying, "Hindsight is 20/20" makes perfect sense. For example, "the Great Depression of the 1930s demonstrated that social and economic forces rather than individual fault created poverty, hitting both the wealthy and the poor laboring classes" (Day, 2006, p. 284). Contemporary federal welfare reform policy defines poverty as an individual failing. Since 1996 with the passage of the Personal Responsibility and Work Opportunity Reconciliation Act (PRWORA) and a series of short-term extensions due to acrimonious debates that stalled its reauthorization until 2006, the mantra of welfare reform has been about self-sufficiency and getting mothers into the work force regardless of whether the wages earned will raise a family out of poverty. How did the Great Depression challenge existing definitions of poverty in that moment? What makes definitions of poverty so different in this moment? What factors might contribute to this shift?

History Helps Us Create Linkages

History connects themes across time. For example, taking a historical perspective on women and work teaches us about women's history of inequality. We discover that women in the United States earned one half of what men earned for similar labor at the turn of the 20th century (Van Kleeck, 1917). Learning that women earn 76.5% of what men earn for equal work today (Institute for Women's Policy Research, 2005) teaches us a powerful lesson about the persistent discrimination women have experienced over the past 100 years. Knowing the snail's pace of progress makes it harder to convince ourselves the fight for women's equality has been won.

History Helps Us Understand How Power Works

History provides a window into how definitions of social problems and the structuring and shaping of institutions and individuals are time-specific and contextually embedded. For example, theories explaining the nature of child abuse were nonexistent until the late 1800s. They evolved based on shifting social constructions of children and childhood throughout the last century and increased faith in the power of science and medicine to cure societal ills. History teaches us how those with the power to shape new meanings come to have their definition of a social problem accepted as truth.

History Inspires Us to Act

History reminds us of possibilities for change created by ordinary people at times when it seemed as if all hope was lost. Think for a moment of Rosa Parks, an

African American woman who left a truly inspirational legacy regarding possibilities for social change. She played a significant role in the Civil Rights movement in Montgomery, Alabama, during the 1950s. As a trained activist, she took a monumental step and created possibilities of gaining power and access to ordinary ways of life for herself and other African Americans by taking a seat at the front of the bus, a place reserved at the time only for whites. Howard Zinn (1970) would describe her behavior as acting "as if" she were free: "Acting as if we are free is a way of resolving the paradox of determinism and freedom, of overcoming the tension between past and future" (p. 283). Zinn claims that assuming one is free is far less risky than assuming one is not free. Adherents to this assumption have moved us toward a more just world. Martin Luther King, Jr., and Gandhi are familiar examples of individuals who acted as if they could make a difference. They faced overwhelming odds yet mobilized the possibilities of freedom. Their compassion and conviction inspire us today to have hope and to take action for social change. What examples do you have from your own life of people who acted as if they could make a difference?

Marginalization of History in Social Work

Now that we have made claims for the importance of a historical perspective for social work education and practice, let us take a brief look at why a perspective that makes such critical and intuitive sense seems to carry little weight in social work. Think what this omission means for social work and the implicit ways in which it shapes practices, programs, and policies. Michael Reisch (1988) claims we are an ahistorical culture. He contends we have become accustomed to fragments of information, instead of what he refers to as the "connective tissue," that is, themes that span time and integrate information across decades, centuries, and millennia. Sound bytes (and text bytes too!) are the stock and trade of the mass media. They influence and shape the very ways we think about and process information. Too often we fail to question these bytes of information as morsels. Instead, we accept them as the whole story. Context falls out along with history. Reisch (1993) comments,

> Unfortunately, our current cultural and political institutions perpetuate our ignorance of the past in order to sustain the perception of the present as a "given," and thereby limit the range of societal choices for the future. What makes this tendency so ominous is the absence of institutions of equal authority to critique the prevailing wisdom and present us with viable alternatives. Sadly, this is true for the field of social work as well. (p. 3)

In general, history has been marginalized in social work education. However, there have been periods when the contributions of historical knowledge and method were valued. For example, Robert Fisher (1999) investigated the emergence in the mid-1950s of the Social Welfare History Group (SWHG), an organization that continues today to promote educational and research activities in social welfare history.[3] Early on, this collection of social welfare historians and social workers formed a network to share their interest in teaching social welfare history and to encourage the use of historical research methods. Karl de Schweinitz, a social work scholar and administrator at the University of California, Los Angeles, School of Social Work, spearheaded the formation of the SWHG. He had this to say about social work education and history:

> I wonder how far we are going to get in education for leadership unless we do more, than I suspect is now being done, to give social workers historical perspective. I covet for our students more philosophic sweep and a wider knowledge of past experience as background for developing the ability to plan and to conceive social programs and social legislation. We are behind other professions in the attention we pay to history. (as cited in Fisher, 1999, pp.192-193)[4]

Fisher notes that in social work's history, a push toward understanding the past generally occurs when conservative political forces exert a repressive influence on the profession. A return to history re-ignites the fires of progressive values and practices. At these times, social workers use history as a "shoulder to stand on" (p. 210). Fisher also speculates that the opposite is true: Liberal political forces dampen tendencies to look inward because social conditions are adequate and do not provoke a call to action. Times like these steer social workers toward planning.

In his critique of social work's neglect of history, Reisch (1988) observes how the theoretical perspectives that guide social work practice rarely consider time as an essential factor. These include the person-in-environment and the eco-systems perspectives, two approaches to social work practice we discuss in Chapter 5. What implications do you think this lack of attention to time has on practice? Take a moment to think about the social work texts you have read. Which ones paid attention to history? Of the possible actors and institutions, what history did the text most represent and whose stories did it leave out?

History as a Tool of Inquiry

The importance of a historical perspective for social workers reaches beyond its use as a means of socialization into the profession. Reisch (1988) claims that history is also a method, an essential tool of inquiry that "cultivates the development of a critical perspective—a problem posing approach—a vital antidote to the flood of misinformation which poisons students' minds on a daily basis" (p. 5). At all levels of social work practice, historical inquiry is a useful tool. It guides social workers to the implicit and explicit meanings of individual and family histories; how organizational, community, and worldviews are shaped; and how powerful themes resonate historically and play out through the life course. It helps us compare fact and interpretation and contextually grounds social research, policy analysis, program evaluation, and individual or community assessment. Take a moment to think of a historical event, even one as recent as the events of September 11, 2001, when hijacked U.S. airliners crashed into the World Trade Center in New York City and the Pentagon in Washington, DC. What happened? How did it happen? Who did it involve? What were the consequences of this event? Through what lens were your ideas about the event influenced? Post 9/11, what alternative possibilities could have emerged for addressing the event and its aftermath? How did the U.S. government's response to 9/11 relate to current sociopolitical and economic contexts?

REFLECTION: **The Multilayered Nature of Time**

Carel Germain's (1994b) work on family development provides an example of history as a tool of inquiry. Germain conceptualizes time in historical, social, and individual layers. *Historical time* refers to the effects of historic forces on groups of people born at particular points in time. *Individual time* reflects how people experience these circumstances, expressed through life stories. *Social time* merges the individual with the collective and intertwines development from one generation to the next. Social time supports the notion that parents and children develop simultaneously, thereby affecting one another's growth. These three conceptions of time help us think about human development in terms of synergistic processes instead of linear, cause-and-effect patterns: "Human life is more aptly conceived as a moving spiral, manifesting predictable and unpredictable twists and turns along its track through physical and social environments" (Germain, 1994b, p. 261).

Take a moment to think of your own family. What historic forces and social changes marked your development and those of your peers as children and as adolescents? Likewise, what historic forces and social changes affected your parents' generation? How did certain transitions you experienced affect and promote changes in other family members and in turn, how did the transitions they experienced affect and change you? How might these notions about family and time inform your practice? What other ways can you think of that you could use historical inquiry to inform practice and policy decisions?

A Historical Perspective Informs the Questions We Ask

What would it mean to claim a historical perspective for social work? How might this perspective transform our modes and methods of practice? What questions would a historical perspective compel us to pose regarding practices, problems, and policies, our personal histories, and the histories of our neighborhoods, organizations, and communities? Here is a list of questions that a historical perspective prompts us to ask:

- How has the nature, definition, and context of a particular social problem, people, or situation changed over the course of time?
- What role does power play in the unfolding of this historical event, social problem, theme, or situation?
- What groups of people had the power to define a particular social problem and to have their understandings of reality accepted as true?
- What possibilities do you see for alternative scenarios?
- How does this history shape the meanings you give to notions of race, class, gender, ability, and sexual orientation?
- What lessons do you learn from this history to guide your practice?

What questions might you add to this list to claim a historical perspective for social justice work? How might posing these questions help you be more effective as a social worker? How might it help those you work with?

Applying a Historical Perspective

One way to begin using history as a tool of inquiry is to apply it to a special social problem or concern that interests you. For example, the history of intelligence has shaped areas of social work practice. If we examine the concept of intelligence from a historical perspective we discover that in the early 1900s terms such as "idiot," "imbecile," and "moron" were used as descriptors in the classification scheme for the Stanford-Binet intelligence test (Gould, 1981). A shift in terminology occurred between 1950 and 1970 when the term "mentally retarded" came into use to describe an intelligence "deficiency." Today we note yet another shift: "Developmentally disabled" or "developmentally challenged" have gradually replaced "mentally retarded." Shifts in the languaging of intelligence give us a potent message about the historical context of meaning, language, and power. Now take a moment to consider what these terms imply and how they might influence your practice as a social worker. What do these words mean to you? What actions might you take or what services might you develop or recommend based on your interpretation of these shifts in the languaging of human intelligence? What issues of power play through these practices?

H. H. Goddard, one of the leading pioneers of hereditarianism in the United States, brought the Stanford-Binet intelligence scale to America from France in the early 1920s. Whereas Binet's vision of the intelligence scale was to use it to identify and assist individuals in their intellectual development, Goddard had a radically different vision in mind. By continuing to develop the scale, he "wished to identify [intelligence] in order to recognize limits, segregate, and curtail breeding to prevent further deterioration of an endangered American stock, threatened by immigration from without and by prolific reproduction of its feebleminded within" (as cited in Gould, 1981, p. 159). While Goddard's plan may assault our present-day sensibilities, it formed an ideological base (theory) that guided action. Around the turn of the 20th century, many newly landed immigrants to Ellis Island in New York were tested and denied admission to the United States based on intelligence scores alone. Ironically, test administrators conducted the test in the English language, a language most immigrants did not speak. Test scores also legitimized the adoption of forced sterilization laws in a number of states. In effect, these laws stripped many people of color and individuals of minority status, deemed intellectually deficient, of their right to bear children. The sterilization of over 7,500 women and men occurred in Virginia alone between 1924 and 1972 (Gould, 1981, p. 335).

Similar examples from more recent history suggest a larger pattern of discrimination and oppression of women and minorities. For example, "public health" campaigns were organized to promote sterilization of Native American and Puerto Rican women during the 1960s and 1970s (Garcia, 1982; Karsten-Larson, 1977; Lawrence, 2000)[5]. Sterilization occurred at times against women's will or without informed consent. These campaigns and their consequences graphically demonstrate the ways in which language masks racist agendas and shapes beliefs about human capacity and public policies that target vulnerable groups. Where do you encounter similar examples of racist, sexist, or heterosexist beliefs shaping understandings of difference and public policies toward "other" groups today? How does language play into these differences? What examples might you find in your local newspaper over the course of the next week?

Now look back at the questions listed on page 67. How has the nature, definition, and context of the notion of intelligence changed over the course of time? What role do you think power played in the unfolding of sterilization as a historical event? How does this history shape meanings we give to notions of race, class, gender, ability, and sexual orientation? What lessons do you learn from this historical snapshot to guide your practice today?

A Historical Perspective

It is better for all the world, if instead of waiting to execute degenerative offspring for crime or to let them starve for their imbecility, society can prevent those who are manifestly unfit from continuing their kind. . .Three generations of imbeciles are enough.

Supreme Court Justice Oliver Wendall Holmes, Jr., in *Buck v. Bell.*

SOCIAL WORK IN THE 20TH CENTURY

Introduction

In this section we take another look at social work's history from its emergence around the turn of the 20th century through the present. Our presentation is brief, partial, and focused. We call attention to the factors that influenced how the profession took shape. We respond here to the following questions: Why did social work emerge when it did in U.S. history? What factors influenced its development? Specifically, what has been the ongoing role of the economy in this development? Historically, what has social work's relationship been to social justice-oriented practice? What erasures and omissions does this historical perspective bring to the forefront? What key lessons can history teach us about social work's legacy of justice-oriented practice and people? As you read this section think of the relevance of the key practice concepts of meaning, context, history, power, and possibility and how these bear on our representation of social work's history.

Setting the Stage: A Context of Social Turbulence

To understand social work and its emergence as a profession, it is important to understand its *context*, or the conditions that helped to influence and shape its development. Social work in the United States grew out of social turbulence around the turn of the 20th century as the country entered a period of tremendous change brought on by rapid industrialization, immigration, and urbanization, and power concentrated in the hands of a few (Day, 2006; Ehrenreich, 1985; Reisch & Wenocur, 1986; Wenocur & Reisch, 1989). These scholars of social work history describe the confluence of factors that created a social crisis at the turn of the 20th century:

Industrialization

The 50-year period following the Civil War was one of massive industrialization in the United States. It changed the face of the economy, the nature of work, and how and what we produced, bought, and consumed. Furthermore, it changed the ways in which people lived and how they defined themselves and their relationships to one another. (We elaborate on the issue of capitalism in the following section on Social Work and the Economy.) To understand these changes, imagine the shift from horse-drawn carriages to the automobile—each mode of transportation embedded in its own culture. Using horses for travel necessitates ranching, training, feeding, breeding, carriage building, and teamsters. Now contrast this image with the automobile, and its culture of gas stations, auto repair, metal smelting, assembly-line production of parts, road building, gas and oil exploration, and massive changes in time and space. Think for a moment how these shifts influence the intricacies and intimacies of people's lives—how long it takes to get from here to there, the types of jobs created, and why a Muncie, Indiana, judge referred to the car as a "house of prostitution on wheels" (Allen, 1957, p. 100, as cited in Ehrenreich, 1985, p. 50). How did the automobile change the face of intimate relationships and perhaps increase the number of children born and prompt marriage? Think for a moment of other industrial, technological creations. What comes to mind? How do these define and structure our everyday lives?

Immigration

The United States was literally built on the backs of immigrants. When we needed railroad track laid or coal mined, immigration was encouraged. When foreign-born workers were perceived as taking away the jobs of the native born, or during times of labor glut, the government enacted quotas to limit immigration. Immigration caused social problems as well. Immigrants were poor and they were different. They spoke other languages and practiced different religions. They were viewed as "altogether a threat to 'decent' values and the structure of the American community" (Ehrenreich, 1985, p. 22).

Mass Emigration and Urbanization

In search of employment, large numbers of people emigrated from rural America to urban industrial centers. Whereas just before the Civil War approximately 60% of the labor force worked in agricultural employment, by 1914, almost 70% of the labor force had nonagricultural jobs. Here again, think of how this shift created enormous change in people's lifestyles, their roles as men and women, and their conceptions of work. Factory work was based on a new set of principles, those promoting scientific management, and the belief that increased efficiency leads to increased profits.[6] Routine and regimentation structured the factory workers' day. Work was accomplished in bits and pieces with no one worker connected to the entire process. This was the beginning of modern-day assembly line production.

Concentration of Power in the Hands of a Few

At the turn of the century, the United States had large numbers of people living in wrenching poverty and a growing middle class. Power was concentrated in the hands of monopolistic corporations owned by 1% of the population, the wealthy elite. Money is power in a capitalist society and commands political influence. Graft and corruption were common concerns of the general population. For example, John Ehrenreich (1985, p. 23) points out that prior to the Civil War the United States claimed only a handful of millionaires. However, by the turn of the 20th century, hundreds to thousands of U.S. citizens had sufficient assets to call themselves millionaires. Ehrenreich estimates that at least 20 of these individuals were U.S. senators.

REFLECTION: Documenting Desperate Times

The social work historians we cite above provide a nuanced, retrospective look at the context, events, and circumstances that shaped the early history of social work. Depth and richness is added to their accounts by examining how this period was viewed at the moment by social critics of the times. Below we highlight the works of Jacob Riis, Charles Loring Brace, and Scott Nearing. What images do they evoke of this period in U.S. history?

***

Jacob Riis (1890) was a photographer, police reporter, and author of *How the Other Half Lives*. His work chronicling tenement-house life in New York City at the turn of the 20th century provides a vivid picture of the human fallout of industrialization, immigration, mass emigration, and urbanization, and the concentration of power in the hands of a few. Riis used photographs and anecdotal material to illustrate how the "lower half" lived. He put a face on poverty for middle- and upper-class citizens and gave them indirect, and therefore safe, access to crowded housing conditions, disease, hunger, and the desperation of poor immigrants. Riis' work illustrated how many who came seeking the American dream found instead a political and economic nightmare:

> To-day three-fourths of its [New York City's] people live in the tenements, and the nineteenth-century drift of the population to the cities is sending ever-increasing multitudes to crowd them. The fifteen thousand tenement-houses that were the despair of the sanitarian in the past generation swelled into thirty-seven thousand, and more than twelve hundred thousand persons call them home . . . We know now that there is no way out; that the "system" that was the evil offspring of public neglect and private greed has come to stay, a storm-centre forever of our civilization. Nothing is left but to make the best of a bad bargain. (p. 60)

At the time, Riis' work did much to expose the underbelly of poverty in the tenements of New York. The middle and upper classes took notice. On the other hand, his work also sensationalized poverty and created images of "otherness." He spoke, for example, of poor men, women, and children in language that evokes images of wild and hungry animals. These images mapped out difference and played on the fears of a middle class uncertain of its own social footing and anxious about slipping into poverty's abyss.

***

Charles Loring Brace (1872), author of *The Dangerous Classes of New York and My Twenty Years Work Among Them,* spoke of impending doom as social, economic, and political factors coalesced in a city of one million near the turn of the 20th century. Like Riis, Brace described the poor in animalistic terms and made a case for addressing the problems of the "dangerous classes." In recalling the street riots in 1863, Brace begged his readers not to forget how quickly the "desperate multitude" rose up like "creatures who seemed to have crept from their burrows and dens to join in the plunder of the city. . .who look with envy and greed at the signs of wealth and luxury all around them, while they themselves have nothing but hardship, penury, and unceasing drudgery" (pp. 30-31). As you can see, these contradictory images of the poor illustrate a moment in the growth of industrial capitalism and concomitant poverty. They also illustrate how constructions of difference intermingled with and helped to shape discourses of helping and concern.

***

Scott Nearing (1916), another author of the period, although often omitted from historical accounts, wrote *Poverty and Riches: A Study of the Industrial Régime.* Nearing, an academic fired twice for his outspoken views on child labor, war, and inequitable income distribution, and an early advocate of socialism, was a master at pointing out the contradictions inherent in industrialization. He firmly supported the belief that democratic ideals should be applied to the processes of industrialization, that human needs must win out over corporate greed:

> Within a century the political functions of society have been pushed into the background, and in their places are the industrial forces, easily dominating, in their importance, every other activity of the community. Large scale industry has come to stay. It is an integral part of social life. It must be made a servant of man. . .The Industrial Régime drives a hard pace; it pays indecently low wages; it racks its leaders as it does the subordinates; it continues poverty in the presence of plenty; it permits piled up riches in the hands of a few. The Industrial Régime evidently has not brought "the greatest good to the greatest number." Low wages, over-work, distorted individuality, poverty and riches have no place in a democracy. (p. 231)

Social Work and the Economy

Social Work and Industrial Capitalism

Social work emerged as a means of bringing equilibrium to an industrializing society in crisis. Therefore, to understand social work we must situate ourselves at its emergence within the context of industrial capitalism. Phyllis Day (2006, pp. 29-32) contends that the polity (the exercise of power in a society) and the economy (the production, distribution, and consumption of goods and services) are the most influential social institutions shaping actions, values, and relationships. According to Day, "In the United States, the polity and the economy are so closely tied that it is difficult to see them as separate, for laws and regulations are based on the ideals of capitalism and the free market and much of the economy is politically supported" (p. 32). Others (Harvey, 1989; Wenocur & Reisch, 1989) emphasize the power of the polity and the economy to influence and shape not only who we are, but also what we value. (We expand on this idea in Chapter 4.) Capitalism influences and shapes people's lives, and it is more of a process than a thing. David Harvey (1989) summarizes this perspective:

> [Capitalism] is a process of reproduction of social life through commodity production, in which all of us in the advanced capitalist world are heavily implicated. Its internalizing rules of operation are such as to ensure that it is a dynamic and revolutionary mode of social organization, restlessly and ceaselessly transforming the society within which it is embedded. The process masks and fetishizes, achieves growth through creative destruction, creates new wants and needs, exploits the capacity for human labour and desire, transforms spaces, and speeds up the pace of life. It produces problems of overaccumulation for which there are but a limited number of possible solutions. (p. 343)

Redressing the Failings of Capitalism

One way to view the emergence of social work is as an attempt to redress the failings of capitalism. Given this interpretation, social work easily falls prey to the trap of being construed as the handmaiden of the political economy. That is, social work serves to mitigate the consequences of capitalism and care for its causalities. Yet at the same time, social workers throughout the profession's history have created spaces of resistance to contest the status quo.

Shortly before social work emerged in the United States, the economy had experienced a series of severe depressions. Ehrenreich (1985, pp. 26-27) recounts how a number of observers believed American markets had more goods than they could sell. They felt the only solution was to look to other countries as potential markets for U.S. products. These countries could also be resources for less expensive raw materials needed for production, including an even cheaper labor force (sound familiar?). Only when the working class fought against these conditions by organizing labor unions and striking did the middle and upper classes take notice. Ehrenreich (1985) cites the concerns of Teddy Roosevelt, who, like others at the time, believed the rich had to take some responsibility for the current state of affairs. His words capture a climate ripe for resistance and revolt as he critiques a privileged point of view:

> I do not at all like the social conditions at present. The dull, purblind folly of the very rich men, their greed and arrogance, and the ways in which they have unduly prospered by the help of the ablest lawyers, and too often through the weakness of shortsightedness of the judges. . . ; These facts, and the corruption in business and politics, have tended to produce a very unhealthy condition of excitement and irritation in the popular mind, which shows itself in part in the enormous increase in the socialistic propaganda. (p. 27)

Political Economy and Professionalism

Stanley Wenocur and Michael Reisch (1989) suggest that, in a capitalist system, the political economy helps to shape a profession's goals, structure, ideology, and the dominant forms of practice. Reisch (1998b) poses a cogent argument for "...why social workers in the United States maintained a focus on clients' needs even as their counterparts in other industrializing nations created policies and practices that emphasized clients' rights" (p. 161). According to Reisch, with the advent of industrialization, business or market methods and values penetrated family life, the nature of philanthropy, and social work practice itself. The logic of capitalism transformed family life by fragmenting traditional support systems. It created new kinds of workers, made it necessary for more women to enter the workforce to sustain family incomes, and produced and reproduced consumers for the goods and services needed to fuel the economy. The first order of business in a capitalist economy is to continually sustain growth. In fact, lack of growth signals a crisis of capitalism. Think for a minute about the ways in which capitalism penetrates the very fabric of social life. In what ways do the mentality of markets and the purchasing of goods and services influence social work?

The Emergence of Social Work: Dichotomies in Practice

Contradictions

Life is full of contradictions, and social work and its practice are no exception. Anthony Kelly and Sandra Sewell (1988) contend that binary logic, or a logic of contradiction, is the dominant mode of thinking in the United States. The tendency in binary logic is to divide things into mutually exclusive or dichotomous groups— for example, black or white, or good or bad. In dichotomous thinking, there are no shades of gray (Kelly & Sewell, 1988). Social work practice mirrors the dichotomous ways in which we view the problems of the poor. Historically, society has grouped poor people into dichotomous categories of worthy or unworthy based on criteria that have persisted over the years. Dating back to the 1600s, the Protestant ethic believed in the godly inheritance of wealth, the wisdom of members of the "ruling class," and the inherent deficiencies of the poor, thus sealing their fate at birth. This belief system persists today as a lingering undercurrent that influences and shapes policies and practices (Day, 2003). Yet around the turn of the 20th century, it bumped up against a newly forming conception of the poor as victims of circumstances and specifically, as victims of capitalism. Additional factors produced shifting perceptions of the poor. For example, a new middle class of professional managers emerged, many of whom were educated women who contested traditional gender roles ascribed to women. They sought to translate their newly acquired knowledge for societal betterment into practice and were less inclined to marry and raise a family. They brought to social work the ideals they learned through formal and religious education (Ehrenreich, 1985).

Mediating Containment and Change

As members of the newly forming profession of social work, these young women became the mediators between the forces of change and the ever-present human need for stability. Mimi Abramovitz (1998, p. 512) refers to these forces as the "twin pressures of containment and change." From its inception, the profession of social work developed methods to forge both change and stability. These tensions have persisted throughout the life of the profession.

As mentioned in Chapter 1, the Charity Organization Societies (COS) and the Settlement House Movement (SHM) were the early forerunners of social work. Administrated primarily by middle- and upper-class women, both the COS and the SHM worked toward stabilizing the crisis of capitalism. However, each operated with quite distinct philosophies and methodologies. Figure 3.1 illustrates some points of comparison.

Charity Organization Societies

The Charity Organization Societies were based on principles of scientific charity, which sought to find a balance between giving handouts to those in need and providing assistance in the form of moral uplift. Agencies distinguished between the worthy and the unworthy poor. The primary goal of charity was to "fix" the poor and make them independent, responsible, and self-reliant. These ends were to be achieved through contacts with "friendly visitors." The visitors provided "not alms but a friend." Their activities included teaching the importance of regular mealtimes and educating about proper nutrition. It was believed that through example, visitors would strengthen their clients' moral fiber. Linda Gordon (1988, pp. 61-64) describes how the COS defined pauperism as hereditary poverty "caused by loss of will, work ethic, thrift, responsibility, and honesty." Ehrenreich (1985) uses an anecdote from a short story entitled "My Own People" by Anzia Yeziersha to illustrate the irony of COS goals and the realities of those living in poverty. The story's heroine, Hannah Breineh, cries out:

> [The friendly visitor] learns us how to cook oatmeal. By pictures and lectures she shows us how the poor people should live without meat, without milk, without butter, and without eggs. Always it's on the tip of my tongue to ask her, 'You learned us to do without so much, why can't you yet learn us how to eat without eating?'(p. 39)

The COS workers' scientific approach was based on principles solidified by Mary Richmond (1917) in her text *Social Diagnosis*. The scientific approach to social diagnosis consisted of documenting contacts with clients, collecting volu-

Contrasting Modes of Practice: Charity Organization Societies and the Settlement House Movement		
Characteristics	**Charity Organization Societies**	**Settlement House Movement**
Key figures	Mary Richmond; Edward Devine	Jane Addams; Lillian Wald
Language of helping	Clients	Neighbors
Method of practice	Casework; Friendly visiting	Group work; Education; Advocacy; Social investigation
Philosophy	Scientific; Expert	Participatory democracy
Power in relationship	Hierarchical	Toward equal and shared
Definition of poverty	Result of individual failings	Result of sociopolitical, economic conditions
Focus of change effort	Individual; Familial	Sociopolitical; Economic; Individual
Professionalization	Primary concern	Not a concern —a distraction
Practice theory	Personal deficits	Political economy

FIGURE 3.1

minous client and family histories, categorizing and assessing areas of concern, and providing each family with an individualized approach. Richmond viewed the case file as a way to keep a record of clients' development for the following purposes: to guide future actions, to provide training material for other caseworkers, to document the numerous ways in which problematic social conditions affect people's lives, and to be used as a basis for statistical and other forms of inquiry (Richmond, 1922, pp. 22-28). How do you see case files being used in your agency? What are the similarities to how they were conceptualized by Mary Richmond? What are the differences?

Gordon (1988), however, makes the point that although reform-minded workers identified the environmental factors contributing to poverty, the persistent undercurrent was one of preventing the undeserving from receiving charitable relief. Karen Tice (1998) describes a variety of ways through which the COS tried to disseminate their message regarding the problems inherent in alms giving. For instance, the Russell Sage Foundation funded and published a three-act play in 1915 entitled "A Bundle or a Boost?" Tice states:

> The performance was designed as a visualization of how to give
> advice over material aid, a preferred charity organization society

practice. The case included the villainous "Father Springfield," whose primary task was to hand out bundles of provisions. In contrast, "Mr. Better Way," the charity organization hero, had no bundles to distribute but "more to give," so ultimately the poor would receive "help so that they won't need relief." The play ended with Mr. Better Way surrounded by a cheerful throng of deserving poor who had been referred to the society by a teacher and truant officer. (pp. 34-35)

In summary, the Charity Organization Societies remained true to its class-based origins. Workers adhered to a definition of poverty that viewed individual failings as the root cause. They sought to produce change in the lives of immigrant poor families by "passing on" the values of the middle class. Through the efforts of Mary Richmond, the COS sought to align itself with the newly emerging scientific movement in an effort to gain increased credibility for the profession of social work. Mary Richmond, along with Edward Devine, director of the New York COS, viewed professionalization as a pathway that would promote necessary changes in COS work without having to question social structures and institutions (Reisch & Andrews, 2001). "Professionalism operat[ed] as a brake on radicalism within social work and as an assurance to the business elite that their hegemony would never be seriously challenged by the growing corps of social workers" (Gettleman, 1975, p. 59, as cited in Reisch & Andrews, 2001).

Nonetheless, Mary Richmond made substantial contributions to the emerging profession of social work. She is quoted as saying, "The radicals think I'm a conservative and the conservatives think I'm a radical, and they're both surprised that I somehow manage to keep in the procession" (Richmond, 1930, p. 15). Unlike many women social workers of the time, Mary Richmond had firsthand experience of poverty. Both of her parents died when she was very young and she received no formal education until she reached the age of 11. Shortly after finishing high school, her aunt who had cared for her since her parents died suffered a breakdown. Mary Richmond cared for her aunt until her death.

Mary Richmond knew hardship and it shaped her conceptualization of social work. She understood the need for what she called "mass betterment" or social reform and "individual betterment" or social case work. For her, these were not opposing perspectives on social work. Together they formed a symbiotic relationship: "Social case work provides many of the facts on which the necessary reform is based, and later it makes the adaptations that render possible the enforcement of a law embodying the reform" (p. 588). Mary Richmond understood that with each passing decade, both aspects of social work gained in knowledge base and together, each served to help social work "come into full possession of itself" (p. 584).

Settlement House Movement

Allen Davis (1967), author of *Spearheads for Reform*, a book that chronicles the Settlement House Movement (SHM) in the United States from 1890-1914, traces the "settlement idea" to John Ruskin, British writer, art critic, and social reformer. Ruskin lectured at the Working Man's College in London, England, where ". . .his lectures and his strange and compelling books had a great impact on a generation of young men and women searching for a means of rebelling against the drab and overpowering industrial city" (p. 4). Davis recounts how Ruskin, a professor of fine arts, looked with disdain at the industrial city and sought to address how industrialization and the division of labor essentially separated urban inhabitants from culture and beauty. It was Ruskin who initially suggested a solution—"that a group of college men live in the slums" (p. 4). Through their connections to wealth, these men instituted necessary social reforms including minimum wage laws, a social security system, and public ownership of transportation.

Although Ruskin lacked the social and political influence necessary to carry out his ideas for reform, others took up the gauntlet and paved the way for what Davis refers to as the "settlement impulse" (p. 26). The settlement impulse was initially driven by religious convictions and beliefs. The desire to serve was strong as was the desire to make significant changes in a landscape where humanitarian values were overshadowed by corporate greed and political corruption. In an early study of 339 settlement workers, 88% reported religion as a major influence in their lives (Davis, p. 27). Many early settlement workers came to the settlement movement following theological training.

On U.S. soil, the SHM emerged in reaction to the moralistic paternalism of the COS and was less stingy in its attitude toward the poor. While still steeped in the middle-class values of the Progressive Era, including the belief that the presence of someone of "higher caliber" would enlighten the lives of those in poverty, the SHM carved out a different location for itself among the poor. Settlement workers believed poverty stemmed from a confluence of social, political, and economic conditions. They moved to poor, immigrant neighborhoods, purchased homes, and opened their doors to their neighbors for cultural gatherings, classes, youth activities, club meetings, and other community events. Settlements supported labor unions and conducted social investigations that addressed issues such as child labor, unsafe working conditions, and wage inequality for women. In her descriptions of the settlement house, Jane Addams (1910), founder of Hull House, a Chicago settlement, stated,

> It aims in a measure, to develop whatever of social life its neighborhood may afford, to focus and give form to that life, to bring to bear upon it the results of cultivation and training; but it receives in exchange for the music of isolated voices the volume and strength of the chorus… (p. 125)

The group work tradition in social work emerged from the Settlement House Movement. Small groups were a context for action, a site for learning and practicing democracy, and an expression of the connection between the individual and the social (Schwartz, 1986). For this very reason Catheryne Cooke Gilman of the Northeast Neighborhood Settlement House in Minneapolis suggested that the motto of the settlements should be: "Keep your fingers on the near things and eyes on the far things" (Chambers, 1963, p. 150). This motto expresses the twin emphases of group work, to pay attention simultaneously to individual need and social reform through the themes of shared control, shared power, and shared agenda. These egalitarian notions alone give us ample indication of the principles that guided settlement house practice. Although settlement houses continued throughout social work's history, beginning in the 1920s they gradually moved away from reform efforts and toward the provision of social services.

Settlement Motto

Keep your fingers on the near things and your eyes on the far things.

Catheryne Cooke Gilman

At the height of the Settlement House Movement, there were 413 settlements located in 32 states. Settlement houses weathered many political storms, and today there are still over 300 settlements in 80 U.S. cities. Howard Karger (1987, p.105) discusses the evolution of settlement houses and their practice beginning in the 1920s. Following World War I and the Russian Revolution, dominant middle-class American society became less tolerant of foreign ideas and cultures, and consequently demanded an uncompromising allegiance to Americanism. Practice within the settlement houses reflected this shift in cultural attitudes and beliefs. Influenced by xenophobic and nativistic tendencies, settlement house workers pressured immigrant neighbors to enter the melting pot of Americanization. Many settlements evolved into neighborhood service centers by the 1930s. While funding for settlements shifted from dependence on philanthropic support to competing for governmental grants, they continue to hold sacred their historic mission of treating poor people as citizens, not clients (Husock, 1993).

Yan (2004) argues for social work's reinvestment in the settlement house as a way to countermand the effects of globalization being experienced by communities worldwide. These effects include the widening gap between the rich and the poor, decreased expenditures for social welfare, increased unemployment rates, and loss of job security as increasingly mobile corporations disinvest themselves on U.S. soil and move to countries where wages are cheaper and environmental standards are less rigorous. Yan reminds us that while the Settlement House Movement appeared to lose momentum in North America in the 1960s, developing countries such as India and China and parts of Eastern Europe are using new forms of neighborhood centers modeled after settlement houses. These provide both social services and community development based on citizen participation.

REFLECTION: The Father of All Settlements

Little history is available in introductory social work texts providing more than a cursory glance at the genesis of the Settlement House Movement in the United Kingdom. (Both the COS and the SHM were based on models transplanted to U.S. soil from the UK.) Because context invariably modifies and transforms concepts, structures, and practices, and is acted upon by people and institutions, it is important to trace the original philosophy of the SHM to its English roots. Perhaps we learn about Toynbee Hall and its founder but rarely do we learn of its namesake.

The first settlement house was located in East London and founded by Rev. Samuel Barnett, a young clergyman who was vicar of St. Jude's, a parish in East London. The area was noted for its extreme poverty, lawlessness, and ethnic conflicts (Picht, 1916). It was named Toynbee Hall in memory of Arnold Toynbee, a young economic historian, student, and lecturer well versed on the effects of industrialization on urban settings. Described as "the leader of the younger Oxford generation who were inspired by social ideals" (p. 11), Toynbee was of frail health and died at the age of 31. Despite his short life, he made a lasting impression on those who knew him and those who heard him speak.

Dr. Werner Picht, author of *Toynbee Hall and the Settlement Movement*, portrays Toynbee as a born leader, intelligent, enthusiastic, and a person who possessed "the gift of language in an uncommon degree, so far as it concerned things which lay near his heart" (p. 15). Toynbee was a deeply spiritual man who criticized the contradictions and dogma of popular, organized religions and sought instead to discover "the dim idea of perfect holiness which is found in the mind of man . . ." (p. 20).

Toynbee's earnest and deeply spiritual persona, his humility, and his fervent commitment to addressing the inhumane consequences of industrialization earned him the title of a "modern-day saint" (Picht, 1916, p. 23). Following his death, a commons was created situated in a working-class neighborhood where university men could affiliate with working-class men, learn about their lives, and contribute through public service. Albert Kennedy, a historian of the U.S. Settlement Movement with a 50-year career as a settlement researcher (Barbuto, 1999), described Toynbee Hall's principal aim:

> The chief beneficiaries were to be the rich and the educated. The well-to-do were to pay in cash for their own education, and 'in kind' for the illumination which the workers were expected to provide. The residents came 'to learn as much as to teach, to receive as much as to give.'" (Kennedy, 1953)

Tensions of Social Service and Social Change[7]

A confluence of events created a deepening divide within social work between casework and social change. A number of factors were at play here. In this section, we look at some distinct moments of tension between social service and social change. We highlight the end of the Progressive Era, the Great Depression, the Rank and File Movement, the McCarthy era, the civil unrest of the 1960s, retrenchment of the 1970s and 1980s, and the tearing of the social safety net throughout the 1990s to present.

End of the Progressive Era

Following World War I, many of the advances made by labor during the Progressive Era were retracted. Increasingly under corporate attack, union membership decreased. Industry and labor regulations fell prey to efforts on the part of business and government to meet their own needs for control, power, and wealth. Social achievements rolled back to restore class relations wherein capital had ultimate control (Ehrenreich, 1985, p. 45). This period witnessed the first "red scare," (fear of socialism and communist political ideology) and "twenty-four states passed 'red flag laws'" (Ehrenreich, 1985, p. 47), which made it illegal to use a red flag in public gatherings, parades, or general assemblies. While this may sound unbelievable or even ridiculous today, courts of law across the country jailed over 350 people for this offense. Methods of repression such as this cooled the fires of social reform and activism that had distinguished the Progressive Era.

As a case in point, Reisch and Andrews (2001) chronicle the developments that followed the drafting of a "spider web chart" in 1922 by a librarian staff member of the War Department's Chemical Warfare Service. The chart implicated 15 women's organizations supporting feminist and pacifist causes such as the Young Women's Christian Association (YWCA), the Women's Trade Union League (WRUL), and the Women's International League for Peace and Freedom (WILPF) in subversive activities whose alleged main objective was to further the spread of international communism. Women leaders with connections to the Settlement House Movement were included most often at the center of the web (e.g., Jane Addams, Florence Kelley, and Julia Lathrop). The pamphlet, including its ever-expanding web of antipatriotic individuals and groups, was circulated to powerful organizations with immense political clout (e.g., the American Medical Association [AMA], the Daughters of the American Revolution [DAR], etc.). Ultimately the pamphlet's message slowed the passage of legislative reforms, dampened social activism, and led social work at the end of the 1920s down a path where its sights turned away from "political danger" (p. 41) toward shoring up its fortress through professionalization efforts.

Repression also helped to shape the nature of social work practice. Think for a moment what it might be like if you believed government was responsible for and to, at least in part, its citizenry. Moreover, what if this way of thinking branded you a communist? And furthermore, how is it that "communism" has been defined in the U.S. context as inherently evil? Ehrenreich (1985, p. 48) tells the story of how the American Medical Association favored national health insurance until 1916. With a change of leadership, the Association challenged this idea as one step on the road toward full-blown communism. If the "red scare" was such a powerful restraining influence on the medical profession, how might its force both contain and energize the social work profession?

Numerous scholars and historians have proposed hypotheses regarding the factors leading to what many assume was the decline of progressive thought and action during this period of U.S. history (Ehrenreich, 1985; Reisch & Andrews, 2001). Some attribute it to a post-World War I social depression when crusading for peace had drained the reformers of their zeal for social change, or that progressive initiatives were merely pipe dreams lacking in real world applicability, or that progressivism was dead of its own success (Chamber, 1967). Others point to the hysteria generated as a result of the Russian Revolution, political conservatism, xenophobia, and isolationism. While perhaps presenting a more optimistic account, Clarke Chambers (1967), a social welfare historian and author of *Seedtime of Reform: American Social Service and Social Action-1918-1933,* cautions against generalizing "one prolonged and uninterrupted slump in reform thought and determination, when the processes were more subtle and more complicated than that" (p. 265). Chambers draws attention to the numerous and varied voluntary action associations that may not have triumphed during this time but who nonetheless kept the reform impulse alive. Associations such as the National Consumer's League, the Child Welfare League, the National Federation of Settlements, the American Association of Social Workers, and the Women's Trade Union League pioneered new methods of social action lead by prewar progressives such as Jane Addams, Paul Kellogg, Florence Kelley, and Lillian Wald. With their groundbreaking work and continued efforts, the New Deal took root. Although noted for its gaps and limitations as well as its focus on providing immediate relief for people, the New Deal marshaled in an innovative approach for addressing social and economic ills never achieved before on such a grand scale. Early on it focused on providing relief for millions of U.S. citizens caught in an economic depression that would not cure itself like all others had up to this point (Ehrenreich, 1985). Programs were created that put people back to work (Civilian Conservation Corp), subsidized state-run relief programs (Federal Emergency Relief Administration), and regulated the banking and securities industries (National Recovery Administration, Agricultural Adjustment Administration). It supported the ideal of entitlement instead of eligibility written into welfare reform policies today. Other social workers, however, would ask if it was enough or if it reinforced the status quo in

Social Work History Resource

Clarke Chambers (1967). Seedtime of Reform: American Social Service and Social Action-1918-1933.

the profession while never fully addressing the root causes of poverty and other problems brought on by the Great Depression.

Day (2006) explains how the Great Depression, different from other economic depressions that had preceded it "was based on 'paper money': stocks and bonds for the rich and easy credit for the poor" (p. 285). The working class had little "real money" to keep up with consumption patterns once the plug was pulled on loans as creditors foreclosed in an attempt to keep themselves solvent. The economic structure buckled under the weight of dropping consumer sales, increasing unemployment, declining income, and production cuts. As this cycle continued to repeat itself between 1929 and 1933, the gross national product dropped to almost half of its all-time peak of $103 billion prior to the stock market crash. Unemployment rates escalated to over 8 million jobless by 1932. Out of every 5 people, one person was on relief (Day, 2006, p. 286). People of color were hardest hit by the economic fallout. For example, 30% of African Americans were receiving some form of assistance by 1935. Near social revolt conditions consisting of demonstrations, strikes, and riots broke loose across the country precipitating federal government response in the form of New Deal legislation.

Rank and File Movement

Many in the social work profession did not escape the economic turmoil of the Great Depression. In an effort to counteract its effects, a group of relief agency employees formed the Social Work Discussion Group of New York. This marked the beginning of the Rank and File Movement. Mostly from outside the social work profession or bachelors-level social workers excluded from joining the American Association of Social Workers (ASSW), they pooled their resources to confront poor working conditions within their agencies such as low wages and lack of job security. As mentioned in Chapter 1, the ASSW, founded in 1921, was the first professional social work organization. From its inception, it allowed membership only to those workers who had an advanced degree (Fisher, 1990).

Rank and Filers were acutely sensitive to the plight of the poor because they shared many of the same concerns. Garnering mutual support from others in the same boat and raising their consciousness about economic and political concerns empowered this group to speak out against oppressive work environments and the social work profession itself. They believed many social workers were content to "adjust" to the economic and social crisis brought on by the Depression instead of taking action (Fisher, 1990).

Bertha Capen Reynolds (1992) was a member of the Rank and File Movement and an educator in the social work program at Smith College. In the 1930s she wrote about the Great Depression and how quickly sentiment toward the poor had changed: "The unemployed now included so many formerly successful citizens that it was useless to pretend that individual fault was responsible for their plight" (p. 73). According to Reynolds, in the early years of the Depression people were asked to donate money to relieve the suffering of the poor; in later years, she noted, the tune changed and played off people's fear: "Give to protect your homes from the public enemies of poverty, disease, and crime! The old note of exclusion of the poor became more menacing: Give, not to protect the poor, but to protect yourselves against them!" (p. 74) With more middle-class wage earners losing their footing on the slippery slope of lingering economic disaster, and taxation reaching staggering costs for public relief, compassion-based giving turned quickly to fear-based giving. Through control of the media, the wealthy recast those in need of relief as cheats and chiselers, thereby effectively driving a wedge between the middle class and the poor.

Contrary to most social workers' beliefs of the United States as a functioning democracy, Reynolds saw the political economic system in the country as an oligarchy of wealth. Individuals with money had the power to influence government, and in fact, she believed individuals with power to influence *were* the government. Reynolds called the poor "victims of economic disaster," a view that reframed beliefs about the causes of poverty from individual failings to structural deficits. In a telling quote, Reynolds speculated on what hindsight might reveal about the "true" nature of this period in U.S. history: "Was the meager provision for relief to be seen, in the long perspective of history, as just enough to keep alive without giving life—in reality as a preventive of really fundamental solutions?" (p. 77) Reynolds and others, such as Mary van Kleeck (whom you will read about at the end of this chapter), believed government-supported relief programs such as the New Deal were a way to appease the masses so the fundamental logic of the capitalist system could go undisrupted.

Reynolds and other members of the Rank and File Movement formed discussion groups, and within 2 years these spread to other large cities in the United States. Rank and Filers disseminated critical knowledge on the labor movement, social welfare policy, social conditions, and world affairs by publishing their own journal, *Social Work Today* (Ehrenreich, 1985). Rank and File numbers grew to exceed the membership of AASW by 1935. More traditional social workers criticized Rank and Filers for being too involved with their clients, lacking professionalism, and being guided more by economic theories than those of personal maladjustment. On the other hand, Rank and Filers criticized mainstream social work for focusing more on professionalization to gain status and prestige than on attention to the concerns of the poor.

Professionalization

By the end of the 1930s, even though Fisher (1990) predicted the Rank and File Movement was "here to stay," it dissolved, and its members reentered the mainstream of social work (Ehrenreich, 1985, p. 120). Many attribute the decline in the Rank and File Movement and the Settlement House Movement to the increased professionalization of social work beginning in the 1930s. Husock (1993) addresses how " the settlement style, with its use of volunteers and emphasis on group activities and recreation, would pale in contrast to a paid, credentialed, apparently scientific helping profession [casework]" (p. 19). Settlements began to lose their community focus and eventually, those that survived were a hybrid, simultaneously offering programs to combat problems, and clubs and group meetings to bring together neighbors with common interests. Professionalization was a double-edged sword for social work. On the one hand, it provided social work with status, a sense of expertise, and professional privilege. On the other hand, many believed social work had sold out to the status quo.

Reisch and Wenocur (1986) define what it means to be a profession and in so doing, explore the power base a group must build and maintain to make such a claim. They believe the compulsion to professionalize rose out of the Industrial Revolution and mirrors the colonizing activities of corporations as they capture new territory and set up the necessary structures, policies, and mandates to ensure their survival. Although Rank and File workers preferred to unionize, social work's predominant middle- and upper-class membership aligned more with the ideology of establishing a privileged position for itself. Before the 1920s, social activism and reform work made up approximately one half of social workers activities. Workers were involved in such diverse areas of practice as child labor reform, women's suffrage, civil rights, peace, social insurance, industrial safety, and labor organizing. By the 1930s, funding streams and dominant discourses on the definitions of social problems supported casework as the preferred method of social work practice. These alterations in social, economic, and political conditions compromised the reformist momentum in social work.

McCarthyism

During the 1940s and early 1950s, the United States was overwhelmed with fear about the potential threat of communism spreading from Eastern Europe and China. Capitalizing on these fears, a young Republican senator from Wisconsin named Joseph McCarthy proclaimed, according to Ehrenreich (1985),

> I have in my hands a list of 205 [government employees] that were made known to the Secretary of State as being members of the Communist Party and who nevertheless are still working and shaping policy in the State Department" (a list he never revealed); and Congress passed the Internal Security Act, which authorized the president to declare an "internal security emergency," permitting the detention without trial of suspected dissidents and setting up a system of detention centers to hold those so detained. (pp. 140-141)

Janice Andrews and Michael Reisch (1997) describe this era as the most oppressive political climate in the United States: "Thousands of workers lost their jobs and millions of others curtailed their political activities out of fear of being labeled a communist or a communist sympathizer" (p. 31). McCarthyism, as it came to be called, had a tremendous effect on narrowing the social action stream of social work. Andrews and Reisch point out how U.S. policy makers, backed by the concerns of big business, do not tolerate beliefs that challenge property rights and free enterprise. They emphasize how McCarthyism was not a grassroots movement but rather "artificially stimulated at the national and local level by competing political elites, and fanned in turn by mass media motivated both by panic and opportunism" (Coute, 1973, p. 320, as cited in Andrews & Reisch, 1997, p. 31).

Andrews and Reisch (1997, pp. 32-33) discuss a book published in the mid-1940s by the Department of the Army entitled *How to Spot a Communist*. It warns that a communist is someone critical of the FBI, the American Legion, and the Daughters of the American Revolution. The book outlines a list of words commonly used by communists and sympathizers such as "progressive," "colonialism," "exploitation," "civil rights," "discrimination," and "unions," to name a few. Many federal- and state-funded institutions and programs required their employees to sign a loyalty oath. Liberals fearful of losing their jobs often went to great extremes to prove their loyalty by introducing legislation that would further curtail the activities of the Communist Party or by informing on co-workers who were involved in organizations that addressed issues such as peace or labor rights.

After passage of the New Deal legislation in the 1930s and through the period shortly following World War II, the welfare state expanded from the pressures caused by economic conditions and global war. Reisch (1998b) contends that the improved economy and prosperity after WWII influenced the nature and development of social work practice for the remainder of the century. The end of WWII signaled the escalating influence of multinational corporations, the spread of consumerism, increased government intervention in the economy, the expansion of the military industrial complex, the postindustrial era, and the shift toward an information-based and service-based economy. These conditions, combined with the repressive politics of McCarthyism, put a major damper on social workers' social activism.

REFLECTION: Blacklisting Social Workers

Many social workers were fearful of taking a stand on controversial issues during the McCarthy era (Andrews & Reisch, 1997; Reisch & Andrews, 2001; Schreiber, 1995). Social activists in the 1930s and 1940s were reluctant to continue their activities openly. At a professional meeting, Bertha Capen Reynolds argued that McCarthyism could be defeated "if plain folks like ourselves" would just demand democracy of the people, by the people, for the people (as cited in Andrews & Reisch, 1997, p. 36). Increasingly marginalized, to the point where she was "let go" from her position at Smith College, Reynolds gradually receded from social work's mainstream. It is interesting to note that although she made incredible contributions to social work practice through the bridging of social action and individual change, social work texts make little or no reference to her enormous achievements in mapping out an early model of integrated social work practice.

Jacob Fisher, a colleague of Reynolds in the Rank and File movement of the 1930s, also found himself abandoned by co-workers and colleagues. In 1954, his employers at the Social Security Administration charged him with being a security risk based on his group affiliations and activities:

> While some social workers publicly supported him most did not. Unable to find social work employment and alienated from his former colleagues, Fisher left the field of social work. Years later, through the Freedom of Information Act, he learned that some of his social work friends and colleagues had informed on him. (Andrews & Reisch, 1997, p. 36)

The McCarthy senate committee investigated Verne Weed, another Marxist member of the Rank and File Movement and a lifelong activist. Many social workers attacked her for her involvement in the peace movement (Andrews & Reisch, 1997). What positions or stances might a social worker in the United States take today that would result in blacklisting? What about resistance to war at a time when peace activism is defined as unpatriotic? What might be the limits of a social worker's freedom of expression in another political context? Think for a moment beyond U.S. borders to the practice of social work elsewhere. How might the rise to power of a dictator and the involvement of social workers in peoples' resistance efforts affect the practice of social work? How do situations such as these provide cause to rethink our notions of the social work profession and its location in a political context?

The 1960s and 1970s

Abramovitz (1998) reminds us that efforts to forge equality, social justice, and an enduring peace have persisted throughout social work's history, albeit influenced and shaped by the political, social, and economic mood of the times. Wars and their aftermath of economic revitalization have caused a waxing and waning of these struggles, as many social workers "settled in" and focused inward on establishing credibility for themselves and the profession. Abramovitz states,

> It took the massive disorders of the 1960s, however, to rekindle the profession's social action spirit fully. Finding social work far behind the social-change curve, critics from within and outside the field accused it of having its head in the sand. (p. 517)

This period bore similarities to the Rank and File Movement of the 1930s. According to Abramovitz, social work students carried the banner of social change during this era:

> Students charged that organizational maintenance interests over-rode addressing clients' needs in agencies. They also lambasted rigid welfare bureaucracies, condemned school curricula as parochial and outdated, reproached social work's view of social problems as rooted in individual development or family dynamics, and protested social work's lack of response to the black revolution. (p. 517)

In the 1970s, posing challenges to social work's intensified move toward professionalization, some social workers joined labor unions and formed groups composed of individuals historically excluded from social work's prestigious professional organizations. They founded organizations of their own such as the Association of Black Social Workers, the Association of Women and Social Work, the Bertha Capen Reynolds Society, and the Radical Alliance of Social Service Workers (Abramovitz, 1998). Even social work's more staid organizations (the National Association of Social Workers and the Council on Social Work Education), called attention to the need for social policy change and mandated curriculum changes in social work education to address questions of peace and social justice.

Furthermore, the combined efforts of social movements promoting gender and racial equality, social justice, and human rights supported what Ehrenreich (1985) refers to as "an expansion of the New Deal pattern" (p. 209) nurtured, in part, by the presidencies of John F. Kennedy and Lyndon B. Johnson. Their approach included legislation prohibiting discrimination based on gender and race; expanding social services, especially directed toward addressing issues of poverty, social exclusion, and urban decay; creating economic stimulation and employment training programs; and at the very least, recognizing the importance of citizen participation in service programs and policy development. The inability of social movements to maintain their momentum became evident during the early 1970s, and without this push from the masses, social work's activist impulse faltered. Ehrenreich points out "that no real social reforms, no major advances in social policy have occurred in twentieth-century America in the absence of pressure from massive social movements of the poor and dispossessed" (p. 212).

Survival of the Profession

By the 1980s, with the retrenchment of federal support for social welfare under the Reagan administration, the growing antiwelfare movement, and the massive privatization of social services, social work turned inward in an attempt to ensure the profession's survival. As the very fabric of the social safety net seemed to tear, the profession became increasingly preoccupied with professional licensure and credentialing for private practice (Reisch & Wenocur, 1986; Specht & Courtney, 1994). Graduate school enrollments expanded as the job market contracted. Many social workers were carving a niche for themselves in the clinical practice market and valuing the knowledge, skills, and professional accreditation that would secure their positions. Social work experienced a crisis of identity: There appeared to be no single organizing basis for unity (Ehrenreich, 1985). Common questions raised in the professional literature during this period included, What is social work? Is it art? Or is it science? Are there any commonalities across what seem to be distinct fields of practice such as child welfare, school or hospital social work, social administration or clinical practice? Do social workers really share a common knowledge base, skills, and values?

Eliminating the Social Safety Net

By the 1990s, "ending welfare as we know it" became the mantra of U.S. social policy regarding the poor. The social safety net continued to be compromised with cuts in federal spending and the "devolution" of social costs to state and local governments and private charities (Schnieider & Netting, 1999; Vidika-Sherman & Viggiani, 1996). Organized labor suffered tremendous losses. "Managed care" became a household word as individuals were forced to bear ever-increasing burdens of the costs of health care. As welfare "reform" legislation moved toward passage, some social workers joined with welfare rights groups to challenge punitive social policy. Some worked within social work organizations to focus attention on the value of social justice.

Some describe social work's response to the impending crisis in social welfare as "too little, too late." Throughout the 1990s increasing numbers of social workers left or never entered public agency work for the lure of private clinical practice and its promise of increased prestige and much higher earnings (Karger, 2004). According to Alice O'Connor (2001), up until the last minute, even some of President Clinton's top poverty advisors assumed he would continue to veto the Personal Responsibility and Work Opportunity Reconciliation Act of 1996. As O'Connor describes, the Act effectively tore a gigantic hole in the social safety net constructed in 1935 by the New Deal which *guaranteed* assistance to families with children: "Demonizing welfare as the root of all evil, House Republicans proposed unprecedented spending cuts and behavioral restrictions, including the strict time limits and federal devolution that eventually made it into law" (p. 286). The (re)languaging of welfare reform harkened back to colonial days when sharp distinctions were made between the "worthy" and the "unworthy" poor. However, in the mid-1990s the poor were stereotyped through gender-biased, racist images as poor, black women living off the dole and rewarded by the welfare system for reproducing more children who would, as portrayed in the media, grow up to live out their legacy as dependents of the state (Abramovitz, 1996, 2000; Albelda &

Withorn, 2002).

With the passage of welfare reform, "the 104th Congress and President Clinton absolved society of its burden of poor, homeless, hungry people" (Day, 2003, p. 413). Monies allocated to the states through federal block grants to address burgeoning issues related to poverty received massive cuts. These included slashing the already straining budgets of programs that had a proven track record of success such as WIC (Special Supplemental Nutrition Program for Women, Infants and Children) and Head Start, which lost $137 million and subsequently served 48,000 fewer children and their families in 1996 (Day, 2003).

Late 20th century social work has been described by those less optimistic about its future as a modern day dinosaur soon to be extinct (Kreuger, 1997). With the increasing disinvestment in human concerns, massive corporate influence on political and legislative processes furthering the interests of the wealthy few, social work has cause to be pessimistic about the future of the profession. (We address 21st century concerns in Chapter 10.) Yet historian Howard Zinn would caution social workers to "act as if" and to draw on history to shine a light on possibilities for the future:

> I can understand pessimism, but I don't believe in it. It's not simply a matter of faith, but of historical evidence. Not overwhelming evidence, just enough to give hope, because for hope we don't need certainty, only possibility. Which (despite all those confident statements that "history shows…" and "history proves…") is all history can offer us. (Zinn, 1997, p. 656)

SOCIAL WORK'S STRUGGLES FOR HUMAN RIGHTS, PEACE, AND CITIZENSHIP

The Howard Zinn quotation above is a reminder of the importance of holding on to possibility as a way to push against pessimism. It also highlights an element of a historical perspective we point out early in this chapter when we discuss how history inspires us to act. We conclude our narrative on social work's history by presenting a brief snapshot of social work's struggles for human rights, peace, and citizenship. We point to the accomplishments of Jane Addams, Mary Church Terrell, Ida B. Wells-Barnett, Addie Hunton, and Jeannette Rankin at a time in our history before women had the right to vote. We marvel at the tenacity of these bold women who held firm to their convictions and stayed in the struggle for a better world.

Jane Addams' Legacy

Congruent with their espoused practice theory, early into the "Great War" (World War I), Hull House residents took an unpopular stand for peace. Given their location in a neighborhood composed of European immigrants, they understood the ravages of war as these played out locally in the lives of their neighbors. During the fall of 1914, two women, one from England and one from Hungary, visited

In speaking of the futility of war, Jane Addams (1922) explained,

It took the human race thousands of years to rid itself of human sacrifice; during many centuries it relapsed again and again in periods of national despair. So have we fallen back to warfare, and perhaps will fall back again and again, until in self-pity, in self-defense, in self-assertion of the right of life, not as hitherto a few, but the whole people of the world, will brook this thing no longer. (p. 121)

Hull House to appeal to U.S. women to lead an international campaign for peace. The Women's Peace Party was formed as a result of the Women's Peace Congress held in New York City in January 1915 and attended by over 3,000 women. Jane Addams was elected as its leader. The resolutions adopted at the Congress were novel at the time or at any time since: "The convention called for the limitation of armaments and the nationalization of their manufacture, organized opposition to militarism in the United States, education of youths in the ideals of peace, and removal of the economic causes of war" (Sullivan, 1993; p. 515). As the Chairperson of the Women's Peace Party, Addams argued against war for its cruelty and inhumanity and because it reversed the function of human relationships, something she saw as the essence of human need (Lee, 1992).

In April, 1916, the International Women's Peace Congress was organized in The Hague, Netherlands. Twelve countries were represented and three Hull House residents besides Jane Addams attended as members of the U.S. delegation: Grace Abbott, Alice Hamilton, and Sophonisba Breckinridge. According to recommendations made by the Congress, Jane Addams, Alice Hamilton, and a number of other delegates visited the capital cities of eight countries that supported the war and two countries that had remained neutral. This contingent of bold women met with and urged leaders of civic government, "that a conference of neutral powers be called for the purpose of beginning negotiations upon which peace terms might be formed" (Hull House Residents, 1916, p. 64).

After returning to the United States from The Hague, Addams and other peace activists felt the harsh sting of the pro-war media as it attacked pacifists relentlessly for expressing their views. In *Peace and Bread*, Addams (1922, p. 133) discloses some regret about taking what she felt was a "conspicuously clear," uncharacteristically left-leaning position regarding war. However, upon reflection she was grateful for having voiced her opinion prior to the time "when any spoken or written word in the interests of Peace was forbidden" (p. 134). Once the United States entered the war, newspapers and journals across the country waged their own war against pacifism. Bearing strong similarities toward sentiments expressed in the media more recently when the United States declared war on Iraq in 2003, the patriotism of those opposed came under question. Another striking similarity deserves mention. Addams believed that those who sought peace were prevented from knowing the allies they had across the United States and therefore the strengths they had in numbers because of media censorship. Similar claims were made by peace activists in our more recent history who protested against the war in Iraq and felt the number of protestors was grossly underreported by the media. Despite all organized efforts launched by Addams and other pacifists, the United States entered the war in May 1917. Shortly thereafter, Congress passed major legislation "which made it criminal to criticize the government, the war effort, or the draft, and also closed the U.S. mail to antiwar propaganda" (Sullivan, 1993, p. 519).

Following the war, the Women's Peace Party regrouped and became the Women's International League for Peace and Freedom (WILPF). Efforts to expand the base of power included forming coalitions with other women's organizations such as the League of Women, the Women's Joint Congressional Committee, and the Daughters of the American Revolution (Sullivan, 1993). Many women peace activists suffered the fallout from their attempts to gain a peaceful solution to war. Jane Addams, who had previously been hailed as a "living saint" for her work at Hull House, was now labeled one of the most "dangerous" women alive. Others lost their jobs. For example, Emily Greene Balch was terminated from her professorship at Wellesley College after 20 years of employment (Sullivan, 1993). After considerable struggle over her role in peace efforts, Addams concluded:

> That ability to hold out against mass suggestion, to honestly differ from the conviction and enthusiasms of one's best friends did in moments of crisis come to depend upon the categorical belief that a man's [sic] primary allegiance is to his vision of the truth and that he is under obligation to affirm it. (Addams, 1922, p. 151)

African American Women for Peace, Justice, and Racial Equality

Until recently, little information about struggles for peace, justice, and equality of early African American women activists and social reformers has been highlighted in the social work literature. Yet the histories of African American and white social workers and social welfare professionals are intertwined in their struggles to achieve sociopolitical and economic change. Drawing on the works of Susan Chandler, Wilma Peebles-Wilkins, Aracelis Francis, and Michelle Rief, we provide a snapshot of the significant contributions made by African American activists—Mary Church Terrell, Ida B. Wells-Barnett, and Addie Hunton—and their struggles for human rights, racial equality, and international peace. We resurrect their histories from marginalized status in social work and social welfare and emphasize the important contributions they made at a time when Black women bore the brunt of "double discrimination," attributable to their womanhood and the color of their skin (Chandler, 2005; Peebles-Wilkins & Francis, 1990).

Mary Church Terrell promoted gender and race equality in her unfailing advocacy attempts to gain women's vote and to promote racial integration. Born to the first African American millionaire, Terrell learned at a young age that race trumped wealth. Her history of activism was shaped by being witness to and the object of racial discrimination throughout her childhood and adolescence. She graduated from Oberlin College in 1884, one of the first African American women to attain a college degree. She quickly gained recognition as a writer and as an outspoken critic concerning the treatment of African Americans in the United States and people of color worldwide. Journalism and public speaking were the tools she used to create social change (Broussard, 2002).

Mary Church Terrell and Addie Hunton were among the first African American women to join the Women's International League for Peace and Freedom (WILPF). Jane Addams invited African American women to join the new peace organizations when none were in attendance during the first meeting of the Women's Peace Party. Terrell quickly took on a leadership role and became one of the earliest executive committee members of the WILPF (Rief, 2004). Following the end of World War I, Terrell attended the second international women's peace conference in Zurich, Switzerland, in May 1919. While 30 delegates from the United States were appointed to attend, the U.S. State Department granted passports to only 15. Ida B. Wells-Barnett's request for a passport was denied. Terrell was the only woman of color at the conference and as a result, she felt the burden of responsibility not only to speak to the concerns of African American people but people of color worldwide. For her and other African American antiwar activists, race relations were at the heart and soul of the actions necessary to secure an enduring peace:

> She informed the international delegates that African American men fought in the war to secure freedoms for others that they themselves did not enjoy. Terrell warned the delegates, "You may talk about permanent peace till doomsday, but the world will never have it until the dark races are given a square deal." (Rief, 2004, p. 212)

Ida B. Wells-Barnett, only one generation removed from the horrors of enslavement, was mobilized by her family history of slavery and turned tragedy into action through her involvement with antilynching campaigns. She viewed the lynching of African Americans as a direct consequence of persistent struggles for equality and freedom and the relentless, uncompromising pursuit of social justice (Pebbles-Wilkins & Francis, 1990), and Wells-Barnett more than exemplified these characteristics and behaviors. She was tenacious and outspoken. Following the lynching of an African American man in Paris, Texas, in 1893 that received worldwide publicity, Wells-Barnett was invited to Europe where she embarked on a speaking tour to disseminate information about racism in the United States and her antilynching campaign. The Society for the Brotherhood of Man was formed by her supporters in Europe as way to publicize her work (Rief, 2004). She was well received and noted as a particularly persuasive speaker. When a city councilman wrote to a British newspaper professing to have little interest in the lynching of African Americans in the United States, Well-Barnett responded to the editor with the following comments:

> The pulpit and press of our own country remains silent on these continued outrages and the voice of my race thus tortured and outraged is stifled or ignored wherever it is lifted in America in a demand for justice. It is to the religious and moral sentiment of Great Britain we now turn. These can arouse the public sentiment of Americans so necessary for the enforcement of the law. The moral agencies at work in Great Britain did much for the final overthrow of chattel slavery. They can in like manner pray, write, preach, talk and act against civil and industrial slavery; against the hanging, shooting, and burning alive of a powerless race. (Duster, 1970, p. 100, as cited in Rief, 2004, p. 205)

Addie Hunton developed her perspective on peace based on her experiences as one of 19 African American women who served in France for the YMCA during World War I and whose role was to establish and maintain "huts" for American soldiers (Chandler, 2005). Huts were similar to coffee houses where soldiers could socialize with others; buy coffee, cigarettes, and chocolate; read; and attend movies and lectures for respite against the discomfort of war. Initially encouraged by France's openness to African Americans, Hunton soon learned the powerful reach of racial discrimination wielded by the U.S. military forces in an effort to regulate the lives of African American soldiers.

Although Hunton was an advocate of war prior to this experience, upon returning to the United States several years later, she was "deeply committed to peace and considerably more political than she had been when she boarded the ship for France" (p. 275). Chandler (2005) explains that while war brought increased opportunities to African Americans, it also heightened intolerance and racial hatred. Hunton and other like-minded African American women took up the charge, moved from their roles as social service providers, and engaged in efforts in the United States and abroad to increase world consciousness about racial hatred in a country claiming to be a social democracy. To realize this goal, they formed organizations for peace and justice, joined white women as members of the Women's International League for Peace and Freedom (WILPF), and created a model for African American women's participation in peace efforts. "At the heart of their peace perspective was the belief that as Hunton wrote, 'there can be no world peace without right local and national relations'" (Plastas, 2001, p. 95, as cited in Chandler, 2005, p. 277). For Hunton, "right local and national relations" meant addressing the relationship between African Americans and whites. As Chandler explains,

> This dialectic between peace, on one hand, and racial equality, on the other hand, was one of the strongest to emerge from the war. To it, African American women added a determination to secure a place for themselves at tables and within organizations that were dominated by African American men and White women. (p. 277)

The Lone Vote for Peace

Jeannette Rankin is another example of an early human rights activist who devoted her life to struggles for peace and equality. She was educated at the New York School of Philanthropy (now known as the Columbia University School of Social Work) where she studied social work and subsequently went on to practice in Montana and Washington. She joined the suffragist ranks and helped win women's right to vote in state elections in California, Washington, and Montana. In 1916, she was the first woman elected to the U.S. Congress. Her slogan was "Peace is a woman's job," and she remained true to her campaign promises when she voted against U.S. entry into World War I. Shortly thereafter, she lost the Congressional election but continued her work through her affiliation with various peace and public interest groups. In 1940 she ran again for congress as a Republican pacifist and was reelected. The day after Pearl Harbor on December 8, 1941, she cast the lone vote against U.S. involvement in World War II. This vote cost her the congressional seat. Once her term expired, she returned to social work and progressive political activities. Throughout the remainder of her life she continued to oppose war and continued to believe in a global society of peace.[8] She moved to Georgia in the 1930s and organized the Georgia Peace Society. Her legacy continues in her hometown of Missoula, Montana, where the building housing the School of Social Work at The University of Montana bears her name and the Jeannette Rankin Peace Center carries on the work she started almost 100 years ago (O'Brien, 1995; Simon, 2002).

History's Challenge to Contemporary Social Work

This snapshot of history reveals that struggles for human rights, social justice, and equality have played out through the organized and concerted efforts of social work movements for change. These efforts call on the participation of social workers and citizens alike, to band together and form a solid, powerful base for change. Wagner (2000, p. 4) makes the point that major positive changes for poor people and people marginalized because of race, gender, sexual orientation, and ability have come not from philanthropy but from social movements. He speculates about what might happen if all the effort and time spent in volunteering and in supporting the work of nonprofit service organizations were channeled into a movement of people to change society for the better. He asks us to imagine what today might be like for us all if Mother Jones or Martin Luther King, Jr., had handed out meals at a soup kitchen, or if they had become therapists or program administrators instead of being leaders of social movements. Wagner also pushes us to consider why we view only the Mother Teresas as a symbol of love, and fear or pass over as "cranks" those individuals who organize against, write about, or protest social injustice. He gives us much food for thought as the social work profession moves into the 21st century.

CHAPTER SUMMARY

In this chapter we have explored the reasons why history and a historical perspective are important to social justice work. We have presented a brief and partial history of social work beginning with its emergence around the turn of the 20th century. We have emphasized the interrelationship between social work and the economy and explored polarities in the philosophies and practice of social work. We have highlighted the contributions of advocates and activists who have been marginalized in many accounts of social work's history. And we have provided biographical sketches of activists inside and outside of social work who have inspired us to question the status quo and pushed us to strive toward increased congruence among our words, values, and actions. In the next chapter we address questions of values and ethics and their relationship to the possibilities of social work practice.

Teaching–Learning Resource: Stories and Scripts from a Century of Activism

A number of individuals have made significant contributions to social work's history of activism and have "consistently kept the voice of change alive" (Abramovitz, 1998, p. 524). It is important to (re)claim these people we hear so little about but whose histories shed light on possibilities for justice-oriented practice today. As Abramovitz (1998) notes:

> Their ongoing fights against the conflicts stemming from the profession's structural location in society, the narrowing forces of professionalization, and the rise of conservative political climates ensured social work remained an arena of struggle throughout the 20th century. Without such political struggles neither social work nor society would have changed for the better. (p. 524)

The following section presents an example of Reader's Theater and brief histories of people in and outside social work who believed they could make a difference. These are individuals with a deep sense of purpose and an abiding commitment to social justice. As you read these vignettes think of the lessons to be learned from their histories. Are there commonalities you see in the actions they took, what they valued, or the issues upon which they took a stand? What set of justice-oriented practice principles emerge and how would you apply them to social work practice today? You may also want to draw on these vignettes in the creation of your own Reader's Theater.

Reader's Theater

The following Reader's Theater scripts were prepared by Janet Finn and Sally Brown, drawing from the life, work, and words of two of social work's "founding mothers." A reader's theater is a brief dramatization in which readers take on the roles of people in the scripts. Janet and Sally performed these scripts for a number of social work audiences, wearing period hats and dresses to bring their characters to life. What other scripts would you add to expand a reader's theater production of the history of social justice work?

Jane Addams and Bertha Reynolds: "The Jane and Bertha Show"

Jane: Let me tell you a bit about myself. I was born in Cedarville, Illinois, in 1860, the same year Abe Lincoln was elected President. I was only 4 when Lincoln died, but he looms large in my memory. He was a man of conscience and integrity, like my father. My mother died when I was only 2. My father was the most important influence in my life. He was a Quaker, mill owner, banker, and for 16 years, an Illinois State Senator. I adored him and tried hard to live up to his example. My father taught me "to be honest with myself inside, whatever happened." I still remember his words of wisdom: "No matter what your role is in the great drama of life, act well your part."

My father encouraged me to pursue my education and a career; he never saw my gender as a limitation. So I went to Rockford Seminary, a boarding school near my home, and planned to study medicine at Women's Medical College in Philadelphia. My dear father died right after I graduated from boarding school, and I felt like my whole life was crumbling around me. I lost all my incentive. I became ill and had to drop out of school. I felt like such a failure. For several years, I was adrift. I was "weary of myself and sick of asking what I am and what I ought to be."

I traveled to Europe with my stepmother. In my day, that was how one cultivated the graces of womanhood. But that was not for me. I made a second trip to Europe in 1887; this time I did not visit cathedrals and galleries but factories and slums. I had seen poverty among rural farmers in the Midwest, but now I came face to face with the suffering and struggles of the urban poor. I attended meetings of the London match girls who were on strike. I saw the hunger and need in the faces of tenement dwellers in London's East End. And, finally, in 1888, I made a visit to a place called Toynbee Hall, the first Settlement House, established in East London. It was an experiment in Christian socialism dedicated to meeting the needs of the poor. It was then and there that I realized that to be true to myself I would have to cast my own lot with the poor.

And so, in the fall of 1889, I moved to an industrial district of Chicago. My school friend Ellen Starr and I found a decaying old mansion on Halsted Street. On September 18, 1889, we opened its doors to all who cared to enter. I remember how my father had never locked his doors, and I decided from the start that the doors of Hull House would always be open to the world. Halsted Street was teeming with immigrants, and with bars and brothels and pawnshops. It was here we began our experiment in social work.

At Hull House, we learned about immigration and community life from immigrants. These were the people making the clothing that Americans wore, growing the food and working in the stockyards to feed Americans. They lived under conditions of oppression, both in the countries they left behind and in their new home in the United States. Yet they also lived with music and art, with joy and laughter. Hull House became a center of community life, struggling with their challenges and celebrating their successes. It became a university, concert hall, gymnasium, library, and clubhouse of the neighborhood. We took pride in the fact that our first new building was an art gallery. Over time at Hull House we established a working girls' home, a day nursery, a labor museum, boys' club, and theater. We were always seeking funding, but we turned down any money with strings attached that would compromise our mission.

We approached our work at Hull House with the enthusiasm of an artist, trying to translate a vision into reality. It was a place where those who have a passion for human joy, justice, and opportunity came together. We were painfully aware of the confusions and struggles all around us, but we also believed that struggle itself might be a source of strength. The Settlement was, above all, a place of tolerance and openness. We had to let go of our preconceptions and open ourselves to learning from and in the neighborhood.

We soon learned that so-called "simple" people are interested in large and vital subjects. Residents and community members became involved in policy and legislative issues, such as child labor laws, and together we conducted investigations of the area's living and working conditions. The investigations carried out at Hull House arose from the problems of peoples' everyday lives. For example, our investigation of sanitary conditions was prompted by the fact that neighborhood residents lived alongside garbage dumps. Our children played in and around huge wooden garbage boxes overflowing in the streets. We initiated an effort to get the boxes removed and began a systematic investigation of the city's system of garbage collection. Members of the Hull House Women's Club came together to discuss the high death rate in our ward. They began to investigate the conditions of alleys in the ward and document violations of health regulations. Because of our dogged efforts, the mayor appointed me garbage inspector for the ward with a salary of $1,000 a year!

Narrator: After the outbreak of World War I, Jane Addams dedicated herself to world peace. She was a founding member of the Women's Peace Party in 1915. She came under severe public criticism for her pacifist position during World War I. She headed the U.S. delegation to the second Women's Peace Conference in 1919. She was elected the first president of the Women's International League for Peace and Freedom. She dedicated herself extensively to international peace issues in the 1920s.

Addams: "I believe that peace is not merely the absence of war but the nurture of human life and that in time this nurture would do away with war as a natural process."

Narrator: In 1931 Jane Addams was awarded the Nobel Peace Prize. Jane Addams was both activist and intellectual, theorist and organizer. She spoke of concern over class division of society and over the incompatibility of industrialism and humanity. She offered a strong critique of society over the years even as she maintained an optimism for the empowering possibilities of a true social democracy. She died in Chicago on May 21, 1935. In one of her last public appearances, at the 20th anniversary celebration of the Women's International League, three weeks before her death, Addams spoke these words:

Addams: People must come to realize how futile war is. It is so disastrous, not only in poison gas used to destroy lives, but in the poison injected into the public mind. We are suffering still from the war psychology. We can find many things which are the result of war, and one war is really the result of past wars… If it became fixed in the human mind that killing was not justified, it would be done away with…

Bertha: My name is Bertha Reynolds. I was born in rural Massachusetts in 1885, about the same time Jane was in Europe learning how to be a lady. I come from a family of very modest means. My father and two of my siblings died when I was quite young. I was raised by my mother, a high school teacher, and her family. I was home-schooled until I was 12, and graduated Phi Beta Kappa from Smith College in Psychology.

My first job was as a teacher in an all-Black high school in Atlanta. It was an important learning experience for me. I was only able to stay barely a year and had to leave the post due to emotional and physical illness. I returned to Boston and after recovering my strength, I entered a one-year certificate program in social work offered by the Boston School of Social Work and Simmons College.

I found my studies fascinating, and I ended up entering the first class for psychiatric social workers at Smith College. I worked for the Boston Children's Aid Society for 5 years, then went on to receive my MSW. Eventually I was offered the position of associate director of the Smith College School of Social Work.

I left the position at Smith over a widening chasm between my approach to social work and that of the prevailing theory and practice at the time. I took a very practical approach, looking at the connections between social work and social living, and thinking about the ways in which social work respected or denied people their full adult status. I looked at problems from an environmental perspective and was concerned about the ways social work was integrated with social change. I didn't fit too well with the Diagnostic School, the more popular social work approach at the time, which focused on individual problems and treatment.

In the 1930s I became an active member of the political left, joined the Communist and later the Socialist party, and got involved in labor organizations. My colleagues and I started the Rank and File Movement, a broad-based organization made up largely of public sector workers without professional credentials. We published the journal *Social Work Today,* a magazine for and about the work of activist social workers. I learned a great deal working with merchant seamen at the National Maritime Union, not your typical social work clients, as we set up social services for the union members. The work helped me develop new theories about what social work should and should not be.

For me, social work must stay the course with a focus on humanitarian concerns and social reform. We, as social workers, need to work as advocates and activists for structural change. I have tried to sum up what social work means to me in five simple principles: (1) Social work exists to serve people in need. (2) Social work exists to help people help themselves. (3) Social work operates by communication, listening and sharing experiences. (4) Social work has to find a place among other movements for human betterment. And (5) social workers as citizens cannot consider themselves superior to their clients. We too, have the same problems.

Narrator: Reynolds professed and practiced social work based on four key values: belonging, keeping full adult status, mutuality, and no strings attached. Her practice wisdom serves us well today. Reynolds died in 1978. The legacy of her work continues through the Social Welfare Action Alliance (formerly the Bertha Capen Reynolds Society), an organization of activist social workers dedicated to progressive social change.

Reclaiming Histories, Voices, and Possibilities

In this section we present brief autobiographies of four inspirational people in the history of social justice work: Mary Abby Van Kleeck, Myles Horton, Mary Harris "Mother" Jones, and W. E. B. DuBois. We invite you to draw on these vignettes to create your own performance. For example, class members could participate "in character" in discussions and debates about social justice issues. Perhaps you could put together a panel of speakers presenting different times in the history of social work or orchestrate a debate among historical figures on a specific topic such as poverty, discrimination, or war. What dialogue can you imagine occurring between Jane Addams and Mother Jones? Between W. E. B. DuBois and Myles Horton? How might these key figures view social work today? What might they recommend for a justice-oriented approach to social work? We encourage readers to learn about other inspirational people who have shaped the history of social justice work. Create and perform your own scripts. It is a great way to inspire others.

Mary Abby Van Kleeck (1883–1972)

I was born in upstate New York and my father was a minister. By the age of 21, I had completed my bachelor's degree from Smith's College. This is when I joined the College Settlements Association, and I began my career as an economist, social researcher, and social reformer. From the very beginning of my research career, I studied issues that concerned labor. For example, I completed a study on children's home labor and three on women's labor as factory workers, milliners, and artificial flower makers. I enjoyed researching these topics because it fit so well with my interest in economics and was such a good way to publicize the plight of working-class people in the United States at the turn of the century. I was well organized and had a knack for getting people to collaborate on a research project.

For several decades, I served as the director of Russell Sage Foundation's Department of Industrial Studies. I like to think that my work helped bring about legislative reform by shedding light on the exploitive work conditions (i.e., long hours, poor equipment, and miserly wages) in various trade occupations. My devotion to the rights of labor, especially women's work, led me to help set the War Labor Policies Board standards during World War I. This really needed to happen so big business would not continue to exploit women working in the war industry.

I was appointed head of the Women in Industrial Service agency established within the Department of Labor. This later became the United States Women's Bureau.

After the war, I returned to Russell Sage Foundation where I took on more research to investigate the underlying causes of job insecurity and labor unrest. With the stock market crash in 1929 and the advent of the Great Depression, my philosophical beliefs and my critical analysis of government, corporate interests, and labor found a home in socialism. A turning point in my life happened in 1933 when I resigned from a new position I had taken with the Federal Advisory Council of the United States Employment Service after only one day on the job. While other social workers and reformers were singing the accolades of the New Deal policies, I had an entirely different way of looking at what I believed was a "three-cornered conflict of interest." This triangle of interests was among those who own and control the economic system; the workers, who were claiming their right to a livelihood in an age of plentiful production; and the government, which has always more closely identified itself with property rights. To attain human rights there must be struggle.

I firmly believed that most people, including social workers, have illusions regarding government and unless we break through this fog, social workers will continue to play down elements of power so essential to maintaining property rights over human rights. I warned other social workers against cooptation by the New Deal and other government reforms. My conviction in these principles shaped my actions as a social reformer. Social workers should have a closer association with workers' groups than with boards of directors and governmental officials. Only then will the practice of social work have the vitality of social purpose that comes out of the genuine experience of life of the underprivileged. I presented some of my ideas at a National Conference of Social Work in 1934 where I received an award for my social activism work. I based my analysis on two theories of government:

> That government stands above conflicting interests in a democracy and can be brought, by majority vote, to decide between those conflicts and compel standards and policies which are in the best public interest. . . Another theory . . . is that government essentially is dominated by the strongest economic power and becomes the instrument to serve the purposes of the groups possessing that power. (Van Kleeck, 1934/1991, p. 79)

I believed communities were composed of groups with conflicting interests rather than common interests and that "(t)he government will then represent the strongest power and will develop instruments of defense of that power—army, navy, militia, and police." While the audience responded to my words with both uproar and exultation, social work went on to accept the New Deal as an interim measure, never fully coming to grips with their illusions of government. Throughout my life I continued to contend that relief programs such as the New Deal were ploys to suppress the possibility of grassroots revolt. They were a way to avoid making fundamental structural change in our social institutions.

In 1948, following World War II, I retired from the Russell Sage Foundation. Shortly thereafter, I ran unsuccessfully for the New York State Senate on the American Labor Party ticket. Through my organizational affiliations with the Episcopal League for Social Action and the Church League for Industrial Democracy, I pursued postwar interests such as disarmament and the peacetime uses of nuclear energy.[9]

Myles Horton (1905–1990)

I was born in Savannah, Tennessee, on July 9, 1905. My parents were both school teachers before the time when it was necessary to have a formal teaching degree. When that changed, they took odd jobs, but we never thought of ourselves as working class or poor—just regular people who didn't have any money. I got some early training from my grandfather that set the course of my life. He was an illiterate mountain man who thought rich people were evil and were going to hell. I took this for granted and didn't understand the meaning of this belief until I started working myself and saw how unfair the wage system really was. Why should one person work so hard and get so little while another hardly works at all and benefits from the other's labor? This question planted the seeds that would later grow into my work as an educator, labor organizer, civil rights activist, and in 1932, one of the founders of Highlander Folk School.

I loved schooling and learning. I saw learning as a lifelong process, and I combined this with a good sense of what was right and what was wrong. I believe I got this from my mother and I took it to another level—it's the principle of trying to serve others and build a loving world. I attended college and Union Theological Seminary. I learned about unionism, communism, socialism, and pacifism but I tried not to let any of these "isms" become a dogma in my life. I went to the University of Chicago in 1930 to learn about sociology and how to help people solve social conflicts and change society. I was really looking for a model for how to work in Appalachia, my home. One day I went with a group of students to visit Hull House. Jane Addams was there and so was Alice Hamilton, the mother of industrial medicine. When asked why each of us had come to visit, all the others talked about their interest in social work. When it was my turn, I came straight out and said I had no interest in what Hull House had become, but I was interested in what it used to be. I wanted to know about the early struggles, how they dealt with being labeled Communist and being put in jail, and about their involvements in the early labor movement. Jane Addams personally asked to speak to me after that day. She helped me get some of my ideas together about the meaning of democracy that led to the next leg of my journey.

In 1927, I spent the summer teaching Bible classes back home in Tennessee. From working with the poor mountain people, I began to formulate my plan to start a school different from other schools. I wanted to help people transform their oppressive life situations into action. I left Chicago a year later and headed for Denmark. I had discussed my ideas about a school with two Danish-born ministers I had met. They thought the Danish folk schools came really close to my descriptions of a democratic education model. This model had originated out of social ferment in Denmark in the mid-19th century. Back in the United States a year later, I pulled together a group of like-minded friends and we started Highlander Folk School in Monteagle, Tennessee. Highlander was known as a hotbed of radicalism.

We taught leadership skills to Blacks and whites in the same classroom, something unheard of and down right illegal at the time, given segregation laws. We stayed true to our convictions. We lived democracy as we tried to change the so-called democratic social, political, and economic structures of government and the institutions of power in the United States. We worked with labor unions, antipoverty organizations, and civil rights leaders. Highlander got a name for itself as the spark that ignited the civil rights movement.

In 1960, right in the midst of the civil rights movement, the Tennessee courts closed Highlander. They said it violated its charter by permitting integration of Blacks and whites. We opened it right up again and called it Highlander Research and Education Center in Knoxville. In 1971 we moved to a 100-acre, mountainside farm in New Market, Tennessee. I'd have to say that one of the biggest learnings of my life was the realization that if we think we have the answers to other peoples' problems then we close the door to the answers they have for themselves. If, on the other hand, we realize we don't have the expert answers, we open up the door to the possibilities for change. I've always believed that people are experts on their own lives.[10]

Mary Harris "Mother" Jones (1830–1930)

I was born in Cork, Ireland, in 1830. My family was poor and had been fighting for Ireland's freedom for generations. My father, Richard Harris, came to America in 1835 and as soon as he became an American citizen, he sent for his family. His work as a laborer in railway construction brought my family to Toronto, Canada. (Although I was raised in Canada, I have always been proud of my American citizenship.) After school, I returned to America to become a teacher. In 1861, I met my husband while teaching in Memphis, Tennessee. He was an iron moulder and an active member of the Iron Moulder's Union. In 1867, a yellow fever epidemic swept Memphis. Its victims were mainly among the poor and the workers. One by one, my four children and my husband sickened and died.

After the Union buried my family, I nursed the remaining sufferers until the plague was stamped out. Afterward, I went to Chicago into the dressmaking business. I worked for the aristocrats of the city and as a result, had ample opportunity to observe the luxury and extravagance of their lives. Often while sewing for the rich who lived in magnificent houses on Lake Shore Drive, I would look out the windows and see the poor, shivering wretches, jobless and hungry, walking alone along the frozen lakefront. The contrast of their condition with that of the people for whom I worked was painful to me.

In October 1871, the great Chicago fire burned up my business and everything that I had. The fire made thousands homeless. Along with many other refugees, I stayed at Old St. Mary's church. Nearby in an old fire-scorched building the Knights of Labor held meetings. During this time, I spent my evenings at their meetings, listening to the splendid speakers. I became more and more engrossed in the labor struggle and decided to take an active part in the efforts of the working people to better the conditions under which they worked and lived.

From 1880 on, I became wholly engrossed in the labor movement as a labor organizer. I went to Ohio and Baltimore to organize railroad laborers, to Chicago to organize lake seamen and dock laborers and to Virginia to organize coal miners. In 1899, I was asked to help the United Mine Workers organize the coalfields of Arnot, Pennsylvania. After five months of striking the men had become despondent. So I told the men to stay home with the children and urged their wives to take their dishpans, brooms, and hammers to the fields. I instructed them to hammer and howl and chase the scabs and mules away when they approached. And it worked, because no scabs went to work that day or any other. The union was victorious.

In 1903 I went to Kensington, Pennsylvania, to strike with textile workers who wanted more pay and shorter hours. At least 10,000 of the 75,000 laborers were little children. I helped to assemble a number of the children who were striking one morning in Independence Park. After a large crowd had gathered, I held up the children's mutilated hands and told the people that Philadelphia's mansions were built on the broken bones, quivering hearts, and drooping heads of the children who worked in the textile mills. When things began to calm down in Kensington, I decided to stir them up again. At the time the Liberty Bell was traveling around the country and drawing large crowds. This gave me an idea. I decided to take the little children from the textile mills on a tour.

We went all over Pennsylvania, New Jersey, and New York, drawing in great crowds and educating people about the horrors of child labor. Not long afterward, the Pennsylvania legislature passed a child labor law that sent thousands of children home from the mills to get an education and kept thousands of other children from entering the factory until they were 14 years of age.

When Mother Jones died in 1930, she was the single most beloved individual in the whole history of the U.S. labor movement. She devoted her life to enhancing the power of working-class people.[11]

W.E.B. DuBois (1868–1963)

I was born in Berkshire County, southwestern Massachusetts, in 1868, five years after the Emancipation Proclamation began freeing American Negro slaves. I learned my patterns of living in Great Barrington, Massachusetts in the town schools, churches, and general social life. As a child, although my schoolmates were invariably white, I had little experience of segregation or color discrimination. I joined quite naturally in and excelled at all games and excursions, and I was in and out of nearly all the homes of my mates and ate and played with them. I understood nevertheless that I was different, that I was exceptional in appearance and that most of the other colored persons I saw, including my own folk, were poorer than the well-to-do whites, lived in humbler houses, and did not own stores.

Early in life I believed that the secret of loosing the color bar rest in excellence and in accomplishment, that the only way colored people could gain equality was to get an education, work hard, and excel. However, by the time I entered high school I had grown more introspective. I began to think and write about the development of my race. At age 15 I became the local correspondent for the *New York Globe*.

In the summer of 1885 I began college at Fisk University, a college for Negroes in Nashville, Tennessee. My formative learning experiences at Fisk solidified my determination to promote the emancipation of my people. I wanted to know the real seat of slavery. I spent my summers traveling and teaching summer school in the rural districts of the South. I witnessed discrimination I had never imagined, and my critical understanding of the race problem in America deepened. I saw first hand the depths of poverty and prejudice, and I also saw people's hunger for education.

It was a piece of unusual luck, much more than my own determination, that admitted me to Harvard. There had been arising in Harvard in the 1880's a feeling that the institution was becoming too ingrown. I saw advertisements of scholarships and submitted applications. I was immediately accepted. In 1888, I went to Harvard as a Negro, not simply by birth, but by recognizing myself as a member of a caste whose situation I accepted but was determined to work from within that caste to find my way out. I pursued philosophy as my life career, with teaching for support at Harvard from 1888 to 1890.

It wasn't until I went to Germany, to attend the University of Berlin, that I began to see the race problem in America, the problems of peoples of Africa and Asia, and the political development of Europe as one. At this time I began to feel that dichotomy which all my life characterized my thought: how far can love for my oppressed race accord with love for the oppressing country? And when these loyalties diverge, where shall my soul find refuge?

From the autumn of 1884 to the spring of 1910, for 16 years, I was a teacher and a student of social science. For two years I taught at Wilberforce, for a year and a half at the University of Pennsylvania, and for 13 years at Atlanta University in Georgia. I sought in these years to know my world and to teach youth the meaning and way of the world. The main significance of my work at Atlanta University during the years 1897 to 1910, was the development of a program of study on the problems affecting the American Negroes. This program produced an encyclopedia on the American Negro that was widely distributed and used by other scholars. Between 1896 and 1920 there was no study made of the race problem in America that did not depend in some degree upon the investigations made at Atlanta University. During this time I also completed and published my now famous books, *The Philadelphia Negro* (1896), *The Souls of Black Folk* (1903), and *John Brown* (1909).

In 1905, I organized a conference in response to the growing philosophical divisions among American Negroes. This was the beginning of the Niagara Movement, whose objectives were to advocate for freedom of speech, an unfettered press, manhood suffrage, the abolition of all caste distinctions based on race, and a belief in the dignity of labor. In 1909 most of the members of the Niagara Movement merged with a group of white liberals concerned with the race problem. The National Association for the Advancement of Colored People or NAACP formed as a result, and I was asked to join the organization as Director of Publications and Research. With some reluctance, I accepted. For 25 years I served as Editor-in-Chief of *The Crisis*, the main publication of the NAACP. Through *The Crisis* I used my words to challenge bigotry, expose the rampant reality of lynching and call for legal action, and demand fair treatment for the Black soldiers who had served valiantly in World War I only to return home to a world of racism and discrimination.

In 1919 I traveled to France to serve as the NAACP observer at the Peace Conference held shortly after the Armistice was signed ending World War I. It was there that I realized what my future held. For Africans to be free anywhere they must be free everywhere. I helped organize the 1921 Pan-African conference. I became dedicated to the power and possibility of Pan-Africanism and remained so throughout my life. Upon my return to the U.S. I found my role with the NAACP no longer tenable, and I returned to teaching and research at Atlanta University. In the following years I completed two major books, *Black Reconstruction* (1935) and *Dusk of Dawn* (1940). I continued to question and challenge the global power of capitalism and imperialism and their intersections with racism. In 1945 I was elected President of the Pan-African Congress. My vocal challenges to the forces of imperialism and racism, along with my stance as an advocate for peace and opposition to nuclear weapons, marked me as "dangerous." In the 1940s I was investigated by the FBI on suspicion of being a socialist. In fact, in 1961, at age 93, I did join the Communist Party, USA.

In 1961 I was invited to Ghana by President Kwame Nkrumah to direct the *Encyclopedia Africana*. With delight, my wife and I seized the opportunity. However, two years later, I was denied a new U.S. passport, and so, at age 95, I became a citizen of Ghana.

DuBois died on August 27, 1963, in Ghana, one day before Martin Luther King Jr.'s "I Have a Dream" speech.[12]

Questions for Discussion

1. What examples of the history of a particular social problem or construct could you use to illustrate the importance of an historical perspective to social work practice?

2. What are some historic or contemporary examples that illustrate the intertwining nature of social work and the economy?

3. What factors account for the differences between the Charity Organization Society and the Settlement House Movement?

4. What factors contributed to the decline of social justice-oriented practice in social work's history beginning in the 1920s?

5. What are some examples in your community that illustrate social work's engagement with human rights, peace, and citizenship?

Suggested Readings:

Addams, J. (1910). *Twenty years at Hull House*. New York: Macmillan.

Arnove, A. & Zinn, H. (2004).*Voices of a people's history of the United States*. New York: Seven Stories Press.

Barbuto, D. (1999). *American settlement houses and progressive social reform: An encyclopedia of the American Settlement Movement*. Phoenix, AZ: Oryx Press.

Deer, A. & Simon, R. (1970). *Speaking out*. Chicago: Children's Press Open Door Books.

Du Bois, W.E.B. (1903/1969). *The souls of black folk*. New York: New American Library.

Edmunds, D. (Ed.).(2001). *The new warriors: Native American leaders since 1900*. Lincoln, NB: University of Nebraska Press.

Ehrenreich, J. H. (1985). *The altruistic magination: A history of social work and social policy in the United States*. Ithaca, NY: Cornell University Press.

Fisher, R. (1999). Speaking for the contribution of history: Context and the origins of the Social Welfare History Group. *Social Service Review, 73*(2), 191-217.

Gould, S. (1981). *The mismeasure of man*. New York: W.W. Norton and Co.

Reisch, M. & Andrews, J. (2001). *The road not taken: A history of radical social work in the United States*. New York: Brunner/Routledge.

Reynolds, B.C. (1987). *Social work and social living*. Silver Spring, MD: National Association of Social Workers.

Sullivan, M. (1993). Social work's legacy of peace: Echoes from the early 20th century. *Social Work, 38*(5), 513-520.

Zinn, H. (2003). *A people's history of the United States, 1492—Present*. New York: HarperCollins Publisher, Inc.

End Notes

[1] From Zinn, H. (1990). *Declarations of independence - Chapter Four: The uses and abuses of history* (p. 86). New York: Harper Collins.

[2] From Horton, M. (1998). *The long haul*: An autobiography (with Judith Kohl and Herbert Kohl). New York: Teachers College Press, (p. 51). Permission to quote courtesy of Teachers College Press.

[3] http://www.historians.org/affiliates/social_welfare_his_group.htm

[4] Karl DeSchweinitz's quotation comes originally from correspondence to Fedele Fauri, September 9, 1955, Council of Social Work Education Manuscripts, Box 7, Folder 24, Social Welfare History Archives, University of Minnesota, Minneapolis, MN.

[5] See Ana Maria Garcia's 1982 *La Operación* that addresses the sterilization of women in Puerto Rico and Jane Lawrence, The Indian Health Service and the Sterilization of Native American Women. *The American Indian Quarterly*, Summer 2000, *24*(3), p. 400.

[6] Scientific management principles were promoted by Fredrick Taylor during the early 1900s. See J. Schriver, *Human behavior and the social environment,* pp. 427-428 for a thorough explanation of Taylor's organizational theory and its main principles.

[7] We borrow from Ann Withorn's seminal work, *Serving the people: Social service and social change.* New York: Columbia University Press.

[8] Based on the Jeannette Rankin Commemorative Booklet, (n.d.) by Joan Hoff-Wilson, Executive Secretary, Organization of American Historians. For more information contact OAH at http://www.oah.org. For further background on Jeannette Rankin see also Mary Barmeyer O'Brien (1995) *Bright star in the big sky, Jeannette Rankin, 1880-1973.*

[9] Adapted from Mary Van Kleeck (1934/1991) Our illusions regarding government. Reprinted in *Journal of Progressive Human Services*, 2(1), 75-86.

[10] Adapted from Myles Horton (1998). *The long haul: An autobiography.*

[11] Based on Jones, M. & Kerr, C. (1996). *The autobiography of Mother Jones.* Ashley Atkinson, MSW, University of Michigan, researched and wrote the biographical sketch on Mother Jones.

[12] Adapted from W. E. B. DuBois (1968). *A soliloquy on viewing my life from the last decade of the first century*, and (1903/1989) *The souls of black folk*. New York: Random House. Ashley Atkinson, MSW, University of Michigan, researched and wrote the biographical sketch on W.E.B. Dubois. Revisions for the 2nd edition of *Just Practice* drawn from Gerald C. Hynes (2003) Biographical Sketch of W. E. B. DuBois accessed 7/12/06 at _http://www.hartford-hwp.com/archives/45a/427.html_ and Wikipedia accessed 6/08/06 at _http://www.wikipedia.org/wiki/Web_dubois_.

Values, Ethics, and Visions

The philosophy of social work cannot be separated from the prevailing philosophy of a nation, as to how it values people and what importance it sets upon their welfare. . . Practice is always shaped by the needs of the times, the problems they present, the fears they generate, the solutions that appeal, and the knowledge and skills available.

Bertha Capen Reynolds (1987), *Social Work and Social Living*

Virtually every caring system we have keeps its eye on the good it hopes to accomplish and blinks at the harm it is doing. As a result, hundreds of thousands— perhaps millions— of people are violated every day of their lives by the encroachments of ostensible benefactors.

Ira Glasser (1978), "Welfare vs. Liberty: Prisoners of Benevolence"

CHAPTER OVERVIEW

In Chapter 4 we explore the concept of values, their formation, and their place in our everyday lives. We develop a historical understanding of values, consider the concept of values in context, and address questions of power in the practice of valuing. How are values and the practices of valuing shaped and challenged over time? How are values entwined in our most basic assumptions about the world and how we relate with others? We explore the relationship between values and ethics and consider the ways in which values are translated into standards for ethical practice. We present frameworks for ethical decision making that enable us to critically engage with the translation of values into practice.

In this chapter we also examine the value base of social work and introduce readers to the core values of the social work profession as described in the Code of Ethics of the National Association of Social Workers in the United States. We then turn to a consideration of ethics and values in context, looking at the history of social work ethics in the United States and changes in the code over time. We consider the challenges and possibilities posed by alternative perspectives on practice ethics in the United States, such as the Code of Ethics of the National Association of Black Social Workers. Moving beyond U.S. borders we draw from an international story of social work as a profession and questions of ethics therein. We locate social work in the context of global struggles to meet human needs and respect human rights.

Returning to the grounded practice of ethical decision making, we consider two frameworks for ethical decision making in social work developed in U.S. contexts. We then expand on those possibilities through consideration of an ethics of participation and a human rights perspective. What possibilities might we open if we were to embrace an ethics of liberation and hope? We conclude with a consideration of the relationship among values, human rights, and social justice work. What are the values that guide social justice work and inform a framework for Just Practice?

WHAT DO WE MEAN BY VALUES?

Defining Values

Merriam-Webster's dictionary (2005) defines value as "a principle, standard, or quality regarded as worthwhile or desirable" (p. 1248). Values are often described as guides to individual and collective action. Values are not provable "truths." Rather, they can be summarized as guides to behavior that grow out of personal experience, change with experience, and are evolving in nature (Johnson & Yanca, 2007, p. 46). Some writers describe values as principles about what we ultimately hold as worthy and good, about desired ends, and about the means of achieving those ends. Values are the principles upon which we base critical reflection and action. Frederic Reamer (1995) describes the attributes and functions of values as follows: "they are generalized, emotionally charged conceptions of what is desirable; historically created and derived from experience; shared by a population or group within it; and they provide the means for organizing and structuring patterns of behavior" (p. 11). Attention to the emotional component is important. People feel deeply about that which they value, and value conflicts can provoke strong emotional responses. As Robin M. Williams, Jr. writes:

> Values merge affect and concept. Persons are not detached or indifferent to the world; they do not stop with a sheerly factual view of their experience. Explicitly or implicitly, they are continually regarding things as good or bad, pleasant or unpleasant, beautiful or ugly, appropriate or inappropriate, true or false... All values have cognitive, affective, and directional aspects. Values serve as criteria for selection in action. When most explicit and fully conceptualized, values become criteria for judgment, preference, and choice. When implicit and unreflective, values nevertheless perform "as if" they constituted grounds for decisions in behavior. Individuals do prefer some things to others; they do select one course of action rather than another out of a range of possibilities; they do judge their own conduct and that of other persons. (1979, p. 16)

Our values are not random (Miley, O'Melia, & DuBois, 2007, p. 66); they have histories. They are learned through our experiences in families, communities, and other social groups. Values are emergent and dynamic, both shaping and shaped by our beliefs about and experience in the world. We learn, internalize, and question our values in historical, political, and cultural contexts. We learn powerful lessons in values through participation in schooling, religious institutions, work, the market place, and from the media. However, the value lessons being learned may be very different from the value lessons purportedly being taught.

Values and moral authority have long been the subject of study and debate by philosophers, religious and political leaders, and everyday people struggling to make their way in the world. Discourses regarding values reverberate throughout human history. As Frederick Ferré (2001) argues, fundamental questions of values came into play with the entrance of people into the world, because humanity is the only species capable of acting irresponsibly toward other species and to the Earth. According to Simon Blackburn (2001) human beings are value-based animals.

> We grade and evaluate, and compare and admire, and claim and justify. We do not just "prefer" this or that, in isolation. We prefer that our preferences are shared; we turn them into demands on each other. Events endlessly adjust our sense of guilt and shame and our sense of our own worth and that of others. We hope for lives whose story leaves us looking admirable; we like our weakness to be hidden and deniable. (p. 4-5)

Plato sought to identify moral values, or "virtues" as he called them, that guide both individuals and societies. For Plato, the morally virtuous person is wise, temperate, courageous, and just (Dobelstein, 1999, p. 27; Peterfreund, 1992, p. 10). In a similar vein, Confucius wrote, "wisdom, compassion and courage... are the three universally recognized moral qualities of men" (Confucius, *The Doctrine of Mean, Ch. XX, 8).*[1] Scottish philosopher David Hume described benevolence and justice as the two great social virtues. French philosopher Denis Diderot saw the capacity for valuing and judgment to be fundamental to humanity. Echoing Diderot, German-born American political philosopher Hannah Arendt wrote: "Thinking, willing and judging are the three basic fundamental activities. They cannot be derived from each other, and although they have certain common characteristics, they cannot be reduced to a common denominator" (*Life of the Mind,* unfinished trilogy in Seldes, 1985, p. 16). How would you define values? Do you agree that there are universally recognized moral qualities of human beings? How would you describe your personal philosophy of human values? Where does your philosophy agree with or differ from those mentioned above?

Many writers have sought to describe "universal" human values that remain constant through time and across human groups. However, the very concept of "value" is socially constructed, imbued with multiple and contested meanings. As Robin Williams, Jr. writes:

> [V]alues operate as constituents of dynamic systems of social action because of their interconnectedness, their informational or directive effects, and their capacities as "carriers" of psychological energy. Values always have cultural context, represent a psychological investment, and are shaped by the constraints and opportunities of a social system and of a biophysical environment. (1979, p. 21)

One of the challenges of social justice work is to both appreciate diverse constructions of values and question the modes of power at work in the process of valuing. As Dobelstein (1999) describes, in the U.S. context:

> [Values] have gradually become associated with nouns rather than verbs or adverbs, as if values were things rather than action. When objects are valued over actions, then much of the moral authority of the value is lost…(T)urning values into things without concern for how the things are achieved empties them of much of their authority to guide morally relevant behaviors. (p. 26)

Thus, value has come to have a different meaning as it has become more closely associated with the goal-driven nature of economic rationality and less with a notion of virtue that guides individual and social actions (pp. 26-27).

Dobelstein (1999) writes that values are based on ideologies, that is, our beliefs about what is "true." As we saw in Chapter 3, values are deeply embedded in our political, social, and economic institutions, creating an ideological foundation for institutional structures and practices that often goes largely unquestioned. For example, in the United States the value of "freedom" is broadly invoked as a fundamental value with the force of moral authority. The dominant concept of freedom in the United States is one grounded in liberalism, capitalism, and positivism, and constructed in terms of individualism and individual rights (Dobelstein, 1999, p. 24). Discourses of individual rights often serve to limit reflection on another value, that of social responsibility. We frequently hear claims for rights to privacy, to bear arms, to choose. These claims seem to drown out discussion of responsibility to the common good.

REFLECTION: Personal Core Values

It does not take long to see the complex nature of values and valuing and the tensions in play as competing values are espoused, practiced, and challenged. Similarly, we encounter tensions and contradictions in our efforts to formulate and practice our own core values. Take a few minutes to reflect on your own core values. Try to identify six core values, ways of being and doing that you hold to be good and desirable. Think about what these values mean to you. Would you describe these as personal values? Social values? Both? Have you experienced a time when two or more of these values were in conflict with one another? What were the circumstances? Were you able to resolve the conflict? What values guided your actions? Now think about a time when your own everyday action in the world has contradicted one of these values. What was the context? How did you negotiate that predicament? What sorts of feelings did it provoke? How did you justify your actions to yourself or to others? As meaning-making beings with the capacity to evaluate and reflect on our actions in the world, we often find ourselves up against conflicts and contradictions. We are, as the country music singers tell us, "walking contradictions."

VALUES IN CONTEXT

American Values?

We often hear talk about "American" values, "societal" values, or "middle-class" values. Such sweeping notions of values suggest that these values are broadly shared and uncontested. They also assume that "America," "society," and the "middle class" are homogeneous groups who would readily agree on a set of shared values. Such value claims are often held up to be both correct and normative, that is, the norm by which "other" values held by "other" groups are to be judged. Such a view of values denies the complexities and conflicts of interests, beliefs, values, and practices within contemporary U.S. society. It creates boundaries between "us" and "them" and contributes to particular assumptions about difference and similarity. These all-encompassing notions of values may reflect the particular interests of dominant groups who wish to maintain the status quo; they neglect the possibility that "others" may share similar values but are denied the resources and opportunities to realize them. Further, individuals and groups may give very different meanings to the same expressed value. Consider, for example, the many possible meanings of "success." For some it may be measured in terms of individual achievement and monetary gain, while for those with a collectivist, noncapitalist orientation, such a measure would be antithetical to their values.

Consider for a moment some of the values we commonly hear described as "American" values. A list of those values might include: freedom, opportunity, individualism, enterprise, pragmatism, efficiency, equality, progress, democracy. What else would you add to the list? These values are deeply embedded in our social, political, and economic institutions and practices. They have evocative force. They are often paired with the value of patriotism and touted as values that "others" should embrace. And yet, as we look at our list, we can point to values that may be in conflict with one another. Moreover, we can identify other values and virtues that are not part of our list, but we could readily argue to be desirable in guiding human action. And we can describe a litany of examples that demonstrate the ways in which individual and institutional practices contradict these values.

Now, imagine for a moment a first-time visitor coming to the United States with little prior knowledge of popularly expressed American values. She has an opportunity to travel, to visit cities and towns, to read newspapers, to watch television, and to participate in other activities of contemporary social life. Based on these experiences, how might she describe "American values?" Perhaps she would describe Americans as placing a high value on size, where bigger always seems to be better. After a trip around the country she may note an American value for mobility, given the impressive amounts of pavement, cars, and trucks. A trip to a few supermarkets may leave her with the impression that Americans highly value choice, packaging, pets, and hygiene. A pass through the checkout stand would confirm suspicions about the valuing of sports heroes, diets, gluttony, political scandal, celebrities, greed, horoscopes, and pop psychology experts. She may be perplexed by reading a headline that says a high court has upheld the fundamental separation of church and state, then paying for her groceries with money that claims, "In God We Trust." A trip to a suburban housing tract may suggest that conformity is more highly valued than individualism. What other impressions of "American" values might our first-time visitor gain? What sorts of contradictions might she encounter? If you were to take a visitor on an "American value tour" where would you go?

Values are also shaped in relationship to social class. For example, how a person gives meaning to "success" or comes to value certain kinds of knowledge and forms of labor may be powerfully shaped by class-based experience. Those who have been involved in working-class struggles for the right to organize may

Contradicting Values

◆ What are some contradictions that come to mind as you reflect on your list of "American" values?

◆ As you compare your list to your experiences of everyday life in the United States?

◆ Where are the contradictions most salient for you?

value solidarity and mutual support over autonomy and assistance. Too often, helping professionals have taken a particular set of "middle-class" values to be the norm and have made faulty assumptions about other persons and groups based on those values. People in different class positions may express values in common, such as the desire for a healthy environment, a comfortable home, and a good job. They may, however, give very different meanings to those values. And their differing access to resources profoundly shapes their possibilities for translating the visions of what they value into reality.

REFLECTION: **The Social Class Questionnaire**

Take a few moments to reflect on your own social class background and the values associated with your class-based experience. Turn to the "Social Class Questionnaire" at the end of this chapter (p. 155). First, take time to respond individually to the questions posed. Then get together with a classmate and discuss your responses. What did you learn about the intersection of values and social class through this exercise?

Family Values?

The concept of "family values" is another case in point. While many people might share a valuing of "family," they may strongly disagree on the definition. Family means different things to different people, and kinship is constructed in a remarkable variety of ways. The concept of family promoted in the "family values" discourse of recent years is based on one very particular family form—the nuclear family—made up of two heterosexual parents and their children, with the father as the authority figure and mother as nurturer. This model is one that serves to justify and maintain gender and generational inequality (Day, 2003; Finn, 1998b, pp. 205-217). The question of what constitutes family values depends on who counts as family. Rather than assuming the nuclear family as the norm, we can learn more about both family and values by appreciating the different ways in which we define and create families and practice family relations. Linda Nicholson (1986) defines family as a historically and culturally variable concept that connects positions within a kinship system and household. Baber and Allen (1992) describe families as powerful socializing institutions, arenas of affection and support and tension and domination between genders and across generations. Heidi Hartmann (1981) keeps her definition simple: "Any two or more individuals who define themselves as family" (p. 8). Take a moment to think about how you define family.

THE PRACTICE OF VALUING

Let's begin to think about "valuing" as a verb that describes the process by which we make judgements about what is desirable and preferred. As cultural beings constantly interpreting and making sense of the world, we are also engaged in an ongoing practice of valuing. Learning to value is part of our broader experience of acquisition of cultural knowledge. Through our everyday interactions in the world, in families, schools, neighborhoods, communities, and cultural groups, we are sub-

REFLECTION: Family and Values

What does family mean to you? Take a minute and write down your definition of family. Get together with a small group of your classmates and share your definitions. See if you can come to agreement on a definition of family. Have one member of each small group write the group's collective definition(s) on the blackboard. Take time to read the definitions. What do the definitions have in common? How do they differ? Is it possible to reach consensus as a class on a definition of family? Do the definitions reflect values about what a family *should* be? Do the definitions reflect your own *experience* of family? How do values shape our understandings of family? How do our experiences in family shape values?

Our differing experiences in families shape the meanings we give to family, which, in turn, shape our understanding of "family values."[2] Take a few moments to reflect on your own experiences of family life. What were some of the messages you received while growing up that indicated what attributes and actions were or were not valued? For example, what and how did you learn about the value of family, work, education, religion, achievement, money, relationships, or helping? From whom did you receive those messages?

The expressions we pass down through families often serve as vehicles for inculcating values. Consider the following common expressions: "A penny saved is a penny earned;" "Time is money;" "Children should be seen and not heard."[3] What values are expressed here? Think for a moment about the expressions you heard while growing up. What did they teach you about family and values?

What messages did you receive about what it meant to be male or female in your family? What messages did you receive about race and racism? About social class? About the valuing of "whiteness?" About heterosexuality and sexual difference? From whom? Can you identify some values that you have incorporated? Values that you have resisted? Can you identify changes in your values over time? What forces or experiences prompted those changes?[4]

jects of, witnesses to, and participants in practices of valuing. Those practices are shaped by the political, economic, social, and historical circumstances of our lives. The lessons in valuing learned by a white boy growing up in an upper-middle class Chicago suburb may be very different from those learned by a Chippewa-Cree boy growing up amidst poverty and unemployment on the Rocky Boy's Reservation in Montana, or those learned by a boy surviving on the streets of Sao Paulo or Seattle.[5]

Families and Valuing

When we shift our attention to valuing as a verb it helps us to think about the many ways that we learn which qualities and behaviors are considered desirable and by whom. Families are powerful arenas for learning to value. From our earliest social experiences we are enmeshed in the practices of valuing. Some of these practices, such as the ways in which resources of time and space are organized and managed in the context of family, are so deeply ingrained in our experience that they go without saying (Germain, 1994b, p. 261). For example, values of individualism and privacy are structured into the design of living space in the United States and are expressed in the middle-class expectation that children have "their own rooms." No matter how small the overall living space, it is divided into units that break up the social group. In other social and cultural contexts, such use of space would be inconceivable both in terms of use of material resources and in terms of the social isolation it would impose on family members who have learned to value the collective rather than the individual. Values shape and are shaped by the social structuring of our lives as well. As Germain (1994b, p. 261) describes, "family paradigms" —members' shared, implicit beliefs about themselves and their social world—profoundly shape one's orientation to and patterns of action in the world. Through the everyday routines, the messages and silences, and the crises of family life many of us learn powerful lessons in valuing.

The Power of Schooling

Families are powerful, but not the only, sources for lessons in valuing. Schools are particularly powerful sites of valuing. Public schools have played a key role in the inculcation of "middle-class" values and in the organization of working-class life (Apple, 1982, 2003, 2004; Ehrenreich, 1985; Willis, 1981). A number of critical education theorists have argued that public schooling plays a key role in socializing children for their class position in capitalist society at the same time that it promotes the myth of classlessness and equality of opportunity to "get ahead" (Apple, 1982; Aronowitz & Giroux, 1985; Shor, 1980). They argue that, in theory, public schools are democratic places of equal opportunity. In practice, they are places where class differences play out and get reproduced, whether in the form of unequal funding for "rich" and "poor" school districts or in the everyday indignities and exclusions experienced by poor and working-class children. A closer look at the history of education in the United States reveals that, while schooling has created opportunities for some groups, it has served as a powerful form of discipline, containment, and social control for others. In the reflection text box below we address the place of boarding schools in the history of Native American education in the United States as a case in point. Boarding schools offer a provocative site for reflecting on questions of values, power, and difference.

REFLECTION: Education and American Indians

For nearly a century (1870-1968) federal government-run boarding schools played a powerful role in the "education" of American Indian children in the United States. In the mid-1800s many American Indian groups were forcibly relocated to reservations to make way for economic development of the western United States. Not long afterward, developers saw that reservation lands themselves had value for logging, mining, and cattle interests, and tribal organization was an impediment to that development. A new thrust in federal Indian policy (through the General Allotment Act) emerged calling for the "assimilation" of American Indians through "reduction to citizenship," establishment of individual property rights, and education into mainstream white culture (Smith, 1985; Takaki, 1979, 1993). Boarding schools played a key role in this federal effort. By 1890 there were 140 federal boarding schools with an enrollment of nearly 10,000 students (Morgan, 1890, as cited in Washburn, 1973, p. 44). Below are two quotes from Commissioners of Indian Affairs regarding American Indians and the value of education. What values are reflected in these quotes? What is the meaning of Indian education to the Commissioners? What might the educational experience have meant to an Indian child enrolled in boarding school in 1890? What questions do these passages raise regarding the relationship between values and social policy? What lessons might we draw as social workers to inform our practice?

He (the Indian) should be educated to labor. He does not need the learning of William and Mary, but he does need the virtue of industry and the ability of the skillful hand... And the Indian should not only be taught how to work, but also that it is his duty to work; for the degrading communism of the tribal reservation system gives to the individual no incentive to labor, but puts a premium on idleness and makes it fashionable. Under this system, the laziest man owns as much as the most industrious man, and neither can say of all the acres occupied by the tribe, "This is mine." The Indian must, therefore, be taught how to labor; and, that labor may be made necessary to his well being, he must be taken out of the reservation through the door of the General Allotment Act. And he must be imbued with the exalting egotism of American civilization, so that he will say "I" instead of "We," and "This is mine" instead of "This is ours."

Commissioner of Indian Affairs John H. Oberly, 1888[6]

****

It is of prime importance that a fervent patriotism should be awakened in their minds. The stars and stripes should be a familiar object in every Indian school, national hymns should be sung, and patriotic selections be read and recited. They should be taught to look upon America as their home and upon the United States Government as their friend and benefactor. They should be made familiar with the lives of great and good men and women in American history, and be taught to feel a pride in all their great achievements. They should hear little or nothing of the 'wrongs of the Indians' and the injustice of the white race. If their unhappy history is alluded to it should be to contrast it with the better future that is within their grasp. The new era has come to the red men through the munificent scheme of education, devised for and offered to them, should be the means of awakening loyalty to the Government, gratitude to the nation, and hopefulness for themselves.

Commissioner of Indian Affairs T.J. Morgan, 1889.[7]

These words of the Commissioners of Indian Affairs and the values they reflect may provoke and disturb us. Some may argue that these accounts are more than a century old and things have changed. Yes, many things have changed. But we continue to see the differential valuing of children by class, race, and gender in our educational systems. As Jonathan Kozol (1991) has shown in his powerful book *Savage Inequalities,* poor children of color in the United States attempt to learn in underfunded, unsafe schools, where there are often not enough books, materials, or teachers to go around. Meanwhile, children of the majority, white, middle and upper classes enjoy the safety of suburban schools equipped with the latest technologies and resources. Every day, children learn lessons in values informed by their differing school experiences. In reflecting on your own school experiences, what are some of the values you were expressly taught? What did you learn through your daily observations and experiences of valuing? Did you face any contradictions between the values taught and the values practiced?

Power, Inequality, and Valuing

Much can be learned about the practices and contradictions of dominant values and valuing from the perspectives of less powerful people and groups. Single mothers raising children in poverty live the contradictions of the "family values" discourse. Children of color who suffer the highest rates of poverty in the United States must wonder what political leaders have in mind when they claim, "our children are our future." Young Black men in the United States see that they are more valued as prisoners than scholars, given that their chances of incarceration are better than their chances of going to college. Millions of the world's poor live (and die) the daily reality of human devaluation and disposability in the "new world order." They have been denied the very basic value of their humanity.

The work of W.E.B. DuBois (1985, 1989) is important in thinking about the contexts of inequality and the questions of meaning and power through which our lessons in values are filtered. (See the Teaching-Learning Resource at the end of Chapter 3 for a biographical sketch). DuBois writes about his experiences with racism in the United States and the ever-present but rarely asked question: "How does it feel to be a problem?" He goes on to describe the "strange experience" of "being a problem" through a story from his childhood school days:

> In a wee wooden schoolhouse, something put it into the boys' and girls' heads to buy gorgeous visiting-cards— ten cents a package— and exchange. The exchange was merry, till one girl, a tall newcomer, refused my card, —refused it peremptorily, with a glance. Then it dawned on me with a certain suddenness that I was different from the others; or like, mayhap, in heart and life and longing, but shut out from their world by a vast veil . . .

He continues:

> . . . the negro is a sort of seventh son, born with a veil, and gifted with second-sight in this American world, — a world which yields him no true self-consciousness, but only lets him see himself through the revelation of the other world. It is a peculiar sensation, this double-consciousness, this sense of always looking at one's self through the eyes of others, of measuring one's soul by the tape of a world that looks on in amused contempt and pity. One ever feels his twoness, — an American, a Negro, two souls, two thoughts, two unreconciled strivings; two warring ideals in one dark body, whose dogged strength alone keeps it from being torn asunder. (1989, pp. 1-3)

What lessons in valuing can we draw from Du Bois' reflections? What connections can you make to the experiences of children of color, poor children, and immigrant children in the United States today?

Valuing and Social Justice Work

Valuing is a dialectical process. Our actions in the world are shaped in part by our valuing of the world. Our experiences in the world, in turn, shape our values. It is important to reflect critically on our values and the processes through which they have been formed and challenged. We continually bring our values and valuing to bear in the practice of social work. A commitment to social justice work demands a constant search for competence, an honest examination of our personal as well as professional values, and a commitment to making our actions fit our words (Freire, 1990). Are our actions consistent with our expressed values? Do our values form the basis for justice-oriented action?

Our values can be thought of as screens through which we interpret actions and give meaning to experience. They are shaped by our power, positioning, and experiences. But our values are never fully determined or determining. There is always the possibility of new understandings and relations and thus alternative values and approaches to valuing.

In summary, valuing is a complex and contested process. We are social beings with interests, desires, and relations at stake. We incorporate, resist, reproduce, and change values over time through the dynamics of our life experiences. The process of valuing cannot be separated from the contexts of power and inequality in which it plays out. We grapple with value contradictions in our everyday lives even as we practice and resist the (de)valuing of others and ourselves. And in the struggle there is always the possibility of transformation.

THE CONCEPT OF ETHICS

Defining Ethics

The concept of ethics is closely linked to that of values. In a formal sense, ethics refers to the branch of philosophy that concerns itself with moral decision making and the principles that guide people in determining right and wrong. In everyday usage, ethics may be thought of as the translation of human values into guidelines for action. Loewenberg and Dolgoff (1996, p. 43) describe two major philosophical approaches that have historically informed ethical decision making—ethical absolutism and ethical relativism. Absolutists stress the importance of fixed moral rules and contend that actions are inherently right or wrong. Relativists reject this stance and argue instead that ethical decision making is contextual and may be judged on the resulting consequences. Peterfreund (1992) summarizes two "great traditions" in ethics. The Greek tradition of ethics centered around understanding the "good life." Ethical inquiry was directed toward the nature of happiness and ways to achieve it. The Judeo-Christian tradition, in turn, emphasized righteousness before God and duty to God and neighbor. An emphasis on duty and rights tends to characterize contemporary approaches to codes of professional ethics.

Ferré describes ethics as a way of thinking, judging, and acting. As a way of thinking it requires adequate relevant data, a keen awareness that we will never have all the "facts," and an openness to the evidence while "seeking to integrate it in a pattern that does it no violence" (2001, p. 8). As a way of judging, ethics links thinking and feeling, such that reason and emotion mutually shape moral sensibility and decision making. Finally, it is this interplay of feeling-laden judgments that makes coordinated action possible. As Ferré argues, "there is no ethical action without thought and feeling, no ethical thought without feeling and potential action, no ethical feeling without conceptual recognition and implications for behavior" (p. 20). Blackburn (2001) contends that ethics—dynamic processes of thinking, judging, and acting—play out in an "ethical environment." He describes this as the "surrounding climate of ideas about how to live. It determines what we find acceptable or unacceptable, admirable or contemptible. It determines our conception of when things are going well and when they are going badly" (p. 1). Margaret Rhodes argues that dialogue is central to ethics. According to Rhodes:

Only through sustained and open dialogue can we develop informed ethical positions. Dialogue of this sort assumes that (1) we can communicate across different views; (2) that we can be open to each other; (3) that we need other views in order to fully reexamine our own. Dialogue of this sort is itself an ethic, best exemplified in the early works of Plato, where Socrates questions the actions and views of his fellow citizens and urges them to rethink what they are doing. The dialogues often end without a conclusion, the conclusion being that we must constantly reexamine our answers. (1986, p. 19-20)

Ethical Theories

As the preceding discussion suggests, a diverse range of ethical theories has been articulated and debated over the centuries. Utilitarian theories, exemplified in the thinking of English philosophers Jeremy Bentham and John Stuart Mill, emphasize actions that bring about the greatest good—and the least harm—for the greatest number. To quote Bentham, "The greatest happiness of the greatest number is the foundation of morals and legislation" (as cited in Seldes, 1985, p. 39).[8] Duty-based theories, such as that articulated by Immanuel Kant, focus on the fundamental respect and dignity owed to every human being. As Rhodes writes, duty-based theory "makes us focus on the value of every individual person and on the respect owed to a person, apart from that person's usefulness and apart from our own desires, a respect essential to human dignity. . ." (1986, p. 32). Rights-based theories emphasize an individual's fundamental right to choose, and they seek to protect individual freedom from encroachment by others. They see humanity as grounded in the dignity of free will. Fairness approaches seek to ensure that all individuals are treated in the same way and view favoritism and discrimination as unjust. Common good approaches view the good of individual members of society as being inextricably linked to the good of a community; they focus on actions and conditions that are beneficial to the community as a whole. Virtue approaches see the goal of individual and collective action as human excellence. Ethical actions are those that promote the full development of humanity and human potential (Rhodes, 1986; Velasquez, Andre, Shanks, & Meyer, 2004). Differing theoretical perspectives lead us to ask different sorts of questions regarding ethical decision making:

- ◆ What benefit or harm might result from a particular course of action? What action will lead to the best overall consequences?
- ◆ Does this course of action respect the dignity of another? Does it treat the person as an end and not as a means?
- ◆ What rights do the affected parties have? Which course of action best respects those rights?
- ◆ Which course of action treats everyone the same, unless there is a morally justifiable reason not to? Which course of action avoids favoritism and discrimination?
- ◆ Which course of action promotes the common good? Which best contributes to the kind of society we want to be?
- ◆ Which course of action develops moral virtues? Which helps us realize the best of our individual and collective potential? (Adapted from

Velasquez et al., 2004).

While each of these questions may be important to guide action, it is equally important to recognize that each is informed by a unique theoretical viewpoint. Velasquez et al. (2004) make the case that we can engage more fully in debate by drawing from each perspective and posing all of these questions in our practices of ethical decision making. In the following section we refocus on social work, explore the values that shape the profession, and consider the ways in which our ethical theories affect our practice.

VALUES, ETHICS, AND SOCIAL WORK

Social Work as a Value-based Practice

Social work is a value-based practice. According to Reamer (1995), social work values shape the mission of the profession; relations with clients, colleagues, and members of the broader society; decisions about intervention methods; and the resolution of ethical dilemmas (p.12). Writers in the field frequently describe social work's value base as a defining feature of the profession's uniqueness. Miley, O'Melia, and DuBois (2007) see human dignity and worth and social justice as the overarching values of social work. Similarly, speaking of social work in an international perspective, Ramanathan and Link (1999) contend that human dignity, worth of the individual, and sanctity of life are transcendent values. Miley et al. (2007) describe values that shape the everyday practice of social work. "They include acceptance, individualization, nonjudgmentalism, objectivity, self-determination, access to resources, confidentiality, and accountability" (p. 56). The Council on Social Work Education embraces these values as guides to professional practice. The Council also addresses values of mutual participation, peoples' right to make independent decisions, and respect for diversity. It calls on social workers to build just social institutions. Social workers have developed ethical codes that translate expressed values into standards for professional practice. As Johnson and Yanca (2007) note, "codes of ethics flow from values; they are values in action" (p. 48).

Core Values: An Overview

The Preamble to the National Association of Social Workers Code of Ethics states in part:

> The mission of the social work profession is rooted in a set of core values. These core values, embraced by social workers throughout the profession's history, are the foundation of social work's unique purpose and perspective.
> ♦ Service
> ♦ Social justice
> ♦ Dignity and worth of the person
> ♦ Importance of human relationships
> ♦ Integrity
> ♦ Competence

> This constellation of core values reflects what is unique to the social work profession. Core values, and the principles that flow from them, must be balanced within the context and complexity of human experience. (NASW, 1999)[9]

We refer you to the National Association of Social Workers (NASW) website for a complete version of the Code of Ethics (www.socialworkers.org/pubs/codenew/code.asp). Virtually every contemporary U.S. social work practice text spells out the core values of the profession as articulated by the NASW. Writers often praise the uniqueness and righteousness of a profession founded on these core values and implore budding social workers to embrace them wholeheartedly and put them into practice. Less attention is given to critical reflection on these values, their meanings, their relationship to the history of social work, the challenge of practicing them within a context of unequal power, and the tensions among them and between this core set of values and one's personal values. Discussion generally sidesteps the practices of valuing within the field of social work. By providing a definitive list of core values and locating "social justice" as one among several values to be embraced we may unnecessarily constrain a discussion of *possible* values that could illuminate a vision of a just world. Take a close look at these six core values. It seems that they could have different meanings for different people in different situations. What do they mean to you? Are they meaningful outside of a context in which they are applied? Do they define a core of social justice work? Are there values you would add, delete, or question?

Social Work Values and Tensions

The NASW preamble states that these six core values have been embraced by social workers throughout the profession's history. However, as we learned in Chapter 3, social work's history reveals a rather awkward "embrace" of the profession's core values. As John Ehrenreich (1985) describes, social work emerged in conjunction with the growth of industrial capitalism. Industrial capitalism was premised not only on mass production but also on mass consumption. It demanded new kinds of workers, consumers, and citizens and required new forms of labor discipline that extended from the factory floor to the regulation of the habits and intimacies of family life (Ehrenreich, 1985; Finn, 2001a; Harvey; 1989). Capitalism in the 20th century forged the reorganization of working-class life and fueled the emergence of a professional middle class (Ehrenreich, 1985, p. 28-30). Social workers played key roles in monitoring working-class life and instructing working-class immigrants in the values conducive to capitalist production and consumption.

The molding and monitoring of poor, working-class, and immigrant family life is another part of social work's history. What values would you say underlie these practices? Rather than brushing this history under the rug, we contend that social workers need to learn from it and consider the inconsistencies between our expressed values and our actual practices. We need to examine the values reflected in these practices and ask how it was that these practices were promoted and justified. What other possible courses of action might social work and social workers have taken that would have been consistent with the profession's core values? What lessons can we take away from this history to help our actions match our words today?

Social Workers and Surveillance of Working-Class Life: Inside Ford Motor Company

Ford Motor Company was on the cutting edge of the making of new kinds of workers, and Henry Ford hired social workers to help. According to David Harvey (1989):

> Ford sent an army of social workers into the homes of his "privileged" (and largely immigrant) workers to ensure that the "new man" of mass production had the right kind of moral probity, family life, and capacity for prudent (i.e. non-alcoholic) and "rational" consumption to live up to corporate needs and expectations. (p.126)

John Ehrenreich (1985) offers a more vivid description:

> When Ford Motor Company introduced its celebrated $5-a-day wages…it set up a Sociology (social services) Department, whose thirty investigators were to screen applicants and monitor the behavior of employees. Gambling, drinking, and, of course, radicalism, and unionism were forbidden; "proper" (i.e. middle-class) diet, recreational habits, living arrangements, family budgets, and morality were taught and encouraged. For the foreign-born, English classes were mandatory, with the text used beginning with the lesson "I am a good American." Symbolizing the school's function was the "graduation" ceremony: walking on stage in the costumes of their native lands, graduates disappeared behind a giant cutout of a "melting pot." After their teachers had stirred the "pot" with long ladles, the graduates appeared on the opposite side of the pot dressed in proper American attire and waving American flags. (p. 31)

The History of Social Work Ethics

Becoming a Profession

As discussed in Chapter 1, social work in the United States was coming to view itself as a profession in the 1920s. Practitioners were turning away from environmental models and urban community work in favor of psychological models that emphasized the individual as the locus of concern and intervention (Day, 2006). Schools of social work were growing in number as was concern with professional training, credentials, and ethical standards of practice. As early as 1919 there were attempts to draft professional codes of ethics for social work (Reamer, 1995, p. 6). Mary Richmond furthered this work in the 1920s. During the 1940s and 1950s professional ethics became a subject of study in its own right in social work, and in 1947 the Delegate Conference of the American Association of Social Workers adopted a code of ethics, thereby formally translating a value base into principles of practice and standards of professional conduct (Reamer, 1998). As discussed previously, the move toward professionalism was a move away from positioned advocacy and political critique.

In a 1957 article in *Social Work,* University of California professor Ernest Greenwood argues that social workers "might have to scuttle their social action heritage as a price of achieving the public acceptance accorded a profession" (Greenwood, 1957, cited in Ehrenreich, 1985, p. 59). Let's take a minute to think about the implications here. What does it mean to say that activism "undermines professionalism?" What values are being embraced here? Does a negation of activism suggest a political commitment to the status quo? Professionalism, defined by unequal relations of power, control of expert knowledge, and technologies of intervention, objectivity, and distance, seems to be at odds with a value of social justice based on participation and committed to challenging social inequality. Is activism antithetical to professionalism, or do we perhaps need to explore other possibilities for understanding and acting as professionals and as activists?

Professionalism and Radical Challenge

The National Association of Social Workers adopted its first Code of Ethics in 1960 (Reamer, 1994, p. 197). That code consisted of 14 proclamations, all in the form of first-person statements, which covered such issues as the duty to put professional responsibility above personal interests, respect of client privacy, and dedication to contribute knowledge and skills to human welfare programs (Reamer, 1998). Seven years later a "pledge of nondiscrimination" was added. Social workers at the time debated the direction of the profession and the merits of professionalizing. As one former NASW president asked, "Are we truly interested in improved public service or are we looking forward to basking in the sun of respectability?" (Reichert, 1965, p. 140).

The historic events of the 1960s forced practitioners to reflect on constructions of ethical practice in the face of the civil rights struggles and the War on Poverty. By 1970 there was also a growing interest in the study of applied and professional ethics and an increase in litigation regarding violations of ethical principles. Some social workers sought a more prescriptive and proscriptive code to guide professional practice. A task force appointed by NASW in 1977 took up the task, and in 1979 a more substantive set of standards for ethical practice was adopted.

Other social workers promoted a more radical approach to practice in the 1970s, much like Bertha Reynolds, Mary Van Kleeck, and others had done a generation earlier. In the United States, community action workers in the War on Poverty and community organizers sought to change social conditions by building grassroots organizations through which poor and disenfranchised people could have a say in the decisions that affected their lives (Naples, 1998). They challenged what they saw as the conservative bias shaping the direction of social work in the United States and advocated for a critical, politicized practice whose goal was transformation of society.

Conceptualization of a Professional Value Base

Despite the radical challenge, the service-oriented model of social work continued to largely dominate the change-oriented approach, and the development of ethical standards reflected this dominance. In 1976 Charles S. Levy published *Social Work Ethics*, a foundational text that sought to articulate the philosophical and conceptual basis for social work ethics. Levy (1973) classified social work professional values in three categories: preferred conceptions of people; preferred outcomes for people; and preferred instrumentalities for dealing with people. Levy's classification of social work values is summarized in Figure 4.1[10].

Levy's Classification of Social Work Values		
Preferred Conceptions of People _Belief in:_ • Inherent dignity and worth • Capacity for change • Mutual responsibility • Need to belong • Uniqueness • Common human needs	**Preferred Outcomes for People** _Belief in society's obligation to:_ • Provide opportunity for individual growth and development • Provide resources and services for people to meet basic needs • Provide equal opportunity for social participation	**Preferred Instrumentalities for Dealing with People** _Belief that people should:_ • Be treated with dignity and respect • Have the right to self-determination • Be encouraged to participate in social change • Be recognized as unique individuals

FIGURE 4.1

Levy's conceptualization is frequently cited in social work texts as the classic formulation of social work values. Levy's schema brings together humanitarian values and a sense of societal obligation to create conditions in which these values can be expressed. He recognizes and articulates the fundamental linkage of the personal and the social, or "person-in-environment" perspective as it is commonly called, that has been central to dominant depictions of social work's professional uniqueness (we elaborate on this in Chapter 5). Levy implies that society has an obligation to the poor and that people should participate in the decisions that affect their lives. Importantly, Levy also speaks to questions of power in the social work relationship and the need to be mindful of that power and its ethical implications. He states, "The social worker's power is a function of the client's vulnerability, and the client's vulnerability is a function of the social worker's power" (1976, p. 70).

However, Levy does not develop a political and ethical critique of the _conditions_ of poverty, inequality, and exploitation, and of the arrangements and relations of power that create and maintain those conditions. Nor does Levy address the discourses of pathology and difference that mask those conditions and justify individualist, deficit-oriented, "professional" approaches to social work intervention. Levy speaks of common human needs, but does not address basic human rights. He speaks to opportunities for social participation but not of struggles for social justice. In contrast to the radical social workers who argued the need to confront structural as well as interpersonal contradictions, Levy's schema stops short. How is it that Levy's formulation has become central to values discussions in social work while the principles articulated by two generations of social justice workers have been erased from or relegated to the footnotes of social work history?

Values and Survival of the Profession

By the 1980s, with the retrenchment of federal support for social welfare under the Reagan administration, the growing antiwelfare movement, and the massive privatization of social services, social work seemed to value professional survival more than anything. The profession was preoccupied with professional licensure and credentialing for private practice (Reisch & Wenocur, 1986; Specht & Courtney, 1994). Graduate school enrollments expanded as the job market contracted. Many social workers were carving a niche in the clinical practice market and valuing the knowledge, skills, and professional accreditation that would secure their positions. The NASW professional Code of Ethics, as revised in 1979, detailed attention to professional-client relations, confidentiality, access to records, payments for services, and responsibilities to professional colleagues. The revised Code reflected the "medical model" of social worker, that is, social worker as professional expert engaged in client treatment focused on change at the personal and interpersonal level. Social workers were not ethically obliged to combat conditions of violence, inequality, and exploitation, nor were they obligated to make the concerns of people living in poverty their priority. It was not until 1983, as the U.S. social context grew bleaker, that the Council on Social Work Education (CSWE), the profession's academic accrediting body, called for the study of oppression and injustice as part of the social work curriculum (Gil, 1994, p. 258).

Welfare Reform: A Challenge to Professional Values

By 1990, "ending welfare as we know it" had become the mantra of U.S. social policy regarding the poor. The social safety net continued to contract with cuts in federal spending and the "devolution" of social costs to state and local governments and private charities. "Managed care" became a household word as individuals were forced to bear ever-increasing burdens of the costs of health care. As oppression and injustice became "talkable" subjects in popular discourse in the United States, some groups within social work began to mobilize in response. Some social workers joined with welfare rights groups to challenge moves toward more punitive social policy. Some worked within social work organizations to focus attention on the value of social justice. In 1992, CSWE put forth a curriculum policy statement that made it the responsibility of schools of social work to teach about social justice and approaches to overcoming oppression more explicit. However, as Gil (1994) notes, "the 1992 revision reflects the fallacious assumption that discrimination, oppression, and injustice affecting women, minorities, and other discrete social groups can be overcome without eradicating their sources in the occupational and social class divisions of contemporary capitalism" (p. 259).

Rethinking Ethics: The Social Justice Challenge

Revising the Code of Ethics

The political realities of the late 20th century and the accompanying tensions and debates among social workers prompted serious reflection on the profession's ethical direction and responsibilities. In 1993 the Delegate Assembly of NASW formed a task force to craft a new code of ethics. Their efforts reflect concern over the mechanisms and consequences of discrimination, oppression, and injustice. In addition, a new scholarly field of applied ethics had emerged over the previous decade, and this, along with the emergence of the field of bioethics, also shaped the direction of the new code. In August 1996, the Delegate Assembly adopted a revised code of ethics that went into effect in January 1997. It was revised again in 1999. In contrast to the earlier code, which summarized social work values to include "the worth, dignity, and uniqueness of all persons as well as their rights and opportunities" (NASW 1979, rev. 1990, 1993), the 1999 code specifically spells out the mission of social work:

> The primary mission of the social work profession is to enhance human well-being and help meet the basic human needs of all people, with particular attention to the needs and empowerment of people who are vulnerable, oppressed, and living in poverty. A historic and defining feature of social work is the profession's focus on individual well-being in a social context and the well-being of society. Fundamental to social work is attention to the environmental forces that create, contribute to, and address problems in living.

> Social workers promote social justice and social change with and on behalf of clients. "Clients" is used inclusively to refer to individuals, families, groups, organizations, and communities. Social workers are sensitive to cultural and ethnic diversity and strive to end discrimination, oppression, poverty, and other forms of social injustice. These activities may be in the form of direct practice, community organizing, supervision, consultation, administration, advocacy, social and political action, policy development implementation, education, and research and evaluation. Social workers seek to enhance the capacity of people to address their own needs. Social workers also seek to promote the responsiveness of organizations, communities, and other social institutions to individuals' needs and social problems.

Naming Poverty, Oppression, and Injustice

The 1999 revised code provides a pronounced shift in attention to questions of poverty, oppression, and injustice. It calls on social workers to take social justice seriously. The ethical standards now spell out social workers' responsibilities to the broader society. Examples of these responsibilities include:

♦ Social workers should promote the general welfare of society, from local to global levels, and the development of people, their communities, and their environments. Social workers should advocate for living conditions conducive to the fulfillment of basic human needs and should promote social, economic, political, and cultural values and institutions that are compatible with the realization of social justice.

♦ Social workers should promote the conditions that encourage respect for cultural and social diversity within the United States and globally. Social workers should promote policies and practices that demonstrate respect for difference, support the expansion of cultural knowledge and resources, advocate for programs and institutions that demonstrate cultural competence, and promote policies that safeguard the rights of and confirm equity and social justice for all people.

♦ Social workers should act to prevent and eliminate domination of, exploitation of, and discrimination against any person, group, or class on the basis of race, ethnicity, national origin, color, sex, sexual orientation, age, marital status, political belief, religion, or mental or physical disability. (NASW, 1999)

The Challenges Ahead

These are daunting standards. They pose challenges and opportunities as social workers make the commitment to translate them to practice. However, as Gil (1994) notes with regard to the CSWE curriculum standards, we cannot overcome the oppression, exploitation, and discrimination experienced by discrete groups without confronting the underlying systemic inequalities. Further, social workers in both the United States and abroad have reported on the insidious damaging effects of marketization, managerialism, and fragmentation of social welfare systems and social work practices in the era of neoliberal globalization (Clarke, Gewirtz, & McLaughlin, 2000; Harris, 2005; Jones, 2005). According to Ferguson, Lavalette, and Whitmore (2005), these forces have contributed to a "'dumbing-down' of social work education and practice, with theory often seen in an instrumental way ('sociology for the workers') and/or as simply one element (often subordinate to 'skills') of employer-driven competencies." Karen Healy (2005, p. 220) warns about the trend toward "reprivatization of public concerns, such as poverty" and the implications for a critical practice of social work. In this new environment of marketization and managerialism, Healy (2001) expresses concern that "social workers face increasingly stringent expectations from funding agencies and service managers to demonstrate cost-effectiveness and evidence of service outputs and outcomes" that may be removed from the profession's core values. Similarly, Dominelli (1996) has expressed concern over the "commodification of social work" that moves the focus of practice away from concern about people and relationships toward a "product that is being purchased from a contractor" (pp. 163-164). Rossiter (2005) asks us to think specifically about the clinical, legal, and ethical implications of social work within the neoliberal global order. She asks: "Can we picture our current students working for a private child protection service owned by an American multinational? Do we know that the GATS (General Agreement on Trades and Services, forerunner to the World Trade Organization) has a Working Group on Domestic Regulation that is busy formulating global competency standards for professions so that professional qualifications are 'no more burdensome than necessary'?" (Gould, 2003; Rossiter, 2005, p. 190). These are serious questions that challenge our values and the integrity of value-based practice.

Here we must return to the beginning of this section and ask ourselves, are social work's stated core values a sufficient guide for the task at hand? We cannot merely claim a revisionist history of social work. Nor can we ignore the very real value challenges of the present. Might our key concepts for just practice—meaning, context, power, history, and possibility—also be thought of as guides for "valuing?"

Guides for "Valuing"

♦ What values might you add to, take from, or question in social work's core?

♦ What values would you draw on in realizing your vision of social justice work?

♦ How would you translate them into standards of ethical practice?

SOCIAL WORK VALUES AND ETHICS: ALTERNATIVE CONCEPTUALIZATIONS

Thus far, we have focused mainly on the values articulated by the National Association of Social Workers, the predominant professional association in the United States. There are, however, alternative conceptualizations articulated in the definitions and codes of practice developed by other social work groups both within and outside of the United States. In this section we will take a look at some alternative conceptualizations within the United States and the questions they raise. In the following section, we turn to an international perspective on social work as a value-based profession and locate the subject of ethics in a global context. We ask you to consider this question: Are we able to talk about the ethical base of social work without talking about the political base of social work?

National Association of Black Social Workers

Several other social work organizations in the United States have developed their own Codes of Ethics. For example, the introduction to the National Association of Black Social Workers states the following:

> In America today, no Black person, except the selfish or irrational, can claim neutrality in the quest for Black liberation nor fail to consider the implications of the events taking place in our society. Given the necessity for committing ourselves to the struggle for freedom, we as Black Americans practicing in the field of social welfare, set forth this statement of ideals and guiding principles.
>
> If a sense of community awareness is a precondition to humanitarian acts, then we as Black social workers must use our knowledge of the Black community, our commitments to its determination, and our helping skills for the benefit of Black people as we marshal our expertise to improve the quality of life of Black people. Our activities will be guided by our Black consciousness, our determination to protect the security of the Black community, and to serve as advocates to relieve suffering of Black people by any means necessary.
>
> Therefore, as Black social workers we commit ourselves, collectively, to the interests of our Black brethren and as individuals subscribe to the following statements:
>
> ♦ *I regard as my primary obligation the welfare of the Black individual, Black family, and Black community and will engage in action for improving social conditions.*
>
> ♦ *I give precedence to this mission over my personal interest.*
>
> ♦ *I adopt the concept of a Black extended family and*

embrace all Black people as my brothers and sisters, making no distinction between their destiny and my own.

♦ *I hold myself responsible for the quality and extent of service I perform and the quality and extent of service performed by the agency or organization in which I am employed, as it relates to the Black community.*

♦ *I accept the responsibility to protect the Black community against unethical and hypocritical practice by any individual or organizations engaged in social welfare activities.*

♦ *I stand ready to supplement my paid or professional advocacy with voluntary service in the Black public interest.*

♦ *I will consciously use my skills, and my whole being as an instrument for social change, with particular attention directed to the establishment of Black social institutions.*[11]

The code calls for workers to commit to the welfare of Black individuals, families, and communities as the primary obligation and to make no distinction "between their destiny and my own." Black social workers are expected to serve the Black community, work as instruments for social change, and promote the development of Black institutions. The code challenges the value of "professional distance" between worker and "client." Importantly, this powerful document written in the charged political climate of 1971 has remained unchanged over the course of 35 years. It rejects notions of social worker neutrality. It calls on workers to make the community's struggles their own and to dedicate themselves to advocacy in, for, and with the Black community. The impassioned tone of the code sets it apart from that of NASW. In the face of the well-documented institutional racism of our criminal justice system and the shameful underbelly of racism exposed to the world in the wake of Hurricane Katrina in 2005, we argue that this passionate call for a political stance against racial injustice still needs to be heard and heeded. Would you agree? What other points of comparison or contrast do you see? How do the values articulated here fit with your values?

Cornel West Considers Katrina and the Aftermath

The following essay by Cornel West appeared in the *London Observer*, September 11, 2005. What ethical questions does West raise? What are the implications for social justice work? How would the NASW Code of Ethics guide your practice in response the issues West addresses? How would the Code of Ethics of the National Association of Black Social Workers guide your practice?

Exiles from a City and from a Nation

by Cornel West (Interview by Joanna Walters)
Published on Sunday, September 11, 2005 by the Observer/UK

It takes something as big as Hurricane Katrina and the misery we saw among the poor black people of New Orleans to get America to focus on race and poverty. It happens about once every 30 or 40 years.

What we saw unfold in the days after the hurricane was the most naked manifestation of conservative social policy towards the poor, where the message for decades has been: 'You are on your own'. Well, they really were on their own for five days in that Superdome, and it was Darwinism in action - the survival of the fittest. People said: 'It looks like something out of the Third World.' Well, New Orleans was Third World long before the hurricane.

It's not just Katrina, it's povertina. People were quick to call them refugees because they looked as if they were from another country. They are. Exiles in America. Their humanity had been rendered invisible so they were never given high priority when the well-to-do got out and the helicopters came for the few. Almost everyone stuck on rooftops, in the shelters, and dying by the side of the road was poor black.

In the end George Bush has to take responsibility. When [the rapper] Kanye West said the President does not care about black people, he was right, although the effects of his policies are different from what goes on in his soul. You have to distinguish between a racist intent and the racist consequences of his policies. Bush is still a 'frat boy', making jokes and trying to please everyone while the Neanderthals behind him push him more to the right.

Poverty has increased for the last four or five years. A million more Americans became poor last year, even as the super-wealthy became much richer. So where is the trickle-down, the equality of opportunity? Healthcare and education and the social safety net being ripped away—and that flawed structure was nowhere more evident than in a place such as New Orleans, 68 per cent black. The average adult income in some parishes of the city is under $8,000 (£4,350) a year. The average national income is $33,000, though for African-Americans it is about $24,000. It has one of the highest city murder rates in the US. From slave ships to the Superdome was not that big a journey.

New Orleans has always been a city that lived on the edge. The white blues man himself, Tennessee Williams, had it down in A Streetcar Named Desire - with Elysian Fields and cemeteries and the quest for paradise. When you live so close to death, behind the levees, you live more intensely, sexually, gastronomically, psychologically. Louis Armstrong came out of that unbelievable cultural breakthrough unprecedented in the history of American civilisation. The rural blues, the urban jazz. It is the tragi-comic lyricism that gives you the courage to get through the darkest storm.

Charlie Parker would have killed somebody if he had not blown his horn. The history of black people in America is one of unbelievable resilience in the face of crushing white supremacist powers.

This kind of dignity in your struggle cuts both ways, though, because it does not mobilise a collective uprising against the elites. That was the Black Panther movement. You probably need both. There would have been no Panthers without jazz. If I had been of Martin Luther King's generation I would never have gone to Harvard or Princeton.

They shot brother Martin dead like a dog in 1968 when the mobilisation of the black poor was just getting started. At least one of his surviving legacies was the quadrupling in the size of the black middle class. But Oprah [Winfrey] the billionaire and the black judges and chief executives and movie stars do not mean equality, or even equality of opportunity yet. Black faces in high places does not mean racism is over. Condoleezza Rice has sold her soul.

Now the black bourgeoisie have an even heavier obligation to fight for the 33 per cent of black children living in poverty - and to alleviate the spiritual crisis of hopelessness among young black men.

Bush talks about God, but he has forgotten the point of prophetic Christianity is compassion and justice for those who have least. Hip-hop has the anger that comes out of post-industrial, free-market America, but it lacks the progressiveness that produces organisations that will threaten the status quo. There has not been a giant since King, someone prepared to die and create an insurgency where many are prepared to die to upset the corporate elite. The Democrats are spineless.

There is the danger of nihilism and in the Superdome around the fourth day, there it was—husbands held at gunpoint while their wives were raped, someone stomped to death, people throwing themselves off the mezzanine floor, dozens of bodies.

It was a war of all against all - 'you're on your own' - in the centre of the American empire. But now that the aid is pouring in, vital as it is, do not confuse charity with justice. I'm not asking for a revolution, I am asking for reform. A Marshall Plan for the South could be the first step.

Dr. Cornel West is professor of African American studies and religion at Princeton University. His great-grandfather was a slave. He is a rap artist and appeared as Counselor West in Matrix Reloaded and Matrix Revolutions. Interview by Joanna Walters, in Princeton, New Jersey

© 2005 Guardian Newspapers, Ltd.

Code of Ethics for Radical Social Service

In 1975, a group of social workers who embraced a structural approach and sought to challenge the dominant social work paradigm put forth the Code of Ethics for Radical Social Service (Galper, 1975). This code developed from the work of radical social workers in the United States who were confronting the contradictions of social work and questioning the logic of capitalism in which U.S. social work had emerged. Radical social workers held that the NASW Code of Ethics contained a conservative bias that did not serve the best interests of clients or workers. In response they put forth a radical code built on 14 planks informed by a critical Marxist perspective. Among the planks are:

♦ I will work toward the development of a society that is committed to the dictum, "From each according to his or her ability, to each according to his or her need."

♦ I will struggle for the realization of a society in which my personal interests and my personal actions are consistent with my interests and actions as a worker.

♦ I will consider myself accountable to all who join in the struggle for social change and will consider them accountable to me for the quality and extent of work we perform and the society we create.

♦ I will use information gained from my work to facilitate humanistic, revolutionary change in society.

♦ I will use all the knowledge and skill available to me in bringing about a radically transformed society. (For full text see Galper, 1975, pp. 224-227).

This code posed its own set of challenges to mainstream social work values and ethics. What points of comparison and contrast do you see? How do the values articulated here fit with your own values? How do they differ? What would social work practice today look like if it were guided by this code?

Feminist Interventions

Feminist social workers have raised questions regarding the ethics of social work and posed alternative conceptualizations of ethical practice (Dominelli & McLeod, 1989; Hanmer & Statham, 1989). For example, Jalna Hamner and Daphne Statham (1989, pp. 139-143) propose a "Code of Practice for Non-sexist Woman-centered Social Work." The code is built around principles for personal awareness, such as awareness of one's own biases and the pervasiveness of interpersonal and institutionalized sexism, recognition of the role of social definitions in causing women's problems, and understanding of the nature of women's survival strategies—and strategies for intervention—such as establishment of nonhierarchical working relationships, use of all-woman groups, and validation of women's strengths. Feminist scholars and practitioners have also engaged in sustained critical analysis regarding the underlying assumptions of notions of justice that inform ethical stances and the workings of power that shape interpersonal relationships and institutional arrangements (Figueira-McDonough & Sarri, 2002; van Wormer, 2001). They have made questions of power central to ethical inquiry, they examine gender as a central axis of power and inequality, and they consider the intersection with other axes such as race, class, and sexual identity (Boris, 1995; Dujon & Withorn, 1996). Feminists have explored the need to problematize women's relationship to both the state and "expert" models of diagnosis and treatment (Gordon, 1990; 1994; Rossiter et al., 1998). Some have called for an ethics of care as a corrective to what they see as an overemphasis on a rights-based ethics (Bubeck, 1995; Gilligan, 1982; Held, 2006) Others, such as Amy Rossiter and colleagues (1998), have called for an "ethics of resistance" that challenges the assumptions and practices of the dominant disciplines and institutions of helping. From the preceding discussion, we can see that ethical questions are also political, cultural, and historical questions. In light of this overview of alternative ethical perspectives, what questions come to mind for you? Do you see your own ethical stance as a social worker gravitating to one or more of these alternative perspectives? What questions does that raise for you regarding practice ethics?

INTERNATIONAL PERSPECTIVES ON ETHICS AND SOCIAL WORK

Ethics and Professionalization

Thus far, we have focused on U.S. social work as a value-based profession. Now let's turn our attention to social work in a global context. What can we learn from an international perspective on the ethics of social work practice? There is a rich 20th century history of social work engagement with the struggles to meet human needs and champion human rights on an international scale that both parallels and challenges the domestic social work story we have addressed. A thorough discussion of that history is beyond the scope of this chapter. We refer readers to Lynne M. Healy (2001), *International Social Work: Professional Action in an Interdependent World,* for an excellent overview of social work history from an international perspective. In the following paragraphs we highlight moments in that story, with particular attention to the evolution of standards of ethical practice therein.

As Healy addresses (2001), early 20th century social work was characterized by two emergent patterns. On the one hand, social work as a profession and the modern social welfare state were emerging across Western industrialized societies in response to the contradictions and fallout of industrial capitalism. Both the settlement house model and the charity organization societies had their roots in London in the late 1800s. Schools of social work education were forming around 1900 in London, New York, Berlin, and Amsterdam. By 1920 we see the efforts to bring social work knowledge and practice to bear to a broader global audience. In the early 1900s, European and U.S. "experts" began to introduce social work theories and methods as correctives to concerns over "modernization" and "development" in parts of Asia, Africa, and Latin America. For example, the first Latin American school of social work, established in Chile in 1925, was strongly influenced by the medical model of practice. A similar pattern characterized the emergence of social work in Argentina, where the first prototype of social work was the "hygiene visitor." South Africa and Egypt hosted the first schools of social work on the African continent, and students were tutored in a charity model borrowed from the United States and Europe (Healy, 2001). The importation of formalized training models led rapidly to a particular form of social work professionalization in this international context.

The professionalization of social work was occurring internationally in tandem with the emergence of the profession in the United States discussed previously. The International Association of Schools of Social Work was founded in 1928, along with the International Permanent Secretariat of Social Workers (IPSSW). These professional entities emerged from the first international social work conference, held in Paris in 1928. The aim of the Secretariat was to "promote social work as a profession with professional standards and ethics" (Healy, 2001, p. 57). The IPSSW was the predecessor to the International Federation of Social Workers (IFSW), which was founded in 1956. The IFSW has served as a vehicle for representing social work perspectives and positions on significant global issues before the United Nations, and it has played a role in human rights advocacy (Healy, 2001).

IFSW Declaration of Ethical Principles

The IFSW adopted the first International Code of Ethics in 1976. The code was substantially revised in 1994 and again in 2004. The current IFSW Statement of Ethical Principles developed jointly with the International Association of Schools of Social Work (IASSW) reads as follows:

1. Preface

Ethical awareness is a fundamental part of the professional practice of social workers. Their ability and commitment to act ethically is an essential aspect of the quality of the service offered to those who use social work services. The purpose of the work of IASSW and IFSW on ethics is to promote ethical debate and reflection in the member organisations, among the providers of social work in member countries, as well as in the schools of social work and among social work students. Some ethical challenges and problems facing social workers are specific to particular countries; others are common. By staying at the level of general principles, the joint IASSW and IFSW statement aims to encourage social workers across the world to reflect on the challenges and dilemmas that face them and make ethically informed decisions about how to act in each particular case. Some of these problem areas include:

- The fact that the loyalty of social workers is often in the middle of conflicting interests.
- The fact that social workers function as both helpers and controllers.
- The conflicts between the duty of social workers to protect the interests of the people. with whom they work and societal demands for efficiency and utility.
- The fact that resources in society are limited.

This document takes as its starting point the definition of social work adopted separately by the IFSW and IASSW at their respective General Meetings in Montreal, Canada in July 2000 and then agreed jointly in Copenhagen in May 2001 (section 2). This definition stresses principles of human rights and social justice. The next section (3) makes reference to the various declarations and conventions on human rights that are relevant to social work, followed by a statement of general ethical principles under the two broad headings of human rights and dignity and social justice (section 4). The final section introduces some basic guidance on ethical conduct in social work, which it is expected will be elaborated by the ethical guidance and in various codes and guidelines of the member organisations of IFSW and IASSW.

2. Definition of Social Work

The social work profession promotes social change, problem solving in human relationships and the empowerment and liberation of people to enhance well-being. Utilising theories of human behaviour and social systems, social work intervenes at the points where people interact with their environments. Principles of human rights and social justice are fundamental to social work.

3. International Conventions

International human rights declarations and conventions form common standards of achievement, and recognise rights that are accepted by the global community. Documents particularly relevant to social work practice and action are:

- Universal Declaration of Human Rights
- The International Covenant on Civil and Political Rights
- The International Covenant on Economic Social and Cultural Rights
- The Convention on the Elimination of all Forms of Racial Discrimination
- The Convention on the Elimination of All Forms of Discrimination against Women
- The Convention on the Rights of the Child
- Indigenous and Tribal Peoples Convention (ILO convention 169)

4. Principles

4.1. Human Rights and Human Dignity

Social work is based on respect for the inherent worth and dignity of all people, and the rights that follow from this. Social workers should uphold and defend each person's physical, psychological, emotional and spiritual integrity and well-being. This means:

1. Respecting the right to self-determination - Social workers should respect and promote people's right to make their own choices and decisions, irrespective of their values and life choices, provided this does not threaten the rights and legitimate interests of others.

2. Promoting the right to participation - Social workers should promote the full involvement and participation of people using their services in ways that enable them to be empowered in all aspects of decisions and actions affecting their lives.

3. Treating each person as a whole - Social workers should be concerned with the whole person, within the family, community, societal and natural environments, and should seek to recognise all aspects of a person's life.

4. Identifying and developing strengths - Social workers should focus on the strengths of all individuals, groups and communities and thus promote their empowerment.

4.2. Social Justice

Social workers have a responsibility to promote social justice, in relation to society generally, and in relation to the people with whom they work. This means:

1. Challenging negative discrimination* - Social workers have a responsibility to challenge negative discrimination on the basis of characteristics such as ability, age, culture, gender or sex, marital status, socio-economic status, political opinions, skin colour, racial or other physical characteristics, sexual orientation, or spiritual beliefs.

* In some countries the term "discrimination" would be used instead of "negative discrimination". The word negative is used here because in some countries the term "positive discrimination" is also used. Positive discrimination is also known as "affirmative action". Positive discrimination or affirmative action means positive steps taken to redress the effects of historical discrimination against the groups named in clause 4.2.1 above.

2. Recognising diversity - Social workers should recognise and respect the ethnic and cultural diversity of the societies in which they practise, taking account of individual, family, group and community differences.

3. Distributing resources equitably - Social workers should ensure that resources at their disposal are distributed fairly, according to need.

4. Challenging unjust policies and practices - Social workers have a duty to bring to the attention of their employers, policy makers, politicians and the general public situations where resources are inadequate or where distribution of resources, policies and practices are oppressive, unfair or harmful.

5. Working in solidarity - Social workers have an obligation to challenge social conditions that contribute to social exclusion, stigmatisation or subjugation, and to work towards an inclusive society.

5. Professional Conduct

It is the responsibility of the national organisations in membership of IFSW and IASSW to develop and regularly update their own codes of ethics or ethical guidelines, to be consistent with the IFSW/ IASSW statement. It is also the responsibility of national organisations to inform social workers and schools of social work about these codes or guidelines. Social workers should act in accordance with the ethical code or guidelines current in their country. These will generally include more detailed guidance in ethical practice specific to the national context. The following general guidelines on professional conduct apply:

1. Social workers are expected to develop and maintain the required skills and competence to do their job.

2. Social workers should not allow their skills to be used for inhumane purposes, such as torture or terrorism.

3. Social workers should act with integrity. This includes not abusing the relationship of trust with the people using their services, recognising the boundaries between personal and professional life, and not abusing their position for personal benefit or gain.

4. Social workers should act in relation to the people using their services with compassion, empathy and care.

5. Social workers should not subordinate the needs or interests of people who use their services to their own needs or interests.

6. Social workers have a duty to take necessary steps to care for themselves professionally and personally in the workplace and in society, in order to ensure that they are able to provide appropriate services.

7. Social workers should maintain confidentiality regarding information about people who use their services. Exceptions to this may only be justified on the basis of a greater ethical requirement (such as the preservation of life).

8. Social workers need to acknowledge that they are accountable for their actions to the users of their services, the people they work with, their colleagues, their employers, the professional association and to the law, and that these accountabilities may conflict.

9. Social workers should be willing to collaborate with the schools of social work in order to support social work students to get practical training of good quality and up to date practical knowledge.

10. Social workers should foster and engage in ethical debate with their colleagues and employers and take responsibility for making ethically informed decisions.

11. Social workers should be prepared to state the reasons for their decisions based on ethical considerations, and be accountable for their choices and actions.

12. Social workers should work to create conditions in employing agencies and in their countries where the principles of this statement and those of their own national code (if applicable) are discussed, evaluated and upheld.

The document "Ethics in Social Work, Statement of Principles" was approved at the General Meetings of the International Federation of Social Workers and the International Association of Schools of Social Work in Adelaide, Australia, October 2004.

What assumptions inform this statement? What values are reflected? How does the declaration compare with the values and principles articulated by the NASW Code of Ethics?

Universalism, Relativism, and Human Rights

Human rights and social justice are the guiding beacons of the current IFSW statement. It stands as a concerted effort to position social work as a profession committed to the realization of these values in practice in a global context. However, the legitimacy of an international code of ethics for social work is not without question and criticism. As Healy (2001, p. 151) has addressed, there have been intense debates regarding the "universality" of social work values, and the predominance of individualistic Western values to the marginalization of other perspectives, especially those that might claim a more communal world view. The fundamental debates between absolutism and relativism that resonate through the long history of human values discourse play out here as well in the tensions between universal human rights and cultural relativism. Healy argues that there is a continuum between universalism and cultural relativism, and she sees the IFSW declaration of ethical principles as a valiant effort to position itself in the middle ground.

These discussions of universalism and relativism are challenging. Drawing from Donaldson (1996), Healy raises the question, "When is different just different and when is different wrong?" Healy does not pose facile answers, but contends that social workers in a global context face the ongoing challenge of "negotiating spaces of moral ambiguity discerning value tensions from intolerable practices that cause harm" (Rao, 1995, p. 168, cited in Healy, 2001, p. 156). Healy brings a dynamic concept of culture to bear in discussing these tensions and the ethical implications for international social work. She defines culture as "a series of constantly contested and negotiated social practices whose meanings are influenced by the power and status of their interpreters and participants" (Healy, 2001, p.156). She poses four questions for evaluating cultural claims:

1. What is the status of the speaker?
3. In whose name is the argument of culture advanced?
4. What is the degree of participation in culture formation of the social groups primarily affected by the cultural practices in questions?
5. What is culture anyway? (Healy, 2001, p. 155, citing Rao, 1995, p. 168)

The tension between universalism and relativism is ongoing in the effort to craft a set of practice principles that meaningfully crosses and bridges complex boundaries of difference. This tension is not the only focus of critique of the IFSW statement, however. Some have expressed concern over its language of professionalism and implicit assumptions of a "client-oriented" model of practice.[12] Critics contend that the IFSW Declaration of Ethical Principles favors an expert model of social work practice over one that promotes participation and social transformation. For example, the Latin American Southern Cone Committee of Professional Social Work and Social Service Organizations voiced their criticism during the process of revising the IFSW declaration.[13] They argue that the understanding of social work embraced by IFSW is disconnected from the social realities and pressing concerns of people in different countries and regions of the world. Members of the Southern Cone organizations developed their own statement of ethical and political principles to guide social work practice. Their statement recognizes their differing social realities and their common concerns regarding social exclusion, violation of human rights, conditions of widespread poverty, and erasure of collective memory. They directly voice concern over globalization and its effects on cultural identity in Latin America. The members criticize the neoliberal economic model of late capitalism, the concentration of economic and political power in the hands of the elites, and the barriers to democratization throughout the region. These forces, they argue, have severely limited social work's historic commitment to social justice. They point to the urgent need for social workers to assume a *political-ethical* position in the face of these forces and engage in the struggle for social transformation.[14]

Latin American Southern Cone Committee of Professional Social Work and Social Service Organizations

Basic Ethical and Political Principles

Based on the values of human emancipation, liberty, social justice, solidarity, and participation, we firmly defend the following basic principles:

1. The defense of the expansion and consolidation of democracy in every State constitution, with independent legislative, executive and judicial powers, a Republican system, as well as creation of new spaces of public participation, the collective control of socially produced wealth, and the defense of human, social, political, civil, cultural and economic rights.
2. The support and promotion of initiatives that expand the guidelines of integration in Mercosur (the trade alliance of the Southern Cone) to go beyond questions of the market economy to social questions, the interests of workers, and the participation of organized civil society in the region.
3. The search for and expansion of means of real access for all persons to socially produced material and cultural goods, of social participation in decisions regarding those goods, and in the collective questions regarding their conditions as citizens, without discrimination on the basis of sex, sexual preference, ethnicity, social or economic condition, religion, etc.
4. The defense of the maintenance and expansion of State responsibility to respond to the social question through universal social policies with the participation of organized civil society in their formulation, implementation and control. And the rejection of the transference of state responsibility for the social question to civil society or to voluntary philanthropy.
5. Respect for the self-determination of persons, groups, organizations, expression, and popular movements.
6. Contribute to maintaining the collective memory of the people.
7. The exercise of professional competence (theoretical and technical) and commitment (ethical and political) in meeting social demands and guaranteeing the quality of services rendered.
8. The creation, defense, and consolidation of legal regulation of the pro-

fession, of codes of ethics and of professional development with common bases in the region, grounded in collectively determined, autonomous, and democratic principles, that guarantee the free exercise of
the profession, with legally recognized rights and obligations.

9. The guarantee of pluralism through respect of the democratic political
and theoretical currents that exist in the professional environment.

10. The Oversight of professional practice, competence, and credentials
according to ethical principles that reaffirm professional responsibility for the consequences of professional intervention.

11. Ongoing professional development and the inclusion of ethics in the
academic curricula in each country.

12. Guarantee of adequate and decent working conditions for professional
practice (salary, social security, working environment, duties, etc) and
respect for professional autonomy.

Finally, we emphasize the right and the obligation to denounce every situation that puts these affirmed principles at risk, whether that be due to
professional practice or to the social reality.[15]

Social Work Ethics in Differing National Contexts

Let's look beyond the IFSW Declaration of Ethical Principles to a few examples of
ethical standards for social work practice in different national contexts. Many social work organizations in diverse parts of the world have adopted standards of
ethical practice regarding professional obligations, competence, and responsibilities to "clients," the profession, and social change that closely resemble those of
NASW. Others address the importance of ethical, responsible behavior by social
workers but do not standardize those value expectations in a code of ethics. We
find interesting and important variations in the ways values and expectations are
expressed. For example, the Canadian Association of Social Workers (1994) recognizes a commitment to the values of acceptance, self-determination, respect of
individuality, and belief in the intrinsic worth and integrity of every human being.
It also acknowledges the obligation of all people to provide resources, services,
and opportunities for the overall benefit of humanity and calls for the respect without prejudice of individuals, families, groups, communities, and nations.[16] The
Canadian Code of Ethics also contains a more explicit statement regarding nondiscrimination on the basis of sexual orientation than does the NASW Code of Ethics.

Challenges to the primacy of an individualist ethic are also reflected in various national contexts. For example, social workers in India have "questioned the
relevance of clinically-oriented Western codes for Indian community development
and prefer the term 'declaration' of ethics for people-centered work" (Desai, 1987,
cited in Link, 1999). The Indian Declaration of Ethics places a priority on social
work's responsibility to advocate for oppressed groups. A questioning of self-determination as a core value has come from diverse national and cultural perspectives in which traditions of communitarianism take precedence over individualism. Denmark is another one of the countries that has embraced a strong ethic of
communitarianism. The Danish Association of Social Workers describes itself as a
professional organization and trade union with an interest in both working condi-

tions and working methods. Their model is reminiscent of that of the Rank and File Movement in the United States, discussed in Chapter 3. The Association practices a strong commitment to international cooperation and solidarity. It is committed to promoting social development in impoverished countries and backing colleagues in these countries in their struggles to organize groups of social workers and develop local social services. For example, the association's solidarity funds have supported exchange programs with Chilean colleagues, a center for victims of torture in Chile, a seminar on human rights and social work in the Philippines, and the development of the Nicaraguan Association of Social Workers. Similarly, social workers in Norway and Finland are organized in trade unions and professional associations and maintain a strong international focus.

The New Zealand Association of Social Work has adopted a Bicultural Code of ethical practice as a concrete commitment to anti-oppressive practice that honors the identity of native Maori people. Social workers are expected to be knowledgeable of the 1840 Treaty of Waitangi, negotiated between Maori and occupying British leaders that guaranteed Maori people's right to independence. Social workers are called upon to advocate for policies and practices that honor the treaty and the rights of Maori people. The code also recognizes the right of Maori clients to have access to Maori social workers and culturally appropriate resources and services (Dewees, 2006, p. 65; Aotearoa New Zealand Association of Social Work, 2006)

In sum, these alternative conceptualizations of social work values reflect the intimate linkage between ethics and politics. They suggest the importance of understanding values in context. And they remind us of the dynamic nature of codes of ethics. Perhaps we can best think of codes of ethics as living, evolving documents, shaping and shaped by the historical, political, social, and cultural context of practice.

FRAMEWORKS FOR ETHICAL DECISION MAKING IN SOCIAL WORK PRACTICE

Our preceding discussion of values and ethics in social work speaks to the complexity of ethical issues that we confront in our practice. How then, should we proceed in the process of ethical decision making? What frameworks might guide us? These questions have been the subject of study and debate by social work ethicists and practitioners over the course of the profession's development. Most fundamentally the key questions that stem from the differing ethical perspectives discussed above may also be a starting point for the process of ethical decision making in social work:

♦ What benefit or harm might result from a particular course of action? What action will lead to the best overall consequences?

♦ Does this course of action respect the dignity of another? Does it treat the person as an end and not as a means?

♦ What rights do the affected parties have? Which course of action best respects those rights?

- Which course of action treats everyone the same, unless there is a morally justifiable reason not to? Which course of action avoids favoritism and discrimination?
- Which course of action promotes the common good? Which best contributes to the kind of society we want to be?
- Which course of action develops moral virtues? Which helps us realize the best of our individual and collective potential? (Adapted from Velasquez et al., 2004).

While these questions may offer a starting point, we are still left with fundamental questions regarding which of these perspectives then take priority in guiding our actions. Some students of social work ethics argue that there is, in fact, a clear order of priorities that should guide our decision making. For example, Loewenberg, Dolgoff, and Harrington (2000) have put forth the "Ethical Principles Screen" and argue that seven core principles can be rank-ordered in guiding decision making. The seven principles, rank ordered, are (1) protection of life; (2) equality/inequality; (3) autonomy and freedom; (4) least harm; (5) quality of life; (6) privacy and confidentiality; (7) and truthfulness and disclosure. At first glance this hierarchy may have a common-sense appeal. On closer examination, however, it seems to be informed by an implicit set of values that may be at odds with those of the individuals and communities with whom we are engaged as social workers. Think for a moment of a situation where you might apply the Ethical Principles Screen. Where might it help guide your decision making? Where might it prove problematic?

Marcia Abramson (1996) has made the case that we as social workers must know ourselves ethically in order to engage in meaningful ethical decision making with others. She sees self-examination as an ethical responsibility for professional practice. To this end, Abramson has developed a framework for ethical self-assessment that challenges us to look inward and see where and how our personal values, beliefs, and experiences filter into our ethical stance as professionals. In so doing, she has drawn from diverse ethical perspectives to pose a series of critical questions to practitioners. Take time to assess yourself in light of Abramson's framework. How might your ethical stance shape your approach to decision making regarding a social work issue such as inter-country adoption or end-of-life care? (see box on p. 144)

EXPANDING THE POSSIBILITIES FOR ETHICAL DECISION MAKING

Human Rights as a Foundation for Ethical Practice

Let's return for a moment to the question of social work and human rights. A number of people have called on social work to use the United Nations Universal Declaration of Human Rights as a foundation for ethical practice (Ife, 2001; Reichert, 2003; Witkins, 1998). The Declaration is a remarkable document crafted in response to the horrors of World War II and the Nazi Holocaust. It was endorsed by

Knowing Yourself Ethically: A Framework for Self-Assessment

Adapted from Marcia Abramson (1996)[17]

Prejudgments: Reflect on your personal value system and philosophy. What do you bring from your own personal and cultural history and background in terms of attitudes, biases, stereotypes, agendas?

Character and Virtue: What is your image of a morally good person, a good social worker, a good member of society? What generates self-esteem or self-approval for you? In what ways do you gravitate toward activities that make you feel good and away from those that make you feel bad? How might that affect your practice as a social worker?

Principles: How do you use and prioritize ethical principles? Where do you stand on these principles? When they come into conflict, which ones take precedence over others? For example, how do you weigh in on the balance of self-determination versus doing good or doing no harm? How do you weigh safety issues against self-determination and autonomy? What are your views regarding distributive justice?

Ethical Theories: Do you hold a utilitarian view that the correctness of actions needs to be weighed in relation to context or outcome? Or do you hold that certain acts are intrinsically good or bad, regardless of consequence?

Free Will versus Determinism: Do you see human beings as free agents, able to choose courses of action, or as determined by their life circumstances? Or as somewhere in between?

Spirituality: Where is the place of religion and spirituality in your worldview and in your understanding of the human search for meaning and purpose?

Individual-Community: Where do your values fall in the balance between individual rights and common good and social responsibility? Are you guided more by an ethics of individualism or communalism?

Voice: How would you describe your moral "voice"? Is it a voice of rights and justice? A voice of relationship, intimacy, and connection? Another voice?

member states of the newly formed United Nations in 1948, who explicitly recognized its principles as the "common standard of decency." Its fundamental implicit principle was that less-powerful people and groups needed protection against those with more power, especially the state (Nagenast & Turner, 1997, p. 269).

The document is a product of the historical and political moment in which it was crafted and ratified. It has been criticized for its privileging of Western conceptions of personhood, individual rights, and citizenship (Jelin, 1996; Link, 1999; Lyons, 1999, Turner, 1997). However, as Stanley Witkin (1998) notes, the declaration is significant for articulating the idea of universal rights that cannot be separated from political, social, and economic arrangements (p. 197). It embraces a philosophy that all human beings are equal in dignity and rights, and it incorporates economic, social, and cultural rights. It addresses positive rights, such as freedom of thought and religion and the right to recognition as a person before the law, and negative rights, such as protection from arbitrary arrest and detention. Its very existence provides a basis for grappling with complex questions of national sovereignty, cultural relativity, collective rights, the nature and extent of rights, the very right to have rights, and the myriad tensions therein.

Elizabeth Reichert argues that social work in the United States has avoided specific integration of human rights documents into the study and practice of social work for too long (2003, p. 249). Witkin (1998) points out that the values articulated in the declaration are central to social work. He contends, however, that a true commitment to human rights is neither visible in social work practice nor integrated into social work education in the United States. Witkin argues that U.S. social work's continued emphasis on individual change and psychological explanations for complex human concerns and noncritical acceptance of capitalism and Western individualism obscure the view of broader human rights issues (pp. 199-200). He calls on social workers to challenge individualist, medicalized explanations of peoples' pain and troubles and to make human rights a part of all aspects of practice, from assessment to intervention and evaluation criteria (p. 201).

The work of Paul Farmer, an anthropologist and physician dedicated to promoting human rights in health care, is instructive for ethics and social justice work. Farmer (2003, p. xiii) argues, "Human rights violations are not accidents; they are not random in distribution or effect. Rights violations are, rather, symptoms of deeper pathologies of power and are linked intimately to the social conditions that so often determine who will suffer abuse and who will be shielded from harm." He frames this structural violence perpetrated against the poor as "structural sin." He calls for a professional ethical stance that works from a "posture of penitence and indignation," honors human rights, promotes morally robust social policy and, in the spirit of liberation theology, embraces the "preferential option for the poor" (Farmer, 2003, pp. 157, 227). Similarly the UN Human Development Report has put forth the ethical principle of "universalism of life claims," which is the belief that no child should be doomed to a short or miserable life merely because the child happens to be born in the "wrong class" or in the "wrong country," or to be of the "wrong sex." Healy (2001) concludes:

> The implications for social work practice and advocacy of an ethical obligation to eliminate discrimination on a global scale have not been explored, yet would be far-reaching. Adopting universal life claims as a social work value would require the profession to commit to improving the lives of children living in misery anywhere in the world and to consider the global implications of equity for its practice, knowledge development, and, especially, policy development and advocacy efforts. (p. 164).

REFLECTION: **Rights, Values, and Social Justice Work**

Take some time to read and reflect on the Universal Declaration of Human Rights (Appendix A). What do you see as its strengths? Its limitations? How do the values encoded in the Declaration fit with the core values of social work? With your own core values? Return to the examples of differing perspectives on social work presented in Chapter 2:

◆ a homeless person turned away from a full shelter for the third night in a row;

◆ a 9-year-old child in a receiving home awaiting temporary placement in a foster home;

◆ a school principal making a referral of child neglect to the local child protection services office;

◆ an undocumented resident of the United States whose young child, born in the United States, is in need of emergency health care;

◆ a TANF (Temporary Assistance for Needy Families) recipient whose monthly benefit has been reduced for failure to provide proper documentation of a part-time day care arrangement.

Select one of these situations and consider it from a human rights perspective. What rights may have been denied or violated? How might your knowledge of human rights inform your response to the situation? How might your response differ from that of a social worker taking a more "traditional" approach? Has your engagement with the Universal Declaration of Human Rights prompted you to think differently about yourself as a social worker or the possibilities for social work practice? If so, how? How would you describe the relationship between human rights and social justice work?

Incorporating Human Rights in Practice

It is easier to talk about human rights than to actively incorporate them in our practice and struggle with the tensions and contradictions therein. As Janet George (1999) notes, "[h]uman rights are rather like motherhood" (p.15). Everyone agrees they are a "good thing." But translating them into practice is another story. Can notions of values and right and wrong be extracted from their cultural, historical, and political context? How do we address the dilemmas inherent in a notion of universal rights and a notion of cultural relativity? How do we support less-powerful people's claims to individual or group rights? Who counts as a "citizen" and who decides what the role of the state should be in protecting and enforcing rights? How do we respect cultural difference and stay critically aware of our own values and assumptions? How do we recognize the historical struggles against structured inequalities within cultural groups? George argues that social workers are not well prepared in the conceptual and practical issues of human rights. Further, social workers seldom have working knowledge of other United Nations Conventions, such as those addressing the rights of the child and social development.[18] She notes that concepts such as human rights imply a value judgment, and thus make it logically impossible to come to full agreement. The process of naming and claiming rights is always emergent and negotiated—a work in progress.

Manuel Garretón (1996, p. 39), writing on human rights in the Southern Cone of Latin America, argues that human rights are basically historical and cultural concepts centering on the right to life. They are constructed hand-in-hand with our ideas of citizenship and the state. He asks how human rights get addressed in situations where the state is responsible for their massive violation. How do we come to terms with massive violations of human rights? What are the tensions and contradictions in trying to translate human rights reparations into remunerative compensation? These are difficult questions that may seem to be beyond the bounds of social work. However, as George (1999) argues, "If social work as a profession espouses a commitment to social justice, then a role in the promotion of human rights is implicit. Developing that role involves considerations that are conceptual, cultural, and political" (pp. 21-22). One of the implications for social work in the United States is that we must move beyond the safety of local and national boundaries and consider the potential political and ethical ramifications of our privileged positioning in the "Global North" and the action generated from that positioning. It means that we must embrace what Rosemary Link (1999, p. 85) calls an "ethics of participation."

Toward an Ethics of Participation

We will explore the politics and ethics of practice and processes of an ethics of participation in more detail in Chapters 7 to 9. We close this chapter with a starting point for an ethics of participation. An ethics of participation demands, most fundamentally, that the people affected by particular issues or circumstances and events need to be present in the process of decision making. Discussions need to take place in people's first language. And people need to have a legitimate voice in all decisions that affect them (Link, 1999, pp. 85-86). Link puts forth a number of universal principles for social workers who seek social and economic justice. She organizes the principles into three broad categories:

1. **Widest perspective for assessment**
   - Before acting, review personal values, history, and cultural bias; ask the question, "How am I influenced personally and professionally by this question or problem?"
   - Review the value base, history, and culture of the other(s) concerned with the ethical question.
   - Question geocentrism and the effect of location of people involved; what would be different if this dialogue were happening elsewhere in the world and why?
2. **Inclusion of the service user in dialogue and decisions**
   - Discuss the "right to reality" of the service user and their family or community; spend time defining this reality.
   - Acknowledge the "power" of the professional.
   - Attend to the use of clear language.
   - Consider the question of "conscientization": To what extent is the immediate ethical tension reflective and part of wider societal and global issues?
3. **Joint Evaluation**
   - Was the outcome lasting in its resolution of the ethical questions in the workers', service users', and community view?
   - Which actions by the workers worked best?

- Which actions by the service user(s) worked best?
- Did all members feel included and respected?
- What would be different in a future instance of this ethical decision? (Link, 1999, p. 90)

Take a moment to consider these principles. Do they provide a starting point for guiding the politics and ethics of social justice work? How might you modify these principles? What would you add, delete, or change? Using these questions and guidelines, take time to reflect on an ethical dilemma you or others have faced as you have engaged in social work practice. Do you see alternative possibilities for understanding the problem, building relationships, and developing courses of action? We will return to specific questions of values, ethics, and participation as we explore the core processes of social justice work in the following chapters.

CHAPTER SUMMARY

In this chapter we have examined the concept of values, their place in our everyday lives, and their role in shaping social work thought and practice. We have considered values in political, historical, and familial contexts, and we have addressed the practice of valuing. We have considered the core values of social work, the relationship between values and ethics, and the emergence of codes of ethics. We have challenged the ethical boundaries of social work in the United States by examining alternative constructions of values and standards of ethical and political practice in diverse organizational and national contexts. We have outlined approaches to ethical decision making and the challenges therein. Finally, we considered the relationship of social work and human rights and put forth ethical and political principles that may guide us in the pursuit of social justice work. In Chapter 5, we turn our attention to theory, the dialectics of understanding and action, and the Just Practice Framework and processes.

Teaching–Learning Resource: Reflections on Questions of Values, History, and Community

The following essay is a reflection on questions of values, history, and community written by University of Montana MSW graduate, Eric Diamond. Take a moment to read and reflect on Eric's story. What feelings does it evoke for you? What questions of values, history, and community does he raise? What lessons for social justice work can you draw from the essay? What stories of your own does it bring to mind?

Yid Vicious
by Eric Diamond

In order to put an end to a six-year meander through the University of Wisconsin, I took a job working nights and weekends as a line cook at a popular Madison steak house called the Hurricane Cafe. I earned the money needed for my few remaining credits by serving up beef, frogs, venison, chicken, snails, and lamb at a breakneck pace to Madison's elite. Lawmakers, University professors, businessmen, and rich kids from the East Coast used the Cafe to avoid their families and flaunt their excess on a regular basis; they flirted with the waitresses while their wives and girlfriends were at home, drank themselves into a stupor, and tossed their food around as if they were already full. Chef Karl used to lecture the waitresses to get the plates out to the tables while they were still hot. "Steam's the best garnish, Tara!" Twenty minutes later, when half of a 16 ounce steak and three-quarters of a potato was slammed into the trash by the dish pit, we'd all shake our heads at the dear price of a good time, the distasteful waste in food, labor, and money in which we were all fruitlessly engaged.

For the most part, the Hurricane Cafe was a way station for drunks, cocaine addicts, pot heads, and students who had not yet developed their professional skills. The cooks, wait staff, and the management traded labor, laughs, cigarettes, booze, and connections on various types of illegal substances for a temporary state of friendship and steady employment. But then again the lifestyle was not conducive to any semblance of normalcy. The Hurricane Cafe opened for business at 5:00PM every evening except Mondays, and stopped serving dinner at 10:00PM. The adjoining bar remained open each evening until 2:00AM. With great frequency, the Hurricane Cafe's staff hustled through their shifts, cleaned up their sections, changed out of their filthy aprons, and snuggled up to the bar for shots and beer, many consuming their meager wages in a matter of hours. Most would have their "breakfast" well into the afternoon on the next day, like one would on New Year's Day, following a long evening of exceptional excess. It was the life of a vampire, and it was one that I found impossible to live. Not long after I had mastered the cracks and crevices of the Hurricane Cafe, I found myself looking for something with a little more meaning and purpose.

Although I stayed on at the steak house (the pay was about as good as I could get), I looked for something useful to do with my Monday afternoons. On the East Side of town there was a Jewish community center that provided all types of services for the small elderly Jewish population of Madison. On Mondays at 12:30 in the afternoon, the community center offered more than 300 seniors a hot kosher meal and an activity. For some of the elderly citizens, the center provided a fanciful break from the norm, a way to connect regularly with neighbors and possible friends, a place to share their stories; for others, it provided the only square meal for the week, and a reason to keep getting up each morning.

My job was to put my limited cooking skills at Ben and Hannah's disposal, a married catering duo that had a veritable strangle hold on all the kosher catering jobs in the Jewish Community. They were like celebrities, receiving hugs, kisses, blessings, and warm smiles wherever they were recognized. In the center's kitchen, they whipped up kosher meals by the hundreds, providing each holiday with the necessary flavor and fare to the delight of all involved.

For the most part, I spent about three hours every Monday working as a prep cook under Ben and Hannah's direction. I cut onions, carrots, and celery for the matzo ball soup, I trimmed the jelly off of the gefilte fish; I rolled blintzes, and breaded shnitzels. I learned quite a bit in the kitchen working with them, and in my own home that knowledge is regularly put to good use throughout the year on various Jewish holidays. It also felt good to be doing something for the Jewish community. Not since my Bar Mitzvah had I even considered stepping foot in a house of worship, and not since my time in Israel had I been in the company of so many Jews. A connection to a "Jewish Community" was something that I never really experienced growing up; my "Judaism" was never at the forefront of my personal thought. It was interesting for me to be around so many people who were Jews before they were anything else.

Chanukah at the community center was a big deal, a real showcase for the services offered to its seniors. Ben and Hannah asked me to come in an hour earlier because the center was expecting to seat some 400 seniors at their annual Chanukah party, and there was a lot more work to do that day. Lunch was going to be roast beef served with latkes (fried potato pancakes) and apple sauce, a traditional Eastern European meal for the holiday. The activity for the afternoon was to be music and dancing; the center had booked a local *Klezmer* group named Yid Vicious to play an array of up-tempo Jewish favorites. It was to be a full afternoon, and I spent the morning grating so many potatoes and onions, my right arm was left in a limp and Jell-O-like state. The next day, I was actually sore from the extensive preparations, the way one is when they spend too much time lifting too much weight in the gym. The apple sauce, thankfully, came out of five or six huge cans, but the latkes all had to be individually fried. Working with six huge frying pans, Ben, Hannah, and I prepared about 1,200 latkes for lunch in about 35 minutes, no mean feat, I assure you. The roast beef was much easier to prepare; after about two hours in the oven, Ben used his knife to shave paper thin slices of meat onto the paper plates, making sure that there was as much food offered to the 390th person as there was to the first.

Amid much commotion, chaos, and noise, the four hundredth plate left the kitchen on a tray and arrived in front of the eagerly waiting seniors sitting around the long rectangle tables covered with the cheap paper cloths. All were served and for the most part rather pleased with the effort and presentation that defined their lunch. I peaked through the circular window on the swinging kitchen doors to see 400 seniors tearing into their Chanukah feasts, for some the best they've had in years. As I was standing there observing the group, and feeling good about myself, Ben handed me a paper plate generously filled with roast beef and latkes and told me to go sit down and take a break. I took off my stained apron, washed my hands, and took my place next to two women seated at the end of one of the tables.

I barely hit my seat before I began to dig into my lunch; preparing so much food had not only made me a little weary, I was famished. I poured a little apple sauce over my latkes and went to work. Not bad, I thought; but you can't really mess up latkes. As I sat and ate my meal (the one tangible perk to being a cook) I became aware of a lively conversation occurring at the table between the two women I had sat next to. I had never heard anything like it. What language were they speaking? I knew a little Hebrew, and as I eavesdropped, I recognized every tenth word or so; I had heard Yiddish spoken many times, and I knew that that wasn't it. I was at a loss.

I sat there and listened to the rambling rhythm of the language, the peaks and valleys of the tongue; it was beautiful. An older man seated across from me, who's rolled up left sleeve exposed a vertical row of greenish blue numbers flashed me a kind smile after taking a sip of grape juice. His stained purple teeth were crooked and worn, like a band saw dipped in ink. I leaned over the table and asked him, "Do you know what language that is?" He answered with a soft nod, "Ladino, my young man, the Yiddish of Spain."

Ladino? The Yiddish of Spain? I had no idea there was such a thing. All I could utter in response was a misplaced and naïve "Wow!", exposing my ignorance to my learned host. But as I regained my thoughts, I realized, why not Ladino. When populations are segregated from others their language patterns embark upon their own unique and culturally specific course. In Spain, as in Poland, Italy, and Germany, Jews lived as a race apart, as a ghettoized community cast aside from the greater culture, habits and favor of the majority. My thoughts quickly moved from not accepting that such a language could exist to disbelieving that such a language could have possibly survived. But in my experience, that is precisely what Jewish crafted things did best. They survived. And here they were, two Jewish women in Madison, Wisconsin, at the end of the 20th century speaking a language that perhaps only a handful of others even knew about. Amazing!

The gentleman and I soon continued our pleasantries. He related that he was from Minsk, and had lost nearly everything when the Nazis invaded. He had moved to Madison to live near his daughter, who was a professor at the University. As I began to tell him my own relatively mundane tale, we were interrupted by a high pitched screech of a sound coming from the end of the table. "Don't talk to him! He's a Stalinist!" A grey-haired woman with a prominent mole on her nose was pointing a crooked and wrinkled finger at my newly found friend. "He supported the Stalinists! *The Stalinists*!" Her voice was the sound of pure venom, one that contained a life of misery and woe, one that needed an outlet no matter how misplaced. With a characteristic smile and a casual shrug, the man retorted, "Better to support Stalin, than Hitler." With that, the conversation was over. The woman dismissed the exchange with a wave of her hand and went back to her latkes. My friend gave me another kind look, leaned into the table and said, "You can't please everyone." With that he excused himself from the table, and went to join perhaps a less politically judgmental group at the far end of the room.

Misery makes for strange bedfellows; and during the chaos and horror of

World War II it made for even stranger political alliances. A Jew caught within the barbed confines of the Nazi death camp knew that Stalin's forces were one of the two on Earth that were capable of liberating him. As one is worked to death in the shadow of his tortured and mutilated brethren, is it any wonder why a Jew might become a Stalinist? I guess it is a function of time and place that determines which murderers we support and which we oppose. For the woman at the end of the table, perhaps her family was one of the millions Stalin slaughtered, displaced, or imprisoned. Doubtless on her side of the fence, he was the very opposite of a liberator. It's all a matter of perspective.

As the group at the table finished their meals, I took a look around the room and noticed that everyone was just about done. I got up and skated back into the kitchen to help Ben and Hannah clean up. I swept the floor, hung up the last remaining pots and pans, and wiped down the counters. I remembered that Yid Vicious was set to play today and decided to stick around for the show; usually I left right after clean up because the activities the center offered regularly were in my mind rather lame. But I am a great fan of *Klezmer* music; and since I had never heard Yid Vicious, I walked back into the hall and propped myself up against the back wall. The band was just setting up and tuning their instruments. I helped the community center staff set up rows of chairs in front of the band. The mood in the room was light and carefree; everyone was well-fed and generally in good spirits.

It took a good while to get everyone over to the chairs from where they had been seated for lunch, but after the center's president introduced the band, Yid Vicious wasted no time and broke into a lively version of *Hava Negilla*, a tune that got everyone singing, clapping, and tapping their feet. After a few opening numbers, the band leader, a bearded chubby fellow playing a forest green colored tuba, signaled a break and addressed the crowd. "*Hag Smeach* everyone! Happy Chanukah! Thank you for having us here today for your celebration. We are Yid Vicious, a local *Klezmer* group." He went on in pedantic fashion to explain to the group of senior citizens that *Klezmer* is the Yiddish word for musician, and that *Klezmer* music was the cultural creation of the *Shtetl*, the small towns set within the Pale of Settlement on Russia's Western border. On and on he droned, telling people what they already knew, relating their own history as if it were only words. He said that *Klezmer* music was practically lost with the near destruction of Eastern Europe's Jewish population during the Holocaust, and that his band was a part of a national *Klezmer* revival sweeping across Europe, America, and Israel. The good people of the center had had just about enough of this self-indulgent horn tooting. They wanted to hear some music. Was this a lecture or a concert?

After about five minutes of this misplaced and unnecessary history lesson, the band leader inquired of the group if anyone knew what their name meant. Yid had been a slur that was thrown around a lot in the faces of European Jews throughout history, and I guess the band wanted to apologize for its usage. A woman in the back row yelled out, "Sid Vicious was a drug addict, a wife beater, an awful man! Why do you honor him with our music?" The nods and grumblings from the crowd nudged the band leader towards uneasiness. "Actually, it is just a play on his name. We are trying to reclaim the word Yid for our community the way other oppressed groups have reclaimed their own epithets." On deaf ears he defended his choice to a group that stood as a veritable cornucopia of Jewish suffering. They saw neither humor nor an opportunity for activism in the word Yid, a word that the majority had escaped to America to avoid. Only the young-those born thousands of miles and decades away from their parents' struggles-would make a joke out of their ancestors' misery; only those who hadn't experienced the brutality and ferocity hiding behind such a word would ever conceive of such a name.

Wiggling out of his discomfort, and trying to reclaim the mood, the band leader shared that they were going to play a traditional Polish wedding song for the joyous occasion of Chanukah. In this song, and in many traditional *Klezmer* pieces, it is tradition to increase the tempo of the song throughout the song at regular intervals. Doing so not only showcased the musicianship of the band, but also was designed to get everyone in a more festive mood. The band leader, unfortunately still talking, told everyone to be on the look out for the tempo changes. As he counted in Yiddish to start the number, he was suddenly forced to stop the count, and signaled with a raised hand for the band to wait. Something was awry. An elderly, hump backed woman in a tattered green shawl tiptoed up to the stage, leading a reluctant man behind her by the hand. She strained to reach her lips to the ear of the band leader, who hunched over and met her halfway. After about 30 seconds of the inaudible exchange, the band leader removed the microphone from its stand and handed it to the elderly woman. She smiled meekly in front of the crowd, which had become awash with whispers and inquiries as to what was going on. The lady flashed a diminutive smile, cleared her throat and spoke: "My husband play drum in Russian Army. He will play one song with group. Thank you. Thank you."

With that, the gentleman took the drummer's seat and arranged himself properly behind the kit. Immediately after he sat down on the stool, he revealed a row of glistening gold teeth below his upper lip, and shared his exuberant joy with his friends and neighbors by making funny faces and waving to the crowd. The song began and the gentleman showed himself to be a master from the start. His style was crisp, progressive, and sharp; his introduction into the group made the band finally a real *Klezmer* group. As was promised earlier, the tempo picked up after each successive cycle, and soon the other members were at a loss to keep up with their new drummer. For the first time that afternoon, people were out of their seats, dancing, reliving old memories, bringing the music ever more so alive. This old grinning Russian drummer was a Jewish pied piper, his crisp and driving beats forced the group to abandon their heavy histories and embrace the up-tempo moment, dancing, laughing, and singing as they did. Eventually, the pace became too fast for the neophyte *Klezmers*, and the song collapsed into a cacophonous melee of noise. As if putting a wounded animal out of its misery, our Russian drummer struck a final cymbal crash, announcing the merciful conclusion to the piece. With one last twirl of the stick, and one last strike at the cow bell, the Russian drummer placed the sticks atop the bass drum, raised himself off of the stool, and rejoined his wife, who had been clapping, singing, and dancing with reckless abandon just a few feet from her husband.

More so than anyone else, Yid Vicious was awe-struck by the Russian's performance. But really, except for me and them, no one else in the hall was. The band immediately began to pack it in, unplugging their amps, collecting their cords, and encasing their fragile instruments. What on Earth could possibly follow such a performance? Not Yid Vicious, that's for sure. I bet the band leader thought that it was better to depart while everyone was smiling, than to risk starting another argument over the word Yid or god knows what else. But really, although the seniors in the hall had enjoyed the last song, none of them were surprised at the quality of the drumming, and the way this lone Russian drummer had made this rather mundane band momentarily great. They were used to greatness. This generation, these senior citizens, true victims in the eyes of the greater community-labeled simply as Holocaust survivors or refugees-all had heroic talents, magical secrets, and fantastic stories to share with anyone who cared to inquire-all of them. Theirs was the upheaval generation, which unlike my own, demanded nothing short of miracles and superhuman strength from those who would dare survive. In every way, they were the best humanity had to offer, forged into greatness by the very fires of hell. And what did we do with them? We house them en mass in "nursing homes." We give them 50 cents off of their bus fares, and two bucks off their movie tickets. We shuffled them into a hall, gave them a few scraps upon paper plates, and asked a motley group of 20-somethings to lecture them about the very culture their friends and family died defending.

I recall the merits of my own generation with a bitter cautiousness, and do not wonder why so many of my friends and acquaintances regularly abuse drugs and alcohol, seek thrills that endanger their lives, and routinely dive headfirst into the shallow pool of our material consumer culture, awash with the glorification of casual sex, violence, monetary wealth, and crime. And while the upheaval generation's world was unsustainable because they were at war, ours is as well because we have accepted a dangerous peace. In vast numbers, the Yid Vicious generation has made peace with an increasingly unequal wealth distribution, an illegal and interminable global war, an arms race the likes of which we have never seen; we've made peace with a slide towards fascism, growing intolerance, cruel and unfair imprisonment, the destruction of our natural world, the enslavement of our own children. And be sure that if we look to the cozy middle class youth taking up space within our national universities, we will find no savior. I am sure that there are no partisans to be found among them.

Instead, let us look backwards. Let us find halls such as those at the community center, unlikely places filled with those that define strength and survival. Let us seek out those who speak dying tongues, those that made deals with devils. Let us learn from the few who wiped the blackened ashes of a lost world from their sleeves and began anew; those whose struggles and trials make ours look almost manageable. In order to go forward, we must learn to look back; we must utilize the upheaval generation's strengths, the myriad lessons they have for us, the thousands of powerful perspectives while there's still time. Let us seek out the lone drummers who with just a couple of sticks and a golden smile can make the mundane into something special. Together we can join in and change the tune.

Teaching–Learning Resource: The Social Class Questionnaire

This questionnaire was used in an undergraduate introductory course at Brown University taught by Professor Susan Smulyan entitled "Basic Issues in American Culture. We find this questionnaire helpful in exploring the intersection of values and social class.[19]

Please respond to the following questions about social class:

1. How would you characterize your family's socioeconomic background? (For example: poor, working class, lower-middle class, middle class, upper- middle class, upper class, ruling class). What tells you this?

2. What was/is your father's occupation (if applicable)? What was/is your mother's occupation (if applicable)?

3. How would you characterize the socioeconomic nature of the neighborhood(s) you grew up in? Of the larger community you grew up in?

4. Pick five values/expectations/orientations that seem to be most valued in your family. Then pick five that seem to be least valued or important.
   Getting by
   Making a moderate living
   Making a very good living
   Open communication among family members
   Going to a place of worship
   Keeping up with the neighbors
   Being physically fit or athletic
   Working out psychological issues through therapy
   Helping others
   Getting married and having children
   Respecting law and order
   Defending one's country
   Staying out of trouble with the law
   Being politically or socially aware
   Recognition
   Community service
   Saving money
   Making your money work for you
   Enjoying your money
   Getting a high school degree
   Getting a college degree
   Getting an advanced or professional degree
   Learning a trade
   Helping to advance the cause of one's racial, religious-cultural
       group

Physical appearance
Being a professional
Being an entrepreneur
Owning a home
Being patriotic
Going to private school
Not being wasteful
Having good etiquette
Others: _____

5. Think of one or two people whom you perceive to be from a different social class from you (someone from high school, from a job, from your university). What class would you say they belong to? What tells you this?
    Besides money, what do you see as distinguishing them from you (or your family from their family)?
    How would you characterize their values or their family's values?
    How are their values the same as or different from yours?

6. What do you appreciate/have you gained from your class background experience?

7. What has been hard for you being from your class background?

8. What would you like never to hear said about people from your class background?

9. What impact does your class background have on your current attitudes, behaviors, and feelings (about money, work, relationships with people from the same class/from a different class, your sense of self, expectations about life, your politics, etc.)?

Questions for Discussion

1. If you were to organize a "value tour" of your community, where would you go? What values would you highlight? What impressions might participants take away from the tour? How would you engage participants in critical reflection on their experience?

3. Reflecting on your own values, what life experiences have posed the greatest challenges to your values? What institutions beyond the family have shaped your values? How have your values evolved or changed as a result?

4. Based on your review of a number of codes of ethics, what would you include if you were to write a code of ethics for 21st century social justice work?

5. How do the five key concepts of meaning, context, power, history, and possibility suggest a framework for valuing?

6. Arrange a viewing of the film "Ladybird, Ladybird" for your social work class. Facilitate a group discussion after the film so that viewers can share their reactions. What emotions does the film evoke? What value conflicts can you identify? What social work values to you see as present or absent in the helpers and helping systems depicted in the film? What issues of human rights are at stake?

Suggested Readings

Adams, M., Blumenfeld, W., Castañeda, R., Hackman, H., Peters, M., & Zuñiga, X. (2000). *Readings for diversity and social justice.* New York: Routledge.

Farmer, P. (2003). *Pathologies of power: Health, human rights, and the new war on the poor.* Berkeley: University of California Press.

Healy, L. (2001). *International social work: Professional action in an interdependent world.* New York: Oxford University Press.

Kozol, J. (1991). *Savage inequalities: Children in America's schools.* New York: CrownPublishers.

Rawls, J. (1995). *A theory of justice* (2nd ed.). Cambridge, MA: Harvard University Press.

Takaki, R. (1993). *A different mirror: A history of multicultural America.* Boston: Little, Brown.

End Notes

[1] The following quotes are taken from George Seldes (1985) (Ed.) *The great thoughts*. New York: Balantine Books. Confucius (p. 92), from *The doctrine of the mean*, Ch. XX, 8; Diderot (p. 108) from "On man, a refutation of Helvetius' work, 1774"; Nietzsche (p. 311) from *Ecco homo*, 1908, Pt. I, 1; Arendt (p.16) from *The life of the mind*, unfinished trilogy, no date.

[2] This side bar is based on excerpts from J. Finn (1998b) "Gender and Families," Chapter Six in Josefina Figueira-McDonough, F. Ellen Netting, and Ann Nichols-Casebolt (Eds.) *The role of gender in practice knowledge: Claiming half the human experience*, pp. 207-208.

[3] See Nakanishi and Rittner (1992) for a discussion of the "Inclusionary cultural model" and exercises that enable students to work through a process of cultural self-definition. The authors address the role of family and childhood lessons in values and valuing as part of the process of cultural self-definition.

[4] This exercise on values and valuing is informed by White and Tyson-Rawson's (1995) work on the "gendergram," a tool for assessing gender role socialization.

[5] Rocky Boy's Reservation in North Central Montana home to the Chippewa-Cree confederated tribes.

[6] From John H. Oberly, Annual Report of the Commissioner of Indian Affairs, 1888, in Washburn (1973, p. 422).

[7] From T. J. Morgan, Annual Report of the Commissioner of Indian Affairs, 1889, in Washburn (1973, p. 434).

[8] Seldes' work is a collection of quotes. The quote from Jeremy Bentham comes from *The Commonplace Book*, Works X, 142. See Seldes, 1985, p. 39.

[9] From the Preamble to the NASW Code of Ethics, approved by the Delegate Assembly in 1996 and revised by the delegate assembly in 1999.

[10] This chart was developed based on Levy's discussion of preferred conceptions of people, outcomes for people, and instrumentalities for dealing with people (Levy, 1973, pp. 38-42).

[11] Text taken from NABS website, retrieved March 10, 2006. Permission to reproduce excerpt from the Code of Ethics of NABSW courtesy of NABSW, Detroit, Michigan.

[12] See the website of the School of Social Work, University of Costa Rica, San Jose Costa Rica, at www.ts.ucr.ac.cr/decla, for an archive of declarations and debates regarding the definition of social work.

[13] The Southern Cone is made of up Argentina, Bolivia, Brazil, Chile, Paraguay, and Uruguay

[14] From the First Regional Seminar on Ethics and Social Work organized by the Comité MERCOSUR de Organizaciones Profesionales de Trabajo Social y Servicio Social en Montevideo, Uruguay, June 1-3, 2000. See the full text of Principles at the website of the School of Social Work, University of Costa Rica, San Jose, Costa Rica: www.ts.ucr.ac.cr/decla-002.

[15] Declaration from the First Regional Seminar on Ethics and Social Work organized by the Comite MERCOSUR de Organizaciones Profesionales de Trabajo Social y Servicio Social en Montevideo, Uruguay, 1-3 junio, 2000

[16] From Canadian Association of Social Workers website, www.casw-acts.ca, 2001.

[17] This framework for self-assessment is based on the model developed by Marcia Abramson (1996) Reflections on knowing oneself ethically: Toward a working framework for social work practice. *Families in Society* 77(4), 195-201.

[18] For more information on Human Rights and links to documents and archives see the Office of the High Commissioner for Human Rights website at http://www.unhchr.ch.

[19] The social class questionnaire is reproduced here courtesy of *Radical Teacher* where it was published in Spring, 1995.

Just Thinking: Theoretical Perspectives on Social Justice-Oriented Practice

Theory enables us to deal with contradictions and uncertainties. Perhaps more significantly, it gives us space to plan, to strategize, to take greater control over our resistances.

Linda Tuhiwai Smith, 1999[1]

I came to theory because I was hurting—the pain within me was so intense that I could not go on living. I came to theory desperate, wanting to comprehend— to grasp what was happening around and within me. Most importantly, I wanted to make the hurt go away. I saw in theory a location for healing.

bell hooks, 1994[2]

CHAPTER OVERVIEW

In Chapter 5 we define and discuss theory and the practice of theorizing in social science inquiry and everyday life. We consider theorizing as a fundamental human activity through which we work to make sense of our worlds, experiences, and relations. We examine theory in the context of social work and present a brief overview and critique of several approaches to social work theory and practice— *ecosystems, structural, strengths,* and *empowerment.* We then introduce readers to a range of critical theoretical contributions that have been developed by people outside of social work who are concerned with questions of social justice and social change. They address questions about the *politics of knowledge development,* the workings of *nonviolent domination* (hegemony), and the *positivist assumptions of objectivity.* They explore the *intersectionality* of race, class, gender, sexuality, citizenship, and age in systems of oppression, and the centrality of language, meaning, and narrative in the crafting of human experience. In Chapter 2 we introduced you to some of the critical theorists who have influenced our approach to social justice work. In this chapter, we reflect on their contributions and the ways they have informed our thinking about the Just Practice Framework. We return to our key concepts—*meaning, context, power, history,* and *possibility*—and argue their relevance for social justice work. We then introduce the seven core processes— *engagement, teaching/learning, action, accompaniment, evaluation, critical reflection,* and *celebration*—through which the concepts are translated into practice.

WHAT IS THEORY?

Challenge of Defining Theory

If social work practice is a house we build, then theory is its blueprint. Explicitly and implicitly, formally or informally, theory is ever present in our practice. Nevertheless, say the word "theory" to many social work practitioners and be prepared to hear of its irrelevance outside the classroom. The dialogue goes much like this: "Theory is what they teach you in school. This is the real world and theory has no use here. We need skills, tools, and methods to guide our practice." Theory is thought of as intangible, highly academic, and entirely intellectual. In school we learn about theory without "doing" theory and we learn theory without recognizing that we have been doing theory all of our lives. The irony here is that theory is *always* in play in our work, whether we take the time to think about it or not. It underscores every action we take as social workers. It informs our behavior, the choices we make, and the interventions we plan and carry out. So what is theory? Is it too abstract? Is it separate from the "real" world of the social worker practitioner? How does it work? And what are its contributions to the profession?

A Child's-Eye View

Theory has multiple meanings, according to the Webster's dictionary: It is the analysis of a set of facts in their relation to one another, a plausible or scientifically acceptable general principle or body of principles offered to explain phenomena, and abstract thought or speculation (Merriam-Webster Online, 2006). The first and second definitions have the tone of scientific formality while the latter speaks more to contemplation and our human sense of wonder and curiosity. Now think of that favorite phrase of toddlers: "But why?" With those two words, children enter into theorizing about the world and their experience in it. They are seeking explanations and trying to grasp cause and effect. They are trying to understand the rules, the way things work.

REFLECTION: Making Theory

Holly Peters-Golden, a medical anthropologist, teaches us about theory and theorizing from the experiences of everyday life. Several years ago, Holly was home caring for her preschool-age daughter, who had a bad case of the flu. As she stroked her daughter's feverish forehead, she said, "Honey, you just feel miserable, don't you?" Her little girl looked up at her and asked: "Mommy, what makes mizzuhble happen?" Her daughter's question is about theory, about trying to understand her pain and give meaning to her experience. She is trying to construct a theory of health and illness.

Reflect on a moment in your own early life experience that you struggled to understand. How did you give meaning to the experience? What information did you draw on to come to your understanding? Did you share your theory with others? Did they share your interpretation of the experience or did they have a different understanding? Did your theory change over time as you gathered more information? What might reflection on your own experience suggest about theory and theorizing more broadly?[1]

The Urgency of Theory

The writer bell hooks, whose quote begins this chapter, speaks to the urgency, emotionality, and, most fundamentally, the necessity of making sense of our life experiences and conditions. Her sense of desperation to grasp and give meaning to the power and pain of her experience contrasts sharply with a sterile notion of theory as separate and separable from "practice." Her understanding of theory parallels that of Antonio Gramsci, the Italian Marxist philosopher who theorized about culture, power, history, and Fascism from his prison cell. Gramsci spent the last 11 years of his life—1926 to 1937—in prison for his participation in working-class movements and his promotion of the dangerous idea that poor and working-class people were capable of critically understanding and collectively changing the conditions of their lives (Forgacs, 1988; Gramsci, 1987). Like hooks, Gramsci wrote about theory with a sense of urgency, filling notebooks from his prison cell. He lived the inseparability of theory and practice and wrote, "so the unity of theory and practice is also not a given mechanical fact but an historical process of becoming…" (Gramsci, 1987, p. 67). He argued the importance of grasping the

> . . . passage from knowing to understanding and to feeling and vice versa from feeling to understanding and to knowing. The popular element "feels" but does not always know or understand; the intellectual element "knows" but does not always understand and in particular does not feel… the intellectual's error consists in believing that one can know without understanding and even more without feeling and being impassioned. (Gramsci in Forgacs, 1988, p. 349)

Theory and Oppression

We quote Linda Tuhiwai Smith (1999), Maori scholar, researcher, teacher, and activist, at the beginning of the chapter. Writing from an indigenous perspective, she notes that the word "theory" is a word that can provoke a broad range of feelings, values, and attitudes. She points out that, in many ways, indigenous peoples have been oppressed by theory. Outsider understandings and assumptions have guided the probing into "the way our origins have been examined, our histories recounted, our arts analysed, our cultures dissected, measured and torn apart…" (p.38). Smith recognizes the power of theory in crafting social reality and making claims about that reality. She reminds us that theory is not made in a vacuum but in the context of cultural understanding and social and political relations. She calls on indigenous people to participate in the theory making that shapes understanding of their histories and experiences. Smith writes:

> The development of theories by indigenous scholars which attempt to explain our existence in contemporary society (as opposed to the "traditional" society constructed under modernism) has only just begun. Not all these theories claim to be derived from some "pure" sense of what it means to be indigenous, nor do they claim to be theories which have been developed in a vacuum separated from any association with civil and human rights movements, other nationalist struggles or other theoretical approaches. What is

claimed, however, is that new ways of theorizing by indigenous scholars are grounded in a real sense of, and sensitivity towards, what it means to be an indigenous person. As Kathie Irwin [1992] urges, "We don't need anyone else developing the tools which will help us to come to terms with who we are. We can and will do this work. Real power lies with those who design the tools—it always has. This power is ours." (1999, p. 38)

Theory as Explanation, Prediction, and Filter

In their most positivist sense, theories explain or predict certain behaviors or particular social phenomenon (Payne, 2005; Robbins, Chatterjee, & Canda, 1999, 2006; Schriver, 2004). Positivism refers to an ideology, or set of beliefs, that assumes there is a stable, "knowable" world, governed by natural laws, that can be discovered through controlled, objective, value-free, systematic inquiry. Theories are thus "based on cognitive abstractions that develop over time and are both a description and generalization from our experiences" (Robbins, Chatterjee, & Canda, 2006, p. 375). In their social work practice text, Bradley Sheafor, Charles Horejsi, and Gloria Horejsi (2006) write that a theory "offers both an explanation of certain behaviors or situations and guidelines on how they can be changed" (p. 51). Patricia Lengermann and Jill Niebrugge-Brantley (1998, p. 2) describe theory as a "lens that directs the eye towards a given reality so that one focuses on some of its features while filtering out others."

Theory as Survival Skill

Charles Lemert (2004) describes theory as a basic survival skill. In so doing, he removes theory from its privileged academic location as "a special activity of experts" (p. 1) and demystifies it by illustrating how ordinary people create theory and do it quite well. He uses an example from Alex Kotlowitz's book, *There Are No Children Here* (1991), where the author tells the story of a young boy trying to survive in Chicago's most dangerous public housing project (contemporary tenement houses). This 10-year old child says, "If I grow up, I want to be a bus driver." Think for a moment of what the word "if" means in this context. Contrast this with the common phrase of the privileged child: "When I grow up. . ." In the story, the boy's mother adds increased depth and richness to social theory through her comments, "But you know, there are no children here. They've seen too much to be children." Lemert tells us this is social theory: "The boy and his mother both put into plain words the social world of the uncounted thousands of urban children whose lullaby is gunfire" (pp. 1-2). What theories of children and childhood do this boy and his mother express? How do they test out these theories every day? Are there other places in the world where this theory might apply? How in these circumstances is theory a basic survival skill as bell hooks recounts in this chapter's beginning quotation?

Theory Guides Social Work Practice—A Historical Snapshot

As we saw in Chapter 3, a historical perspective helps us better understand the relationship of theory to social work practice. It helps us step back for a moment and contemplate the power and importance of theory to guide our practice as social workers. Near the end of the Progressive Era, social work practice gravitated toward the "objectivity" of scientific methods. It was a time when science claimed and colonized social work and other professions with its promise of finding the right and true solutions to address the struggles and challenges of the human condition. Mary Richmond (1917) (re)languaged social casework to reflect this scientific allegiance and further the advancement of a professional standard for social work. Richmond spoke of "social diagnosis" instead of "investigation" and forged the marriage of social work and medicine through what she called "medical-social service." Bringing medicine to bear on social work provided it with credibility. This was an act of (re)theorizing social work. Medical theory reconfigured practice. It defined and reflected the familiar power relationships of doctor and patient, expert and the uninformed. This configuration established the basis of the casework relationship. It also guided workers to look for the source of problems within individuals and less so in environmental circumstances and structures. Even settlement house work, once predicated on the principles of participatory democracy, showed signs of theoretical infiltration and alteration as the language of clients, problems, and needs circumvented that of citizen, participation, and rights.

This historical snapshot helps us to imagine how theory influences and shapes the very essence of our work as social workers, from deciding the location of our work and its rules and regulations, to defining the very nature of the relationships we establish and how these are predicated on our understandings of the process of change. Theory steers us to develop particular kinds of programs and services or even to think in terms of programs and services as the means through which we conceptualize that which we believe to be helpful. They underlie the strategies we use and our formulations of change. Some of our theories reduce people to needs and problems. Others view them as active participants in shaping their own reality.

REFLECTION: The Lobotomy—From Preferred Practice to Cruel and Unusual Punishment

Differing theoretical perspectives can have profound consequences for practice. Between 1930 and 1970, a surgical procedure called the lobotomy was the preferred mode of treatment for a number of debilitating mental health problems such as schizophrenia and chronic depression. The procedure consisted of the following: "After drilling two or more holes in a patient's skull, a surgeon inserted into the brain any of various instruments—some resembling an apple corer, a butter spreader, or an ice pick—and, often without being able to see what he was cutting, destroyed parts of the brain" (Valenstein, 1986, p. 3). A theory legitimizing lobotomies claimed that pathologically fixed thoughts localized in the brain's prefrontal lobe caused the patients' symptomatology. Fixative surgery destroyed these abnormal pathways, thus releasing patients from agonizing mental disorders (Valenstein, 1986, p. 84). Some practitioners contested use of the lobotomy over the course of its 40-year history. Nevertheless, even though the theories it was based on were discredited, many accepted claims of its success. In 1949, the Nobel Prize was awarded for its discovery. In contrast, Nolan Lewis, director of the New York State Psychiatric Institute had this to say about "successful cases":

> *Is the quieting of the patient a cure? Perhaps all it accomplishes is to make things more convenient for the people who have to nurse them. . . . The patients become rather childlike. . . . They act like they have been hit over the head with a club and are as dull*

as blazes. . . . It disturbs me to see the number of zombies that these operations turn out. I would guess that lobotomies going on all over the world have caused more mental invalids than they've cured. . . . I think it should be stopped before we dement too large a section of the population. (as quoted in Valenstein, 1986, p. 255)

While the lobotomy is certainly a dramatic example of a practice that did more harm than good, might we look back from some future vantage point and be appalled at our acceptance of some of our "best" practices today? Might we judge them as inappropriate, insufficient, cruel, and inhumane? What examples come to mind?

The Social Construction of Theory

Theory and Values

Robbins et al. (1999, 2006) remind us that theory is socially constructed. This means that we are all born into a pre-existing society and its cultural context of norms and patterns of acceptable behavior. From generation to generation, we socially transmit our notions of reality and internalize these through socialization processes. This socially and culturally transmitted knowledge that we acquire from infancy equips us with systems of language, screens of meaning, patterns of practice, and shared assumptions through which we engage in the world and from which we come to question, explore, and theorize about the world. Our theories about human behavior and processes of change are intimately linked to these broader systems of values, meanings, assumptions, and practices that shape our worldviews. Rarely do we question this taken-for-granted knowledge. Remembering that all knowledge is socially constituted allows us to understand theory as an expression of values and as such, representative of different ideological systems of thought (Berger & Luckman, 1966).

The Case of Psychosocial Development and Moral Reasoning— Erickson, Kohlberg, and Gilligan

Holding on to the idea of theory as socially constructed, we explore how values shape the development of theory and also how they influence practice. Erik Erikson's (1963) theory of psychosocial development is an excellent example. Perhaps you learned of this theory in an introductory psychology course or in a social work course in human behavior in the social environment (HBSE). Erikson postulated that human development occurs in sequential stages, predetermined steps, if you will. He called these the "eight ages of man" and wrote about them in his seminal work published in 1950, *Childhood and Society*. Erikson based his theory on research conducted on white, heterosexual, middle-class males. The theory made an important contribution to the linkage of psychological processes and social experience, and it challenged us to think about human development as a process that continues through the life course.

Thirty years later, Carol Gilligan (1982), informed by a growing body of feminist theory, critiqued Erikson's work for portraying male development and experience as the norm. She asserted that Erikson's theory ignores differences among people in the developmental process, and represents and privileges a white, middle-class, male notion of the meaning of development. Furthermore, she criticized the work of her colleague Lawrence Kohlberg, who along with Erikson, was a faculty member at Harvard. Similar to Erikson, Kohlberg's research on moral development, justice, and rights focused primarily on samples of privileged white men and boys (Women's Intellectual Contributions, n.d., ¶3-4). Through her research Gilligan illustrated how a partial view of the world, based on a privileged masculine "positionality" shared by Western white male theorists, researchers, and subjects, was assumed the norm and presented as a universal model of human psychosocial development. In short, she pointed out that both Erikson and Kohlberg were not theorizing from an objective and omniscient position but rather from a particular *standpoint*, informed and limited by their social location and experience. In an interview recapping her research for the *Psychotherapy Networker*, Gilligan had the following to say:

> I used to tell women graduate students, half-seriously, that the role of slightly rebellious daughter was one of the better roles for women living in patriarchy. And as I loved my father, I felt very warmly toward both Erik and Larry. Larry wrote a blurb for my book. But if I had to paraphrase what they thought, I'd say: "I like her, she's bright, she writes well, she's fun to be with, and it's important for women to study women. But change my theory—you've got to be kidding. (Wylie, n.d., ¶ 48)

Regardless of Gilligan's work, the theories developed by both Erikson and Kohlberg continue to set the standard for how others assess psychosocial and moral development, respectively. Women's experience was not seen as an issue and was subsumed under the male model of experience articulated by Erikson and Kohlberg. It is important here to consider how the values, history, and context (positionality) of the theorists (Erik Erikson and Lawrence Kohlberg) influenced and continue to influence notions of normalcy and deviance in present-day society. Given these considerations, how do you think power bears on theory? If we base our practice on either of these theories, how might we inadvertently set standards of human and moral development that are inherently classist, sexist, and racist? What other examples come to mind of ways in which theories of human behavior and moral development "normalize" and "universalize" the experience of particular, privileged groups? Whose experiences count and whose are discounted? What might be some practical consequences of such universalizing theories?

The Case of Loss and Grief

Theorizing about loss and grief provides yet another example of the intertwining nature of theory and practice. Many of us may be familiar with the theory of loss and grieving developed by Elisabeth Kübler-Ross. Based on her work with and observation of people in the process of bereavement, she developed a model for understanding the stages of loss and the tasks of grieving.

Stages of Loss and Grief

Kübler-Ross (1970) describes the initial reaction as one of shock and denial, followed by a series of emotional stages, moving from anger to sadness and depression, and finally to a place of acceptance of the reality of the loss. Her model has been broadly applied in processes of healing and support, not only for people who have lost loved ones to death, but also for understanding and addressing other losses such as divorce, loss of a job, and loss of capacity due to illness or injury. Kübler-Ross's stage model of loss and the grieving process has been criticized by other scholars and researchers for its individualist focus and its failure to take in to account multiple environmental factors that influence how people deal with loss. For example, Mark Marion (1996), in his important work on AIDS and loss, argues that Kübler-Ross's model is not sufficient for understanding the progressive, multiple loss and trauma experienced by gay men in the face of the AIDS epidemic. Marion explores the trauma associated with losses that continue and accumulate over time. He argues that the experience of multiple loss can shatter one's assumptions about self-worth, the meaning of life, and a just world. He writes that, for multiple-loss survivors, "(l)ike a tiny boat in a pounding surf struggling to find its moorings, more trauma and loss keeps pounding away at the sense of self-worth, sense of safety in the world, and sense of meaning" (Marion, 1996, p. 65).

The Global Loss Model

Prior to the availability of effective treatment reducing AIDS mortality by 80% in the United States (Clinton, 2006), being diagnosed HIV-positive was a death sentence. Drawing on the experiences of gay men with AIDS in the decade preceding new medical advancements, Marion developed the concept of "global loss" to comprehend their experiences that could not be contained even within the concept of "multiple loss." With the experience of global loss, "no aspect of life or identity is unaffected...there is a loss of community," and "there is no safe haven" (1996, p. 65-66). Gay men and gay communities had been experiencing "losses too big to grieve." Marion described four symptoms of coping he had witnessed among gay men struggling with global loss: psychological fatigue, depression, survivor guilt, and shame (p. 68). He argued that we needed to develop a new language to describe global loss that encompassed its profound grief and trauma. He proposed a circular model of denial, anxiety, anger, depression, and adaptation to begin to articulate the experience of global loss that had no defined beginning or end. Marion stressed that this was a model about living and wrote, "In fact, gay men surviving and thriving in the global loss of AIDS are doing just that: living in a community where traumatic loss is ongoing and creating ways to live passionate and meaningful lives in the midst of it" (p. 80). Take a minute to think about the practice of theorizing here. Marion constructed new ways of thinking about the social reality he confronted. He tried to give meaning to human pain and struggle. And he engaged with theorizing as a survival skill. His concept of global loss is profound. What thoughts and feelings does the concept provoke for you? In what other contexts might a theory of global loss be applied today? How might practice guided by a concept of global loss differ from practice guided by Kübler-Ross's more linear model of loss and grieving?

Weaving Together the Personal and the Political

Kübler-Ross theorized loss and grief on an individual level. Marion theorized loss and grief on individual and community levels. If a theory of loss and grief accounted for more than individual familial and community pain and suffering, how might this shape practice? June Allan (2003) asks us to question our taken-for-granted assumptions about death, dying and loss, primarily shaped by individualistic, pathologizing approaches, and consider theorizing the individual within a broader context. Acknowledging "the deep penetration of social arrangements, culture and history into people's emotions and intimate internal experiences" (p. 170), she asks us to think of loss and grief as social experiences. To understand her argument, think of the event of 9/11 and the indelible mark it left on the American psyche; disasters such as Katrina that uprooted and displaced thousands of people from their homes; or the tsunami that provoked such unimaginable, catastrophic human loss on multiple levels as it crashed on to the shorelines of Thailand, Malaysia, Indonesia, India, and Sri Lanka. How do time limits on grieving ("get on with it," "get over it") apply to these situations or how do labels such as "complicated bereavement" fit with new advances to theory development in this area that indicate there are no established pathways through loss? New approaches suggest that "a sense of community is important for those who grieve" (p. 182). Allan comments on alternatives to Western individualistic approaches that include community partnerships formed in Malawi to confront the losses directly related to HIV/AIDS; bereavement recovery work conducted by UNICEF to address the profound trauma and loss from genocide and "ethnic cleansing"; and memory boxes created by mothers diagnosed HIV-positive containing important items from their lives as a remembrance for their children (see pp. 182-183).

In summary, theories are not facts. As tools of inquiry, theories aid in the study of human behavior, provide us with ways in which to explain how the world works, and help us build frameworks, models, and guidelines for practice. Theories, however, are this and much more. They are value-laden social constructs, the process and products of our search for meaning, and part of our human repertoire of survival skills. They emerge at particular points in history, are molded and shaped by that history, and serve to transmit values and ideology. Thinking of theory in these ways reminds us that we must search for the meanings others create and make no assumptions of how others construct their worldviews. It also compels us to look critically at our own thinking and practice.

MAKING THEORY

Making theory is something we all engage in every day of our lives as we act in and reflect on the world. In our work, play, and relationships we use theories to interpret our experiences. We "gather data" from the trial-and-error experiences of everyday life, sometimes changing our practices and sometimes changing our thinking along the way. We apply our "folk theories" about the body, health, and illness as we take our family cures for hiccups or the common cold or as we adopt and invent new remedies. Parents apply and develop theories of child rearing as they put personal and cultural knowledge into practice each day. Likewise, children develop their own theories about the meaning of adulthood and the practice of parenting based on their experiences. Their respective theories of childhood and adulthood may be sharply contrasting, given their very different "positionalities."

Developing Alternative Perspectives

The making of new theory is often rooted in both the appreciation and critique of existing theoretical perspectives. As we addressed earlier in this chapter, Carol Gilligan used the theories of Erik Erikson and Lawrence Kohlberg as a springboard into alternative theory development. She appreciated their work and also critiqued the gender-bound limits represented in their approaches to research. Her theory added a different voice to human development theory as she stretched the boundaries of traditional approaches to include and reflect the unique experiences of females. In her research, she uncovered two different modes of thought, not necessarily gender-based but reflective of individualization and rights on one hand, and connectedness and responsibility on the other. She criticized traditional developmental approaches for their depiction of females as inferior rather than stressing the limitations of the theory. Gilligan made new theory from critical engagement with previously existing theory.

Carol Stack—Rethinking Moral Development

Anthropologist Carol Stack (1990) crafted new theoretical insights as she critiqued the limitations of Gilligan's theory in explaining moral reasoning among working-class African American adolescents and adults.[2] While Gilligan paid attention to gender, Stack showed how Gilligan failed to attend to the intersectionality of gender, race, and class. Stack's work talks back to feminist theories that take gender as a serious issue but fail to question their own assumptions about the universality of white, middle-class experience. For five years, Carol Stack lived and worked with African American return migrants —men, women, and children moving back to their home places in the rural southern United States. She was especially interested in children's movements back and forth between family ties in the urban North and rural South and the real-life moral dilemmas they faced regarding where to reside, with whom, and the responsibilities therein. Her findings paid particular attention to differences of class and race as well as gender in the practice of moral reasoning. She found that both men and women, adults and adolescents alike, were equally oriented toward both justice and caretaking. The data from Stack's study suggested that men's and women's shared experience of oppression "informs both self-identity and group-identity among return migrants and these converge in the vocabulary of rights, morality, and the social good" (1990, p. 24). Further, she found that boys and girls alike were aware of the "tyranny of racial and economic injustice" from an early age. She writes:

> Likewise, the interviews with children reveal a collective social conscience and a profound sensitivity among young people to the needs of their families. The children's voices tell a somber story of the fate, circumstances, and material conditions of their lives. Their expectations about where they will live in the coming year conform to the changing needs and demands of other family members, old and young, and family labor force participation. (p. 25)

Anti-oppressive Practice from Whose Perspective?

Linda Tuhiwai Smith, discussed earlier in this chapter, asserts that indigenous people should create theory based on their own experiences. Making new theory can be rooted in feelings of social exclusion, marginalization, and oppression. Making theory can be a form of resistance. Anne Wilson and Peter Beresford (2000), both academics and both "psychiatric system survivors," contest the omission of people who use social services in the development of anti-oppressive practice. As defined by Lena Dominelli (1998), anti-oppressive practice is an approach to social work practice that emphasizes "highlighting social injustice and finding ways of eradicating at least those forms of it which are reproduced in and through social work practice" (p. 5). Although Wilson and Beresford make their commitment to the claims of anti-oppressive practice perfectly clear, they unpack the complexities of mental health system work where social workers engage in social control as they classify, categorize, and label service users while speaking the language of equality. They explain how people who use services are invited to speak at social work classes where their experiences are mined and add to understandings of anti-oppressive practice from a service user point of view. However, they are never named as partners in the theory-making enterprise. They are omitted from meaningful participation in discussions in which they could critique and help in the ongoing development of anti-oppressive practice. How does anti-oppressive practice oppress through the exclusion of those who use services in the theory development process? What shape might theory take if those who use services were asked to participate in discussions to evaluate professionals' existing explanations of their behavior? How might their input guide practice in different ways? How might this practice lend itself to the teaching-learning process we discuss at the end of this chapter on p. 199?

Revisiting the Concept of Positionality

Rather than accepting white, middle-class experience as the norm, Stack (1990) showed how theory can be broadened, challenged, and enriched by considering social reality and relations from diverse "positionalities." As we mentioned above, Wilson and Beresford (2000) propose including the voices of people who use services to achieve these ends. Let's return for a moment to the subject of "standpoint" and "positionality" that we introduced in Chapter 2 and have been discussing here. As engaged human beings we bring our histories and experiences with us as we act in and make sense of the world. Our positionalities are shaped through ongoing processes of identification. By this we mean that, as social actors, people are at once claiming identities, being labeled by others, and experiencing the world in terms of those multiple identities such as race, gender, age, class, citizenship, ethnicity, and sexual orientation. As Reed, Newman, Suarez, and Lewis (1997) note:

> Some of these identities give us, almost automatically, and certainly at times unconsciously, certain privileges and stakes in power; alternatively, some of these identities work to produce us as oppressed.... Positionality underscores the necessity that each of us locate himself or herself along the various axes of social group identities. We must begin to articulate and take responsibility for our own historical and social identities and interrogate (challenge or questions and work to understand in an ongoing way)

how they have helped to shape our particular world views. (p. 58)

Implications for Theory—Theories Reflect Standpoints

So what does this mean in terms of theory? Proponents of various standpoint theories argue that people with different positionalities acquire differing standpoints, positions from which they view and experience reality and from which alternative views may be obscured. Just as people acquire differing standpoints, so do the theories they construct reflect their standpoints (Harding, 2004; Hill Collins, 1990; hooks, 1984; Swigonski, 1994).[3] According to Patricia Hill Collins (1990), standpoint theory argues that group location within the context of unequal power relations produces common challenges for individuals in those groups. Further, Hill Collins contends, those shared experiences shape similar angles of vision leading to group knowledge or standpoint that is essential for informed political action. Philosopher Sandra Harding (2004) also defines what standpoint is and what it is not. She argues:

> Its concern is not to articulate women's or some other marginalized group's perspective about the group's lives, though this frequently is an important step in its process. Rather, it ambitiously intends to map the practice of power, the ways the dominant institutions and their conceptual frameworks create and maintain oppressive social relations. . . . it does this by locating, in a material and political disadvantage or form of oppression, a distinctive insight about how a hierarchical social structure works. . . . it takes more than recording what women or members of some other oppressed group in fact say or believe to identify their distinctive standpoint insights. Oppressed groups frequently believe the distorted representations of social relations produced by dominant groups; we can change our minds about what our experiences were or how we want to think about them. . . . Finally, standpoint theory is more about the creation of groups' consciousnesses than about shifts in the consciousnesses of individuals. An oppressed group has to come to understand that each member is oppressed because she or he is a member of that group—Black, Jewish, women, poor, or lesbian—not because he or she individually deserves to be oppressed. The creation of group consciousnesses occurs (always and only?) through the liberatory political struggles it takes to get access to and arrive at the best conception of research for women or other oppressed groups, among the other goals of such struggles. Thus, feminist standpoint projects are always socially situated and politically engaged in pro-democratic ways. (pp. 31-32)

According to some standpoint theorists, people in oppressed social positions experience a different reality from those who enjoy positions of privilege. As W.E.B. DuBois (1989) has argued, oppressed people develop a critical consciousness as part of their survival strategy. They must be attuned to the dominant rules and vigilant in their social practice. As a result, people in positions of oppression develop a more critical and complex view of social reality, a "double consciousness," so to speak. As critical race and gender theorists have argued, the crafting of theory from the standpoint of the oppressed is not simply an intellectual exercise but a matter of survival (Hill Collins, 1990; hooks, 1984; Mohanty, 1991; Moraga & Anzaldua, 1983). For instance, Patricia Hill Collins, addressing Black feminist consciousness, calls on Black women to claim their standpoints, recognize the power in their positioned knowledge, and make their critical knowledge of the world a base for transformative action (1990, pp. 21-33).

REFLECTION: Your Standpoint
Reflect for a moment on the many facets of your own "positionality." What are some of the identities and experiences that shape your positionality? How would you describe the standpoint you have acquired? How has knowledge gained from your standpoint aided you in surviving and negotiating your way in the world? What might be some of your "blind spots"?

Grounded Theory

The kind of theory we have been discussing has been built from the ground up. Qualitative researchers who study cultures, peoples, institutions, and practices to uncover and explore lived experiences and their meanings call this "grounded theory" (Strauss & Corbin, 1990). Grounded theory is derived inductively instead of deductively through traditional scientific methods. That is, theory is built bottom-up, from the concrete, empirically grounded realities of people's lives, experiences, and narratives, rather than top-down from general, abstract principles (Lengerman & Niebrugge-Brantley, 1998, pp. 40-43). Carol Stack (1990), for example, grounded her critique of Gilligan's theory of moral reasoning in concrete knowledge gained from her observations and conversations with people differently positioned than those in Gilligan's study. Now we can also begin to see points of connection between the concept of grounded theory and that of standpoint theory. Both attend to and emphasize the importance of what we might call "local knowledge," or knowledge that is explanatory and particular to certain people at particular points in time. Both validate the importance of *relationship* in the generation of knowledge. Both ask, "How do we build knowledge about the world through concrete engagement with people's experiences in the world?" The making of grounded theory calls for an appreciation of the "positionalities" of the researcher and the subjects of study and a recognition of the limits of one's hands-on knowledge.

Examples from Our Experiences

We offer some examples from our own experiences as researchers to better illuminate the notion of grounded theory. Here is Janet Finn's story:

> *In the early 1990s, I spent three years tacking back and forth between two copper mining towns, Butte, Montana, and Chuquicamata, Chile. The towns had been the copper-producing hubs for the Anaconda Copper Mining Company for the better part of the 20th century. I wanted to learn how residents imagined and built community together with and in resistance to a powerful corporation. Most accounts of mining towns and their histories focus on men's experiences. I was especially interested in learn-*

ing about community history and practices from the perspectives and experiences of "working-class" women—the wives, mothers, and daughters of miners, many of whom were workers themselves. I spent time living in both towns, talking and working with women, and recording their stories of community support, struggles, and survival. Women in Butte told stories about the temporal structuring of their lives around 3-year labor contracts as they maintained a vigilance of family and community life during times of employment and mobilized networks of friendship and kinship to hold the "body and soul" of community together during strikes. In contrast, women in Chuquicamata told stories of the spatial structuring of their lives as they got up at dawn to stand in line at the company store every day in order to provide for their family's needs. The lines shaped the social space of women's lives, where they came together, shared their stories, and built solidarity and support. Their critical consciousness of their positionings as women and of the possibilities for collective action was honed through their everyday struggles for family and community survival. Drawing from their stories, I began to develop a theory of gendered social practice grounded in women's experiences of "crafting the everyday." Women crafted a sense of the ordinary to hold family and community together during hard times. They used their material and emotional resources to create community and a sense of the possible. They were craftswomen, using the tools and supplies at hand to create new meanings and purpose. (Finn, 1998a, p. 176)

Maxine Jacobson's (1997, 2001) story of grounded theory springs from her research on multidisciplinary teams that investigate child sexual abuse:

I became interested in multidisciplinary teams because of my experience as a team member on three different teams in Montana in the 1980s and early 1990s. When I began my research, I was interested in how teams from different locations in the state made sense of the causes of child sexual abuse and what connection, if any, these theoretical underpinnings had for how teams practiced. In other words, how did theory and practice intersect and were there differences based on location or context? I discovered that teams made sense of child sexual abuse through a multitude of explanations ranging from individual causes such as low self-esteem, sexual deviance, and learned family patterns to broader societal causes such as the acceptance of violence against women and children, patriarchy, and poverty and other environmental stressors. Although unarticulated as such, teams operated from dominant theories on the nature of child sexual abuse but their practice was shaped and constrained by the availability of community service resources, community culture, and beliefs about the efficacy of treatment as a panacea for the child sexual abuse problem. The most rural team in the study, the team I called the "frontier team," stood out in this regard. This team had limited access to services for the treatment of child sexual abuse but this was business as usual in a remote rural community in Montana. Team members made do with what they had, and ingenuity and creativity highlighted their practice. For example, one team member shared the following story:

> *We do some creative sentencing—We had an old man who had to be 80 years old. He had a long history and every once in a while he would chase little kids and flash. What we did with him—we knew that there were no programs that would touch him so we told him he had to report to the sheriff's office once a week, and we gave him a 2-year sentence. We never told him when his sentence was over so he reported to the sheriff's office once a week until he died—and I bet it was 5 or 6 years—and we never had any trouble with him as long as he had that reminder that he had to go to the sheriff's office. (Jacobson, 1997, p. 209)*

The frontier team was situated at least 200 miles away from residential, foster care, and psychological services. Besides having limited access to services, frontier team members expressed concerns regarding the efficacy of a costly 30-day treatment regime as the answer for the child sexual abuse problem. Instead, they questioned dominant professional beliefs about the nature of "treatment," and individuals as "points of intervention." Although connected to other teams across the states through policy mandates and prescribed team structures, local knowledge and local resources shaped team practice:

> *I think we just see some things being used that you wouldn't see otherwise. Maybe you've got an adolescent that's getting in a lot of trouble and needs some structure that he's not getting at home with his mother and father—whatever. You happen to know someone whose husband does fencing in the summer and who likes to hire youth to do that. So let's see if we can get this kid hitched up for the summer—do some hard work and get him straightened out—something like that. So that might not seem ethical— you know I'm going to set that kid up with my cousin who does fencing but in a situation like this when there are no other alternatives, it would probably be real helpful—and it could probably work out well. (Jacobson, 1997, p. 209)*

Theory and Meaning Systems

Dennis Saleebey (1993, 1994) provides another example of grounded theory. He brings the workings of theory to a generative level, that is, discovering with practitioners through dialogue the theoretical/practice linkages they make. This implies an inductive approach to theory and compels us to start from the ground up to look for understandings in people's lived experiences. Saleebey looks at theory as the meanings we construct to explain our reality. He sees culture as the raw material from which we construct these meanings. Saleebey asks social workers to look for theories in the meaning systems people create such as stories, narratives, and individual and collective versions of myths. This pushes us to look at the meanings conveyed in peoples' words and actions and to see these as the embodiment of theory.

In sum, theorizing is a critical and creative process of making sense of and giving meaning to the world and our experience in it. Theorizing is a survival skill that enables us to bring a sense of coherence to the demands of everyday life. Theorizing is part and parcel of our social practice. We have attempted to bring the process of making theory to light in order to systematically reflect on it and examine the relationship between theory and practice. In the following section we turn to the dominant theories that guide social work practice and discuss their contributions and limitations. To lay the groundwork for thinking about alternative theory, we discuss critical thinking and its connection to informed practice and ongoing theory development. We introduce a set of questions we have found helpful in the process of critiquing theory.

THEORY AND CONTEMPORARY SOCIAL WORK

Thinking about theory and being able to engage critically with theory requires applying the skills of critical thinking. In their seminal work *Social Work Futures: Crossing Boundaries, Transforming Practice,* Robert Adams, Lena Dominelli, and Malcolm Payne (2005) remind us that social work practice is much more than the work we do in face-to-face encounters with individual clients, families, or community groups. Much like a theater production where the bulk of the work happens behind the scenes—conceptualizing, refining and writing the script, creating the set design, and rehearsing—"Practice also entails reflection, reflexivity and being critical in and through action" (pp. 6-7). Adams, et al. refer to this as "complexity thinking," a process whose importance is often underestimated. They refer to the following five ways of thinking as critical components of complexity thinking:

1 *Being reflexive*: standing aside to observe and act from both inside and outside the situation thus allowing for the identification of taken-for-granted assumptions concerning the way things work;

2 *Contextualizing*: giving thought to the wider context of social relations and policy in which practice in a particular situation takes place;

3 *Problematizing*: debating, discussing, and deliberating about policy and law to inform us that the present agendas, language, and situations should not be assumed as the truth;

4 *Being self-critical*: accepting that our actions and those of our agencies are never entirely separate from the problems we identify;

5 *Engaging with transformation*: identifying barriers and divisions in social relations that lead to oppression and helping people move beyond self-blame, guilt, and shame to consider possibilities for change. (p. 11)

Thinking about and critiquing theory is one of social work's behind-the-scenes practices. As you read about the different theories that inform social work practice in this section, we want to equip you with some tools so that you can engage in your own critique of theory. We present nine questions to guide your critical reflection on theory. We invite you to join us in using "complexity thinking" to assess the contributions and limitations of the range of theories that inform and guide contemporary social work in the United States. In the following section on critiquing theory we incorporate the critical thinking components of complexity thinking in the questions we pose.

Critiquing Theory

Given theory's inherently ideological, socially constructed nature, it is important to analyze it in depth. It is equally as important to consider what implicit theories are at play in particular social work practices and "interventions." Although these underpinnings are implicit, they are powerful determinants of practice. As you read through the list of questions provided below, think of particular examples of theories that inform social work practices of "intervention," and then subject them to analysis and critique.

♦ What contextual aspects or forces does this theory address (individual, relational, familial, communal, political, cultural, economic)?

♦ How congruent is this theory with the values and ethics of social work practice?

♦ Does this theory support or promote particular values or assumptions about human behavior, human nature, and how the world should be?

♦ At what particular point in time is this theory historically situated? When did it develop and what was its contextual surround?

♦ Does this theory contribute to preserving and restoring human dignity?

♦ What truth claims support this theory (empirical, heuristic)? What is the power of this theory to define, explain, and interpret reality?

♦ Does this theory recognize the benefits of and celebrate human diversity?

♦ Does this theory assist us in transforming our society and ourselves so that we welcome the voices, the strengths, the ways of knowing, and the energies of us all?

♦ Does this theory reflect the participation and experiences of males and females; economically well off and poor; white people and people of color; gay men, lesbians, bisexuals, heterosexuals; old and young; and people with disabilities?

(Adapted from Schriver, 2004 and Robbins et al., 2006)

Will these questions help you actualize the five components of critical thinking introduced by Adams, Dominelli, and Payne? Are there other questions you might add? Do these help you apply your critical thinking skills? Next we present an overview of dominant social work theories, their contributions, and a summary of the critiques leveled at them from social work scholars. We encourage you to offer your own critique based on the questions listed above.

Systems

Overview

For the past 25 years, social systems or ecological (ecosystems) perspectives have dominated social work theory in the United States. The systems approach argues that individuals are complex living systems and that human behavior needs to be understood in its broader systemic context. A system is defined as "an organized whole made up of components that interact in a way distinct from their interaction with other entities and which endures over some period of time" (Anderson & Carter, 1990, pp. 266-267). Social systems theory argues that human needs must be understood in light of the larger systems in which people function. Systems maintain boundaries that give them their identities, and they tend toward homeostasis, or equilibrium (Hutchinson & Charlesworth, 1998, p. 44), which means they try to maintain a balance between sameness and change. Systems theorists view systems holistically such that, "All systems are parts of larger systems and, at the same time, are made up of smaller systems" (Anderson, Carter, & Lowe, 1999 as cited in Dubois & Miley, 2005, p. 59). Proponents contend that the systems perspective provides a means for considering the total social situation and intervening accordingly. Systems theories shifted attention from the past to the present, focusing on possibilities for creating change rather than on "why things happened" (Strom-Gottfried, 1999, p.7). Take a minute to consider why social systems theory was so readily taken up by the social work profession. How does a systems perspective help to link the individual and the environment? What social work practices have you read about thus far that are particularly aligned with systems thinking?

Person in Environment

Systems theories attracted support in social work for their fit with a "person-in-environment" perspective (Germain, 1994a, p.104). For example, in their classic 1973 text, *Social Work Practice: Model and Method*, Allen Pincus and Anne Minahan applied systems theory to social work practice. They argued for an integrated approach to problem assessment and planned change that addressed the role of systems as well as people in the helping process. They put forth a conceptual model for social work practice that identified four systems central to the change process:

 The *change agent system* includes the social worker, the agency, and formal and informal resources they bring to bear.

2 The *client system* contracts with the worker to engage in a process of planned change.

3 The *target systems* are those individuals and/or groups that the client and worker seek to change or influence in order to achieve the client's goals.

4 The *action system* includes all those involved in the change effort. (Pincus & Minahan, 1973, p. 63)

Systems theories were readily adopted into social work understandings of human behavior in the social environment and practice with families, groups, and communities (see for example, Hartman & Laird, 1983).

Toward an Ecosystem Perspective

By the 1980s, systems theorists had begun to incorporate the language of human ecology in order to conceptualize more specifically the dynamics of exchange between people and their social and physical environments (Germain, 1979, 1983; Germain & Gitterman, 1995). In 1980, Carel Germain and Alex Gitterman published *The Life Model of Social Work Practice.* They embraced an ecological approach, promoted the "person-in-environment" language and perspective, and identified both persons and social systems as contributing to the problem-solving process. The emerging "ecosystems" perspective "suggests that the nature of the transactions between people and their environments is the source of human needs and social problems" (Dubois & Miley, 2005, p. 62; Germain & Gitterman, 1980, 1995). According to Brenda DuBois and Karla Miley (2005), the ecosystems perspective

- ♦ Translates the principles of ecology to the relationships between people and their social environments;
- ♦ Conceptualizes stress as the discrepancies between individuals' needs and capacities and environmental qualities;
- ♦ Promotes understandings of stress as related to life transitions, environmental pressures, and interpersonal processes;
- ♦ Frames problems as a lack of "fit" between the person and the environment;
- ♦ Conceptualizes all interaction as adaptive or logical in context;
- ♦ Provides a number of entry ways into solutions for change that include change within persons, their social groups, and in their social and physical environments. (pp. 62-63)

Key Contributions

The ecosystems perspective constructs human interaction with the social environment in terms of resources, niches, carrying capacity, adaptation, and competition. It emphasizes the integrated nature of human behavior, the interplay of multiple systems, and the "fit" between people and their environments. It takes a "transactional" view of "dysfunction" that might arise as persons and environments strive for mutual adaptation (DuBois & Miley, 2005, p. 62). By 1986, James Whittaker, Steven Schinke, and Lewayne Gilchrist (1986) proclaimed that social work had a new "paradigm"—the ecological paradigm. Paradigms refer to worldviews, ways of thinking, or systems of belief that denote certain methods of practice (Lincoln & Guba 1985, p. 15; Maguire, 1987, p. 11; Patton, 1975, p. 9).[4]

Since the 1980s the ecological or "ecosystems" paradigm has powerfully shaped social work thought and practice in the United States. Let's consider some of the contributions of the various systems, ecological, or ecosystems approaches. These approaches point to the fundamental importance of context and draw attention to the person-environment relationship. They provide a theoretical basis for social work's professional uniqueness, which is predicated upon the grasp of this relationship. Systems and ecological approaches challenge understandings of social problems based on a "medical" or "personal deficiency" model that emphasizes individual problems or deficits. They look beyond the individual person in crafting solutions and they point to social work's historic concern for environmental conditions, as evidenced in the Settlement House Movement. What do you see as other contributions of an ecosystems approach? Return for a moment to the nine questions for critiquing theory presented in the previous section. How would you rate systems theory or an ecosystems perspective? What additional information do you need to respond to these questions?

Critiques

Despite its continued prominence in the field, the ecosystems perspective has also been criticized on a number of fronts. Some critics see the perspective as so vague and general that it can be broadly applied yet gives us very little specific guidance for practice. Its focus on the here-and-now situation and possibilities of intervention has resulted in a neglect of history. Critics also argue that the emphasis on "fit" tends to support the status quo rather than question the dominant order of things. Ecosystems perspectives emphasize strategies for adaptation to, rather than transformation of, existing structural arrangements. Questions of power and conflict, so important to considerations of practice, are not addressed. For example, Amy Rossiter (1996) argues that the ecosystems perspective incorporates an uncomplicated view of both person and environment, assuming that both are stable, knowable, and nonproblematic concepts. Furthermore, the perspective assumes a fundamental distinction between the person and society rather than seeing the dialectical, mutually constituting relationship between people and society (Rossiter, 1996). In their more recent writing on the ecological or ecosystems perspective, Germain and Gitterman (1995) have responded to some of these concerns. They have called for consideration of dimensions of power, history, and life course development in the definitions and dynamics of person-environment transactions. Take a minute to think about these critiques. Are these critiques that you agree with? Are these critiques you would challenge? What arguments or evidence would you bring to bear?

Structural Social Work

Overview

The structural approach (also referred to as a political economy or conflict approach) to social work is part of a larger radical social work movement. Structuralists view the problems that confront social work as a fundamental, inherent part of the present social order wherein social institutions function in ways that systematically work to maintain social inequalities along lines of class, race, gender, sexual orientation, citizenship, and so on (Carniol, 1990; Moreau, 1979; Mullaly, 1997). Informed by Marxist theory, structuralists place questions of conflict and exploitation at the center of social work theory. They see personal problems as resulting from structural injustice and the resulting unequal access to means and resources of social and economic production. From the structuralist perspective, clients are viewed as victims of systemic inequality and exploitation. Structuralists raise questions about the historical and material conditions through which inequalities are structured and experienced.

Key Contributions

The structural approach has made significant contributions to social work practice. Structuralists have placed questions of power and inequality at the center of theory and practice. They have challenged social workers to see personal problems as resulting from structural injustice and have advocated for systems changing interventions. Structuralists have engaged in a critique of the relationship between social work and capitalism and have contended that the goal of social work practice is the transformation of the social structure to a new order grounded in social justice, egalitarianism, and humanitarianism (Bailey & Brake, 1976; Coates, 1992; Galper, 1975).

Critiques

While structural social work has long been a prominent voice in Canadian, Australian, and British social work theory and practice, it has largely been marginalized in the United States. Structural social workers have been criticized for being "too political" in their sympathies for a socialist alternative to the dominant political order and unrealistic about the possibilities of achieving structural change. The structural approach has also been critiqued for its emphasis on people as "victims" of structural inequalities rather than as actors capable of participation in processes of personal and social change and its reliance on a "universal discourse of structural oppression which does not necessarily account for cultural differences (Fook, 2000; Ife, 1997, as referred to in Allan, Pease, & Brickman, 2003). What do you see as possible strengths and limitations of a structural approach? What evidence would you bring to bear?

Strengths

Overview

In recent years a strengths perspective has gained prominence in social work in the United States. The strengths perspective emerged as a corrective to social work's problem-focused approach, arguing that, to be true to the value base of the profession, we need to begin by recognizing people's capacities and the potential of their circumstances. The strengths perspective "presents a shift from an emphasis on problems and deficits defined by the worker to possibilities and strengths identified in egalitarian, collaborative relationships with clients" (Saleeby, 2006, p. 38). Social workers are encouraged to attend to the resource potential of the environment and appreciate human resiliency, creativity, and capacity for survival in the face of adversity. The basic premises of the strengths perspective are as follows:

♦ Clients have many strengths.
♦ Client motivation is based on fostering client strengths.
♦ The social worker is a collaborator with the client.
♦ Avoid the victim mindset.
♦ Any environment is full of resources (Saleebey, 2006).

Key Contributions

Working from a strengths perspective, the social worker seeks to identify, facilitate, or create contexts in which people who have been silenced and isolated gain understanding of, a voice in, and influence over the decisions that affect their lives. The perspective promotes belonging, healing, and relationship building through dialogue and collaboration. Rather than asking, "What's wrong?" the social worker, operating from a strengths perspective asks, "What's possible?" (Cowger, 1994, Saleebey, 2006).

Critiques

Proponents of the perspective point to its compatibility with an ecosystems approach. Rather than challenging the fundamental tenets of the ecological model, the strengths perspective is generally seen as offering an enhanced lens through which to view the person-environment nexus. The strengths perspective has been praised for recognizing human capacity and agency. It has been criticized for underplaying constraints and the often overwhelming struggles that poor and oppressed people face in their everyday lives (Barber, 1995; Coates & McKay, 1995; Fisher, 1995; Gutiérrez & Lewis, 1999; Howe, 1994; Margolin, 1997). What do you see as possible contributions and limitations of a strengths perspective? Take a minute to return to our nine questions about critiquing theory and ask them of a strengths perspective.

Empowerment

Overview

The empowerment approach in social work has been gaining prominence over the past decade. The empowerment approach is premised on a recognition and analysis of power, group work practices of consciousness raising and capacity building, and collective efforts to challenge and change oppressive social conditions (see, for example, Dubois & Miley, 2005; Gutiérrez, 1990; Gutiérrez & Lewis, 1999; Simon, 1994). This approach makes linkages between the personal and the political. It builds on the traditions of self-help, mutual support, and collective action. Empowerment theorists frequently speak of personal, interpersonal, and political levels of empowerment and advocate forms of social work practice that engage all three. Lorraine Gutiérrez and Edith Lewis have developed empowerment approaches to social work with women of color (1999). They write,

> The three types of empowerment (personal, interpersonal, political) are unified by a central belief, namely that social work's primary goal is to help individuals, families, groups and communities develop the capacity to change their situations. The social worker's role is to help people change the situation and prevent its recurrence. The effects of powerlessness occur on many levels, so change must be directed toward both large and small systems; it is insufficient to focus only on developing a sense of personal power or providing skills or working toward social change. Practice at all three levels when combined comprises empowerment practice. (p. 12)

According to Gutiérrez and Lewis (1999, p. 18-20), the key methods for empowering social work practice are education, participation, and capacity building. Following Freire (1974), they see education as a critical process of raising consciousness. To develop critical awareness, one must engage in a power analysis of the situation wherein connections are made between the immediate practice context and the distributions of power in society as a whole.

Key Contributions

Empowerment approaches build on the social work traditions of self-help, mutual support, and collective action. Some empowerment theorists have drawn on both feminist and critical race theories in critiquing the limitations of competing approaches and articulating an alternative direction for social work. For example, Gutiérrez and Lewis (1999) argue that social work can work toward greater social justice by simultaneously building on individual and social transformation. They recognize the possibilities of human agency and the significance of cultural and political knowledge and histories.

Critiques

Empowerment perspectives have been praised for bringing questions of power to the center of social work theory and practice and for recognizing the mutual constitution of individual and society. Concepts of empowerment have been criticized for being so broadly applied to such diverse practices that the term itself becomes meaningless. More recently, we have seen the appropriation of the term "empowerment" to describe punitive practices. For example, time limits imposed by welfare reform under Temporary Assistance for Needy Families (TANF) Program have been described by proponents as "incentives" that "empower" poor people to "get off welfare." This use of the term masks the power relations in play in the politics of welfare and makes poverty a personal problem that can be ameliorated through "self-help" without structural change. Critics have argued that social workers may be more likely to embrace the language than the practice of empowerment. Leslie Margolin (1997) contends that most empowerment perspectives fail to fully acknowledge social work itself as a type of power, a way of seeing things. He points to the ways in which a language of empowerment may mask practices through which social workers "stabilize middle-class power by creating an observable, discussible, write-aboutable poor" (p. 5).

What do you see as the strengths and limitations of the empowerment approach? How have you witnessed the appropriation of the term "empowerment?" How do the nine questions on critiquing theory help you gain a better understanding of the empowerment approach?

REFLECTION: **Meanings of Empowerment**

Think for a moment about where you have heard the word "empowerment" used. For example, we now have "empowerment zones" in urban areas struggling for economic survival. Welfare reformers talk about "empowering the poor" to help themselves. Women's organizations around the United States have mobilized action empowering women to stand collectively against violence and fear and "take back the night." In what other contexts do you hear people talk of "empowerment?" Are there differing meanings of empowerment being used in these differing contexts? What does the idea of empowerment mean to you? What might be an example of a situation in which you were empowered? Disempowered? What are some of the feelings that you associated with those situations? What did you learn from the experiences? How did the experience limit or enhance your sense of possibility?

REFLECTION: Comparing Approaches

Review the approaches to social work practice we have presented thus far, then get together with your classmates in a small group and consider the following scenario:

Lynn, a single mother of three, is 27 years old. She and her children live in a small older mobile home located in a trailer park near the edge of Middleton, a community of 40,000. Lynn grew up in Middleton and graduated from high school here. She had her first child, Bobby, at age 16. She married Rob, the baby's father, the following year. Lynn and Rob were together for 8 years, and they moved frequently in that time. Lynn had two more children, a boy (Brandon) and girl (Heather), now ages 8 and 5. She and Rob returned to Middleton when Lynn was pregnant with her youngest child. Rob has been both physically and verbally abusive to Lynn during their time together. After a particularly serious assault, Lynn left briefly with the children, and threatened to get a restraining order. Lynn and Rob reconciled for a time, then separated 18 months ago. Rob left town shortly thereafter to take a construction job. He sends an occasional support check.

Lynn's mother died when Lynn was 19, and her father abandoned the family when she was in grade school. Lynn has one older brother who lives in Middleton. He has recently remarried. Between his work and family time, he has seen little of Lynn in the past few years. Lynn has lost touch with many of her high school acquaintances since returning to Middleton 3 years ago.

Lynn has been working day and evening shifts in a local restaurant. Money is tight, and Lynn is behind on several bills. Lately, she has had to go to the community food pantry for help by the end of the month. Lynn's boys are in school, and Heather attends a Head Start full day program. A neighbor woman in the trailer court watches the children at times when Lynn is at work. Occasionally, Lynn has to rely on Bobby to take care of the younger ones for a few hours in the evenings and on weekends when she has to work. Lynn has been trying to work extra shifts in order to get caught up on bills. The children have missed several days of school this year. Bobby seems listless and distracted. He has been falling behind in his classes, and Lynn has not responded to attempts from the school to set up a meeting with her. You are the school social worker, and you have received a request from Bobby's teacher to follow up on the situation at home. How will you proceed in assessing the situation?

Now chose two of the approaches to compare in assessing the case. For example, you could compare the systems approach with the structural approach or the strengths approach with the systems approach. Respond to the following questions in your comparison:

1. How does each approach differently define the problem?
2. Who is responsible for resolution of the problem? (i.e., the individual, society, or both)
3. What is the focus of the intervention?
4. What is the role of the social worker in the assessment plan?
5. What is the role of the client in the assessment plan?
6. How would you describe the nature of the social work relationship?

Take 15-20 minutes to consider the direction your assessment and intervention might take. How do the approaches you chose to compare differ? Where do they differ? How do the theories you chose for understanding human problems shape your approach to assessment and intervention? How do the approaches differ in what you consider important and what you leave out of the process? What do you see as the limits of the approaches you used? Of the two approaches, which one do you see as most compatible with your knowledge and values? Why? If you were to develop a third approach that addresses some of the limitations you encountered in the two approaches you used to complete this exercise, what would it look like? What would you call your approach?

EXPANDING THE THEORETICAL POSSIBILITIES

In contemporary U.S. social work, ecosystems, strengths, and empowerment constitute the field's most widely taught theoretical perspectives. Unfortunately, too much of our practice still seems to be guided by the medical or personal-deficit model that reduces social problems to personal troubles. What are some possibilities for challenging the limits of theory and practice and realizing the possibilities of social justice work? We turn to the diverse and challenging terrain of critical social theory to address this question.

Understanding Critical Social Theory

Social work is not alone in grappling with questions about the production and practice of knowledge. Over the past two decades there has been considerable attention to the "crises" of theory throughout the social sciences (Agger, 1998). Critical social theorists have questioned ideologies of scientific objectivity and have explored the social construction of knowledge. They have challenged notions of determinist, universal social laws and pointed to the possibilities of changing history. A number of these theoretical debates have filtered into social work. We have already introduced you to several theories and theorists that have influenced our thinking about social justice work. It has been through our long-term engagement with the dominant theories of social work, exploration of alternative theoretical possibilities, and reflection on our own practice that we have come to craft a new framework for social justice-oriented social work. In this section we further explore some of these contributions and point out ways in which they have shaped our development of the Just Practice Framework.

The concept of "critical social theory" as used here encompasses a range of perspectives, including feminist, poststructural, postmodern, and critical race theories. The significant differences among these perspectives are beyond the scope of this chapter, and they have been addressed elsewhere (see, for example, Agger, 1998; Allan, Pease, & Briskman, 2003; Dirks, Eley, & Ortner, 1994; Figueira-McDonough, Netting, & Nichols-Casebolt, 1998; Hick, Fook, & Pozzuto, 2005; Hill Collins, 1990; Lemert, 2004; and Weedon, 1987). They have in common a critique of positivism ("a family of philosophies characterized by an extremely positive evaluation of science and scientific method" (Reese, 1980, p. 450, as quoted in Lincoln & Guba, 1985, p. 19); a concern for questions of power, difference, and domination; attention to the dialectics of structure and human agency; and a commitment to social transformation (Agger, 1998). Critical social theorists address the mutual constitution of forms of knowledge and relations of power (Foucault, 1977, 1980). These common themes form the foundation of our thinking. In the following discussion, we highlight some of these influences and ideas that have shaped our thinking about social justice work. First, we address the concepts of "discourse," "domination," "globalization," and "oppression" as they relate to our thinking about social justice work. These concepts are essential to understandings of critical social theory. We then turn to the work of feminist, critical race, and practice theorists and discuss their influence on our development of the Just Practice Framework. We find this material both "hard to think" and "good to think." We argue that engagement with ideas that push us out of our comfort zones is part of the process of social justice work.

Discourse

Some critical theorists have focused on questions of language, discourse, and power in the construction of social reality (Derrida, 1976; Weedon, 1987). The concept of *discourse* as used here is about more than language and "talk." It refers to ways of constituting knowledge together with social practices, forms of subjectivity, and relations of power. Chambron (1999, p. 57) writes: "More than ways of naming, discourses are systems of thought and systematic ways of carving out reality. They are structures of knowledge that influence systems of practice." Thus, the concept of social work discourse brings critical attention to the mutual constitution of systems of knowledge—what counts as "truth," and systems of practice—what count as problem and intervention. For example, Leslie Margolin (1998) writes about the power of social work discourse in constructing both "clients" and their "problems." He writes:

> My point is that social work's original clients, consisting largely of foreigners who swelled American cities at the turn of the twentieth century, were not allowed to read what investigators wrote about them. They were not allowed to offer corrections, or monitor the uses to which their biographies were put. Entering into social workers' language "for their own good" made clients subordinate objects in it. They were engaged in a mass of records that captured and exposed them. . . . And because written words are more easily controlled than speech, fine distinctions can be drawn between those who should have access and those who should not, between those who can make additions and corrections and those who cannot. Recordkeeping, in other words, is the mechanism that assures the differential distribution of power. (p. 37)

The concept of discourse has helped us think more specifically about the ways in which knowledge is constructed and the relationship of power and inequality therein. It allows us to move from a more abstract level of theoretical, political, and ethical concerns to the concrete realities of the power of language and the ways we carve out terrain of the "talkable" and that which goes without saying. For example, how is it that only certain kinds of social benefits are construed as "welfare"? How did "welfare" come to be thought of as a dirty word, associated with the "dependency" of the poor? And how is it that "dependency" is constructed as a bad thing, pitted against the "correctness" of "independence?"[5] What are the social and political consequences of omitting discussion of interdependence and social as well as personal responsibility from the welfare debates? These are questions of discourse.

Wendy Limbert and Heather Bullock (2005), for example, draw on critical race theory to deconstruct contemporary discourses of welfare reform. Critical race theory is "interested in studying and transforming the relationship among race, racism and power" (Delgado & Stefanic, 2001, p. 2, as cited in Limbert & Bullock, p. 254). Limbert and Bullock point to recent debates concerning the reauthorization of the Personal Responsibility and Work Opportunity Reconciliation Act of 1996 (PRWORA) and the astonishing similarities to the debates preceding its initial passage. These evoke images of African American women as lazy people who have no incentive to marry because they continue to have "out of wedlock" children to boost their monthly welfare allotments. Limbert and Bullock dispel popular stereotypes of welfare recipients by citing research indicating that "most poor families have at least one member working outside the home. . ." and the "strongest predictors of anti-welfare attitudes among Whites were perceiving welfare recipients as 'underserving' and Blacks as lazy" (p. 260). They ask important questions to rock the foundation of firmly entrenched dominant discourses by wondering out loud about who benefits from framing poverty issues in terms of personal responsibilities and how "restricted welfare benefits and punitive sanctions against poor families help maintain systems of privilege that benefit elites" (p. 265).

Domination

Other critical theorists have pursued the relationship among practices of knowledge production, the making of social subjects, and the logic of capitalism (Harvey, 1989; Rouse, 1995; Thompson, 1966; Williams, 1977). They have returned to the work of Antonio Gramsci, who we introduced at the beginning of the chapter, for guidance. These questions were central to his work. Gramsci asks us to think not only about the structure of capitalism as an economic model based on the production of profit for the few through the extraction of "surplus value" from the many. He asks us to also think about how it is that the many come to accept a logic that seems to serve very particular interests. How is it that those in less powerful positions come to accept as "common sense" and to participate in the systems of domination and exploitation that conflict with their interests? What is the role of economic systems in producing particular kinds of social and cultural subjects and shaping their interests, dispositions, and desires? Through posing and reflecting on these sorts of questions, Gramsci put forth his notion of "hegemony" to describe processes of nonviolent domination and the ways in which people become participants in systems that continue to oppress them (Gramsci, 1987; Williams, 1977, 1980). And he explored the ways in which the everyday practices of capitalism worked in shaping people's dispositions and desires as particular kinds of producers, consumers, and citizens. As John Ehrenreich showed us in Chapter 3, many social workers became partners with industrial capitalists in the making of "good workers" during the early 20th century. We find Gramsci's insights to be provocative for social work theory and practice today for the following reasons:

♦ He offers analytical tools for thinking critically about the ways in which the logic and workings of the economy penetrate our everyday lives and sense of self.

♦ He provides us with the means for exploring how nonviolent forms of domination work and what their human consequences may be.

♦ We can draw on his insights to help us see how the social production of social work knowledge and practice—the framing of theories, problems, interventions; the structuring of "worker-client" identities and relations; and the location of the profession in society—is intimately implicated in the workings and logic of the larger economic system.

We have found Gramsci's work very important in helping us think critically about questions of meaning, power, and history in the making of social problems and interventions. He reminds us that we are never outside of the political, cultural, and economic systems that shape our experiences, interpretations, and actions. He challenges us to question received "common sense" and to pose questions that may help us come to an alternative common sense regarding root causes of social problems and the words and actions that both mask and justify structured inequalities.

REFLECTION: Crime and Punishment

Below is the mission statement for "Critical Resistance," an organization dedicated to challenging the "justice" behind the burgeoning prison population in the U.S. Take a moment to read the mission statement and reflect on the questions that follow:

> Prisons and incarceration have become the panacea for all our social ills. Where once the U.S. looked to the welfare state to alleviate social problems, today the U.S. looks to prisons, prisons, and more prisons. Critical Resistance (CR) uses the term Prison Industrial Complex (PIC) to encompass both this phenomenon and the corresponding reality that capitalism flourishes from locking people in cages.

> CR recognizes that an integral component of the PIC is the dramatic increase in the incarceration of people of color, women and the poor, along with the continued imprisonment of political prisoners. CR is strongly committed to challenging the existing structure of "criminal justice" which is about revenge, punishment, and violence. As part of the emerging international movement for penal abolition, we envision a society where fundamental social problems are no longer "solved" through the mass warehousing (and periodic torture) of human beings, the overwhelming majority of whom are poor people of color and non-violent. CR's mission is to build a national campaign to challenge the Prison Industrial Complex.[6]

Think about the term "prison industrial complex." What images does it bring to mind? What questions might it spark regarding the production of "crime," "criminals" "prisoners," and "justice"? How is it that U.S. prison populations have exploded in recent years? How is it that people of color are vastly over-represented in prisons? What "common sense" is at work here? How does the discourse of crime and punishment work to construct not only a certain "common sense" but also an economic industry of the keepers and the kept? What "alternative common sense" is suggested by the work of Critical Resistance?

Globalization

More recently the shift in attention to neoliberal, market capitalism characterized by the global reorganization of work and the making of new social subjects (such as "flexible" workers, "displaced" workers, "migrant" workers, and refugees) and new strategies of resistance, has raised further critical questions for social work (Dominelli, 1999; Harvey, 1989; Ife, 2001; Rouse, 1995). Critical theorists of late capitalism have drawn attention to globalization as both an *ideology*, or set of beliefs, regarding the "inevitability" of the new world order, and a *political strategy*, a systematic effort to consolidate power, create "flexible" workers, and open borders to the movement of corporate interests (Piven and Cloward, 1997; Korten, 2001). They recognize the transnational penetration of "neoliberal" economic politics and practices as a driving force in the production of new forms of social exclusion and political conflict (Alvarez, Dagnino, & Escobar, 1998; Lowe & Lloyd, 1997). Critical understanding of and attention to these processes are essential to social justice work, even in its most "local" and "personal" forms.

David Korten, in his book *When Corporations Rule the World,* succinctly addresses the issue of globalization and what is at stake (2001, pp. 27-32). Over the past two decades we have experienced accelerating social and environmental degradation and rising rates of poverty, unemployment, inequality, and violence on a global scale. This has been accompanied by a fivefold increase in economic output since 1980 that has pushed human demands on ecosystems beyond sustainability. The continued quest for economic growth has intensified the competition between the rich and poor for scarce resources, and the poor have been the losers. Korten further argues that national governments have been incapable of responding. The result is a crisis of governing

> born of a convergence of ideological, political, and technological forces. . . . [that is] shifting power away from governments responsible for the public good and toward a handful of corporations and financial institutions driven by a single imperative—the quest for short-term financial gain. This has concentrated massive economic and political power in the hands of an elite few whose absolute share of the products of a declining pool of natural wealth continues to increase at a substantial rate—thus reassuring them that the system is working perfectly well. (Korten, 2001, p. 22)

The logic of neoliberal, market capitalism and the forces of globalization have profoundly shaped social conditions, social welfare policies, and social work practice. We are witnessing the shrinking of the social safety net accompanied by the privatizing of social work and the increasing complexity of human problems that transgress national borders. Social justice workers need the theoretical and political capacity to grapple with questions of discourse, globalization, domination, and oppression in order to be effective players on this challenging terrain.

Oppression

Fully comprehending the concepts of discourse, domination, and globalization requires knowledge about how oppression works because oppression is implicated in, embodied by, and plays through each of the other concepts. We define oppression in Chapter 2 (p. 39) and we explore its key variables such as power, exploitation, deprivation, and privilege (van Wormer, 2004). Critical theorists grapple with these key variables as they attempt to make sense of the ways in which oppression works. Practitioners have created anti-oppressive perspectives to "draw attention of social workers to the more focused objective of challenging structural power dynamics in order to eradicate various forms of oppression" (Sakamoto & Pitner, 2005, p, 437). Oppression is a complex concept, difficult to fully grasp, especially by people born into positions of privilege. Peggy McIntosh (1995) points to the invisible hand of oppression when she states,

> As a white person, I realized I had been taught about racism as something that puts others at a disadvantage, but had been taught not to see one of its corollary aspects, white privilege, which puts me at an advantage. I think whites are carefully taught not to recognize white privilege, as males are taught not to recognize male privilege. (p. 76)

Margaret Anderson and Patricia Hill Collins (1995) suggest *shifting the center* as a stance "that illuminates the experiences of not only the oppressed groups but also those in the dominant culture" (p. 2). This requires putting groups who have been socially excluded at the center of our thinking. Anderson and Collins argue that by not shifting the center we keep ourselves blind to the intersections of race, class, and gender and how we are all implicated in the production and reproduction of oppression.

Feminism and Critical Race Theories

Feminist perspectives and practices have presented an important challenge and corrective to contemporary social work. And as women entering into our adult professional lives in the midst of what has come to be called the "second wave" women's movement of the 1970s, we (the authors) have been influenced by feminist theory, practice, and politics. Feminist movements have challenged the political, social, and economic marginalization of women and the systems of thought and practice that have informed and justified women's marginality and inequality. Feminist theorists and activists have sought to raise consciousness of the many forms of women's oppression, whether it occurs in the home or workplace, in schools or on the streets.

Accomplishments of the Women's Movement

The accomplishments of the women's movement have been far-reaching. Feminists have made gender an issue and have examined the workings of patriarchy in the family and larger society that systematically structure women's subordination (Jaggar, 1983; Ortner & Whitehead, 1981; Rosaldo & Lamphere, 1974; Smith, 1990). They have addressed the connection of the "personal" and "political" and critically examined the politics of family and everyday life that have contributed to women's oppression. In social work, feminist scholars have explored the assumptions about gender, women, marriage, and family that have informed and continue to inform social welfare policies (Abramowitz, 1998; Gordon, 1990). Feminist scholars have questioned the assumptions about motherhood and the "good mother" that underlie child welfare policies and practices (Armstrong, 1995; Finn, 1994, 1998b; Gordon, 1988). In their discussion of the integration of gender and feminist thought into social work practice knowledge, Figueira-McDonough, Netting, and Nichols Casebolt (1998, pp.19-20) have articulated a set of intellectual and practice guidelines that reflect principles of feminism and critical theory. These eight principles also undergird our thinking about Just Practice:

1. Recognition that gender is a complex social, historical, and cultural product.

2. Rejection of the study of unique histories and specific social formations as universal.

3. Recognition of institutionalized perceptions and patterns of behavior that are diverse and changeable without falling into polarizations or homogenized categories.

4. Promotion of methodologies that allow for the study of the relative salience of other divisions within gender.

5. Analysis of gender embeddedness so that other forms of patterned inequality can be assessed.

6. Recognition, exploration, and valuation of women's experience as a precondition to understanding the effect of different and unequal contexts on identities.

7. Initiation of a process of integration in knowledge construction guided by praxis.

8. Awareness that the end of subjugation, not difference, is the target of action.

Challenging "Scientific Racism"

Critical theorists have also challenged "scientific racism," the bodies of knowledge about "race" produced within biological and social sciences and designed to "prove" the inferiority of people of color. They have addressed the social construction of race, ethnicity, and racist ideologies; processes of *racialization* (assignment of racial meaning to a previously neutral event); and practices of everyday racism as well as the social and institutional structures of inequality. They have examined the mutually constituting relationships among race, difference, discourse, and inequalities (see for example, Gates & West, 1996; Gilman, 1985; Marable, 1997, 1999; West, 1993). Important linkages between race and gender theories have been addressed in the work of "third-world" feminists, women of color, and critical race theorists (see, for example, Hill Collins, 1991; hooks, 1984; Mohanty, 2003; Mohanty, Russo, & Torres, 1991). They have challenged the limits of "liberal," "radical," and "socialist" feminisms articulated by white women; have spoken to the super-exploitation of women of color, and have addressed the importance of narrative and experience in voicing the feminist stories of women of color (see Jones, 1984; Moraga & Anzaldua, 1983). The contributions of Black and Latina feminists, for instance, have encouraged us to listen to and respect stories of survival and strength rather than pathology in understanding cultural diversity in the constructions of family and gender (Segura & Pearce, 1993; Zavella, 1987). They have addressed the need to examine the specific historic, economic, and cultural contingencies and the gendered strategies for responding to those circumstances rather than falling back on simple generalizations about ethnicity, class, and gender that may tell us very little.

Theories of "Practice"

A Different Way of Thinking about "Practice."

The Just Practice Framework we develop here is grounded in a reconceptualization of "practice" informed by critical social and cultural theory. The term "practice" in contemporary social theory does not have the same meaning as practice in the traditional social work sense of a series of planned interventions. Rather, practice refers more broadly to social action carried out in the context of unequal power relations (Dirks, Eley & Ortner, 1994; Ortner, 1984, 1989, 1996).[7] According to Sherry Ortner (1994), a fundamental premise of practice theory is "that society is a system, that the system is powerfully constraining, and yet that the system can be made and unmade through human action and interaction" (p. 403). Practice theorists have attempted to place human agency and social action at the center of new social theory. In explaining the concept of human agency, Albert Bandura (2006) states, "To be an agent is to influence intentionally one's functioning and life circumstances. . . People are self-organizing, proactive, self-regulating, and self-reflecting. They are not simply onlookers of their behavior. They are contributors to their life circumstances, not just products of them" (p. 164). Bandura identifies four core properties of human agency or agentic properties possessed by human beings:

1. **Intentionality**: People have the ability to form intentions which include creating action plans and developing strategies for achieving them.
2. **Forethought**: People have the ability to create cognitive representations or images of the future which when brought to the forefront, act as guides with potential for motivating behavior.
3. **Self-reactiveness**: Once people adopt an intention and an action plan for achieving it, people have the "ability to construct appropriate courses of action and to motivate and regulate their execution."
4. **Self-reflectiveness**: People have the capacity to reflect on their own functioning, to evaluate their thinking, abilities, actions, and motivations and to make adjustments, if necessary. (see Bandura, pp. 164-165)

Bandura emphasizes that people's behavior is never fully determined by circumstances: "Rather, human functioning is a product of a reciprocal interplay of intrapersonal, behavioral, and environmental determinants" (p. 165). Practice theorists are responding to what they see as overly deterministic structural approaches that ignore human actors, and overly "actor-oriented" approaches that neglect attention to the structural forces that shape and constrain human action (Giddens, 1979). They draw our attention not only to large scale evidence of people resisting seemingly overwhelming structural forces in social movements such as civil rights, women's rights, and immigrant rights, but to everyday forms of resistance where people assert their human agency.

The Interplay of Culture, Power, and History

Practice theorists are concerned with the interplay of culture, power, and history in the making of social subjects and in the processes of social reproduction and change (Bourdieu, 1977; Dirks, Eley, & Ortner, 1994). A number of practice theorists have drawn on the work of French philosopher Michel Foucault in thinking about the disciplinary practices at work in the shaping of positionality, discourses, and social relations. Foucault paid particular attention to localized, institutional contexts, such as clinics and prisons, where one could witness the power of what he termed "disciplinary practices," those that contributed to the production of particular kinds of social subjects. He was concerned with the power of modern scientific reason, of objectivity, measurement, classification, and evaluation at work in the disciplining of bodies and making of particular kinds of social subjects. Foucault argued that power is not ultimately in the strong arm of the state, but rather it is a productive force exercised through relations between people when questions of power, authority, and control over the definitions of reality are constantly being negotiated (Foucault, 1977, 1978, 1980).

Although the language of practice theory may sound unfamiliar to social work, we argue that the issues practice theorists are grappling with go to the theoretical and practical heart of the profession. The practice perspective attends to the mutual constitution of the person and society; points to the irreducible connection of structure and practice; and addresses the power of discourse in the construction of the terrain of the thinkable, talkable, and doable. Working from a practice perspective, we are challenged to consider the cultural and political *processes* and historical *contexts* in which we construct social problems; imagine "clients," "helpers," and their respective "roles" and relationships; and develop social policies and intervention technologies. Importantly, then, a practice perspective makes power, inequality, and transformational possibility foci of concern, thus offering a theoretical bridge between the concept of social justice and the practice of social work.

REFLECTION: Thinking about Community Food Security through Different Theoretical Lenses

Throughout this chapter we have discussed theory as an embodiment of human values that steers us to develop particular kinds of programs and services, or to even think in terms of programs and services as a way to conceptualize how to promote change. So how does practice theory with its emphasis on both human agency and social structure, help to guide particular forms of practice? Or better yet, how does practice theory translate into thinking about and working with individuals, groups, and communities? We use the example of community food security to illustrate how social work's dominant perspectives might conceptualize the issue. Then we use the Finding Solutions to Food Insecurity (FSFI) project as an example of a community-based participatory research project whose primary objective is to investigate barriers to food insecurity in Missoula County, Montana (see Chapters 6 and 7 for additional information about FSFI). Maxine Jacobson tells the story about the thinking that went into creating the FSFI project and how practice theory helped to guide the way.

***

Social work's primary approach to addressing food insecurity is to depend on food banks and other systems structured and marked by charitable giving as the solution to the problem. Social work practice, in this case, focuses on hungry people as the root cause of food insecurity and helps them cope by giving them food, generally on a limited basis. After reading about the social work theories that inform practice in this chapter, one must ask what role even the dominant theoretical perspectives play when it comes to understanding and addressing issues concerning community food security. A system's perspective would direct us to look to the *community food system* to find our solutions, the broader field of vision that includes not only food consumption, but production, processing, distribution, and waste. We would ask questions about where our food comes from, who grows it, the mechanisms in place that connect local farmers with consumers, and the barriers to and opportunities for food security that exist at the community level. We would not ask why more than 85% of the food we eat is shipped into our communities or why we have lost so much farm land in the United States to development. In this perspective these are questions that link us to the past, and history does not count when we view food security through a system's lens. Analyses of power regarding, for example, whose voices count in the policy decision making processes are not brought to the table either.

The empowerment approach, another dominant social work theoretical perspective, guides practice in yet another direction. It pushes us to engage in consciousness raising, capacity building, and collective efforts to challenge the unequal access to food in our communities. However, empowerment has different interpretations and has been appropriated by policy makers and program developers in back-handed, often punitive ways that promote "getting people to work" as the answer to community food insecurity. This interpretation of empowerment downplays the structural barriers such as low paying jobs, high rents, and steep utility costs that compromise people's ability to eat well. Using an empowerment perspective as a guide for practice has helped to create innovative approaches to food security that include community supported agricultural programs (CSAs) that link low-income people to community farms where they trade farm work for fresh, nutritious vegetables. However, this approach does little to address barriers to program participation such as transportation, child care, disability accommodations, or even more fundamentally, the unequal power relations that keep people separated by race, class, gender, ability, and so on. The empowerment approach espouses the idea that people need to participate and be perceived as actors in addressing issues in their own lives. However, the approach has primarily been developed *for* people who have experienced social injustice not *with* them. As a result, it fails to consider what empowerment means and what empowerment practices might look like if shaped by the experiences of people who encounter, for any number of reasons, social exclusion and inequality everyday.

How does practice theory inform an approach to community food security? I think it starts with the following questions (and these are predicated on a belief in human agency - the idea that we are never fully determined by our circumstances - that we are all social actors who possess the ability to act intentionally with forethought, planning, and reflectivity). "What helps people participate in the decision making that concerns their livelihood and wellbeing?" Why aren't more low-income people involved in shaping practices and programs at the community level?" "What have been the results of policies and programs that have not included the voice of experience?" A common assumption is that people who struggle to put food on the table have too many other problems that prevent them from being social actors in creating solutions. Or in the words of a gatekeeper for a local foundation I spoke with during the project's fund raising efforts, "*Those* [emphasis added] people have not been taught what it means to give back to society like you and I have." Instead of blaming the poor for their plight and trying to fix them as the solution, what if we looked to ourselves as part of the problem for not asking the right questions and what if we did some thinking along these lines - What factors exclude people from having an active role in shaping their life circumstances, and how can we address these to create a space for participation and solution building?

My own response to these questions was very basic. I participate in the community as part of my employment as do other people who sit on boards, steering committees, and coalitions. I get paid. My time is valued in the form of monetary reimbursement along with the vicarious satisfaction I receive from being an active, engaged member of my community. Being paid helps me shore up the infrastructure that supports my participation - I can hire a baby sitter, purchase gas for my car to get to a meeting, or have enough money to pay the bus fare. Not all people who become involved in community change work are paid. However, if we took a survey of community volunteers, I am certain most, if not all of them, have the means which allows their participation without undue hardship. This would not be the case for most people living from pay check to pay check who struggle to make ends meet. So it is not a question of people not wanting to be involved but more a question of how to support their involvement.

Based on how practice theory challenges and reminds us to consider the cultural and political processes and historical contexts in which we construct social problems, we (re)conceptualize the social worker's role and her relationship to people who have generally been considered "clients." We are co-workers learning to commit to a shared agenda and to make power a talkable subject. We prepare ourselves for the unpredictable, rewarding, complex, unnerving, and transformative work of addressing how power plays through our positions as representatives of the university, the food bank, and the homeless shelter and how so much of what we learn is informed by a middle-class sensibility that devalues and discounts the importance of experiences informed by daily struggles for survival. To understand food insecurity, not from our positions as people who have no problems with food access but from the positions of those who face multiple, complex barriers within the community, we recruited a steering committee of community members experiencing food insecurity to inform all aspects of the project from its beginning. To provide an infrastructure to sustain their participation over the long haul and to place cultural value on time spent at meetings, the FSFI project pays steering committee members for their time spent in monthly meetings. We also developed a system with the newly forming cooperative food market to reimburse members through food vouchers for the time they spend outside meetings conducting research. We provide child care, transportation, and food at each meeting. Beginning with the first meeting, steering committee members have been encouraged to and have taken on the role of planning the agenda and helping to facilitate meetings.

Practice theory pushes us to let go of our preconceived notions, some built in by training, about people's capacity to be community organizers and leaders. It focuses our attention on human agency and that people, as Bandura (2006) argues, are "contributors to their life circumstances, not just products of them" (p. 164). Practice theory reminds us how power is produced and reproduced and how relationships of inequality are a dominant model in social work practice and a force to contend with and disrupt in the struggle for social justice. It never lets us forget that people assert their human agency in everyday forms of resistance to overcome what seems like insurmountable structural forces. Practice theory gives us hope.

We have covered much conceptual ground in this section. Our abbreviated discussion does not do justice to the richness and complexity of the theoretical terrain. Our journey across this terrain continues. Our purpose in this section has been to point to some of the important influences on our thinking and to offer readers some theoretical benchmarks to guide your own journeys.

JUST PRACTICE: FRAMEWORK AND PROCESSES

An Integrated Approach

These significant, critical interventions have posed challenges to dominant modes of social work theory and practice. Concerns over questions of meaning, power, and knowledge in social work have been variably addressed by empowerment, narrative and social constructionist, and "postmodern" approaches. Some of these approaches have emphasized questions of meaning, others have addressed relations of power and inequality, and a few have attended to questions of history (Guitérrez & Lewis, 1999; Laird, 1993; Leonard, 1997, Mullaly, 1997; Parton, 1996; Payne, 2005; Pease & Fook, 1999; Rossiter, 1996; Swingonski, 1994). However, none of these have articulated an *integrated* approach to social work that theoretically and practically links themes of meaning, power, and history to the context and possibilities of justice-oriented practice. As we reflected on these diverse, challenging, and at times problematic theoretical influences, we began to build our own critical thinking around the five key themes of just practice. What were we pulling from these influences that helped us envision social justice work? Could these five themes be the necessary and sufficient elements for a foundation? As we held these five independent themes in relation and explored their interconnection, what new possibilities for thought and practice might emerge? We began to explore those possibilities.

In crafting the Just Practice Framework we have organized our thinking around five key terms: *meaning, power, history, context,* and *possibility.* In articulating the framework, we attempt to incorporate the critical insights of practice theorists and bring the meaning and power of transformative possibility to the fore in shaping struggles for social justice-oriented social work. As we have argued above, the challenge of social justice work calls for challenging ways of thinking and the disruption of our certainties about the world. We argue that the Just Practice Framework offers not "answers" but a model for critical inquiry that enables us to disrupt assumed truths, explore context, and appreciate ways in which social location may shape interpretation. To recap, the five key themes provide the basis for question-posing to inform and shape the practice of social justice work. How do people give *meaning* to the experiences and conditions that shape their lives? What are the *contexts* in which those experiences and conditions occur? What forms and relations of *power* shape people and processes? How does *history* make people and how do people make history as they engage in struggles over questions of meaning and power? How might an appreciation of those struggles help us imagine and claim a sense of *possibility* in the practice of social justice work? These questions are translated into action through *seven core processes* that link theory and practice: *engagement, teaching/learning, action, accompaniment, evaluation, critical reflection,* and *celebration*. In this section we address each of the core processes and consider how they work with the five key themes of the Just Practice framework. This foundation provides the theoretical and practical support for the subsequent chapters in which we develop the processes and present concrete skills and exercises that help us think about and engage in social justice work.

The Core Processes

The theory, politics, and ethics of social justice work are translated into practice as participants in the change process engage in the *praxis* of action and reflection for personal and social transformation.[8] It is possible to think of the core processes as a series of actions, or steps that, when taken together, move us toward this goal. However, the seven core processes do not necessarily imply linear, sequential movement. It may be helpful to envision them as overlapping and mutually informing processes, like waves, shaping and washing over one another. It is in this sense of nonlinear movement that we can better grasp the dynamics of change produced through the ebb and flow of ideas, reflections, and actions (Smith, 1999, p. 116). In the following paragraphs we outline the core processes.

Engagement

Engagement is the process through which the social worker enters the world of the participant(s) and begins to develop a working relationship. It entails entry into both context and relationship. It is a process of listening, communication, translation, and connection that seriously addresses questions of trust, power, intimacy, difference, and conflict. The social worker begins from a place of openness and curiosity and acknowledges the partiality of her knowledge. Through the engagement process the social worker anticipates the work ahead by reflecting on the participant(s) in the change process and coming to an appreciation of the other's situation. Engagement also calls for critical reflection on one's own positionality and the ways in which it may shape the relationship and the process of change.

Teaching–Learning

Teaching-learning is a participatory process of discovery and critical inquiry. In part, it entails the process of data collection, assessment, and interpretation and reframes them as collaborative activities. Teaching-learning connotes a two-way street and a relationship of interchange among participants. We teach at the same time that we are taught. We engage in mutual question posing, use various means to collaboratively collect information, identify resources and supports, discuss root causes of presenting concerns, teach and learn skills of assessment, and discover personal and collective capacities for critical practice, both our own and others.

Action

Action is the process of carrying out plans and sustaining the momentum. Action consists of recognizing and activating, brainstorming, decision making, planning, organizing, and putting these efforts in motion. It includes animating, facilitating, maintaining impetus, awakening the spirit and sense of possibility, advocating, and taking responsibility to speak for the values of social justice. Action is informed by reflection. It demands vigilance and a commitment to the ongoing search for one's own competence (Freire, 1990). Action calls for critical and respectful attention to resistance.

Accompaniment

Accompaniment is the actual people-to-people partnerships through which action is realized. In its simplest sense, accompaniment means to go with, to support and enhance the process. It reflects a commitment to being part of the journey over the long haul. The process entails ongoing critical dialogue regarding difference, power, and positionality among participants. It keeps us mindful of the challenges of collaboration and the need for conscious work in building alliances, mediating conflicts, and negotiating power.

Evaluation

Evaluation is an ongoing process consisting of stepping back, taking stock at different moments in the change process, and assessing the effectiveness of our efforts. Evaluation is interwoven with reflection and teaching/learning. In evaluation, we systematically examine the process and outcomes of our efforts. Evaluation is a collaborative process done *with* rather than *to* others. It is a process of documenting, scrutinizing, and sharing the results of our efforts so that we can learn from one another and produce the changes that we have envisioned.

Critical Reflection

Critical reflection is a dialogical process of learning together from our experiences. It is a structured, analytic, and emotional process that helps us examine the ways in which we make sense of experiences and circumstances. Through critical reflection, we systematically interpret our individual and collective experiences, question taken-for-granted assumptions and reframe our inquiry to open up new possibilities. Critical reflection enables us to challenge "common sense," make connections and explore the patterns that connect.

Celebration

Celebration is the act of commemorating the successes, big and small, in the process of change. It consists of the activities and performances that allow us to have fun with and in the work. Celebration is a process of bringing joy to the work and honor to the workers. Celebration, as a process, is rarely examined or practiced, but it is a fundamental way in which we can give voice to the beauty and power of our work. We borrow this process from other cultural contexts in which people integrate work and play and see celebration as an essential component of a just world and the struggle to achieve it.

Putting it All Together

We envision the Just Practice Framework as a guide for critical question-posing throughout the change process. It enables us to structure the process of being, doing, and becoming in light of the values and principles of social justice. As we engage in each moment and facet in the praxis of social change, the Just Practice framework keeps us critically mindful of the interplay of forces at work shaping the process. In the following matrix (p. 202), we illustrate the possibilities for question posing and critical reflection that emerge as the Just Practice Framework is brought to bear in carrying out the core processes. The questions we pose here are by no means exhaustive. Rather, we offer them as a starting point for your own critical reflection and action.

CHAPTER SUMMARY

In this chapter we have taken a close look at the concept of theory and the making of theory. We have explored the dominant paradigms that have shaped social work practice in the United States, particularly in the last half of the 20th century. We have drawn from a range of critical social and cultural theory to pose challenges to the dominant paradigm and suggest alternative possibilities for thought and action. Through ongoing dialogue about these ideas and reflection on our practice, we came to articulate the Just Practice Framework, which we have outlined here. In chapters 6 to 9 we develop each of the seven core processes and address the skills needed to carry them out.

Just Practice Matrix: Applying the Framework to the Core Processes

Framework and Processes: Critical Questions	Engagement	Teaching/ Learning	Action and Accompaniment	Evaluation, Critical Reflection and Celebration
Meaning	What is the significance of the encounter and relationship? How do the parties involved interpret the experience?	What and how do we learn from one another's interpretations? Create new meanings and understandings?	How does partiality of knowledge shape action? How do differing meanings constrain or promote differing courses of action?	How do we appreciate meaning via reflexivity? How do we validate the meaning of our work? Give meaning to social justice?
Context	How do interpersonal, organizational, social contexts shape relations and trust building? How can the context be changed in order to facilitate engagement?	How does context inhibit or facilitate possibilities for mutual learning? How does the teaching/learning process challenge the interpersonal, organizational, and social context?	How does context shape the pathways for action, access to resources, patterns of practices, social work roles, nature of partnerships? How do our actions expand contexts for social justice work?	What is context specific about the process? What can be applied to other contexts? How can reflection on the context be a catalyst for contextual change? What forms of celebration fit the context?
Power	How do differing positionalities of participants shape engagement? What forms of power need to be addressed in the engagement process? How do we use the power available to promote justice in relationship?	What can we learn from a power analysis of the situation? How can the process of teaching/learning challenge power inequalities among participants and promote social justice?	What access is there to power and resources? How do we remain mindful of power differences in the change process? How do they challenge accompaniment? How do actions contribute to empowerment of participants?	How do we evaluate redistribution of power in the change process? How do we measure individual, organizational and community empowerment? How do we both appreciate and celebrate new forms and practices of power?
History	How do past histories and experiences of participants shape the encounter and process of relationship building? What prior knowledge and assumptions might promote or inhibit the process?	How do we teach/ learn from and about our histories? How do our histories shape the ways that we know and experience the world? How do we learn from those who came before? How do we learn from what is historically possible?	How do histories become resources and catalysts for action? How does historical consciousness inform future action? How do we bridge differences of history and forge alliance for action? How do actions challenge inscriptions of historic injustice?	How do we evaluate change over time? How do we account for historical conditions? How does reflection on where we have been inform where we are going? How might a reclamation and celebration of our histories animate future efforts?
Possibility	What are the possible relationships that can be formed and strengthened in this change effort? What spaces of hope can be opened?	What can we learn from this other person/group? What can we contribute? What new ways of knowing might emerge from this experience? How can this learning promote other possibilities for social justice work?	How might we expand our repertoire of roles and skills? What possible courses of action are available? How can our efforts enhance future possibilities for empowering action?	How do we select among the possibilities at hand? Assess possible courses of action? Expand the terrain of the thinkable, talkable, and do-able? Reflect on decisions made and opportunities lost? Celebrate creativity?

FIGURE 5.1

Welfare Reform and Structural Adjustment

In this case study we define briefly what welfare reform and structural adjustment mean, and then we outline the neoliberal economic logic that underlies both practices. Once you have completed reading these two vignettes, reflect on the following questions: How do welfare reform and structural adjustment tie into globalization? What are the commonalities and differences in these two concepts? Does a difference in language mask common practices? What might be the patterns and the logic that connect these discourses and practices?

***

The words "welfare reform" stand for the latest in a string of federal welfare policies meant to decrease the "chronic dependency" of people, mostly women and children, from government "hand-outs" and provide "incentives" to get folks into the job market where they can achieve "self-sufficiency." The Personal Responsibility and Work Opportunity Reconciliation Act (PRWORA), signed into law by President Clinton in 1996, was a response to his campaign promise to "end welfare as we know it." And he did so with the support of Republicans and Democrats alike. Ann Withorn (1998, p. 277) refers to PRWORA as "pubic policy at its most controversial" and with these words, she sums up general public sentiment on this piece of legislation. Welfare reform has been hailed as a great success by those who measure success in terms of numbers of people off the "dole." Others, those most intimately aware of the realities of living in poverty in the United States, call it an abysmal failure. Peter Edelman (1997) resigned from his position as the assistant secretary for planning and evaluation at the Department of Health and Human Services in protest of the bill's passage. He argued the bill would increase rather than decrease the rates of poverty, pushing more families with children below the poverty line. Senator Edward Kennedy (as quoted in Edelman, p. 45) voted against the bill and described it as "legislative child abuse."

Welfare reform set into motion new policy directives such as mandatory work requirements; strict lifetime limits on how long someone could receive public assistance (5-year maximum); the elimination of public assistance as entitlement; punitive sanctions for policy noncompliance (e.g., missed appointments with case worker) resulting in reductions in or termination of welfare benefits; incentives for those who married or chose to stay married; and the creation of block-grant funding that, in effect, transferred responsibility for welfare reform from federal to state governments. Each state, within certain parameters, decides how to spend its welfare dollars.

Since the passage of welfare reform policy over a decade ago, significant changes have been noted in the lives of families and children living in poverty. The Urban Institute, located in Washington, DC, is a center whose primary function is to "analyze policies, evaluate programs and inform community development to improve social, civic, and economic well-being." Originally initiated by President Johnson in the mid-1960s, the center represents a nonpartisan analysis of social problems facing U.S. cities. We highlight some of the changes noted by The Urban Institute based on an examination of the experiences of low-income families (The Urban Institute, 2006):

♦ Welfare caseloads were cut in half between 1996 and 2000 and continued their decline through the 2001 economic recession (4.6 to 2.1 million families by 2002).

♦ Many former welfare recipients work in low-wage jobs, with median hourly wages hovering around $8.00 in 2002, and only one third of these workers have health insurance through their jobs.

♦ Fifty percent of families who have left welfare and are working earn wages below the federal poverty line.

♦ The proportion of low-income single-parent families with an employed parent has increased significantly. Full-time employment with employer-provided health benefits did not increase in this group.

♦ Child poverty increased in the United States from 2000 to 2004.

♦ Children in low-income families—whether receiving welfare or not—consistently fare worse than children in more affluent families on measures of child well-being, family environment, and sociodemographic risk. (pp. 1-5)

The law authorizing TANF expired in 2002 and it was subsequently extended, as is, periodically over the last 4 years because of a stalemate in Congress. The stalemate concerned significant issues that would affect the welfare of recipients, including proposals to increase the work requirement hours and restructure the food stamp program so unlimited amounts of funding could be shifted to other programs. TANF was reauthorized in 2006.

***

Structural Adjustment Programs (SAPs) have been central to the economic policies of the International Monetary Fund (IMF) and the International Bank of Reconstruction and Development, or the World Bank, since the early 1980s. SAPs were designed to help developing countries emerge from their debt crises. They involve a set of conditions or obligations with which countries have to comply in order to have their existing loans rescheduled and to be eligible for future loans. To understand structural adjustment one must understand the economic logic of neoliberalism. Green (1995) tells us that the word neoliberalism is confusing. Liberal usually connotes support of human rights and community values, but in the case of neoliberalism it has economic, not political connotations. In neoliberalism the ideology of the free market and economic rationalism reign. It is rooted in the belief that "unfettered free markets will promote economic growth resulting in development" (Ecumenical Coalition for Economic Justice, 2001, p. 1). The basic tenets of neoliberalism are:

1) decrease state intervention,

2) decrease regulation of industry,

3) decrease government spending,

4) build up private sector industry, and

5) stabilize the economy by curbing inflation.

In neoliberal eyes, the way to fight inflation is . . . by reducing the growth in the money supply by cutting government spending and raising interest rates. Wage controls are also used to reduce demand in the economy (Green, 1995, pp. 2-4).

Green contends that structural adjustment promotes stabilization by:

> . . . getting the prices right, removing artificial distortions such as price controls or trade tariffs and allowing the unregulated market to determine the most efficient allocation of resources. Because of its role in distorting prices and generally interfering with the free operation of the market, the state is seen as part of the problem, not part of the solution, and the economy has to be restructured to reduce the state's role and unleash the private sector. (p. 4)

Critics argue that structural adjustment policies actually increase poverty. For example, the privatization of government enterprises are typically associated with layoffs and pay cuts for workers. Cuts in government spending result in reduced health, education, and welfare services available to the poor. The imposition of user fees for government services from health care to clean drinking water makes these basic services inaccessible to the poor.

> Countries have also been regularly required to "privatize" government-owned functions, such as utilities and water. In most cases these essential services have been purchased by private companies, sometimes from the north, whose primary interest has been profit, sometimes with subsequent cuts in essential services to populations unable to afford market pricing. (Polack, 2004, p. 283)

Measures that force countries to increase their exports are often associated with the displacement of people from land and subsistence economies. And the elimination of tariff protections for industries frequently results in massive layoffs. Ultimately, structural adjustment entails cutting the labor force to reduce labor costs. Employers achieve these ends by hiring more part-time labor and decreasing the number of full-time employees to avoid paying the costs of expensive benefit packages (Essential Action, 2001, p. 1). Structural adjustment also includes cutting wages, increasing working hours, and sidestepping minimum wage requirements (Polack, 2004).

Women have been especially hard hit by SAPs. When unemployment increases, women are often first to lose their jobs. Increased food prices and decreased subsistence agriculture leave women unable to meet their family's basic needs. Cuts in health and welfare services leave women in multiple jeopardy. They are expected to care for the sick, the old, and the young and are left with few resources to do so. In short, women serve as "shock absorbers" for the social effect of economic adjustment (Ecumenical Coalition for Economic Justice, 2001, p. 2).

Questions for Discussion

1. What does it mean to say that theory can influence and shape racist, classist, and sexist notions of people, groups, and societies?

2. Why is it important to think of theories as value-laden constructs?

3. What is positionality, and why is this concept important to the understanding of theory?

4. Where would you begin to build your own theory of social justice work? What key principles would guide your theory?

5. How do theories of practice differ from dominant theories of social work?

Suggested Readings

Freire, P. (1990). A critical understanding of social work. *Journal of Progressive Human Services, 1*(1), 3-9.

Gutiérrez, L. & Lewis, E. (1999). *Empowering women of color.* New York: Columbia University Press.

Harvey, D. (1989). *The condition of postmodernity: An enquiry into the origins of cultural change.* Oxford: Basil Blackwell.

Korten, D. (2001). *When corporations rule the world.* West Hartford, Conn: Kumarian Press.

Lemert, C. (2004). *Social theory: The multicultural and classic readings.* Boulder, CO: Westview Press.

Leonard, P. (1997). *Postmodern welfare: Reconstructing an emancipatory project.* London: Sage.

Margolin, L. (1998). *Under the cover of kindness: The invention of social work.* Charlottesville, VA: University of Virginia Press.

Pease, B. & Fook, J. (1999). *Transforming social work practice: Postmodern critical perspectives.* New York: Routledge.

Smith, L. Tuhiwai (1999). *Decolonizing methodologies: Research and indigenous peoples.* London: Zed Books.

END NOTES

[1] Thanks to Holly Peters-Golden, medical anthropologist at The University of Michigan, and her daughter Becca for permission to use this story.

[2] While Carol Stack did find more similarity than difference in moral reasoning among African American women and men returning to the rural South, she did find striking difference in ways of acting. She notes: "Men and women in these rural southern communities differ in their assumptions of the work of kinship, in the roles they perceive as wage-earners, and in their political actions" (Stack, 1990, p. 25). We recommend this essay to readers, and also invite you to explore other works in Faye Ginsberg and Anna Lowenhaupt Tsing's important collection, *Uncertain Terms: Negotiating Gender in American Culture* (Boston: Beacon, 1990).

[3] Nancy Naples (1998) offers a helpful distinction regarding the broad tradition of feminist standpoint epistemologies. She writes:

> Those writing within this broad tradition of feminist standpoint epistemologies draw on three different definitions of standpoint: standpoint viewed 1) as embodied in particular knowers who possess certain racial, ethnic, class and gender identities as in certain aspects of [Patricia Hill] Collins' approach; 2) through communal or relational processes through which a standpoint is achieved, as in [Donna] Haraway's approach; and 3) as an axis point of investigation as in [Dorothy] Smith's "everyday world" perspective. (p. 224)

[4] Lincoln and Guba (1985, p. 15) state that paradigms represent what we think about the world (but cannot prove). Historically and contextually embedded in fundamental belief systems about how the world works, approaches to inquiry shift with time. Paradigms therefore have the power to enable and constrain:

> The power of a paradigm is that it shapes, in nearly unconscious and thus unquestioned ways, perceptions and practice within disciplines. It shapes what we look at, how we look at things, what we label as problems, what problems we consider worth investigating and solving, and what methods are preferred for investigation and action. Likewise, a paradigm influences what we choose not to attend to; what we do not see. (Maguire, 1987, p.11)

[5] For further discussion of the concept of "dependency" see Nancy Fraser and Linda Gordon's important article "A genealogy of *dependency*: Tracing a keyword of the U.S. welfare state," in *Signs: Journal of Women in Culture and Society,* 1994, 19(21), 309-336.

[6] This quote comes from the Critical Resistance website: www.criticalresistance.org

[7] Our idea of practice is informed by a range of contemporary anthropological and sociological inquiry (Bourdieu, 1977; Giddens, 1979; Ortner, 1989, 1996; Sahlins, 1981; Sewell, 1992).

[8] The term praxis refers to the ongoing systematic process of action and critical reflection.

Just Get Started: Engagement

CHAPTER OVERVIEW

In this chapter we develop the meanings, contexts, and skills of engagement; consider power, history, and participants in the engagement process; and address the challenges and possibilities therein. Although we will develop each core process separately throughout the next three chapters, we ask that you keep the matrix presented in Chapter 5 (p. 202) in mind to guide you in thinking about the framework and processes as a whole. Engagement provides the entrée to social justice work in cultural, community, organizational, and interpersonal contexts. We explore skills of anticipatory empathy; observation, noticing, and bearing witness; body consciousness; listening; and dialogue that are central to engagement. We raise questions regarding power, difference, and forms of resistance that may constrain and contradict engagement. And we attend to the place of group work and popular education in expanding the possibilities of engagement for social justice work. We have devoted an entire chapter to engagement in order to do justice to its importance. However, we ask that you think of engagement not as a discrete process readily separable from teaching-learning or the other core processes, but as an ongoing practice integral to all aspects of social justice work.

Throughout this chapter we ask you to try to imagine the intertwining and mutually informing relationship between engagement and teaching-learning. One image that we have found helpful is that of a dance with partners responding to one another as they execute complex patterns and improvise new possibilities of form and expression. Through engagement, we bring both preparedness and openness to bear on the teaching-learning moment. As we learn more about one another and our social realities we construct shared meanings and histories and reshape the nature of our relationships and the processes of engagement. The "dance" of engagement and teaching-learning may grow more intimate, confident, and creative over time. The pacing and rhythms may shift over time. Likewise, we may make mistakes and stumble and need to regroup and reflect on the limits of our engagement and learning. What might be another image that captures the dynamics of engagement and teaching-learning?

THE MEANING OF ENGAGEMENT

Understanding Engagement

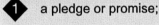
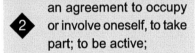
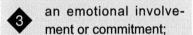
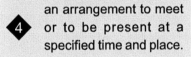

MEANINGS OF ENGAGEMENT

1 a pledge or promise;

2 an agreement to occupy or involve oneself, to take part; to be active;

3 an emotional involvement or commitment;

4 an arrangement to meet or to be present at a specified time and place.

According to the dictionary, "engagement" has a number of meanings: (1) a pledge or promise; (2) an agreement to occupy or involve oneself, to take part; to be active; (3) an emotional involvement or commitment; and (4) an arrangement to meet or to be present at a specified time and place. The process of engagement in social work encompasses all aspects of this definition and more (American Heritage Dictionary, 2000). Engagement is a socio-emotional, practical, and political process of coming together with others to create a space of respect and hope, pose questions, and learn from and about one another. As we engage, we begin building a base of knowledge and a place of trust from which to discover, reflect, and act. Many social work texts describe engagement as the first step in a helping process in which the social worker seeks to establish rapport with her "client" and to clarify her professional role as a representative of a social service agency and the purpose for her involvement. For example, Naomi Brill and Joanne Levine (2002, p. 126) describe engagement as "involving oneself in the situation, establishing communication, and formulating preliminary hypotheses for understanding and dealing with the problem." Pamela Landon (1999, p. 103) describes engagement as "the communicative activity characterized by mutual development of a beginning relationship between the social work response system and the client system." We argue that these depictions of engagement are useful, but limited. The abstract language of problems and systems too easily distances us from the fundamental human connection at the core of engagement. The Just Practice approach asks us to think of engagement as both an intentional *process* and an ongoing *commitment*. It is a process shaped by critical curiosity, humility, compassionate listening, and respect. It requires a commitment of our energies to be present, open, and willing to struggle with our own preconceptions and worldviews so that we can allow space for alternative possibilities. In short, engagement is a process of being, doing, and becoming (Kelly & Sewell, 1988). It is about being fully present and open to another's story, doing the communicative and relationship-building work, and becoming transformed in the process. This is a simple, yet profound statement. Social justice work demands that we as social workers open ourselves to ongoing growth and change; we, too, are transformed through our participation with others in purposeful, dynamic relationships.

Importance of Relationship

Marty Dewees (2006) defines engagement as "the process of building a relationship among the worker, the client, and the client's environment" (p. I-5). In so doing she speaks to a resonant theme in the history of social work practice and a core social work value, the importance of relationship. Jane Addams sought to build meaningful, lasting relationships with the residents of the Hull House neighborhood. Bertha Capen Reynolds believed that social work operates by communication, listening, and sharing experiences—the building blocks of relationship. Helen Harris Perlman (1979) describes relationship as the heart of social work. Perlman writes, "What is the common element, the red thread, that seems to run through every successful effort by one person to influence another in benign and enabling ways? The answer seems to be 'relationship' (p. 12). . . We become human beings and grow through the nurture of relationship" (p. 30). According to Perlman, the relationship that gives social work its uniqueness is one characterized by an emotional bond rooted in warmth, concern, and, most fundamentally, acceptance. Social workers have drawn on the humanistic psychology of Carl Rogers in promoting relationships based on three qualities: empathy, genuineness, and unconditional positive regard (Rogers, 1951). Rogers and his colleagues hold that these core qualities facilitate a climate in which a relationship of dignity and respect can develop and in which challenging work can be tackled (Rogers, Gendlin, Kiesler, & Truax, 1967). Building a relationship grounded in love, dignity, and respect is not something to be taken lightly. Our own humanity is deepened as we engage in what philosopher Martin Buber terms an "I-Thou" relationship; and, through compassionate connection to mutual personhood an "I-Thou-We" relationship is created (Kelly & Sewell, 1988).

＊When we fail to engage with love, dignity, and respect we not only risk diminishing the humanity of another, but also find that our own personhood begins to atrophy (Deegan, 1996, p. 7). The result, as Patricia Deegan describes in her important work on professional helpers and mental illness, is a breaking of the spirit that robs both clients and helpers of their full humanity (Deegan, 1990). In contrast, Deegan invites us to think about engagement as entry into a "conspiracy of hope" wherein we "refuse to reduce humans beings to illness"; challenge radical power balances between professionals and those labeled as "clients," "patients," or "consumers"; and craft relationships marked by "true mutuality" (1996, pp. 2-3). A social-justice approach to engagement calls on us to honor the dignity and full personhood of all participants in the change process. In so doing, we must think critically about the ways in which concepts such as "client," "patient," "consumer," or "member" are used in our social work practice and how the ways in which people are named may shape perceptions of their personhood, competence, and capacity to participate in the decisions that affect their lives. Thus, an examination of the meaning of engagement raises the question, "Who participates?"

Participants in the Engagement Process

Social workers have struggled with the languaging of practice. We speak variously of consumers, participants, members, clients, patients, collaborators, allies, and constituents. Each term carries a certain cultural freight and suggests particular kinds of relationships. At times, a language of participation may serve to mask relationships of unequal power rather than reflect a spirit and practice of mutuality. There is a fundamental politics of naming at work in our practice, and it is important to explore and acknowledge the ways in which the language used to name social work relationships and activities shapes practice. The practice of social justice work challenges us to reflect critically on models of helping that place the social worker as expert and "client" as victim or problem. We also recognize that much of social work practice, at least in the United States, operates on a problem-focused model and is carried out in systems that focus on one-to-one intervention with clients. Too often, our understanding of "clients" reinforces a notion of the problem being located within the person and thus limiting our cognizance of the social conditions that contribute to and exacerbate individual pain and struggle. The labels of helping systems often keep social workers from seeing the full personhood of those with whom we work. This, in turn, leads us to making assumptions about a person's capacity for participation in the change process, thereby limiting his role from the moment of engagement. We argue that there is space for social justice work within dominant systems and that through the practice of social justice work we can challenge the limits of these spaces and expand their possibilities as spaces of hope.

Power in the Process

As part of the engagement process we need to consider the contextual and structural arrangements, the conditions in which people come together, the nature of our social work practice, and the social, political, and organizational forces that shape our roles as social workers and the roles of those with whom we work. Power relations are in play in any relationships formed for the purpose of creating personal, social, or political change. The social work relationship is an examined one in which we think from the start about who is included in the process and why and who is excluded and why. The very definition of who counts as part of the change process from the start is informed by theoretical, organizational, political, and practical factors. As critically reflective practitioners we need to continually consider the ways in which assumptions about the nature of the social work relationship and about who participates in the relationship often "go without saying"—as part of the unspoken rules of a particular context of practice. The answer to the question, "Who participates?" reflects our views of and respect for human agency. The answer will shape how we come to see the situation, how we envision the possibilities of action and the direction of the work, how we mobilize resources, and ultimately how we realize our roles as social justice workers.

Throughout the following chapters we use examples of practice that illustrate diverse ways of responding to the question "Who participates?" We invite readers to consider how the processes and outcomes might differ if we had started from a different answer to the question. One of our goals in consciously addressing the question of participation is to examine assumptions regarding agency-based worker-client service delivery as the primary mode of practice and imagine alternative ways of framing and engaging in relationships and change efforts. When entering into the process of engagement we ask that you keep in mind the questions of power posed in the Just Practice matrix on p. 202: How do differing positionalities of participants shape engagement? What forms of power need to be addressed in the engagement process? How do we use the power available to promote justice in relationship?

The opening quote for Chapter 6 speaks to issues of power and positionality in the engagement process. Stephen Rose, a white, middle-class social worker, is describing his encounter with Michael, an angry Black teenager (Rose, 2000). Rose describes his personal epiphany when he realized that his social work training had taught him strategies for distancing himself from Michael, drawing on his expertise to interpret the meaning of Michael's anger, and using his professional power to name Michael's experience. Rose recalls,

> I was trained not to share power in constructing or producing what we worked on together, in not perceiving him worthy or capable of partnership with me… In other words, my professional status included the illusion of ownership of meaning of another person's experience through the delegated power to interpret it. Professional knowledge was built into my packaged identity, the medium through which domination reigned. (p. 404)

As Rose opened himself to listen to and learn from Michael, he faced a personal and professional crisis: "I knew that my reality and my identity—place, position, privilege—were being challenged" (p. 405). Rose describes his encounter with Michael as an explosive learning experience in which Michael was the teacher who transformed his safe, knowable world into an "active contradiction:"

> Michael implies, powerfully, that authentic communication with him could not occur in the agency; it had to happen in his lived reality. . . We existed in relation, Michael and me; we were not discrete entities linked in a linear equation, but relationally connected parts of a larger social world whose requirements created both Michael's suffering and rage and my position to respond to it. (pp. 405-406)

As Rose reworked his assumptions, not only was his relationship with Michael transformed, but also his relationship with social work. Rose began to confront the contradictions embedded in social work and explore the possibilities of empowerment-based practice. Rose describes:

> The challenge was to create relationships in which meaning was being produced, not received, where the participants were equally valid contributors to defining and shaping the process, product, and purpose of their interaction, not simply functional consumers of concealed, still dominated relationships, and where action derived from the entire dynamic and reflected its values. Later, Parsons (1991) articulated this experience, discussing how trust built among people changed their dialogue which, in turn, changed their perceptions of themselves as isolated people, and changed their capacity to generate action strategies. (p. 411)

In sum, Rose offers a poignant example of the challenges of engagement and the transformative possibilities that emerge when we take questions of power, positionality, and participation seriously in building empowering relationships.

REFLECTION: Who participates? Who is the expert?

Take a moment to consider the images that come to mind when you think of the term "expert." Many of us have been socialized to see experts as privileged outsiders who have amassed a body of specialized knowledge about a specific topic and who objectively bring that knowledge to bear in making judgments and predictions, directing interventions, and evaluating outcomes. From this perspective many invisible communities of experts—those affected by poverty, mental illness, violence, or disability—are rarely recognized for their expertise. They are more likely to be planned for as targets of intervention rather than part of a meaningful process of engagement. At best, tokenism tends to define the dominant model of participation. What might happen if social workers drew on expertise of those affected by oppression and marginalization from the start? Patricia Deegan is a clinical psychologist and founder of the National Empowerment Center. Deegan has been diagnosed with mental illness and has dedicated herself to "pressing back against the strong tide of oppression" experienced by people labeled with mental illness. Drawing from her expertise and that of others diagnosed with mental illness, Patricia Deegan argues that,

> it is not our job to pass judgment on who will and will not recover from mental illness and the spirit-breaking effects of poverty, dehumanization, degradation, and learned helplessness. Rather our job is to participate in a conspiracy of hope. It is our job to form a community of hope which surrounds people with psychiatric disabilities. It is our job to create rehabilitation environments that are charged with opportunities for self-improvement. It is our job to nurture our staff in the special vocations of hope. It is our job to ask people with psychiatric disabilities what it is they want and need in order to grow and then to provide them with the good soil in which a new life can secure its roots and grow. And then, finally, it is our job to wait patiently, to sit with, to watch with wonder, and to witness with reverence the unfolding of another person's life. . . We must stop exercising 'power over' the people we work with . . . we must begin to think in terms of having 'power with' or 'creating power together'... we must stop using the phrase, 'I judge this to be in the client's best interests,' and instead ask people what they want for their own lives and provide them the skills and support to achieve it. . . . . we must commit ourselves to removing environmental barriers which block people's efforts towards recovery and which keeps us locked in a mode of just trying to survive (1996, pp. 9-10).

Drawing from the expertise of people who have been diagnosed with mental illness, Deegan poses the following questions as a starting point for those working in mental health settings to critically examine their own practices:

♦ Are the people we work with overmedicated? Too often apathy, lack of motivation, indifference or "resistance" are the results of drug effects.

♦ Are consumers/survivors in both community-based and hospital programs involved in evaluating staff work performance? Who better knows how effective a staff person is than those receiving services from that staff person?

♦ Are program participants and hospital inpatients receiving peer skills training on how to participate in and effectively get what they want from a treatment team? Are we allowed to sit through the entire treatment-planning meeting and are staff committed to speaking in plain English so we can understand the conversation? Are there peer advocates who are available to come to the treatment planning meetings with us? Are there opportunities to meet prior to the team meeting in order to strategize what we want to get out of the meeting and how to go about presenting our ideas?

♦ Are there separate toilets or eating space for staff and program participants? If so, they should be eliminated. This is called segregation and creates second-class citizens.

♦ Who can use the phones? Who makes what decisions? Who has the real power in this program? Information is power and having access to information is empowering. What are the barriers to getting information in the program?

♦ Do we understand that people with psychiatric disabilities possess valuable knowledge and expertise as a result of their experience? Do we nurture this important human resource? Are peer-run mutual-help groups available? Are we actively seeking to hire people with psychiatric disabilities and to provide the supports and accommodations they may request?

Which of these questions have relevance for your own work or practicum setting? What other questions come to mind? How does the participation of people diagnosed with mental illness as critics as well as consumers of programs, policies, and practices challenge dominant notions of expertise? How might the critical participation of those affected challenge and change the "rules of engagement" in other contexts of social work practice?[2]

The Challenge of History

In Chapter 3 we explored questions of history in relationship to contemporary social work practice. Now we invite you to think about those who have historically been excluded from the process of making decisions about their lives and about the ways in which oppression has systematically silenced some voices—children, women, people with disabilities, the poor, people of color, immigrants—and legitimated the power of others to speak for them. Histories of marginalization and exclusion have profoundly shaped and constrained practices of engagement. As Patricia Deegan has addressed in the context of mental illness, people with psychiatric disabilities are never free from the problematic history of labels, stigma, fear, and containment that have characterized public perceptions and professional interventions (Deegan, 1990, 1996). In a similar vein, Romel Mackleprang and Richard Salsgiver (1996) argue that troubling historical constructions of disability as a form of spirit possession, punishment from God, mark of deviance, or source of shame filter through contemporary constructions that continue to focus on weakness and pathology. In a qualitative study of individuals with disabilities and their experiences with social workers, Stephen French Gilson, John Bricout, and Frank Baskind (1998) found that social workers treated respondents as if they had categorically fewer aspirations and rights than nondisabled people. Social workers tended to make prejudgments about capacity based on their personal assessment of the level of visible disability. They tended to establish an instant one-way familiarity while failing to really listen, recognize uniqueness of the individual, or seek the expertise of individuals with disabilities themselves. Overall, the respondents characterized social worker engagement as demeaning and paternalistic (Gilson et al., 1998). In other words, their "expertise" limited their capacity to engage. In short, long-standing histories of oppression and marginalization have played out in very immediate, felt ways in the process of social work engagement, revealing "the ways forms of oppression create problems out of difference" (Dean, 2001, p. 269).

Hilary Weaver (1998) speaks powerfully to the challenges of history as part of contemporary practice with indigenous people. She writes, "Historical trauma and unresolved grief are a legacy that many Indian people struggle with today. Although discussed less frequently than the Holocaust in Europe, the genocide was no less devastating. American Indian nations experienced decimation of their numbers and sometimes complete extermination" (p. 205). Weaver details the forced relocation, land dispossession, and subordination of Indian people that marked 19th century federal policies and practices in the United States. She describes the shift from physical to cultural genocide and the break-up of Indian families through the boarding school system and, later, systematic removal of Indian children through foster care and adoption that characterized late 19th and 20th century policies and practices. Weaver cites Brave Heart-Jordan and DeBruyn (1995) in describing the generational trauma and unresolved grief experienced by many Native Americans. Weaver writes:

> Suspicion and mistrust are natural outcomes and important survival skills for people who have experienced attempts at genocide. Many interactions with the dominant society have had dire consequences for Native Americans. Practitioners and program planners who seek to work with Indian people must realize that their helping interventions may be viewed within this context. (1998, p. 206)

As Weaver's discussion suggests, history cannot be bracketed out of the engagement process. Instead, we as social workers must be mindful of the ways in which personal, political, and cultural histories shape our positionalities as well as those with whom we work. "Helping" systems of the state or dominant culture have served as institutions of power and control over oppressed groups. Distrust and resistance are often healthy responses to such systems, and social workers within these systems need to approach the engagement process with a sensitivity to the palpable presence of history and an appreciation of resistance as both a right and a survival skill. Furthermore, participants frequently enter the engagement process with little shared history. Those histories cannot be assumed. Rather, the art of engagement entails making space and time where experiences can be shared, stories told, and trust built in the process of co-creating relationship. When entering into the process of engagement, we ask that you keep in mind the questions posed in the Just Practice Matrix on p. 202: How do past histories and experiences of participants shape the encounter and process of relationship building? What prior knowledge and assumptions might promote or inhibit the process?

THE CONTEXT OF ENGAGEMENT

As the previous discussion suggests, engagement is embedded in context. Participants come together in a specific time and space that is shaped by personal experiences, historical and political influences, and current social circumstances. The process of engagement plays out in cultural, community, and organizational contexts that serve as both resources and constraints. In this section we address the cultural, community, and organizational contexts of engagement. We locate engagement as an interpersonal process that is shaped powerfully by the contexts in which it plays out. At the same time through the dynamics of engagement, participants encounter and create possibilities for transforming the very contexts in which their relationships emerge.

Engagement requires ongoing critical reflection on one's own *positionality*. That is, where are we, as social workers, coming from? We discussed the concept of "positionality" in Chapter 5. Our positionalities are shaped by the multiple identities through which we experience the world and through which we acquire or are denied certain privileges and stakes in power. In the following sections, as we focus discussion on cultural, community, and organizational contexts of practice, we also reflect on our positionalities therein.

Cultural Context of Engagement

The NASW Code of Ethics calls on social workers to engage in culturally competent practice. The profession has struggled over time with the challenge of both defining and realizing "cultural competence" (Lum, 1999). Some efforts examined questions of diversity and proposed strategies for "ethnic-sensitive practice" (Devore & Schlesinger, 1981). Much of the early work on ethnic diversity focused on characterizations of and intervention strategies for presumably discrete "groups" viewed as culturally "different" (See for example, Atkinson, Morten, & Sue, 1989; Sue, 1981). While caveats were given regarding the significance of individual differences, these approaches often relied on rather simplistic understandings of "cultures" as homogeneous entities identifiable by common history, language, customs, values, belief systems, and practices. The audience for the early writings on ethnic sensitivity and diversity in U.S. social work were generally assumed to be members of the dominant, white majority who needed tools for working with the ethnic "other." Over time, the profession has come to appreciate a more complex and nuanced understanding of culture and its interplay with power and history (see, for example, Healy, 2001; Lieberman & Lester, 2004). Social workers have been challenged to recognize diversity as inseparable from issues of social and economic justice. Diversity cannot be decoupled from the mechanisms of privilege and oppression through which some forms of difference are constructed as deviant (Van Soest & Garcia, 2003, p. 3). The work of David Gil (1998), for example, has been critical in examining forms and practices of oppression and their relationship to the production of notions about difference and deviance. Dorothy Van Soest and Betty Garcia (2003) argue that understanding of cultural diversity demands a focus on power and privilege; they insist that "diversity issues include everyone in the equation: both those who benefit from oppression and those who are marginalized" (p. xi).

Considerable attention continues to be paid to the question of cultural competence and to the preparation of social workers to engage in culturally competent practice (Anderson & Carter, 2003; Lum, 1999). For example, one current social work practice text describes cultural competence as:

> fluency with cultures different from one's own. This means that learning as much as possible about the cultures of our clients is critical, particularly in terms of theories, techniques, and skills that are culturally sensitive. It also means learning about all aspects of diversity including gender, sexual orientation, race, ethnicity, and other characteristics that affect clients. (Boyle, Hull, Mather, Smith, & Farley, 2006, p. 73)

While well-intentioned, this understanding of "cultural difference" tends to reproduce notions of the client as "other" and culture as a set of traits or characteristics that one possesses. It suggests that one can become competent through mastery of a particular "diversity content." It does not mention the relations and arrangements of power or forces and mechanisms of oppression through which beliefs about differences and their consequences are constructed, justified, and reproduced. It does not address the social worker's responsibility to examine critically her own "culture" and positionality and their relation to systems of privilege and inequality in which her practice is embedded. Nor does it emphasize the importance of historical context and intergenerational dynamics in understanding people's strengths and struggles (Van Soest & Garcia, 2003, p. xii).

Some social workers have challenged the assumption that one can attain "cultural competence." They suggest a more humble appreciation of the ongoing struggle to grasp another's experience. Cultural engagement entails opening ourselves not only to hearing another's story but also to appreciating potentially very different systems of meaning and values and ways of organizing and making sense of basic concepts—such as personhood, family, health and illness, faith, and social organization. For example, Ruth Dean (2001) writes persuasively about the *myth* of cross-cultural competence and encourages social workers to recognize our "partiality of knowledge." Dean writes:

> . . . the concept of multicultural competence is flawed. I believe it to be a myth that is typically American and located in the metaphor of American "know-how."

> It is consistent with the belief that knowledge brings control and effectiveness and that this is an ideal to be achieved above all else. I question the notion that one could become "competent" at the culture of another. (p. 624)

Rather than assuming cultural competence as an achievable goal, Dean and others encourage social workers to practice from a place of "cultural humility" and "not knowing" and to take responsibility for ongoing learning about difference and about one's own "cultural baggage" (Dean, 2001; Laird, 1993b; Zayas, 2001). Dean encourages social workers to develop a historical knowledge base, examine critically their cultural freight, consider the ways their values and assumptions shape the relationship, and engage in sociopolitical analysis of intersecting forms of oppression and their effects (2001, p. 628).

Given the centrality of cultural competence in contemporary social work debates, we want to probe further into the concepts of "culture" that inform our thinking regarding the cultural context of engagement. In Chapter 4 we noted the dynamic understanding of culture put forth by Lynne Healy to guide ethical practice in a global context. In Chapter 5 we provided an overview of practice theory, which offers a dynamic understanding of the ways people both shape and are shaped by cultural meaning systems and social institutions. In the following discussion we draw from cultural anthropologists who have helped us to see culture not as a fixed set of traits and customs but a complex and contested process of meaning-making embedded within relations of power. Anthropologists of the late 20th century have critiqued a concept of culture as a shared system of meaning, a unified "whole" of the customs, practices, language, symbols, and institutions of a group. Rather, attention has been drawn to the permeation of power relations, forms of resistance, the contested and contingent nature of culture, the role of hegemony, and the active practice of cultural agents. For example, anthropologist James Clifford describes culture as "always relational, an inscription of communicative processes that exist, historically, *between* subjects in relations of power" (1986, p. 15). Clifford contends that:

> Cultures are not scientific "objects" (assuming such things exist, even in the natural sciences). Culture, and our views of "it," are produced historically, and are actively contested. . . . If "culture" is not an object to be described, neither is it a unified corpus of symbols and meanings that can be definitively interpreted. Culture is contested, temporal, and emergent. Representation and explanation—both by insiders and outsiders—is implicated in this emergence. (pp. 16-18)

From this point of view, the process of engagement invites us to start from a place of not knowing and to open ourselves to the ethnographic experience of "learning from other social worlds" (Aull Davies, 1999, p. 77). It is a process of entering into "another history of interactions," and that can pose for the social worker what Charlotte Aull Davies calls "the problem of memory"—we enter without a shared history and without being privy to the collective memory of which other participants are a part; therefore, we have to have a heightened sensitivity to the limits of our knowing and the dangers of facile interpretation. We are, in many ways, having to learn a new language of relationship that both draws on the language of the other party(ies) and that is co-constructed through the relationship. When we put it in the frame of learning another language it helps us keep that sense of humility about the limits of our knowing and the possibilities for making "cultural mistakes."

When we speak of the cultural context of engagement, we speak to the dynamic interplay of meaning and power among the worldviews of the social worker and the other participants in the change process. It is helpful to think of the engagement process itself as a cultural encounter in which the participants struggle to hear and be heard, to understand and be understood. If we approach the engagement process as "cultural workers," we start from a recognition of the partiality of our knowledge, we bear witness to another's experience, we continually examine our own cultural baggage, we seek to co-create meaning, and we remain ever vigilant to the workings of power and privilege and the possibilities for mitigating the effects of past and present inequalities. The work of anthropologist/physician Paul Farmer, whom we mentioned in Chapter 4, is instructive here. Farmer warns against the danger of confusing structural violence and cultural difference. Too often, he argues, those in positions of privilege and power invoke notions of "cultural relativity" to "explain "difference" without acknowledging the underlying structural inequalities and impoverishment that shape so much of human experience. We need to be wary of simplistic explanations of difference as "part of their culture" or "in their nature." According to Farmer (2003) such explanations reflect a cultural essentialism used to explain away assaults on the dignity and suffering of others. Farmer argues:

> Such analytic vices are rarely questioned, even though systematic studies of extreme suffering suggest that the concept of culture should enjoy only an exceedingly limited role in explaining the *distribution* of misery. The role of cultural boundary lines in enabling, perpetuating, justifying, and interpreting suffering is subordinate to (though well integrated with) the national and international mechanisms that create and deepen inequality. Culture does not explain suffering; it may at worst furnish an alibi for it. (pp. 48-49)

One of the challenges of engagement, then, is to be at once attentive to cultural context, sensitive to cultural difference, and mindful of the role of structural violence in shaping both.

Community Context of Engagement

Meanings of Community

The process of engagement also calls on us to be cognizant of our personal and organizational location within a larger community. The concept of community itself has multiple meanings. As Yan (2004) notes, it is one of the most vague and elusive social concepts. Community may refer to a political entity, a circumscribed and identified social and geographic space, or a group of people with common interests or concerns. Rhoda Halperin (1998), in her ethnographic study of Cincinnati's East End, writes,

> Community is circular—sometimes spherical with many layers. Community must be understood in the round—in multiple dimensions of ups and downs, of intergenerational ties—of politics personal and bureaucratic, of children and elders, of getting food and the other stuff of livelihood, of home and heritage (p. xi). . . Community is a common ordinary word. We think we know what it is. We take it for granted. We assume its presence or lament its absence. We know why we need it; yet we question it at the same time—where is it, what is it? (p. xii). . . Community is not just a place, but a series of day-to-day, ongoing, often invisible practices. These practices are connected but not confined to place. (p. 5)

Mark Homan defines community as follows:

> Community consists of a number of people with something in common that connects them in some way and that distinguishes them

from others. This common connection could be a place where members live—a city or a neighborhood. It may be an activity, like a job, or perhaps their ethnic identification provides the connection. When I use the term community I do not presuppose any particular size or number of people. (Homan, 2004, p.9).

As the above quotes illustrate, community is a complex concept. It has been the subject of considerable study. We highlight a few studies of community to provide tools for thinking about the community context of practice and its significance for engagement. Sociologist Ferdinand Tonnies (1957) sought to understand the changes in societal relations as a result of industrialization. He described the shift as one from *Gemeinschaft* to *Gesellschaft*, that is, from communities based in informal, integrated, organic relationships characteristic of small-scale pre-industrial life to those based in complex relations of specialization of function and formalization of structure. Some would argue that this continues to be reflected in rural/urban differences in social relations. Others contend that the notion of small harmonious communities reflects a nostalgic ideal rather than a historical or contemporary reality. They point to the complex nature of both rural and urban communities in the context of globalization. Nevertheless, images of community, belonging, and connection continue to play a key role in social work thought and practice.

Community power structures have also been an important subject of inquiry. Studies of community power have addressed the forms and distribution of power; formal and informal power structures; ways in which power is held, wielded, and perceived; identification of power holders and brokers; and strategies for community empowerment (Homan, 2004; Hunter, 1953; Kelly & Sewell, 1988). Theorists of community power and political systems have examined types and sources of community power and the ways in which power is made visible in times of community conflict (Kirst-Ashman & Hull, 2001, pp. 280-282). Community power dynamics and the location of our social work practice therein form an important backdrop to the engagement process.

Systems perspectives have also been used to understand community dynamics. From a systems perspective, "every community can be viewed as a *social system* with all the associated characteristics, including boundaries, homeostasis, stressors, task and maintenance functions, and subsystems (Kirst-Ashman & Hull, 2001, p. 267). Roland Warren's (1963) classic conceptualization of communities as social systems with multiple functions provides food for thought on the process of engagement. Warren considers community as a locality-based set of social relations intimately connected to external systems. He is interested in *how* communities carry out five necessary functions: (1) production-distribution-consumption, (2) socialization, (3) social control, (4) social participation, and (5) mutual support. Warren examines the relationship between vertical patterns—ties to external structures and systems, and horizontal patterns—ties within the community. He offers a framework for exploring patterns of community participation and the ways in which needs of members are variably addressed or neglected. When we consider differences in personal or group experiences across these five dimensions we may come to appreciate how people living in physical proximity may be part of very different communities and how systems of power and privilege shape the meaning and experience of community and access to community resources. Social justice work challenges us to bring to the engagement process a permanent critical curiosity about the dynamics of community in which our practice is located. Patterns of social relations, structures of power, and community functions are not necessarily forces of constraint; they are also sources of possibility for transformative engagement.

In sum, communities are made, maintained, and modified through the ongoing negotiation of belonging and difference (Finn, 1998a). We may be members of multiple communities and may have varying degrees of identification with and investment in them. As social justice workers, we need to be cognizant of our own communities of connection and concern, of the communities in which our practice is based, and of the communities affected by our work. We do not parachute in to our social justice work "from nowhere." We come from a community context and bear the markers of that context as we begin to engage with others. As we enter into relationships with individuals and groups we engage in a process of reading and interpreting one another's markers and making judgments regarding belonging and difference.

Global Challenges

Questions of engagement and community are becoming increasingly complex in the face of globalizing trends and the concomitant dislocation and movement of people. For some, technological advances have opened the way for creation of countless virtual communities of engagement that transcend cultural, political, and geographic borders. For others the relentless downward pressure of structural adjustment policies and the consequences of "free trade" agreements have contributed to the dissolution of longstanding ties to land and place, loss of sustainable life ways, and movement into the precarious circuits of global labor migration (Bigelow & Peterson, 2002; Lowe & Lloyd, 1997; Yan, 2004). Migrant and refugee "communities" are straddling borders in diverse parts of the world. Communities in the Philippines, Mexico, Central and South America, and other parts of the globe are becoming home to the very young and the very old as men and women emigrate to work and send remittances back home to support their families. Undocumented workers live in the shadows, fearful of encounters with "officials" and distrustful of "helpers." Language differences and differing social and cultural norms and expectations further complicate the process. Traditional notions of communities as stable, homogeneous, place-based entities are becoming anachronistic as more and more people negotiate complex global circuits of interaction and obligation just to survive (Chin, 2003; Macklin, 2003; Mendoza Strobel, 2003). Our knowledge seems to become more partial by the day as the situations we confront grow more complex. In spite of and because of this complexity, community still matters to people. As Ife (2000) asserts, community is still an important buffer to the effect of globalization on people's lives (as cited in Yan, 2004, p. 55). We have a responsibility to engage across boundaries of difference. In so doing we can learn how people define and practice community, cultivate a sense of belonging, meet social obligations, negotiate barriers, and stake claims to their rights as community members. Engaging with others as members of communities is a measure of respect for their full personhood and for the power of relationships.

From Outside and Inside the Community Context

Cindy Hunter, MSW and member of the social work faculty at James Madison University in Harrisonburg, Virginia, describes the powerful experience of learning about self, community, and difference with residents of San Martin, El Salvador.

My husband, two young children (with one on the way) and I arrived in San Martin, El Salvador, in 1995, just 3 years after the U.N. brokered peace accords were signed to bring an end to the brutal civil war in which 80,000 people died. A white, North American family, we had been searching for an overseas assignment to learn from and work among people who struggle to survive, as much of the world's population does. My Peace Corps experience 10 years earlier had taught me that people in the developing world have much to teach. My own cultural assumptions allowed me to feel the privilege of using the earth's resources without much thought and it seemed crucial that my family and I reevaluate our assumptions. We also wanted to use our skills in areas of great need.

The Mennonite Central Committee (MCC), a faith-based relief, development, and peace-building organization, accepted us as volunteers. They assigned us to do "community development" in a bustling urban community with people who had fled the war and found refuge along the unoccupied strips of land flanking the railroad tracks (La Linea) as squatters on the outskirts of town.

The post-civil war political climate was tense and fraught with violence and criminality. The rampant violence and gang footholds had become the new form of terror. People even talked about the good old days of the war when one knew who the enemy was. In La Linea, people had either aligned themselves with, or escaped persecution of either side of the conflict, and so lived among neighbors who may have been from the opposing faction. Sometimes the neighbor's kids were in the local gang. Trust was a serious impediment to developing a sense of community.

For the residents of La Linea, sharing the little one has is also a way of life. For example, when Andrea discovered a 12-year-old boy in the market who had lost his parents months before, she took him in, even though there was already too little food in the house to support her own family. When Martina, who was raising several children and grandchildren on her own, offered one of only two mangoes she had in the house, I had no choice but to humbly accept that gift because it was offered out of love.

Our experiences taught us that cultural "competence" seems unrealistic. One must enter a new culture with a great deal of humility. The local people (the "insiders") were forever patient with my own cultural assumptions. There is a story of a young North American who, upon quizzing a peasant farmer about the economics of his bean field, calculated that the farmer could buy beans for about the same as it cost to grow them. He asked why the farmer continued to farm. There they stood on the edge of the bean field, one who was raised to be independent, increase his wealth, and weigh cost versus benefit, and one whose people for thousands of years have fed their children by the hand plow and the bean seed. Neither could comprehend the meaning of that question for the other. This story has been a constant reminder to me about the assumptions I carry.

The first couple of years of our time in El Salvador were very difficult. We were slow learning the language, didn't understand how things worked in the community, who the leaders were, how people got things done, how trust was built. And the community did not trust us either. At 18 months we were so discouraged that we considered going home. I went to speak with Bernarda, a wise older woman, who asked me, "How long have you been here, a year?" "No!" I responded, "A year and a half!" "That's the reason," she explained, "You really have to be here at least a couple of years to gain the trust of people." She was right. By the two-year mark we were sufficiently fluent, people trusted and wanted to work with us. We finally had a grasp on how to do things effectively, in such a way that people were empowered and took leadership, while we assisted and facilitated, and all were happy with the results. The next two and a half years for us were very productive.

Trusting relationships took months and even years to develop. There was no false sense of being an insider. People were always kind and unfailingly offered many unearned privileges. Trust, however, happened through presence. Passing time and being there for whatever. To listen to horrific details of war, to sit for hours at the funeral gathering of a 5-month-old baby and listen to the laments of the stream of other mothers who had lost children, to open a door at midnight to a neighbor fleeing her husband's drunken wrath…was to risk another sleepless night with a broken heart. Only by entering into the pain and joys of community life did we slowly gain trust. Professional distance would not have been understood in this context.

Most often, when someone was in deep pain, there was nothing we could actually do to change the situation, and no one seemed to expect that either. Salvadorans have a word *acompañar*, to accompany, which they use frequently. They see "being there" as an active form of caring. They chuckle at North Americans who, in the middle of a conversation about someone's illness, might glance at their watch and excuse themselves to be somewhere on time rather than finish listening to their friend. Relationships in the present moment take priority. Raising children, attending funerals, arriving shortly after a new birth, washing clothes by hand, attending community meetings, shopping in the market—are intentional acts. Each act, in the context of relationship with another person, allowed for deeper trust and connection.

Besides the power of relationships, we learned about the empowering process of education. Popular education is political, and it was threatening to the established government in El Salvador in the 1980s. Peasant farmers learning to read and discuss politics and religion led to discomfort and unrest with the system and in turn to a brutal oppression by the government of the uprising poor. Anyone hearing firsthand accounts of that civil war could begin to understand the sacrifice and danger of "empowering the masses." "Solidarity," like the brutal days of forming labor unions in my own country, was a concept that held people together and a vision that helped them prevail throughout incredible suffering. As outsiders in that process, my team members and I had to always be aware of the possible consequences of any of our actions to the people with whom we worked. A role for us was to be the questioners and learners.

Being the outsider had its advantages in the teaching-learning cycle. Ignorance of the community allows for seemingly obvious information to be examined. The inquiries (who lives in houses, who owns them, who has income, where the water is and who controls it, who chooses whether or not there is electricity) not only inform the questioner but create a space for the informers to reflect on deeper issues in a way that is new. When small groups of people agree or disagree on the answers, it promotes dialogue. Community members verbalize, sometimes for the first time, what is unique about their setting and situation.

The questions we asked in La Linea proved revealing. One discovery was that, in high foot traffic areas where people live in houses of mostly discarded tin roofing and woodscraps, there is very little sense of security. Almost always, one person stays home to guard the few household items and attend to the children while others work outside the home. Many women pass time at home learning crafts that might bring them some extra income. Few had enough money to buy raw materials for projects other than what someone might commission them to do. I took on the task to invite several artisans who had learned crafts from various church projects to come together as a group to share resources and market their products together. We saw this as a micro-enterprise (small business) project that would allow women to increase their income while still being home with their children. I spent three years with this small group, *Las Mujeres Tiñecas*. Most of my job was to encourage them to try something new, like going into the city and meeting with the manager of a fair trade shop, or making a phone call to see if there were any new orders, or risking using their own ideas to improve a product, or encouraging them to work through their differences and not dissolve the group at every threat of conflict. Employing popular education techniques, we started every meeting reflecting on the actions we had taken during the week. We wrestled with disagreements over missing money and how to spend profits, we had fun with kids and adventurous trips, and we cried and had our own ceremony when one of the members died.

The business side was tenuous. Though there were times that the money flowed, it was admittedly due to my own ease and privileged status in making contacts to sell to foreigners and visiting church delegations. So I was not surprised when, the year after we left the country, I received an apologetic email from one of the members stating that the group was not doing much work these days. I *was* surprised, however, to see a video tape that MCC produced after the great earthquakes of 2000 that featured the same *Mujeres Tiñecas* in San Martin leading the effort to rebuild each others' homes in a cooperative fashion. No, they were not crocheting purses or needle pointing t-shirts. But there were the women handling skill saws and measuring for roof beams!!!

Perhaps the real work we did together was building a sense of community and leadership ability. With each interaction we learned to reflect, process, and improve our situation. Skills and confidence increased as together we made decisions on who would buy supplies or keep money or lead the meetings or even who would make those decisions. This proved to be foundational for ongoing community change as women transformed those group skills into organizing reconstruction. It was in the context of the *Mujeres Tiñecas* that insiders most invited me into their lives. Group members frequented our home. Often, with one or more of my own kids in tow, I would spend hours visiting members in their homes to compare earring designs or thread colors. In either setting, the talk unfailingly turned to kids, health, food, and then to community, national, or world events. We watched how each other parented, we laughed endlessly about silly events or misunderstandings, we compared reactions to illnesses, we lamented over prices, we cried over brutal husbands or loss of family members.

Having the opportunity to live and learn and contribute in another culture, is, in itself, a privilege. It is hard to experience without being transformed. El Salvador affects me in my everyday interactions with people. I try to ask more questions and understand the big picture. I make more decisions based on how the decision affects others on a local and global level. I often find it hard to do justice to the lessons learned in San Martin. My current reality does not always allow for me to show up late because I was listening to a friend. My family stays connected to our Salvadoran friends through calls and visits. Keeping an open door, a room, and food in our home for new friends from all walks of life is an intentional act of creating space for relationships and community. We have learned that we can live with much less than we imagined and our ecological footprint has been greatly reduced.

Central America transformed my social work practice in the US. Interpreting the Code of Ethics, I am not encouraged to spend hours in clients' homes or certainly not to invite them into my own home for hours of discussion of life events that may or may not be related to the "presenting problem." Traditional worker/client roles, with the built in power difference, are questionable. Concepts like "noncompliant" and "resistant" give way to an understanding of what might make someone choose a different direction for themselves. I constantly question "professional boundaries" and opt for a collaborative effort. Finding work environments that focus on fostering community rather than "delivering services" has allowed for experimenting with new ways to do social work.

Even trying to separate the lessons between work and life seems artificial. I strive for "cultural humility" rather than an air of "cultural competence" in work or play with others different from myself. Maybe most importantly, I look for the justice factor in my actions, try to stay open to continued growth, and as verbalized by my colleague Dr. B. J. Bryson, I even have to question my own altruism.

Organizational Context of Engagement

The process of engagement also calls for reflection on our location as social workers in an organizational context. Most social work practice is carried out under the auspices of state-based human service systems, voluntary not-for-profit organizations, community- or neighborhood-based associations or, occasionally, for-profit corporations. Rarely are social workers autonomous agents of change. Therefore, we argue that engagement requires critical reflection on the organizations in which we work. What can we learn by reflecting on our positioning within organizations and the ways in which organizational context may variably constrain and enable our social justice work?

Theorizing Organizations

From Classical Theory to Human Relations

First, let's consider some theoretical perspectives on organizations. The classical organizational theories of the early 20th century were grounded in the belief that "people and organizations act in accordance with rational economic principles" (Netting & O'Connor, 2003, p. 104). These theories emphasized scientific management of human activity to maximize productivity, specialization and division of labor, and centralization of authority (for example, see Taylor, 1947). Sociologist Max Weber is well-noted for his depiction of the "ideal type" of bureaucratic organization whose features included official authority, hierarchical structure, standardized record keeping, specialized functions and training, establishment of clear roles and responsibilities, written rules, concept of career, impersonal relationships among organizational members, and managerial authority over resource allocation (Netting, Kettner, & McMurtry, 1998, pp. 196-197; Weber, 1947). Human relations theorists, in contrast, have argued that human motivation is more than economic and that human relations complicate the bureaucratic "ideal." They have emphasized the importance of attention to the individual worker, positive social relations, and the power of informal social groups in achieving organizational efficiency and productivity (Argyris, 1970; Mayo, 1933). Various systems theorists have characterized organizations as complex systems of information, control, and decision making; some have favored more mechanical, functionalist approaches while others have applied ecological systems principles to understanding organizations.[3]

Power and Conflict

Conflict theorists have taken power as a central theme in organizational analysis and have addressed the importance of informal power and politics within organizations (Netting & O'Connor, 2003, p. 45). Some have examined the interpersonal dynamics of conflict as well as the oppressive effects of organizational structures and systems of compliance. Others, such as Rosabeth Moss Kanter (1977, 1979), have brought a feminist lens to organizational inquiry, conducting gender analyses both of dominant theory and of the ways in which formal and informal practices in organizations work together to produce, maintain, and justify relations of power and inequality.

Culture and Sense-Making

Theorists of organizational culture and sense-making have brought questions of meaning to the fore. Schein (1992, p. 12, cited in Netting & O'Connor, 2003) defines organizational culture as:

> a pattern of shared basic assumptions that the group learned as it solved its problems of external adaptation and internal integration, that has worked well enough to be considered valid and, therefore, to be taught to new members as the correct way to perceive, think, and feel in relation to those problems. (p. 43)

Organizational culture theorists emphasize the shared experiences among organizational members that merge over time into a shared pattern of beliefs, values, practices, language, and everyday rituals. They argue that these patterns eventually become internalized and adhered to, even though individuals are not consciously aware of them. These patterns become part of a taken-for-granted way of being and doing within the organization that shapes not only internal practices but also the ways in which organizational members perceive and interact with "outsiders." Over time, as these implicit patterns and practices become individually and collectively ingrained, it becomes harder for members to explain how the organization works to outsiders and insider-outsider communication becomes more limited. The organizational culture may differ dramatically from that of a person seeking services from the organization. The outcome may be a collision of meaning systems and power relations that results in the "outsider" being labeled as deviant, defiant, or undeserving.

Closely related to theories of organizational culture are theories of sense-making in organizations, which explore the ways in which people within an organization seek to understand the organization. Weick (1995, p. 13) describes sense-making as an active process through which people "generate what they interpret" as they try to bring a sense of order and manageability to organizational ambiguity. While theories of organizational culture see "culture" as a system of shared meaning, sense-making speaks to human agency in organizations and the ways in which people struggle to give meaning to conflicts and contradictions as well as shared patterns of practice.

In the preceding discussion we have briefly introduced some theoretical perspectives that have informed thinking about the organizational context of practice. Our intent here is to spark the process of critical inquiry into our location within organizations as part of the engagement process. We find these ideas about structure, power, culture, and sense-making useful in developing awareness of ourselves as organization-located actors and in engaging with others in the organizational context. From a practice theory point of view, we must be mindful of the interplay of these aspects of organizations to understand how we shape and are shaped by the organizational context of practice. In Chapter 7 (p. 291) we present a guide to "Getting to Know Your Organization" drawn from these insights.

Learning from Experience

Janet Finn offers an example from her social work experience to illustrate ways that organizational context shaped the practice of engagement and ways in which she was both constrained and transformed by her experiences:

One of my first paid social work positions was as a "group life counselor" in a state institution for girls and young women who had been adjudicated "delinquent." I was 21 years old and fresh from college when I took the job. The institution resembled a country boarding school, with several residential cottages, a cafeteria, gymnasium, and school. Underneath its welcoming façade was a tightly controlled system of discipline, rules, and surveillance. I was a shift worker charged with overseeing cottage life in the afternoon and evenings, one of the least powerful staff positions in the institution. I was barely older than many of the young women under my "supervision." In many ways, it was by not-so-simple twists of fate that I was the one with the keys. But with those keys came power and responsibility. Those keys marked my privileged posi-

*tion as a well-educated white woman. They symbolized a boundary of difference be-
tween me and young women who had used the resources at hand to escape violent
homes and abusive parents and partners, who had survived on the streets by plying
their wits and selling their bodies, and who had sought comfort or oblivion in glue and
booze and dope. The keys gave me access to everything from deodorant and hairspray
to cigarettes and aspirin— all securely locked away from my young charges. They
symbolized my everyday power to withhold privileges and offer rewards—"Yes, you
can call home this weekend... No, you cannot leave campus with your aunt on Sunday." They symbolized the power of my voice in decisions about life beyond the institution. In effect, the job was an ongoing negotiation of the nuances of power, trust, and
intimacy. I worked to build trust and to be clear about my responsibilities and the
limits of my authority. But the institution's policy manual did not prepare me for the
everyday challenges that negotiation posed. There was so much I did not know—about
myself, the young women, and the structural inequalities of justice systems. I made lots
of mistakes, usually when my own lack of confidence and fear of failure pushed me to
wield my authority and restrict possibilities, when what I really needed to do was listen
more carefully. I felt my own sense of powerlessness as a young woman in a male-
dominated system. And yet the young women in my cottage saw the many sources of
power at my fingertips that separated me from them. I came to appreciate my privileged positioning as one with potential to advance in the system due to my degree while
my co-workers often had more limited options. With time, I learned to suspend my
disbelief, tether my precarious authority, and listen more carefully and respectfully to
the young women's stories. Their stories of tenacity, survival, courage, and longing
were their gifts to me. As I became more cognizant of both the limits and possibilities of
my position, I sought ways to push the boundaries of the possible. I began to find my
own voice as I learned to advocate on behalf of the young women in staff meetings and
court reports where their voices were too often silenced. When I left my position after
two years, I did not know enough to thank them for all they had taught me. Thirty years
later, I continue to draw lessons for engagement through critical reflection on the organizational context of that profound experience.*

Engagement as an Interpersonal Process

We have highlighted various contexts in which we engage with others in the process of change. Keep in mind, however, that while engagement is embedded in
multiple contexts it is, as we discussed at the start of the chapter, fundamentally an
interpersonal process that demands commitment to building relationships. Person-
to-person relationships provide the foundation of social justice work. Regardless
of whether we work with communities, families, neighborhoods, groups, or organizations, we are called upon to build and maintain interpersonal relationships. We
can think of the interpersonal context of practice as one that cross-cuts all facets of
social justice work. As we noted previously, social workers have paid particular
attention to the importance of building and maintaining relationships based on
respect for human dignity and worth. We have claimed this as a hallmark of the
profession. Bertha Reynolds (1987) has challenged us to get close to people and
honor the inseparability of social work and social living. This closeness implies a
relationship that respects the whole person, encourages a sense of belonging, and
recognizes people as much more than "bundles of problems and needs."

In recognizing the central place of relationships in social justice work, we acknowledge that relationships have value in themselves; they are not merely means to an end. Rather, relationships are the bedrock of our humanity (Finn, 2001b, p. 193). We can think of the process of justice-oriented change as one of being in relationship with others, doing the work, and becoming transformed through the process. As we work to build meaningful and productive relationships we are likely to be confronted with differences in our power and positionalities and with the limits of our partial views of the world. Dynamic, change-oriented relationships create possibilities for shifting our positions and expanding our views. This is hard work that demands humility, commitment, and reflection. In the following section we address the skills of engagement that enable us to form partnerships, build trust through dialogue, and create an interpersonal context that contributes to justice-oriented practice.

Finding the Private Self

Genevieve Hatcher describes how we are "joined in our humanness" as we struggle to communicate across boundaries of difference. In her essay, "Finding the Private Self: James' Story of Joining," Genevieve describes her experiences in her second-year practicum when she met and worked to connect with James, a 33-year-old man diagnosed with schizophrenia. Hatcher remembers,

> I have learned that most mental health therapists are not sitting around in staff meetings trying to learn the language of schizophrenics. I often watch James as he struggles with his language, tries to find his tongue, and searches for it, as it lies there limp. I see his frustration that he desperately tries to hide. I see his pain and sadness over wanting his life to be different. (p. 333)

Genevieve struggled with her own frustration to reach James.

> I realized quickly that I needed to be able to develop both a new way of communicating and a new kind of patience—one that allows for a slow process of giving and taking, one that has an undefined agenda. I realized this was going to be different from anything I had ever done before. I knew that I needed to be open to his way of communicating and trust that perhaps a new language would occur, but I had no idea what that would be like. . . . I found myself asking, How can I connect to a man whose whole world is a sweep of confusion? How was I going to help him with his frustration and anger when I could not understand him? . . . We worked hard at creating our own language. . . We practiced weekly and slowly created our own informal dictionary: me, helping him to talk about his feelings; he, helping me to build confidence as a practitioner. We did build, one stone at a time, and were creating a strong foundation of trust. . . The more I sat back and listened to his words, the clearer they became. His words began to sound like poetry, a rhythmic, art-like song of mixed-up words. At times they were confusing, but, at others, the images and feelings were clear. (p. 334)

Genevieve began to create poetry from James' words, capturing his sadness and struggle, and reflecting them back to him. Genevieve learned so much from James. She writes, "His fragmented words shaped his inner roadmaps, and, by creating these poems, I found it possible to follow his trail and help him understand his own road signs." (p. 338)

Excerpt from Genevieve Hatcher (2000). Finding the Private Self: James' Story of Joining. *Families in Society, 81*(3), pp. 333-338.

SKILLS AND PRACTICE OF ENGAGEMENT

In this section we develop a range of skills to draw on in the process of engagement. These include (1) anticipatory empathy, (2) observation, noticing, and bearing witness, (3) body consciousness, (4) listening, and (5) dialogue. We do not see this as a definitive list of techniques to be mastered but as an entry point into building genuine relationships. We draw on the practice knowledge of social work and communication studies, the teachings of social justice workers who have challenged and expanded our thinking, and our own practice experience. We invite you to add to and refine these skills as you create your personal tool kit for social justice work.

Skills of engagement are fundamentally about communication. As Floyd Matson and Ashley Montagu (1967, p. 6, cited in Johnson & Yanca, 2007, p. 171) describe, the purpose of communication is "not to 'command' but to 'commune' and that knowledge of the highest order (whether of the world, of oneself, or of other) is to be sought and found not through detachment but through connection, not by objectivity but by intersubjectivity, not in a state of estranged aloofness but in something resembling the act of love." Our human capacity for meaning making has resulted in the production of multiple meaning systems, diverse languages and linguistic conventions, a rich and emergent capacity for expression, and the possibility of error and misinterpretation. In every communication process, the attitudes, feelings, and positionalities of both receiver and sender are vitally important. As Baum (1971, p.42) writes, "we are created through ongoing communication with others." Differences in age, gender, cultural background, class positioning, and racial and ethnic identification all affect the communication process. Awareness of these differences and relations of power inherent in them is crucial to effective communication.

SKILLS OF ENGAGEMENT

 anticipatory empathy

 observation, noticing, and bearing witness

 body consciousness

 listening

 dialogue

Anticipatory Empathy

Engagement calls for "anticipatory empathy"—a process of preparation through critical reflection on the possible situations, concerns, and interests of the other participants in the change effort. In this process we are mindful of the question, What is the significance of this encounter and relationship? What does it mean to me and to the other participants? It is a process of readying ourselves for an encounter with others, focusing our energies and attention, and opening ourselves to new learning. In many ways it is a time of transition wherein we move away from the phone calls and email and other demands of our work and create a space for intentional reflection. We start from a place of not knowing and uncertainty and allow ourselves to wonder. What information do we have thus far? What sort of partial picture is beginning to emerge? Who has provided us with the information? How might the people we are about to encounter tell their story? How can we best open ourselves to hearing their stories and receiving them as gifts? What might the other person (people) be feeling or thinking? How might our differing histories and positionalities influence the encounter?

Anticipatory empathy may entail very concrete preparation for a specific encounter or meeting. It creates time and space to think about the *purpose* of our engagement and our *role* in the process. It provides an opportunity to consider our own expectations and those of others. Who will be present? Who else should participate? What resources are available? What may be some of the constraints? What do you hope to accomplish? What might others hope to take away from the meeting? It is a time to consciously reflect on the cultural, community, and organizational contexts in which you are coming together with others and to think about the ways in which these forces might infiltrate the emergent relationship. Returning to the insight of Ruth Dean (2001), anticipatory empathy entails reflection on the cultural, political, and historical forces that may have shaped our own and another's experience. It is a time to take stock of the cultural freight we carry with us so that we enter the encounter from the humble position of "not knowing." It is a time to think about the multiple forms and processes of oppression that may have left and continue to leave their marks on the participants, ourselves included. To paraphrase Stephen Rose (2000), we are not discrete entities linked in a linear equation, but relationally connected parts of a larger social world whose requirements created both another's suffering and rage and our position to respond to it. It is a time to reflect on the ways in which our differing locations within broader community and organizational contexts may come into play.

REFLECTION: Engaging in the Difficult Situation

Take a moment to reflect on a social work situation that you would find very difficult to engage in emotionally. Perhaps your own experiences (or lack thereof) with death and dying make it difficult for you to contemplate engaging with persons who are terminally ill. Perhaps you have experienced abuse in your own childhood or adulthood and find painful memories and emotions sparked by the stories of others who have been victimized. Try to allow yourself to feel and to identify some of the feelings that are stirred. It may be very hard to come close to those feelings. Perhaps, in this moment, the most important thing you can do is honor the distance. Sometimes the distance from our own feelings is a good measure of our distance from the feelings of others. Anticipatory empathy calls on us to actively grapple with our own feelings, to appreciate the power of our feelings in shaping the possibilities of engagement, and to make a commitment to bridging the distance to the best of our abilities through honest dialogue.

Anticipatory empathy is also a time to consider the possibilities and strengths of people and communities. As we open ourselves to new learning from and with participants it is important to think not only in terms of struggles but also in terms of capacities, resilience, and creativity. We often only see that which we are conditioned to see, so part of the process may involve preparing ourselves to "see" in different ways and learning to recognize social, emotional, and material resources that may be outside of our own experience. It is helpful to ask ourselves these questions: What new knowledge and understanding might I take away from this experience? How might I be changed by my participation in this process and relationship? Too often, we assume change is about "others." In social justice work, we recognize that change is also about *us*.

Anticipatory empathy is not only a time of intentional preparation for engaging with "others." It is also a time for getting in touch with one's own feelings and biases. The structural violence confronting people in poor communities, dangerous neighborhoods, and hot and crowded apartments; the human drama of a hospital emergency room; the dank air of a jail cell or nursing home—these sensory realities can tap into our histories and memories in a visceral way that is beyond words. They pummel our emotions and wrench our guts. Anticipatory empathy requires time and space to feel and to be honest with ourselves about what we feel, especially difficult feelings such as fear, anger, or revulsion. Even as we prepare to approach what we anticipate to be "comfortable" encounters, it is important that we allow space for feelings of uncertainty, anticipation, and perhaps excitement. Recognition of the emotional context of the work prepares us to engage with our hearts as well as heads and hands.

The practice of self-reflection in anticipation of the encounter is a crucial component of the engagement process. Unfortunately it is often neglected in practice. As the demands for "efficiency" and "productivity" and the overall businessing of social work increase, anticipatory empathy is too often construed as a luxury. We often hear social workers lament, "Who has time to sit and think. . . I have too much work to do!" We argue that reflection is a necessary part of the work, but organizational constraints are real and they impose barriers to reflection. How do we carve out spaces for contemplation in our work places? What organizational changes might be necessary to legitimize the importance of reflection time? These are essential questions to pose, especially as we consider the linkage between reflection and anticipatory empathy.

Anticipatory empathy puts us in touch with both pain and possibility. It is through genuine connection to our own humanity that we open ourselves to tap into and engage the dignity and worth of others. It situates us in a mutually informing process of being, doing, and becoming. Anticipatory empathy is not a "one-time" exercise carried out before engaging with a person or group for the first time. Rather, it is a process we engage in as we move in and out of particular contexts of communication and action. It prepares us to enter the world of the participant(s) and develop and strengthen the working relationship. Each participant in the change process approaches the encounter from the complex context of everyday life and brings the weight of history and memory to bear in crafting a new context.

Observation, Noticing, and Bearing Witness

A fundamental communication skill is that of observation. The social work setting, whether it is a kitchen table, community hall, hospital room, or boardroom, presents both possibilities and constraints that shape the process of relationship building. It is important that we be tuned in to the immediate context of practice so that we can best appreciate and address both limits and possibilities. Our initial observations give us a very partial sense, a rough sketch of the context, but it is a beginning. In addition to taking in the physical context of our work, the communication process is also shaped by our observations of the social context. How do other participants in the change process initially respond to us, to one another, and to their surroundings? How do we interpret the mood or tone of the setting? What sorts of patterns of social interaction are in play? What unspoken rules seem to govern people's social relations and actions?

Honing Your Observation Skills

A C T I O N

Social workers can learn a great deal from cultural anthropologists about the power and practice of observation. Cultural anthropologists learn about cultural diversity through ethnographic fieldwork. Ethnography provides an account of particular cultural contexts or practices. One technique central to ethnography is firsthand observation of the details of everyday life. Ethnographers seek to understand the patterns and rules that shape the most taken-for-granted aspects of social life. This exercise introduces you to ethnographic observation.

Select a public setting where you can observe some aspect of everyday social interaction (a sporting event, an airport luggage claim, a restaurant, a bus terminal, the entrance to your campus Student Union). Spend one hour observing the details of social life. Record your observations. Write a brief report describing your observations, noting patterns, and probing the unspoken rules that seem to underlie these patterns. Try to suspend your pre-existing understanding of what is going on. Focus on what you observe. Did you see any patterns in people's social behavior? Did you find yourself "seeing" the setting differently over the course of the hour? How did it feel to be an observer? Did the exercise offer you any new insights or surprises regarding everyday social interactions?

In our everyday interactions we are observers of people and social groups. We give meaning to social interactions as we take in content, "read" nonverbal expressions, and interpret feelings, attitudes, and intentions (Brill & Levine, 2002). We hone our observation skills as we become cognizant of the aspects or levels involved and systematically attend to them. In the context of social justice work, however, observation is not a detached process. It is a mindful process wherein we are actively *noticing* what is going on within and around us. Dewees (2006, p. 48) describes noticing as "both a political and pragmatic act" wherein we pay attention to everyday indignities of racism, sexism, homophobia, and other forms of violation and exclusion; to the subtleties of our own practice, from tone of voice to sense of time and style of dress; and to the myriad barriers large and small that can block participation—lack of gas money or public transportation, child care, or confidence. Noticing is the practice of critical, compassionate observation in which we are probing the connections between personal struggles and public issues (Witkins, 1998).

Noticing entails attention to time as well as to people and place. Barry Locke, Rebecca Garrison, and James Winship (1998, p. 18) use the Greek concepts of time, *chronos* and *kairos*, to capture a distinction that social workers need to keep in mind. *Chronos* refers to chronological time, and *kairos* refers to readiness or timeliness. Mindfulness to an individual or group's readiness to engage in a process of change is critical. Readiness is not simply a matter of individual "motivation" but a complex phenomenon shaped by levels of trust, structural constraints, available resources, levels of acceptance, and cultural norms, in addition to individual or collective felt need for change. Attention to readiness draws on skills of empathy as well as analysis.

Noticing may also entail the practice of *bearing witness*. Paul Farmer (2003) suggests two ways of bearing witness, and he sees both as essential to the process of social justice work. One is to observe, document, and speak out about the suffering of others that we have seen with our own eyes. In this sense one bears witness by making the connections between personal pain and structural violence. A second way is to stay present with what Farmer terms the "surface silence"—a silence perhaps conditioned by poverty, oppression, exclusion, and concomitant distrust—and respect the profound eloquence that lies beneath it (2003, p. 26). We may be tempted to scratch the surface and trigger that painful eloquence, and at times that may be helpful. At other times it may be more respectful to bear witness through honoring the silence and engaging in pragmatic solidarity to address the immediacy of that suffering and its consequences (Farmer, 2003).

Observation is a two-way process, shaped by relations of power. We are both observers and observed in any social work relationship. Our initial and ongoing observations provide us with data from which we can engage in dialogue for co-learning. We also provide other participants with "data" regarding our comfort level and preparedness in the situation. As our impressions and understandings become more textured and detailed, we may find that interpretations based on initial observations were faulty. Careful, respectful observation is a skill that we can hone through practice.

Body Consciousness

Honest, respectful communication starts from a place of openness, curiosity, and partiality of knowledge. We need to be mentally and emotionally present and attentive. We convey that readiness through our bodies and physical presence as well as through our words. Our responses and emotions are coded on our faces and bodies and through our carriage and gestures, as well as through our spoken and written words and silences. As Brill and Levine (2002) describe:

> Nonverbal messages are conveyed through the person and the setting. Age, sex, color, speech, personal appearance—physique, posture, body odor, dress, tension, facial expressions, behavior, silence or speech, tone of voice, gestures or movements, eye contact, touch, body sounds—all convey messages to the receiver, as does the physical setting—its appearance, aesthetic quality, comfort, and privacy (or lack of them), and general climate. The ways in which we convey nonverbal messages about ourselves are endless. Once workers know where to look and what to listen for and to sense in both self and client, their sensitivity and ability to understand will increase. (p. 92)

Take a minute to think about conversations you have had when you have felt as if the other person was really listening to you. How did she convey that attentiveness? How did she position herself? How did her body indicate openness? What were the cues that indicated this person was paying attention and that what you said mattered? Take a minute to become aware of your own body and practice that physical attentiveness. How would you describe your posture? Do you feel comfortable? Try taking a deep breath in and out, relaxing and opening yourself to the person and situation as you do so. How would you describe your posture now? Do you feel ready to listen and engage?

Now take a moment to think about conversations you have had where you have felt shut out and ignored. How did that person's body convey her inattentiveness or resistance to your words? Take a minute to practice that physical inattentiveness. How would you describe your posture? Your breathing? Do you feel comfortable? Take a deep breath in and out, and then return to your posture of openness. How would you describe the difference between the two? Each of us brings particular sociocultural knowledge and patterns of practice to the communication process. The process is a complex one of expression, reception, translation, and interpretation through screens of cultural meaning. The process is fraught with possibilities for misunderstanding. However, we can become more critically conscious participants in the process as we learn to appreciate the communicative power of our own bodies. When we are uncomfortable in the process, our bodies become physical blocks to effective communication. So, the first rule of thumb for respectful communication is to **remember to breathe!** As we remind ourselves to breathe we create the possibility of releasing the block and opening ourselves once again to respectful listening. Yes, we will make mistakes and misinterpret even when we are attending as best as we can. But as we come to better understand our capacities for communication we can better address the mistakes and craft a space of understanding.

Mirroring Exercise

A C T I O N

Get together with one of your classmates. Arrange your seats so that you are facing one another and a comfortable distance apart, as if you were going to engage in conversation. Sit facing one another in silence for 3 minutes. Take time to observe one another without words. Be mindful of breathing. Try to mirror the rhythm of your partner's breathing, without forcing it. At the end of 3 minutes, talk to your partner about your response to the exercise. Did 3 minutes seem like a long time? Did the exercise make you feel uncomfortable? What were some of your observations? How did it feel to focus attention on breathing? If you do this exercise as a class working in pairs, you probably found it hard to maintain 3 minutes of silence. Most likely, bursts of laughter rippled through the class a time or two. Many of us lack experience or comfort in being present with another person without words. What reflections on communication could you draw from this exercise?

It is also important to keep in mind that the concept of body consciousness goes beyond awareness of "body language." From a social justice perspective, we are called on to be mindful of the ways in which forces of oppression insinuate themselves and shape one's physical as well as psychological being. Janet Finn recalls her group work with young survivors of sexual abuse. One girl had virtually no memory of her life without violation of her body as a part of it. She had learned to curl into herself, rarely standing or sitting erect. At age 12 she had the curved posture of an elderly woman. While her experience of violence and survival was deeply personal, it also played out in a society that maintains high tolerance for violence against women and children and in a nation that still refuses to recognize children as bearers of rights. We need to continually examine the relationship between structural violence and individual experience. In the words of Paul Farmer (2003, p. 30) we need to keep asking: "By what mechanisms, precisely, do social forces ranging from poverty to racism become *embodied* as individual experience?"

Listening

Perhaps the most important skill of communication is that of listening. It is a skill we have been developing since birth, and, as a result, we often take our listening skills for granted. For example, in various communication situations we may find ourselves tuning out what others say or busying ourselves thinking about what we would like to say next. Or we may find ourselves listening to those whose knowledge we value and failing to hear alternative views. Listening is a powerful skill, one that takes considerable discipline and a willingness to hold our own needs at bay. Listening gives voice, affirmation, and confidence to those individuals and groups who have been typically ignored, marginalized, and oppressed. It is through respectful listening that a group develops a sense of belonging and community and members see themselves as speaking subjects worthy of voice (hooks, 1994, pp. 148-150). As bell hooks (1994) describes, teaching people how to listen is part of a pedagogy of liberation. We have to learn how to hear one another, suspend disbelief, and take what another person says seriously.

People often use the term "active listening" to describe the focused, intentional process of listening. In "active listening" we use words and gestures to show the speaker that we are attending to her words. A nod of the head may indicate that we are understanding, or perhaps encouraging the speaker to continue. We might reflect feelings we have been picking up back to the speaker or summarize the content of the story to both demonstrate that we are listening and to see if we are grasping the speaker's intended meaning (Shulman, 1992). We might ask the speaker to tell us more so that we have a better grasp of the context. However, beneath all of the tricks to demonstrate that we are "actively" listening, we need to be honestly listening. If we are busy thinking about what we will say or do next we often fail to listen deeply and fully to the other person's words.

Murphy and Dillon (1998) describe the importance of "listening intently" to what people say and how they say it. Through a practice of listening intently, "(w)e listen to our own inner process and the relationship process. We listen to what is happening in the work and what is happening in the surrounding world" (p. 10). They point to the importance of listening to silence as well as speech and of listening for the "behavior, feelings, thoughts, contexts, and meanings that constitute the client's story" (p. 67). Similarly, Anderson and Jack (1991) note the importance of learning to "hear the weaker signal of thoughts and feelings that differ from conventional expectation" (p. 11). They contend that respectful listening calls on us to shed our own agendas and resist the temptation to leap to interpretation too soon. They remind us that what and how we hear is shaped by our cultural constructs and historical experience. A challenge, then, of listening intently is to try to understand another's story from his or her vantage point. This requires "listening with a third ear."

Marty Dewees (2006) describes listening skills as those needed to truly hear another's story. She encourages social workers to engage through the practice of "radical listening," which recognizes clients as experts on their own lives (p. 94). Dewees (2006, pp. 94-95), drawing from Weingarten (1995), addresses radical listening in terms of four processes and skills: attentive listening, deconstructive listening, perspectival listening, and listening to bear witness.

Attentive listening "requires the social worker to listen for and hear the client's story, not for symptoms or insight, but rather for the experience and what it meant to the client" (p. 94). Deconstructive listening is a process through which the social worker helps the client consider alternatives to his or her understanding of the story. Perspectival listening is a circular process wherein worker and client uncover and explore ways of viewing the situation from the perspectives of the other. In listening to bear witness, the social worker allies with the client in "recording and taking a stand on the experience of hardship, discrimination, or violence (for example) that she or he has endured" (p. 95).

A Short List of Interpersonal Communication Skills

◆ **Clarify:** Check in with the other person to make sure you are understanding what she is telling you. Invite the other person to seek clarification from you.

◆ **Paraphrase:** Restate the other person's story in your own words to make sure you are grasping the content.

◆ **Reflect**: Check in with the other person regarding the feelings associated with what he is telling you.

◆ **Encourage Elaboration:** Invite the other person to tell you more about her situation or experience.

◆ **Reach for Feelings**: Invite the other person to reflect on his emotional response to what he is telling you.

◆ **Check in:** Take a moment to reflect on the here-and-now. How is the other person doing? Does she have questions or concerns?

◆ **Allow for Silence:** Give the other person time and space to collect his thoughts and feel his emotions.

◆ **Summarize:** Take a minute to highlight both the content and feelings that have been expressed.

◆ **Acknowledge Mistakes and Ask for Feedback:** Remember that you are human and will make mistakes. Take responsibility and apologize. Give the other person a chance to tell you how you are doing.

◆ **Respect Resistance:** Remember that change is not easy, and honor ambivalence.

◆ **Point Out Contradictions:** If you are picking up discrepancies between what someone is telling you in words and what you are reading in nonverbal communication, respond directly and encourage reflection.

What other skills would you add to this list? What skills are needed for bridging possibilities of communication across boundaries of difference?[4]

Dialogue

Engagement calls for dialogue. Whether working in one-to-one situations or in the context of groups, social workers need skills in listening and dialogue in order to build a sense of safety, trust, and hope. As Hope and Timmel (1999, V. 2) write:

> Building trust and dialogue in society cannot be done by pronounce-
> ments nor by some "magical waving of a wand." Dialogue begins
> at the local level, in small units and thus in groups. . . Dialogue is
> based on people sharing their own perceptions of a problem, of-
> fering their opinions and ideas, and having the opportunity to make
> decisions or recommendations. (p. 3)

Paulo Freire (1974) reminds us that dialogue "requires an intense faith in man [sic], faith in his power to make and remake, to create and recreate, faith in his vocation to be fully human, which is not the privilege of an elite, but the birthright of all people" (p. 79). Freire believed that honest, genuine dialogue is founded on love, humility, and faith. It cannot exist without hope. Nor can it exist without critical thinking and the possibility of transformation. Dennis Saleebey (2006) has drawn on Freire in articulating his beliefs about dialogue and collaboration that inform a strengths perspective in social work. Saleebey states:

> Humans can only come into being through a creative and emer-
> gent relationship with others. Without such transactions, there can
> be no discovery and testing of one's power, no knowledge, no
> heightening of one's awareness and internal strengths. In dialogue,
> we confirm the importance of others and begin to heal the rift
> between self, other, and institution.

> Dialogue requires empathy, identification with, and the inclusion
> of other people. Paulo Freire (1973) was convinced, based on his
> years of work with oppressed peoples, that only humble and lov-
> ing dialogue can surmount the barrier of mistrust built from years
> of paternalism and the rampant subjugation of the knowledge and
> wisdom of the oppressed. "Founding itself upon love, humility,
> and faith, dialogue becomes a horizontal relationship of which
> mutual trust between dialoguers is the logical consequence" (pp.
> 79-80). A caring community is a community that confirms other-
> ness, in part by giving each person and group a ground of their
> own, and affirming this ground through encounters that are egali-
> tarian and dedicated to healing and empowerment.

> The idea of collaboration has a more specific focus. When we work
> together with clients we become their agents, their consultants, stake-
> holders with them in mutually crafted projects. This requires us to
> be open to negotiation and to appreciate the authenticity of the views
> and aspirations of those with whom we collaborate. Our voices may
> have to be quieted so that we can give voice to our clients. Com-
> fortably ensconced in the expert role, sometimes we may have great
> difficulty assuming such a conjoint posture. (pp. 14-15)

It is this understanding of dialogue that creates the possibility for social justice work.

Introductions and Openings

Dialogue is the basis for building and sustaining relationships. We need skills in initiating dialogue. Whether we are meeting with a single individual, a family, or a group we need to address basic questions of why we are here and what each of us hopes to accomplish. The change process is structured and purposeful, and it requires that each participant have a voice in defining the purpose and creating the structure. The social worker can take responsibility for initiating the process by (1) introducing herself and her organizational position, (2) clearly stating her understanding of the reason for coming together and inviting others to do the same, (3) and asking questions and seeking clarification. It is a process of *welcoming* and *naming* ourselves, our concerns, and our hopes. Together, participants seek to establish a common understanding of purpose. The process of getting started in face-to-face meetings is often easier said than done. It is a tentative process of feeling one another out and trying to get a sense of where others are coming from. It is important that we pay attention to the physical surroundings of the meeting and try to make the context conducive to dialogue. For example, is the seating arrangement conducive to open communication? Do others know the layout of the space and facilities available to them? If we are meeting in someone's home, how can we be sensitive to issues of space and privacy? If the meeting space poses challenges—too hot, too cold, too big, too small—can we make adjustments before the meeting gets underway? If not, how might we address the limitations of the space and be cognizant of the ways it may affect people's participation? Part of the social worker's responsibility is to set the stage and the tone and facilitate the process of opening dialogue. We can begin by acknowledging that first meetings can be difficult, especially if the participants do not share common knowledge or histories. We can encourage people to ask questions and seek clarification, and we can do the same. As facilitators of communication, we help others recognize and express their understandings, attitudes, and feelings and put them into words. We do so by encouraging elaboration of experiences, perceptions, and context. Our job is to create opportunities for participants to tell their own stories in their own words, let people know that they have been heard, and to seek clarification to build mutual understanding.

Openings: Creating Dialogue

The BRIDGE (Building a Race and Immigration Dialogue in the Global Economy) project has developed a great popular education resource guide for immigrant and refugee community organizers. They have developed "Our Names, Our Stories" as an opening activity to engage participants in dialogue around immigration. We present the exercise below and invite your suggestions for additional topics. For example, Janet Finn has used the exercise as a starting place for group members to share self-descriptions and get acquainted, express interests in social work, and name the personal effects of globalization. What might be other possibilities?

Our Names, Our Stories

Why do it?	To use as an icebreaker and introduction
	To get participants moving around
	To form a personal connection to the topic of immigration
	To gauge how participants feel about the topic of immigration

Time   20 minutes (more for groups larger than 20)

Materials   Sheets of paper, one for each participant
              Markers or pens for all participants
              Tape
              Easel paper

Directions 1. Hand out a piece of paper and a marker to each participant. Ask each participant to write her or his name in big letters vertically, going down the center of the page.
2. Ask participants to think about immigration for a few moments. Then ask participants to use each letter in their name to write a word that describes their views, feelings, or experiences with immigration. Participants can use the letters at the beginning, middle, or end of a word, in any language. For example:

co**M**munity

tr**A**nsition

f**R**eedom

fam**I**ly

dignid**A**d

3. After participants finish, they should take their paper and tape it to their shirt, as if it were a "giant name tag." Ask participants to walk around the room, and to talk to other participants about the words that they wrote on their paper (5 minutes).
4. When participants have been able to meet and talk to most or all of the other participants, bring the group back into a large circle. Ask each participant to introduce herself or himself, and to name *one word* on their paper that they would like to share with the group. As participants name their words, write the words that the participants have named on a large sheets of easel paper.

Source: BRIDGE Authors: Eunice Hyunhye Cho, Francisco Argüelles Paz y Puente, Miriam Ching Yoon Louie, and Sasha Khokha. (2004)

REFLECTION: **Challenges to Introductions and Openings**

Introductions and openings create challenges for workers and those with whom they work. They require clarity of role and purpose on the part of the social worker. Think for a minute about the child protection services worker sanctioned to investigate allegations of child abuse and neglect and the need to respond to stressful situations and circumstances that might entail the removal of children from their home. What must the worker know about the limits and requirements of her role and how might these limits and requirements be communicated to set the foundation for subsequent action? How might personal values and beliefs about parenthood, the disruption of children's lives, and the sanctity of family life conflict with the prescribed functions of the child protection worker mandated by state and organizational policies? Also think about how the word "participant" fails to capture the true nature of coming together in this particular circumstance. How can the worker prepare for the resistance posed by "involuntary" contacts, those with individuals who did not seek out the contact? What ethical dilemmas and political issues might shape communication? How might these issues be addressed in introductions and openings? How does the process of coming together change given these circumstances? What preparatory work must the worker engage in to be effective?

Closings and Transitions

Each meeting and encounter, whether it is a first meeting with a teenager in a youth shelter or with a newly forming advocacy group at a homeless shelter, becomes a micro context where questions of meaning, power, history, and possibility are at play. Part of the communicative work of engagement is to value that context, acknowledge what has been accomplished in it, and prepare participants to move beyond it at its close. To do so, we need to be able to summarize both the content and process of the encounter and seek feedback from participants. What did we accomplish? Where are our points of agreement and difference? What are people thinking and feeling about the process? Where do we go from here? Who takes responsibility for what?

It is important to recognize people's participation, to thank them for their presence, to honor their silences as well as their words, and to address the challenges posed in getting started. Just as we emphasized the importance of creating time and space to prepare for engagement, it is important to give time and space to disengagement and transition. That may entail acknowledging the emotions people express and creating an opportunity for both letting go of and holding on to those feelings as participants move out of this context and into other spaces of their work and lives. It may mean giving participants the "last word." It may involve giving yourself a few minutes to absorb and reflect on the process and the responses it stirred for you. What do you take away from this "closing" that informs the next "opening"? What did you learn about yourself, others, and the possibilities for social justice work in this encounter? Thus, the basic skills of communication provide us tools for tacking back and forth between action and reflection.

CHALLENGES OF ENGAGEMENT: POWER, DIFFERENCE, RESISTANCE

Power

Effective social justice work requires us to be able to acknowledge and address issues of trust, power, and difference in the relationship-building process with individuals and groups. Given differing past histories and experiences, participants often have reason to be distrustful of "helpers" and processes of change. We need to start from the point of distrust and work to build trust rather than assume that it exists. For example, Lorraine Gutiérrez and Edith Lewis (1999) address the troubling history of misdiagnosis and mistreatment of people of color by professional helpers. They write, "This mistrust has been exacerbated by the lack of attention to gender, ethnicity, race, economic status, and environment as variables influencing the engagement process for both service providers and service consumers" (p. 26). We need to honestly and directly speak to mistrust and invite participation in the ways we can collectively build trust and understanding. In order to do so we need to make power, authority, and difference "talkable themes." Too often, these are taboo subjects that we shy away from even as they play out in and shape the dynamics of a meeting or relationship. We can facilitate this conversation by speaking honestly to our own power and authority and its limits in the context at hand. For example, if, in our social work capacity, we have the authority for particular types of legal or social sanction that others do not have, it is important that we speak honestly about our authority, responsibilities, and their limits, invite questions from other participants, and respond candidly to their concerns. We can also initiate a discussion of power and engage in an analysis of power as part of the process of co-learning. Finally, we need to acknowledge difference as an issue and create space for dialogue about differences that shape our meanings, interpretations, and actions.

Difference

How do we respond when our authority and assumptions are challenged? It is one thing to talk about power, trust, and difference. It is another to honestly reflect on our ability to open ourselves to challenge, especially if we come from positions of privilege where dominant views have been part of our "common sense." How do we stay open to listening and learning when faced with differences of experience and perspective that disrupt our certainties? Perhaps we respond defensively, asserting our authority in the face of challenge and attempting to discredit or dismiss the challenger. Communication across and about differences that disrupts our comfort zones is a key part of the labor of social justice work. In the following sidebar, social worker, scholar, and activist Deborah Bey draws from her own experiences to challenge her colleagues about the meaning and power of difference.

REFLECTION: Difference is Political and Personal

The following is an excerpt from an essay by Deborah Bey, a doctoral student at the University of Michigan, reflecting on her lived experience and the politics of belonging and difference she has encountered in social work education. What challenges does she pose? What feelings does the essay provoke? How do we move beyond talk of collaboration and tackle the tough realities of difference?

After I had decided to leave my comfortable job and go back to school and earn my Ph.D., my therapist at the time asked me what my motivation was. Getting my Ph.D. would not mean more money, and I would be dirt poor for the next 5 years. Besides, it would only bring prestige if I published a lot of books and became a careerist. My reply to that inquiry was that I was almost 30 and I wasn't dead or dying so I might as well make good on this promise I made to myself when I graduated from undergrad and go back to school to get my Ph.D.

By this point you might be thinking, "Does she have cancer?" "Is she HIV positive?" "Why would she be thinking she would be dead at age 30?" To explain that I have to go back to my childhood and my experience in the world.

When I was 12 I figured I would be dead by 30, and I might as well live my life like 30 was the ending point. Being dead by 30 made plenty of sense; most of the people in my neighborhood never saw 30 or they celebrated their 30th birthdays in prison. Or they were so cracked out that they might as well be dead. At 12 years of age I saw no prospects for the future, so I saw no reason to plan for it.

Besides all that, by age 12 I was homeless and living on my own in Detroit. You see, I was a ward of the State of Michigan, and I had liberated myself from one of the many foster homes they had shipped me to. So, at 12, I was on the streets, trying not to get caught by the police or my social workers, and sure as hell not my mother, especially not my mother, because she would have liberated my ass for bringing protective services into her life. Eventually, protective services caught me and shipped me out to another foster home in Saline, Michigan (about 50 miles from my home town), and the foster cycle would start again. They would put me in a home and either I would liberate myself or the foster parents would ask the social worker to come and get me, and then it would be off to a new placement. In between there would be stints with my mother if she were off drugs and out of her crazy relationships. But it was mostly crazy foster homes until I turned 20. With a life like that, reaching 20 seemed like a pipe dream.

This is why I wanted to go back to school, to do research in an area that really touched my life— foster care. The reason I chose the University of Michigan is because it was close to my family, and I was trying to re-establish ties, and it was away from the streets of Detroit that I had hung out on.

Now that I am at the university, I question my decision to return to school every day. I sit in classrooms with people who want to "help" the poor, or who just want to deliver psychotherapy to middle-class suburbanites, or best yet, future community organizers who want to organize communities as long as they do not have to live in them, or have their values questioned by those people they are trying to save. Which begs the question: Do the people these social workers want to work with want to be saved, helped, or patronized? Not everyone is like that— a large majority, but not everyone. There are some good Liberals (big L not little l) trying to earn their "I am sensitive to the suffering of others" Brownie points. Of course, no one wants to talk about issues of oppression—folks will start to cry and feel uncomfortable. And, as Rodney King put it, "Why can't we all just get along?"

When I buck that "can't we all get along" trend, I am constantly told that I am too judgmental, and I should cut folks slack. . . I have to wonder about this. When other graduate students go home and take off their clothes for bed, do they bear scars of growing up literally on the streets? Do they have the scar from a knife wound, where some crazy girl stabbed them in the leg? Do they have the bullet wound from when they were at a party that turned ugly? When they look at their faces, do they see scars from fights, when someone cracked a beer bottle over their head, just because? Have they been thrown through plate glass windows in fights because their cousin did something to someone else's man. . . ?

Have these students experienced what it is like to be homeless and hungry? Sleeping in cars and bushes and abandoned buildings, because you knew you were vulnerable just walking the streets? Have they had to fight their way out of gang attacks, because a group of men realized you were blossoming into a woman, and you were just a street kid anyway, so no one would care if they took some? Have these students experienced what it is like to come home and find the house empty because their mother or her boyfriend has taken everything to the pawnshop so they can get their drugs? Have they witnessed their mother getting her needle ready to shoot up because her cravings were so strong she did not realize that they were in the room? And, finally, have they experienced 11 years at the hand of the state, who said it was going to protect them, but instead screwed them more? Where they were treated more like cattle than like a person? The only thing the state helped with was to prepare you for prison or welfare once you aged out. Do they have dreams at night about living through things so horrible that they had to open their eyes just to not relive it? When they go home to their parents for the holidays, do they go to a one-bedroom apartment, shared by their mom and two siblings (when they are out of jail), with crumbling walls and floors you could fall through? To a neighborhood so rough that you keep a shotgun beneath your bed?

I don't think many of the people in social work know what this is like. So I will not cut them some slack. My job is to challenge the future social workers in the world because when they look at that and deal with me, they are dealing with their future clients. So if they can deal with my shit, they can deal with any shit...[5]

Honoring Difference

As we have addressed throughout the text, issues of difference and power profoundly shape our experiences and positionalities in the world and the perspectives from which we see, make sense of, and act in the world. Operating from our particular locations and partial views of the world, we give meaning to new experiences and interpret new information in differing ways. Thus each person engaged in a relationship and process for change has a somewhat different experience of the process. We "hear" things in different ways. We grant importance to some information and interactions and discount or ignore others. As a facilitator of open dialogue and effective communication, the social worker has a teaching responsibility to help other participants see that differing meanings and interpretations will emerge. Effective communication depends on helping participants seek clarification of one another's interpretations, respect differing meanings, and recognize common ground. This is a socialization process that the social worker can initiate by speaking directly to difference, acknowledging the ways difference shapes trust and dialogue, and making respect for difference and the negotiation and clarification of meaning part of the change process in which all participants are engaged.

These issues are particularly challenging in cross-cultural and multilingual contexts. We run quickly into barriers to understanding when attempting to bridge differing meaning and belief systems or interpret a discussion to speakers of different languages. For example, people from different cultural backgrounds may have very different assumptions regarding fundamental issues such as the meaning of family, decision-making authority, and privacy. As we discussed in Chapter 5, our cultural meaning systems shape our beliefs about fundamental issues such as the nature of the body and bodily integrity, causality, and health and illness. Further, our linguistic systems are rich in nuances of expression that are often not directly translatable. Readers who have had experience in multilingual settings know that it takes very skilled interpreters to assure that meanings, not just words, are communicated. Such is the case in professional "linguistic groups" as well. We can think of a multidisciplinary planning team as a multilingual context wherein representatives of different professions may require an interpreter so that they are not talking past one another as they speak in the jargon of their respective professions. Professional language is a source of power, which can exclude those who do not speak the language. Part of the challenge of social justice work is to interrupt practices of exclusion and advocate for skilled interpretation that promotes open, intelligible communication across multiple "languages" and boundaries of difference.

Engaging with Resistance

Throughout this discussion of engagement we have emphasized that different parties in the change process bring differing meanings, positionalities, interests, and concerns to bear. We have also pointed out that people in less powerful positions and people who have experienced oppression and discrimination may have very little reason to put their trust in "helpers" and "helping systems" and have very good reason to be suspicious and guarded about becoming participants in the process. In other words, as social justice workers we need to be both mindful and respectful of resistance.

Let's think for a moment about the meanings of resistance. Resistance is defined as "a force that tends to oppose or retard motion" (American Heritage Dictionary, 2000). In systems theories resistance is described as a force that helps systems and organisms remain stable in the face of other forces. In a psychological sense resistance is viewed as a defense mechanism that we use to avoid and cope with stress and change (Wade & Travis, 1999). It is often more popularly interpreted as a deficit, a person's refusal to open up, admit to her difficulties, and engage in the work of personal change. In literature on oppression, resistance describes the many subversive, often indirect strategies through which oppressed people assert their agency in the face of dehumanizing circumstances (Scott, 1985). In literature on privilege, resistance connotes a person or group's reluctance to reflect critically on the benefits of their positionality (Fine, Weis, Powell, & Wong, 1997; McIntosh, 1995). What other meanings and images of resistance come to mind? In the practice of social justice work, it is important to consider the many facets of resistance and to consider resistance as a skill for personal and cultural survival.

In social work, a great deal has been written about "resistant clients," referring to those who are unwilling to open up in the engagement process, acknowledge particular definitions of the "problem," or participate in prescribed courses of action. "Resistance" is often the defining feature of the "involuntary client," one who is required to participate in an intervention and treatment effort as a result of legal order or other institutional sanction. Often, the person's resistance becomes defined as pathology, a symptom of her inability or unwillingness to make prescribed changes. It is possible, however, to take alternative views regarding the meaning and power of resistance. For example, Paul Carter (1986, 1987) offers a psychological interpretation of the meaning of resistance. He argues that our capacity to resist points to our need for a balance between holding on and letting go. People need contexts of safety in order to take the risks that a change process demands. Thus, a deep sense of ambivalence often lies behind processes of change. Carter argues that while people may be consciously agreeing to participate, they may be resisting change at an unconsciousness level. Change forces people to give up something of their familiar here-and-now experience and engage with uncertainty. Even if current life circumstances cause pain, there may be a degree of comfort in the familiarity and predictability of those circumstances. Carter argues that each person has resources and potential that can be tapped into during the change process. Resistance can stem from the worker's failure to recognize and use a person's uniqueness.[6]

Reframing Resistance

Carter's approach offers an opportunity for reframing resistance at the personal level. However, he does not address the larger social, political, and economic context or histories of oppression and discrimination that shape action and resistance. From a cultural perspective, resistance may be seen as a survival strategy invoked when powerful forces threaten to invade, invalidate, or erase one's history, knowledge, and experience. Beverly Bell (2001), who has documented the lives and words of Haitian women living in contexts of extreme violence and violation, describes survival itself as a form of resistance, a determined claim to the fundamental right to life in the face of forces attempting to extinguish their last breath. Bell writes, "Survival can be a purposeful act of defiance against the many components of life in Haiti, from assassination to disease to despair, that impel the destruction of body and spirit. For example, the preservation of something as seemingly intrinsic as moral integrity or dignity—given the exertions of will required—can be a triumph" (pp. 5-6). Bell offers the testimonies of many Haitian women to illustrate their many forms of resistance, including: "maintaining survival and psychological integrity; enacting personal, political, and cultural expression; battling for political and economic justice; fighting gender oppression; and transforming the nature and application of power to create a new civil society and polity" (2001, p. 7).

A person resisting participation in the change effort may not be demonstrating pathology but may be actively asserting her right to protect herself, lay claim to her experiences and fears, and challenge those threatening to misinterpret her experience and silence her voice. There is a rich array of cultural literature that examines the creative resistance of less powerful people and groups to the oppressive forces of dominant cultural systems (e.g., Guzman Bouvard, 1994; Ong, 1987; Scott, 1985). We have also seen evidence of resistance to social work interventions on the part of people who have very different understandings of what constitutes a problem and for whom. The policies, procedures, goals, and expectations of social service agencies are often culturally foreign and at times antagonistic to the values, beliefs, and practices of those they serve. Resistance to intervention is born of a struggle to retain one's autonomy and beliefs in the face of powerful countervailing forces.

We must also examine the other side of the coin—the resistance of individuals and institutions ensconced in relations of power and privilege. Rather than thinking of resistance as a marker of the pathology of an individual, it may be more instructive to examine the resistance of those invested in their particular modes of expertise and wedded to forms of knowledge and intervention that reinforce the correctness of their worldview, distance them from the targets of their actions, and maintain patterned inequalities between "professionals" and their "clients." As social justice workers we need to *notice* how resistance is talked about in our work. Does the label of resistance become another form of violence perpetrated against people in positions of vulnerability? How might we draw on our knowledge of context in exploring how resistance is identified and addressed? In locating resistance in an individual, what other forms and practice of resistance remain invisible and unaddressed? Think for a moment about your own work or field site. Where have you seen resistance in the organizational context? How has it been addressed? How has it been experienced by workers? By "clients" or other organizational participants? What have been the consequences? Who has borne the burden of resistance?

Respecting Resistance

The Just Practice Framework provides a guide for recognizing and respecting resistance through posing critical questions regarding meaning, context, power, history, and possibility. Consider the following questions, for example. Are the policies, practices, goals, and language of your organization meaningful to the person with whom you are working? How do you know? What have you done to check this out? What is the context of your encounter? Under what circumstances did you come together? How do those circumstances, as well as the physical context of your meeting, contribute to or reduce resistance? What are the relations of power that affect the encounter? What forms of power do you as the social worker bring to bear? How might the other person perceive your power and his own in relation to you? Have you explored the issue of power as it affects the encounter? Are there alternatives open to you that could shift the balance of power? What prior history with the organization or with "helpers" does the other person have? How might this history, along with other experiences and feelings of powerlessness, contribute to resistance? What are the nonnegotiable aspects of the relationship (e.g., a person may be required to participate in a court-ordered treatment plan in order to regain custody of a child, avoid incarceration, etc.)? Where are the spaces of possibility for negotiating a process that recognizes and respects the other person's values, beliefs, and interests? How might the plan not only acknowledge but also challenge and change the power differences among agency, social worker, and "clients"?

EXPANDING THE POSSIBILITIES: ENGAGING GROUPS

In this section we return to the practice of group work and its significance for social justice-oriented practice. We provide background on the group work tradition in social work, and explore the benefits of group work. Breaking with the individual-focused, person-changing approaches to intervention, social justice work emphasizes the power and possibilities of collective effort to produce change. The basic communication skills outlined above apply to both one-to-one and group contexts. In this section, however, we further develop issues, skills, and possibilities for engagement with groups. We conclude with an overview of popular education as a practice of group work.

The Group Work Tradition

Social work has a lengthy history of attention to group work beginning with the Settlement House Movement. Early settlement house workers forged collaborative relationships with neighborhood immigrant populations through group work. Together social workers and community members addressed child labor laws, unsafe working conditions, and health concerns. Groups were a vehicle for policy advocacy, education, and mutual aid and support. Jane Addams (1910) envisioned groups as helping people learn about democracy through participation in democratic group dynamics. She eloquently addressed the need to exchange "the music of isolated voices [for] the volume and strength of the chorus" (as cited in Schwartz, 1986, p. 12).

Schwartz (1986) reminds us of the group work tradition initially crafted by early settlement house workers: ". . . to help needy people in their own milieux, surrounded by their peers and working in an atmosphere of mutual aid" (p. 7). People came together in groups to address mutual interests and concerns, to gain support from others when they faced overwhelming personal problems, and to learn from and teach one another new skills to improve the quality of their lives. Schwartz describes some of the common features of group work and how they shape the relationship between the worker and the group members. These features include sharing information between members, instead of confidential information being held between worker and "client," and sharing leadership and supportive functions so the worker's power is diffused in what Schwartz calls "the network of relationships that goes to make up the pattern of mutual aid" (p. 8). He emphasizes how early group workers found the language of "client" distasteful and preferred to call group participants "members." Through the practice of shared control, shared power, and the shared agenda, group members create support systems whereby they empower themselves to take collective action to address personal, interpersonal, and social concerns.

Benefits of Group Work

Throughout social work's history, social workers have noted the importance of group work and the beneficial dynamics and processes groups help to support. We outline some of these dynamics and processes below:

◆ Groups provide the milieux in which the social worker becomes one of many helpers (Schwartz, 1986).

◆ Groups create opportunities for developing critical consciousness (Freire, 1974, Gutiérrez, 1990).

◆ Group dialogue helps to break "cultures of silence" and helps people gain confidence in themselves and find their voices (Freire, 1974).

◆ Groups provide people with the opportunity to become conscious of power relationships, the differing effects of social inequalities on different social groups, and their own location therein (Garvin & Reed, 1995; Gutiérrez & Lewis, 1999).

◆ Groups offer spaces for mutual support and collective problem-posing, action, and reflection (Schwartz, 1971; Shulman, 1992).

◆ Groups help us structure the time and space of co-learning and unite our change efforts (Schwartz, 1994).

Thus, as social justice workers we need to develop our own capacities as group workers and to teach skills of mutual aid and collective action to others.

Creating a Climate for Group Work

In order to engage people in a group process, we need to create a welcoming learning climate. Issues of trust and intimacy, power and authority, and difference and commonality are at the very heart of group work. We need to start by honoring feelings of distrust and ambivalence (Shulman, 1992) and recognizing that people in marginalized or vulnerable positions have good reason to be suspicious of "helpers." Reflect for a moment on your own experiences in a group context. How did you feel at the first meeting of the group? What questions and concerns did you have? What did you know about or wonder about other members of the group? Did you have a sense of common purpose? Perhaps you felt exposed or resistant. Perhaps you felt wary, not knowing what was going to be expected of you or what you could expect of others. Perhaps you had concerns about how others would respond to you and whether they would respect your contributions to the group. Reflection on our own experiences provides a helpful entry point for engaging other people in the process of working in groups. What sorts of concerns can we anticipate? How can we address those concerns honestly and openly?

We can begin building trusting relationships among participants by starting from a place of "not knowing" and acknowledging distrust. As group members share knowledge, histories, and experiences, they develop a basis for trust. Similarly, as people begin to trust that others are committed to respectful participation, they are more likely to offer more of themselves and their experiences to the process. As engaged participants, they are better able to recognize and respect differences and seek possibilities for common ground. Over time, a sense of collective wisdom and intimacy emerges. As facilitators, we also have the responsibility of engaging with questions of power and authority as they play out in the group. How does our organizational position shape our role in the group process? How do others perceive our power? If we are in the position of primary facilitator of a group process, how do we both acknowledge and share the power of that position? What forms of power do other group members bring to bear in the process and how do we acknowledge them? For example, a member may use the power of silence or silencing in ways that inhibit communication. Others may use the power of blocking, which is finding reasons to stall or stop the progress of the group. Members may draw on outside or intimate knowledge related to the group as a source of power. These various means of bringing power to bear are not inherently "wrong" or "right." Rather they are part of the group dynamics that facilitators must address openly.

REFLECTION: Thinking about Community-Based Research as Group Work

Maxine Jacobson tells the following story of her experience with a community-based participatory research (CBPR) project whose goal was to investigate the policy barriers to food insecurity in Missoula County, Montana, and simultaneously gain a voice in the policy decision-making process for community residents experiencing hunger and food insecurity (Jacobson & Hassanein, 2004; Jacobson, in press). CBPR addresses the social justice mission of social work by engaging marginalized community residents as valued participants and collaborators in decision making and community solution processes that concern their lives. It is fundamentally a group process through which participants problematize their social reality and build collective capacity to challenge and change that reality (Finn, Jacobson, & Dean Campana, 2004; Freire, 1974; Jacobson & Rugeley, in press).

***

The Finding Solutions to Food Insecurity (FSFI) project began in August 2005 with funding from a USDA Community Food Solutions Grant (the project is ongoing at the time of this writing). The project sought to include low-income people in all aspects of the work. We started with a six-member coordinating committee composed of representatives from a food bank, a soup kitchen and shelter, a school of social work, and a community development corporation located in Missoula's lowest-income neighborhood. For the first 4 months we met weekly to develop strategies for engaging low-income county residents with firsthand knowledge of food insecurity for a steering committee, to conduct interviews, and to recruit the steering committee. The project has a core group of eight steering committee members. From the beginning we laid the groundwork for a group process that would sustain our efforts; help build leadership capacity; deal effectively with issues of race, class, gender, and ability; and help us achieve our goals. We meet at a local church where we have wheelchair access, a child care facility, and a kitchen to prepare food.

The steering committee meets monthly. Members share strategies for coping and surviving on limited incomes. As a group we uncover the inequities in the system, where depending upon the "luck of the draw," case workers and eligibility technicians *may* inform us about important resources and programs. We teach from our experiences and learn from the experiences of others—the stigma attached to needing services and asking for help, living with a mental illness or a physical disability, working as paid caregivers but not making enough money to feed our own families, and feeling undervalued in a system that never once acknowledges the importance of our lived experiences and asks us for help in making it better. We learn about and inform each other about what constitutes the "poverty line," hidden or hardly visible resources to tap to promote food security, strategies for conducting research, the cost of living in Missoula County, the importance of getting out the vote to increase the minimum wage initiative, how to create allies instead of enemies when fine-tuning interview questions for administrators and caseworkers at the Office of Public Assistance, and strategies for a series of town meetings to generate solutions to address the increasing costs of utilities, housing, health care, and transportation in the country.

We make power a *talkable* subject. We challenge ourselves to speak about feeling left out or left behind by the process. We talk about how reams and reams of handouts, chocked full of the written word, may not be the best method to communicate with one another about the project, especially for those of us who have not been inculcated with the dominant educational methods of the university. So we draw pictures, charts, concept maps, and diagrams to examine our trajectory and map out the path we need to follow next. We support and challenge ourselves to assume power—to talk in front of the group, to speak our minds when evaluating the meetings, to take on leadership by facilitating a section of a meeting, and to ask for direction when feeling lost.

I envision our project as a site where an amazing amalgamation of social work methods and skills must come together and play out effectively to inform the process: Community-based participatory research requires knowledge of community organizing, research, social planning, coalition building, leadership development, and most fundamentally, group work. In fact group work is the component that links each of these methods (Jacobson & Rugeley, in press). Schwartz (1986) spoke of the dual functions of group work—to attend to individual need and to achieve both personal and social transformation. Informed by social work's legacy of group work in the Settlement House Movement, participants in the FSFI project are learning about and teaching each other how to share control, share the agenda, and share power. We are realizing the potential of mutual aid while conducting research for community change.

Now think about the elements of creating a climate for group work discussed in the section preceding Maxine's story. What elements come through in the FSFI story? Return to this story once you have read about the mutual aid dynamics in Chapter 7 on pp. 276-277. What examples of mutual aid dynamics as described by Lawrence Shulman do you see illustrated in the FSFI project?

Developing Group Ground Rules

As members of a social work practice class, you are being asked to participate in a group learning process, take risks, and develop your repertoire of skills. The experiences may leave you feeling exposed and vulnerable. What sorts of ground rules do you want to have in place that will help create a context of safety in which you can take risks? Think about the difference between "safety" and "comfort" here. The risk taking associated with new learning may create discomfort. Risk taking in a group setting may also expose challenges of difference in the classroom. By virtue of "positionality" some class members may enjoy a greater degree of taken-for-granted "safety" and "comfort" in the classroom than others. Some class members might find unacknowledged "comforts" of privilege challenged by those who have been denied those comforts. Questions of difference may play out in very personal and emotional ways. How can the classroom become a safe enough place to be uncomfortable and to learn through that discomfort? Prepare your own list of ground rules for group learning that would allow you to take risks. Get together with a small group of classmates and share your lists. See if you can come to agreement on a set of ground rules. Now get together as a class and consider each group's ground rules. Where are the points of agreement? Where are the differences? See if you can reach consensus as a full group on the ground rules for group process.

A C T I O N

A key part of the engagement process is the socialization of group members about the dynamics of group work. By preparing people for what lies ahead, inviting candid dialogue about trust, power, and difference, and modeling openness, we help them become committed partners in the process. In order to engage meaningfully in a group process, members need to have a sense of belonging and a voice. They need to feel their experiences and perspectives are valued despite differences and disagreements among members. And they need to feel both a sense of responsibility and a sense of possibility in the process. The principles of popular education outlined below provide a valuable base for engaging groups in the process of personal and social transformation.

POPULAR EDUCATION

As previously mentioned, the National Network for Immigrant and Refugee Rights (NNIRR) has developed BRIDGE—Building a Race and Immigration Dialogue in the Global Economy—a Popular Education Resource for Immigrant and Refugee Community Organizers (2004). The organizers share their beliefs about a popular education model:

What do we believe is popular education? We believe that:

♦ Popular education **draws on the direct lived experiences** and knowledge of everyone involved—including participants and facilitators.

♦ Popular education encourages **active participation** to engage people in dialogues, fun, and creative activities, and draws on the strength of our diverse cultures. We learn in many ways—by seeing, hearing, talking, doing, creating, or a combination of these modes. We include dialogues and learning experiences that engage all of our senses, emotions, perceptions, and beliefs.

♦ Popular education draws on these **multiple modes** of learning. Discussion, drawing, writing songs, making sculptures, or acting out a skit gives us tools to express ourselves and communicate at all levels of our human experience.

♦ Popular education creates spaces for **trust and participation.** All education takes place within a larger context of behaviors, attitudes, and values. The ways in which we feel "safe" in a space depends on our own circumstances—our class, our race, gender, sexual orientation, age, immigration status, disability, and many other variables. As facilitators, we cannot remove these differences, but we can acknowledge their existence in order to open a space of more direct dialogue.

♦ Popular education is clear about its **agenda.** All education reproduces a set of values, ideologies, and attitudes. Popular education is not neutral, but holds a commitment to liberation from oppression at its ethical cores.

♦ Popular education is **accessible** to all participants, and actively works to explore and challenge ways that create unequal access to participation, such as language barriers, disability, and group dynamics.

♦ Popular education **connects our lived experiences to historical, economic, social, and political structures of power.** When our personal experiences are placed in larger contexts and patterns of power, our personal realities are transformed.

♦ Popular education **explores our multiple identities and experiences** of inclusion and exclusion, oppression and privilege. The underlying truth of popular education is of the existence of oppression: Racism, classism, sexism, homophobia, heterosexism, and transphobia are a reality in all of our lives. Popular education is not about building tolerance, but about building respect, acceptance, equality, and solidarity.

♦ Popular education **empowers individuals and groups to develop long-term strategies** to transform structures of power and to build a more just society. Popular education and organizing should not be reduced to short-term campaigns, mobilizations, or events, but rather, a democratic process based on values, connected and accountable to concrete needs of a community.

♦ Popular education **develops new community leaders** to build movements for social change. Popular education is a way to develop new leaders, who will in turn develop other leaders. This kind of leadership will be based upon concrete experiences of collective action and organizing.

♦ Popular education **results in action** that challenges oppression, and helps develop political spaces that are democratic and equal.

♦ Popular education **affirms the dignity** of every human being.

Engaging Community and Possibility: Life Lessons from La Pincoya

Rosemary Barbera, a social justice worker and professor of social work at Monmouth University, tells her story of engagement, community, and transformation in La Pincoya, a *población* of Santiago, Chile.

At the time I began "social work" in the United States in the 1980s, I was studying for a master's degree in theology. I began reading about Liberation Theology coming from Latin America and I was inspired. I wondered how people who faced so many obstacles, not just systemic poverty, but violent repression from military regimes supported by the United States, could still find hope and energy to organize and protest. I was also inspired by the collective focus on resolving problems and organizing to change social realities. I was working with people living on the streets of Philadelphia and in the prison system and I did not witness that hope in the United States, nor was there a collective focus to make change happen. I decided to move to Chile to learn about what motivated people to risk their lives and organize for social change. I wanted to see what we in the United States could learn from the global south. I found out that we have a lot to learn!

In Chile I lived in the *población* (shantytown) La Pincoya and engaged in human rights work at different levels. I worked with survivors of torture and in the Sebastian Acevedo Movement against Torture protesting the practices of the Pinochet regime; I worked with 11 local *ollas comunes* (common pots); and I worked with a grassroots human rights group and base Christian community. In all of this I learned that one of the key components to action for liberation and hope was being part of a community—knowing that we are not alone and that there are others supporting our work and ideals. While this may not seem revolutionary at first glance, it is certainly counter-cultural in a society that focuses on "ownership" and individual success. Almost everything about U.S. society screams individualism, but what I learned in Chile was that in order to make true change on behalf of human rights and social justice, we must be willing to let go of our selfish individualistic perspective and form part of a community. This can be so difficult to do since from the day we are born we have been indoctrinated to think that to be successful, we have to be independent. Yes, we talk about interdependence, but usually in a utilitarian way—how can I benefit from this relationship? I learned what interdependence really means in Chile, and it was not an easy lesson. I also was able to witness and be a part of a process of liberation—liberation that necessitates partnerships and mutual relationships, relationships that are critical to the exercise of effective social work practice.

For the past 15 years I have brought students to La Pincoya, to work in partnership with youth to plan and carry out an *Escuela Popular* (Freedom School). While in Chile, they too experience hope and community in ways that they find missing in the United States. Invariably, upon return to the United States, the students fall into a type of depression—after living and working in a community for a few weeks, they feel alone, isolated, and lonely once back in the United States. They also are not sure how to explain what they experienced in Chile to folks in the United States who do not see a problem with their isolation. Through our reflections over the years we have come to realize that the only way to really engage in true social work—social justice work—is through communities committed to liberation for all. If, as *Funk & Wagnall's Standard Desk Dictionary* says, liberation is defined as "setting free, as from bondage or confinement" (1984, p. 372), then we must work together to free ourselves from our isolation, creating caring communities where liberation for all is the goal.

CHAPTER SUMMARY

In this chapter we have explored the many facets and dynamics of engagement. We have considered the significance of organizational and community context in the process of engagement. We bring our histories with us to each new relationship, further shaping the possibilities and limits of engagement. We have addressed the interpersonal context of practice and the importance of anticipation, observation, respectful listening, and dialogue in building mutual knowledge and trust. Social justice work calls for strong skills in interpersonal communication and the ability to engage people in teamwork. We have considered both specific skills and the larger questions of meaning, power, difference, and resistance that we need to bring to bear simultaneously in the practice of engagement. The process of and commitment to engagement prepares us for the work of teaching-learning that we address in Chapter 7.

Essay: Making Sense of Just Practice

Chuck Wayland

Social justice worker Chuck Wayland wrote the following essay as an MSW student in response to the following question: How do you personally make sense of the five key concepts discussed toward the end of Chapter 2? His response also goes to the heart of engagement - relationship.

It is a damp and dark morning in the Absorka-Beartooth wilderness. The rain that let up briefly when we woke the kids an hour ago has intensified. The rain and cold make getting out of a sleeping bag, packing, eating, and hitting the trail for another long day of hiking a daunting challenge, even for the staff. However, for 14-year-old Jodie, the challenge appears impossible and she is refusing to get up. The entire trip has been a struggle for her, and this day she has decided to take a stand. When I ask her what is wrong, she replies that she does not feel well. When I push her for a deeper understanding of what she is experiencing emotionally, she becomes defensive and shuts down. When I attempt to figure out for her the meaning of her refusal to get up, I cross a line. After a barrage of expletives and name-calling, she exclaims that I do not know who she is and can never understand her world or life experiences. I pause and take a deep breath. I know she is right. I have learned an important lesson in humility.

I have come to realize that at that moment it did not matter how well-intentioned my prodding was. It made no difference that I already knew that Jodie had seen and done things that no 14-year-old should have to see or do. Nor did it matter that I knew that Jodie's mother struggled to raise her children despite chronic battles with alcohol and drug addiction. My knowledge of attachment theory informed me that the adult caregivers in Jodie's life were unable to provide an emotionally safe environment in which she would develop the skills to form healthy attachments. However, that knowledge was not helping me in that moment. What mattered most at that point in our relationship was that we were still seeing each other through the lens of our differing positionalities. If she could tell me more, I would not have to assume what she was thinking. However, she was not ready to open an emotional connection with a college educated 35-year-old, middle-class male whom she had known for only a few days. In fact, on the first day she quickly determined that I held power and authority over her because I was making decisions about her physical and emotional safety in the backcountry. She did not like many of those decisions because of the limits they placed on her freedom and choices.

As I sat in the rain outside Jodie's shelter, I came to acknowledge the accuracy of her comment that up to that point in our relationship I did not know her well enough to make assumptions. Reflecting on this encounter, after learning the role that positionality plays in how each of us makes meaning of events in our lives, the boundary that I crossed with Jodie seems more obvious. I was not in a position at that point in our relationship to offer her my advice or interpretation about her experience of poverty, parental neglect, drug abuse, and risky sexual behaviors. She was correct in saying that I did not know her well enough to make assumptions about her thoughts and feelings. In fact, it was downright arrogant of me to do so. I believed my years of experience working with teenagers in wilderness programs entitled me to make some assumptions about what was best for her in the backcountry. In hindsight, what I really wanted from Jodie as I confronted her was for her to get out of her sleeping bag so the group could start hiking. I was rushing a process of relationship-building to suit my own needs. I was over-relying on my position of power and authority as the group leader to guide our interaction.

For Jodie, power was a means to manipulate the world around to shield her from having to deal with the pain and sense of unworthiness that lingered beneath her tough façade. As the trip progressed, I realized that if I was asking her to make changes in her life, then I needed to engage in self-reflection as well. It was my task to re-frame power in our relationship so that it looked to her like "power with" rather than "power over." I needed to present my expectations of Jodie in a way that ensured her safety, both physically and emotionally, that also removed the pressure to change so that it came from her willingness rather than from meeting my needs. I had to examine how success was defined for the students within the context of this "therapeutic" program. In doing so, I came to understand how the fear of not measuring up to an adult's definition of success activated the defenses of the youths in the program and led to suspicion of our motives. I came to learn that much of this defensiveness arose as a result of previous negative experiences in therapy. Was I contributing to another "bad" experience of therapy for them? Though I was not a therapist, some of the teenagers clearly thought of me as someone trying to change them, and they were very resistant to my approach.

As I reflected on this experience, I reasoned that if Jodie could begin to see that my intentions were born of a compassionate desire to help her rather than from an exercise in power designed to change her, then the process of building a trusting relationship could begin. The relationship improved when I was able to assure her that I was not passing judgment on her character or any behaviors she had engaged in. I learned to separate out the behaviors in the field from the context and emotion from which I believed she was acting. I could see that the context in which she made meaning of her life contributed to her poor decision making. Her experiences contributed to a diminished sense of possibility and every story she told about her life's history confirmed that she was a victim. She saw the world as a dark and foreboding place and interpreted events, people, and circumstances through a lens of self-loathing, hate, and anger. When I allowed more room for this in my interpretation of her actions, the relationship improved. I knew we had turned a corner in our relationship when she began to invite my feedback while trying to problem-solve and self-reflect. I noticed signs of her expanded sense of possibility when she began to conquer mountain peaks and long hikes that she previously thought impossible. I offered hope and praise liberally upon these achievements to help her solidify the new meanings she was making

I came across a quote from one of my favorite authors, Terry Tempest Williams (2004), that helps me put perspective on lessons of that day, as well as what I am currently learning about integrating the concepts of meaning, context, power, history, and possibility. In reflecting on what she calls the "open space of democracy," she says, "We are in need of reflective activism born out of humility, not arrogance. Reflection with deep time spent in consideration of others, opens the door to becoming a compassionate participant in the world" (p. 25). Humility paves the way for thoughtful, reflective introspection of one's own values, assumptions, and uncertainties. Consideration of others will force us to ask questions about how our positionality and constructions of difference affect the views that color our perceptions of one another. If we are to become "compassionate participants in the world," we will seek to redress the sociopolitical and economic structures of power that contribute to inequality and injustice. Social justice work compels us to empower others through self-advocacy, while teaching them to make meanings that are compatible with the dignity and human rights of every individual. If we are to learn from history, as I did with Jodie, we must expose the arrogance that assumes it knows best and replace it with humility and the possibility that we can learn how to better support one another through compassionate action.

Reference: Williams, T. (2004). Commencement. *Orion*, 23(2), 18-25.

Questions for Discussion

1. Describe anticipatory empathy in your own words. In what situations have you made use of this skill before? How would you describe the relationship between anticipatory empathy and social justice work?

2. How do the concepts of power, trust, and difference affect communication? What examples illustrate your point?

3. Return to the description of "radical listening" on p. 239. What examples can you think of to illustrate the act of radical listening?

4. Where have you encountered resistance as a survival skill? As a manifestation of power and privilege? As a form of cultural expression? What example can you think of that expands the notion of resistance to include social, political, and economic contexts or histories of oppression and discrimination?

5. What are some challenges you have faced as a member or facilitator of a group? How do these experiences affect how you might approach a new group experience?

Suggested Readings

Anderson, K. & Jack, D. (1991). Learning to listen: Interview techniques and analyses. In S. Berger Gluck & D. Patai (Eds.)., *Women's words: The feminist practice of oral history.* (pp. 11-26) New York: Routledge.

Cisneros, S. (1984). *The house on Mango Street.* New York: Vintage Books

Dean, R. (2001). The myth of cross-cultural competence. *Families in Society, 82*(6), 623-630.

Deegan, P. (1990). Spirit breaking: When the helping professions hurt. *The Humanistic Psychologist, 18*(3), 301-313.

Fine, M. Weis, L. Powell, L, & Wong, L.M. (Eds.). (1997). *Off white: Readings on race, power, and society.* New York: Routledge.

Hope, A. & Timmel, S. (1999). *Training for transformation: A handbook for community workers,* Volumes 1-4. London: Intermediate Technology Publications.

Schwartz, W. (1986). The group work tradition and social work practice. *Social Work with Groups, 8*(4), 7-27.

Scott, J. (1985). *Weapons of the weak: Everyday forms of resistance.* New Haven: Yale University Press.

End Notes

[1] From Stephen Rose (2000) Reflections on empowerment-based practice, *Social Work,* 45(5): 403.

[2] Excerpts adapted from Patricia Deegan (1996) Recovery and the Conspiracy of Hope. Paper presented at the sixth Annual Mental Health Services Conferences of Australia and New Zealand, Brisbane, Australia, 1996. Copyright Patricia E. Deegan, 1996.

[3] See Netting and O'Connor (2003, pp. 99 - 118) for a more detailed discussion of diverse theories of organizations.

[4] This list of communication skills draws from the work of Shulman (1992), Brill and Levine (2002) and Miley et al. (2007).

[5] Excerpt from "When the academic becomes personal and the personal is academic," text of presentation by Deborah Bey, University of Michigan, 2000.

[6] This discussion of resistance is taken from the work of Paul Carter as presented in his "Parts Work" workshops in Nelson, British Columbia and Edmonton, Alberta, Canada in 1987.

7

Just Understanding: Teaching–Learning

> *Tell me and I forget. Show me and I remember. Involve me and I understand.*
>
> Chinese proverb

CHAPTER OVERVIEW

In Chapter 7 we examine the teaching-learning process. We challenge the one-way flow of information that characterizes most social work approaches to data collection, assessment, and interpretation. We reframe the process as one of co-learning in which the social worker and other participants in the process recognize their wisdom and the limits of their knowledge, consider the knowledge they need to inform action, identify ways to gather data, and draw on their collective wisdom in rendering the data meaningful in the context of their work. Together participants gather data, identify resources and supports, discuss the root causes of presenting concerns, and discover their own personal and collective capacities. We consider strategies for setting the teaching-learning climate, the development of critical awareness, and the importance of collaboration in the process. We examine a variety of assessment techniques and tools, including both "classic" social work tools and alternative approaches. We ask you to apply your critical thinking skills to assessing the assessment tools and to constructing and or modifying assessment approaches to reflect understandings of social justice-oriented practice.

TEACHING–LEARNING: CONCEPT AND PROCESS

Thinking about and Defining Teaching–Learning

In thinking and talking through the organization of this book, we struggled with ways to frame and name this collaborative process of gathering "data," learning about people and places, needs and resources, problems and possibilities. Most guides to social work practice speak of "assessment" as a key phase in the change process that follows initial engagement. Assessment refers to the collection and interpretation of information needed to inform change-oriented action. We see assessment as a central part of the teaching-learning process, but we did not feel that the word captured the sense of collaboration and co-learning that is fundamental to social justice work. Moreover, assessment has often been construed as a one-way process in which the "expert" gathers data, makes interpretations to the "client," and provides a "diagnosis" and course of "treatment" or "intervention." The process has largely been problem-focused, resulting in a discourse of deficits and shortcomings (Iverson, Gergen, & Fairbanks, 2005). We sought a concept that disrupted a unidirectional view of "assessment" and emphasized a participatory process.

In their important work on an empowering approach to social work practice, Miley, O'Melia, and DuBois (2007) locate assessment as part of the "discovery phase" of the change process and emphasize assessment of resources and strengths rather than "problems." Similarly, Cowger (1994, p. 265) supports strengths-oriented assessments that build a base "for an examination of realizable alternatives, for the mobilization of competencies that can make things different, and for the building of self-confidence that stimulates hope." We agree with their emphases on partnership, possibilities, and strengths. However, the idea of "discovery" suggests that we "find" some truth or resource either "out there" or within. It does not speak to the social construction of knowledge, the emergence of critical consciousness, or the creation of new possibilities through dialogue and praxis.

The Teaching-Learning Process

In an effort to address the shortcomings mentioned above and embody both the spirit and practice of a dialectical exchange, we conceptualize this process as one of "teaching-learning." Iverson et al. (2005) speak of "a collaborative inquiry into transformative possibilities" and an "appreciation of the not-yet-seen, the yet-to-be-storied" (p. 704). We envision teaching-learning as a dynamic process that goes beyond discovery. It includes *learning to learn from others* through which we recognize multiple ways of knowing, challenge dichotomous thinking, question assumptions, and probe the contradictions among words, actions, and consequences. It entails systematic inquiry into questions of meaning, context, power, and history in which both problems and possibilities are embedded.

Each party to the process brings knowledge grounded in personal experience and cultural history. Together we begin to map out what we know, consider what we need to learn more about, seek out knowledge, consider underlying forces and patterns that shape experiences, and bring our collective wisdom to bear in translating data into a meaningful guide for action. We draw inspiration from Freirian principles of popular education that contrast interactive problem-posing and search for solutions with a "banking" approach to learning (Freire, 1974). A banking approach posits the "teacher" as expert who deposits information (currency) into those with empty bank accounts. A banking approach is perhaps the most common form of information transfer and it is based on the assumption that the "teacher" knows everything and the "student" is a blank slate (Freire, 1974).

In contrast, as social justice workers we act as animators, facilitators, and researchers who recognize the limits of our own experience and the partiality of our knowledge. We work to create a climate that promotes co-learning. We support and encourage the process of critical reflection about people's concerns and what we need to know through question-posing. And we help people *systematically* examine the information at hand, *theorize* about problems and possibilities, and *strategize* courses of action. Together we can create new meanings and labels that can help us think and act differently (Reed et al., 1997). We are both learners and teachers in the process. We are learning in the context of partnership with those who possess the wisdom of lived experience. And we are teachers, helping others develop knowledge and skills in research and planning so that they can carry out their own assessments and develop action plans in the future.

Power and the Teaching–Learning Process

In the discussion of context and positionality in Chapter 6, we addressed the need for social workers to be clear about the extent and limits of professional power and authority. By virtue of our positions, we may have the power to attach labels to others, access resources, impose sanctions, and make recommendations with significant legal and social consequences. We need to be critically self-aware regarding the sources, forms, and limits of our power and to be able to communicate that honestly to others. Likewise, we need to be critically conscious of the various forms of informal power we may assume or that others might attribute to us, such as the power of credentials, titles, or access to information. People and groups who have been excluded from arenas and processes of decision making may be very wary of both the formal and the informal power of the social workers. People socialized to respect the power of the expert may defer to the authority of the social worker as advice-giver and decision-maker. For social workers, an integral part of the teaching-learning process is, therefore, learning to acknowledge the power and expertise we have; learning and teaching the skills of participation so that our power and expertise is brought to bear honestly, effectively, and justly; and learning and teaching modes of leadership that challenge top-down models of authority and promote participation.

Authentic teaching-learning must be predicated on understanding how oppression works to silence, devalue, denigrate, and otherwise stigmatize individuals and groups of people based on perceived differences in terms of race, class, gender, sexual orientation, ability, and age.

REFLECTION: Power and Powerlessness

The purpose of this class exercise is to promote personal understandings of power and powerlessness and to begin to draw out how these affect the teaching-learning process. On a large piece of paper using markers, crayons, or colored pencils, draw a line down the center of the paper. On one side of the paper draw a situation that has made you feel powerful. On the other side, draw a situation that has made you feel powerless. Even if you do not feel confident about drawing, it is important to express yourself in this exercise through symbols instead of words. Having to think creatively about how to express ourselves in a nonverbal way can enable us to see experiences differently through fresh eyes. The quality of the artwork is not important to the exercise so feel free to draw stick figures or symbols to express yourself.

After everyone has completed their drawings, divide into small groups of four or five members.

Appoint someone to be a scribe to write down group members' descriptions of their drawings and a reporter to summarize what the group learned about teaching-learning by completing this exercise for the entire class. In the small group everyone takes turns explaining their drawings, while the scribe jots down their responses. After everyone is finished take at least 15 minutes to discuss the following questions:

1) What images and words were used to describe powerful and powerless experiences?

2) What did you learn about the teaching-learning process from this exercise?

3) How does what you learned translate into a set of practice principles for teaching-learning?

This exercise was adapted from:

VeneKlasen, L., & Miller, V. (2002). A *new weave of power, people & politics*. Oklahoma City, OK: World Neighbors.

Engaging in a Power Analysis

Fundamental to the teaching-learning process is an analysis of power. Engaging in a power analysis is a prerequisite for understanding our own sources of power, identifying the forms of power working against us, and determining the same for individuals, families, groups, and communities we work with to affect change. In their development of an empowerment approach to practice with women of color, Lorraine Gutiérrez and Edith Lewis (Gutiérrez, 1990; Gutiérrez & Lewis, 1999) describe engaging in a power analysis as an essential component of empowering people in the context of a collaborative helping relationship. We summarize the important steps and strategies they find useful in analyzing people's power base and determining what sources to draw from to engage in empowering forms of practice:

♦ Analyze how conditions of powerlessness are affecting the client's situation.

♦ Identify sources of potential power in the client's situation.

♦ Dialogue with the client about the social structural origins of the current situation.

♦ Focus the client's analysis on a specific situation, either the client's own situation or a vignette developed for the intervention.

♦ Think creatively about sources of potential power, such as forgotten skills, personal qualities that could increase social influence, members of past social support networks, and organizations in the community.

♦ Make connections between the immediate situation and the distribution of power in society as a whole.

♦ Engage in consciousness-raising exercises to look beyond the specific situation to problems shared by other clients in similar situations.

♦ Beware of adopting feelings of powerlessness from clients.

♦ Learn to see the potential for power and influence in every situation. (1999, p. 19)

Gutiérrez and Lewis (1999, pp. 38-51) describe how individual practice can be transformed into an empowering process by honoring the other person's social reality, walking with rather than directing a person through the helping process, and providing mechanisms for acknowledging and responding to experiences of oppression and discrimination. They address the centrality of relationship to empowering practice, and they recognize spirituality as an empowering resource in many people's lives. We can enrich the power analysis by teaching participants about dimensions of power (see Townsend et al., Chapter 2, p. 45) and learning how they claim and confront power in their everyday lives. We also see the need to take the power analysis further by making the power and authority of the social worker a talkable theme in the process. How do the participants in the process variably perceive the social worker's power? How comfortable is the social worker with the power, authority, and responsibility of her position? How does her power factor into the larger power dynamics of the presenting situation and the change process? These are key questions of the teaching-learning process.

The Matrix of Power Relations

Often forgotten in models emphasizing emancipatory perspectives on practice are the conditions within social work practice that demand attention to social workers' use of authority, specifically in situations where people's rights have been violated such as in cases of sexual assault and domestic violence. Jerry Tew (2006) presents a nuanced framework for analyzing different forms of power that acknowledges the potential of power to be damaging and productive. He discusses how the framework's concepts translate to a practice level and helps to address the often dicey, tension-wrought issues social justice workers face around the use of power and the limits and reach of their authority. He grapples with the complexities inherent in situations in which an individual's use of power has violated the rights of others. He provides us with no easy answers but with considerable food for thought.

Tew illustrates how "power over" and "power together" or what Townsend et al. (1999) refer to as "power with," have both productive and limiting dimensions. Productive modes of power open up or help to create opportunities, whereas limiting modes of power close off opportunities. Tew defines "opportunity" as involving "anything from accessing resources and social or economic participation, to developing personal identities and capacities, expressing needs, thoughts and feelings, and renegotiating relationships" (p. 40). Tew emphasizes the importance of a multidimensional understanding of how power works and he calls our attention to the "complex and contradictory ways" (p. 40) in which power operates:

> People may be involved in more than one mode of power relations at the same time: for example, an interpersonal relationship may offer opportunities for co-operative power while simultaneously retaining aspects of oppressive inequality in how it is structured. (p. 40)

THE SKILLS AND PRACTICE OF TEACHING–LEARNING

Overview

In this section we elaborate on the skills and practice of teaching-learning. We look at teaching and learning in community, organizational, familial, and interpersonal contexts. We begin by discussing *sistematización* and consider a number of approaches to systematic inquiry. We present some examples of the basic assessment tools widely used in U.S. social work. We highlight their strengths, pose questions about their limitations, and consider their fit with the teaching-learning process of social justice work. We also illustrate how a number of these tools have been adapted to address a broad range of issues with diverse groups of people. We also introduce tools from popular education, feminist practice, and international and cross-cultural contexts that can facilitate the practice of social justice work.

Systematic Inquiry

Sistematización

Teaching-learning involves the "systematization" of experiences. This is not a word in the English vocabulary. We borrow it from the Spanish, *sistematización*. Popular educators in Latin America, influenced by the work of Paulo Freire, describe *sistematización* as a rigorous, ordered process of taking concrete, lived experience into account, looking for generative themes (we describe this process on pp. 280-283), and sharing with others what we have learned from it. It is a participatory process in which people critically examine and interpret their experience and social reality in order to arrive at a more profound understanding. The process involves detailed deconstruction, examination, and reconstruction of the elements, context, and forces shaping the experience (Jara, 1998).

The key themes of Just Practice provide a foundation for *sistematización,* or systematic inquiry into experiences, conditions, and possibilities for change: How do the participants in the process variably describe and give *meaning* to their experiences, interests, and concerns? What constitutes a "problem" and for whom? What is the *history* of the problem, and how does it intersect with the histories of the participants? What is the *context* in which participants are coming together? How is it connected to the larger contexts of their lives? What can we learn from a *power* analysis of the situation that addresses questions of power over, power with, power within, and power to do? Where and what are the *possibilities* for transformative action? What possibilities can be realized and how? What can we learn from the process that will transform our thinking and inform future practice?

"Diagnosis" and Analysis

In developing a popular education course on democratic participation and the exercise of local power in Costa Rica, Cecilia Díaz (1995) describes the "diagnostic" process that enables people to critically and systematically analyze their social

REFLECTION: A Note on Standardized Assessment Tools

There is no shortage of standardized tools for diagnosis and assessment that are available to and used by social workers. By standardized we refer to instruments that have been tested on large numbers of people and that provide practitioners general guidelines for problem diagnosis. Most standardized instruments used by social workers focus on the individual and not on the context of her life experience. Most are administered and interpreted by the practitioner who then uses the results to inform action. While the tools may yield useful information, we see them as fitting within the "social worker as expert" model of practice. We agree with Gutiérrez and Lewis (1999, p. 31) that social workers need to be cautious in the use of standardized instruments whose "standards" may not take into account the social reality of the person being assessed. From their very conception, these assessment instruments are based on particular assumptions about people, what is important to know about their lives, and how this information will inform predetermined strategies for change based on available services and programs.

Hilary Weaver (2005) tells the story of lessons learned from Tamil refugees from Sri Lanka who were seeking refugee or asylum status while traveling through Buffalo, New York. Weaver explains that due to its proximity to the Canadian border and large cities such as Montreal and Toronto with diverse international populations, Buffalo is often a pass-through place for populations in transition: "The purpose of the project was to develop a culturally appropriate assessment tool for Tamils who have fled ongoing civil war in Sri Lanka and relocated to North America" (p. 239). Along with other researchers, Weaver helped modify a standardized assessment tool, the Harvard Trauma Questionnaire (HTQ) to make it culturally appropriate. The HTQ contains items that gather information about issues such as brainwashing, torture, and sexual assault. Although the tool has been translated and used extensively in other countries, researchers had never adjusted it to reflect cultural differences. Weaver reports that "The wording of an assessment tool must be framed with explicit consideration for the cultural and gender norms of the targeted population" (p. 239). She highlights important information learned from the project that challenged stereotypes of working with Asian women, namely that issues of modesty and shame would prevent them from discussing sexual abuse. On the contrary, women in the study discussed sexual abuse, and participants including men and women preferred to discuss issues of trauma and torture in the presence of at least one male relative or a male interpreter. Weaver shares lesson learned from the project that include the willingness to listen to clients and modify procedures to ensure comfort and participation and to examine long-held beliefs based on Western ideology that may need to be rethought when working with people from non-Western cultures. This story helps us understand the importance of thinking about the teaching-learning process through a cultural lens and challenges us to question the underlying assumptions embedded in prepackaged or standardized assessment tools. Weaver reminds us that "We need to question broad generalizations that lump diverse groups of people under one heading, like Asians or Hispanics" (p. 244). Think for a moment of how standardized instruments "lump" diverse groups of people under one heading. In what situations and for what purposes might they be useful? Where might their use cause more harm than good? While standardized instruments can provide valuable data, we will not be addressing them here. Instead, we focus on tools that facilitate participation, consciousness-raising, and critical action and provide room

reality in order to discover possible solutions and make informed collective decisions. It is a process that addresses three levels of analysis:

 Context: the population, economic, cultural and natural resources, mode of production, service infrastructure, and so forth.

2 Practice: what has transpired in the life of our group or community; what have been significant moments, events, achievements; how have we been transforming our reality; and

3 Values and subjectivity: why we act as we do, believe in working for change; why participation is important; what dreams inspire us; why we think what we think. (p. 2)

Díaz describes a five-step process of analysis. It is a process with a wide range of applicability:

1 Describe: We start by recognizing things as they present themselves to us. What are the visible, exterior signs of our reality? How does our social reality present itself before our eyes? We may gather this information through interviews, group conversations, observations, review of existing data, surveys and questionnaires, and through testimonials. This is our starting point.

2 Organize: Then we try to classify what we have described and organize the elements into aspects of our reality, such as economic, cultural, social, and political aspects.

3 Prioritize: We give preference to some aspects over others as we consider those that are most significant in contributing to the situation that concerns us. The criteria by which we set priorities might include most urgent, most serious, that which affects the most people, the most deeply felt, and so on.

4 Analyze: We reflect on the different aspects, analyzing them separately. We seek to understand causes and consequences of each of those aspects that we have set as priorities. Then we integrate the different aspects and look for relations among them.

5 Draw Conclusions: We return to the basic points that emerged from the analysis—the most consistently named concerns and affirmations, the common elements across seemingly diverse problems or needs. At this point we begin to orient ourselves toward possible courses of action. (Díaz, 1995, pp. 8-11)

The process brings us to new points of arrival, which then become points of departure for further reflection and analysis.

Teaching and Learning in Groups

Much of the social work literature divides discussion of group work into broad categories of individual change (e.g., therapy, support, psycho-educational, and self-help groups) and task groups (e.g., community and social action, interdisciplinary teams, coalitions, steering committees) (Garvin, Gutiérrez, & Galinsky, 2004; Garvin & Seabury, 1997, pp. 231-32). We argue that social justice work calls for an integrated approach to group work that brings the dynamics and skills of mutual aid, analysis of power, and a commitment to the equality of participants to bear as

Applying Díaz's Five–Step Process

Get together with a few classmates and select an issue relevant to social work that is currently being debated in your community, for example, housing and homelessness, access to affordable health care, disability access on campus, access to public transportation. Over a period of 2 to 3 weeks, gather relevant and readily accessible information on the issue (e.g., newspaper and other media reports, agency reports, etc.). Identify key stakeholders in the issue and consider what their interests may be. Role play a session in which members of your group take on the roles of people struggling for improved access or services. Carry out the five steps of diagnosis and analysis outlined by Díaz. What did you learn from others? What were you able to teach? Where did you find common ground? Important differences? What difficulties did you encounter? Were you able to work through them? If so, how? What feelings did the role play evoke for you? Now, role play a session in which each member of your group takes on the role of a different stakeholder (e.g. landlord, property owner, single parent in need of decent affordable housing, housing authority director, housing advocate, director of local homeless shelter, etc). What do you learn from the expression of different points of view? Where did you find common ground? What difficulties did you encounter in the teaching-learning process? Were you able to work through them? If so, how? What feelings did this role play evoke? Did it differ from the first? If so, how? Does this exercise challenge assumptions regarding difference and commonality? What lessons did you learn about the teaching-learning process?

A C T I O N

part of the teaching-learning process. Groups provide a site for ongoing processes of collective critical reflection, and within them lie the potential for transformative action and social change (Finn, Jacobson, & Dean Campana, 2004).

Teaching and learning happens in dialogue with others. Groups provide a space for teaching and learning where people can take risks, experiment with new ideas, and build a powerful base for change with the support of others. Groups form a base and a place for learning about effective membership and for building leadership capacity. A well-facilitated group process ensures that decisions are made collectively. Power is distributed among members and not solely concentrated in the hands of one group leader. To work effectively with and in groups, it is important to understand about group work and group dynamics (Abramson & Bronstein, 2004).

Processes of Mutual Aid

In Chapter 6, we introduced William Schwartz's concept of mutual aid as a basis for collective support and action. Let's return to the processes of mutual aid and the implications for social justice work. By conceptualizing the group as a mutual aid system, we locate all participants, including the social worker, as learners, teachers, and facilitators, or "animators." We also recognize the dialectical relationship between the individual members and the group as a whole in the process (Shulman, 1986, p. 52). As participants learn and practice the skills of mutual aid they contribute to a climate of trust and intimacy in the group that supports individuals in assuming the risks and opportunities of teaching-learning. Let's take a closer look at these processes and the elements of teaching-learning at work in carrying them out. Drawing from Lawrence Shulman (1986, 2006), we offer a description of each of the processes. As you read about the processes, reflect on the questions, "How can we as social workers facilitate the process? How does the process promote co-learning?" We offer our thoughts on these questions in our description of sharing data, the dialectical process, exploring taboo subjects, and the "all in the same boat" phenomenon. We invite you to do the same with each of the processes.

Sharing Data

Groups provide a context for members to be resources to one another by sharing ideas, data, and strategies for survival and change. We can facilitate the process by teaching groups about the value of sharing data and serving as resources to one another, giving members opportunities to share data, recognizing members for their contributions, and checking in with members to see what data they have put to use and what the results have been. The process allows each member opportunities to teach from his experience and learn from the experience of others.

The Dialectical Process

This process consists of members engaging the debate of ideas with members variably putting forth a thesis and antithesis and finally arriving at some form of synthesis. The process can help members explore contradictory forces and discourses that shape everyday life. And it can help members grapple with the pushes and pulls of ambivalent feelings. In short, as tensions and contradictions emerge and are addressed in the group, each member has an opportunity to recognize internalized contradictions. We can facilitate the process by recognizing tensions and contradictions as key parts of social experience and by naming and honoring the process when group members are engaged in it. It is especially important that facilitators be able to frame the dialectical process as a healthy part of group work and not as a "problem" between members. The process illustrates the fundamental give and take of teaching-learning.

Exploring Taboo Subjects

The group context creates a space where members can address issues that are silenced and topics whose honest discussion is avoided in other social contexts. For example, groups can be powerful places to approach questions of sexuality, terminal illness, racism, and other topics often considered taboo in dominant social discourse. Groups may experience the power of trust and intimacy as members find the courage to "speak the unspeakable." Again, we can facilitate the process by encouraging participants to approach difficult subjects and by helping members establish ground rules that help create a context of safety needed for risky discussion. The process teaches members about the possibilities in risk taking and helps to build the trust needed for more difficult learning.

The "All in the Same Boat" Phenomenon

Realizing that one is not alone and that others share similar concerns and struggles is a powerful dimension of group work. As facilitators, we not only recognize and respect difference but also take opportunities to make connections and encourage others to reflect critically on the patterns that connect and the forces that shape both individual and group experience. We can both pose and invite questions that may help break down a sense of personal isolation or deficit and help people move to another level of questioning: "But why are we in this boat?" The process expands the critical awareness of the group beyond the teaching and learning of individual members.

Emotional Support

Group members can provide a range of immediate, direct support to individual members dealing with pain, trauma, and loss. Rather than encouraging a person to "cheer up," members can recognize and honor difficult emotions and experiences. Members can provide a gift of emotional support by sharing their own feelings and experiences and letting the other person know that his or her pain is respected, even if it may not be fully understood.

Mutual Demand

Support is only one dimension of the dynamic of group work. Members need a context of support and a base of trust in order to take the risks necessary for social and personal transformation. Thus, effective groups are also places where participants make demands on one another and hold one another accountable for responsible participation and follow-through on work. Working in a context of trust and intimacy, participants are able to confront one another on the contradictions between their words and actions.

Mutual Expectation

Hand in hand with mutual demand is mutual expectation. Individual members come to feel a commitment to one another and to the group as a whole. Trust develops as the group places expectations on its members to follow through on commitments and honor the ground rules. Likewise, members strengthen their sense of belonging as they live up to those expectations.

Helping with Specific Problems

Groups can move back and forth between general concerns of the group as a whole and the specific concerns of individual members. Members can assist one another in concrete problem solving. Successes of individual problem solving can become resources for the group as a whole.

Rehearsal

The group setting provides members with an arena for practicing alternative responses, difficult interactions, and challenging tasks. Members provide both support and critical feedback and bolster individuals' confidence in the process.

Strength in Numbers

The group experience not only breaks down isolation, it also helps members overcome feelings of powerlessness and envision the possibilities of and the strength in collective action.[1] Shulman (1992) comments, "An individual's fears and ambivalence can be overcome by participating in a group effort as one's own courage is strengthened by the courage of others" (p. 312).

As members engage in these processes over time, they develop their knowledge of group work, skills of teaching-learning, and both individual and collective capacity for critical reflection and action. The processes support group work that integrates the possibilities of mutual aid and social action. The dynamics that foster teaching-learning in the early stages of new groups include creating a climate conducive for the development of sharing data and power, helping participants see their commonalities and shared humanity and recognizing the importance of learning from and teaching others. Refer back to Maxine Jacobson's story about the Finding Solutions to Food Insecurity project on pp. 253-254 in Chapter 6. What mutual aid dynamics can you identify?

REFLECTION: Mutual Aid Potential of Focus Groups

We generally think of a focus group as a research tool for gathering information to assess people's attitudes, beliefs, concerns, and ideas about solutions to community problems (Jacobson & Goheen, 2006; Jacobson & Hassanein, 2004; Krueger, 1994; Krueger & King, 1998). For these purposes, focus groups are composed of individuals who do not know one another, who are brought together usually for only one meeting, and who provide a range of varying opinions on a particular subject. Focus groups operate on the philosophy that group dialogue helps to spark a synergistic process in which people build on others' ideas. A group climate is created that promotes discussion of diverse beliefs and attitudes without fear of reprisal. Focus groups have been used extensively in business and marketing as a data collection tool to gauge the opinions of select groups of people regarding particular products and criteria for product development.

Focus groups have also become a popular research tool in the social sciences. For example, social work researchers have used them to gather information from domestic violence survivors (Davis & Srinivasan, 1995), child welfare workers (Gold, 1998), people experiencing food insecurity and hunger (Jacobson & Hassanein, 2004), and social work faculty and students for program evaluation purposes (Jacobson & Goheen, 2006). Irene Chung (2003), a social work researcher and faculty member at Hunter College School of Social Work in New York City, discusses the creative use of focus groups to provide healing and support to residents of Chinatown following the attacks on the World Trade Center in September 2001. The original intent of the focus groups was to investigate the service needs and mental health issues of three generations of Asian Americans, which included elderly people, dislocated workers, and children. Chung explains how the Chinatown community is less than 10 blocks from what has since become known as Ground Zero. Community residents experienced extended disruption in their daily lives because of school and business closures and residents' immediate connections to people who had lost their lives in the attacks.

Although focus groups are generally structured for single sessions and require the advanced preparation of protocols that include questions and probes to elicit more detailed information, Chung allowed herself to be present in the moment. She discovered that the focus groups were the first opportunity for residents to collectively share their stories of emotional trauma experienced as a direct result of 9/11 and its aftermath. Adhering to the philosophy of "starting where the client is at," group facilitators attended to focus group participants' recall of traumatic events (sights, sounds, smells) and personal experiences. Chung explains, "In addition to meeting the focus group's mandate to gather information from participants, it was more important to seize the window of opportunity to provide healing through the facilitation of a mutual aid group process" (p. 5).

As noted above in our description of mutual aid group dynamics, finding common ground or gaining a sense that everyone in the group is "all in the same boat" helps participants share their vulnerabilities, bond with others around a common experience, learn new ways of coping, and "exchange empathy in the supportive environment of the group" (p. 6). Chung highlights the mutual aid dynamics that occurred within the context of the focus groups. These included sharing personal information and feelings, validation of common concerns and rendering of mutual support, and collective problem-solving efforts. Although Chung never uses the term "teaching-learning," she describes the process. She indicates how important it is for the group facilitator to adopt "an inquisitive stance to allow the group members to articulate their concerns and develop their own insights and solutions. . ." (p. 18). The group facilitator achieves these ends "by relinquishing her role as leader and authority figure, and by showing acceptance and respect for minority clients' perceptions of their needs and feelings, the worker is offering validation of these clients' ethnic heritage and strengths" (p. 18). Think for a moment of how a research tool fulfills a dual purpose—gathering information and bringing together people isolated in their own pain to share experiences and ways of coping with trauma and grief, and perhaps to take collective action. In this situation, everyone is both a teacher and a learner.

Open Space Technology—Group Work for Policy Change

Another group work approach that promotes dialogue in the teaching-learning process is called Open Space Technology (OST).[2] This tool has enormous potential for social justice work as a vehicle for creating policy change. OST was originally developed in the 1980s by Harrison Owen (1997a, 1997b), a conference organizer and facilitator who experienced the informal conversations outside of the formal agenda (during the coffee and meal breaks) at conferences as far more productive and rewarding than those that happened within the confines of the conference. After witnessing a 4-day rite of passage ceremony for young men in a western Africa village where 500 people seamlessly managed to organize themselves and all aspects of the event, Owen's insights led him to conceptualize a group dialogue process based on informality and people's ability to structure themselves: "Open Space has since become the operating system beneath some of the largest self-organising meetings the world has seen" (Bojer, Knuth, & Magner, 2006, p. 49).

OST meetings can last for 2 hours, an afternoon, or an entire weekend. The meeting begins in a large circle with one facilitator who welcomes participants to the OST, introduces the main theme, and explains how the agenda will be shaped by participants during the first hour who will propose sessions on topic areas they are passionate about and willing to take responsibility for. After discussing the four principles of OST and the one main law listed below, participants sign up for the small group discussions they have suggested and the process gets underway. Participants reconvene in the large circle near the end of the allotted time frame to share information across groups.

OST operates on the following four principles:

1 *Whoever comes are the right people*: Those who care enough about the need to enter into a dialogue about a particular subject will attend. This principle helps people let go of the idea that meetings should be attended by power brokers or experts.

2 *Whenever it starts is the right time*: Although meetings start at a specific time, creativity and inspiration are not time-bound dynamics.

3 *Whatever happens is the only thing that could have*: This principle gives people permission to let go of their expectations about meeting outcomes. It asks us to be present and to attend to what is happening and emerging in the moment.

 4   *When it's over, it's over*: Who can really predict how long it will actually take to address an issue? OST supports the notion that the issue is more important than the time frame. If the issue is not addressed in the time allotted, the group can self-organize another meeting time to continue with their work.

OST also has one law—"the law of two feet." According to this law everyone present is responsible for his or her own learning. If participants are in a small group where they are not learning or not feeling able to contribute, they are encouraged to move to another small group where they can "add more value, and feel more engaged" (p. 50). OST has been used internationally, in corporations, in townships, and in dialogue between countries in conflict. According to Harrison Owen,

> Open Space works best where conflict is present, things are complex, there is huge diversity of players and the answer was needed yesterday. The personal investment is critically coupled with a real sense of urgency among participants. The greater the diversity, the higher the potential for real breakthrough and innovative outcomes. (Bojer, Knuth, & Magner, 2006, p. 51).

Take a minute to think about OST and its potential to promote both teaching and learning in a group context. What do you envision as its teaching-learning potential? What might be some of its challenges and constraints? What values are this dialogical process based on? What facilitation skills would it require? Where might you implement OST?

Teaching and Learning—Communities

We addressed the importance of the community context of practice in Chapter 6. How do we learn about the communities in which we live and work and come to understand the commonalities and differences among concerns and interests of the residents? How do our ideas about what constitutes community shape the questions we ask and the strategies we use to learn about the community? And how do we teach the community skills helpful to promote community change? A number of community practitioners have created useful guides, strategies, and approaches for learning about the community context of practice. We highlight some of their important work here to illustrate possible approaches to build from and adapt to other situations.

Homan's Guide

Mark Homan (2004, pp.153-167) offers a helpful guide for getting to know your community. He writes, "the information you need to know about your community can be organized into five categories":

 1   Basic community characteristics (e.g., physical features, social features, landmarks, demographics, meeting places)

REFLECTION: Using OST to Set the Agenda for State Disability Planning

The following case example illustrates one way OST can be used to include the participation of people with disabilities in affecting policy change at the state level. As you read this story, think of the many and varied ways in which OST can be modified and applied to foster the participation of people in policy planning processes who are generally excluded from these efforts. What groups come to mind?

Elizabeth Lightfoot, Vicki Pappas, and Jeffrey Chait (2003) challenge the predominance of disability advocates, professionals, and agency representatives in policy planning processes meant to serve the interests of people with disabilities. The Developmental Disabilities Services and Facilities Construction Act of 1970 requires every state to have a Developmental Disabilities Council (DD Council) where 50% of the membership should be composed of people with disabilities or their family members. The Council's function is to create a state plan to guide funding and program decisions every 3 years. Light, Pappas, and Chait explain, however, that in general, Council membership is rarely in accordance with the requirements of the Act:

> The planning committee typically devises the goals and objectives of the plan and then asks citizens—often through public hearings or public forums—if they have anything to add to the final version of the plan. Although this certainly is a legitimate and efficient means of gaining public input, it provides little opportunity for people at the grassroots level to affect the initial development of the goals and objectives. (p. 7)

Although OST was not developed as a policy-making tool, the authors adapted it to create the space necessary for people with disabilities to participate meaningfully in the front end of the policy planning process in a Midwestern state. They provided more details to participants about the purpose of OST, used a facilitator at the initial phase of OST where discussion topics were generated, included a facilitator and scribe at each small group meeting, and added more structure to large group report-outs at the end of the session. Direct advantages and indirect benefits of using OST included:

♦ Increasing front-end participation in a nonthreatening policy-making process;

♦ Allowing for participation from people who have limited, if any, policy experience;

♦ Providing a nontechnical approach for people with disabilities to name issues relevant to their own experience;

♦ Creating a space for a broader range of potential issues to be addressed;

♦ Developing advocacy skills among people with various forms of disability including individuals with developmental disabilities, and;

♦ Educating participants about policies that directly affect service provision.

In the end, a significant portion of the state plan reflected input from the OST process. Lightfoot, Pappas, and Chait caution their readers about using this modified version of OST for appearances' sake alone, for example, where a session for people with disabilities is followed by one with the "experts." To protect against this possibility, they recommend having a multiple citizen-review process for the draft plan.

2 How the community functions to meet its members' needs (physical needs, social and emotional needs, economic needs, educational and communication needs, political needs)

3 Unmet needs (e.g., for services, resources, information, action)

4 Community resources (human, material, natural, intellectual, etc.)

5 Capacity for and disposition toward purposeful change (constraints and possibilities, desire, motivation, past experience, etc.)

These five categories provide a useful outline for initiating collective inquiry into community.

Henderson and Thomas's Guide

Henderson and Thomas (1987) have developed a guide entitled "Getting to Know Your Community" for neighborhood workers. They write, "We suggest that the following scheme be used by workers as a guide or checklist in their data-gathering activities, and not as an analysis to straitjacket their own perceptions of the particular and unique, community in which they find themselves working" (1987, p. 57). The six major categories they include are:

1 **History**: "Issues and problems of an area are connected to people, organizations and events in the past. Local people are often the best sources of historical data…" (p. 58)

2 **Environment**: Includes data on administrative and natural boundaries, population density, public space, transportation facilities, land use, and so forth.

3 **Residents:** Includes data on demographics, housing, employment, and general welfare, as well as information on community networks, people's perceptions of the area, and values and traditions.

4 **Organizations**: Includes data on local and central government, economic activities, religious organizations, and voluntary and civic associations.

5 **Communications**: Newspapers, radio and TV, information technology, people-to-people communication via posters, leaflets, and conversations.

6 **Power and leadership**: Includes business and organized labor, elective politics, administrative politics, civic politics, community politics. (pp. 57-68)

Generative Themes as a Guide

Another helpful approach to getting to know the community is by collecting and assessing generative themes. Communities of individuals have issues that resonate for them based on the shared, contextual nature of their experience (Freire, 1974). To understand the concept of generative themes think, for example, of a group of villagers in India who depend on the land for their livelihood. Now consider the issues and concerns that connect the villagers based on shared histories and experience. What might be some of the common issues and concerns raised by this group if, for example, the government proposed the construction of a dam that would flood their farm lands, displace them from their community, and threaten to wash away daily patterns and experiences and uproot relationships nurtured and sustained for generations? Might the villagers express a common felt affinity toward the land? And might these emotions wrapped in and layered with memories of births, deaths, and rituals evoke strong enough feelings to propel villagers to act?

Generative themes are issues that bring strong feelings to bear on the possibilities for sustained action. Tapping into these themes and eliciting their emotional content is one way of breaking through the barriers of apathy and powerlessness that keep people immobilized and incapacitated and prevent them from experiencing hope. Hopelessness is not a natural human condition (Hope & Timmel, 1999, V. 1). However, thwarted attempts at achieving a goal eventually create apathy. Looking for generative themes is one way to break the silencing power of oppression and stigmatization and channel this new-found strength toward creative action.

Think for a moment of generative themes that might resonate for you and the community you form with other students. Maybe you work long hours each week, parent children alone, and have a full course schedule at school. What stresses and strains do these conditions create for your well-being as a student and family member? What of tuition increases and the mounting price of textbooks? What common themes tie you together as a group?

Creating, identifying, and reflecting on common themes is an important part of the teaching-learning process. Identifying generative themes adds to the development of critical consciousness that links personal issues with the context of lived experiences (Freire, 1974; Hope & Timmel, 1999, V. 1). The process begins with an informal listening survey. To conduct a listening survey we must first learn to listen for the issues that resonate with the strongest emotions in people's lives. As Ann Hope and Sally Timmel note, "Only on issues about which they feel strongly will people be prepared to act" (1999, V. 1, p. 53). We highlight key steps, considerations, and guidelines for conducting a listening survey below. We refer you to Hope and Timmel (1999) for a more thorough explanation (see V. 1, pages 53-68).

♦ Whether you are working with an individual, a group, a neighborhood, or a community, the following questions should guide your inquiry: What are people worried about? Happy about? Sad about? Angry about? Fearful about? Hopeful about?

♦ Think of the survey as a team effort, and decide whom to include in the process based on specific training and attention to diversity. Be sure to include people who have insider information on the community, group, or individual level (e.g., relevant family members, local shop keepers, hairdressers, etc.).

♦ Remember to gather background information as well. This information could include statistics on community demographics, economic indicators, and previous studies completed that document community life.

♦ Conduct unstructured interviews that allow participants to tell their stories and feel relaxed in the process.

♦ Listen for themes that address basic needs such as housing, food and shelter, safety and security, love and belonging, self-respect, and personal growth.

♦ Make sure you cover six areas of life that concern people's well-being: meeting basic physical needs, relationship between people, community decision-making processes and structures, education and socialization, recreation, and beliefs and values. Remember to approach these issues sensitively with regard to cultural differences.

♦ Take advantage of listening sites where you can capture community members' spontaneous discussions. Sites could include grocery stores, sports and other recreational events, hairdressers, bars, places where people have to wait (i.e., doctor's offices, grocery store lines, movie theatre lines), and times before and after public meetings and events.

♦ Let people you interview know the full purpose of your questioning and what you intend to do with the information you gather.

♦ Gather facts as well as feelings. Remember that tapping into the emotional content of people's stories requires active listening.

♦ Most often, the strongest feelings will emerge in connection to the six areas of life. For example, changes in the local economy will have implications for employment and people's relationship to changing personal identities.

♦ Get back together with the team and identify themes that resonate most for the community, group, or individual.

♦ Analyze these themes critically as a group, paying particular attention to basic needs, community decisions, and values and beliefs. Then decide the relative importance of each theme.

♦ You might do this by using a chart, table, or grid. What do people comment on with the most frequency? What themes are most important? Which carry less weight? How do the themes connect to one another and create a picture of community residents' lives?

♦ Move through each theme and then decide upon one theme and brainstorm ways in which this theme could be presented visually through a play, picture, chart, or graph.

♦ In deciding on your visual representation for this particular theme think about the situation, the feelings involved, the difficulties, the problem, the obstacles, and the contradictions.

♦ Create a dramatization or drawing of the theme and decide what questions you would pose for discussion.

Hope and Timmel remind us that developing critical awareness begins with connecting peoples' lived experiences to "the structures of society that keep things the way they are. . ." (p. 53). The listening survey is one step in this process. They recommend that its results be combined with research already completed to provide documentation and statistics related to community life. In what particular situations might you find the listening survey useful? Are there ways you might adapt it to better suit your needs? How would you rate the listening survey as a potential teaching-learning tool? What might be its strengths and challenges?

You now have three frameworks to help you get to know a community. What do they have in common? How do they differ? How might they be used in the teaching-learning process? What steps would you take to facilitate a participatory process of community assessment? How would you decide what data to gather? Where would you look for information? What steps would you take to facilitate interpretation of the data?

REFLECTION: Conducting a Community Food Assessment

Maxine Jacobson describes a community food assessment (CFA) she helped facilitate with students, faculty, and a steering committee of community residents and key elements of the process (Jacobson, in press; Jacobson & Hassanein, 2004). A CFA is an integrated approach to addressing community food security that appreciates the connections between different aspects of the food system, which includes growing, harvesting, processing, packaging, transportation, marketing, consuming, and disposing of food. It is a tool that helps identify food-related issues, plan what to do about them, and gather local support to take action to address them. It is an integrative, systematic, and participatory process that combines many of the methods generally associated with social work practice such as community organizing, social planning, research, coalition building, and organizational and community development.

***

The Missoula County Community Food Assessment began in the spring of 2003 as a joint (ad)venture between a faculty member from the School of Social Work (myself) and a faculty member from the Environmental Studies Program at the University of Montana who shared interests in food issues and community-based participatory research. Initially, the approach was twofold: (1) to bring together a steering committee of community food system stakeholders to guide the process and provide community input and ownership, (2) and to design and teach a graduate-level course, experiential in nature, in which students would learn about the local food system and community-based research by helping conduct a food assessment. Under faculty supervision and guidance from the steering committee, students carried out much of the data collection and analysis for the food assessment. They learned valuable skills and earned course credits while making an enormous contribution to a community-based research project.

We used and modified some of the steps outlined by Kami Pothukuchi, Hugh Joseph, Andrew Fisher, and Hannah Burton (2002) in *What's Cooking in Your Food System? A Guide to Community Food Assessment* as a framework for the project. I touch briefly on the steps we followed below:

Learning about Other Community Food Assessments: We collected and reviewed a number of community food assessments that had been completed across the United States. They provided us with information on how others had tackled community food issues, limited their scope, decided research methodology, disseminated findings, and followed through with action strategies.

Recruiting Community Participants: We recruited a steering committee of 19 members representing different aspects of Missoula County's food system (e.g., food bank network, faith-based ministry, community development corporation, land trust, local farming, welfare rights advocates, etc.).

Defining Participants' Roles: Roles were clarified at the first steering committee meeting. Faculty were responsible for overseeing the research, facilitating the group process, keeping the project on course, and fund-raising. Students helped conduct the research, wrote reports, and contributed to decision making. Steering committee members attended monthly meetings, contributed expertise on various aspects of the food system, and helped identify and access resources.

Defining Assessment Purposes and Goals: We engaged the steering committee in a series of group exercises intended to help us identify what we wanted to achieve and the methods we would use to get there.

Planning and Facilitating the Process: We met for 2 hours each month with the steering committee and weekly with students. The amount of time it took to plan a meeting always exceeded and sometimes doubled or tripled the actual meeting time itself. The process took intense planning and well-thought-out facilitation to achieve an atmosphere in which people's time was respected and valued.

Limiting the Scope: This is probably one of the more difficult tasks—how to limit the effort, establish parameters, and stick with them. We focused strictly on Missoula County even though we were well aware that our food system crosses county borders. However, data indicating the current state of the food system is generally available at the county level.

Identifying Funding and Other Resources: We conducted the food assessment on a small budget ($6,500). Funds were used exclusively for materials, food, and events.

Planning and Conducting the Evaluation: We winnowed the number of questions we wanted to investigate from 70 to 2 that encapsulated the concerns of the entire committee. We developed surveys for consumers, conducted focus groups with low-income community residents and Hmong farmers, and conducted telephone interviews with local ranchers and farmers. Students and faculty conducted the research and steering committee members helped with the analyses.

Disseminating the Results: We got the word out about the community food assessment results through radio, newspaper, and television media, hard copy reports disseminated to agencies in the county, posters, a website (www.umt.edu/cfa), and community forums.

Evaluating and Celebrating: We shared food often, thanked people profusely for their help and support, and marveled at the community's wholehearted enthusiasm for the project. We evaluated each meeting and community forum.

Taking Action: Four major change actions were a direct result of the Missoula County Community Food Assessment: (1) the adoption of a joint city/county government resolution to increase the security of the local food system; (2) the formation of a multi-stakeholder, food policy coalition (Community Food and Agriculture Coalition) to address community needs related to food and agriculture in a comprehensive way; (3) the formation of a group of county residents who are organizing a public education campaign to address issues concerning the human right to food and how to increase resources to build a sustainable, self-reliant community food system; (4) and a USDA grant award for $200,000 to provide the infrastructure to develop and maintain a strong community-based food policy council; to bridge the gap between local producers and consumers by increasing consumers' access to nutritious local food and expanding markets for producers; and to organize groups of low-income people to identify shared concerns, inform policy change efforts, and build their capacity for participation in decision-making processes concerning community food security.

What do you think of the steps in the community food assessment process? Are there any you would add or leave out? In what ways could these steps be modified to address other community issues? How does this assessment compare to the other tools introduced in this chapter for getting to know your community?

Community Mapping

While not a framework per se, we introduce community mapping as a useful tool for getting to know the community. John L. McKnight and John Kretzmann (1990) have made important contributions to our understanding of assets-based community development. In their work on mapping community capacity they challenge "needs-oriented" approaches and focus instead on strategies for recognizing and promoting the capacities, skills, and assets of low-income people and their neighborhoods (p. 2). They frame "assessment" as a process of mapping the building blocks for community regeneration. Whereas McKnight and Kretzmann use mapping to illustrate community assets, others involved in community change use it to achieve alternative purposes (Amsden & VanWynsberghe, 2005; Chambers, 1997; Nelson & Baldwin, 2004; Phadke, 2005).

Comprehensive neighborhood mapping (CNM) has been used to address issues of children's safety in Edinburgh, Scotland, in a marginalized neighborhood where a high proportion of children and single mothers live (Nelson & Baldwin, 2004). The philosophy of CNM is rooted in the belief that local knowledge can illuminate the connections between different forms of harm to children and the development of effective strategies to address their protection. CNM "is a technique for imaginatively gathering and interpreting information relevant to young people's safety within a given geographic area which involves agencies and communities in partnership in identifying problems and seeking solutions" (p. 415). The CNM process is an attempt to augment the work of the child protection system by building in additional safeguards informed by neighborhood residents. Besides enumerating the risks of sexual abuse, the mapping also identified dangerous physical environments, including unsafe buildings. The process also focused on neighborhood strengths such as informal networks of communication and support, a history of involvement in the arts and drama, and a tradition of community activism and campaigning. Project results revealed common concerns among agency stakeholders and community residents and a commitment to co-learning. As a whole the process and results were easily understood by all residents, easier to apply than survey methods, and reflected the priorities of residents more accurately than other approaches to understanding the community.

Amsden and VanWynsberghe (2005) report on a project in which youth living in Vancouver, B.C., used community mapping as a participatory research tool to learn about and evaluate health clinics in the area. The authors premise their work on recognition of the failure of the current social welfare system to adequately meet the needs of an increasingly diverse and "socially divided" population. Operating from a policy model whose primary goal was to support, include, and empower citizens, the project's work was guided by the following questions: "What supports and what challenges your health as you grow to adulthood?" . . . "What is an ideal health service?" (p. 360). The authors define community mapping as a "visual and relational data-gathering technique that can be used to document not just geographical, but also other forms of abstract data" (p. 361). They outline steps in the map-making process, which include establishing an atmosphere of trust, creating an empowering space, setting a clear focus, creating an open space, and encouraging collaboration. Once supplied with colored pencils, magic markers, and crayons, youth responded to the research questions by drawing graffiti-style images, features of an ideal health clinic including a swimming pool, dance hall, and waiting rooms equipped with computers and televisions. Youth, along with an adult advisory committee, created the maps, coded the symbols represented on the maps, and summarized the information. The issues most relevant to youth concerned the accessibility of health services; the creation of a friendly, inviting atmosphere where differences were accepted and medical staff were open, nonjudgmental, and good listeners; and where "receptionists don't treat me like a criminal when I ask for help" (p. 365). What uses could you make of a community mapping approach to teaching and learning about the community? What might be some of the strengths of this approach? What challenges might you have to confront?

REFLECTION: Whose Voices Count?

Rinku Sen, in her article on "Building Community Involvement in Health Care" (1994), challenges the absence of the voices of poor people of color in shaping the public health care system in the United States.[3] Viewing the national health care debates through the lens of People United for a Better Oakland (PUEBLO), a community-based direct action and service organization, she poses critical questions: Will we ever have enough power to care for ourselves as we should? What is the role of government in providing for the basic human needs of all members of a society? How do we fight for reform that will allow greater local and cultural control over health care options and practices? How can we build an investment in the notion of "community" and the skill level in community members themselves that will lead us to solutions to the myriad health problems that plague our communities? Sen documents the efforts of poor people of color, working collectively, to challenge and change the power relations between themselves and the health care system. PUEBLO's approach to improving health care was based on three goals: (1) building a sense of community by collectivizing problems and defining common solutions, (2) challenging the institutionalized behavior and practices of health care providers and administrators, and (3) developing indigenous leaders well-versed in different aspects of health care. PUEBLO members invited community residents to come together in neighborhood churches and schools, identify common and immediate problems people were experiencing in health and health care, identify concrete differences in the ways people wanted to experience their health care, and advocate for institutional change. PUEBLO won a number of local victories: Parents are able to get their children immunized for free on weekends and evenings; the county hospital is providing translators for non-English speaking people to communicate with health care workers; and early diagnosis and abatement of lead poisoning is underway.

Based on her experiences with PUEBLO, Sen proposes a people's movement-based approach to envisioning and designing a new health program. The first step would be to recruit credible community organizations committed to health care issues to take on the project. Lead organizations would coordinate face-to-face visits with community members to learn about their health care needs, current access to care, their overall health, their wishes for how things could be, and the kinds of home remedies and cultural practices they and their families use to deal with health problems.

Sen writes: "As we meet people for initial purposes of the interview, we would recruit them to join the organization and help us to find out the same things from other people. We would work through whatever structures gave the most access to people's time: through door knocking, at house meetings, on long supermarket lines in poor communities (our supermarkets have the longest lines) or at the local check-cashing place. I would get children in schools to draw pictures and write essays about their families' experiences with health care. With time from students, community-health practitioners, volunteers, and whoever else I could put out in the community, this process could take anywhere from 2 to 6 months.

"When we finished the process we would tabulate the results, including anecdotes and examples of great health care and terrible health care. I would gather people locally to examine the results of those interviews and collectivize our experiences, including firsthand testimony from people willing to share. I would then hold a meeting with key leaders and staff from each of the cities to compare research experiences and data.

"The next step would be to relate our findings to a wide range of surrounding questions. What kinds of practices can we imagine to address health needs? What kinds of health practices exist locally or elsewhere that would address our problems? How do our culturally established cures compare with the practices of modern Western medicine? What are the current public health institutions doing that works and doesn't work? Which institutions are closest to the community and which are removed? How should health care in our community be funded, regionally and nationally? What kinds of changes would we make in key institutions for increased access and improvements in quality? What would it cost to test, then establish our ideas into programs, and how would we finance them? What other kinds of resources could we engage?

"I would get to these questions through a series of discussions or study groups, each discussion informed by local and broader research conducted by members, each discussion designed as a tool for simultaneous use by the lead organizations to raise consciousness, analysis and proposals for change...."

Based on her community-based experiences with PUEBLO, Sen proposes that a process that really engaged communities of color would result in a list of ideas that would include the following:

♦ Comprehensive programs for peer education.

♦ Free or low-cost food programs that provide fresh, nutritious food.

♦ Health-care options indigenous to cultures of color, generally ignored or blatantly dismissed by the American medical establishment.

♦ Open space and organized (non)competitive and individual athletics activities, particularly for girls.

♦ Attractive, clean, and prolific public transportation.

How does Sen approach the process of teaching-learning? What strategies for participation does she use? What elements of "systematization" and "diagnosis" can you identify here? How does her approach fit with the practice of social justice work? How does her vision of health care fit with or challenge your own?

Learning about Organizations

Social work happens in and with organizations. The primary place of employment for most social workers is within the context of an organization, and organizations can take many shapes and forms depending upon practice method, philosophy, and area of focus (e.g., children and families, community development, etc.). Similar to families, every organization has a unique culture and its own specific way of functioning based on history, community context, and particular patterns, rituals, and procedures. These elements affect our work with people. For example, what message is conveyed in an organization offering assistance to children and families when front office staff are located behind bullet-proof glass partitions? In the following section we describe several frameworks for learning about organizations. Think about the types of information each framework would provide. How do these differ? What about them is the same? What important elements might be left out? What underlying assumptions are communicated about the nature of organizations? What values?

Appreciating Organizations

Sarah Michael's (2005) field research using Appreciative Inquiry (AI) opens up new possibilities for learning about organizations. AI is a teaching-learning tool that can help an organization renew a commitment to reflect upon itself, create ideas about its future, and inspire a group of people to move in that direction. Michael explains,

> AI is founded on the *heliotropic principle* borrowed from biology and the common amateur gardener, which notes that plants grow towards their source of light. It is believed that, in the same way, people and organisations move towards what gives them light. As such they will be drawn towards positive images of the future and positive actions, based on the affirming, energizing moments of their past and present" (p. 222).

As part of her research in Senegal, Tanzania, and Zimbabwe on the power of local African NGOs (nongovernmental organizations), Michael crafted a set of interview questions to ask organization directors to provide her with rich information about organizational history, experiences, and external relationships to stakeholders. Her list included 22 questions all framed from AI perspective. For example, she asked directors, "What's your favorite memory of working here?" "What part of your work are you most proud of?" "What do you like best about your job?" Michael's initial concerns were that an AI approach would fail to produce information representative of the dynamic, sometimes troubling and tense, environments characteristic of organizations pushed and pulled by the current economic and political climate. Michael asks:

> Would the appreciate approach I was using give interviewees the impression that I understood nothing about the realities of their work and wanted only to hear the now commonplace rhetoric on the importance of NGOs and what a great job they do? Would they perceive my appreciative questions as belittling their difficulties and seeking to cast a rosy glow over them? (pp. 224-225).

After completing 60 interviews she discovered that directors "were eager to tell their stories; offered dynamic and unrehearsed information; and spoke more openly, with less defensiveness or fear of reprisal" (p. 226). Some directors even reported enjoying the interview and having fun.

Getting to Know Organizations through Appreciative Inquiry

Take some time to read Michael's article to more fully understand the underlying philosophy of Appreciative Inquiry and the questions she crafted for her interviews. Then, together with classmates, develop an interview protocol to learn about the social work organizations in your community. What questions do you develop based on an AI philosophy? Test out your protocol by slecting a handful of organization directors to interview. Once you have completed the interviews, share your experiences with your classmates. Were your experiences similar to those described by Michael? What comments did directors make about the interview process? What did you learn about the organizations by using an AI approach? Were you still able to gather information about organizations that provided you with an impression of their strengths as well as their challenges? What does an AI approach teach you about teaching-learning?

A
C
T
I
O
N

Guide to Getting to Know Your Organization

We draw on the theoretical insights of practice theory discussed in Chapter 5, to develop a guide to getting to know your organization. Consider the questions in Table 7.1 (p. 290) from the perspective of your work or practicum setting. As you respond to these questions do you find you have a better grasp of the organization and your location within it? These questions help us flesh out issues of meaning, power, history, and possibility that shape and are shaped by the organizational context of practice. Our social work positioning is never neutral, and we need to be cognizant of our organizational location as we learn about how it functions and how we can function within it.

How does the guide help you with learning certain aspects of your organization? How would you rate it as a tool for getting to know your organization? How does it compare to the framework described by Michael? What assumptions about organizations are embedded here?

Learning about People in Interpersonal, Familial, Communal, and Historical Contexts

Let us now turn to approaches to learning about people's contextual experience. Considerable attention has been paid to an ecosystems approach to individuals in the context of family, with assessment focusing on two broad dimensions: family history and relationship to other systems in the environment (Garvin & Seabury, 1997, p. 216). Social workers have developed and used a number of assessment tools grounded in an ecosystems perspective and designed to help us learn about people's experiences in families and communities. We introduce and describe two commonly used tools here—the ecomap and the genogram. We provide examples of how others have interpreted these tools and expanded upon their application. Recall from our discussion of theory in Chapter 5 that once a framework is developed, it lays the groundwork for ongoing development as social work practitio-

Getting to Know Your Organization

Mission	What is the mission of the organization? How does it define its meaning and purpose? Has the mission changed over time?
History	What is the organization's history? Where does it fit in a larger political, social, and economic context?
Structure	How is the organization structured? What is the system of governance? How are decisions made?
Power	How is power defined and distributed? What are sources of formal and informal power? Does the organization have the power of legal authority or sanction? Does it have the material power to provide or deny resources?
Participants	Who are the people likely to be involved with the organization? As employees? As "clients," "members," "recipients," etc.? What distinctions are made among different participants?
Communication	What are the formal channels of communication in the organization? How does information flow? What are the informal channels and sources?
Activities	What kinds of activities are associated with the organization's work? Are they broad-based or specialized? Where do they occur? How do they relate to the mission?
Funding	How is the organization funded? How does funding influence organizational activities?
Resources	What resources are available to the organizational participants? What resources are lacking?
Perceptions	What are the public perceptions of the organization? How is it seen by outsiders? How is it seen by employees? By its clientele? What does it mean to be associated with the organization as a "worker," "patient," "inmate," "member," "volunteer," "client," etc.?
Your Position	Where are you located within the organization? What is your role and the scope of your responsibilities? What is the purpose of your position? How does it relate to fulfillment of the organizational mission?
Supports	Where are your sources of formal organizational support? Of informal support? Where might you find support beyond the organization?
Barriers	Where have you encountered barriers in the organization? What activities or opportunities have they blocked? How have you attempted to address them? Have you been successful?
Values	What values are officially expressed by the organization? What values are demonstrated in everyday practice? Where have you encountered value tensions?
Possibilities	Where do you see possibilities for social justice work in this organizational context? Who might join with you in pursuit of social justice work?

TABLE 7.1

ners, and researchers build upon the contributions to knowledge completed by others by filling in the gaps and revising tools based on alternative perspectives. Think about how you might do the same based on your own areas of interest. [4]

The Ecomap and Some Adaptations

The ecomap provides an opportunity for identifying, illustrating, and examining key aspects of a person's social context, sources of support and stress, flows of energy and resources, and patterns among them (Hartman & Laird, 1983). Generally, the tool is used in a context of dialogue between social worker and "client." With the help of prompts and questions posed by the social worker, the client maps out her current situation. Figure 7.1 below illustrates the ecomap.

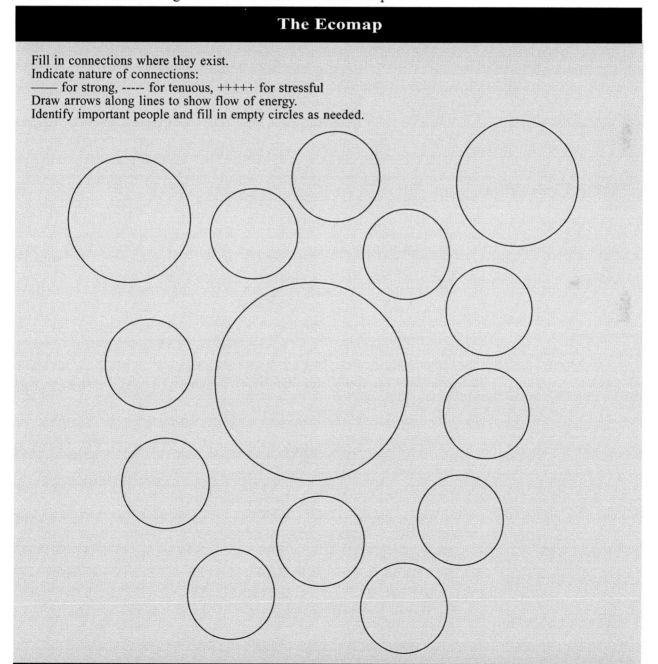

The Ecomap

Fill in connections where they exist.
Indicate nature of connections:
—— for strong, ----- for tenuous, +++++ for stressful
Draw arrows along lines to show flow of energy.
Identify important people and fill in empty circles as needed.

FIGURE 7.1

In the map, the "client" (large circle in the center) identifies people and social systems that are part of or that affect her current life situation. She links the systems to herself and possibly to one another with lines that mark the direction of energy and resource flow in the relationship and the nature of the relationship. For example: a solid, bold line (——) indicates a strong relationship; a dotted line (-----) indicates a tenuous relationship; and a slashed line (+++++) indicates a stressful or conflicted relationship. Arrows are used to indicate the directions of energy and resource flow (toward the client, away from her, or a two-way flow). The ecomap provides a visual window into the person's current life circumstances.

The map imposes little and allows for the person drawing it to illustrate her own social relationships and consider the patterns that connect. It can create openings for teaching-learning dialogue. However, the ecomap only gives us a glimpse of a moment in time, with little sense of history or of the larger structural arrangements and practices that may have shaped the immediate context and relationships illustrated in the map. Take a moment to think about the ecomap as a resource for social justice work. Where do you see its possibilities? Its limitations? How might you modify this tool to fit particular teaching-learning situations?

We include several examples to help spark your imagination. David Hodges (2005) points to the increased recognition of spirituality as a necessary component of the assessment process by social workers and other helping professionals. He describes spirituality as a "core animating principle in client's view of reality" (p. 314) and a source of and window into client strengths and coping strategies during times of stress. Once spiritual resources are identified, these can provide the basis for treatment planning. Hodges has developed a number of assessment tools to assist in gathering information about clients' spirituality. These include spiritual histories, lifemaps, genograms, ecomaps, and ecograms (Hodges, 2005). We highlight Hodges' spiritual ecomap and refer you to his work for descriptions of these other tools and their strengths and limitations.

Similar to the ecomap developed by Hartman and described above, the spiritual ecomap focuses on the client's present spiritual assets and the family system's connection to spiritual systems or domains in the family's immediate environment. Hodges reports that the ecomap can be used "to explore clients' relationship with God or transcendence, rituals, faith communities, and transpersonal encounters" (p. 320). Circles outside the domain of the family therefore could include churches and other places of worship, fellowship groups and other groups whose underlying purpose is to connect people with similar faith-based beliefs, and transpersonal encounters. The core of the spiritual ecomap is assessing the relative strength or weaknesses of a client's relationship to spiritual resources. Spiritual ecomaps are strength-based, provide a focal point for discussing spiritual matters, and may help clients "externalize" their problem to the broader systems functioning in their lives. On the other hand, spiritual ecomaps, similar to other diagrammatic approaches to assessment, may simply create a barrier between client and worker and prevent the earnest exchange of information related to spirituality. As client and worker attend to the piece of paper between them, important human connections can be lost.

Nancy Vosler (1996) uses the ecomap to identify family issues related to economic stress. Whereas some families may have developed ingenious methods for coping with financial distress such as tapping into the resources of extended family networks, others may not have access to or developed these resources.

Vosler's (1990) theoretical framework rests on understanding the effects of the larger political, social, and economic environment on families and "the link between symptoms and chronic stress from lack of basic economic resources" (p. 434). Figure 7.2 shows a household ecomap we have created that illustrates a situation wherein a single-parent family lacks sufficient connections to resources. Vosler (1990) indicates "how symptomatic families [such as the one described in Figure 7.2] are easily blamed for their inability to provide for the basic needs of family members" (p. 435). How might this particular focus of an ecomap on economic, financial issues, and connections (or lack thereof) to social service resources help in the teaching-learning process?

Household Ecomap: Family Unconnected to Resources and Stressed

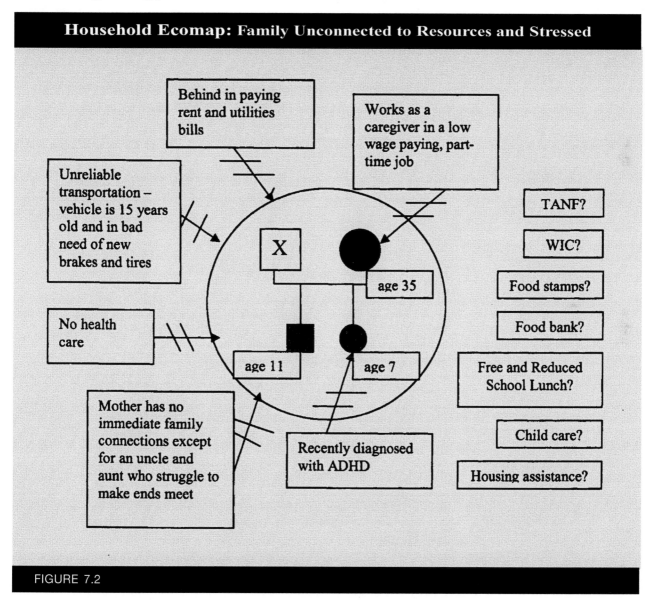

FIGURE 7.2

Janet Finn shares a teaching-learning experience that offers yet another way to envision the ecomap:

> In my first year of teaching an undergraduate social work practice course, I spent one class period introducing and discussing the ecomap. The class members were to prepare their own ecomaps

over the course of the next week. One of my students was a young woman who was blind. We had previously discussed ways to make the classroom and the learning experience more accessible. She had already taught me a great deal about being a better teacher for all students in the class, not only those with disabilities. She stopped me after class and said she would like to try her hand at reinventing the ecomap. She wanted to explore ways to make it meaningful for other people who are blind. The following week she returned with an ecomap that captured the attention and imagination of the entire class. She had created a mobile with index cards and paper plates indicating people and systems. Interlocking paper clips lent material force to conflicted relationships while rubber bands linked people and systems in flexible and reciprocal relationships. Delicate threads represented tenuous connections. Each plate and card contained information in Braille about the person or system. The student became the teacher and gave her classmates and me an opportunity to see the ecomap from a different perspective. Her creativity sparked that of others who began to wonder out loud about alternatives. For example, class members talked about the potential to engage children in creating their ecomaps in the form of mobiles or other creative designs. We not only gained knowledge about a single tool, but we also gained knowledge of the possibilities that emerge from co-learning.

The Genogram and Some Adaptations

Another commonly cited social work tool for learning about individuals in the context of family is the genogram. The genogram borrows from anthropological kinship studies and focuses on the mapping of intergenerational family relationships (Hartman, 1978). Proponents of the genogram see it as an important complement to the ecomap. The genogram contributes a historical perspective lacking in the ecomap. It can also serve as the base for exploration and discussion of family relations, cultural practices, and traditions. The genogram focuses on the intergenerational extended family, and it is represented visually as a "family tree." The genogram is created in a collaborative teaching-learning process with social worker and "client." It includes basic information including the ages of family members, marriages, divorces, separations, and deaths. It may be elaborated to include additional information such as place of birth, employment, and so forth. The product represents a "client-centered" perspective on her family and her relation to family members.

Figure 7.3 gives an example of a genogram representing three generations. The following symbols are used in creating the genogram: Males are represented by squares and females by circles. A straight horizontal line connecting two people indicates a marriage (_____). Cross slashes through the line indicate divorce (//). Some people use a dotted line to indicate cohabitation as opposed to marriage (. . . . .). The children of a particular union form the next tier of circles and squares and are listed oldest to youngest from left to right.

The genogram can provide a foundation to facilitate discussion about family relations, history, patterns, struggles, and support. Some people improvise with the

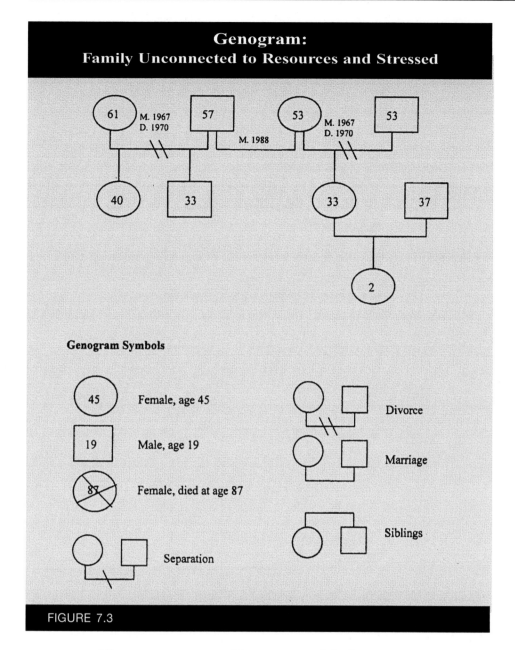

Genogram:
Family Unconnected to Resources and Stressed

FIGURE 7.3

genogram, adding on components of the ecomap and finding ways to visually represent additional information. According to Garvin and Seabury (1997, p. 228), the genogram is helpful in gathering the following assessment information:

◆ What behavioral patterns have occurred in the family that have persisted through several generations?

◆ What are the sources of mutual reinforcement of values in the family as well as sources of value conflict?

◆ What resources exist that are or could be of help to the family subsystem incorporating the client system?

◆ What are the kinds of issues related to the family's beliefs and common experiences that function either to limit the family's problem solving and decision making or to enhance it?

Numerous scholars and practitioners have experimented with the genogram's potential as an assessment tool, created new formats and procedures, and highlighted different foci for its use. Sandy Magnuson and Holly Shaw (2003) review the relevant literature in this area and in so doing, map out the historical evolution of the genogram. They describe the genogram's use with couples to explore family-of-origin issues concerning sexuality, intimacy, and gender dynamics and how these influence decision making, communication patterns, and rules established to address them. For example, in the process of creating a genogram a couple might be asked questions such as, "What were you taught about sexuality as a child?" (Hof & Berman, 1986, p. 43, as cited in Magnuson & Holly, 2003, p. 48),. "Does intimacy occur most frequently during fights or during quiet times?" (Sherman, 1993, p. 92, as cited in Magnuson & Holly, p. 48), and "What did your father/mother teach you about being male/female?" (White & Tyson-Rawson, 1995, as cited in Magnuson & Holly, p. 48). Magnuson and Shaw also discuss, for example, how genograms have been used in the treatment of alcoholism to help stepfamilies understand the complexities of family structure and relationships, to address issues of grief and loss, to document the multiple foster care or residential placements of children, to identify family strengths, and to increase trainees' awareness of and sensitivity to cultural diversity. In what ways might you apply the genogram or modify this tool for relevance in another area of practice other than those suggested above? What seems to be missing in these discussions of the genogram?

Mapping Your Family Story

ACTION

Take time outside of class to prepare your own genogram. Feel free to make it as simple or elaborate as you wish, according to what best represents your concept and experience of "family." After you have completed the genogram, take time to reflect on the feelings this exercise evoked for you. Are there gaps in your knowledge of family history? Do you have questions about who counts as "family" and where to draw the boundaries? Does the exercise bring back memories of loss? What have you learned from your own experience in completing the genogram that may heighten your critical awareness about using this tool with others?

Janet Finn notes, *Class discussions around the genogram have been provocative. Some have chosen to map their genogram on a 3 x 5 index card, while others have used yards of newsprint. Some people have found themselves profoundly moved by memories of a deceased loved one. Some have found the exercise to be an opening for hearing the untold stories of their ancestors. Others have found it difficult to map ties to family that have been fraught with tension. People whose experience in family has been one of numerous separations and recombinations have difficulty mapping their complex histories. They have said they would need color-coded transparencies to do justice to their "family tree." Some have chosen to include social or "fictive" kin—close friends and neighbors who have become part of family through ties of reciprocity and social support. Those with histories in adoptive and foster families have sometimes found themselves wary of a genogram—who and what counts as "family"? To whom? Other students have commented on marriage and heterosexual partnerships in the textbook illustrations of genogram, thus indirectly communicating a norm of what counts as a "proper" family. Take a few minutes to reflect on your genogram in light of these experiences. Which ones resonate for you? Why? What can we learn here from others' experience with the genogram about diversity and difference?*

Assessing Individual Strengths

In Chapter 5 we discussed the strengths perspective and its contributions to social work practice. Assessing collective or individual strengths is grounded in a philosophy that contests the dominant approach to labeling, diagnosing, and otherwise identifying deficiencies and deficits as the basis for assessment and planning (Saleebey, 2006). Social workers are recognizing the importance of identifying abilities, values and interests, cultural beliefs/practices, life contributions, and protections and supports as potential sources of information that provide a balanced approach to assessment with elder clients. In reaction to assessment of the elderly using tools heavily influenced by the medical model, Helen Kivnick and Shirley Murray (2001) present a framework for gerontological assessment that balances problems and assets to help with intervention planning. They display graphically the personal assets and problems elicited during interviewing by using a balance scale to illustrate that aging is not necessarily synonymous with asset loss. They report that while the elderly are teaching the practitioner about their strengths and limitations, they are also learning that their strengths are not confined to the past and can be reactivated in the present. We include Kivnick and Murray's guide for conducting an assessment with elderly clients.

Strengths Assessment Interview Guide

1. What makes a day a *good* day for you? What do you hope for at the start of a new day?

2. What are the things you do, each day or each week, because you really want to, not because you have to? When you get totally absorbed, forget about everything else, and the time seems to fly?

3. What are you good at? What kinds of things did you used to be good at? What about yourself has always given you confidence or made you proud?

4. What kinds of exercise do you do regularly? What kinds could you do to help you feel better?

5. What kinds of help, service, or assistance do you give? To whom? What help or service would you like to give?

6. When you get out, what do you like to do? Where do you like to go? What would you like to do? Where would you like to go?

7. What lessons have you learned about how to cope with life from day to day? Are there ways you wish you could cope better?

8. Who are the people that are especially important to you these days? Tell me about these relationships.

9. What physical things or objects do you have that are most precious to you? What things do you save? Or take special care of? If you had to relocate, what things would you take with you? (Kivnick and Murray, 2001)

What other questions might you ask to learn about an elder person? Are there some listed you might omit or modify? If so, why? In what other ways could you apply the guide? How could you modify it for other areas of practice?

REFLECTION: The Diagnostic Strength Manual[5]

An assessment tool that many social workers are likely to become intimately involved with, especially if they enter the field of mental health, is *The Diagnostic and Statistical Manual* (DSM-IV-TR) compiled and produced by the American Psychiatric Association. The DSM presents a classification system of mental disorders used by mental health professionals in the United States and elsewhere around the world. The primary intent of the DSM is to clearly and categorically differentiate one mental disorder from another. It offers a list of specific behavioral criteria, the degree of severity, and the duration of symptomotology necessary to label and render a specific diagnosis or assessment of an individual's mental state. The DSM-IV is a powerful tool that informs the language base of psychological assessment and popular culture. It creates a common nomenclature for those engaged in mental health work directly or indirectly, which includes the pharmaceutical industry, law, and health insurance companies.

Dennis Saleebey (2001) comments on the enormous popularity and extraordinary influence of this assessment tool despite the fact that "it provides an insufficient and hard-to-operationalize conceptualization of mental disorder" (p. 183). He points to the disturbing absence of alternative explanations for depression when, for example, about 80 or 90 physical illnesses include symptoms of depression. He makes a similar point with the diagnosis of Attention Deficit Hyperactivity Disorder, better known as ADHD. Saleebey argues that the diagnostic framework of the DSM makes it virtually impossible to consider or make an accounting of the assets, talents, capacities, knowledge, survival skills, personal virtues, or the environmental resources and cultural treasures such as healing rituals and celebrations of life transitions that a person might possess—despite or, in some cases, because of their difficulties and trauma. (p. 184)

Saleebey provides an accounting of client strengths and resources all but forgotten in the DSM's quest to pinpoint deficits and deficiencies. These include, for example, qualities such as persistence, insight, patience, and a sense of humor; the ability to tell stories of healing and perseverance, falls from grace and redemption; the skills to play bagpipes, garden, cook and juggle. Based on a student's suggestion, Saleebey recommends that all students working in a mental health placement should complete "a strict accounting of the merits and strengths of clients and the resources in their environment" (p. 185). Saleebey offers a counter narrative to the DSM by developing what he calls Code 300: Estimable Personal Qualities. We include several examples of Saleebey's version of a strength-based diagnostic tool below:

301.0   Trustworthiness
   A.   For at least 6 months, nearly every day, the individual has exhibited at least three of the following:
   - has done what he or she promised
   - kept at a task that had many snares and difficulties
   - did not reveal a confidence
   - stuck by a relative, friend, or colleague during a rough time
   - did more than expected.
   B.   This is not better explained by codependency or a pathological desire to please.
   C.   Such behavior must have improved the lives of other people.
   D.   Rule out the possibility of a self-seeking desire to cash in on these loyalties later.

302.0   Patience
   A. For at least 6 months, nearly every day, the individual has exhibited at least three of the following:
   •   held his or her own wishes in abeyance while allowing a young child or a dependent to struggle to master a behavior
   •   demonstrated forbearance in the face of a serious delay, not of his or her own doing, in achieving an important goal
   •   calmly endured serious challenges and stresses occurring in the environment
   •   exhibited tolerance and understanding when confronted with a personal situation that defied personal values and standards of taste
   •   maintained equilibrium and steadfastness in the midst of a situation of rapid change and transition.
   B. This is not better explained by sedative, hypnotic, or anxiolytic abuse.
   C. Such behaviors have a positive, calming effect in stressful situations.
   D. Such behaviors do not interfere with taking assertive action when it is required.

Besides trustworthiness and patience, what additional personal qualities could you highlight that would be important to a comprehensive, "whole-person" assessment process? How do these examples from Saleebey's version of a diagnostic strengths manual, although "a bit frivolous" (in his own words), make a point about the heavy reliance on assessment tools to label and pigeonhole behavior, emotion, and life experience? Saleebey asks social workers to consider what practices might look like if equal effort were expended toward "understanding life's real problems and the virtues of the people who suffer them" (p. 186).

Challenges of Teaching–Learning

As we stated at the beginning of this chapter, teaching-learning is an ongoing process that requires openness to multiple ways of knowing and critical awareness of the partiality of our knowledge and experience. Remaining open to co-learning is no small task in a Western context replete with messages about the need to make rapid-fire decisions and to "move on" and "get it done" for the sake of efficiency and expediency. The teaching-learning process is ripe with rewards for increased awareness of self and others. However, it is a humbling, time-consuming process that requires considerable attention to how to sustain the effort, how to balance contributing our knowledge without taking over the process, and how to admit we are wrong when our ideas are challenged. Teaching-learning demands that we grapple with meanings of power on both personal and professional levels and come to understand how it works in our own lives.

Expanding the Possibilities of Teaching–Learning

Throughout this chapter we have encouraged a collaborative approach to teaching-learning that appreciates different ways of knowing and being in the world. We agree with Reed et al. (1997) that social justice work demands that we move beyond "diversity" and actively engage with the meaning and power of difference. Encounters with radically different worldviews and belief systems remind us of the partiality of our knowledge and challenge us as learners. In the next section of this chapter we include several examples of assessments that challenge us to consider, for example, economic structural arrangements that affect family well-being; positive, appreciative ways of engaging with and learning about community; and learning from and through difference. We hope they promote critical reflection and discussion about the possibilities of co-learning that emerge once we break out of our taken-for-granted assumptions about how the world works. We begin with a tool that helps us consider the economic effect on family functioning.

Family Access to Basic Resources

Nancy Vosler (1990, 1996) has developed a number of important assessment tools that highlight *structural stress* and how this plays out in the lives of families. She points to the plethora of assessment tools developed to address "multiproblem," "troubled," "at-risk," "dysfunctional," and "multideficit" families and the absence of assessment tools to assess how broader structures in the environment affect family functioning. Vosler makes no assumptions that the "services and structures necessary for healthy family functioning are in place and simply need to be accessed and mobilized by the family. . ."(1996, p. xii). She critiques, for example, family therapy, a model of practice based on white, middle-class families as the norm. To address this oversight Vosler developed a tool referred to as the Family Access to Basic Resources (FABR). We summarize elements from the assessment tool here and encourage you to refer to it in its entirety (Vosler, 1990, pp. 436-437; Vosler, 1996, pp. 191-192). We include it here as an example of an assessment tool based on the theoretical premise that families living through economic hard times experience stress. Stress manifests itself in a wide variety of behaviors that go into the production of the labels highlighted above. Vosler pushes us to get at root causes.

Areas Included in the Family Access to Basic Resources (FABR)

- **Monthly expenses for a family of this size and composition**
  Work expenses (transportation, child care, taxes)
  Purchases for basic needs (decent housing, utilities, food, etc.)
  Health care (medical, dental, mental health, etc.)
- **Potential monthly family resources**
  Money income (wages, child support, income transfers)
  Credits, goods, and services (housing, food, clothing, education, etc.)
- **Current resources (access to resources last month)**
  Money income
  Credits, goods, and services (housing, food, clothing, education, etc.)
- **Resource stability (How stable was each resource over the past year?)**
  Wages
  Child support
  Income transfers
  Housing
  Food
  Clothing
  Personal care and recreation
  Health care

Education
Family and developmental services
Procurement (bus, car, etc.)
Other comments and reflections

In explaining how the FABR works, Vosler states,

> This vital knowledge will enable the family and the social worker
> to understand specific stressors, because family members are likely
> to blame themselves or other family members when resources are
> not available. Few family members or professionals have been
> taught to look for stressors in the structured lack of access to ad-
> equate resources. (1990, p. 438)

How does Vosler's approach to family assessment support a social justice-oriented practice? What does she think is important to learn from families? What might using this information teach families about their situation given the focus of the questioning? How does this approach differ from other approaches to family assessment you have used or know about? Let us now turn to an assessment tool based on the principles of Appreciative Inquiry you were introduced to by Sarah Michael in this chapter, only in this example the focus is on developing a community profile.

Rethinking Community Health Assessments

Brenda Talley, Alison Rushing, and Rose Mary Gee (2005) use a process called unitary appreciative inquiry (UAI) developed by Richard Cowling (2001) to capture patterns of wholeness or what he refers to as *overarching panoramic aspects of life patterns* innate in persons, families, groups, and communities. As Cowling explains, to appreciate pattern is to "perceive, be aware of, sensitive to and to express the full force and delicate distinctions of something while sympathetically recognizing its excellence as experienced in gratefulness, enjoyment, and understanding" (Cowling, 2001, p. 19). Talley et al. describe four forms of knowledge generated through the UAI process:

1. *Experiential knowledge* occurs through the immediacy of participation and relationship with another, a place, or a thing. It may manifest as descriptions of everyday experiences in unique ways or through mutually shared or created group expressions.

2. *Presentational knowledge* emerges from expressing meaning and significance through such forms as art, music, images, movement, films, drama or the like, or any combination of these.

3. *Propositional knowledge* consists of ideas or theories expressed in informative statements. This form of knowledge emerges from a synopsis/synthesis of shared information and helps to form the basis for factual claims that are unique to the phenomena.

4. *Practical knowledge* involves identification of information that may be useful in developing skills or competencies. It allows for the

establishment of purposive strategies to achieve capacity building, leadership development, and personal and community empowerment. (p. 32)

Talley et al. used the UAI process with RN-BSN students enrolled in a community health nursing practicum to create a community profile. The authors began by conducting a meditation exercise with students to prepare them for "entry" into the community. Students were asked to do the following:

♦ Check out their attitude about the community. Acknowledge any prejudices, fears, concerns and put them out of your way.

♦ Practice noticing. Hear what people have to say, what they talk about, think about and what they mean.

♦ Relax and allow the community to tell its story to you. Engage with the community.

♦ Feel yourself immersing into the community and connecting with the people who live there.

♦ Look at them with eyes of respect and with a valuing approach. Be thankful for them and what they can share with you. Appreciate them and their way of life.

♦ Also value your own intuition and your own ways of knowing.

♦ Find joy in the experience and keep it with you. (pp. 32-33).

Students began the inquiry by walking around the small rural community, exploring shops and just generally "hanging out." They collected community information on demographics, statistics, infrastructure, newspaper headlines, photos, stories, and sounds. And they collected more subtle information, some of which we outline in Table 7.3 on the following page.

Together, students, faculty, and community members created a synthesis of the information gathered. In this case, they wove it together into a story about the community that made use of poetry, music, and photography. How could you make use of UAI as a tool for getting to know your community? What questions might you ask? The next teaching-learning tool and the story that precedes it provides some challenges to our culture-bound notions about health, illness, and medicine.

Difference and the Cultural Meaning of Illness

While we may verbalize an appreciation of cultural difference, the proof is in the practice, when our most deeply held and unquestioned beliefs are challenged. In this section we consider a case in which fundamentally different systems regarding the meaning of health and illness collide, with tragic results. Understandings of health, illness, prevention, and treatment are embedded in cultural systems. They cannot be understood outside of an appreciation of those meaning systems. Cultural meaning systems shape how we learn to categorize "symptoms" into an illness, where we look to explain causality, and who we turn to for cures.

	Examples of Questions for Community Health Assessment Using UAI
Spirit	What do you feel as you walk through town? Do people greet you with a cheerful "good morning!" or do they smile or stare at you silently?
Flow	Does the community feel closed off from other communities? Is there a feeling of "insider-outsider?"
Experience	What has happened in the community? What are people proud of? Has this community experienced disaster—has the only manufacturing plant closed and now many are unemployed?
Expectations	Do residents see this community as dying, or do they see it staying much the same or growing? Are things going to get better.....or worse?
Attitudes	How do residents feel about change in their community? How do they feel about strangers and about each other? How do they define being healthy or being sick? Do they "take care of" their own?
Values	What behavior is okay and what is not? Are people expected to work if they are able to or is it okay (or even expected) to be on social programs?
Esthetics	Look at the buildings. How are the streets and homes kept? How important are esthetics to the community?
Rhythms-Movement	How do things happen every day? Can you "set your watch" by the behaviors?
Time Sense	Is the past a frequent reference or do people speak of the future?
Hopes and Fears	Do residents speak of a bright vision for the future or do they fear for the survival of their children?
Relationships	How important is family? What is meant by family? Who talks about whom? Do there seem to be divisions along economic, racial, or ethnic lines?

Source: Talley, B., Rushing, A., & Gee, R.M. (2005). Community assessment using Cowling's Unitary Appreciative Inquiry: A beginning exploration. *Journal of Rogerian Nursing. 13*(1), 27-40.

TABLE 7.2

In her book *The Spirit Catches You and You Fall Down* (1997) Anne Fadiman tells the poignant story of Lia Lee, a Hmong child diagnosed with "epilepsy," and the cultural collisions that occur between her family and her American doctors as they give meaning to and seek to treat her illness. Her newly arrived refugee parents understand illness as "soul loss." They seek aid from Shamans; but also, as they struggle to make a life in the United States, they try to follow some "American" expectations regarding illness and healing. Lia's California doctors understand illness through the belief system of Western biomedicine and intervene based on their own expertise. While both the family and the doctors want the best for the child, the lack of understanding between them has tragic consequences.

Fadiman educates readers about the culture and history of the Hmong people.

She examines critically the power of medical institutions and state bureaucracies to force compliance when the dominant view of proper intervention is challenged by cultural difference. Fadiman sought out help from a medical anthropologist in trying to understand and perhaps bridge the gulf of incomprehension that separated the Lee family and the practitioners of Western biomedicine. Fadiman writes:

> Trying to understand Lia and her family by reading her medical chart (something I spent hundreds of hours doing) was like deconstructing a love sonnet by reducing it to a series of syllogisms. Yet to the residents and pediatricians who had cared for her since she was three months old, there was no guide to Lia *except* her chart. As each of them struggled to make sense of a set of problems that were not expressible in the language they knew, the chart simply grew longer and longer, until it contained more than 400,000 words. Every one of those words reflected its author's intelligence, training, and good intentions, but not one single one dealt with the Lee's perception of their daughter's illness. (p. 260)

The "Patient's Explanatory Model"

Fadiman turned to the work of physician and medical anthropologist Arthur Kleinman to better understand the difference of cultural meanings and the meaning of cultural differences here. Kleinman (1980) has designed a set of eight questions to help elicit the "patient's explanatory model." The questions are simple and seemingly obvious. And yet, they are seldom asked. Taken-for-granted assumptions about the problem and the possibilities of intervention too often get in the way. However, posing these questions to the patient or patient's family can open a new terrain of teaching-learning. The answers can be rich in material to promote understanding of cultural difference and disrupt the certainties informed by a Western biomedical view. Here are Kleinman's questions:

- What do you call the problem?

- What do you think has caused the problem?

- Why do you think it started when it did?

- What do you think the sickness does? How does it work?

- How severe is the sickness? Will it have a short or long course?

- What kind of treatment do you think the patient should receive? What are the most important results you hope she receives from this treatment?

- What are the chief problems the sickness has caused?

- What do you fear most from this sickness? (Kleinman, 1980, as cited in Fadiman, pp. 260-61).

Take a minute to reflect on these questions. What fundamental issues of difference do they address? What basic assumptions do they challenge? What are some implications for teaching-learning in a context of cultural difference? What sorts of questions do they suggest for use in the context of social justice work?

Assessing the Assessment Tools

This exercise gives you an opportunity to learn about the ways practitioners in your community assess problems and strengths. As a class, identify five or six areas of social work practice that you want to learn more about (e.g., child welfare, aging, mental health, school social work, etc.). Break into groups, with each group focused on one of the identified practice areas. In the small group, identify several local agencies or groups that address this area and divide the list among group members. Each member takes responsibility for contacting an agency or organization, arranging a time to discuss the assessment process with an organizational representative, and requesting copies of tools, forms, or guidelines used in making an assessment. Reconvene in small groups to assess the assessment tools. The following questions serve as a guide; however, new questions may arise from the group discussions.

- ◆ What values are reflected in the tool?

- ◆ What assumptions are made about the cause of problems and directions for intervention?

- ◆ What assumptions are made about the person or group being assessed (e.g., assumptions about age, gender, ability, etc.)?

- ◆ What aspects of a person's life are addressed? What aspects are not addressed?

- ◆ Does the tool take a problem-focused approach?

- ◆ How are strengths addressed?

- ◆ What is the norm against which "deviance" is assessed?

- ◆ What sort of language does the tool use?

- ◆ Does the tool promote participation in the assessment process?

- ◆ What do you see as the possible strengths of this tool? The possible limitations?

- ◆ How would you assess the tools in terms of the criteria outlined by Rosemary Link in Chapter 4 (pp. 147-148)?

A C T I O N

CHAPTER SUMMARY

In this chapter we have developed the concept of teaching-learning—a collaborative process through which we give meaning to experience, learn about concerns, and systematically develop, share, and reflect on knowledge of those concerns. We have addressed the importance of teamwork in the teaching-learning process and outlined the foundational skills for effective group work. We have examined questions of power and power relations in the teaching-learning process and have pointed to the importance of making power a talkable theme. We have introduced a number of approaches for systematic inquiry into organizational and community contexts of social work practice and for learning about people in familial, communal, and historical context. We have challenged readers to question taken-for-granted assumptions regarding notions of family and offer possibilities for systemically learning about gender, culture, power, and difference in the context of family. In Chapter 8 we consider the possibilities for translating the process and outcomes of teaching-learning into concrete action plans. As Cecilia Díaz (1995) reminds us, action and reflection will yield new understandings and bring us to new points of departure for further teaching-learning.

Life and Death in Libby, Montana[6]

C A S E   S T U D Y

Libby, Montana, is nestled in a valley in the northwest corner of Montana, alongside the Kootenai River. For generations many of Libby's 11,000 residents have made a living in the timber and mining industries. Over the past two decades, Libby has fallen on hard times. First, the local saw mill closed and then the W. R. Grace & Company's vermiculite mine shut down. Residents have tried to rebuild their economy around the possibilities of tourism and the hopes of selling their enticing scenery and their proximity to prime fishing and hunting spots and the famous landscape of Glacier National Park, only a couple of hours away. But a more troubling danger lurked in the shadows of Libby's history, one that was taking its toll in the lives of hundreds of residents.

For the past 40 years, disease has claimed the lungs and lives of residents throughout the valley. Many miners and their family members were suffering and dying from asbestosis, a terrible disease resulting from asbestos exposure that causes a thickening of the lungs and slow death from suffocation. Others were suffering from tumors, cancers, and other respiratory illnesses. Miners at the W.R. Grace vermiculite plant would come home from work each day with their clothes and bodies covered in a fine white dust. The dust settled in their homes, on their furniture, and on the bodies of their loved ones. Their wives breathed it in even as they tried to clean it up. Their children inhaled it as they hugged their fathers and played on the living room floor. W. R. Grace told its workers the dust was merely a nuisance. What the company knew and did not reveal was that the dust was actually microscopic asbestos fibers that would settle in their lungs and eventually sentence them to death (Vollers & Barnett, 2000).

Nearly 200 asbestos related-deaths have been documented in Libby since the 1960s, and approximately 1,200 other residents suffer from some form of asbestos-related illness (Jalonick, 2005; U.S. Department of Justice, 2005). In December 1999, after hundreds of people had been stricken with lung problems, and after a local family filed suit against W.R. Grace over their mother's death, the Environmental Protection Agency launched an investigation. Their evidence pointed to the W. R. Grace mining operation as the source of Libby's massive health crisis. While the mine and mill workers suffered the greatest exposure, the rest of the town also got daily exposure. Mine dust was dumped down the mountainside and poured into the air from the plant's ventilation stack. "By W.R. Grace's own estimates, some 5,000 pounds or more of asbestos were released each day. On still days, some of it settled back on the mine site. When the wind blew from the east, a film of white dust covered the town" (Vollers & Barnett, 2000, p. 55).

Moreover, vermiculite ore packed with lethal concentrations of asbestos was packaged for export at a plant next to the town's baseball diamonds. The area was surrounded with piles of discarded ore. Libby residents, unaware of the risks, carted bags of the discarded ore home for their gardens. Vermiculate itself is harmless. It has been used in insulation and in potting soil. But the vermiculite deposit at Libby is laced with tremolite—the most toxic form of asbestos. W.R. Grace & Company knew the dangers of asbestos. Corporate memos dating to the 1970s document that 63% of the mine employees with more than 10 years of service tested positive for lung ailments and that a number of young men suffered from "obvious asbestos disease." W.R. Grace officials did not inform the people of Libby, and they did not offer effective safeguards to miners and residents. In fact, their own company memos recommended stall tactics to delay further investigation of and action on the health hazards posed by the mine operations (Grand Jury Indictment, 2005).

Over the past 7 years, Libby residents have been submitted to medical screenings to determine the state of their health. The EPA has continued to assess the extent of the damage done to people and the environment. In 2000, under pressure, the company agreed to pay for the medical expenses for residents affected with asbestos-related diseases. A nonprofit clinic, the Center for Asbestos Related Disease (CARD), was set up in Libby to care for the hundreds of sick and dying residents (Johnson, 2006). And year by year, the numbers of confirmed cases of asbestos-related ailments have increased. CARD sees approximately 20 new patients a month. Kimberly Rowe, a nurse and clinical coordinator at CARD, states, "We're seeing more and more people, and younger people, but our clinical resources are the same" (quoted in Johnson, 2006, A, 3, p. 1)

As the extent of human and environmental devastation came to light, some political leaders expressed their outrage that an entire community had suffered from the unconscionable acts of a single company. Others met behind the scenes with company executives and tried initially to find a "quiet" solution to the toxic problem that would not hurt business interests and relations. Libby residents themselves have struggled with the toxic realities of the asbestos contamination and the implications for individual, family, and community survival. Some have taken a fatalistic approach and argued that mining has historically been dangerous work, and this is one more story in the tough saga of labor history. Some who have been untouched by the illness worry that the problem may be blown out of proportion. Some watch their loved ones struggling for each breath or witness the telltale signs in X-rays of their own lungs, and wonder when the inevitable symptoms will begin. Many simply want their town cleaned up and fear that the ongoing media attention to Libby's toxic troubles will further endanger an already precarious local economy.

Since 2000, there has been ongoing debate regarding responsibility for cleaning up the town and responding to the residents' health care needs. While there was nearly unanimous agreement that W.R. Grace must be held accountable, few trusted the company to take charge of the cleanup. In fact, as the EPA began to take action, W. R. Grace responded by obstructing the investigation and filing for bankruptcy to avoid responsibility for the personal injury claims stemming from asbestos exposure. In 2001, the Libby mine and related W. R. Grace properties were designated a Superfund cleanup site, and the EPA has spent over $120 million to date in the cleanup effort (Johnson, 2006). In 2005 Montana Senator Max Baucus introduced legislation that would force the company, by then operating under bankruptcy protection, to put $250 million in a health care trust fund for the victims of asbestos exposure in Libby (Jalonick, 2005). The U.S. Department of Justice has gone further, bringing criminal charges against W. R. Grace and its top management. In February, 2005, a federal grand jury indicted W. R. Grace and seven current and former executives for "knowingly endangering the residents of Libby,

Montana, and concealing information about the health effects of its asbestos mining operations" (U.S. Department of Justice, 2005). The federal criminal trial has been set for the fall of 2006. The corporate machinations continue, from requests for change of trial venue to actions on the part of the company's medical plan administrator to obstruct the operations of CARD (Johnson, 2006). Residents of Libby continue to live with the toxic consequences of asbestos, the uncertainty of their future health, and the fear of losing access to health care. The following account is a case in point:

> Two asbestos-diseased Libby residents have been forced to live out their retirement in the Kirkland home of their daughter where every day is nothing more than a struggle to survive. . . The husband worked in the vermiculite mine in the 1950s before leaving to pursue a different line of work. The family eventually returned to their home in Libby by 1966, where they lived until 2005. While the husband was faced with asbestos exposure on a daily basis via mining operations, his wife believes her only source of contact came from washing his clothes and living in the overwhelming shroud of asbestos dust cast over the town from the W.R. Grace & Co. mining operation.
>
> Fortunately for this asbestos-diseased couple, they maintain a private insurance plan; however, between Medicare deductibles and prescription drug costs, they are still paying in excess of $1,000 per month in expenses. Originally hoping to spend their retirement years together enjoying the twilight of their lives, the couple is relegated to a room in their daughter's home where they struggle for each and every breath. Their only escape from the confines of the house is the frequent doctor/hospital visits that consume increasing amounts of their time and energy. (MESORFA, 2006).

There is no doubt that asbestos has taken a tremendous physical, social, economic, and political toll. What is less clear is how those affected can best participate in the multiple levels of decision making that affect their health and lives. What issues of social justice work can you identify here? What questions of meaning, context, power, history, and possibility come to mind? What might be possible roles for social justice work in the community? What issues of difference might you confront? Develop a plan for conducting a participatory community assessment. Which of the frameworks introduced earlier in this chapter for getting to know a community might you use? What criteria would you use to make your decision about the best approach to use in the teaching-learning process? What issues of cultural difference would you most likely have to address in preparation for your assessment? Where and how would you look for additional information? What obstacles might you encounter? How would you involve community members in the process?

For further discussion and action, arrange a showing of the film *Libby, Montana*, a powerful 2004 documentary by Missoula, Montana-based filmmakers Drury Gunn Carr and Doug Hawes-Davies. The film captures the character of the residents, the history of mining, and the struggle for accountability in the wake of this toxic tragedy. For more information visit the High Plains Films website at http://www.highplainsfilms.org/.

Questions for Discussion

1. How would you proceed in developing a plan for building community involvement in health care in your community? How would you assess the situation? Who would you involve? Why?

2. Choose one of the methods of systematic inquiry discussed in the chapter and explain how you would apply this method in practice.

3. Use one of the family assessment tools presented in this chapter. What do you see as its strengths? What do you see as its weaknesses?

4. In what ways have your beliefs about health and illness been informed by a Western biomedical view? In what ways have your beliefs been informed by differing perspectives on health and illness? Think for a moment about some of the "folk" practices of medicine in your experience, such as your cure for hiccups. What beliefs inform these practices?

5. You have had the opportunity to apply Díaz's Five-Step Process to a current issue in your community. In what other contexts might you use the process? Give an example.

Suggested Readings

Barber, J. (1995). Politically progressive casework. *Families in Society: The Journal of Contemporary Human Services*, 76(1), 30-37.

Fadiman, A. (1997). *The spirit catches you and you fall down.* New York: Farrar, Strauss, andGiroux.

Solomon, B. (1976). *Black empowerment.* New York: Columbia University Press.

Stack, C. (1974). *All our kin: Strategies for survival in a black community.* New York: Harper and Row.

Townsend, J., Zapata, E., Rowlands, J., Alberti, R., & Mercado, M. (1999). *Women and power: Fighting patriarchies and poverty.* London: Zed Books.

Werner, D. (1977). *Where there is no doctor.* Palo Alto: Hesperian Foundation.

End Notes

[1] Permission to present skills of mutual aid, based on excerpts from Lawrence Shulman (1999) *The skills of helping individuals, groups, and families* (3rd ed.). Courtesy of F.E. Peacock Publishers, Itasca, IL.

[2] Marianne Bojer, Marianne Knuth, and Colleen Magner (2006) completed a research project whose goal was to profile dialogue tools and processes for social change. The project's report describes twenty-five tools and case examples to illustrate how many of these have been applied, some cautions and challenges, and a matrix outlining the purpose for which each tool is best suited. We refer you to this concise yet thorough compilation of resources for facilitating the teaching-learning process in a group context. www.pioneersofchange.net

[3] Permission to reprint excerpts from Rinku Sen (1994), "Building community involvement in health care," *Social Policy*, 24(3), 32-43, courtesy of *Social Policy*. Copyright by Social Policy Corporation.

[4] Permission to utilize adaptation of ecomap courtesy of Ann Hartman and Joan Laird. This is a very brief introduction to the ecomap. We refer readers to Ann Hartman and Joan Laird (1983) *Family-centered social work practice*, New York: Free Press. For a concise guide to a range of frequently used social work tools see also Kim Strom-Gottfried (1999) *Social work practice: cases, activities, and exercises*. Thousand Oaks, CA: Pine Forge Press.

[5] Title and excerpts are from: Saleeby, D. (2001). The diagnostic strengths manual. *Social Work*, 46(2), 183-187.

[6] This case study is based on Maryanne Vollers and Andrea Barnett (2000) "Libby's Deadly Grace," *Mother Jones* (May/June): 53-59, 87; Kirk Johnson (2006) "In Old Mining Town, New Charges Over Asbestos," *The New York Times*, April 22, Section A, Column 3, National, p. 1; U.S. Department of Justice Press Release, February 7, 2005, "W. R. Grace and Executives Charged with Fraud, Obstruction of Justice, and Endangering Libby, Montana Community," www.usdoj.gov; Mary Clare Jalonick (2005) "Baucus bill would force W. R. Grace to Provide health Care for Libby Residents," *Billings Gazette*, September 28, 2005, www.billingsgazette.com/newdex.php?display=rednews/2005/09/28/build/state/18-wrgrace.inc ; Mesothelioma Research Foundation of America (2006) Patient Stories: Libby, Montana: A Town Rife with Asbestos Disease (www.mesorfa.org/patient/patient6.php); and Josh Cable, (2005) "Grand Jury Indictment: W. R. Grace Lied About Dangers of Asbestos Exposure," February 8, 2005, *Occupational Hazards* www.occupationalhazards.com/articles/12965.

8

Action and Accompaniment

> *"It was so important. It was really a beautiful thing, women coming together to work together. We started small and we learned everything. We learned we were capable, we could do this. We talked and laughed and it was so special. It was a road to a new life of learning. It was a beautiful experience working and learning together, block by block, helping each other"*
>
> Pobladora (1999), Villa Paula Jaraquemada, Chile[1]

> *We are not passive objects which professionals are responsible for "rehabilitating." Many of us find this connotation of the word rehabilitation to be oppressive. We are not objects to be acted upon. Rather we are fully human subjects who can act, and in acting change our situation… Recovery does not refer to an end product or result. It does not mean that one is "cured" nor does it mean that one is simply stabilized or maintained in the community. Recovery often involves a transformation of the self wherein one both accepts one's limitations and discovers a new world of possibility."*
>
> Patricia Deegan (1996), Recovery and the Conspiracy of Hope

CHAPTER OVERVIEW

In this chapter we explore the interwoven processes of action and accompaniment. Action entails the diverse activities of planning, supporting, decision making, mobilizing resources, motivating participants, challenging barriers, and following through in creating change. Action occurs in the company of others. A challenge of social justice work is the integration of being in relationship with others, doing the work, and becoming more critically aware and capable in the process. It is in this spirit of being, doing, and becoming that we pair action and accompaniment. We want to challenge a view of action as technical implementation of a series of "interventions" and consider it instead as always carried out in the context of social relationships. So we emphasize accompaniment as part of the change process as a reminder once again that we are not "Lone Rangers." The relational aspect of social justice work demands ongoing attention and respect. We address the concepts, processes, and contexts of action and accompaniment and the roles of social justice workers therein. We draw examples from social workers across diverse arenas of practice to illustrate the possibilities. We explore challenges and questions of power and difference involved in action and accompaniment. We present skills and practice of action and accompaniment and the possibilities for their integration on multiple fronts in pursuit of social justice.

CONCEPT AND PROCESS OF ACTION

We are very intentional in the use of the word "action" here. As Kelly and Sewell (1988) remind us, social work is about the work—the hands (and feet) that put ideas to practice. Action is inseparable from thought and feeling, but thought and feeling devoid of meaningful action is at best insincere and at worst one more form of violence and violation. We recognize the place and possibilities of multiple participants in processes of change. We have also chosen the word "action" as a way of distinguishing the process from what most social work texts refer to as "intervention." We do this for two reasons. First, "intervention" carries with it a connotation of the expert acting on a passive subject (Allan, 2003; Deegan, 1996; Ife, 2001). In keeping with a model of mutuality and dialogue we have developed thus far, we contrast the Just Practice approach with this sort of top-down model. As Patricia Deegan suggests in the opening quote, those who carry the stigma of "diagnoses" and bear the weight of labels such as "client" and "patient" are so much more than that. By speaking of action we honor the human agency of all participants in the process. Second, "intervention" suggests the application of technologies and techniques; action, on the other hand, is a more fluid concept, suggestive of the emergent and dynamic nature of "making plans and dreams real," of translating critical consciousness into concrete claims, or of resisting oppression (Locke, Garrison, & Winship, 1998). Action simultaneously encompasses the personal and the political, doing and becoming—the grounded work and the transformational potential.

Many social workers who approach practice from a strengths, empowerment, or critical perspective have challenged top-down, unilinear models of intervention with the social worker as expert. Rather they speak of the "praxis" of social work—the ongoing interplay of action and critical reflection. They frame action in terms of liberation, transformation, and empowerment (Allan, 2003ab; Blundo, 2005; Saleebey, 2006). Dennis Saleebey, for example, writes of strengths-oriented action in terms of liberation, empowerment, hope, and the heroism of everyday life (pp. 7-8). Working from an empowerment perspective, Miley, O'Melia, and DuBois (2007, p. 108) describe the ways in which *dialogue* (engagement) and *discovery* (teaching-learning) build toward *development*, or action, which may include activating resources, creating alliances, expanding opportunities, recognizing success, and integrating gains. Action includes a vision of a future and of an alternative reality (Allan, Pease, & Briskman, 2003). Structural social workers such as Maurice Moreau have framed the action of social work in terms of three registers of practice: (1) *immediate tension relief*, which entails helping people cope with the concrete situation at hand through practices of support, education, brokering, mediation, and advocacy; (2) *group tension relief*, which entails longer-term collective efforts to address conditions that are adversely affecting people through practices of consciousness raising, mutual aid, and collective action; and (3) *working toward elimination of oppression* through work carried on outside the bounds of human services organizations, such as labor solidarity work, human rights campaigns, and peace and justice movements (Moreau, 1977, as cited in Allan, 2003a, pp. 55-56). Our concept of action broadly encompasses these understandings and also challenges us to look toward elimination of oppression and promotion of social justice *within* the bounds of human service organizations.

Action, then, can take many forms. It may be manifest in caring, protection, support, and nurturance. It may be realized through teaching of skills and political education; through exercises in consciousness raising; in confrontation and demands for work; in brainstorming, planning, and decision-making activities; through mediation, negotiation, and conflict resolution; in advocacy, organization building, and direct action campaigns; and through collaborations, coalitions, and legislative initiatives. Resistance and refusal may also constitute powerful forms of action. Whatever forms our actions take, a distinguishing feature of just practice is that we do not "guard" our actions and the skills that inform them as professional "secrets." Rather, we share them with others, thereby expanding the capacities and skill repertoire of all participants. Later in the chapter we explore forms and skills of action, illustrating how they cut across arenas and contexts of practice.

CONCEPT AND PROCESS OF ACCOMPANIMENT

Accompaniment is the actual people-to-people partnerships through which action is realized. It represents another facet of practice where we are once again reminded of the commitment to collaboration and dialogue over the long haul and to the interplay of power and possibility that shapes practice. Traditional approaches to the change process in social work often refer to the "monitoring" of intervention. The notion of monitoring positions the social worker outside the process and in the role of overseer. It places the burden for action on others and suggests that the worker retains the power of scrutiny. The language of monitoring disconnects the worker from her relationship to the participants in the process. We find the notion of accompaniment more conducive to the values and assumptions of social justice work.

In its simplest terms, accompaniment means to go with, to support and enhance the process. We often hear this word used in reference to music. The dictionary defines accompaniment as "a vocal or instrumental part that supports" the principal part (American Heritage Dictionary, 2000). While this definition alludes to accompaniment as secondary to the principal part, it would not be the principal without support. Each part complements the other and together produce a richer and more complex whole.

We develop our notion of accompaniment from the work of Canadian social workers and educators Elizabeth Whitmore and Maureen Wilson, both of whom have extensive practice experience in Nicaragua. They were inspired by the work of their Latin American colleagues in collaborative efforts of community change (Whitmore & Wilson, 1997, p. 57-58). Whitmore and Wilson describe the relationship of social justice workers to the communities, groups, and individuals with whom they are engaged as one of "*acompañamiento,*" a Spanish term that best translates as accompanying the process. Whitmore and Wilson, describing their work as North American social worker/scholars working in collaboration with colleagues in Nicaragua, write, "We are attracted to this way of expressing such a relationship precisely because of its inherent clarity about who owns and controls the process: our partners do; it is *we* who accompany *their* process" (p. 58). They have identified a set of principles of accompaniment, which have applicability to a variety of settings. These include

1. nonintrusive collaboration,

2. mutual trust and respect,

3. a common analysis of what the problem is,

4. a commitment to solidarity,

5. equality in the relationship,

6. an explicit focus on process, and

7. the importance of language (Wilson & Whitmore, 1995).

Wilson and Whitmore argue that these principles parallel both feminist principles and the attributes of a good social worker. They advocate an approach to accompaniment that combines both "structural and conjunctural analysis with the interpersonal skills so essential to effective collaboration" (Whitmore & Wilson, 1997, p. 58). They contend that a true partnership of equals calls for the democratization of information flow, collaborative knowledge development and dissemination, and action networking. Participation cannot be confined to "local" arenas but must also engage political activity in broader arenas. Accompaniment calls for a deep appreciation of process and a sense of dignity and hope. It is a process of "participatory alignment" that attends to the ways in which marginalized people become critical agents of transformation, going beyond personal troubles to public issues (p. 61). Accompaniment demands ongoing critical attention to questions of power and the power differences among the participants in the change process. Accompaniment is a process of joining across diverse borders to build mutual trust, explore possibilities for cooperative work and division of labor, and create a two-way movement of people, knowledge, and power (see also Whitmore & Wilson, 2005).

The rich understanding of accompaniment presented by Wilson and Whitmore resonates with a number of other conceptualizations of the relational component of action. For example, as noted in Chapter 6, Paul Farmer powerfully describes the practice of bearing witness to the suffering, humanity, and determination of those most violated by the forces of oppression and inequality. His concept of bearing witness links practices of engagement and accompaniment. Farmer argues that human rights abuses are best understood from the point of view of the poor. Those of us committed to social justice work must, then, work in solidarity with the poor; bear witness to the ways in which "large-scale forces become embodied as sickness, suffering, and degradation" (2003, p. 19); and commit our voices and actions to the elimination of what Farmer terms "pathologies of power."

Reflection on Accompaniment

Scott Nicholson, a social worker and human rights activist who works in western Montana and in Colombia, has worked in solidarity with union organizers in Barrancabermeja, Colombia, accompanying them as a human rights "witness" to try to ensure their safety in the face of persistent death threats. For Scott the personal and the political are absolutely inseparable in his human rights action and his deep bonds of love for the activists and their families with whom he works. Scott tells his story below.

I'm accompanying leaders of social organizations in the state of Arauca in Colombia. These leaders have been threatened with death by the right-wing paramilitary groups—which have close relations with the Colombian military. They're also at risk of being imprisoned or killed by the government security forces. Our compañeras and compañeros ("beloved companions") have requested this accompaniment because the paramilitaries and the military are less likely to take action in the presence of international witnesses. Ironically, because the U.S. government is financing this paramilitary and military repression ($3.8 billion in military aid to Colombia from 2000 to 2006) I enjoy a relative degree of protection. If the paramilitaries or the military were to harm someone from the U.S., that could jeopardize their funding.

For me, international accompaniment is a life-transforming gift that I'm receiving from our compañeras and compañeros. They're risking their lives to construct peace with social justice. The radiance of their example touches the depth of my being and inspires me to be in solidarity with them in their struggle. The intensity of the situation forges deep relations of love and solidarity that are more difficult to encounter in the U.S. and take longer to develop there—but that are equally beautiful. I believe that these relationships are the heart of the "just practice" of social work and of genuine spiritual experience.

A central component of accompaniment is bearing witness to the suffering caused by U.S. economic and military intervention, and then transmitting this reality to the people in the U.S. so that we can take action to transform those policies. It's also important to experience and transmit the joy and celebration of our compañeras and compañeros, and the ways in which they're implementing their vision for justice. The goal is not to leave us depressed and overwhelmed, but to inspire us to join together in the creation of social justice.

My vocation is to be a bridge for our compañeras and compañeros in reaching out to the people of the U.S. I take photos and write their "testimonios" (declarations of their lived experiences) and share these via e-mail. I then use these words and images to give presentations in the U.S. One of my favorite activities of bridge-building is organizing U.S. speaking tours for some of these amazing and inspiring community activists. I have the privilege of interpreting their words into English as they touch our hearts with their testimonios and inspire us to join in solidarity with them.

Last evening, I was speaking with Graciliano Carrillo. He described how the Colombian military killed three social leaders from Arauca—Alirio Martinez, Jorge Prieto, and Leonel Goyeneche—on August 5, 2004. "Their physical being died but their spirit lives on in the seeds they left behind—those of us that are continuing their struggle for justice."

In love and solidarity,

Scott Nicholson
Saravena, Arauca, Columbia, July 14, 2006

Brief description of Arauca:

Arauca is one of the most war-torn regions of Colombia. Occidental Petroleum has a huge oilfield and pipeline that is being protected by the Colombian and U.S. military. More than one hundred community leaders have been killed in the past 4 years (2002 to 2006), and more than a hundred others have been imprisoned on charges of "rebellion" (source: Joel Sierra Regional Human Rights Committee). The people of Arauca have a long and inspiring history of organizing and resistance, and they're continuing forward with their struggle to achieve peace with social justice. The slogan of the social organizations is "Arauca exists, insists, and resists!"

Accompaniment is also central to the practice of hospice care, in which volunteers join with the person who is dying and share in the journey. Through her MSW practicum experience in hospice care, Melanie Trost, a graduate of the University of Montana School of Social Work, made the connection between the process of accompaniment in *Just Practice* and that of companioning the dying. Melanie taught us about the work of Alan Wolfelt (2004) on companioning and shared some of the tenets:

♦ Companioning is about walking alongside; it is less about leading or being led.

♦ Companioning is more about curiosity; it is less about expertise.

♦ Companioning the dying is often more about being still; it is not always about urgent movement forward.

♦ Companioning is about being present to another's emotional and spiritual pain; it is not taking away or fixing it.

♦ Companioning is about going into the wilderness of the soul with another human being; it is not about thinking you are responsible for finding a way out.[2]

A notion of accompaniment is also present in Bonnie Benard's (2005) discussion of the significance of caring relationships in the stories of resilient survivors of child sexual abuse. According to Benard, survivors talk about relationships characterized by "quiet availability," "fundamental positive regard," and "simple sustained kindness." Caring people who conveyed compassion and demonstrated "active genuine interest" played important roles in nurturing and sustaining the resilience of survivors (p. 200). In this sense, we can imagine accompaniment as the ongoing melding of relationship and action. Catherine Faver (2004), in turn, provides further food for thought on the process of accompaniment. In writing about women's relational spirituality and social caregiving, Faver describes ways in which women of faith talk about the fundamental connectedness of spirituality and social justice in their lives and work. Faver writes, "many described a sense of sacred companionship that pervaded their lives" (p. 244). Thus, for some, social workers and participants alike, accompaniment may have a spiritual as well as a social and political dimension. Action and Accompaniment go hand in hand, whether in the group solidarity of a march for peace and social justice, or in the quiet availability of one-to-one connection with another person.

ACTION AND ACCOMPANIMENT IN CONTEXT

We have developed the concept of *context* and explored ideas about diverse contexts of social work practice in earlier chapters. We ask readers to keep questions of context in mind as we explore action and accompaniment. Our actions and relations are always embedded in contexts, which shape the nature of the interpersonal encounter, the power relations among participants, the goals and pathways of action, the available resources, and the outcomes. Social justice work calls for the affirmation of context, as opposed to the "context stripping" that has characterized too much of traditional, problem-focused social work. As Saleebey (2006) argues,

> When we transform persons into cases, we often only see them and how they fit into a category. In this way, we miss important elements of a client's life—cultural, social, political, ethnic, spiritual, and economic—and how they contribute to, sustain, and shape a person's miseries, struggles, or mistakes. The irony here is that, in making a case, we really do not individualize. Rather we are in the act of finding an appropriate diagnostic niche for the individual, thus making the client one among many and not truly unique. All individuals suffering from bipolar disorder hence become more like each other and less distinctive. In doing this we selectively destroy or at least ignore contextual information that, although not salient to our assessment scheme, might well reveal the abiding distinctiveness of the individual in this particular milieu. It might also indicate important resources for help and transformation as well as problem-solving. (p. 6)

Challenging Oppression and Creating Contexts of Support

Questions of trust, power, and authority and courses of action may look very different in the context of child protective services than in the context of housing rights advocacy or hospice care. We argue, however, that a social justice approach to action calls on us to first and foremost honor human rights and dignity, *especially* in those contexts where we are working with those whose rights have been violated and with those who have violated the rights of others (Ife, 2001; Skegg, 2005). Furthermore, it is our responsibility to contribute to the creation of supportive contexts—caring communities, engaged families, welcoming schools, and learning organizations. In so doing, we need to be constantly mindful of the ways in which oppression plays out in diverse institutional, organizational, and community settings as well as the ways interpersonal relationships and family or group dynamics may be shaped by practices of power and oppression among members.

For example, Katherine van Wormer and Robin McKinney (2003) address the oppressive power of heterosexism in public schools in the United States, Europe, and Canada, producing a "toxic environment for gender-nonconforming girls and boys" (p. 410). They cite examples of oppression in schools, from the heterosexist view of sexuality embedded in abstinence-only sex education, to the prevalence of antigay epithets and verbal and physical harassment that goes unchecked. They conclude, "The reluctance of school officials to protect gay students and to punish perpetrators of harassment shows, at the very least, their tacit acceptance of homophobia. High levels of personal prejudice, ignorance, and fear result in negligible intervention by teachers, counselors, administrators, and school board members when homophobic attacks occur" (van Wormer & McKinney, 2005, p. 411; Uribe & Harbeck 1991).

Van Wormer and McKinney argue that action on behalf of gay/lesbian/bisexual youth must be both context-relevant and context-changing. It is not enough to attend to the individual pain of an adolescent client trying to survive in this context. Rather, they call for a harm-reduction approach that encompasses preventive measures aimed at helping all youth with issues of sexual identity; public consciousness-raising about sexuality, sexual identity, and nondiscrimination; group work with young people to build support through gay/straight alliances; teacher training in crisis intervention; acquisition of library materials that speak to diverse experiences of sexual identity; program development to create school-wide antibullying programs; community organizing with parent-teacher associations to promote a culture of support; and advocacy work to redress discriminatory school policies. In short, they support integrated action that addresses the intersections of multiple forces of power and oppression that shape young people's lives in the everyday context of schooling and recognizes the rights of youth to safe learning environments and to expression of sexual identity. Social justice work entails concerted action on multiple fronts to respond to individual suffering and develop welcoming school climates for all students. It also creates opportunities for accompanying those most affected by oppressive contexts through processes of environmental as well as personal transformation.

Risk and Rights

The previous example illustrates that action and accompaniment may have diverse starting points: with individuals, families, organizations, governmental bodies, or community groups. By practicing contextually we are constantly mindful of the connective tissue linking people's lives to larger histories and systems. As with sexual identity, people who bear the labels of mental illness or physical disability live the context of stigma and discrimination as part of everyday life (Deegan, 1996; Sayce, 2005; Warner, 2000). Thus practice must critically address this context through both mindfulness of rights and challenge to discriminatory approaches to risk that jeopardize rights. As Patricia Deegan (1996) has argued, people diagnosed with mental illness have the right to take risks, the right to try and fail (and succeed), whether at work, in relationships, or in community living, just as do people who do not bear a diagnostic label. Likewise, Liz Sayce (2005) calls for social workers to challenge the stereotypes that underpin unfair risk-thinking in mental health, to interrupt the discourse of "us" and "them" that sustains the stigmatizing of labeled persons, and to champion the rights of labeled persons to participate as equals in the decisions that affect their lives (pp. 176-77). Vivienne Cree and Susan Wallace (2005) contend that social work should be about maximizing welfare, not minimizing risks (p. 127). We ask you to return to Tew's (2006) discussion of power in Chapter 7. What forms of power in the social work relationship serve to reproduce stigma and limit participation? What forms of power support the right to take risks?

Much of social work practice plays out amid contexts and discourses of risk and notions of who is deemed to be "a risk" or "at risk." "Risk assessments" are routinely conducted in child protection cases, mental health crisis interventions, and adult protective services. Practice in these contexts of risk often involves "nonvoluntary" participants. It may also call on us to engage with people who have acted toward others in brutal ways—people who have committed rape, battery, or homicide, for example. We do not check social justice at the door when facing these challenges. Cree and Wallace (2005) argue that social justice work in relation to risk and protection needs to be grounded by four cornerstones of practice: 1) legislation, 2) policy, 3) procedure, and 4) rights. Social workers need firm knowledge of the relevant legislation regarding their area of practice, such as child and adult protection, criminal justice, domestic violence, or mental health. Furthermore, social workers need to be aware of "procedural legislation as it applies to specific work activities" (Cree & Wallace, 2005, p. 117). For example, what is the procedure for investigation and action in cases of child sexual abuse? What is the procedure for making an assessment of imminent harm to self or others? Social workers need to be aware of government policy directives that affect practice. As Cree and Wallace note, such directives often emerge as the outcome of high-profile cases, for example, requirements for registration of sex offenders or professionals' "duty to warn" regarding a person's risk to self or others. Additionally, social workers need to continually update their knowledge regarding internal organizational policies and procedures through which larger mandates are enacted and monitored. What is the agency protocol for assessing risk in determining a child's removal to out-of-home care? What is the procedure for responding to a report of suicide risk regarding a client of a mental health facility or resident of a group home? Too often, however, while workers are attending to the three corners of responsibility, attention to rights falls by the wayside. When we lose sight of rights we lose cognizance of another's full humanity. Further, attention to rights may provide grounds for questioning the assumptions informing legislation and the ways in which it is translated into policies and procedures. Concern for rights can provide the basis for ground-up advocacy for social justice.

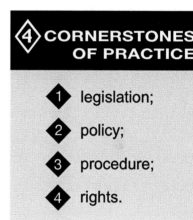

CORNERSTONES OF PRACTICE

1 legislation;

2 policy;

3 procedure;

4 rights.

Both those considered to be "at risk" and those considered to present a risk have rights, and it is our duty to ensure that those rights are honored. In the United Kingdom, the Human Rights Act of 1998 "guarantees all citizens certain absolute and qualified rights, which all public bodies in the UK (including social services, social work, and probation departments) must adhere to when dealing with the public" (Walden & Mountfield, 1999, as cited in Cree & Wallace, 2005, p. 118). In many countries of the world, the UN Convention on the Rights of the Child provides the basis for ensuring children's rights. In the United States, where the Convention on the Rights of the Child is not ratified and there is no Human Rights Act ensuring recognition of social, economic, and cultural rights, social workers are more limited in their options for rights advocacy. It is thus critically important that we understand both the extent and limits of rights—especially the rights of children—and work to educate people about their rights and to ensure their right to representation in procedures, hearings, or legal actions that affect their lives.

Context, Power, and Echoes of History

The preceding discussion suggests the power of dominant discourses of "normalcy" to both shape social experience and to render invisible or deviant (or both) those who do not "fit" within the context of dominant schema and scripts. It also suggests the power of "risk" discourse to overwhelm that of rights, thus driving action justified in terms of protection of the "best interests" of people deemed to be vulnerable. Contemporary discourses contain within them the echoes of history, oftentimes histories of disempowerment, exploitation, and forced dependence of marginalized persons and groups. Therefore action in the present contains within it reverberations of the past. The history of "intervention" with Indigenous People in North America and beyond offers painful lessons in the perpetuation of violence and violation in the guise of "helping." Margaret Waller (2005) sums up this troubling history as follows:

> As Standing Rock Sioux scholar Vine Deloria (2004) points out, much of the professional and popular literature about Native Peoples is a tangled web of distortions suffused by the influence of colonialism. For example, most social science research related to Indigenous Peoples focuses on social problems (Riding In, 1996). This is true even in social work, a profession purportedly committed to the strengths perspective (Hepworth & Larsen, 1982; Towle, 1945; Waller, Risley-Curtiss, Murphy, Medell, & Moore, 1998). With professional helpers whose model is a conglomeration of negative stereotypes, who needs enemies? (p. 47)

For many years private and state-based social work organizations in Australia, Canada, and the United States participated in the systematic removal of Native children from their families. For the most part, these practices were carried out secretly and invisibly, with the actions of professionals protected by rules of confidentiality (Briskman, 2005). This history of violence and violation has been challenged through the organized efforts of Indigenous People on multiple fronts. For example, in the United States the 1978 Indian Child Welfare Act sought to interrupt ongoing practices of cultural genocide through which Indian children were routinely labeled as "at risk" and placed in non-Indian foster and adoptive homes for what was deemed their "best interests." In 1997 the Australian Human Rights and Equal Opportunity Commission published findings of a national inquiry of the systematic abuses of Aboriginal people at the hands of the state. The report provoked public outcry, which served to further point out the longstanding "invisibility" of the racist treatment of Aboriginal people in the eyes of the white majority (Briskman, 2005, p. 212). As Linda Briskman argues, social work's implication is hard to address since practice remains shrouded in the cloak of professional confidentiality. Briskman points out the sharp contrast between professional silence around current and past practices with aboriginal children and families and the vocal public advocacy by Indigenous People of Australia to "change hearts and minds," "expose the locked cupboard of history," and prevent ongoing oppressive practices (2005, p. 213). We bring this history to bear here as a powerful reminder that our claims and actions regarding issues such as "best interests," "confidentiality," and "protection" are not chaste. They are embedded in historical, cultural, and political contexts that have been infused with violence and violation. We cannot assume a common understanding of these concepts, or the correctness of our beliefs. Instead, part of our responsibility in taking action is to bring these loaded issues forward and create the space to listen and learn, to address them transparently and candidly, and to be willing to challenge and change our practice in ways that honor another's experience, rights, and dignity. Thus our action is always political in the sense that it is conceived and carried out in the context of dynamic relations of power. It is interpreted, and often contested, by the various meaning-makers involved. And it carries with it weight of history. Action continually tests our courage and integrity.

Echoes of History: *Rabbit-proof Fence*[3]

Host a viewing of the film *Rabbit-proof Fence*— a powerful account of the forced removal of Aboriginal children from their families—for your social work class or a campus-community audience. Facilitate a discussion following the film to engage the audience in a discussion of state power, ideas about risk and best interests, and the power of racism in shaping child welfare policies and practices. What new learning do you take from the film? From the discussion?

REFLECTION: Coming to Action

Social work is about change, and change means taking action. Change can provoke feelings of excitement, empowerment, and elation, but it can also churn up feelings of insecurity and fear. What does it mean to take action for the people with whom we work and ourselves? Gaining a better sense of how this works personally can help us come to a better understanding of what change and taking action might be like for those with whom we work.

Pick one of the exercises below as it applies to you and your situation.

 Think of a time when you were compelled to take action on an issue of concern. Perhaps you had a talk with an employer about getting a raise in pay. Perhaps you took the car keys away from a friend who had too much to drink. Or maybe you wrote a letter to the editor of your hometown newspaper voicing concern about welfare reform policies that pushed people into low-paying jobs and did nothing to raise them out of poverty. What emotions propelled you into action? What decision-making process did you go through that got you to this point? How did others respond to your action, and how did this affect you?

Certainly, many of us *think* of taking action against troubling policies, procedures, or events that have life-altering affects on peoples' lives. However, we stop ourselves short by thinking the issue is much too big to tackle or that someone else will take care of it for us. Think of a time when you noticed something that disturbed you in your community or neighborhood. Maybe it was the litter scattered along the highway, or the need for a traffic light at a particularly dangerous intersection. What issues or concerns come to mind? What emotions kept you from taking action? What decision-making process did you go through that got you to this point? Were there any responses to your decision, and if so, how did these affect you? Discuss these exercises in class in small groups. Those who did Exercise 1 can generate a list of reasons people get involved in action and those in who completed Exercise 2 can generate a list of reasons people use to stop themselves from taking action. Remember to catalogue both the intellectual and emotional responses to your scenarios of action and inaction. What did you learn about taking action in your discussion?

RETHINKING SOCIAL WORK ROLES

We have painted an intense picture of action and accompaniment thus far. We turn now to a consideration of the different parts social justice workers may play in taking action for change. Social workers are generally prepared to play a variety of professional "roles," shaped by both organizational mission and the worker's position and responsibilities therein. Roles are also shaped by the definition of the "problem" and determined course of action. Most likely, you have been introduced to a number of social work roles such as broker, counselor, and case manager (see, for example, Sheafor, Horejsi & Horejsi, 2006, p. 55-67). We want to first reflect critically on the concept of "roles" and then outline what we see as approaches for enacting social justice work.

Discussion of roles generally addresses the workplace-related position a social worker assumes and the related expectations and activities. The role is thus viewed as separate from the particular person who fills it and carries out its "functions." It defines and delimits the activities that the worker engages in. Questions of power and meaning seldom enter into the discussion of social work roles. However, as John Coates (1992) describes, particular social work roles are associated with particular understandings of people and society, interpretations of social problems, and dynamics of power in the social work relationship. For example, Coates depicts the medical model as accepting the hierarchical nature of society and locating problem definition and intervention at the individual level. The social work relationship is top-down with a one-way flow from the social worker as "expert" and "therapist" to the passive "client." Thus, as Coates illustrates, social work roles are not neutral.

The approaches social workers take to enact their responsibilities are shaped in part by organizational expectations and job descriptions. They are also powerfully shaped by the social worker's positionality, values, and critical understanding of societal arrangements, problems, and possibilities for intervention. A role is only realized through its practice, and in that practice social workers bring their own histories, interpretations, power, and sense of possibility to bear. We outline ten roles for social justice work. We think of roles as ways of enacting our responsibilities and commitments. We argue that these roles are relevant for all contexts of social work practice. By rethinking our roles in light of the demands of social justice work, we can better address questions of power, promote meaningful participation, and expand the possibilities for transformative action.

Roles for Social Justice Work

♦ **Learner:** Our most fundamental and constant role is that of learner, approaching situations and relationships with openness, humility, and critical curiosity. As learners we are committed to the ongoing search for our own competence (Freire, 1990).

♦ **Teacher:** We not only bring our knowledge and skills to bear in the change process, we share them with others so that individuals, groups, and communities are better equipped to confront new challenges in the future. To do so we need to be effective teachers, able to engage learners and impart ideas clearly and effectively to diverse audiences.

♦ **Collaborator:** Co-labor is the foundation of social justice work. Our actions need to match the language of partnership. Social justice workers are not remote "advice givers." They are team members, engaging in the give and take of dialogue and action and accepting responsibilities and risks.

♦ **Facilitator:** With teamwork as a central tenet of practice, social justice workers require skills in facilitating group communication, decision-making, planning, and action. Whether the group in question is a family, a mutual aid group, an advisory committee, or a board of directors, skilled facilitation is key to building trust, addressing power and authority, promoting participation, and engaging in change-oriented action.

♦ **Animator/Activator:** We borrow the notion of animator from its French and Spanish uses as one who brings life to the change process and sparks motivation and mobilization for action. The English term "activator" captures some (but not all) of this spirit. The animator "stresses the individual as a shaper of his/her own destiny" (Reisch, Wenocur, & Sherman, 1981, p. 115). The animator helps sustain action through facilitative skills that recognize the power of groups coming together to create change.

♦ **Mediator:** Social justice work demands recognition of and respect for difference. Social justice workers will be called on to serve as mediators, working to bridge differences, craft bases of dialogue, and build critical alliances.

♦ **Advocate:** Social justice workers speak for the rights of those who have been historically excluded from decision-making arenas. We speak against policies, practices, and social arrangements that exacerbate, mask, or justify social injustice and inequality. This does not mean that we speak *in the place of* those living the daily realities of discrimination and oppression. Rather we stand and speak in solidarity with others.

◆ **Negotiator:** Critical awareness of power implies the capacity to confront conflict. As positioned actors embracing a political and ethical stance, social justice workers will face the question, "Which side are you on?" We will be called on to act as negotiators seeking the best possible outcomes for those we represent. We need to be clear about our positioning and what is at stake.

◆ **Researcher:** Social justice work is an integrated approach that demands ongoing critical reflection on and evaluation of our practice. The role of researcher is not something we turn over to those in the university or something we append as an afterthought. Rather it is part of everyday practice.

◆ *Bricoleur:* French anthropologist Claude Levi-Strauss (1966) envisioned cultural meaning making as a process of *bricolage,* the creative process of crafting new meanings and purpose from the cultural materials at hand. People are *bricoleurs,* cultural beings with the wherewithal and imagination and sense of discovery and possibility needed to adapt and transform human and material resources in response to new challenges. We think the concept of the *bricoleur* is an apt one for social justice work, and we elaborate on its meaning in Chapter 9. We are constantly challenged to engage with the circumstances and resources at hand, be inventive, and expand the spaces of hope.

Expanding the Possibilities

The 10 social worker roles described above are derived from critical reflection on our own practice and from insights gleaned from others engaged in social justice work. The naming and describing of social work roles is a work in progress. As we encounter new perspectives and learn from the experiences of others, we find our repertoire of roles expanding. For example, Paul Farmer's (2003) work speaks to the importance of the role of *witness* in social justice work. As you put your own vision of social justice work to practice, pay attention to the roles you are learning and enacting along the way. How would you name these roles? Describe and teach them to others? What do these roles allow you to accomplish?

Animating and Activating the Change Process

We want to develop further the idea of the social worker as animator and activator in the change process. The role of animator and method of animation are relatively foreign to social work practice in the United States. The concept is more frequently associated with popular education and other liberatory social change movements.

Michael Reisch, Stanley Wenocur, and Wendy Sherman (1981), drawing from Brun (1972, pp. 60-71), describe animation as "a method of work which attempts to assist social groups seeking their own mode of expression and which promotes social programs addressed to needs defined by the group" (Reisch et al., 1981, p. 115). It is "both a form of practice and a social movement" (p. 115). Animation involves encouragement of autonomous group development (e.g., skills of mutual aid), promotion of critical consciousness among members (conscientization), and stimulation of group action toward control over those environmental forces and resources that shape the group's development. The ultimate goal of animation is the liberation or empowerment of oppressed and marginalized people or groups. Reisch and colleagues argue that, for the goal of animation to be realized, "Social workers must be trained, therefore, to develop a new form of worker-client relationship based upon the establishment of trust in the motivation of others and a willingness to utilize nontraditional forms of cooperative action to produce change" (pp. 115-116). Thus, the social worker as animator acts as a catalyst, sparking consciousness that informs action and facilitating the social relations and material conditions that enable people to act. As animator, the social worker also attends to the organizational structure and infrastructure necessary to support the activation of plans. Animation and activation are at once socio-emotional, organizational-logistical, and political-ethical practices.

The animator role is grounded in genuine, caring relationships. Animators open up possibilities for meaningful participation; pose critical questions; coach participants through the risk taking, skill building, and rehearsal of new learning; and validate participants' contributions. Animators do not impose problem definitions and directions for action. Rather they encourage and nurture people's critical reflection on their own reality, validate the wisdom of lived experience, and help people envision and plan their own journeys. They remind people of their accomplishments and the importance of celebrating successes large and small. Animators attend to the orchestration of the parts and the whole, the balancing of the known and unknown, and the cultural-political questions of timing and pacing.

Drawing from the experiences of women's community-based organizing (Finn, 2001; Finn, Castellanos, McOmber & Kahan, 2000; Naples, 1998; Townsend et al., 1999), we also argue that animation involves nurturing and attention to the human spirit. *Anima*, the root word of animation, is the Latin word for soul. The stories of women community workers often contain references to the importance of healing body and soul as part of the change effort, of finding and giving inspiration, and of nurturing activism through relationships of love and support. Thus, the possibilities of animation are grounded in the meaning and power of caring human relationships.

"Reverse Mission": An Opportunity and Challenge

Social work practice with "other" groups has at times embraced a missionary model—imposing the "truth" of a dominant belief system and way of organizing social life, from education to child rearing to caring for the sick and dependent to forming families, on the less powerful. In this sense, social workers have assumed the role of "missionary." Faye Y. Abram, John A. Slosar, and Rose Walls (2005), writing about the politics and practice of international social work, call on the profession to adopt a "reverse mission," which entails a commitment to building long-term relationships with other groups and communities, learning about others' beliefs systems and ways of organizing social life, and learning the effects of histories of interventions, from missionization to colonization, to the neocolonialism of "development" and, more recently, to neoliberal globalization and its concomitant demands for structural adjustment. Our charge as social justice workers, then, is to enact a "reverse mission," to take what we learn from other national, cultural, and political contexts and put our individual and collective energies to work in changing the policies and practices of dominant states and international powerhouses such as the World Bank, World Trade Organization, and International Monetary Fund. Take a moment to imagine yourself in the role of "reverse missionary." What personal and professional challenges would the role pose for you? What visions of possibility come to mind? What actions might you take in carrying out this role?

SKILLS AND PRACTICE OF ACTION AND ACCOMPANIMENT

As we rethink the possibilities of social work roles we also need to rethink the skills of practice. We have addressed skills of historicizing knowledge and practice in Chapter 3; valuing and ethical decision making in Chapter 4; theorizing and critical thinking in Chapter 5; anticipatory empathy, listening, communicating, and relationship building in Chapter 6; and teaching-learning in Chapter 7. In the following sections we address skills and practice of action and accompaniment, with examples for practice with individuals, groups, and families, in organizations and communities, and in diverse arenas of decision-making. Some of these examples illustrate the integration of direct practice skills with those of advocacy, education, policy work, and community building. Others point to the possibilities for cross-fertilization of knowledge and skills. These become part of our repertoire as *bricoleurs* creating possibility from the resources at hand.

Principles and Practices of Group Process

Whatever our starting point for action, much of our work is carried out in a group setting. Work with individuals generally entails involvement with families or with important systems immediately affecting their lives, such as schools, hospitals, mental health centers, social welfare organizations, and housing administrations. We continually put knowledge and skills of group process to work through participation in interdisciplinary teams, in workplace staffings, in action planning, and in community organizing. Sometimes we may be officially charged with the task of group facilitation. At other times we may be able to draw on our facilitation skills as a member of the group to promote meaningful participation and ensure that those with less power in the setting have their rights honored and voices heard. The Center for Conflict Resolution in Madison, Wisconsin, offers a summary of practice principles and skills for group facilitation that we can draw on in diverse group settings. They stress the importance of question posing in groups, reminding us to (1) avoid leading questions, (2) phrase questions in a positive manner, and (3) prepare questions in advance. They describe the group facilitator's job as "keeping the discussion focused on the topic, clarifying (or asking for clarification) when something seems confusing, and helping create and maintain a situation where everyone can participate in a cooperative manner" (Center for Conflict Resolution, cited in Highlander Research and Education Center, n. d., p. 37).

Suggestions for Effective Group Process

◆ Every member should know what the discussion is about and what the purpose is for having it.

◆ Give participants room be involved.

◆ Be a model; your own behavior can demonstrate to members how they might participate.

◆ Ask questions to stimulate discussion.

◆ Invite opportunities to brainstorm and use listing to document ideas generated.

◆ Go around the room and give each participant an opportunity to respond.

◆ Write things down—have a recorder to keep track of material generated, and use this for the basis of further discussion.

◆ Relate the discussion to people's immediate experiences.

◆ Use humor to break tension or boredom.

◆ Use your intuition in choosing an approach to engage particular groups.

◆ Strive to equalize participation among members.

◆ Keep on the subject.

◆ Use your skills at clarification and interpretation. Check out meanings and ask for feedback.

◆ Use summarizing to pull together various parts of the discussion and to state progress made.

◆ Be mindful of timing and pacing—how is the group proceeding and when is it time to move on?

◆ Help group members work well together on an interpersonal level. Invite participants to talk to one another. Give feedback about

> interpersonal dynamics when appropriate and offer possible
> interpretations and alternatives.
>
> ◆ Provide members with opportunities to express their feelings and hear
> each other's feelings.
>
> ◆ Seek feedback from the group.

Making Plans

Action for change entails planning and decision making. Social justice work calls
for the participation of all of the stakeholders in the planning process. In this section we present participatory approaches to planning and decision making that can
be used in a broad range of practice contexts. We introduced the work of Cecilia
Díaz (1995) on *sistimaticazión* in Chapter 7. We present here her description of
participatory planning as part of the practice of democracy when people seek common interest from their individual and collective needs and work together to improve the quality of life for all (Díaz, 1997). It is a process that promotes critical
consciousness and self-determination. It strengthens individual and collective capacities and promotes a sense of collectivity. And it provides participants opportunities to hone and practice skills in negotiation, advocacy, and program development. Díaz (1997, pp. 15-23) describes the process of participatory planning in
terms of eight "moments":

 Diagnosis: What is happening, what is the situation, who are we, and
what do we have? (See discussion of diagnosis in Chapter 6).

- What is our reality? What are our needs and problems?
- What are the causes?
- What can we resolve ourselves? What can't we resolve ourselves?
- What resources and capacities do we have to confront the situation?

 Who is involved: Who are the various actors? What are their concerns,
conditions, and interests? Where might be the common ground and
important differences? This may include:

- Residents and local social organizations
- Local government
- Nongovernmental organizations
- Private sector

 Where do we want to arrive? What is our desired outcome? This is
directly related to our hopes and values. Knowing where we want to
arrive brings direction and clarity to the process of setting goals and
objectives.

 Formulating goals and objectives: What are our general goals for
more fundamental, structural change? What do we want to accomplish
in the long run? What specific objectives do we have to meet in order
to get there? How viable is our general goal in light of these specific
challenges? What time frame can we meet these objectives in? What
will be the specific measures of our objectives? What are the concrete

conditions that we need to achieve?

 What path are we going to take? What is our vision of the overall journey, and what are the possible routes that we can take to get there? What route will we select and why? Who will be part of the journey? We need a vision of the parts, of the whole, and of the final goal. This involves action, tasks, responsibilities, people, and resources. For every action we need to determine what needs to be done, who is responsible for what, and what resources are needed. It involves the participation of those affected in the negotiation and decision-making process.

 What do we need to do in order to achieve our objectives? What is our action plan? Díaz offers a guide for action planning:

- **What?** Defining the action or work theme.
- **Why?** Defining the objective. What do we want to result or where do we want to arrive?
- **With what?** What resources (human and material) do we have, what do we need, how are we going to get them?
- **How?** What steps and assignments have to be completed?
- **Who?** Who are responsible?
- **When?** What is the time frame for completion of each step and for the overall plan?

 Taking action: Get to work! In order to carry out the plans we have to engage organizational capacity and decide on a division of labor. We need to make decisions about how the implementation will be organized and overseen. Will we work in committees or task groups? How, when, and to whom do we report? Who coordinates the overall effort? How do we maintain momentum and commitment? The action is also accompanied by ongoing analysis—are we getting the work done? What is at stake in terms of risks and opportunities? Do we need to rethink our route? This is a process of both action and reflection, wherein the information gathered along the way continually informs the action process.

 Evaluation, systematization, and projection of the action: As we undertake the journey, we need to stop along the way to reflect on and learn from the experience: What gains have we made? How successfully have we fulfilled our roles and assignments? How are we confronting difficulties and conflicts? Are we meeting the goals and objectives? Díaz poses three "permanent questions" that permit us to reflect along the way: How are we doing? Are we heading where we want to go? What do we need to change? These questions may lead us to further diagnosis and systematization.

This model for participatory planning has broad applicability. It can be used in making plans with individuals and families, agency committees, advocacy groups, and community organizations. The eight "moments" follow the logic and sequencing of "top-down" approaches to planning. However, the test of a participatory model is in the practice. Is the process truly inclusive such that diverse stakeholders have a meaningful voice? Díaz presents the steps for participatory planning in inclusive, accessible language. Participatory planning efforts need to be free of jargon. Each step of the process is also a place for dialogue and teaching-learning. What does the step entail? How can its practice be illustrated with examples and images? Like most popular educators, Díaz pays close attention to these issues. She illustrates each moment with examples and figures, and she offers practical suggestions, such as the use of discussion groups, drawings, songs, newspaper murals, and sociodrama as part of the participatory process (Díaz, 1995, pp. 12-14; 1997, pp. 15-23).

Participatory Decision Making

The change process is full of decision-making moments. Frequently, we make decisions by default as we move in a direction that "goes without saying" and fail to question our underlying assumptions. One of the most basic skills of decision making is learning to recognize *when* and *how* we are making decisions. Social workers make seemingly mundane decisions every day, from the order in which phone calls are returned to the reports that do and don't get written, to the decision to follow up by phone or in person with a colleague or "client." Each one of these decisions is shaped by questions of meaning, context, power, and history. They, in turn, shape future possibilities. It is useful to reflect from time to time on the "micro decisions" of our everyday practice. What can we learn about our assumptions, our practice, and ourselves? The organizational contexts of social work practice also have histories, cultures, and protocols of decision making. Perhaps there is a history of decision making by decree of a director, or by default where the path of least resistance is followed. Some organizations may pride themselves on their democratic process, with decision making by majority vote. It is important to consider what questions are put forth for a vote and the nature of the data and discussion that informs the vote. What informal relations of power might shape the voting process? Who has the right to vote, and who are affected by the outcomes? Other organizations may pride themselves on their attention to each participant's view and embrace a model of decision making by consensus. Again, it is important to consider what questions are put forth for decision. What data and discussion inform the process? What informal relations of power might shape the consensus building process? When is silence interpreted as agreement? How is dissent addressed?

According to Sam Kaner and colleagues (1996), inviting diverse voices into the decision-making process and purposefully struggling to understand those voices is really the best hope for solving difficult problems. Kaner's approach honors the fact that the "shift from conventional values to participatory values is not a simple matter of saying, 'Let's become a thinking team.' It requires a change of mindset—a committed effort from a group to swim against the tide of prevailing values and assumptions" (Kaner et al., p. xv). Conventional groups, according to Kaner, consider a problem solved "as soon as the fastest thinkers have reached an answer"; participatory groups will not consider a problem solved until each person present (and who will be affected by the decision) understands the process and the logic and has systematic opportunity to weigh in with his or her point of view. Kaner contends that full participation in the decision-making process strengthens indi-

GREAT RESOURCE!

Check out the *Facilitator's Guide to Participatory Decision-Making* by Sam Kaner with Lenny Lind, Catherine Toldi, Sarah Fisk, and Duane Berger (San Francisco: John Wiley & Sons/Jossey-Bass, 2007, 2nd ed.). It's a "must have" resource for social justice work!

Who Plans?

Join together in small groups and return to the case study of "Life and Death in Libby" presented at the end of Chapter 7. Go through each of the eight planning moments and consider who should participate and how you might proceed. What roles of social justice work are you likely to practice here? What might be the nature of your organizational participation as a social worker? Now, take time to assign members of your small group to play out the roles of the various participants in the process, with one of you assuming the position of social worker. Take time to think about how the reality of the situation appears from the vantage point of your particular "positionality." What are your concerns? How do you see the problem? What is at stake for you here? What do you need in this context in order to feel safe enough to speak to your concerns? How do you see your power vis a vis that of other participants? Where do you want to arrive? What path do you see to get there? Where might you encounter barriers and sources of conflict? The social worker has the job of facilitating initial discussion among the participants and trying to move the group through the first moment of the process. Engage in the process for 20 to 30 minutes and then take time to debrief. What challenges did the social worker face? What challenges did other participants face? Did issues of meaning, power, and history come to the surface in this context? How so? Were you able to identify and negotiate common ground and important differences? What sorts of decisions were you faced with? What were the possible plans? What feelings did the process stir for you?

viduals, develops groups, and fosters sustainable agreement. According to Kaner, participatory decision making is grounded in four core values: (1) full participation, (2) mutual understanding, (3) inclusive solutions, and (4) shared responsibility (2007). These principles of decision making mirror the principles for social work practice put forth by Bertha Capen Reynolds (See Chapter 2). Kaner illustrates participatory decision making as a diamond where groups move from the narrow space of business as usual into the wide, uncomfortable "divergent zone" where diverse perspectives disrupt familiarity, and then into the struggle of the "groan zone" where members grapple with a broad range of foreign or opposing ideas and often find themselves frustrated and defensive. Passing through the turbulent waters of the groan zone with the help of skilled facilitation, members find a wellspring of possibilities around which new convergent thinking can coalesce in reaching a collective decision point.

Taking Action: Transforming Direct Practice

In talking with social workers about social justice, we have found that many practitioners have an image of social justice work as a form of "macro practice," seeking to effect change at the level of larger systems through mass mobilization and social action. While that may be a form social justice work takes, we have argued throughout that social justice and human rights need to be the centerpiece of all practice—from the most intimate spaces of one-to-one relationships to participation in large-scale social movements. However, as we truly embrace social justice work at the interpersonal level we cannot ignore its implications for the transformation of organizational practice, social policies, and dominant belief systems. In this section we explore practice with individuals and families, develop examples of social justice work in action, and illustrate relevant practices and skills.

Just Therapy

Charles Waldegrave and colleagues at the Family Centre in Wellington, New Zealand, have developed a model for "Just Therapy," which makes social justice the heart of direct practice (Waldegrave, 2000). The approach is characterized by three main concepts: *belonging, sacredness,* and *liberation.* Waldegrave describes the emergence of Just Therapy in a "reflective environment" in which diverse stakeholders came together and critically examined the ways in which helping systems and demands of help-seeking have served to reproduce inequalities and experiences of marginalization. Participants in the process included women and men, family therapists and community workers, Maori, Samoan, and white. They began to question the dominant systems of knowledge that had informed health and welfare structures and their practice therein. Thus, the practitioners started with a process of consciousness raising regarding their place in systems that valued particular ways of knowing while relegating other "forms of meaning creation, such as gender, cultural or class knowledge" to an "inferior anecdotal status" (2000, p.153).

Just Therapy is a form of practice developed to address these repeated failings of dominant models and systems. It is centered around values of equity and justice, and it recognizes that many mental health and relationship problems are consequences of power differences and injustice (p. 154). Waldegrave describes Just Therapy as a demystifying approach that involves a wide range of practitioners in addressing the deep social pain experienced by people who have been systematically marginalized. They questioned professionally imposed meanings of "problems" that failed to engage sociopolitical analysis or honor the perspectives of those seeking help. They asked how it was that spirituality was largely missing from professional discourse and practice while it was central to the lives of Centre participants. They examined the ways in which a "colonial mentality" played out in the details of organizational practice. Together they articulated a coherent theory that "provides tools for reflection, analysis, and action" and involves a shift in power and meaning (p. 158). As they reconceived their practice they found that a reconception of their organization went hand in hand.

The Family Centre has not sacrificed direct practice for "bigger issues." Rather it has developed a "congruence between casework and the rest of the work" (p. 161). Waldegrave argues that social workers are more effective at helping families with their immediate needs when the workers have hands-on knowledge of and involvement in the issues beyond the office. Just Therapy staff reject the stigmatizing label of "multi-problem family" and try to honor poor people's stories of survival. One of the tasks of the social worker is to help people examine the "problem centered webs of meaning" they bring with them to the Centre and to "weave new threads of meaning and possibility" together. As Waldegrave describes:

> For us the therapeutic conversation is a sacred encounter, because people come in great pain and share their story. The story is like a gift, a very personal offering given in great vulnerability. It has a spiritual quality. It is not a scientific pathology that requires removal, nor is it an ill-informed understanding of the story that requires correction. It is rather a person's articulation of events,

and the meaning given to those events, which have become problematic. The therapist honors and respects the story, and then in
return gives a reflection that offers alternative liberating meanings that inspire resolution and hope. (p. 162)

Just Therapy has much in common with empowerment, person-centered, and
strengths-based approaches that reframe practice in terms of liberation and transformation. All have emerged from critical dialogue among participants—both users and providers of services—who have directly experienced or witnessed unjust
practices and their effects. Empowerment models have been informed and shaped
by the knowledge and experiences of women of color and of people diagnosed
with mental illness. Person-centered practice has grown out of the disabilities rights
movement; strengths-based practice has emerged in response to the pathologizing
power of problem-focused, medical models. Practitioners working from these perspectives offer concrete suggestions for transforming our practices and our organizations.

Empowering Practice, Transforming Recovery

For example, Lorraine Gutiérrez and Edith Lewis (1999; Gutiérrez, 1990) have
put forth an empowerment approach to practice with women of color. They start
from the assumption that the experience of being a member of a group with little
social or political power has personal as well as social costs. The goal of practice is
to increase personal, interpersonal, or political power. The process may take place
on the individual, interpersonal, and community levels. They identify four subpro-
cesses that comprise empowerment practice: (1) develop critical consciousness,
(2) reduce self-blame, (3) assume responsibility to participate in change process,
and (4) enhance self-efficacy, which entails both the capacities and confidence to
take effective action. Action strategies for change include:

- Build a helping relationship based on collaboration, trust, and shared
  power.

- Use small groups.

- Accept "client's" definition of concern.

- Identify and build on strengths.

- Raise consciousness around issues of gender, class, race, and power.

- Actively engage participants in the change process.

- Teach specific skills (e.g., communication skills; self-advocacy skills;
  organizing skills, etc).

- Use mutual aid groups.

- Share power within the helping relationship.

- Mobilize resources and advocate for change (Gutierrez, 1990, Gutierrez
  & Lewis, 1999).

In addressing mental illness and mental health practice, Patricia Deegan (1996)
advocates for a transformational *recovery* model that challenges dominant views
and practices regarding *management* of mental illness. She argues that first and

foremost we must be committed to changing the environment that people are being asked to grow in. Daniel Fisher and Judi Chamberlin (2004) of the National Empowerment Center have put forth an action plan to do just that—consumer-directed transformation to a recovery-based mental health system. They outline "how survivor/consumers can catalyze a transformation of the mental health system from one based on an institutional culture of control and exclusion to one based on a recovery culture of self-determination and community participation" (p. 3). Fisher and Chamberlin put forth the following values as the basis for a recovery-based mental health system:

♦ Self-determination

♦ Empowering relationships based on trust, understanding, and respect

♦ Meaningful roles in society

♦ Elimination of stigma and discrimination.

The change process calls for the cooperation of consumers, their allies, practitioners, and policy makers in leading national and state-based recovery initiatives, whose work would entail recovery-based education, policy development, research, services, and supports. The action would entail launching of a nationwide antistigma campaign; consumer-led planning for development of model recovery policies; engagement of consumers as research partners in evaluating performance of mental health systems; and consumer-driven transformation to a system of recovery-based services and supports based on the five principles of self-determination (Nerney, 2004):

1 **Freedom:** the opportunity to choose where and with whom one lives as well as how one organizes all important aspects of one's life with freely chosen assistance as needed.

2 **Authority:** the ability to control some targeted amount of public dollars.

3 **Support:** the ability to organize that support in ways that are unique to the individual.

4 **Responsibility:** the obligation to use public dollars wisely and to contribute to one's community.

5 **Confirmation:** the recognition that individuals with disabilities themselves must be a major part of the redesign of the human service system.

Fisher and Chamberlin make the case for person-centered planning wherein supports and services are individualized and people can fashion their own recovery goals. This calls for flexible funding mechanisms for the purchase of appropriate services and supports and an expanded range of choice in those services and supports. In particular, they advocate an increase in the involvement of consumers in peer-provided services through four major roles:

1 **Peer professionals:** mental health professionals who have also recovered from personal experience of mental illness and bring both academic and experiential knowledge to bear.

2 **Peer specialists:** people who have recovered or are in recovery and have received specialized training in peer support.

3 **Peers as staff in consumer-run programs**, such as drop-in centers, housing programs, and "warmlines."

4 **Peer involvement in mutual support** on one-to-one basis and in support, discussion, and advocacy groups.

Their plan is not a pie-in-the-sky idea. Rather, there are "conspiracies of hope" across the country making these plans and dreams real. For example, in Florida, a pilot Self-Directed Care Program has been initiated that provides consumers with individual budgets to select and purchase services to fulfill individual recovery plans. In Georgia a Medicaid Rehabilitation Option has been implemented that allows for reimbursement for some peer-provided services. Peer-run drop-in centers are in operation around the country. For example, the Ruby Rogers Advocacy and Drop-In Center in Somerville, Massachusetts, has a 22-year history as a freestanding, consumer-run advocacy program, which receives funding from the Massachusetts Department of Mental Health. The budget includes funds for a director, who must be a person who has recovered from mental illness, and for a number of staff positions that have allowed members to take on leadership roles without losing benefits (Fisher & Chamberlin, 2004). The Western Montana Empowerment Project located in Missoula, Montana, is a grassroots support, education, and advocacy organization developed by people with the experience of mental illness. Participants have developed a peer support network outside of the mental health system. They present sensitizing workshops on mental illness and stigma for diverse audiences, and they advocate for the rights of individuals and for state-level policy change. In addition, members are active in Missoula's flourishing environmental and arts communities.

Like Minds Campaign: Lessons from New Zealand

Like Minds is a public health campaign developed to reduce the stigma of mental illness and the discrimination that people living with mental illness experience every day. The project was initiated in 1997 by the New Zealand Ministry of Health. It works on multiple levels to end discrimination against people with the experience of mental illness. Participants have developed a resource directory that includes workshops, training manuals, fact sheets, posters, videos, and CDs—all aimed at countering the stigma of mental illness and the concomitant discrimination. Twenty-six Like Minds providers across the country are engaged in promotional and educational activities in local communities. Among their actions is a media campaign that features well-known public figures who live with mental illness. To learn more about Like Minds visit their website at: www.likeminds.govt.nz.

REFLECTION: Seizing the Moment and Making (Radio) Waves

Social justice worker Nancy McCourt takes to the airwaves to challenge the public polices and popular images that stigmatize and oppress mothers and pregnant women who experience addiction and mental illness. While working as a supervisor in a community mental health facility Nancy had borne witness to the daily struggles her clients faced. Drawing on her experience with popular education and Iris Marion Young's "Five Faces of Oppression" (see Chapter 2), Nancy seized the opportunity to offer an editorial commentary on KUFM Public Radio in Missoula, Montana. Following is the text of her commentary:

> Mothers and pregnant women are expected to undergo and tolerate extensive public scrutiny. All women are supposed to become adequate mothers while factors of race, age, and socioeconomic privilege are ignored.
>
> Pregnant women who experience addiction problems and mothers with severe mental illness are parents who have increased chance of being on the receiving end of social services— and social judgments. We need to develop positive, effective services that support mothers who have addiction and/or severe mental illness to parent.
>
> Let's look at how oppression plays out in the lives of these mothers. Then let's ask ourselves what sorts of community responses and supports can best meet the needs of all members of our community.
>
> Writer Iris Marion Young offers a way to help us identify the ways oppression appears in the day-to-day interactions between social groups. These include exploitation, marginalization, powerlessness, violence, and cultural imperialism.
>
> Exploitation concerns the social value of work and compensation. Women with mental illness and/or addiction often live in poverty and may be exploited through prostitution. Vocational training programs for recovering drug addicts are primarily targeted toward basic, low-pay jobs. Mothers with mental illness may quality for disability benefits. The limits on personal assets to qualify for these benefits may actually reduce the incentive to set meaningful career goals, reinforcing exploitative policies. In many states, including Montana, women who have been convicted of a felony drug offense are banned for life from welfare benefits. These factors increase the likelihood of further exploitation as the mother seeks to make a livelihood through illegal means.
>
> Marginalization is the process of creating second-class citizens. When unable to live up to the cultural and social standards of motherhood, moms with mental illness and/or addiction are seen as faulty, bad, or unworthy. They have their parenting scrutinized, and they may have "normal" parenting dilemmas attributed to their diagnoses. These mothers generally have the same aspirations, goals, concerns, and challenges as their parent peers who are not diagnosed with these conditions. Addiction is recognized as a disease, yet women known to use drugs while pregnant are more likely to be punished, receive stricter penalties, and lack treatment options when compared to male and non-pregnant female drug offenders. This is marginalization within our justice system. Marginalization occurs when programs lack child care for women seeking treatment. Focusing upon the individual aspects of illness can increase marginalization by ignoring social factors that exacerbate or even cause symptoms of mental illness or addic-

tion. Mothers with mental illness may find a system intended for them, a system intended for their children, but typically mental health and child welfare systems lack the overlap necessary to serve families sufficiently.

Powerlessness is connected to reproduction. You need to have control over your reproduction in order to freely develop and fully exercise your potential. Mental health systems neglect to ask about client sexual activity or use of birth control. Mental health professionals can fail to address immediate parenting concerns despite the significance of child custody issues for these mothers. The shortage of treatment programs for pregnant women who are addicted results in pregnant women sitting on waiting lists far longer than the human gestation period. Expectations that pregnant women possess magical powers of self-control and can quit an addictive habit simply by trying are unrealistic and destructive. Punishment for failure to control an addiction ignores the disease.

Ovulation and conception are not conscious efforts. Yet it is culturally assumed that every woman wants every baby that her body can possibly conceive. Mothers who recognize their own limitations and wish to prevent unplanned or unwanted pregnancies lack access to birth control and abortion. In rural communities privacy concerns can prevent a woman from seeking birth control from the local health provider or retail outlet. Our government has reduced dollars allocated to comprehensive reproductive health care in favor of abstinence-only programs.

According to National Advocates for Pregnant Women, three quarters of American women who need publicly funded family planning services are going without those services. And an estimated one million women living 250% below the poverty level are not using any form of birth control, even though they are at risk of an unintended pregnancy.

Cultural imperialism is when a dominant group imposes its value system and traditions on all parts of a society. Western culture encourages competition and judgment, sometimes in subtle ways, of mothering, including pregnancy, where store clerks, waiters, and passersby feel free and even obligated to pass judgment upon parents. The concept of the nuclear family and individual autonomy is culturally imperialistic. The extended family and use of community as the family support network were once common parts of American lifestyle. Today families are busy with individual jobs, sports, activities, cell phones, laptops, each with his or her own bathroom to avoid interaction. We judge families who don't look like individual autonomous, self-supporting units. Above all, assumptions that all women want to parent and the limiting of birth control access because "those women" should not be having sex are imperialistic.

Violence can be an intense, disturbing, and often destructive action or force. Family violence frequently factors in the history of women who become addicted. Putting addicts in prison is a violent response to addiction. The punitive approach to mothers who use drugs perpetuates the cycle of violence. Some states allow the court-ordered removal of a baby who tests positive or whose mother tests positive for drugs at birth. Taking a child from its mother, regardless of the reason— even if warranted— is a covert act of violence. Overmedication is passive violence, as are selective prescription coverage policies by insurance programs.

Perhaps the greatest act of violence against these oppressed mothers is the ongoing apathetic response by society, by voters, and by our elected officials to the very obvious causes of their greatest troubles. Continuing to fund weaponry and tools of mass destruction while millions of poor mothers lack access to adequate addiction treatment or treatment for mental health is federally sanctioned violence against families.

Over and over mothers with mental illness and addiction state that mothering is the most grounding part of their lives. Mothering is the socially normal thing to do, and it allows them to feel there is something more to their identity than a diagnosis. So how do we want to see these families function in our community? Continued lack of supports for parenting combined with increasingly limited access to relationship education, birth control, and abortion most certainly will lead to increased demand on child protective services, corrections, and other crisis-based reactive approaches. The state Addictions and Mental Disorders Division, in partnership with our community of qualified mental health providers, must take a lead role in studying and developing effective programs to keep families who experience addiction and/or mental illness together while also keeping them safe and healthy.

Inside Prisons: Challenges and Possibilities

Social justice principles and practices grounded in dignity, respect, and transparency offer direction for working in the most constrained spaces. U.S. prisons provide perhaps the most glaring example of a context of top-down power and control. The United States has an incarceration rate of 748 people per 100,000 (as compared to 88 per 100,000 in France and 52 per 100,000 in Finland) ("Prisons," 2006, p. 14; Holt, 2004).The United States accounts for 5% of the world's population and 25% of its prison population. Black men between the ages of 25 and 29 are seven times more likely than their white counterparts to be in prison or jail (Human Rights Watch, 2006). As Josefina Figueira-McDonough and Rosemary Sarri (2002) have argued, the social work profession has largely neglected criminal justice in general and prison work in particular even as issues of basic human rights and social justice have increasingly come to public attention. There are, however, some inspirational examples of healing, support, and advocacy in the prison context that demonstrate possibilities for social justice work. For example, social worker Jack Sternbach (2000) learned profound lessons in action and accompaniment through work in a men's prison. He writes, "I want to focus on what I learned about men together with other men under conditions so oppressive and brutal you would expect to find the worst kinds of male aggression, dominance, and exploitation. There was that, in abundance. What is more important is how much I learned of the positive and affirming ways so many men found to be with each other even under such conditions" (p. 414). Opening himself to being both learner and teacher, Sternbach learned about mutuality, transparency, risk taking, openness, and vulnerability—lessons that continue to inform his professional practice (p. 413). Some of these lessons include:

♦ What we have to offer others has little value unless it is embedded in mutuality.

♦ Let people speak for themselves.

♦ Learn about and honor limits and boundaries that shape and are shaped by the context of practice.

♦ Accept the other man where he is right now in the moment.

♦ Take the first step of self-revelation to facilitate honest, open interaction.

♦ Physical affection between men is all right.

♦ Good intentions do not provide magical protection—we are not invulnerable or special.

♦ Goodbye, Lone Ranger—ask for help. Use colleagues and community resources.

♦ Find the courage to be transparent, honest, and open to mutual relationships in our work.

Sternbach describes how prison work transformed his practice of social work. He gives insight into ways he found and supported the nurturing of humanity against the odds. Others, such as advocates for restorative justice, are seeking fundamental changes in the philosophy and practice of criminal justice. A restorative justice perspective sees crime as "primarily an offense against human relationships and secondarily a violation of law" (Claassen, 1996). Advocates argue for a practical approach that involves the community, focuses on the victim, and promotes inclusive processes toward justice, healing, and reconciliation. The process emphasizes acknowledgment, apology, and forgiveness. Some describe it as a new paradigm for doing justice that starts at the grassroots with ordinary members of the community as well as victims and offenders, inclusive of all whose lives are affected by wrongdoing. The approach seeks to hold offenders directly accountable to the people and communities they have violated, restore emotional and material losses of the victims, and provide opportunities for dialogue, negotiation, and problem solving. The goal is to achieve a greater sense of community safety, social harmony, and peace for all involved (Bazemore & Schiff, 2001; Claassen, 1996; Perry, 2002). Katherine van Wormer (2005) argues that restorative justice should be a central part of the knowledge and practice repertoire for social justice work. Here, too, we see hopeful efforts developing around the world, from community mediation centers and sentencing circles to peace and reconciliation commissions.

The New Abolitionist Movement

We introduced Critical Resistance (CR), a grassroots organization dedicated to ending the prison industrial complex, in Chapter 7. CR argues that reducing the prison population and prison spending is the only way to create genuine public safety. According to CR there is a movement afoot across the United States to change the course of corrections and move in the direction of community-based treatment. States across the country are planning to reduce rather than expand the number of prisons and overall population. There is also a movement seeking to get rid of all prisons, calling themselves "abolitionists." Abolitionists argue that the justification for prisons does not hold up well in theory or practice (Holt, 2004). Their goal is decarceration. Finland is their real-world model of possibility. Until the 1970s Finland had a highly punitive correctional system, modeled after the Soviet Union. In rethinking the system, they opted for transformation rather than reformation. Inmates live in dorms and address guards by their first names. Innovative therapeutic techniques have been encouraged. Today, Finland reports a low crime rate and the smallest imprisonment rate in Europe.

The number of women incarcerated in the United States has grown exponentially in the past 15 years. The United States is now "number one in both incarceration and overall correctional control of women in the world" (Pimlott & Sarri, 2002, p. 59). Nearly 70% of women in prison are mothers, and most are incarcerated in facilities far from their homes and children (Beck, Karberg, & Harrison, 2002). While policies such as the Adoption and Safe Families Act of 1997 push social workers toward expedience in termination of parental rights when parents face lengthy sentences, groups of women across the country are coming together in solidarity and support for women in prison and their children (Ascione & Dixson, 2002). For example, Joyce Dixson, MSW, mother of two, and formerly incarcerated woman, organized SADOI (Sons and Daughters of the Incarcerated) in 1996. She has been providing innovative services to youth in southeast Michigan and helping develop programs in other states ever since. As Dixson describes,

> I never truly knew how badly my children had been hurt by my incarceration until I sat down and had a serious talk with them after my release. They were 6 and 8 years old when I entered prison. The stories they told me were worse than I could have imagined or believed. They talked about how hard it was for them to go to school; how the other children teased and taunted them. They spoke about the many times they would be the last ones to be picked up for the baseball game, and how badly they felt whenever a teacher spoke in class about the "bad people" who live in prison. They spoke about the many times they were told they were not welcome in the homes of their friends; and when they did visit, they would always be reminded (whenever they did something mischievous) that they would end up in prison just like their mother. Their feelings were hurt a lot, and they often wondered what they had done to cause people to treat them so badly. (Ascione & Dixson, 2002, pp. 271-272)

In response to the struggles faced by her children and those of other incarcerated women, Dixson put her energies into SADOI, a group-support program for children who have an incarcerated parent or close family member. SADOI provides a safe and nurturing environment where youth come together in small, age-set groups to talk openly about the experience of their parents' incarceration and its effect on their lives (Acsione & Dixon, 2002, p. 286). The groups provide both support and skill-building for their young members. They address important topics such as grief and loss; stigma; emotional expression; building strong relationships, communication and coping skills; self-esteem; critical inquiry into the causes and effects of incarceration; and what happens when parents come home (p. 287). SADOI also offers training for social workers and educators to help them understand the effects of parental incarceration on children.

Michigan Battered Women's Clemency Project:
A Conspiracy of Hope

Feminist artist and activist Carol Jacobsen grew up in the shadow of Michigan's Jackson Prison, the world's largest prison. Her activism for peace, justice, and women's rights took her around the globe and into the world of photography and film making. Eventually her journey brought her back to the confined space of a prison cell and the stories of women's lives therein. As Carol listened to the life stories of women in prison the barriers of "us" and "them" broke down—she saw herself in their words. Carol turned her camera on the prisons to bear witness to women's accounts of prison experience, positioning women as both narrators of their own lives and critics of the justice system. Her "Women in Prison" project, begun in 1990, consists of numerous documentary films and video installations. In the early 1990s Carol joined with Susan Farr, founder of the Michigan Battered Women's Clemency Project, and a small group of dedicated women—an attorney, a social worker, and former prisoners—to advocate for the release of battered women who had been wrongly convicted for the murder of their abusers.

Carol, a professor of art and women's studies at the University of Michigan, brings student volunteers into the project each year, sparking consciousness of the state of women in prison, learning about human rights through action, and providing hands-on opportunities to practice skills of advocacy. Every Sunday afternoon a team gathers at Carol's home to further work on petitions, write letters to women in prison, report on case and legal research, and arrange film showings, talks, and other public relations events. The Clemency Project has been successful in freeing two women from life sentences, not through clemency, but through the courts, and assisting others in obtaining early paroles. Twenty petitions submitted by the Clemency Project were denied by Michigan's Governor in 2006, but the project continues to resubmit them, adding one or two new ones each year. For more information on the Michigan Battered Women's Clemency Project visit the website at: www.umich.edu/~clemency.

Michigan Battered Women's Clemency Project Rally [4]

Rethinking Family Practice

The Family Centre in New Zealand has provided us with a rich example of social justice work in action. Nancy Vosler (1996) offers a complementary perspective on rethinking family practice. We introduced Vosler's contributions to teaching-learning in Chapter 7. Vosler challenges the assumption in many family "intervention" approaches that if the family system changes, all significant problems can be resolved. She contends that assumption is flawed because it fails to account for the impact of structural issues related to poverty, unemployment, inadequate housing, crime, and lack of accessible services and resources on families. Based on her professional experience in child welfare and juvenile justice, Vosler argues that our actions toward change need to go beyond the family and address these systemic forces as well. She calls for multilevel thinking and action that appreciate the challenges of economic stress on families and the labor involved in maintaining family well-being. Vosler invites us to make links between family systems and the larger social, political, and economic environment. We would then be better able to attend to family stress and coping strategies in an uncertain economy as well as to sources of family resiliency that can be further supported. Social work action with families then would entail immediate stress relief; recognition and support of family strengths; holistic program development and evaluation that considers the needs of families in context; policy practice through advocacy, lobbying, coalition building; and research to promote effective programs and initiatives. It would also include engagement in collaborative practice research to identify and track changes in family demographics and problems, available resources, changes in larger systems that impact families, and innovations in services and support that can strengthen family resilience.

Similar to Waldegrave (2000), Vosler challenges us to look beyond the family in order to understand the conditions that impact well-being. Strengths-based practitioners also remind us to look both to and beyond families for resources and sources of strength. Bonnie Benard (2006, p. 214) calls for practice that recognizes and taps into family resilience. She offers the following principles for strengths-based practice with families:

- ◆ Listen to their story.

- ◆ Acknowledge the pain.

- ◆ Look for strengths.

- ◆ Ask questions about survival, supports, positive times, interests, dreams, goals, and pride.

- ◆ Point out strengths.

- ◆ Link strengths to family members' goals and dreams.

- ◆ Link family to resources to achieve goals and dreams.

- ◆ Find opportunities for family members to be teachers and paraprofessionals.

Benard discusses the growing family support movement in the United States from school-based family resource programs to free-standing family centers. These strengths-based efforts share common ground. According to Benard, they are all based on caring relationships of staff to family, faith in the family's innate resilience and the capacity to grow and change, and commitment to strengths-enhancing practice. (p. 215). Family Support America, a national resource organization for the theory, policy, and practice of family support, promotes the development of strengths-based programs around the country, and they have developed the following principles for working with families from a strengths perspective (cited in Benard, p. 215)[5]:

CHECK IT OUT ON THE WEB!

Would you like to learn more about family resource centers?

Visit the website of Family Support America at www.familysupportamerica.org.

Would you like to learn more about strengths-oriented, community-based practice with families?

Check out the resources developed by the Policy Institute for Family Impact Seminars at www.familyimpactseminar.org.

♦ Staff and families work together in relationships based on equality and respect. Participants are a vital resource.

♦ Staff enhance families' capacity to support the growth and development of all family members.

♦ Programs affirm and strengthen families' cultural, racial, and linguistic identities and enhance their ability to function in a multicultural society.

♦ Programs are embedded in their communities and contribute to the community-building process.

♦ Programs advocate with families for services and systems that are fair, responsive, and accountable to the families served.

♦ Practitioners work with families to mobilize formal and informal resources to support family development.

♦ Programs are flexible and continually responsive to emerging family and community issues.

♦ Principles of family support are modeled in all program activities, including planning, governance, and administration.

Where do you see commonalities to a Just Practice approach? Are there other principles you might consider to further the possibilities of social justice work?

ORGANIZATIONAL PRACTICE: CHALLENGES AND POSSIBILITIES

The preceding examples demonstrate that social justice work holds implications for the organizational context of practice. Social justice practice will be constrained within organizational contexts where "business as usual" entails top-down practices that separate the worker from the client, reproduce relations of power, and value limiting concepts of "expertise" that exclude the grounded knowledge of those experiencing, pain, stigma, and oppression. The ideal organizational context is the learning organization—where there is ongoing search for organizational competence. The learning organization "adopts a climate of openness and trust; people are unafraid to share their ideas and speak their minds. Barriers between managers and employees are eliminated and, ideally, everybody works together to support the collective well-being (Bennett & O'Brien, 1994, p. 44, as cited in Kirst Ashman & Hull, 2001, p.163). However, the reality of human service work is increasingly pushed toward privatization, managerialism, and a market ethic (Ferguson, Whitmore, & Lavalette 2005; Healy, 2005). As Karen Healy notes, "In this new environment social workers face increasingly stringent expectations from funding agencies and service managers to demonstrate cost-effectiveness and evidence of service outputs and outcomes" (Healy, 2002, 2005, p. 222). Thus, a serious challenge for social justice work is to critically engage with these "new imperatives" on human service organizations (Healy, 2005, p. 223). This is no easy task. It calls for action on multiple fronts, including building alliances of solidarity among workers and other program participants that cross and bridge organizational boundaries. In facing these challenges we can draw inspiration from the Rank and File Movement discussed in Chapter 3.

Functional Noncapitulation

Social justice work may also challenge us to "practice against the grain" in our organizational contexts. "Functional noncapitulation" is one strategy for individual action in the organizational context. Reisch, Wenocur, and Sherman (1981) define functional noncapitulation as a means of conflict management wherein workers position themselves as active decision makers with both a right and responsibility to influence the organization and work to reverse the downward organizational pressure that contributes to powerlessness. Reisch and colleagues develop this concept in their discussion of power and empowerment in the worker-client relationship and the worker's organizational location. They note that social work clients often feel powerless to address their problems and that their sense of powerlessness is often intensified by virtue of long histories of experiences of discrimination, devaluation, and exclusion. The social worker, on the other hand, often stands between the client and the sponsoring organization that possesses resources that both the client and worker need. Yet the worker's own power may be limited in terms of ability to access those resources and respond to needs. The worker may come to incorporate feelings of helplessness as well. The authors argue that workers need to understand power and empowerment both conceptually and experientially in order to help clients gain power and control over their lives and to engage meaningfully in the teaching-learning process. Further, workers need to be able to use the power available to them effectively and communicate their grasp of power and power dynamics to clients. They argue: "To pursue such ends successfully, social workers have a responsibility to reverse the process of disempowerment. In this regard it is essential that workers learn to manage conflict, rather than attempt to resolve conflict permanently or ignore it altogether" (p. 111). According to Reisch et al. (1981) the stance of functional noncapitulation:

> requires workers to maintain a willingness and capacity to negotiate continually the conditions of their work. In this position, workers will have to take calculated risks to achieve their goals. The worker's posture of functional noncapitulation encourages the same stance among clients, rather than shared dependency and powerlessness. (p. 112)

The authors argue that in order to establish this stance the worker must become aware of and comfortable with the many sources of available power, including legal power, the power of information, situational power, expert power, coalitional power, and even negative power—the power to make the agency look bad (p. 112). Thus, the analysis of power is not limited to the power dynamics of the client's situation or of the particular context of the worker-client relationship. Rather it is part of the social justice worker's critical positionality in human service organizations.

REFLECTION: **Using Social Work Roles**

We can also draw on our repertoire of social work roles for working for change from within organizational contexts. Return for a moment to the discussion of social work roles on pp. 325-356. Think of ways in which you would use each of these roles in working with colleagues and administrators. How might you engage in teaching-learning with colleagues? Where might you find potential collaborators? How might you seize the opportunity to facilitate group discussion within the workplace that may promote critical consciousness and action? Where might you find opportunities to mediate difference and promote dialogue among co-workers? How might you animate co-workers and spark motivation for creative action? When might you need to mediate difference and negotiate power relations? How might you draw on a commitment to ethical, rights-based practice as grounds for an alternative course of action? Where might you find potential to raise your voice as an advocate for change from within your organization? How might you draw on the rich base of research on power and participation to inform suggestions for change in organizational policy and practice? Where can you support "organizational *bricolage*" that enables you to take the best of what your organization is currently about and use it as the resource for transformation?

Supervision as a Practice of Mutual Aid

Many of you will find yourselves assuming supervisory roles in social work organizations. We find Freda Brashears'(1993) concept of supervision as mutual aid to be a good fit for social justice work. Brashears suggests that the principles and dynamics of mutual aid create a sound basis for realizing worker potential in the organizational context. According to Brashears, conceptualizing supervision as a practice of mutual aid:

1) Challenges the false dichotomy that separates supervision from practice.

2) Envisions the workplace as an environment in which to realize worker potential.

3) Reframes supervisors as change agents working on behalf of staff to promote just practice.

4) Reframes the work unit as a mutual aid group with common interests and common tasks—service to and empowerment of program participants.

5) Counters agency hierarchy.

6) Creates a form of supervisory practice that is consistent with social work values.

7) Realizes the values of advocacy, empowerment, and self-determination in the workplace.

8) Provides a framework for team work, participatory decision making, and group problem solving.

9) Harnesses the creative energy of the group members.

10) Provides the base for creating organizational change.

Think about your own experiences as a supervisor or supervisee. What have been some of the positive aspects of that experience? Negative aspects? Have your experiences encouraged you and others to engage in social justice work? If so, how? Have your experiences fit with Brashears' concept of supervision as mutual aid? If so, how? Do you see possibilities for incorporating supervision as mutual aid in your workplace? What would you add to Brashears' points in order to promote a model of supervision as social justice work?

Building Social Justice Organizations

A group coming together to "promote social justice" does not suggest that justice-oriented, learning organizations "just happen." The history of the Kensington Welfare Rights Union (KWRU), a powerhouse advocacy and action organization, offers important lessons in the challenges and possibilities of building and sustaining social justice organizations. KWRU "is a multiracial organization of, by, and for poor and homeless people" (KWRU, 2006). Founded in 1991 in Philadelphia, the organization is dedicated to ending poverty and realizing economic human rights. KWRU spearheaded the National Poor People's Economic Human Rights Campaign, and members have been on the frontlines in the fight against regressive welfare policy. Their approach to building a people's organization consists of "Five Main Ingredients" (KWRU, 2006):

1. **Teams** of indigenous organizers

2. **Bases** of operation

3. **Voices**—lines of communication

4. **Networks** of mutual support

5. **Committed cores** of leaders.

Ongoing critical reflection and action are key parts of organizational practice. Members of the Narratives Study Group of the KWRU Education Committee have researched and written about the experience of building a social justice organization and movement (Baptist, Bricker-Jenkins, Gentry, Johnson, & Novak, 2006). They conducted in-depth interviews with KWRU members and emerging leaders to learn "(1) how they developed a political consciousness that led them to become involved in the movement, and (2) the organizational factors that sustain their work" (2006, p. 222). Their research pointed to three interlocking themes in people's accounts of the pathways to political consciousness. These include (1) experiencing a sense of injustice in the world, (2) shifting the dominant narrative about poverty from one rooted in personal blame to one that questioned structural arrangements, and (3) nurturing hope that change is possible. In their study of organizational factors that sustain participation they found that people needed the op-portunity to choose among a variety of roles with differing levels of risk (p. 231). Education, a key component of KWRU structure and culture, was found to be an important organizational factor in sustaining participation. Members value oppor-tunities for both developing specific skills—such as listening, mediating, and pub-lic speaking—and political education "through self-study, dialogue, and analy-sis—particularly of history and social forces" (p. 233). KWRU has incorporated the use of study groups and buddy groups as part of a dialogical educational pro-cess, and participants have found them to be invaluable venues for developing consciousness and sustaining participation. Members also spoke of the importance of group identity at KWRU where they experience a sense of family, recognize the collective power of the group, and share a critical analysis and vision (p. 234). KWRU is also a place that sustains participants in personal ways, through friend-ships, family support, and resource sharing. This study of the organization by the organization offers a model of a "learning organization" in action.

> The Kensington Welfare Rights Union (KWRU) is **a multiracial organization of, by and for poor and homeless people.** We be-lieve that we have a right to thrive - not just barely survive. KWRU is dedicated to organizing of welfare recipients, the homeless, the working poor and all people concerned with economic justice.
>
> -KWRU, 2006
>
> To learn more about the Kensington Welfare Rights Union and the Poor People's Economic Human Rights Campaign, visit the KWRU website at: www.kwru.org

CONFLICT—CHALLENGES AND POSSIBILITIES

Social justice work calls on us to engage with conflict as part of the work. Struc-tured inequalities and disparities of power shape and are shaped by conflicting interests. Likewise, differing histories and experiences shape divergent and at times conflicting worldviews. Conflict can be both a source of constraint and possibility. If one looks at a dictionary definition of the verb form of the word "conflict" one finds descriptors such as to fight, contend or do battle, clash or disagree. Its noun form relates to strife, controversy, struggle, quarrel, antagonism, or opposition. Conflict carries negative connotations in our culture. Nowhere does the English language define conflict as a learning edge or an opportunity to question our own assumptions, and create better understanding of ourselves and others as intellec-tual and emotional human beings. The issue of conflict comes down to how we deal with it. Do we flee from controversial topics or conflictual issues? Or do we look to conflict as a battle to be won? Perhaps some of us have been rewarded for "not making waves," for keeping things "on an even keel," or for being the good child who never complained or caused any trouble. Others of us have taken pride in never conceding an issue and always having the last word in a disagreement. But somewhere in the middle of these two polarities is the notion of conflict as opportunity.

Conflict opens a space for learning. Conflict helps us to see different sides of an issue. It reminds us that there are different ways of defining problems and it provides the opportunity to seek alternative solutions. Conflict tells us many perspectives are being shared and that people are not agreeing just to agree. Conflict makes for better decision making in the end, but in the short run it can cause discomfort. Conflict is about learning to negotiate and value difference.

REFLECTION: Dealing with Conflict— Fight, Flight, or Opportunity

Take a minute to think about what the word conflict means to you. Is it something you avoid at all costs? How did members of your immediate family deal with conflict? How easy is it for you to disagree with someone? Is it easier to disagree with some people and not others? How differently do you handle conflict depending upon particular situations and circumstances? Now think about conflict on a much grander scale, say between countries concerning issues of war and peace, nuclear disarmament, or matters related to racial and ethnic cleansing, or the clash of religious beliefs. Recall a recent incident or event where you seriously disagreed with someone else. What was the disagreement about, and how did it feel to be engaged in a struggle? How do we create an environment where it is safe to disagree, where expressing differences is viewed as a growth-producing moment?

Controversial Issues

A C T I O N

The National Coalition Building Institute (NCBI), located in Washington, DC, was founded by Cherie R. Brown in 1984. Since its inception, NCBI has devoted itself to reducing prejudice and ending oppression that results from racism, sexism, and other forms of "otherism" that prevent peoples and communities from realizing their full potential. One of the primary missions of NCBI is to train people to address these issues in their communities. Maxine Jacobson completed the NCBI training and conducts NCBI training events on The University of Montana campus. One particularly powerful exercise from the NCBI training is included below:

In dealing with a controversial issue involving two parties, you may find the following six-step process developed by Brown and Mazza (1997, pp. 63-64) helpful in moving the disagreement forward. The exercise requires a third person to act as facilitator to negotiate and guide the process. We quote directly from their work below:

1. Without interrupting or planning a rebuttal while the other person is speaking, listen carefully to what the person is saying.

2. Repeat back to the person who has just spoken—in the exact words, if possible—the precise reasons the other person gave for her opinion.

3. Next, ask her a question that communicates that you value her opinion and

want to know more about how she sees the issue. For example, you might ask, "Please tell me more how you see this matter—is there anything from your own background that has led you to this conclusion?"

4. The parties then switch roles and repeat the first three steps.

5. Write down the concerns of both, checking with them to make sure that the recorded concerns accurately reflect their respective positions.

6. Review both persons' concerns, pointing out the areas of agreement. Then, propose a reframed question that takes at least one concern from each side into account. A reframed question often follows the format, "How can we do X, while at the same time doing Y?" For example, in [an] abortion dispute, you might ask, "How can we guarantee that young disadvantaged women are not burdened by pregnancy and child care, while taking measures that will keep abortion from becoming a population control policy that ultimately devalues human life?" The reframed question moves the controversy forward, inviting fresh thinking on the issue by incorporating each side's concern.

Controversies do not have to degenerate into polarization. A well-formulated, reframed question can ensure the development of policies that take into account the best thinking of all sides (Brown & Mazza, 1997).[6]

In groups of three, take some time to try out this conflict resolution model. Two people decide on an issue and the third person acts as the mediator, ensuring that the principles of the approach are followed. After completing this exercise, reflect on process and product. How difficult was it to adhere to the model? Were some topics easier to address than others? What were the challenges? What were the outcomes? What can you learn from this model about dealing with difference and conflicts that arise from difference? Develop a list of best-practice principles for resolving conflict and present these to the class.

Addressing Anger

Throughout the book we have addressed questions of difference and the relations of power therein. In Chapter 6 we explored the concept of resistance, and in the previous section we focused on conflict and controversy. We have not, however, considered the emotional underpinnings of these issues or the place and expression of anger associated with histories and experiences of exclusion and oppression. In much of the literature on helping, anger is addressed as an emotion to be "expressed" appropriately or somehow "managed." People, especially women and children, are acknowledged as needing permission to feel anger. Men are often the targets of "anger management" programs. The high incarceration rates of young men of color in the United States perhaps speak to the power of racially coded images of rage that can only be "contained" through imprisonment.

Anger and Cultural Expression

Certain social, cultural, and psychological parameters are often laid out regarding the proper expression of anger. Discussions of anger and emotions in general often assume that human emotions are universal—instinctual, if you will—and that their modes of expression are modulated through screens of cultural meaning. Cultural anthropologists have questioned assumptions about the universality of core human emotions and have helped us to see the production of emotion—the experience and its interpretation; the modes of expression; the range of identification of emotion and the rules of positionality, context, and expression—as culturally constructed (Briggs, 1970; Rosaldo, 1989). Neither anger nor other emotions necessarily fit into the neat scripts for expression and management that have been constructed in the helping professions.

We draw attention to anger here in the context of social justice work. People and groups with long-standing histories of oppression, exploitation, and discrimination may also have deep individual and collective experiences of anger, frustration, and distrust. The emotions and lived experience connected to histories of exclusion, abuse, and marginality and to the everyday indignities of "otherness" are not readily contained in individual models of emotional capacity, expression, and management. To strip powerful feelings from their larger context and locate them within the bodies of individuals is to distort the depth and complexity of their meanings, power, and histories. Social justice work calls for the expression and honoring of anger and frustration, rather than their containment. Working effectively with difference means allowing for anger and engaging with conflict as a valid and valued part of the work.

Skills for Defusing Anger

Let's take a look at one approach to dealing with anger developed by Charles Confer in his book *Managing Anger: Yours and Mine* (1997). Confer writes about five "defusing skills,"

1 Listen: The other person is angry for a reason: he is trying to get his needs met. It is important to listen not only to his words but also to the message behind his words. Respect his point of view even if you do not agree.

2 Acknowledge the anger: Acknowledge the person's anger by paraphrasing and summarizing what he is telling you. Acknowledge the anger without communicating blame and criticism.

3 Apologize: One way to reduce anger is to honestly and genuinely apologize for the pain and suffering the person may be experiencing.

4 Agree with the angry person: There is some truth behind most people's anger. Listen for that truth and agree with it. Perhaps you can agree with the facts of the situation, or the principles at stake, or with the other person's right to his opinion and feelings.

5 Invite the angry person's criticism: By inviting criticism you are communicating that you want to understand the person's point of view and identify what he would like to have happen.[7]

Let's reflect for a moment on Confer's approach to anger. Confer presents interpersonal skills that parallel a number of skills addressed in Chapter 6. For example, he focuses on respectful engagement with the angry person. But what seems to be missing here? What is the history behind this interaction? What are the positionalities of those involved, and how do they shape the power dynamics of the encounter? Whose "truth" counts? How might an approach aimed at "defusing" anger also depoliticize it? By seeking to defuse the emotional energy might we, in effect, be deactivating a possible catalyst for change? Perhaps, for the practice of social justice work, we could draw inspiration from the Spanish term *coraje*, which translates as both "rage" and "courage." How might we conceive of anger as a resource for social action rather than a time bomb to be defused? What possibilities for individual and collective action may open up as we reframe the meaning and power of anger?

Conflict Transformation

Now let's consider another perspective on conflict and resolution. What if we were to think in terms of conflict transformation? The National Network for Immigrant and Refugee Rights (NNIRR) acknowledges that conflict is a common outcome in efforts to build social and racial justice in communities. In developing their popular education resource, BRIDGE—Building a Race and Immigration Dialogue in the Global Economy, NNIRR developed a model for "conflict transformation" that begins by reframing conflict itself. They argue that conflict is an inevitable part of our lives, and so we need concrete strategies to integrate conflict transformation as part of our practice repertoire. They argue that conflict transformation can be a tool to establish a relationship based on equality and mutual respect (Cho et al., 2004, p. 267). The developers state,

> While conflict often stirs up unpleasant emotions and reactions for everyone involved, moments of conflict can also become important learning opportunities. As social justice activists, we need to practice what we preach within our own organizations, so when conflict happens within our organizations or movements, we need to develop ways to address it in a constructive way. Conflict transformation can become an important tool to increase our own capacity as organizations, communities, and individuals to fight for justice.

> Engaging in conflict transformation can address local challenges that can lead to the development of new alliances. Conflicts that our communities experience at the local level take place within a wider social and historical context of oppression and exclusions, as well as resistance and struggle for survival and liberation. For example, what appears at the local level as competition for jobs or services has the potential to be redefined as common ground in the struggle for shared human rights. Examples of this include hostility between African-Americans and immigrant communities, tensions within communities between U.S.-born or permanent residents and undocumented immigrants, as well as conflict within our own organizations. Learning to integrate our values and vi-

sions of social justice with conflict resolution is not only a matter of personal, psychological, organizational, and political survival. It's also a critical part of resistance and movement building.

Without an intentional approach to conflict resolution, we can reproduce the methods and values of dominant cultures, focusing on only "winning" or "losing," or overpowering and destroying our opponents. In many cases, conflict occurs within our own organizations, communities and movements, and when handled badly, results in a collective loss. (p. 266)

NNIRR has developed a series of activities for conflict transformation that encourage groups to name conflict, visualize personal experiences in conflict and steps to conflict transformation, and use theater and role play techniques inspired by Augusto Boal's *Theatre of the Oppressed* (1985) to change the conflict script and visualize solutions. We include here some ideas put forth by NNIRR for conflict transformation. Take time to consider some situations when you might have benefited from putting these steps to practice. Might you be able to draw from these ideas for conflict transformation in addressing conflicts in families, groups, and social service organizations?

Steps for Transforming Conflict Between Community Members

1. Allow people to name the problem, express how it has impacted them personally and as a community.

2. Explore the historical or larger context of the conflict.

3. Listen to how the problem has impacted the other side and recognize the humanity and rights of the other side.

4. Acknowledge your own role in the conflict.

5. Search for shared experiences that you have with the other side, such as shared hurts and suffering, cultural or spiritual sources of understanding and support, common humanity, etc.

6. Recognize the connections and interdependence between communities.

7. Determine what's appropriate for your situation. Is it building a short term, task-oriented solution to defuse a dangerous conflict or a more longterm alliance to address deeper levels of interests?

8. Work together to elaborate win/win solutions that are mutually beneficial to all parties.

9. If necessary, develop a formal agreement to capture the spirit of the unity people reach.

10. Identify mechanisms and parties who will be responsible for convening another dialogue or problem-solving process to resolve any conflicts that may arise in the future in a mutually positive way.

11. Figure out ways to publicize and mobilize people in the broader community in order to implement the agreement or new understanding.

Source: National Network for Immigrant and Refugee Rights (NNIRR), 2004

CRITICAL EDUCATION: CHALLENGES AND POSSIBILITIES

Throughout the book we have addressed the importance of raising critical consciousness about privilege, power, oppression, and inequality as a central aspect of social justice work. This entails an ongoing practice of critical education. In this section we address political education and popular theater as possibilities for social justice-oriented action.

Political Education

Activist and organizer Rinku Sen describes the process of political education as one in which "we have to read, share information, understand history, bring people to speak to our groups, and talk with people in other places. We have to think about our theories of how society is organized, why it is organized that way, and how change will come" (2003, p. 21). As Sen notes, political education has a rich history in labor and community organization. Members of the Kensington Welfare Rights Union have taught us about the importance of political education in building and sustaining both their organization and a broader movement for social justice (Baptist et al., 2006, pp. 221-240). Similarly, Sen argues that political education helps build and strengthen progressive organizations in three ways (2003, p. 166):

1. Political education helps organizations hold on to members — It helps people make connections to issues and history.

2. Political education supports long-term strategic planning - It helps participants and leaders grasp and negotiate organizational complexities and be good allies of other constituencies, a critical aspect of movement building.

3. Political education helps prepare groups to get their ideas into the world - It helps build "media literate" organizations and members who can educate, advocate, and defend their positions.

Take a moment to think about an issue you are concerned about, yet feel poorly informed about. Perhaps you are concerned about housing and homelessness, Social Security, immigration, or the AIDS crisis in sub-Saharan Africa. How might you take a political education approach to action? Perhaps you could form a social work study/buddy group and begin a local process of consciousness raising. What steps might you take to get started? What might be the possibilities for linking critical education and action?

Popular Theater

We introduced popular education in Chapter 6. Popular education makes use of a variety of tools to help people gain deeper understanding of cultural, economic, and political influences on their lives. Political education can be thought of as one form of popular education. Another form of popular education is *popular theater*, which uses performance as a tool for dialogue, consciousness raising, and transformation (Bates, 1996, Boal, 1985, 1998; Srikandath, 1991). Popular theater "covers a wide range of theatrical activities, including drama, dance, puppetry, and song. These theatrical techniques engage people in examination of issues that affect their lives, facilitate communication and interaction that spark awareness of collective oppression, and encourage development of viable strategies for action" (Finn, Jacobson, & Dean Campana, 2004, p. 328). In popular theater performances the boundaries between actor and audience are challenged, and the audience is encouraged to take an active role in the process of performance and critical reflection.

Popular theater links performance, education, and change. It has deep roots in centuries-old political movements as a strategy for consciousness raising. However, popular theater is most closely associated with noted Brazilian director, activist, and educator Augusto Boal who took Freirian principles and translated them into the medium of theater as a tool for creating knowledge and change among people living in conditions of poverty and oppression (Bates, 1996). Boal's *Theatre of the Oppressed* (1985) develops the philosophy and practice of popular theater and offers examples of this strategy for change in action. The use of theater and performance has come to play an important role in popular education. Boal (1998) has also written about the use of popular theater as a strategy to change social policy. Through the use of "legislative theater," a form of popular theater, participants research social issues and use performance as a means of education and advocacy. For instance, legislative theater played a key role in the passage of progressive geriatric health care legislation in Rio de Janiero in 1995 (Boal, 1998).

Social justice workers around the world have embraced popular theater as a strategy for social change. For example, Tom Magill, founding member of Creative Training Solutions in the United Kingdom, uses popular theater to offer social workers new ways of working that link critical analysis and creative expression (Houston, Magill, McCollum, & Spratt, 2001; Spratt, Houston, & Magill, 2000). In December of 2000, Tom Magill and Mark McCollum, then coordinator of the Community Arts Company, worked on the government-funded Community Employment Project, which sought to reach poor, unemployed communities in rural Donegal County, Ireland. Their goal was to "use theatre as a means of enabling socially and economically marginalized communities to participate in wider society through a realization of their social and economic potential" (Houston et al., 2001, p. 287). Magill and McCollum facilitated a group process that helped project participants uncover common experiences of oppression by offering popular theater as a method for sparking critical consciousness.

The original project participants were unemployed adults, and although their life experiences differed, through group dialogues it was revealed that they all shared the common experience of being bullied. The group used this as the basis for constructing a play depicting childhood encounters with bullies, to be performed in Donegal County schools. Participants worked together to create characters and a story line that presented their shared experience of oppression to which their audience could relate and respond. The result was a play about a child who is continually confronted by a bully at school and further victimized by peers. In the school performances audience members were informed that the play was not finished and that they were to help write the ending. After watching the story unfold, children in the audience were transformed into what Boal terms "spectactors"—at once spectators and actors with no boundary between the two. As such they were encouraged to propose possible endings, and they were given the opportunities to take to the stage and act out those possibilities. Through both the play and the following discussion participants were able to name bullying as a form of oppression, critically reflect on its impact, and strategize individual and collective possibilities for change-oriented action.

Trevor Spratt, Stan Houston, and Tom Magill (2000) have taken their pioneering work further to demonstrate the potential for cross-disciplinary work in social work, theater, and cultural studies. For example, they have used popular theater to engage social work students and practitioners in grappling with the contradictions in child protective services work and in envisioning positive and realistic strategies for change. Through use of popular theater they help participants identify and analyze oppressive bureaucratic structures and their dehumanizing effect and craft images of a child welfare system grounded in respect for rights, citizenship, and participation (Spratt et al., 2000; Houston et al., 2001, p. 291).[8]

Andrew Boyd, author of *The Activist Cookbook: Creative Actions for a Fair Economy* (1999), catalogues a rich collection of "recipes" for social action based on the principles of popular theater. The recipes highlight the importance of art and culture "[at] the heart of any movement, any moving of people. . ." (p. 2). Boyd provides a number of sample recipes for popular theater performances and playfully teases the reader to "Help yourself. Spice to taste. Play with your food" (p. 28). We include a sample here to further whet your appetite for popular theater and to stimulate your creative juices. Boyd calls this popular theater performance *War of the Worlds, Part II*:

> A skit based on Orson Welles' famous 1930's-era radio play—but instead of Martians, transnational corporations take over the Earth. Samples: "They're hideous to behold; cold and calculating, their tentacles reaching out everywhere...can nothing stop them...?" "Their dark ships hovering over government buildings, their deadly lasers striking out without warning, aaaarrrrggg, oh my God! They've burned a Mickey Mouse symbol into the White House lawn..." (p. 28)

Boyd and his colleagues at United for a Fair Economy (formerly Share the Wealth) organize themselves and others to draw "public attention to the dangerous consequences of growing income and wealth inequality . . ." (p. 93). How might you use or adapt the *War of the Worlds, Part II* "recipe?" In what context might this particular brand of acting out your message be helpful? What might be the constraints or the fall-out? Are there similar situations of economic disparity in your own community that might be addressed through this kind of public message?

**REFLECTION: Creative Acting Out—
The Social Justice Action Network**

In 2005 a group of MSW students at The University of Montana School of Social Work came together to form the Social Justice Action Network (SJAN) as a vehicle for translating their concerns for social justice into concrete collective action. Among its goals, SJAN sought to address policy change through popular education and advocacy. SJAN was in its formative stages as massive federal budget cuts loomed in the fall of 2005. Members used popular theater techniques to make connections between federal budget cuts and the implications for Montana families. SJAN's first public action was a campus-based popular theater performance showing how the proposed federal cuts were balancing the budget on the backs of the poor. Along with the performance, the group set up an information table with fact sheets on the federal budget, sample letters for contacting congressional representatives, and cell phones for people to place a direct call to their representatives. This first action gave participants a concrete opportunity to put knowledge and values to practice, engage in a group process of consciousness raising, and try out possibilities of popular theater.

Meet with other students in small groups and see if you can come up with some imaginative ways to get a message across. What areas of concern could be demonstrated well using these methods? How might you feel about educating others and yourself by acting out? What might be the constraints or drawbacks?

COMMUNITY BUILDING: CHALLENGES AND POSSIBILITIES

The cumulative actions of social justice work contribute to the building of dynamic, resilient, learning communities. In this section we highlight action related to collaboration and coalitions, both central to community building. We reflect on the challenges and possibilities of working with and across difference in the practice of community building. And we explore the skills of policy practice that are essential to organizational, community, and societal change efforts.

Coalition Building and Collaboration for Change

Defining Coalitions

Coalitions are forged when the power base of a small group of people acting to create change is much too small to accomplish the task on its own, especially when resources are insufficient (Homan, 2004, p. 381). You can think of coalitions as organizations of organizations. There are different kinds of coalitions, and each serves a different purpose and outcome. For example, many coalitions are ad hoc, which means they emerge over an expressed need, and once the task is accomplished they disband. Other coalitions are more permanent. They emerge and become instituted around a specific problem area such as homelessness, hunger, or poverty. Homan points out the benefits to a change effort of forming coalitions to a change effort. He tells us we can think of the organizations that compose a coalition as arms that spread out to capture necessary resources to get the job done. Many arms can gather more resources than one alone. When people are gathered together in coalitions, resources are more abundant. These resources consist of credibility, funding, people power, volunteers, support staff, office equipment, and different ways of thinking about and perceiving situations. Increased resources enlarge the power base of a change effort.

Guidelines for Building a Coalition

Homan (2004) outlines a number of guidelines for assembling a coalition and building alliances across organizations and groups (pp. 383-384). We summarize from his work below and add some of our own thoughts regarding coalitions:

1. Determine whom you would like to have involved in the coalition. Think first about organizations and groups with whom you already have existing relationships and then ask the critical questions, Who is most likely to join? Which organizations are most affected by the issues we intend to address? What talents, skills, and competencies are important to the work we hope to accomplish? Who has what we need? Besides the obvious resources such as money, expertise, and sheer numbers, who can relate best to the different publics you want to influence?

2. Contact these individuals and emphasize how the issue affects their self-interest. This is best accomplished face-to-face. This allows you the opportunity to clarify, answer questions, and explain the benefits of collaboration.

3. Secure a commitment to the coalition, preferably through a written contract that spells out obligations and clarifies roles and procedures. As an alternative to a written contract, you could get a letter of support written on the organization's stationary. Securing a commitment allows you to list this organization's name as part of your group.

4. Involve the new members in organizing an initial meeting and use this as an opportunity to build further support and enthusiasm for your work.

5. Don't expect that all members will attend each meeting, but keep members on board by apprising them of the group's progress. However, don't be afraid to personally ask specific members to be involved in the accomplishment of certain tasks.

6. Effective communication among coalition members is crucial to the effort. Never forget the importance of appreciating people's work.

What are some examples of effective coalition building for social justice in your community? Where do you see possibilities for expanding the efforts?

Collaboration

Nancy Claiborne and Hal Lawson (2005) present a framework for collaboration among social service organizations. They describe collaboration as a collective form of action involving two or more entities who have a stake in working together in response to complex and interdependent issues that affect their organizational efforts and participants. In order to successfully organize, build a common agenda, mobilize resources, sustain action, and obtain results, collaborations must meet the following criteria:

♦ Develop equitable relations amid difference in their power and authority.

♦ Negotiate their difference and resolve their conflicts.

♦ Reinforce awareness that they fundamentally depend on each other.

♦ Identify shared interests, responsibilities, and action-oriented theories.

♦ Promote norms of reciprocity and trust.

♦ Reconfigure and realign rules, roles, boundaries.

♦ Develop shared language.

♦ Promote a collective identity.

♦ Share resources.

♦ Take into accounts salient features of the local context.

♦ Pursue opportunities to develop join accountability for results.

What are some examples of effective collaboration for social justice in your community? Where do you see possibilities for expanding the efforts?

Community Building: Global Possibilities:

The Child Friendly Cities Initiative was launched in 1996 to take action on a resolution passed by the second United Nations Conference on Human Settlements calling for cities to be livable places for all and places that promote the well-being of children. The Initiative, spearheaded by UNICEF, seeks ways to put the UN Convention of the Rights of the Child to practice at the local level throughout the globe. Fundamentally, the initiative promotes children's participation in the issues that affect their lives. A Child Friendly City "is a local system of good governance committed to fulfilling child rights for all its young citizens. A Child Friendly City involves children and youth in initiatives concerning their lives; fosters participative planning, implementation and good governance processes; encourages child participation in family, community, and social life; extends basic services such as health care, education, shelter, safe water, and proper sanitation to all; protects children from exploitation, violence, trafficking and abuse; maintains safe streets and places for socialization and play; provides green spaces and playgrounds; controls pollution and traffic; supports cultural and social events; and ensures that all children live as equal citizens with access to every service, without discrimination related to age, gender, income, race, ethnicity, cultural origin, religion, and/or disability" (CFC, FAQ, p. 1; 2006). Promoters contend that a child-friendly city is friendly to all. The UNICEF Secretariat for Child Friendly Cities has developed a framework for defining and developing a Child Friendly City, based on Nine Building Blocks:

1. Children's participation

2. A child friendly legal framework

3. A city-wide Children's Rights Strategy

4. A Children's Rights Unity or coordinating mechanism

5. Child impact assessment and evaluation

6. A Children's Budget

7. A regular State of the City's children Report

8. Making children's rights known

9. Independent advocacy for children

To learn more about this exciting initiative, find examples of CFC's around the world, and access a Framework for Action, visit the CFC website at http://www.childfriendlycities.org

REFLECTION: Bridging Difference—Skills of Multicultural Practice

Effective social justice work requires the ability to recognize, honor, and bridge differences. As we have just discussed, coalition building is a sensitive and strategic process of finding common interest, creating common ground, recognizing differences, mobilizing alliances, and valuing participants. Social justice work also requires the capacity to build and sustain organizations in which people with different histories, experiences, and interests can come together, pool knowledge and resources, and make a commitment to the work together over the long haul. John Anner (1996) offers the following thoughts on building successful multicultural social justice organizations:

♦ Build personal relationships among members from different backgrounds.

♦ Actively engage in solidarity campaigns, actions, and activities with social justice organizations in other communities.

♦ Challenge bigoted statements and attitudes when they arise.

♦ Hold regular discussions, forums, "educationals," and workshops to enhance people's understandings of other communities and individuals.

♦ Work to change the culture of the organization so that members see themselves as "members of the community" first instead of members of a particular part of the community.

♦ Develop issues, tactics, and campaigns that are relevant to different communities and that reveal fundamental areas of common interests.

♦ Conduct antiracism training to get people to confront and deal with their biases.

♦ Examine and change the organization's practices in order to hire, promote, and develop people of color.

♦ Confront white privilege and nationalism.

♦ Hire, recruit, and train more people of color for leadership positions.

What examples of putting these tactics to practice can you draw from your own experience? How successful were they? Where were the sources of support and resistance? What would you add to the list?

POLICY PRACTICE: ANALYSIS AND ADVOCACY FOR SOCIAL JUSTICE

Linking Policy and Practice

Josefina Figueira-McDonough (1993) reminds us that social policy has long been a neglected side of social work practice. She poses the question that perhaps professional identity precludes social workers' engagement in policy activities. Others (Chapin, 1995; Jansson, 1999) concur with Figueira-McDonough's claim and note that the profession favors "direct intervention" work over policy practice and separates out policy work as "indirect" service. However, this bifurcation of practice into categories of "direct" and "indirect" ignores the fact that initiating new policies requires the same skills of relationship building, communication, and negotiation as does traditional work with individuals, families, and communities. The importance of policy practice to social work is difficult to overlook. The nature and direction of social work practice and the structure and activities of social welfare organizations are shaped by social policy. In turn, individuals, groups, and organizations "make" social policy as they interpret, respond to, resist, and translate policies into practice. Thus social policy issues are at the heart of social work practice. Social justice work calls for the critical integration of policy and practice and recognition of the ways in which policy and practice are mutually constituted.

At their most basic level, policies are rules, guiding principles established to maintain order in the social sphere. Policies are generally thought of as statements about how we as a culture define social problems. Implicitly, they represent beliefs and values about a given social condition (Tropman, 1984). Rosemary Chapin (1995, p. 506) asks us to rethink the notion of policy built on "careful problem definition." She critically examines the emphasis on personal deficits and pathology written into social policy and advocates policy development and analysis that address problems in terms of environmental barriers and inadequacy of resources. Chapin contends:

> . . . this problem-centered approach to policy formulation with its intense focus on definition and assessment has not been coupled with similar attention to assessment of the strengths of the people and environment that the policy targets. (p. 506)

While this approach may sound good in theory, Chapin cautions us that bringing a strengths perspective to policy development, analysis, and advocacy requires addressing the social construction of knowledge and how a problem-centered approach may meet the needs of people in power. Rappaport, Davidson, Wilson, and Mitchell (1975, as cited in Chapin, p. 508) suggest that, in order to provide alternative approaches, we need to look to people who know their communities and who are ultimately affected by policy decisions and see them as partners in the policy development and analysis process. Integrating a strengths perspective into the policymaking process starts by redefining our ideas about policy. A new definition of policy would view it as a tool to help people meet their basic needs for food, shelter, health care, and protection.

Deficit– versus Strengths–Based Approaches to Policy

Chapin (1995, p. 510) presents an informative comparison between deficits-based and strengths-based approaches to policy. We include her model here and ask you to think about the potential of the strengths perspective as an alternative to a problem-centered, deficits-focused approach to policy development. What differences do you see between these two approaches? What challenges does a strengths approach to policy development pose? How does this model attend to the key themes of meaning, context, power, history, and possibility? Are there any areas you might expand on to make the strengths approach outlined by Chapin more congruent with the Just Practice Framework?

Comparison of the Problem-Centered and Strengths Approaches to Policy Formation

Problem-Centered Approach	Strengths Approach
Problem definition	Identification of basic needs and barriers to meeting needs Definition negotiation
Problem analysis—causes and consequences	Identification of the ways that barriers are currently overcome by clients and through programs (best practice)
Informing the public	[Direct participation in the policy process by those affected][9]
Development of policy goals	Identification of opportunities and resources necessary for people to meet their needs Policy formulation
Consensus building	Negotiating consensus on policy goals
Program design	Program design
Implementation	Implementation
Evaluation and assessment	Evaluation and assessment of client outcomes

Four Methods of Policy Practice

Social policy shapes and is shaped by the practice of social work. For example, Figueira-McDonough (1993) contends that taking the profession's core value of social justice seriously means making a commitment to "policy practice." She outlines four methods of policy practice: 1) legislative advocacy; 2) reform through litigation; 3) social action; and 4)social policy analysis. We summarize these methods here, provide examples from practice, and refer you to Figueira-McDonough's article (see pp. 181-186) for an expanded description of each.

Legislative Advocacy

The task of legislative advocacy is to gain access to needed resources and social goods. Figueira-McDonough points out that legislative advocacy usually takes the

METHODS OF POLICY PRACTICE

1. legislative advocacy;

2. reform through litigation;

3. social action;

4. social policy analysis.

form of lobbying in traditional U.S. social work. Lobbying is the act of trying to influence legislators and other government officials to support particular perspectives with their colleagues. Lobbyists can wield considerable power and influence, especially if they are backed by interest groups with large sums of money and connections to other sources of support. For example, representatives of NASW and CSWE join forces and collaborate to amass strength in numbers and lobby for particular causes and concerns relevant to the profession and those individuals it serves. However, these efforts are generally top-down approaches initiated by organization officials, and they often fail to include those most affected by policy decisions. Legislative advocacy efforts can also include the voices of the citizenry.

Reform through Litigation

This form of policy practice receives the least attention in the social work literature perhaps because it requires a certain amount of legal shrewdness and is a slow way of achieving social reform (Figueira-McDonough, 1993, p. 182). Anyone who has dealt with the judicial system knows it has its own time clock, and cases can drag out for months and even years. Yet reform through litigation has some inherent characteristics that make it exceptionally well suited for addressing issues of minority groups:

> (1) the process is initiated by the interested party, not the court, and (2) the decision is made exclusively on the basis of legal antecedents and evidence—both brought to the court by the involved parties. Openness of access and equal chance in defining the issue put the parties on a level playing field (Figueira-McDonough, 1993, p. 183).

Social Action

Figueira-McDonough calls our attention to the civil rights movement of the 1950s and 1960s as an example of social action and its potential to promote social change. Checkoway (1990) describes social action as a way to "create change by building powerful organizations at the community level" (p. 12). When compared with other methods of policy practice addressed in this section, social action is by far the most participatory. Social change is forged from the ground up and relies, almost entirely, on the involvement of ordinary people in addressing their concerns. It seeks to create structural change in society's institutions and addresses issues of inequality and injustice.

Social Policy Analysis

Figueira-McDonough outlines an analytic framework for policy analysis that attends to questions of values, knowledge, and effectiveness. To achieve these ends one focuses on the fit between the stated goals of the policy and the proposals for its implementation, the accuracy and reliability of the knowledge informing the policy development and the means of implementation, and the costs of the proposal, both in human and financial terms. Sarri (1988, as cited in Figueira-McDonough, p. 186) provides an example of policy analysis that focuses on these particular areas of concern: "Before leaving office in 1989, President Reagan supported a policy requiring mothers on welfare to work for their benefits. Because no guaranteed provision of child care was included and the benefits these mothers receive are not sufficient to pay for child care, the anticipated result is deterioration in the supervision of their children." This policy analysis illustrates how policy can fail to consider the consequences of its implementation and that cost-saving initiatives may actually be more expensive (both monetarily and socially) in the end.

Think for a moment of the methods of policy practice summarized here. How realistic is it to envision social workers as policy practitioners? What do you see as some of the constraints and challenges of policy practice in community and organizational contexts? What do you see as some of the possibilities? What values and beliefs do these methods support? How do these methods fit with the key concepts of the Just Practice Framework? Where are the gaps?

RESOURCE: SUMMARY OF SKILLS FOR FAMILY–CENTERED POLICY PRACTICE

Katharine Briar-Lawson (2001, pp. 290-292) offers the following summary of skills for family-centered policy practice. She notes that the list is also "suggestive of the change-agent roles that accompany family-centered practice" (p. 290).

Agenda Setting and Analysis

- Naming and framing
- Reframing and promoting new discourses
- Creating public concern (kids counts, family counts, and elder counts)
- Promoting and using family impact analyses
- Calling for a study committee
- Developing a policy brief with cost-of-failure, benefit-of-success data, along with expenditure shift strategies

Appealing to the Public

- Holding a press conference
- Issuing a press release
- Writing letters to editor, op-ed columns
- Developing relations with the media, for example, seeking media coverage for an issue, an action step, a conference

Mobilizing People for Collective Action

- "Deputizing" and mobilizing others for action
- Using the Internet to persuade, organize, and mobilize others
- Promoting shared leadership among as many individuals and families as possible to build a movement
- Working with local organizations to mobilize them and the families they represent.

Developing an Action System

- Convening a problem-solving group

- Convening a collaborative team or several teams
- Building innovative coalitions and alliances
- Developing interagency working agreements, interpersonal working agreements (contracts)
- Turning a work or task group into a problem-solving and policy-oriented change group

Collective Advocacy with Public Officials and the General Public

- Testifying before governmental officials and private sector leaders
- Holding a conference
- Meeting with representatives of various levels of a hierarchy to put them on notice regarding an issue, ways they can help, what should change
- Proposing a legislative initiative
- Lobbying

Grassroots Change in Laws

- Knowing human rights and using this knowledge to frame needs as legal issues
- Initiating legal action to address rights violations and needs related to family well-being

RETURN TO ACCOMPANIMENT

It's All about Relationship

We have taken a whirlwind trip through the complex terrain of social justice action in this chapter. We conclude with a return to accompaniment and a reminder that it is all about relationship. First let's revisit the work of Maureen Wilson and Elizabeth Whitmore, who introduced us to the process of accompaniment. They learned important lessons in accompaniment through their participation in a 5-year, collaborative social development project funded by the Canadian International Development Agency and involving the Schools of Social Work at Managua's Universidad Centroamericana and the University of Calgary, Canada. The goals of the project were to strengthen the capacities of social work teachers in the Universidad Centroamericana and to develop a social action documentation center. The experience taught them about *how* one engages in the process of accompaniment. It requires the skills and attitudes of good social work: empathy, respect, a nonjudgmental approach, openness, tolerance for ambiguity, and ability to facilitate interaction. Further, they argue that meaningful structural change comes through collaborative action in coalitions and networks where people join to challenge forms and practices of domination. Accompaniment includes the ability to be an active, supportive member of coalitions and networks and to understand one's stake and positionality therein.

As Canadians working in Nicaragua, Wilson and Whitmore needed to be constantly mindful of North-South power imbalances and the implications for their work. Issues and pressures of time shaped the process. While Whitmore and Wilson had a block of time to be present and work with their colleagues, their Nicaraguan counterparts were juggling the many time and resource demands of their everyday lives. The Nicaraguans had also had previous experience with well-intentioned foreigners presenting ideas and proposals that never materialized. Wilson and Whitmore had to guard against taking over the process by virtue of their access to resources and by the nuances of language. For example, many of the conceptual frameworks that shaped their assumptions were developed in English and reflected a "long ideological history and way of life" that were not readily translatable to the Nicaraguan context (1997, pp. 66-67). They found a participatory research methodology most conducive to collaborative knowledge development in this context. Based on their experiences they conclude: ". . .sympathetic listening, engaged questioning, nondirective suggesting, and solidarity in the face of setback are the stuff of accompaniment" (p. 68).

Accompaniment and Alliance

Effective accompaniment demands reflection on what it means to be an ally and how we build alliances. For example, in documenting the contributions and possibilities of young people as competent community builders, Janet Finn and Barry Checkoway (1998) found that a common theme among many thriving community-based youth initiatives was the role of adults as allies. Successful, sustained, youth-directed initiatives often have strong intergenerational ties and longstanding relationships with adults who offer counsel and mentoring, support their efforts without usurping them, and help facilitate access to other networks and resources. Effective allies are engaged in ongoing critical reflection on the balance of power and the importance of autonomy as well as connection.

Gloria Anzaldúa speaks powerfully about allies from her perspective as a Chicana lesbian feminist. She writes:

> Becoming allies means helping each other heal. It can be hard to expose yourself and your wounds to a stranger who could be an ally or an enemy. But if you and I were to do good alliance work together, be good allies to each other, I would have to expose my wounds to you and you would have to expose your wounds to me and then we could start from a place of openness. During our alliance work, doors will close and we'll have to open them again. People who engage in alliances and are working toward certain goals want to keep their personal feelings out of it, but you can't. You have to work out your personal problems while you are working out the problems of this particular community or the particular culture. (Anzaldúa, 1994, as cited in Adams et al., 2000, p. 495)

Anzaldúa challenges those who mask practices of tokenism in the language of alliance. She asks those in positions of relative privilege to reflect critically on their motives for building alliances. Are they looking to assimilate the "other" voice? Are they trying to avoid charges of elitism and racism? She warns that the biggest risk in forming alliances is betrayal:

> When you are betrayed you feel shitty... And betrayal makes you

feel like less of a person—you feel shame, it reduces your self-esteem. It is politically deadening and dangerous; it's disempowering. (1994, as cited in Adams et al., 2000, p. 496)

Margaret Ledwith and Paula Asgill (2000) propose the concept of *critical alliance*, which they argue is vital to the future of community work and collective action for social justice. They draw from their identities and collaborative work experiences as an African Caribbean woman and a white British woman in attempting to articulate the crafting of alliance across difference. They begin with acknowledgement of their differences and critical reflection on the sociopolitical context in which they are coming together. They take seriously questions regarding the unspoken privileges of whiteness and questions of "'black rage,' which is silenced within this whiteness" (hooks, 1995, p. 11, as cited in Ledwith & Asgill, 2000, p. 291). They argue that effective alliances need to address the complexity of identities as "emergent histories which are located at the critical intersection of our lived experience within the social, cultural, and economic relations of our time, shifting, not fixed" (Ledwith & Asgill, 2000, p. 293). They contend that effective community work calls for honest engagement with these knotty issues. They write,

> Our position is one of locating community work at the heart of liberation by defining and contextualizing its critical potential. The feminist challenge is that, by a process of democratisation based on mutual accountability and collective action, alliances of difference can transform those social institutions that entrench prejudice, discrimination and exploitation as legitimate. (p. 294)

Ledwith and Asgill speak to the challenge of dialogue across difference, and the need to explore the anger, the silences, and the misunderstandings between them through ongoing, honest conversation. They echo Anzaldúa's contention that developing alliances is a painful process, but that the naming and exposing of pain is essential to transformative action.

**A
C
T
I
O
N**

Personalizing Accompaniment

This exercise can be done individually, in pairs, in small groups, or with your entire class. Find a comfortable position, take a few deep breaths, and let yourself relax. Now imagine you have embarked on a journey with a potential partner or partners. Allow yourself to create a detailed picture of your partner(s). Where do you go on your journey? The possibilities are infinite. Perhaps a hike in the woods, a canoe trip down the river, or off to a country you have never explored before. How do you make this decision collectively and what do you do to form an alliance with your partner(s)? Do you do this through dialogue or nonverbal signs? Given your choice of partner(s), what feelings does accompaniment evoke? Comfort? Constraint? Anticipation? How do you negotiate these feelings? Now take a minute to investigate your surroundings. Where does your journey take you and what happens along the way? Do obstacles surface that slow you down, or is it smooth sailing? How do you illustrate through your actions the key themes of accompaniment? Once you have arrived at your destination, you meet someone there who gives you and your partner(s) a "gift" that embodies the key principles of accompaniment. You bring this gift with you on the return trip home. Who is this gift-giver? Does the exchange happen nonverbally or through dialogue? What does the gift look like? What lessons does the gift teach you about accompaniment? You and your partner(s) make your way back to where you began. Take time to process this imagery.

CHAPTER SUMMARY

Throughout this chapter we have examined ways in which the knowledge and values of social justice work are translated into concrete actions for change. We have explored the meaning and power of accompaniment in diverse contexts of practice. Drawing inspiration from critical and creative practitioners around the world, we demonstrated ways of engaging in and promoting Just Practice across diverse social work arenas, from direct practice with children and families, to prison settings, to community change efforts. We recognized that the "proof" of social justice work is in the meaningful participation of those affected in challenging and changing the conditions of their lives. To that end we addressed skills and strategies for participatory planning, decision making, and action. The practice of social justice work calls for a reconceptualization of social work roles in order to address questions of power and positionality, a commitment to critical curiosity, the challenges of collaboration, and the possibilities of creative intervention. We have emphasized the significance of the social worker as animator, engaging people in meaningful action and weaving the connections of head, heart, and hand. We have probed the linkage of policy and practice and argued that social justice workers need to grasp and engage with their integration. People-to-people partnerships that respect difference pose both challenges and possibilities. Conflict is part of the process. As social justice workers we need to be able to confront strong feelings, both our own and others, and give time, space, and value to the recognition and expression of feelings. The process of accompaniment can never be taken for granted. Partnerships need to be nurtured, respected, and energized. We invite you to return to the questions regarding action and accompaniment that we outlined in the Just Practice matrix at the end of Chapter 5 (p. 202). How might these questions guide you in developing action plans and building critical alliances and supportive partnerships? What questions would you add to the matrix? As we noted in Chapter 2, action and reflection are dialectical, mutually informing processes. As we take time to evaluate and reflect on our practice and celebrate our achievements, we open up new possibilities for action. In Chapter 9 we explore the processes of evaluation, reflection, and celebration.

Action and Accompaniment: Learning from Fuerza Unida[1]

C A S E   S T U D Y

Fuerza Unida's mission is to educate, empower, and organize workers to become advocates for social change, organizers for economic justice and full participants in the democratic process. Our purpose is to advance the rights of women, workers and low-income communities by providing education, training, guidance, and accessible information so that they may protect their rights and those of their families and communities. We are rooted in the struggle for systemic change in the workplace, communities, and environment of workers and women locally, and reach out to our compañera/os worldwide. Through our collaborations with organizations and coalitions, we build a united force, *una fuerza unida,* that emphasizes the voices of people of color, women, youth, and immigrants within the working class.

(*Fuerza Unida*, 2006)

On January 17, 1990, the Levi Strauss plant in San Antonio, Texas, closed with no warning. Managers announced that in order to "stay competitive" they were moving the factory to Costa Rica. Over 1,000 people, 80% of them Mexican American women, lost their jobs overnight. For Viola Casares, a single mother and garment worker with no organizing experience, the closure opened her eyes to injustice. "Things happen for a reason" she recalls. Viola and her co-workers were outraged. For too long, Levi Straus had viewed women as simply part of the machine, paid them low piece-rate wages, and considered them expendable when labor could be purchased cheaper elsewhere. Now the women needed to take a stand, say "enough is enough," and challenge the company's divide-and-conquer strategy where women's bodies were paying the price for company profit.

The women began to talk with one another and compare their experiences of work-related injuries, bonuses promised and never received, and day-to-day struggles for family and community survival. They started questioning why some women were receiving benefits and others were not. They learned that Levi Strauss had used their pensions for collateral to purchase other plants. With the help of the Southwest Public Workers Union, the women began to organize. They formed *Fuerza Unida* (United Force) to fight for their rights as workers and women. The women launched a boycott of Levi Strauss and filed a lawsuit to reclaim their stolen benefits.

Over the past 17 years *Fuerza Unida* has developed into a formidable organization that contributes to meaningful change in women's lives. Although the lawsuit was ultimately not successful, the organization has a remarkable array of accomplishments. They have kept ongoing public pressure on Levi Strauss regarding its employment practices and working conditions. They have worked in solidarity with women in the *maquiladoras* of Mexico and Central America on issues of wages, benefits, and health care. And they have expanded their efforts from the factory floor to the larger community through their popular education, food bank, and youth projects. Their women's sewing cooperative, established in 1996, created a space where women can use their well-honed skills in production of quality handmade items for sale in the community and through online marketing. Revenues from the cooperative fund their food bank program. *Fuerza Unida* is committed to empowering women and other members of the community through workshops on issues such as domestic violence, adult education, globalization, environmental justice, water rights and quality, military contamination, and advocacy for undocumented workers. And, importantly, it remains a place where women can come together to "talk, cry, laugh, and give back to the community."

As Viola describes, her experience at *Fuerza Unida* has made her a better mother: "I have shown my children that I can be something better than just be part of a machine… My children are proud. It takes something to open your eyes and see that you can make changes in your community. Little changes are the ones that matter…. I have something to give to my grandchildren, too. I can give them a history they are not taught in schools." Viola has drawn on her organizing experience to help other women from Honduras to South Africa.

Petra Mata is a mother, grandmother, and for many years a garment worker for Levi Strauss. She immigrated to San Antonio from Mexico when she was newly married, and she got a job in the Levi Strauss plant. Over time she worked her way to supervisor. Petra witnessed and experienced the stresses of the job. Women were exposed to chemicals, and to injury as they tried to meet production demands. Nearly 70% of the women suffered from carpal tunnel syndrome. But the women were afraid to ask questions and speak out against the company. Petra sees organizing as a necessity. Between 1985 and 1990 Levi Strauss closed 26 plants, and no one challenged their actions until *Fuerza Unida*. Petra describes the importance of making connections, organizing in collaboration with networks of women workers, and building alliances across borders. She speaks to participation in *Fuerza Unida* as a source of personal and collective empowerment: "We are strong women fighting together for communities and families."

> Since 1990, our journey has given us both the challenge and opportunity to become resourceful human beings and community-based leaders. A lifelong lesson that we, the women of *Fuerza Unida*, have obtained and continue to teach is that organizing is key to creating solutions and implementing change for working-class women and communities. This is why we proceed to think and act both locally as well as on a global front since we know that we are part of a larger social movement. We work to effect long-term institutional change by taking direct action and expanding community control over economic, social and environmental decisions affecting our community. (*Fuerza Unida*, 2006)

Fuerza Unida continues to expand and solidify its organizational base. The members are committed to ongoing dialogue and learning from and with the community. They work organically, valuing feelings, learning to listen, and giving all participants a chance to express themselves. *Fuerza Unida* has been working hard to include young people in the work of community building. Recently, *Fuerza Unida* has experienced success in raising awareness regarding CAFTA (Central America Free Trade Agreement), meeting with key legislators and explaining the negative effects of such trade policies on working-class women of color. Similarly, they are exploring avenues for greater youth participation wherein young people have a meaningful voice in the issues that affect their lives. *Fuerza Unida* is crafting new organizational possibilities as it both embraces a model of organization as family and challenges assumptions of gender, power, and patriarchy both in the community and on the factory floor. If you would like to learn more about *Fuerza Unida* and how you can join in solidarity with their work, visit their website at www.lafuerzaunida.org.

Questions for Discussion

1. What roles of social justice work are likely to be practiced using Díaz's process of participatory planning (i.e., eight moments)? Who would be important participants in the process?

2. In your own words, describe how you would use the role of animator and methods of animation. What would be a specific situation that called for the skills of animation?

3. How would you define popular education? How would you apply the principles of popular education in your social work practice?

4. How would you describe policy practice? What factors do you think have made it difficult for social workers to realize Figueira-McDonough's meaning of the policy practitioner?

5. Provide an example of accompaniment in social work. Where do you see possibilities for accompaniment in your social work practice?

Suggested Readings

Boal, A. (1982). *Theatre of the oppressed.* New York: Routledge.

Boyd, A. (1999). *The activist cookbook. Creative actions for a fair economy.* Boston, MA: United for a Fair Economy.

Brown, C. & Mazza, G. (1997). *Healing into action: A leadership guide for creating diverse communities.* Washington, DC: National Coalition Building Institute.

Figueira-McDonough, J. (1993). Policy practice: The neglected side of social work intervention. *Social Work, 43*(4), 335-345.

hooks, b. (1995). *Killing rage: Ending racism.* New York: Henry Holt.

Jansson, B. (1999). *Becoming an effective policy advocate: From policy practice to social justice.* Pacific Grove, CA: Brooks/Cole Publishing Co.

Kaner, S., Lind, L., Toldi, C., Fisk, S., & Berger, D. (2007). *Facilitator's guide to participatory decision-making* (2nd ed.). San Francisco: John Wiley & Sons/ Jossey-Bass.

End Notes

[1] From Janet Finn (2001b). "The women of Villa Paula Jaraquemada: Building community in Chile's transition to democracy." *Community Development Journal,* 36(3), p. 183

[2] Tenets of companioning from A. D. Wolfelt (2004). *The understanding your grief support group guide.* Ft. Collins, CO: Companion Press, cited in G. Yoder (2005). *Companioning the dying. A soulful guide for caregivers.* Ft. Collins, CO: Companion Press

[3] Rabbit-Proof Fence (2002) is an Australian film directed by Phillip Noyce, written by Christine Olsen, and produced by Miramax.

[4] Rally photo courtesy of Carol Jacobsen.

[5] Note: The Family Resource Coalition, cited in Benard, has changed its name to Family Support America.

[6] Permission to print excerpt on dealing with controversial issues from *Healing into action: A leadership guide for creating diverse communities*, (pp. 63-64) courtesy of National Coalition Building Institute, Washington, DC.

[7] Permission to print summary discussion of "Defusing Skills" from Charles E. Confer (1997), *Managing anger: Yours and mine.* Courtesy of American Foster Care Resources, Inc. King George, VA.

[8] This discussion of popular theater is taken from Finn, Jacobson, & Dean Campana, 2004, pp. 331, 335-336, where we offer a more in-depth examination of popular theater.

[9] We add this missing element of direct participation to Chapin's chart. Otherwise, the chart is taken verbatim from text.

[10] The case study is excerpted from an article in the "Women Creating Change" column of *Affilia: Journal of Women in Social Work,* with updated information provided by *Fuearza Unida.* The article, written by Janet L. Finn, is based on a presentation by Viola Casares and Petra Mata for the Affilia board in San Antonio in 2002. The block quotes are from the *Fuerza Unida* mission statement, published on the organization's website, retrieved from http://www.lafuerzaunida.org/ June 15, 2006. Photo courtesy of *Fuerza Unida* and Jana Birchum.

9

Evaluating, Reflecting On, and Celebrating Our Efforts

> *Knowledge emerges only through invention and re-invention, through the restless, impatient, continuing, hopeful inquiry men [sic] pursue in the world, with the world, and with each other.*
>
> Paulo Freire (1974), *Pedagogy of the Oppressed*[1]

> *This project was unforgettable for what it left behind. Both the houses and our capacity to have done this. Now you walk down the street and see what we have accomplished. I see things that are, in truth, so beautiful, and that we had the knowledge and skill to create it. It is something that doesn't happen everywhere. Here is a humble group of folks like us and we've achieved such a valiant effort... We'd gone through all of these problems with lights, sanitation, and water, and now we have left behind something important.*
>
> Pobladora (2001), Villa Paula Jaraquemada, Chile[2]

CHAPTER OVERVIEW

In Chapter 9 we elaborate on the Just Practice core processes of evaluation, critical reflection, and celebration. We begin by defining evaluation and considering its importance for social justice work. We look at different approaches to evaluation and highlight a participatory approach that involves people in addressing the concerns that affect their lives. We discuss the strengths and challenges of participatory evaluation. We present the concept of *catalytic validity* as a way to assess the effectiveness of research efforts and their capacity to promote social justice-oriented action. Guidelines are presented for the participatory design of evaluation tools and processes. We explore the time and resource constraints that can often hamper such efforts. Drawing from practice examples, we show how participatory evaluation can contribute to personal, organizational, community, and sociopolitical empowerment, and how the processes and outcomes contribute to critical theory and practice knowledge.

In Chapter 9 we also identify characteristics of the reflective thinker and explore ways to build capacity for critical reflection. We conceptualize critical reflection as both a tool of inquiry and a constant companion of evaluation practice. We discuss problem-posing as a way to initiate, sustain, and enrich critical reflection. We consider the kinds of questions the Just Practice Framework asks us to reflect upon in order to make meaningful connections between personal struggles and larger social, political, economic, and cultural forces. We discuss the importance of critical reflection in guiding us to question the structures and relations of power embedded in the definitions of personal and societal concerns. Critical reflection demands vigilance on the part of the social worker to look for potential pitfalls and barriers to our actions. We address the core process of celebration and argue the importance of recognizing successes, appreciating contributions, and relishing in the learning that happens at rough spots along the way. We introduce notions of ritual and play as essential elements of social justice work. Finally, we draw attention to the aesthetics of practice and the importance of finding joy and beauty in the work we do.

EVALUATION

Defining Evaluation

We define evaluation as the act of taking stock and determining the significance, effectiveness, or quality of a change effort. It is also about asking questions that appraise the effort and assess whether actions were consistent with the values of social justice work. Striving toward congruence in values and action is of critical importance here. Evaluation is an integral and ongoing part of social justice work that shapes and is shaped by teaching-learning, action, and accompaniment. One can think of evaluation in a number of ways:

1. *Evaluation as research.* Evaluation is a form of research that follows a systematic process. The process consists of planning, implementing the plan, collecting information, making sense of the information, and disseminating the results. Evaluation has three major thrusts: (1) assessing process, the ways and means of meeting goals and objectives; (2) assessing outcomes or the effects of particular change strategies; and (3) assessing the strengths, skills, and challenges of workers and others involved in the change effort.

2. *Evaluation as a benchmark.* Evaluation needs to be continuous. It should happen at various checkpoints in the change process, not only at the end. Checkpoints create stopping-off places where participants can reflect on cumulative change, make comparisons to other checkpoints, and appreciate the distance covered in understanding and altering attitudes and events. As Díaz (1997) notes in Chapter 8, evaluation is a point on our journey where we step back and consider the place we want to reach and the path we are taking. It is a point where we ask: Are we moving in the direction that we want to go?

3. *Evaluation as an individual and group memory process.* Evaluation is the act of recording lessons learned, thus enabling history to become a basis for ongoing learning. Frances Moore Lappé and Paul Martin Dubois (1994) describe this as a process of creating individual and

group memory. Having a sense of history helps us learn from experience. Through the sharing of experiences among participants in the change process, we develop critical consciousness and collective memory of our histories, struggles, hopes, and actions that can both inform the process and motivate the participants.

4 *Evaluation as a statement of assumptions and values.* Behind every evaluation method or strategy is a set of assumptions about people, human nature, power, and the nature of reality. It is important to think about these assumptions and how they influence and shape evaluation practice. Just as we spoke of valuing as an ethical and political practice in Chapter 4, we can think of evaluation as the systematization of valuing.

5 *Evaluation as private and participatory processes.* Evaluation is a private, personal, reflective act. Paulo Freire (1990) describes the progressive social worker as someone who is on a lifelong search for competence. Self-evaluation is key to this search. Evaluation is also a participatory process, not something *done on* others, but *with* others. Thinking of evaluation as a collaborative project is a way to value the contributions of others and open up possibilities for new solutions to old problems. We elaborate on evaluation as a participatory process throughout this chapter.

6 *Evaluation as accountability.* Evaluation is a process of demonstrating accountability to participants in the change process, to those affected, to our organizations, and to funding sources. Participatory approaches to change and to evaluation of change efforts are demanding and time-consuming. They require dedication and commitment from all parties involved. Evaluation gives us pause to consider whether people's time has been well spent with results to show for their work. Has the process enhanced their skills and capacities? Has the process made the most of available resources? Has it strengthened organizational capacity and sparked the imagination of funders? Has it challenged or silenced critics?

Why Evaluate?

The Wisdom of Evaluation

"The best way forward is to take one step back" illustrates well the wisdom of evaluation. Evaluation allows time for rethinking and reorganizing change efforts and strategies based on reflection, interpretation, and analysis. Evaluation calls on participants to see gains, growth, and successes in organized efforts and to use these as a springboard into subsequent action. Evaluation also calls attention to the challenges of our change efforts and provides a process to address these challenges and build new knowledge to forge subsequent efforts. There is also subsidiary knowledge gained from a participatory evaluation process that has little to do with programs or policy but everything to do with people. Involving people in a partnership to investigate social reality is an empowering and transformative process for all.

Taking Evaluation Seriously

Social work texts address other reasons why we should take evaluation seriously (Kirst-Ashman & Hull, 2006, pp. 256-263). Political and economic forces call on program administrators to measure their contributions. Social work programs, services, and projects are fund-driven enterprises, and governmental and foundation funders require results to illustrate that their money is well spent. Social workers are accountable to these funding streams. A move toward increased accountability in a context of a diminishing social contract influences the landscape of social work practice and can constrain efforts at individual, group, and community change or forge new possibilities for action. Community organizations that typically conduct evaluations indicating the number of "client hours," or cases administered over a year's time, are being called upon to evaluate the outcomes of their interventions to assess effectiveness. At the same time, consumers of services want to know if they are receiving a "tried and true" product, one with a demonstrated track record of positive results that will assist them in meeting their needs. Karen Kirst-Ashman and Grafton Hull (2006, pp. 256-263) also stress the importance of social workers knowing the outcomes of their efforts. They argue that this point is less attended to than other factors advocating the need for evaluation for the following reasons:

1 Evaluation opens social workers up for scrutiny, leaving them vulnerable.

2 Most human service work is crisis-driven and stressful. Caseloads are high and time for conducting evaluations is at a premium.

3 Many organizations fail to emphasize the importance of evaluation. Evaluation is often an add-on, poorly thought out, and rarely integrated into the structuring and day-to-day practices of many community organizations.

Evaluation and Constraints

As you can see from this discussion, evaluation is very important to social work. However, there are also personal, organizational, and external constraints that pose barriers to implementing evaluation processes within community organizations. While Kirst-Ashman and Hull illustrate some of the systemic reasons for the devaluation of evaluation, we argue that social work education must also assume part of the responsibility for the lack of attention given to evaluation in social work practice. Evaluation is often taught in schools of social work as an add-on, poorly integrated into the curriculum, and limited to classes in research. A number of authors on the subject locate the problem with the research curriculum itself and note the failure to link research tools to the real-life problems students must address in practice (Anderson, 2002; Epstein, 1987; Reese, 2004). Others comment on the disconnect between research and practice and the need to engage in research methods that more closely resemble the processes inherent in social work practice (Scott, 2002) and align best with the core values of the profession (O'Connor & O'Neill, 2004). The principles of social justice work support collaborative methods in research design, implementation, and analysis, thus requiring social workers to use the skills they learn in practice courses to conduct research (Jacobson & Goheen, 2006). Participatory approaches to research require knowledge of relationship and trust building, skills of leadership and effective communication, and the creation of knowledge useful to the worker, participants, and the community. Given this discussion, it is interesting to note the results of a study conducted by Lindsey and Kirk (1992) in which they assessed research use by NASW members and found that only 5% read journal articles to inform their practice. What do you make of this disconnect between social workers and research? Why might so many social workers place so little value on research? Or should we be asking another question entirely? How does time, or the lack thereof, devoted to reflection on practice within agencies affect attitudes about research? What kinds of research would be the most relevant to practitioners? What reasons can you think of that address why so few NASW members use research to inform their practice?

Different Ways of Thinking about Evaluation

Positivist Assumptions

Evaluation principles and methods derive from two very different ways of thinking about knowledge development. Each approach is a value statement that shapes and guides different practice possibilities. As we discussed in Chapter 5, *positivism* has been the dominant philosophy and ideology guiding research and evaluation in social work and the social sciences in general. Although there are many versions of positivism, it is generally described as rooted in assumptions of objectivity—the idea that there is indeed a single, stable, and ultimately "knowable" reality outside ourselves that we can break into controllable parts called "variables" and subject them to inquiry. In the interest of objectivity, the researcher maintains distance from the subject of the research to prevent contamination and bias. In effect, the researcher is separated from the researched—the object of inquiry (Maguire, 1987). Positivism seeks to make generalizations about reality that are truth claims, free from context and time, and therefore applicable to other times and places. Positivism attempts to control and isolate reality to uncover causes and effects in linear fashion. If one's methods are thought to be objective, then it follows that these methods control for the personal values and assumptions of the researcher. Inquiry based on a positivist perspective is thus considered to be value-free (Denzin & Lincoln, 1994; Lincoln & Guba, 1985; Maguire, 1987; Neuman & Kreuger, 2003; Rubin & Babbie, 2005).[3]

Participatory Assumptions

Participatory approaches to knowledge development question positivist assumptions. They challenge notions of objectivity and value-free inquiry and practices that separate the researcher from the researched. They are more interpretive in nature, recognizing the importance of local knowledge and experience in developing a grounded understanding of social reality. As reported by Finn (1994a, p. 26), the basic tenets of participatory research include "the meaningful involvement of people in addressing the concerns that affect their lives; recognition of knowledge as power; and commitment to a process of critical action and reflection" (Fernandes, 1989; Gaventa, 1988; Maguire, 1987).

Participatory approaches hold that meaningful research is only possible through cooperation and involvement with those from whom one seeks to gain information (Finn, 1994a; Finn, Jacobson, & Dean Campana, 2004; Hall, 1975, 1981; Park, 1993, 1997). Time and place are viewed as shapers of knowledge and, therefore, inextricable from the process of meaningful research. Participatory approaches see reality as mutually constituted and mutually shaping, thereby making it impossible to separate cause from effect. All inquiry is embedded in values and assumptions that underlie each step of the research process from conception through implementation and interpretation. Participatory researchers make values explicit, expose personal assumptions and perspectives, and openly contend with how these influence their choice of methods and modes of analysis. They strive for critical awareness of their own subjectivity in the research situation and process and in their effects upon it. Evaluation is viewed as a social process and the participants have a role and an effect in the process. It is, nonetheless, a systematic and rigorous practice that attempts to account for the ways in which values, positioning, and perspective may shape the method (Lather, 1986, 1991; Maguire, 1987; Park, 1993, 1997).

Proponents of participatory approaches to research understand that research produces knowledge and that knowledge is power. For this reason, "Research can never be neutral. It is always supporting or questioning social forces, both by its content and by its method. It has effects and side effects, and these benefit or harm people" (Reason & Rowan, 1981, p. 489, as cited in Maguire, 1987, p. 24). In sum, participatory research is about people, power, and praxis (Finn, 1994a). As Janet Finn, Maxine Jacobson, and Jillian Dean Campana (2004) write:

> Participatory research calls for the meaningful involvement of people in the coproduction of knowledge to address the concerns that affect their lives; it challenges the separation of researcher and "subject," and it takes power and inequality as central themes. (p. 327)

Qualitative versus Quantitative Approaches?

Participatory approaches value both qualitative and quantitative methods of inquiry. In social work, as well as the social sciences, there has been ongoing debate about the relative merits of *qualitative* research, that is, research that emphasizes "processes and meaning that are not rigourously examined, or measured (if measured at all), in terms of quantity, amount, intensity, or frequency" (Denzin & Lincoln, 1994, p. 4). On the other hand, *quantitative* research is said to "emphasize the measurement and analysis of causal relationships between variables, not processes" (Denzin & Lincoln, 1994, p. 4). When we explored the history of social work in Chapter 3, we discussed the dichotomies that have at times served to polarize the profession into two distinct camps (e.g., distinctions between casework and community-based practice). We prefer to move beyond these dichotomies in our discussion here and remind the reader that qualitative and quantitative research approaches can be quite complementary (Firestone, 1986). Each method brings its own strengths to the process, and they can be effectively combined. In fact, part of a participatory process may involve decisions to gather very specific quantitative information or use existing quantitative measures in order to evaluate ways in which particular programs, policies, or practices affect certain groups. Using multiple methods provides the opportunity to "triangulate," that is, to make comparisons of the data across methods. As Jicks (1979) contends, triangulation "can improve the accuracy of [researchers'] judgments by collecting different kinds of data bearing on the same phenomenon" (p. 602). Triangulation also adds to the richness and depth of the inquiry by providing a means to accommodate multiple perspectives.

Questions of Reliability and Validity

Defining Reliability and Validity

Claims against participatory modes of inquiry call it undisciplined and too subjective to count as "real" research. Critics contend that "legitimate" research must be reliable and valid. These terms may be familiar to you if you have already taken a research methods course. Reliability and validity relate to the trustworthiness of the research knowledge and its results (Lincoln & Guba, 1985). Richard Grinnell and Yvonne Unrau (2005) contend that the test of reliability is whether an evaluation tool measures the same variable repeatedly, with consistency, and produces the same results. The concept of validity relates to:

> the ways in which the research design ensures that the introduction of the independent variable (if any) can be identified as the sole cause of change in the dependent variable . . . and the extent to which the research design allows for generalization of the findings of the study to other groups and other situations. (p. 194)

For example, in studying whether drug abuse causes domestic violence, the independent variable is drug abuse and the dependent variable is domestic violence. Internal validity asks how we know that changes in domestic violence (dependent variable) are a result of drug abuse (independent variable) and not a result of other factors. External validity asks how can we be sure that the information we have gathered reflects only respondents' information and not the researcher's biases or judgments (Marlow, 2005). Can we generalize our information to other circumstances and situations? The ideal study is thought to be one whose research design attempts to control both internal and external threats to validity.[4]

What is "Right" and "True" in Research Today

These notions of what is right and true in research are under question today. In an effort to bridge schools of thought, some have referred to research inquiry as "objectively subjective" (Lincoln & Guba, 1985). For example, Yvonna Lincoln and Egon Guba argue for rigor in qualitative approaches to research and present a set of techniques to ensure validity and to establish the reliability or trustworthiness of the results. One of these techniques is member checks (pp. 314-316).[5] Individual research team members appraise and analyze information alone before discussing their findings with the entire research team. Agreement and working out disagreements ensure some measure of truth in the data. How to achieve reliability and trustworthiness of the data are issues of ongoing debate and dialogue.

Particia Lather (1986, 1991) takes on the controversial subject of reliability and validity and looks at particular criteria that best serve research with a participatory approach and a social justice aim. She argues that researchers who blend theory and justice-oriented action (praxis) may want to consider the less well-known notion of *catalytic validity* as a guiding principle. Lather defines catalytic validity as "the degree to which the research process re-orients, focuses and energizes participants toward knowing reality in order to transform it . . ." (Lather, 1991, p. 68).[6] She ties this in with the Freirean concept of conscientization, meaning that all involved in the knowledge generation process (research) and changed through this process, "gain self-understanding and, ultimately, self-determination through research participation" (p. 68). Lather emphasizes that participatory inquiry can stand up to the test of rigor and relevance in research and must do so to promote the emancipatory possibilities of participatory research and evaluation.

Bricoleur—The Role of the Researcher

What is a Bricoleur?

In our discussion in Chapter 8 of social worker roles, we highlight the role of researcher in social justice work. Our definition stresses the importance of ongoing critical reflection on and evaluation of one's practice. We emphasize incorporating this idea of research into our daily practice rather than excluding those we work with and ourselves from a process that lends itself readily to teaching-learning. In Chapter 8 we also introduce the notion of the *bricoleur*, a role we borrow from the field of anthropology. Noted French anthropologist Claude Levi-Strauss defines *bricoleur* as a "Jack of all trades or a kind of professional do-it-yourself person" (Levi-Strauss, 1966, p. 17, as cited in Denzin & Lincoln, 1994, p. 2). We revisit the notion of the *bricoleur* in this chapter to make some important linkages between this role and doing research (Denzin & Lincoln, 1994, pp. 2-3). Imagine someone who improvises, makes use of the material and expertise at hand, combines multiple methods in which to achieve solutions, and adds to her repertoire of skills and techniques as the situation demands:

> If new tools have to be invented, or pieced together, then the researcher will do this. The choice of which tools to use, which research practices to employ, is not set in advance. The "choice of research practices depends upon the questions that are asked, and the questions depend on their context" (Nelson et al., 1992, p. 2), what is available in the context, and what the researcher can do in the setting. . . The *bricoleur* is adept at performing a large number of diverse tasks, ranging from interviewing to observing, to interpreting personal and historical documents, to intensive self-reflection and introspection. (Denzin & Lincoln, p. 2)

Interpreting and Representing the Results

The *bricoleur* is mindful of the subjective nature of inquiry (Denzin & Lincoln, 1994, p. 3). Norman Denzin and Yvonna Lincoln remind us that all facets of the research process, from planning to analysis, are influenced by the positionality of the researcher and in the case of participatory approaches to inquiry, the positionality of others involved in the process. Issues concerning personal history, race, social class, and gender shape the ways in which those involved in the process arrive at questions to pose, the means and methods through which these questions will be addressed, and the strategies for analyzing the information collected. The process and end product of the *bricoleur's* work is what Denzin and Lincoln call the *bricolage*—"a collage-like creation that represents the researcher's images, under-standings, and interpretation of the world or phenomenon under analysis" (p. 3). Think for a moment of how evaluation results could be represented based on the intended effect you wish to make. Who could be influenced or changed by the results? Through what means (codes, graphics, skits, photos, video, etc.) might you realize your intentions?

What Needs to be Evaluated?

Think for a moment of the varied work situations social workers find themselves in and the multiple functions of social work within particular settings. What should we evaluate and why? What would be important for the child protection services worker to evaluate, for example? Or what might be an important question for a school social worker to pose of a school program that seeks to facilitate parents' increased involvement with their children's education? Hope and Timmel (1999, V. 2, p. 124) suggest that we need to evaluate the following areas, although not necessarily at the same time. We add social justice and human rights to their list and pose questions for you to think about as they relate to each area:

- **Aims:** Given the original mission and purpose of the organization or the goals laid out by participants, where are we now? Are we far adrift from these aims or right on the mark?

- **Ethics:** Are practices and procedures ethical and by whose standards? Who is included and who is left out and why? Are we adhering to the principles of social justice work? Do practices and procedures reflect a commitment to social justice?

- **Participation:** Who is involved in the organization's decision making? Are the voices of those the program was meant to benefit valued? Who participates and how?

- **Methods:** Are methods used consistent with the values of social justice work? Do procedures, policies, and practices allow for the contributions of those most directly concerned with the issues we wish to address? How do these methods deal with or address the issue of difference? Do any methods discriminate based on race, gender, sexual orientation, class, ability, and age?

- **Content:** Does the program or project address participants' expectations? Does the program or project address the root causes of concerns?

- **Animators and Administrators:** What are the leadership skills of the project facilitators or program administrators? What are their strengths and challenges?

- **Follow-up:** How is the program or the project assessed when the work is completed? At checkpoints down the road? Is there a mechanism in place to conduct follow-up?

♦ **Time and Money:** How much time and money goes into this program or project? Has the time and money produced visible, sustainable results? Is sufficient time and money put toward the effort? Would a different allocation of time and money produce better results?

♦ **Planning, Coordination, and Administration:** What is the quality of program or project planning? How would you rate the level of coordination among participants, projects, programs, and other community groups and organizations? How are programs and projects administered? What are the strengths and challenges of planning, coordination, and administration?

♦ **Decision Making:** How does the project or program make decisions? Are these top-down, bottom-up, or a little bit of both? What process is used to make decisions? Is this process collaborative? Whose voices contribute to the decision-making process?

♦ **Social Justice and Human Rights:** How does the project or program address issues of social justice and human rights (Ife, 2001; Witkin, 1998)? Are domestic social justice issues viewed within a larger global framework (Link, 1999; Polack, 2004)?

Evaluating Course Methods of Evaluation

ACTION

Think about the evaluation tool you are administered to assess the college courses you take. Write a list of the types of questions and the kinds of information this tool attempts to elicit. In small groups, brainstorm with others the ways in which you might reconfigure the tool to identify what you think are the essential components of your teaching/learning experience. Course evaluation tools generally attempt to assess the "teacher." For example, you might be asked whether your teacher came to class prepared or if instructions were clear and easy to understand. Rarely do these tools ask you to assess yourself as a learner/teacher or to make comments about your participation in the learning process. Develop a tool with your classmates that you think fills the gaps in these evaluation tools. Now, think about how your learning is evaluated. Most teachers assess your learning by administering tests or quizzes or writing assignments. Brainstorm alternative ways in which your learning could be assessed and evaluated. Present your list to the class for discussion. What did you learn about the meaning of evaluation through this exercise? How does evaluation link to questions of power? What changes would you recommend? What resistance might you meet and why?

PARTICIPATORY APPROACHES TO EVALUATION

As discussed earlier, positivist-oriented evaluation practices generally do not include the involvement of participants in a change effort or project. Instead, evaluation tends to be a top-down approach, conceived of by program administrators and conducted by outside experts. At times the participation of direct service providers and "outreach" workers is sought assuming they grasp the reality of what it is like "out there." But most often social workers and those they work with are the researched. Evaluation is something done *to* them, not *with* them. We imagine evaluation differently. We see it as a participatory process whereby all participants are afforded opportunities to reflect on programs, projects, and policies, the mission and aims of the organization, and their own and others' involvement in change efforts. Evaluation is something done *with* people, not *on* people. Positive outcomes of conducting evaluations *with* people include a greater likelihood the results will be accepted by program personnel and incorporated into practice, increased sensitivity to the social and political context of the organization (Cherin & Meezan, 1998), and much higher rates of effect on organizational decision-making (Rossi & Freeman, 1993). In this section we elaborate on participatory approaches to evaluation and present background information on their history, objectives, principles, and methods. Case examples of evaluations guided by participatory assumptions are presented to provide you with possibilities for your own evaluation practice.

Origins and Objectives

Scholars of participatory approaches to research describe their emergence in the 1960s in countries such as Latin America, India, and Africa where understandings of power and domination forged resistance to knowledge development and research methods based on the positivist paradigm (Parks, 1993). For example, survey research is generally constructed with researcher-predetermined, forced-choice questions. Often this type of research fails to consider the race and class biases built into the structuring of questions. They are languaged for white, middle- and upper-class respondents and allow no room for the richness and depth of understanding that ordinary people bring to the issues that shape their daily lives. To address these and other omissions, early participatory researchers developed alternative strategies for information gathering and analysis that valued and included people's lived experience in every stage of the research process (Hall, 1993). Research by the people and for the people is a powerful tool for addressing power imbalances and other forms of inequality that shape people's lives. Attention to issues of power in knowledge generation and to the exploitive history of research on the lives of Native Americans and other groups of indigenous people is forging new approaches to research that attend to issues of culture and history and highlight assets and strengths (Christopher, 2005; Smith, 1999).

In social work's own history, attention to issues concerning people's everyday lives and the glaring need to address growing social inequalities shaped approaches to research (Altepeter, Schopler, Galinsky, & Pennell, 1999). Early settlement house workers around the turn of the 20th century engaged in participatory research methods by enlisting neighborhood residents as research team members (Addams, 1910). They gathered information about the disparities between women's and men's wages, infant mortality rates and their connection to unsanitary living conditions, and the inadequate working conditions of female-dominated employment settings. They designed and implemented survey research to assess community needs and conditions (Kellogg, 1914; Van Kleeck, 1913, 1917; Zimbalist, 1977). Their methodology was shaped by the historical, political, and economic context at the turn of the 20th century, a context similar to conditions that influenced the momentum toward inclusive, empowering research methods in Latin America, India, and Africa beginning in the 1960s.

REFLECTION:	Conducting a Survey of a Neighborhood

The first systematic attempt to describe an immigrant neighborhood at the turn of the 20th century in the United States culminated in *Hull-House Maps and Papers* (Hull-House Residents, 1895). The text was a compilation of articles written about living and working conditions in the neighborhood surrounding Hull House in Chicago, Illinois, one of the first U.S. settlement houses. Along with reports on social investigations such as "Wage Earning Children," "The Sweating System," and "The Cook County Charities," the volume contains elaborate, color-coded maps identifying the location, nationality, and wage earnings of immigrants from 18 different countries around the world who lived in the neighborhood immediately east of Hull House (Barbuto, 1999; Bryan & Davis, 1990; Hull-House Residents, 1895). We encourage you to visit the websites listed in the endnote section of the text so you can view the maps and read Agnes Holbrook's introduction to the volume. She describes the neighborhood and the results of the survey settlement house workers constructed to gather information on wages and nationality.[7]

What might a color-coded map of your own neighborhood look like? What questions would you ask on a survey to produce a color-coded map of your neighborhood? What issues would be important to display using these methods? How might you use the results to affect neighborhood change?

Principles of Participatory Evaluation

Participatory evaluation has a number of distinct assumptions that differ from those underlying traditional forms of evaluation. We addressed these earlier in the chapter. Based on these assumptions, participatory evaluation is guided by the following principles.

The Dialogical Nature of Participatory Research

Dialogue is the distinguishing feature of participatory research. As we have seen in the preceding chapters, *dialogue* is the conduit of knowledge. Participatory evaluation brings individuals most affected by an issue together with administrators and researchers to pose questions and arrive at solutions. People learn from each other through collective interaction. For example, in participatory evaluation questionnaires are not mailed out but used instead as a "vehicle of dialogue" (Park, 1993, p. 12). Through dialogue, we come to know our communities and ourselves. Park comments on dialogue as a tool of research:

> Dialogue produces not just factual knowledge but also interpersonal and critical knowledge, which defines humans as autonomous social beings. This is an essential reason for the people's participation in research. It is not just so they can reveal private facts that are hidden from others but really so they may know themselves better as individuals and as a community. (pp. 12-13)

Collective Investigation, Education, and Action

Program or project participants also learn the skills of collecting, analyzing, and disseminating evaluation knowledge. Action plans and strategies implemented collectively feed into the evaluation process and initiate change in research methods and strategies and in the participants themselves. Patricia Maguire (1987) states,

> Collective investigation, education, and action are important to the re-humanizing goal of participatory research. By treating people as objects to be counted, surveyed, predicted, and controlled, traditional research mirrors oppressive social conditions which cause ordinary people to relinquish their capacity to make real choices and to be cut out of meaningful decision making. The collective processes of participatory research help rebuild people's capacity to be creative actors on the world. (p. 30)

Attention to Issues of Power

Participatory research challenges the lack of attention to *power* in traditional research. It assumes that everything we do is embedded within a political context, and this context shapes the questions we ask and the kinds of research we conduct. Participatory evaluation disrupts the idea of expert knowledge and research as a tool solely of the "educated." It holds that all people have the capacity to better understand their lives and shape their own reality. Theoretically, participatory evaluation shares common ground with social work's empowerment perspective. Both seek to promote social justice and equality through full participation in society. Both seek to build individual, organizational, and community capacity.

People and Participation

Ideally, participatory projects originate from the people whose lives are most affected by particular concerns. Pragmatically speaking, given the powerlessness that keeps many people from organizing, participatory projects most often originate through an external agent such as a community agency, a university, or a church group. Getting people involved is the next step. People's participation starts with the formulation of the research questions. The research team makes decisions collaboratively. They decide what information needs to be gathered and then they divide research tasks among participants. Social workers facilitate this process by gathering people together, conducting small and large group discussions, and helping to formulate the problem in such a way that it can be researched. Participants play active research roles, instead of merely being the providers of information as is typical in most evaluation efforts. Participants help to decide the research design and method used to carry out the evaluation. People learn research skills by actively participating in the evaluation process (Jacobson & Rugeley, in press).

Diverse Methods Used to Conduct Participatory Evaluation

Participatory evaluation can take many different shapes and forms. It borrows its methods from a variety of social science tools used to conduct other types of re-

REFLECTION: **Diverse Methods Recommendations for Conducting Research with Native American People**

Suzanne Christopher, faculty member at the Department of Health and Human Development, Montana State University in Bozeman, Montana, has been involved with the Messengers for Health project on the Apsáalooke (Crow Indian) Reservation since the mid-1990s. The primary objective of this community-based participatory research (CBPR) project is to decrease barriers to cervical cancer screening, to increase the number of Apsáalooke women receiving Pap tests, and to increase awareness of and knowledge about screening and prevention of cervical cancer (Watts, Christopher, Streitz, & Knows His Gun McCormick, 2005). Based on her long-term involvement with the community, Dr. Christopher outlines recommendations for conducting research with Native American people (Christopher, 2005):

1. Researchers must work to know and understand the effect of historical relations between the U.S government and Native Americans on the present-day attitudes of Native People and research.

2. Researchers must show knowledge of the issues specific to tribes being studied and avoid the common mistake of grouping all tribes together.

3. Native American individuals and communities must be invited to be involved with research.

4. Native communities must receive information back from researchers and have access to data collected from them.

5. Native communities must receive benefits from research.

6. Researchers must address assets and broader social issues.

7. Researchers must place the needs of the community ahead of their own interests.

How do these principles relate to the key concepts and social justice-oriented social work practice? How are they relevant to practice and program evaluation as it concerns working with indigenous peoples and other groups who have been socially excluded and marginalized? Are there any recommendations you might add?

search. However, some methods are modified to allow increased interaction between those administering the methods and those providing information. Below we outline some evaluation methods. Can you think of specific situations when different methods might be helpful or where they might be counterproductive?

Written Questionnaires

Questionnaires are the most common method used for participatory evaluation because of their versatility. They can be used when evaluating efforts with individuals, groups, neighborhoods, and entire communities. Through a collaborative process, participants tailor questionnaires to the investigation at hand by prioritizing questions and making sure the wording is clear and easy to understand. Questionnaires generally include both closed- and open-ended questions, which value information respondents choose to give. However, each type of question has its advantages and disadvantages (Neuman & Kreuger, 2003). Questionnaires can be used as a tool to stimulate dialogue. Deciding to mail out questionnaires or administer them directly depends upon the particular aims of the research and the context. For example, administering questionnaires face-to-face provides an opportunity to become familiar with a community or group of people affected by a particular issue. Face-to-face administration also increases response rates. While mailed questionnaires might be more expedient and cost-effective given the resources you have at hand, response rates are generally lower (Neuman & Kreuger, 2003; Reinhartz, 1992; Rubin & Babbie, 2005).[8]

Informal Interviews

Conducting informal interviews is another useful way to gather information. They are especially useful at the beginning of an evaluation project when there is a need to gather preliminary information. Perhaps the research team is not quite sure what they need to evaluate or what strategies might be best, or what questions to ask. Conducting informal interviews can be a good way to begin (Neuman & Kreuger, 2003; Reinhartz, 1992; Rubin & Babbie, 2005). Informal interviews provide a format in which people can discuss their experiences in their own words and highlight the issues of most importance to them.

Structured/Semistructured Interviews

As the group becomes more familiar with the issues and concerns, more focused interviewing can take place. With structured and semistructured interviews, the interviewer asks questions beginning with the general to the specific and from the least personal to the personal. The research team plans the questions beforehand. Structured and semistructured interviews are appropriate for repeat interviews, once rapport and trust are developed and once the focus of the evaluation is narrowed down (Neuman & Kreuger, 2003; Reinhartz, 1992; Rubin & Babbie, 2005). The interview process itself may be a catalyst for change (Brown & Tandon, 1978).

Small and Large Group Discussion

Discussion groups are the *sine qua non* of participatory evaluation. Group discussion allows for maximum participation. Groups fulfill other purposes as well. They can be a source of support as well as a venue for addressing differences and conflict. Focus groups are a good example of small group discussion as an evaluation research method (Krueger, 1994; Krueger & King, 1998; Morgan, 1988). Krueger defines the focus group as a special kind of group that values participants' experiences, attitudes, and opinions. The open, semidirected format allows participants a voice in the issues that concern their lives and creates a space where responses to questions can be open rather than constrained by a yes or no response. Moreover, when people are gathered together in a group context they learn from and can be further stimulated in their thinking from the responses of other participants. This allows the discussion to reach greater depth than would be possible in a structured or semistructured one-to-one interview. Typically, focus groups consist of no more than 6 to 10 people. They can be conducted in a series to allow for richer discussion and a more thorough purview of the issue at hand. Community members familiar with the focus group participants can be trained to facilitate the meeting, thereby maximizing the potential for trust to develop more rapidly. For example, Richard Krueger and Jean King (1998) elaborate on the virtues of using focus groups for participatory research, and they discuss ways in which to involve volunteers in the facilitation process and the advantages therein.

Surveys

Although surveys typically conjure up images of telephone interviews, survey methods can be rethought to include participatory components. For example, Roy Carr-Hill (1984) argues that survey research can be "radicalized" and transformed into a process in which the inquiry creates a catalyst for participation and change. Hope and Timmel (1999, V. 1, p. 24) describe the use of the listening survey. This approach is quite different from typical survey work in which questions are decided beforehand by a group of "experts." They use the listening survey to develop a program based on the issues most salient to the community. However, this approach can be modified to fit the needs of program or project evaluation. We present our version of a listening survey adapted for the participatory evaluation in The Evaluator's Tool Kit section at the end of this chapter.

Case Studies

Case studies are becoming more common in evaluation research (Yin, 1994). They best address the "how" and "why" research questions, making them well suited to evaluation. "How does the program or project deal with difference? Why does the program or project work so well?" Cases can be programs, projects, processes, neighborhoods, whole organizations, and communities. While case studies zero in on a specific entity, such as a program or project, they view this entity within its context (Stake, 1995; Yin, 1994). They also attend to history as a shaper of present-day structures and practices. Case study methodology considers the multiple systems at play that affect organizations and projects, thereby enriching evaluation information and making it contextually relevant. Case studies use multiple methods such as interviewing, participant observation, focus groups, and questionnaires to achieve these ends.

Illustrated Presentations

Slides, photos, or drawings help to catalogue the history of a program, a project, or an individual change effort. They can evoke a historical perspective, aid in the recall of significant memories, signify points of comparison, and serve as a jumping-off place for critical reflection. Posing questions about the effort brings successes and challenges to bear upon future efforts. For example, community researchers have invited participants in collective change processes to illustrate the effects of their participation through "before" and "after" photographs. How did they see their life situations before becoming involved? How do they envision themselves and their social realities after becoming active contributors to a community change effort? Participants are then invited to tell their stories of participation and describe the meanings of their before and after images. This approach, which is referred to as *photovoice* in the literature, has been used with increasing regularity as a participatory evaluation method with a strong action component (Wang & Burris, 1997). For example, Latino adolescents living in a rural town in North Carolina with documented high drop-out rates routinely described the quality of their lives as poor and felt typecast and funneled into filling low paying, dead-end jobs in industrial poultry processing plants (Streng et al., 2004). Armed with camera equipment and training to learn how to use the equipment, Latino students engaged in a photovoice project where they visually captured and expressed what they perceived as the barriers to inclusion and career fulfillment. Their photo display drew the attention of school administrators and provided an opportunity to address inequities in school policy and for Latino students to publicly voice their concerns.

Skits, Dramatizations, and Other Visual Representations

Enacting the change effort using prepared scripts or impromptu dramatizations is an exciting and energizing way to get body and spirit into the evaluation process. Visual representations of efforts create pictures or images of the work accomplished, its surprises, successes, and challenges. When captured on video or camera, these representations provide the means for instant replay. Ongoing learning occurs through repeat performances. Another visual method for conducting participatory evaluation is presented by Gallagher (2004) in a description of the *Our Town* project that involved low-income urban children in designing and building an intervention in their neighborhood. Children, assisted by architects, community planners, education representatives, and neighborhood residents, first assessed the neighborhood and represented their findings in drawings. Based on what they perceived as the deficiencies and strengths of their neighborhood, the children then designed an ideal living environment. From their ideal images and constructions and based on what they identified as needs, they built a park that brought neighbors together and served as a site for concerts, community events, and other neighborhood venues. The project not only helped create a needed neighborhood space informed by the perspectives of children, it challenged assumptions about children's participation in community planning and evaluation efforts.

Testimonials

Individual and/or group testimonials are yet another way to bring the voices of those involved in the process to bear on analyzing efforts, support and appreciate the work, and create a memorable moment for all participants. When getting the research message out is of timely and critical importance, testimonials are a way to put a human face and a human voice to the message. We describe this process and refer to it as *bearing witness* in Chapter 6.

Participatory evaluation methods must be tailored to the particular context and include consideration of available resources and the assets participants bring with them to the effort. It is important to assess each method for its strengths and limitations. We encourage you to consider the five key concepts of meaning, context, power, history, and possibility as you undertake this assessment. For example:

- Does this method allow for the expression of multiple *meanings* of objects, events, and situations? And does it fit with the experiences and capacities of the group?

- Does this method help connect personal problems and their larger political, economic, and sociocultural *contexts*?

- Does this method consider *power* as it affects relationships among participants? Is this method empowering?

- Does this method allow for points of comparison so *history* can be a source of learning?

- What creative uses can this method be put to and what *possibilities* for evaluation does it bring to mind?

As this discussion suggests, there are multiple ways in which to engage in the development of knowledge. Each strategy for collecting information has its strengths and limitations. Consideration must be given to how a certain strategy will fit, given a particular context, and the resources in terms of time, money, and expertise that will be needed to carry it out. It is also important to consider that each strategy by itself gathers a partial picture of the phenomenon under study. We suggest that you think of ways you can incorporate different strategies to enrich and deepen the quality of information you collect. Recall from our earlier discussion, a mixed-methods approach also provides an opportunity where data can be triangulated, thereby increasing its reliability or trustworthiness. We present these strategies here as possibilities for further exploration and ask you to add to this list and think of ways to combine approaches with ideas of your own.

Making it Participatory

A C T I O N

Interview an administrator or supervisor of a local service, advocacy, or social action organization. Your task is to find out what evaluation means to the organization and what methods the organization uses to evaluate its programs, projects, and personnel. To prepare for this process, in class divide into small groups of three and draw up a tentative list of interview questions you could ask an administrator or supervisor of the organization. What questions might you ask and why? After you have conducted your interview, bring the results with you to class for discussion. What methods does the organization use to evaluate itself? What does it evaluate? People? Policies? Practices? How often? By whom? How are the results used? What is the degree of participation in the process?

Try applying the Just Practice five key concepts of meaning, context, power, history, and possibility as a framework for critique. What *meaning* does evaluation have for the organization? What is the *context*(s) in which it occurs? Who has the *power* to make decisions regarding what to evaluate and which methods to choose? How has *history* affected these decisions and methods? What other evaluation *possibilities* exist? Now think about how you might transform this organization's evaluation strategy to be empowering and participatory. What would you do differently? How would you do it? How does your transformation incorporate the key concepts and what role do they play in building your evaluation process? How do the values of Just Practice translate into a working model of evaluation when you bring the concept of collaboration to bear on your reflections? What might be some of the challenges and constraints of implementing your model in an organization? What might be some of its successes?

Participatory Evaluation in Action

Case examples depicting the realities of participatory evaluation are helpful to draw from when imagining the depth and breadth of this approach in terms of participants, objectives, and potential outcomes. As you read through the case examples think about the ways you could engage in evaluation practice that value the experience of those typically thought of as "clients" or the receivers of services.

Understanding Homelessness and Promoting Community Change

As described earlier in the chapter, photovoice is a community-based participatory research method that involves community members in identifying, representing, and helping build community through photo-taking, critical reflection, and disseminating the results (Wang & Burris, 1997). Caroline Wang, Jennifer Cash, and Lisa Powers (2000) describe the Language of Light project, which involved homeless men and women living in shelters in Ann Arbor, Michigan. The project's primary objective was to provide participants with an opportunity to represent, through photographs, their living conditions and their everyday struggles and strengths. Ultimately the project sought to inform policy makers and increase their awareness of the realities of homelessness from the perspective of those living this social problem every day.

The steps in the project included (1) training facilitators in the project's goals, methodology, group process skills, and how to use a camera; (2) recruiting participants from the city's homeless shelters; (3) conducting training workshops for participants; and (4) disseminating information gathered to policy makers, the media, and the community at large. In reflecting on one of his photographs called "Good Times, But We're Not Feeling It," depicting a clock and digital display on Main Street, a 55-year-old male participant commented,

> Not only does it tell the time, but it also shows the Dow Jones as high as it has ever been. Why is the Dow Jones so high? Everyone is making a bundle of money on the stock market; but even though many of us at the shelter have jobs, we can barely find a hamburger to eat sometimes. (p. 85)

The project resulted in a number of outcomes, some unintended but nonetheless important to the participatory evaluation process. It provided participants with a common purpose and a group experience arranged around this purpose as they shared survival skills and processed the effects of social exclusion and discrimination on their every day lives. Participants, in effect, formed a mutual aid group and benefited from both emotional and tangible support they received from others in the group. Involvement in the project also served to enhance participants' sense of efficacy and self-esteem and provided them with a means to give voice to their experiences of homelessness as well as promoting understandings of homelessness within the community and being valued by the community for their efforts. Although the project appeared to have little effect on proposed plans to build a new homeless shelter on the periphery of town where barriers to service access would be increased, the project, "enabled board members, planners, community people, and community leaders to rethink issues from the perspective of the homeless" (p. 85.)

Involving Children in Evaluating Change

ACTIONAID Nepal's mission is the eradication of absolute poverty through empowerment of women, men, and children. In 1993-95 they carried out participatory research enabling children to share their experiences and opinions. Their work showed that children need to be integral in the process, their voices and views heard, and their rights and needs considered in order to ensure that interventions truly address and improve their quality of life. The researchers began by bringing groups of children ages 11 to 15 together to analyze their social reality and to serve as ongoing consultants to AAN's planning process. Children were also involved in an evaluation of AAN's efforts in two sectors where projects have been underway for 4 years. Boys and girls from the children's groups participated. The techniques used included focus group discussions about changes, diaries to record children's daily activities, and social maps to show how children went to school. Children's thematic drawings presented graphic images of their life circumstances, and they also provided a base for evaluating changes in those circumstances. Rapport between children and facilitators was key to meaningful participation.

> By forming groups the right of children to have a space to discuss their issues has been formally acknowledged. Adults in the community and AAN are beginning to listen to these groups, and participation in these groups has allowed children to develop skills, knowledge, experience, and confidence . . . A key problem identified by the groups was children being sent for wage labor, which prevented them from attending school. Their groups have raised awareness, for example through street drama, about girls' rights to education. They have directly persuaded male household heads to send girls and women to school…" (p. 93)

Participants in one of the children's groups write, "In the past we were innocent and no one would listen to us, and the adults sometimes used to scold and dominate us. Now the situation has changed. We are able to read, write, and speak … we are able to solve our problems ourselves" (Hill, 1998, p. 92-94).

BSW Students as Program Evaluators

Social work research is recounted in the literature as the most dreaded course in the curriculum for social work students (Adam, Zosky, & Unrau, 2004; Epstein, 1987; Nasuti, York, & Henley, 2003; Royse, 1999; Wainstock, 1994). In an effort to foster students' involvement in research, to simultaneously address the Council on Social Work Education's requirement for ongoing program assessment and revitalization, and to create an opportunity for the School of Social Work at The University of Montana to engage in organizational learning, over the course of several years, students in an introductory, undergraduate research course engaged in the evaluation of their own program (Jacobson & Goheen, 2006). Applying the principles of community-based participatory research, students developed surveys to assess the program's effectiveness and administered them to fellow students, faculty and staff, practicum supervisors, and program alumni. They conducted individual interviews with faculty and focus groups with social work majors and practicum supervisors. They experienced the use of both qualitative and quantitative data collection methods and analyses, which allowed them to translate abstract research concepts into practice. They also made the connection between research and practice and were afforded an opportunity to apply the skills they had learned in previous practice courses to their work as program evaluators (i.e., observation, individual interviewing, small group facilitation, and establishing the reliability of evidence).

The project culminated in a research forum held at the end of the semester and attended by faculty, social work students, program alumni, practicum supervisors, family, and friends. Students presented the evaluation results and their recommendations for change. They engaged attendees in a discussion regarding the need for more challenging course work, less repetition of course content across the curriculum, more "real-life" experience prior to the practicum, and an appreciation of the program's strength-based approach and the friendly, family-like environment fostered by faculty and staff. Program stakeholders assured students their work was much more than a course project and that their recommendations would be addressed. As a direct result of their feedback, the structure for senior practicum seminar was changed to better reflect their learning needs. Overall, student responses to the evaluation project were positive. One student summarized her sentiments toward the project by stating, "When you participate and are able to see the results you have a sense of ownership and involvement. I feel that what our class did will make a difference in the future of the BSW program" (p. 97). Another student commented that she now realized "how much research and evaluation can be used to create change" (p. 97).

The Challenges of Participatory Evaluation

Cautions, Considerations, and Challenges

Participatory evaluation is not without its challenges. Evaluation tools and the ways we structure the process of evaluation carry assumptions, values, and standards for how we presume to operate. It is important to consider these assumptions in order to assess whether a particular tool or method is appropriate in another context. In other words, is participation always the best way to go? While the rewards are great, participatory evaluation takes time, and a considerable proportion of this time must be spent in reflection. As we learned early in this chapter, evaluation falls low on the priority list for many organizational administrators and workers. Given the context and culture of most social work organizations, the primary mode of operation is one of reactivity, not reflection. Social workers respond to long-neglected societal problems, but they often do so through programs established to pick up the pieces instead of addressing the root cause of problems and intervening before they get out of control. In these situations, workers find themselves with little time for reflection. Credibility and political expediency are two other factors worth mentioning that need to be addressed depending upon the purpose and nature of the evaluation process. The dominant research paradigm claiming neutrality and objectivity is, in many situations, viewed as producing the most credible information. However, increasingly participatory approaches are gaining voice in the social work literature. Furthermore, for particular audiences and sometimes for the sake of political expediency, a participatory approach to evaluation would be far too time-intensive to pursue.

Responsibility, Risk, and Commitment

Participatory evaluation demands responsibility and commitment to the process. The three major aims of participatory research—to investigate, to educate, and to take action—require versatile, risk-taking participants who are comfortable playing the roles of researcher, educator, activist, and *bricoleur*. For example, think about the amount of time it would take you to get to know, more than superficially, your community, the key power players, and those excluded from meaningful participation in the decisions that concern their lives. Also, consider how difficult it might be to get the most oppressed people to participate, people who spend most of their time and energy meeting their basic survival needs. Given the intensive time requirements of participatory research, how might you get these people involved? And what would it take to keep you committed and involved? Furthermore, consider also the lack of access you and your group might have to support from financial and institutional resources, all of which are necessary to push a project forward and keep up the momentum. Given these challenges, the default solution is often to return to more top-down models of evaluation. Here is a place where social justice workers can exercise "functional noncapitulation" that we discussed in Chapter 8. The social worker may not have control over the decision making regarding the evaluation process. She can, however, raise questions regarding who participates, what is being measured, and whose voices are or are not being heard in the process.

A C T I O N

The Universal Declaration of Human Rights in Your Community

In Chapter 4 we suggested using The Universal Declaration of Human Rights (UDHR) as a foundation for ethical practice. In this exercise, you will be using the UDHR as an evaluation tool. Divide your class into small groups and have each group pick articles from the "plain language version" of The Universal Declaration of Human Rights included below. You will be evaluating the human rights climate in your community. Each group completes three tasks:

1. Read the articles you chose together, discuss their meaning, and be prepared to explain their meaning to the main group when you report on your discussion.

2. Decide to what extent people in your community enjoy these human rights: Everyone, Most People, Some People, A Few People, No One?

3. If everyone does not enjoy a particular right, write down who is excluded.

Share your small group evaluations with the larger group and discuss how you might go about developing an evaluation instrument to assess the human rights climate in your community. How might your evaluation steer social justice-oriented practice? How could you use your results to stimulate action in your community? How would you disseminate your findings?

Universal Declaration of Human Rights (plain language version)

1. Right to equality

2. Freedom from discrimination

3. Right to life, liberty, and personal security

4. Freedom from slavery

5. Freedom from torture and degrading treatment

6. Right to recognition as a person before the law

7. Right to equality before the law

8. Right to remedy by competent tribunal

9. Freedom from arbitrary arrest and exile

10. Right to fair public hearing

11. Right to be considered innocent until proven guilty

12. Freedom from interference with privacy, family, home, and correspondence

13. Right to free movement in and out of the country

14. Right to asylum in other countries from persecution

15. Right to a nationality and the freedom to change nationality

16. Right to marriage and a family

17. Right to own property

18. Freedom of belief and religion

19. Freedom of opinion and information

20. Right of peaceful assembly and association

21. Right to participate in government and free elections

22. Right to social security

23. Right to desirable work and to join trade unions

24. Right to rest and leisure

25. Right to adequate living standard

26. Right to education

27. Right to participate in the culture life of a community

28. Right to a social order that articulates this document

29. Community duties essential to free and full development

30. Freedom from state or personal interference in the above rights [9]

CRITICAL REFLECTION

What is Critical Reflection?

Evaluation goes hand-in-hand with reflection. We begin this section by looking at the meaning of reflection and then comparing the differences when we add the word "critical." Mezirow (1998, pp. 185-186) defines reflection as a "turning back" on experience, but he contends it can mean many things. It includes simple awareness of objects or events or states of being. It can also mean the act of considering something, letting our thoughts wander and contemplating alternatives. As humans, we have the capacity to reflect on ourselves reflecting. Reflection, however, does not imply *assessing* the object of contemplation, and herein lies the crucial difference between reflection and critical reflection. Mezirow argues that critical reflection "may be either implicit, as when we mindlessly choose between good and evil because of our assimilated values, or explicit, as when we bring the process of choice into awareness to examine and assess the reasons for making a choice" (p. 186).

Critical reflection includes questioning taken-for-granted beliefs that relate to different aspects of our experiences. These beliefs may be about how the world works economically, politically, philosophically, psychologically, and culturally. Think for a minute of a belief that you once held firm but no longer believe in its truth-value. Perhaps you assumed, "a woman's place was in the home," or "real men don't eat quiche" or "children should be seen and not heard," or "marriage should be between a man and a woman." Think of the reasons you used to bolster your faith in this belief. Now recall the process or events that occurred that made you question this long-held assumption.

Critical reflection is a structured, analytic, and emotional process that helps us examine the ways in which we make meaning of circumstances, events, and situations. Critical reflection pushes us to interpret experience, question our taken-for-granted assumptions of how things ought to work, and reframe our inquiry to open up new possibilities for thought and action. Posing critical questions is key to critical reflection.

Critical Reflection and Social Justice Work

There are a number of reasons why we include critical reflection as a core process of justice-oriented social work practice. Our list below is far from inclusive, so think of other reasons you might add:

◆ **Critical Reflection Promotes Continuous Self-Assessment:** Posing questions of our own performance is key to social work practice that takes social justice seriously. Assessing personal, emotional, and intellectual challenges and successes and addressing them through augmenting or changing the ways in which we work increases personal and professional competence and integrity (Freire, 1990).

◆ **Critical Reflection Fosters Connections and Linkages between Personal and Social Concerns:** The dominant mode of thought in U.S. culture is based on individualism. The tendency is to look only within ourselves for causes of our concerns. Critical reflection demands we look at the linkages between personal issues and the ways these are influenced and shaped by systems much larger than ourselves.

◆ **Critical Reflection Legitimizes Challenging Dominant Explanations and Observations:** Engaging with issues in a critical way means questioning the power structures and the structuring of power embedded in the definitions attributed to social problems and concerns. Think of some unquestioned myths you adhered to and later discovered you simply lacked sufficient information for an informed opinion. How were these myths perpetuated?

♦ **Critical Reflection Opens Up and Strengthens Spaces of Possibility:** As discussed earlier, binary logic or the logic of "either/or" is the dominant social logic in U.S. culture (Kelly & Sewell, 1988). The primary limitation of this particular mode of thinking is that it narrows choices. For example, something is either right or wrong—there are no shades of gray. Kelly and Sewell remind us that "trialectic" logic or the logic of wholeness provides a space to "grasp the wholeness which emerges" (p. 22-23) when we consider relationship among factors in terms of threes instead of twos.

♦ **Critical Reflection Links to Problem-Posing:** At the heart of critical reflection is problem-posing. Certain types of questions promote critical inquiry. Posing the subject matter as a problem or what Freire called "problematizing the ordinary" connects us to the work of evaluation and systematization. We are engaged in an ongoing process of examining the conditions of our lives, identifying concerns, asking the "but why?" questions, and looking for themes and patterns that connect. These become the foundations for developing action plans.

The Critically Reflective Thinker

John Dewey (1910, 1933), early 20th century educator and philosopher, emphasized the importance of reflection and understood it as both an intellectual and an emotional endeavor:

> Given a genuine difficulty and a reasonable amount of analogous experience to draw upon, the difference, *par excellence*, between good and bad thinking is found at this point. The easiest way is to accept any suggestion that seems plausible and thereby bring to an end the condition of mental uneasiness. Reflective thinking is always more or less troublesome because it involves overcoming the inertia that inclines one to accept suggestions at their face value; it involves willingness to endure a condition of mental unrest and disturbance. Reflective thinking, in short, means judgment suspended during further inquiry; and suspense is likely to be somewhat painful . . . To maintain the state of doubt and to carry on systematic and protracted inquiry—these are the essentials of thinking. (Dewey, 1910, p. 13)

The goal then of critical reflection is to promote tension and uncertainty. As Dewey suggests above, we must be prepared to deal with the discomfort that comes from having one's long-held assumptions open for question. Dewey (1933) identified three characteristics of the reflective thinker that negotiate the "mental unrest and disturbance" resulting from the contradictions between old and new ways of thinking. He called these *open-mindedness*, *responsibility*, and *wholeheartedness*.

Open-mindedness is the desire to hear more than one side of an issue, to listen to alternative perspectives, and to recognize that even the most engrained beliefs are open to question. *Responsibility* connotes the desire to seek out the truth and apply new information learned to troublesome situations. *Wholeheartedness* encompasses the emotional aspect of reflective thinking. It implies that, through commitment, one can overcome fear and uncertainty to make meaningful change and marshal the capacity to critically evaluate self, others, and society.

Building Critical Reflection Capacity

Dewey's characteristics of the reflective thinker are not innate, inborn attributes bestowed on some of us and not on others. In fact, these characteristics and the skills of critical reflection can be developed. Here are five suggestions for fine-tuning your critical reflection skills.

1. **Dialogue:** As we addressed earlier, engaging in participatory learning is the primary way we develop critical reflection capacity. Discussing our ideas, thoughts, and feelings with others externalizes our thinking and helps us engage with others and work on open-mindedness. It is also one of the most viable ways we learn. True dialogue occurs when we open ourselves to new learning and challenge ourselves and change in the process.

2. **Critical Friend Dyads:** Hatton and Smith (1995) describe the use of critical friend dyads and how these relationships help to develop higher levels of thinking. A critical friend is someone who is not afraid to disagree, who will challenge your viewpoint and question your assumptions about reality. Think for a moment what it might be like if the expectation of the "critical friend" was part of your work in a community organization. How might the notion of critical friend change the ways in which we think about our work and how might this notion of continual critique provide permission for altering structures towards more just and equitable arrangements?

3. **Research:** As we have addressed earlier in this chapter, research nurtures reflective practice and critical reflection skills. The research process itself mirrors the critical reflection process. First, a hypothesis is formulated or a topic of inquiry to investigate is decided. Then literature addressing the topic area is searched. Next, decisions are made regarding how to collect and analyze the information. Finally, conclusions are drawn and decisions are made concerning how to disseminate the results of the research.

4. **Writing Experiences:** Journaling and other forms of reflective writing are ways to keep a record of personal growth and changing perceptions. There are a number of approaches to journal writing that range from unstructured narrative to focused writing on specific topics with specific intent. Journals can be used to catalogue and reflect upon critical, perplexing incidents or to examine in-depth, particular case studies. Journals can also provide the means for linking theory and practice.

Artistic Reflection: Photos, artwork, and theater can be used to stimulate critical thinking in their production and presentation. For example, students in Maxine Jacobson's class on Women and Social Action in the Americas completed an assignment in which each student proposed and completed a special project that spoke to students' individual interests regarding women and social action. One student captured her experience at the World Trade Organization protest in Seattle through photographs depicting the human elements of protestors' struggles. When presented to the class, these powerful black and white images of personal and collective anguish, elation, intimidation, and solidarity evoked critical discussion on the more intimate elements of social injustice and struggles for social change.

Learning Letters Home

Think of a close friend or a relative with whom you can share your most intimate thoughts. Compose a letter to this person that addresses the following questions: (1) What are you thinking and how are you feeling at this point in your course work about choosing social work as a career? (2) What are you learning that challenges your thinking about social work and yourself as a potential social worker? (3) What have been some key areas of personal, emotional, and intellectual growth? This letter need not be shared with others. In class, discuss with others what the process of reflection was like for you and how you brought the key themes of critical reflection to bear on the completion of this exercise.

A C T I O N

CELEBRATION

Why Celebration as a Core Process?

Scour the social work literature and you will find hardly a mention of celebration as a core process of social work practice. Yet on the other hand, conduct a literature search on burnout and be prepared to find an abundance of articles written on the subject. How do you make sense of this—a mere oversight or is celebration a concept incongruent with the practice of social work? While our inclusion of celebration as a core process in the Just Practice Framework may make us appear too idealistic or out of touch with the "real" world of practice, we believe it fits well in a model of social justice-oriented practice. We hope to challenge traditional meanings and practices of social work and nurture idealism in others and ourselves. We see celebration as a key component of practice that allows us to look beyond the present and keep our sights on a vision of a just world. Typically, traditional meanings of social work highlight the drudgery of practice and emphasize social workers' proclivity for "burnout." Even the media's attention to social work through television programs such as "Judging Amy" paint a picture of the social worker (Amy's mother) as a brittle and at times, emotionally confused woman, who knows what is right for everyone else but is somehow continually thwarted by bureaucratic rules—the perpetual mother, the perpetual martyr.

Celebration as an Integral Part of Practice

What would it mean to bring the notion of celebration into our work as social justice workers? How might celebration reconfigure the ways in which we envision practice? Lappe and Dubois (1994) remind us that the most effective organizations see celebration and appreciation as integral to their work. Celebration and appreciation breathe new life into the work and recharge the batteries; at the same time they build loyalty and strengthen relationships. Lappe and Dubois provide a list of suggestions or "how-to's" to brush up on our celebration and appreciation skills. We share some of their wisdom on the following page.

- **Celebrate the Learning, Not Just the Winning:** "We don't always get what we want. But out of every effort comes learning to be appreciated. After one citizen group's legislative campaign failed, we noticed that their newsletter celebrated how much their members had learned about both the issue and the citizen lobbying process. So by 'celebration' we don't necessarily mean throwing a party. We also mean acknowledging and expressing satisfaction in what has been accomplished, even when an intended target is not met."

- **Create a Celebratory Spirit:** "Colored balloons. Noisemakers. Streamers. Amusing props. Live music. All these features create a mood of celebration, even in a public gathering dealing with deadly serious problems. Each time we've attended public meetings held by the Sonoma County Faith-Based Organizing Project, for example, our moods are lifted as soon as we enter the auditorium. These techniques infuse their meetings with a spirit of celebration, despite the fact that this group faces such difficult issues as affordable housing and school reform."

- **Show Appreciation of Your Adversaries as Well as Your Allies:** "The most successful groups that we know acknowledge their volunteers at events in which the particular contribution of each individual is described. As members hear what others do, appreciation becomes a means of building a sense of interdependence within the group . . . letters and calls of thanks (even when you disagree with the person), do not signal weakness. You'll establish your credibility as a person or group with strength, who knows you'll be around for the long haul."

Now we add a few of our own:

- **Animation:** Think of the animator role (discussed in Chapter 8) in part as one that sparks the celebratory spirit and brings joy to life. It may be through gestures such as remembering participants' birthdays, celebrating organizational anniversaries and milestones, and recognizing successes along the way—the first time a participant speaks in public about an issue she cares about or a child's first month in a new school. It may be taking time to recognize events and transitions that shape personal and collective history and memory, such as the naming of a group, move to a new home, and so on.

◆ **Celebration as Resistance:** Celebrating rights is a way of claiming voices, time and space, and resisting forces trying to silence and threaten. Celebration of social holidays and religious feast days mark the right to practice and to honor histories. For example, during the 1980s the people of La Victoria, a poor *población* (community) in Santiago, Chile, publicly celebrated International Women's Day as a form of resistance to the military dictatorship. The celebration was a way of enabling residents to move beyond the fear and into the streets. It was both a celebration and a strategy for community mobilization (Finn, 2005; Finn, Rodriguez & Nuñez, 2000).

◆ **Celebration Also Means Finding Joy in the Work:** Townsend et al. (1999), in writing about women and power in Mexico, acknowledge the importance of enjoyment in women's discovery of power from within. Women take and express pleasure in their achievements, in "getting out of the house" and coming together with others. Likewise, the women of Villa Paula Jaraquemada, another Santiago *población*, joined together to build community from the ground up through a housing auto-construction project, express a sense of joy in both the process and products of their work: "I love it, that's why I do it. As you learn something new you get more enthused about learning. I love it. I love the learning. I love seeing results. That's what keeps me coming back" (Finn, 2001b, p. 191). They speak often of the "beauty" of the experience of participation, and they celebrate the beauty of their successes large and small. They talk of the positive outlook they now have and their faith in their own capacity to create change.

Celebrating Small Steps

With your class, brainstorm what the word celebration means to the members of your group. How do you celebrate birthdays, holidays, and rites of passage such as moving from adolescence to adulthood or the end of a long week in school? Brainstorm another list of successes and challenges you have experienced individually and as a group that spring from your involvement in class this term. Decide as a group how you might celebrate your work together.

**A
C
T
I
O
N**

CHAPTER SUMMARY

In this chapter we have developed the Just Practice core processes of evaluation, critical reflection, and celebration. We defined evaluation, explored different approaches to it, and highlighted participatory approaches for their congruence with social justice-oriented social work practice. We examined questions of reliability, validity, and trustworthiness as they relate to current debates about what is right and true in research. We provided case examples of participatory evaluation and explored participatory processes, and we have asked the reader to examine these examples and processes for the key principles that underlie social justice-oriented practice. We emphasized the role of *bricoleur* for its fit with the principles and objectives of participatory approaches to evaluation. We outlined what we need to evaluate and a set of strategies or methods that can be used alone or in combination to promote critical inquiry into the problems of everyday life, and examples of traditional and alternative tools for research practice. We defined critical reflection and its importance to social justice work and addressed methods for developing one's critical reflection capacity. Finally, we introduced and defined celebration as a core process, and we presented strategies that draw attention to the need to see the beauty in our work and help us sustain the momentum necessary for Just Practice. In Chapter 10 we close the circle on our journey through the principles and practices of social justice work. We reflect on the future of social work, and we revisit and expand on the challenges facing the profession as we move into the 21st century. Finally, we summarize key principles we have discussed throughout this text.

Resource: The Evaluator's Tool Kit

In this section, we present a tool kit for evaluators. It contains ideas and examples helpful for conceptualizing and conducting practice and program evaluations. As you read through these, consider how they translate into social justice-oriented practice. What contradictions do you find and how might you alter the tools so they better reflect the values of social justice work?

Getting Started

In their description of evaluation and its applicability to participatory democracy, Hope and Timmel (1999, V. 2, pp. 121-133) suggest how workers might enlist people's participation in reflecting critically on their own projects, programs, aims, and leadership. They start by conducting a workshop with potential participants in which they define evaluation, discuss potential pitfalls, and learn when to conduct evaluations, why these should be conducted, and various evaluation methods and strategies. The final step is to develop a plan for how the group will implement the participatory evaluation process. Hope and Timmel use the following questions to initiate this process:

1. What aspects of your program do you aim to evaluate?

2. What methods will you use for each of the aims you have mentioned? What indicators and what questions are important to include?

3. Who will do what, when, and where? Make out a time, place, and person chart to indicate your plan.

The final step is sharing all plans with the whole group. (p. 130)

Simply Simple

Lappe and DuBois (1994) outline some simple questions they believe are powerful tools for change when applied to small and large group evaluation processes:

1. How do you feel about what happened? (Answers can be in one-word descriptions of emotions: upset, happy, relieved, angry, energized. No intellectualizing allowed.)

2. What worked?

3. What didn't work?

4. What could we do better? (p. 281)

Elegant in their simplicity, these questions provide a framework for group discussion. Responses can be tape recorded, or written out on flip chart paper. This preserves the discussion for later reflection so history can become a basis for continued learning.

Listening Survey for Program Evaluation

Earlier in this chapter we addressed the listening survey as a way to conduct participatory evaluation. We use the model presented by Hope and Timmel (1999, V. 1) and adapt it for program or project evaluation. A listening survey for program evaluation might look something like this:

1. First, the research team listens to unstructured conversations with program or project participants, board members, or other key players with information relevant to an evaluation.

2. Next, the research team takes information from the survey, looks at it critically, and analyzes it for themes. Pertinent questions might include: What are people speaking about with strong feeling? Are project or program issues mainly dealing with problems of exclusion, difficulties with accessing resources, or contradictions between the stated mission and modes of doing practice?

3. Next, the research team prepares problem-posing materials, based on the survey information, to stimulate discussion in learning groups. These could be bulleted points typed on handouts or graphic or pictorial representations of themes or problematic issues. Hope and Timmel (1999, V.1, p. 24) call these "codes" and contend that the better the code, the more people in a learning group will learn for themselves.

4. Next, the learning environment must be conducive to learning. Simultaneously, people must be supported and people must be challenged to allow for critical reflection. Establishing guidelines for participants assists with the development of group safety and trust. The group leader's role is to facilitate discussion, summarize when necessary, and build on the contributions of participants.

5. Last, the research team decides on ways they want to present their codifications.

Building Community Capacity through Empowering Evaluation

Steven Mayer (1996) runs a nonprofit organization called Rainbow Research. The purpose of Rainbow Research is "to assist socially concerned communities and organizations in responding more effectively to social problems" (p. 332). The organization's primary task is to disseminate valuable information about what works to build leadership capacity. Mayer suggests three key features of empowering evaluations that assist programs and projects in building capacity. We summarize them as follows:

1) *Help Create a Constructive Environment for the Evaluation.* A constructive environment is one conducive to action that helps the community use the evaluation process to develop its commitment, resources, and skills.

   a. Minimize the distance between evaluator (as expert) and program participants (as ignorant).

   b. Recommend a policy by which negative evaluation findings do not lead directly to punishment by program funders or directors.

   c.   The intention of an evaluation should be to strengthen community responses, not punish. Move away from faultfinding to identify opportunities for improvement.

2) *Actively Include the Voices of Intended Beneficiaries.* Capacity-building projects should lead to improvements in the systems for service communities. It stands to reason, then, that the voice of community members should be included in the evaluation process.

   a.   Intended beneficiaries should have a voice in deciding not only the methods of evaluation, but also the sources of information and the interpretation of the findings.

   b.   Include their experience, wisdom, and standards of excellence. They should be thought of as the ultimate source for assessing the merits of a program or project.

   c.   Include those not normally included. Bridge the divide between the helpers and the helped.

3) *Help Communities Use Evaluation Findings to Strengthen Community Responses.* Evaluators and others wanting to help communities build capacity can help make sure that community voices are heard, not just in designing and conducting the evaluation but in helping communities and other audiences (such as policymakers) move forward with the findings.

   a.   Help spread the lessons learned. Evaluation findings that stay on the shelf are worthless. Consider spreading the word through the media in some form or fashion.

   b.   Help create links among people who can use the information. All too often community work is compartmentalized, segregated into departments, regions, agencies, and professional groups. Evaluation may have implications across boundaries and borders. Consider your audience broadly.

   c.   Help communities and their organizations build on gains. Recommendations should be written that allow community organizations to mobilize and strengthen the commitment they bring to their work, increase the financial and other resources usable for strengthening their work, and further develop the skills needed to make their work effective. (pp. 335-337)

Questions for Discussion

1. We have described one of the roles of social justice work as that of the "bricoleur." What is the significance of this role for the process of research and evaluation?

2. What are the common linkages between participatory approaches to evaluation and social work's theory base discussed in Chapter 5?

3. Are there other suggestions you might have for building critical reflection skills beyond those discussed in the chapter?

4. Given your current practicum, practice, or volunteer setting, how could you evaluate the effectiveness of your practice? How could you make it participatory?

5. What suggestions or "how-tos" would you add to celebrate and take joy in our work?

Suggested Readings

Altepeter, M. Schopler, J. Galinsky, M., & Pennell, J. (1999). Participatory research as social work practice: When is it viable? *Journal of Progressive Human Services, 10*(2), 31-53.

Fetterman, S., Faftarian, J., & Wandersman, A. (Eds.). (1996). *Empowerment evaluation: Knowledge and tools for self-assessment and accountability.* Thousand Oaks, CA: Sage Publications.

Johnson, V., Ivan-Smith, E., Gordon, G., Pridmore, P., & Scott, P. (1998). *Stepping forward: Children and young people's participation in the development process.* London: Intermediate Technology Publications.

Lappe, F. M. & DuBois, P.M. (1994). *The quickening of America: Rebuilding our nation, remaking our lives.* San Francisco, CA: Jossey-Bass, Inc.

Lather, P. (1991). *Getting smart: Feminist research and pedagogy with/in the postmodern.* New York: Routledge.

Maguire, P. (1987). *Doing participatory research: A feminist approach.* Amherst, MA: The Center for International Education, University of Massachusetts.

Park, P. Brydon-Miller, B, Hall, B. & Jackson, T. (Eds.). (1993). *Voices of change: Participatory research in the United States and Canada.* Westport, CT: Bergin & Garvey

Zimbalist, S. (1977). *Historic themes and landmarks in social welfare research.* New York: Harper & Row.

End Notes

[1] From Paulo Freire (1974) *Pedagogy of the oppressed.* New York: Continuum.

[2] From J. Finn (2001b) "The women of Villa Paula Jaraquemada: Building community in Chile's transition to democracy." *Community Development Journal,* 36(3), p. 192

[3] For a more thorough description of positivism we refer you to the following sources for additional information - Denzin, N. & Lincoln, Y. (1994). (Eds.). *Handbook of qualitative research* (pp. 5-6). Thousand Oaks, CA: Sage Publications; Lincoln, Y. & Guba, E. (1985). *Naturalistic inquiry* (pp. 19-28). Newbury Park, CA: Sage Publications; Neuman, W. & Krueuger, L. (2003). *Social research methods: Qualitative and quantitative approaches* (pp. 70-75). Needham Heights, MA: Allyn & Bacon; Rubin, A. & Babbie, E. (2005*). Research methods for social work* (pp. 39-41). Belmont, CA: Wadsworth/Thompson Learning.

[4] There are numerous threats to internal and external validity. Articulating these goes beyond the scope of this text but we refer you to the following sources for additional information (Grinnell & Unrau, 2005; Marlow, 2005; Neuman & Kreuger, 2003; Rubin & Babbie, 2005).

[5] For further techniques that address the reliability and validity of qualitative data, see Yvonna Lincoln and Egon Guba's comprehensive volume entitled *Naturalistic inquiry* (1985), Newbury Park, CA: Sage Publications. They expand on techniques such as peer debriefing and negative case analysis that also help to ensure the credibility of research findings (see chapter eleven "Establishing Trustworthiness"- pp. 289-331).

[6] See Reason and Rowan (1981, p. 240) and Brown and Tandon (1978) for additional information on catalytic validity.

[7] The following website has additional information on Hull-House Maps and Papers: http://www.uic.edu/jaddams/hull/urbanexp/geography/

Just Futures: Social Justice–Oriented Practice in the 21ˢᵗ Century

> *Hope, as it happens, is so important for our existence, individual and social, that we must take every care not to experience it in a mistaken form, and thereby allow it to slip toward hopelessness and despair. Hopelessness and despair are both the consequence and the cause of inaction and immobilism.*
>
> Paulo Freire, *Pedagogy of Hope*, 1999[1]

> *If, as most of us believe, we have the power to shape the world according to our visions and desires then how come we have collectively made such a mess of it? Our social and physical world can and must be made, re-made, and, if that goes awry, re-made again. Where to begin and what is to be done are the key questions.*
>
> David Harvey, *Spaces of Hope*, 2000[2]

CHAPTER OVERVIEW

In this chapter we reflect on the future of social work and the challenges facing the field in the coming years. We return to some of the issues confronting social work in the 21ˢᵗ century that we identified at the beginning of the book. How will social work configure itself against this newly forming landscape? Perhaps this is a question to be posed to social workers in the United States and internationally as we confront the lived realities and growing uncertainties of the "new global order" (Caufield, 1996; Ferguson, Lavalette, & Whitmore, 2005; Mayadas & Elliott, 1992; Polack, 2004). We argue that the Just Practice Framework provides an approach to critical thought and action as we build future paths for social work while walking them.

We summarize a number of principles for social justice-oriented practice, drawing from themes highlighted throughout the text. We invite readers to join us in articulating principles of social justice work and putting them into practice. We close with examples of the possibilities of social justice work in action. We hope this ending marks a transition to many new beginnings.

THE FUTURE OF SOCIAL WORK

The coming of the millennium brought forth myriad predictions of both hope and doom regarding humanity's future. Social work was certainly not immune to millennial musings. In fact, over the past decade a diverse range of social work academics and practitioners have engaged in serious reflection on social work's past, present, and future. They have considered the emergence, movement, and maturation of social work over the past century and probed its possible futures. Let's take a brief look at some of their predictions for the state of social work practice and social welfare systems in the 21st century.

Children Are Our Future?

A number of U.S. writers have addressed the acceleration and businessing of everyday life and the implications for social work of rapid changes in work, family, and community. Martha Ozawa (1997) points to the challenges posed by demographic changes that include a burgeoning elderly population and a nonwhite majority of children by 2050. She predicts that children of color will be worse off by mid-century than they are today. Similarly, Stephanie Hochman (1997) predicts continued increases in the percentage of children living in poverty in the United States. Her prediction bears weight as approximately 17.8% of children residing in the United States currently live in poverty and this number has been increasing since the year 2000 (U.S. Census, 2004). She argues that disparities between the rich and poor will continue to be exacerbated in education. As federal and state dollars and tax bases for public education erode, poor children will attend poorer schools, and the poor will continue to be blamed for their inability to "get ahead."

Peter McLaren and Ramin Farahmandpur (2006) write about the No Child Left Behind Act, a disturbing piece of legislation passed in the United States in 2001. The Act embodies neoliberal social and economic policies and plays these out in the context of schooling in which principles of business and management rule and schools are expected to perform in the same way as corporations: The Act favors "outsourcing and downsizing methods of production in the name of flexibility and efficiency" (p. 94). It speaks the language of "underperforming schools and students," and regards teachers as "efficiency technicians" and students as "learning managers." If the language itself is not Orwellian enough to scare us, then the immediate repercussions should be:

> In California, where 3,800 teachers and 9,000 other school employees received pink slips last year, districts have cut textbook purchases, summer school, bus routes, maintenance, athletics, student newspapers, and electives. Half of the school districts in Kansas have cut staff, several districts have gone to a 4-day week, and 50 schools in Kansas now charge students to participate in extracurricular activities. In Michigan, funding for gifted and talented students is down 95 percent; Buffalo, New York, has been forced to close eight schools and eliminate 600 teaching jobs over the past years. (Goodman, 2004, p. 43, as cited in McLaren & Farahmandpur, p. 98)

According to *"The State of the World's Children 2006: Excluded and Invisible"* (UNICEF, 2005), children around the globe are experiencing the devastating consequences of exploitation, discrimination, and exclusion. While a primary emphasis of social work practice has been child welfare and addressing issues concerning protecting children from all forms of abuse and neglect, the global, structural manifestations of abuse and neglect are overwhelming to consider. Millions of children are growing up without parental care, living on the streets, and fending for themselves. Hundreds of thousands are estimated to be forcibly abducted or otherwise drawn into armed conflict in countries such as Sierra Leone and Uganda (UNICEF, 2005). Whereas social workers fought for the eradication of child labor at the turn of the 20th century, in the 21st century globalizing economic forces have created similar conditions in which an estimated 171 million children worldwide work in hazardous conditions operating dangerous equipment. Current predictions see little change in these trends (UNICEF, 2005).

Race Matters

Mark Stern (1997) voices concern regarding the solidification of physical, socio-economic, and ideological barriers between low-income Americans, a disproportionately high number of people of color, and the white middle and upper classes. He is hopeful, however, that growing multiracial demographics may challenge the bipolar view of race that has dominated in the United States. James Midgley (1997, p. 61), on the other hand, argues, that "problems such as the exploitation of women migrants (particularly in domestic service), the harsh treatment of illegal migrants, and the growing attachment of racist sentiment to social policy issues affecting migrants" are ones that social work needs to address directly. Stephanie Hochman (1997, p. 267) sees growing racism as a trend that accompanies reduced funding and increasing poverty as key issues in schools. A number of observers have also critically addressed growing incidents of xenophobia in response to immigration and movements of people across diverse borders (Karger & Stoesz, 1998; Mayadas & Elliott, 1992).

For example, recent events regarding immigration in the United States paint a vivid picture of racism and social exclusion, although history tells the story of U.S. borders variably opening and closing based on the need for cheap labor for a rapidly expanding capitalist society (Day, 2003; Zinn, 2003). The latest injustice did not go unnoticed as a bill was quietly passed by the House of Representatives in December 2005 authorizing the construction of a 700-mile fence across the Mexican-U.S. border, raising the crime of illegal immigration to felony status, and criminalizing any acts of assistance given to illegal immigrants, including providing food and water (McFadden, 2006). Spurred by aborted attempts to gain citizenship status, human rights, and protections in the workplace, immigrants astonished lawmakers and the American public in general as demonstrations erupted in cities across the United States to protest passage of the bill as it made its way to the Senate. In an article published in the *New York Daily News* on March 28, 2006, Juan Gonzalez (2006) comments about the magnitude of the protests: ". . . more than 50,000 Latinos gathered in Denver; 20,000 marched in Phoenix and Milwaukee last week, and an estimated 100,000 filled downtown Chicago on March 10" ("Latino Giant Awakens, 2006). These issues will not quickly recede beneath the radar screen in U.S. politics. They will become more contentious as economic conditions worsen. Understanding immigration requires getting at the root causes fueling the dislocation of people across borders rather than just the domestic consequences (Polack, 2004).

"Global Graying"

Janet George (1997) draws attention to what she terms "global graying," referring to the growing aging population. As Karen Lyons (1999, pp. 69-70) indicates, researchers are seeing a universal increase in the number of individuals over the age of 65. Elizabeth van Wormer (2006) states that "Not only is population aging universally, but it also has been unprecedented historically. For the first time in history, people over age 60 will outnumber children 14 and younger in industrialized nations" (p. 377). In fact, predictions say that by 2025, 1.2 billion people will be 65 and older. Moreover, the fastest growing age group is that of individuals 85 and above. The effects of global graying will be felt in business, politics, education, and pension and health care systems. How these issues are addressed will vary from country to country depending upon social, political, and economic structures and cultural values attributed to aging.

However, while much of the world is aging, some of the poorest sectors face a shortened life expectancy as the deadly effect of the AIDS epidemic continues. Hardest hit are those countries struggling with crippling poverty. For example, in sub-Saharan Africa, life expectancy rates have dropped significantly over the last ten years. A child born today has a life expectancy of 45 years, compared to 55 years only a decade ago (United Nations Development Programme, 2005, p. 26; World Bank, 2004).

The Businessing of Human Services

Cynthia Franklin (2000) contends that the devolution of federal and state responsibilities to local communities and the private sector will continue. The effects of privatization will be increasingly felt in health and mental health service systems in which "managed care" will dominate and service providers will find themselves competing for scarce resources. The infiltration of managerial oversight and market principles on health and mental health work demands increased efficiency and cost containment and calls upon workers to practice brief, solution-based modes of treatment in an effort to cut work short.

Imagine, for example, the privatization of prisons in the United States and how the businessing of prisons plays out in what has been referred to as the prison industrial complex (Davis, 2001) or Incarceration, Inc. (Abramsky, 2004). "The prison industrial complex is not a conspiracy guiding criminal justice policy behind closed doors. It is a confluence of special interest that has given prison construction in the United States a seemingly unstoppable momentum" (Schlosser, 1998, p. 52). President Dwight D. Eisenhower warned the American public in his farewell speech delivered in January of 1961 about potential military spending driven by missile contractors fanning the flames of fear about the armament gap between the United States and Russia. Eric Schlosser (1998) points out the parallels to the present-day industrial zeitgeist to build more prisons. Between 1995 and

2005 in the United States, there was a 30% increase in the number of adults either incarcerated or on probation or parole. This translates to 7 million people, with whites making up the majority of probationers yet the minority of those imprisoned (Carroll, 2005, *The Boston Globe*). "The United States now imprisons more people than any other country in the world—perhaps half a million more than Communist China" (Schlosser, 1998, p. 52).

A report in *Alcoholism and Drug Abuse Weekly*, February 14, 2005, indicates that profits are rising as shares climbed from $34 to $42 for Tennessee-based Corrections Corporation of America, one of the largest private prison corporations constructing and managing prisons in Canada, South Africa, Australia, and the U.K. Prisons are big business ("Private Prisons See Rising Profits," 2005). They are springing up in "job-starved" rural communities across the United States (Abramsky, 2004, p. 22). Predictions indicating that the construction of private prisons will continue to increase in the future raise important questions for social justice work: How do market principles play out in this shift from state- or federal-run prison facilities to the private sector? Who gains and who loses? What is at stake here? What are the effects of cashing in on incarceration or the commodification of crime?

Growing Disparities

Nancy Rose (1997) and David Korten (2001) argue that we will see a widening income gap as a result of corporate restructuring, economic globalization, increasing un- and underemployment, and a growing propensity toward elitism in social and economic policies. Sharon Keigher and Christine Lowry (1998) address the "sickening implications" of these global disparities as manifest in infant mortality, AIDS and other epidemics, environmental disasters, and the growing numbers of refugee populations: "It is estimated that about 3,900 children die each day because of disease transmitted through dirty water or poor hygiene" (United Nations Development Programme, 2005, p. 32). The negative consequences of Structural Adjustment Programs are likely to contribute to even more dire conditions for people living in extreme poverty.

Ray Boshara (2003) reminds us not only to look at income disparities when assessing the inequalities wrought by economic globalization but also to look at the wealth gap. He notes that "By the close of the 1990s the United States had become more unequal than at any other time since the dawn of the New Deal— indeed, it was the most unequal society in the advanced democratic world" (pp. 93-94). Those households in the top 20% control 83% of U.S. wealth and even more alarming, the top 1% owns 38% of the nation's wealth. Although income is certainly important, if not essential, to the livelihood of everyone living in a capitalist society, wealth is fundamental. It is about stocks, bonds, and property, those financial assets that really separate the haves from the have-nots. Thus, addressing issues of disparity in the future requires thinking about ways to increase people's wealth or what Boshara refers to as "asset-building policies" (p. 94).

> The vast majority of people who live in rich countries have access to the financial resources, technologies, and services that prevent or, for diseases like AIDS, at least postpone death. Conversely, the vast majority of people in poor countries—especially if they happen to be poor—do not.
>
> United Nations Development Programme, p. 32

Death of Social Work?

Lawrence Kreuger (1997) envisions a grim scenario for the future of social work. He predicts the profession's demise in the 21st century, arguing that "hypertechnologies" and the genetic-chemical revolution will make social work intervention obsolete. Kreuger also predicts the collapse of the "grand narratives" upon which social work has premised its knowledge base. Notions of modernity, progress, and the role of the state that informed 20th century social welfare projects will be replaced by the logic and practice of privatization. In short, his prediction is one of social implosion: radical economic dislocations accompanied by the breakdown of traditional political boundaries and the geosocial space of neighborhood and community. By 2100, argues Kreuger, social work will no longer be.

Others assess social work's relevance and argue that the profession has abandoned its public persona or what Howard Karger and Marie Hernández (2004) refer to as the role of the "public intellectual." They highlight social workers' influence on key public policy issues in the early 20th century and, in contrast, the absence of social workers' presence today in setting standards and agendas to address important social issues such as health care, crime, poverty, and welfare reform. They advocate infusing social work from the outside by disrupting its professional boundaries, and by

> . . . inviting dissident scholars, activists and intellectuals into the profession—much as they were in the early 1900s—some of the intellectual vitality missing in modern social work can be restored. This cross-fertilization can also help cultivate a cadre of public intellectuals able to effectively address social issues. (p. 59)

MEETING THE CHALLENGES AHEAD

Perhaps many social workers do not share Kreuger's vision of the end of social work or the views of Karger and Hernández who chastise the profession for creating and maintaining a culture of exclusivity. However, they do agree that the challenges ahead call for fundamental rethinking of the nature and direction of practice as we come to grips with the rapidly changing environment in which we do our work. Let's consider some of those directions for practice and the knowledge and skills they demand for social workers in the 21st century.

Critical Community Practice

Lisbeth Schorr (1997) reminds us that the most successful programs never forget that the individuals and families they work with are part of a much larger community context. These programs teach the difficult and often-ignored lessons that solutions imposed from outside local structures fail to grasp. They value the importance of local *meanings* and the immediate *context* of practice and of people's lived experience. They recognize *power* as both a constraining and enabling force for community change. They appreciate *history* in shaping current patterns of living. And they are open to the *possibility* of new ways of looking at and addressing both human needs and human rights given varying levels of and access to social supports and resources. In short, they advocate an integrated approach to practice in which social workers are equipped with facilitation, animation, mediation, advocacy, and coalition-building skills. Social workers must also be experts at engagement and collaboration and willing to learn from neighborhoods and the community and to understand and reconfigure community practice skills for a devolution environment.

Internationalism

In light of the challenges of globalization, a number of social workers are calling for a greater emphasis on internationalism (Ferguson, Lavalette, & Whitmore, 2005; George, 1997; Hokenstad & Midgley, 1997; Lyons, 1999; Ramanathan & Link, 1999; Sarri, 1997; van Wormer, 2006). Transnational institutions and global actors, such as the World Bank, International Monetary Fund, and World Trade Organization, exert increasingly powerful influence on domestic social policies (Hokenstad & Midgley, 1997). Practice in the 21st century needs to understand and attend to these influences. Taking internationalism seriously pushes social workers to move away from simplistic and often paternalistic solutions to global problems such as "giving aid," to considering the strengths and capacities that can be drawn on through "mutual aid" and meaningful accompaniment. Thinking of social work in international terms also provides a wealth of new theoretical possibilities to support alternative forms of practice and the exchange of creative and innovative ways of thinking and acting with social workers around the globe.

The Political Dimensions of Practice

Michael Reisch (1997) contends that, in order to speak to possible futures of social work, we first need to examine trends that have been shaping the field. He addresses three interlocking political trends: changes in ideological context of politics, changes in the distribution of political power, and changes in popular attitudes about politics and the role of government. Reisch argues that a "mythology of simplicity" has shaped both public policy debates and analysis of those debates, thus obscuring a much more ambiguous and complex reality. Social workers, Reisch contends, need to incorporate a political dimension into their practice and to serve as *interpreters* of environments to both policy makers and the public, as advocates for those who lack power, and as mediators between communities and institutions in the public, nonprofit, and for-profit sector. Reisch (1997) writes,

In the 21st century the survival of the social services, the well-being of clients and communities, and the ability of social workers to derive satisfaction from our careers depend on the integration of political action into a broader pro-social welfare strategy. Political knowledge and skills should become as much a part of every social worker's repertoire as skills in assessment and intervention with individuals and families (Abramovitz, 1993; Fisher, 1995). (p. 81)

Theorizing for Transformation

Steven Hicks, Jan Fook, and Richard Pozzoto (2005) argue for serious engagement with postmodern critical theory (see Chapter 5) as a prerequisite for addressing the complexities of 21st century practice. They envision social work as an emancipatory project that legitimizes personal and political struggles against oppressive structures and practices. They argue that to achieve these ends, social work needs to transform itself by moving beyond dualisms; challenging notions of objective truth and value-free knowledge; building theory from the grounded realities of practice; deconstructing the truth claims of traditional social work; demonstrating commitment to political struggles; engaging with questions of difference, power, and oppression; and creating an alternative social work discourse.

Karen Healy (2005) reminds us, however, that the tasks laid out above may not be so easy to achieve: Practitioners continue to find theory inaccessible for helping them better understand and improve their practice. This appears to be especially true for critical theory. Achieving praxis, that is, bridging theory and practice, may sound good but in reality its translation is compromised by rapidly changing conditions in social service organizations brought on by globalization and its corporatizing effects on all aspects of the social workers' world. Healy argues for, now more than ever, attention to the complexities in translating theory into practice and the need for

> . . . dynamic and collaborative approaches to knowledge building that draw on the understandings of stakeholders in the critical social work enterprise, whether they are situated as "academics," "practitioners," or "service users." These approaches require all stakeholders to forego their certainties about the "truth" of critical practice while recognizing that each has much to contribute to the ongoing reconstruction of critical social work. (p. 227)

People, Partnership, and Participation

Frank Ashley and John Gaventa (1997) argue that a commitment to social justice demands the democratization of processes of knowledge development, and they call for new forms of partnership and participation to realize this. Korten (2001) echoes this claim, arguing that meaningful, justice-oriented change comes through promotion of the right and possibility for people to control their own resources, economies, and means of livelihood. Rosemarie Sarri (1997, p. 394) challenges social workers to ask ourselves: How genuinely are we committed to the principle of people's participation? A challenge to social justice workers, then, is to advocate and open spaces for people's meaningful and empowering participation in the decisions and decision-making arenas that affect their lives.

JUST PRACTICE: A GUIDE FOR THE FUTURE

Revisiting the Framework

We contend that the Just Practice Framework makes a significant contribution to reconfiguring social work thinking and practice so that we are better equipped to meet these challenges. The five key themes of *meaning, context, history, power,* and *possibility* bring together many of the concerns addressed above regarding the future of social work and the challenges therein. The framework provides a means for appreciating and reflecting on the complexities of 21st century social work practice as we hold these themes in relationship and consider the dynamics of their intersection. The core processes of *engagement, teaching-learning, action, accompaniment, evaluation, critical reflection,* and *celebration* presented in Chapters 6 to 9 invite participation, reflection, nonlinear movement, collaborative knowledge development, and attention to the mutual interplay of the personal, historical, cultural, and political. The Just Practice matrix (refer to Chapter 5, p. 202) offers a guide to question-posing and critical inquiry that engages with contextual complexity, provides a means for mapping constraints and possibilities, and creates space for dialogue to inform action grounded in the concrete circumstances at hand.

Crafting a Flexible Frame

In developing the Just Practice approach, we have attempted to speak to the concerns and challenges of 21st century social work. The Just Practice approach begins with the assumption that our knowledge of the world is partial and shaped by our perspectives and positionalities. Social work knowledge development is an emergent, dialogue-based process gained through engagement with changing contexts and the forces that shape them. We have tried to craft a "flexible" frame that helps us structure inquiry and action and remain open to challenge and possibility. This question-posing approach serves to disrupt our "certainties" and keep us engaged as humble and curious learners.

Addressing Fundamental Issues of Power

Many of the concerns addressed above regarding social work in the 21st century speak to fundamental issues of economic and political power and inequality. By recognizing power as a key theme in social justice work, we have attempted to bring questions of power and inequality to bear in every context of social work practice and to challenge social workers to seriously and honestly address the many micro practices of power in play in every change process. We concur with Reisch (1997) that social workers need to incorporate a political dimension into their practice, not as an "appendage" but as the heart of our work. The Just Practice Framework does not stand without questions of power at its foundation.

Disrupting Nationalism

We have also attempted to disrupt the bounded nationalism of U.S. social work and engage with a greater internationalism here. The critical thinking and practice of social workers and other theorists and activists beyond our borders have challenged and informed our thinking over the past several years as the seeds of ideas for this book were being planted. The Just Practice Framework is, in many aspects, a product of concrete engagement with context, histories, knowledge, and practices beyond the United States. We have tried to incorporate these influences into the model and craft an approach that better enables us to think outside the box and beyond the borders of familiar experience. Fundamentally, social justice work calls on us to ask, "Social justice for whom?" and to constantly question the ways in which we circumscribe the boundaries of justice in our practice.

Strengthening Democratic Participation

In line with the directions advocated by a number of critical social work scholars (Hicks, Fook, & Pozotto, 2005; Pease & Fook; 1999), we have attempted to move beyond dualisms, craft an alternative discourse, and encourage new forms of partnership and participation. We concur with Ashley and Gaventa (1997) that collaborative partnerships that strengthen democratic participation offer "lessons of humility, care, and equity... lessons, at least in part, that return us to the importance of social capital... "(p. 51). Ashley and Gaventa encourage us to see social capital:

> . . . less as a substance than as a network. We see social capital as consisting of connections between and among groups and individuals—connections built incrementally through shared histories of activity and interchange; more like a circulatory system than like the liquid flowing through it. (p. 51)

We find the Just Practice Framework and processes to be a helpful guide for making and strengthening these connections. However, our own view is at best partial. We encourage readers to challenge us, help us see the limits, and suggest directions for enhancing and transforming the knowledge and practice of social justice work.

REFLECTION: Personalizing the Just Practice Key Concepts

Understanding the Just Practice key concepts and beginning to apply them sometimes starts best by thinking about their meaning on a personal level. In the following example, Bonnie Buckingham interjects personal meaning into the key concepts as she contemplates her historic and familial connection to Christianity and her struggle to make sense of her sexual identity.

***

The image of a vessel was lifted up in Church today. It is a timeless image that has been used in the Christian tradition all of my life. How do we fill up our vessel? With what do we fill up our life, and what flows out of the vessel as a result? I think it is an image that I carry with me and bring to mind when thinking about my life. And it came to me again in thinking about how I make sense of the key concepts of integrative social work practice. The history, meaning, context, power, and possibility of my life are those things that are within my vessel—which are put there as I travel through life and added to as time passes. They are also the source from which my responses to life and my experiences emerge.

I grew up in a very traditional and fundamentalist Christian home. My parents were, and remain today, very certain of their beliefs. The uncertainties of life were always weathered by their unfailing belief in their God and his direct interaction with their life. Black-and-white principles of Godliness were very evident and taught with conviction and certainty. At the same time, they raised their children to think for themselves and question what the world had to offer. One of my father's favorite sayings is, "Don't always believe everything 'they' tell you." Imagine my surprise when it became evident to me that I did not really fit into the "right" type of Christian I had been raised to become. What very slowly emerged for me was that I would not embrace the wife and mother role that my sisters had. I would not have the same love for the traditional home life that I was "supposed" to enjoy according to the traditional Christian community in which I was a member.

In my early twenties I moved across the country to go to a small private Christian College in the Minneapolis area. While I was there, I was challenged to think beyond what I had been raised to believe and to question all that I knew. I went through a very difficult time of soul searching, and a remaking of what was at my core. I could no longer look at life in the same way. I was a changed person—one who continued to question each "truth" when presented, to test its merit—perhaps not in the same way my father had encouraged.

A few years later, after my first lesbian relationship ended, I moved into my grandfather's home and attempted to live a more normal life. I attempted to fit into the role of active church member, loving and attentive daughter and granddaughter. After some time, however, I could not really continue to ignore what I knew was my reality. I was living in denial and not at all true to whom I knew myself to be. However, there was a huge gap between my Christian beliefs and the reality that I was a lesbian. I could not make my two realities mesh—Christianity simply did not allow for my "condition." I was either able to live a Christian life, or a lesbian lifestyle. There seemed to be no room for the two within me. I went through many long months trying to figure out how I could be this way—was I giving into something that was a sin, or was I being true to whom God had made me? What was my reality, played out in my own life—in the person that I am?

Fortunately for me, I was not alone. I became involved with some new friends, and a new Church community that lifted up the person I was, and honored my split personality. They encouraged self-examination while uplifting the process of change within me. I found that I could accept the two seemingly opposing beliefs in who I am, and I grew stronger as an individual because of that process.

I share this story as a way to understand the key concepts discussed in Chapter 2 of *Just*

Practice. These two aspects of my experience are obviously not the only things that have shaped my life either. Growing up in poverty, moving frequently and into many different cultural spaces, as well as my work with those in poverty, have all had a profound effect on how I view my world and how I move through it. These complicated histories of conflicting beliefs have merged within me and shaped the person I find in me today. It is in this context of rejection and rejuvenation that I come to the communion table and to the place of caring for those I encounter each day. I was a rejected person who found a way to look at life a bit differently—a way that gives my life meaning and purpose. Having come to terms with my Christian status as a lesbian gives me power to confront hatred and bigotry and do so in a loving manner. I see real possibility in the ability to make change happen. If I can be a vessel of change by the way I live my life and help others to realize their potential because of the experiences I have had, then I see the real possibility of a new view of life and equality for all persons, regardless of their perceived status. I personally embody the integration of Christianity and that which the right-wing vocal church says is an abomination, but which I feel is actually a strong example of God's diversity. I can stand confidently in the torrent of their hatred and show that we are not so very different or threatening to their world. The possibility of change encourages and drives me to continue to speak for those who have no voice and no hope.

I think again of that image of the vessel, and how that long tradition of Christianity, the history of my life, and the contexts of my particular situation flow into that vessel: me. Then it all gets mixed up together, and out of that meaning flows the possibility of change and acceptance, and the power to be and to do and to make change happen—not only within me, but around me as well.

***

How does Bonnie's story make sense of the key concepts meaning, context, power, history, and possibility? What thoughts and feelings did her story evoke for you? How would you incorporate the key concepts on a personal level? What story would you tell?

SIXTEEN PRINCIPLES OF SOCIAL JUSTICE WORK

Throughout this text, we have been bridging social work and social justice and seeking ways to translate our visions of social justice work into concrete principles and practices. In this section we summarize 16 principles for social justice work that we have highlighted throughout the text. These principles are interrelated and mutually informing. We see this set of principles as a work in progress that will be shaped over time through dialogue about our diverse efforts to engage in social justice work. We invite readers to add to the list.

 Take a Global Perspective: Social justice work challenges us to look both to and beyond the immediate context of our work and consider the larger structures and forces that bear on the situation. By taking a global perspective, we challenge our assumptions about borders and boundaries in their many forms. In taking a global perspective seriously, we are challenged to address questions of human rights and consider the ripple effects of our actions. A global perspective also serves as a reminder of the partiality of our knowledge and of the many ways of seeing and knowing refracted through the lenses of cultural and historical experience. Even in our most "micro" or "local" practice of social work it is possible to think and act from a global perspective.

2 **Understand How Poverty Works:** Understanding how some maintain social privilege at the expense of those viewed as different from others is fundamental to social justice work. As discussed elsewhere in this text, definitions of social problems are contested terrain. They guide practice. Those who hold the key to problem definitions have the power to have their understandings accepted as "truth." Poverty conceptualized in its most narrow sense helps when measuring its scope or frequency because it is considered a material phenomenon (i.e., income level, wages earned, number of people living in the household, etc.). But if we fail to go beyond this numbers approach to understanding poverty, we ignore its complexities. Ruth Lister (2004, p. 177) cogently argues for a "bifocal" understanding of poverty that includes a broader portrayal that recognizes the importance of relational and symbolic dynamics. This conceptualization of poverty locates it in discourses of human rights and capabilities, social inclusion, citizenship, democracy, and social well-being. We must know how poverty and the languaging of poverty work. Do we rely on images of passive recipients of welfare, dependent on society for their existence to forge our policies and practice? Or do we think of people who live the consequences of social exclusion, those locked out of full participation and otherwise "othered" based on marital status, race, class, gender, or ability? Understanding how poverty works, its social, economic, political, psychological, and cultural manifestations, is imperative for a social justice-oriented approach to social work.

3 **Appreciate Interconnectedness:** Social justice work challenges us to explore the patterns that connect, often across seemingly disparate contexts and experiences. In order to meet the complex challenges of 21st century social work, we cannot limit our efforts to the safety of narrow specialization. We need to grapple with the relationships between individual, family, and community struggles and broader political, social, and economic arrangements. Likewise, we need to maintain the connectedness of head, heart, and hand in our work such that our actions are guided by both grounded knowledge and by a felt connection and commitment to human dignity and relationships. As we explore and appreciate the patterns that connect, we may discover opportunities for new partnerships and networks to support social justice work.

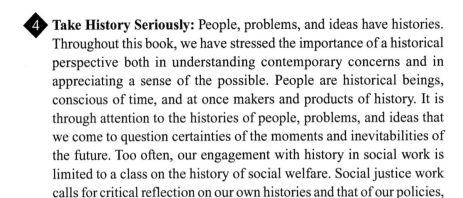

4 **Take History Seriously:** People, problems, and ideas have histories. Throughout this book, we have stressed the importance of a historical perspective both in understanding contemporary concerns and in appreciating a sense of the possible. People are historical beings, conscious of time, and at once makers and products of history. It is through attention to the histories of people, problems, and ideas that we come to question certainties of the moments and inevitabilities of the future. Too often, our engagement with history in social work is limited to a class on the history of social welfare. Social justice work calls for critical reflection on our own histories and that of our policies, practices, and certainties as part of the work.

5 **Challenge Our Certainties:** Social justice work demands that we be willing to constantly question our assumptions, especially those that we hold most dear. We cannot effectively open ourselves to new ways of hearing, seeing, and thinking without ongoing reflection on what and how we know. Moreover, social justice work calls on us to let go of our certainties and be willing to embrace ambiguities and engage with contradictions. In so doing, we open ourselves to learning about the ways others attempt to negotiate the conflicting and often contradictory expectations of everyday life and make sense of their experiences in the process. It is often in the slippery spaces of ambiguity and contradiction that the possibilities for transformational change emerge.

6 **Learn through Dialogue:** In contrast to approaches that value the "expert" role, social justice work asks us to begin from a place of uncertainty, of not knowing. We enter into each new relationship and change process as learners, with humility and openness, cognizant of the partiality of our knowledge and the limits of our worldview. It is through dialogue that we come to appreciate new meanings and interpretations and alternative ways of seeing, being, and acting in the world. This does not imply that we necessarily come to accept or adopt others' interpretations of social reality as our own. Rather, it is through respectful dialogue that we probe, question, and disagree as well. Social justice work involves the art of diplomacy, wherein we help bring to light diverse views and interests, identify important differences as well as common ground, examine the power relations at stake, and seek courses of action that value human dignity and rights.

7 **Confront Questions of Power:** Social justice work recognizes the importance of thinking and talking about power in its many forms. Possibilities for meaningful change emerge when people come to recognize and analyze the forms and relations of power that constrain their lives and realize personal and collective forms of power—power to be, to act, and to join together. We have pointed to the power of discourse in the construction of both problems and interventions. We have examined the power of labels to define and, in effect, stand for the person and the power of the expert to diagnose and treat. We have also demonstrated the power of people to create change as they join together, question their life circumstances, develop critical awareness, build personal and group capacity, and use collective knowledge and capacity to challenge and change the conditions of their lives. Social justice workers exert their own power to question, resist, and act in ways that open spaces of hope and possibility.

8 Recognize and Embrace the Political Nature of Social Work: As Freire (1999) reminds us, social justice workers are not neutral agents. We are positioned and acting in contexts of power and inequality. In so doing we need not only to acknowledge but also embrace the political nature of the work and prepare ourselves to carry out our work with integrity. The commitment to social justice work is both an ethical and a political commitment. Exercising this commitment demands knowledge of the power relations in which our practice is situated, an understanding of strategies and tactics that enable us to effectively engage as players, and the will and skills to enable others to participate in the work of justice-oriented change.

9 Value Difference and Address the Production of Difference: A critical understanding of difference is central to social justice work. The production of difference—different ways of interpreting, organizing, and acting in the world—is part of our capacities as meaning-making, cultural beings. Encounters with difference can challenge our most deeply held truths about the world and our place in it and our abilities to remain open to alternative ways of thinking, feeling, being, and acting. Moreover, social justice work challenges us to grapple with the politics of difference. By this we mean the processes, mechanisms, and relations of power through which particular forms of difference and inequality are produced, maintained, and justified. We need to both value the meaning and power of difference and also question the construction and representation of differences and the multiple meanings and values attached to them. For example, the American Anthropological Association Statement on Race presented in Chapter 2 helps us to understand the historical and political context in which ideas of race and difference in America were produced and reproduced. Social justice work calls on us to ask, "What differences make a difference here and to whom?"

10 Be Cognizant of Positionality: The social work profession has always recognized the significance of self-awareness for social workers. Self-awareness most often takes on the meaning of reflecting on the "baggage" the worker brings to the work, that is, thinking about personal attitudes and beliefs and how these might get in the way of working with particular clients or specific situations. Positionality, however, encapsulates this notion of knowledge of the self and expands it to include awareness of the powerful shaping influences of gender, class, sexual identity, and race, how these shape attitudes and beliefs, and how these locate the worker differently in reference to differently positioned clients. Fully comprehending this idea of positionality is a humbling endeavor. It serves as a constant reminder of one's social/ political location, the challenges and strengths inherent in one's location, and the partiality of one's worldview. It keeps us from making broad generalizations about the way things work and calls on us to see each situation as unique.

11 Promote Participation: We make a bold statement by claiming that there is no such thing as empowerment without participation. We must be vigilant in our search for ways to encourage the participation of people in the full range of change endeavors, from the interpersonal to the social. When in doubt, we must ask ourselves who is included, who is excluded, and why. We must also begin the process of evaluating programs and projects based on the criteria of participation, and, for social justice work, this means giving people a voice in the issues that most directly concern their lives and their well-being.

12 Keep the Social in Social Work: As we have tried to illustrate throughout the book, social justice work is a collective endeavor. We cannot readily "go it alone." We have pointed to the importance of raising critical consciousness through dialogue and building team work and coalitions for change-oriented action as central components of social justice work. This holds true not only for our actions with individuals, families, and communities, but also for building support, solidarity, and quite literally, a movement of social justice workers. It can be very intimidating to pose critical questions in the context of our everyday practice. If we are attempting to engage in "functional noncapitulation" in isolation from others, we can become frustrated and overwhelmed. As social justice workers, we need to build relationships with one another, through intra- and interorganizational networks, with local, national, and international social justice organizations, and with the "rank and file" activists and advocates in our own communities. Together we can nurture our relationships and ourselves and fuel our sense of possibility and commitment to praxis.

13 Build and Share Leadership: Social justice work is about building capacity and sharing leadership. Reaching back to the participatory democracy exemplified in the work of Jane Addams and other social reformers at the turn of the 20th century, a pattern emerges and weaves its way through social work history. This pattern is one of having faith in the capacity of humans, even under the most severe conditions, to challenge the conditions of their lives and participate in its transformation. Thinking of our practice, at least partially, as a way to create opportunities for participation and leadership development, provides us with a clear goal upon which to set our sights. It forces us to pose the following questions: How do I do my work in such a way that I build and support new forms of leadership? What forms and shapes might practice take should I strive to build the leadership capacity of those with whom I work?

14 **Take "Bold and Courageous Action"** (Roby, 1998): Homan (2004) reminds us that, "It is the lack of will to confront the barriers, real and imagined, that preserves conditions that should be changed" (p. 398). Confronting barriers mean confronting unfair policies and practices in welfare agencies that prevent some people from moving out of poverty through postsecondary education and training. It means organizing a rally for laborers overlooked in recent legislation passed by Congress that provides funding and tax relief for corporations hurt by economic recession but ignores the plight of common laborers who have far fewer resources at their disposal. It means getting angry and sustaining anger as a motivating force, choosing your battles well, and taking bold moves with others as a base of power and support. Pamela Roby (1998) contends that, "Moment to moment we have complete freedom to decide our actions" (p. 13).

15 **Create a Spirit of Hope and Spaces of Possibility:** A major theme of social justice work is attention to creating spaces of hope and possibility through visions of a more just tomorrow. Throughout history, others have shared and acted on similar visions and sought to carve out the possible from seemingly impossible situations and circumstances. These individuals and groups understood that without hope there is no purpose and in some cases, loss of hope meant loss of life itself. While for some, this notion of the possible spurred on dreams of a better world, for others it meant contemplating and acting upon alternative ways of being and doing in the world at that very moment. We must continually challenge ourselves to ask how we can infuse our work with this same sense of purpose and recognize the dialectical relationship of hope and possibility—hope brings possibility and possibility brings hope.

16 **Find and Create Joy in the Work:** In Chapter 9, we discussed how social workers in the United States rarely think about or take the time to celebrate the joy and beauty of their work. We continue to question why the concept of celebration is foreign to our work in the U.S. We consider the possibilities that emerge for programs, practices, and relationships when celebration is embraced. We (the authors) learn from our students who teach us that the core process of celebration is one they embrace to combat societal stereotypes of social work as drudgery and "the burnout profession" and social workers as society's "street sweepers" and "garbage collectors." They appreciate the permission that celebration gives to carve out space for patting themselves on the back, supporting each other in the hard work that they do, and giving new meaning to social work that elicits pride and renewed commitment.

REFLECTION: Just Practice

Take a moment and review the 16 principles of Just Practice listed above. Which of these makes the most sense to you and why? Which of these makes the least sense to you and why? Meet with a group of classmates and discuss your choices. What do you learn about others from this discussion? What do you learn about yourself? Now think about some of the voices we have learned from throughout the text (e.g., John Brown Childs, pp. 54-58).What more can we learn from their stories? What can we take from their stories that strengthen our commitment to social justice work? What principles of social justice work do these voices exemplify?

CHAPTER SUMMARY: SOCIAL JUSTICE WORK IN THE REAL WORLD

We opened this chapter with a snapshot of the challenges facing social workers in the 21st century. Some readers may argue that, in the face of these overwhelming demands and increasingly scarce resources, our vision of social justice work is simply too idealistic. Some might argue that the idea of social justice is all well and good but the realities of everyday practice demand attention to more immediate and pragmatic concerns, such as responding to crises, getting clients access to benefits, and keeping our jobs in the era of downsizing. We do not underestimate the daily stresses and struggles of social work practice in a context of increasing complexity of problems and scarcity of resources. We take them quite seriously. In fact, we contend that, given these pressures, the need for social justice work is all the more urgent, and that possibilities await us in every practice setting. The Just Practice Framework offers an alternative way of thinking about our practice settings, relationships, possible courses of action, and, fundamentally, ourselves. Many social workers in hospitals, prison settings, schools, refugee camps, child welfare offices, and other settings are realizing their own possibilities for social justice work in ways large and small everyday. We have offered here a framework with which to embrace that energy and creativity, build on the possibilities, and hopefully bring together the knowledge, power, and commitment for a new collective vision and practice of social work that is grounded in the best of our history and up to the task of 21st century challenges.

REFLECTION: Final Reflection Exercise

This final reflection exercise calls forth the Just Practice Matrix we included at the end of Chapter 5 (p. 202). Now that you have finished reading the entire *Just Practice* text, find an example, perhaps from your own experience, of Just Practice in action. Are there programs or practices in your own community where you see Just Practice in action? Have you read about or discussed in your other classes, examples of social work practice that take social justice seriously? How do these programs or practices draw from the 16 principles outlined above?

Applying the Just Practice Framework: Final Project

The purpose of the final project is to help you apply, in a real-life situation, what you have learned from the material presented in Chapters 6 to 9 in the text. In a paper no longer than 10 to 12 pages, first develop a case study, 1 to 2 pages in length, similar to those presented in the text (e.g., Life and Death in Libby, Montana). A case study is a description of the individual, family, group, or community and the issue or challenge you will be addressing. Draw from your practicum experience or from areas of interest or concern in creating your case study.

The following questions may help with the organization of your paper:

♦ How would you address the problem, issue, or challenge by using the core processes as a basic guide for your work?

♦ What skills and tools of practice discussed in Chapters 6 to 9 would be helpful to your work, and what would be your rationale for using them?

♦ What considerations would you give to the concept of positionality in shaping the change process?

♦ How would you address issues of difference, inequality, and oppression?

♦ Which principles of social justice work outlined above would you highlight in your work and why?

♦ What might be some of the constraints and points of resistance related to applying the principles?

♦ How might you mitigate these?

♦ How does your work exemplify social work practice from an integrated perspective?

♦ What new possibilities for practice do you envision in this area?

Social Justice Work in Practice

Let's look at an example of social justice work in practice. In writing this book, we have gained a deeper appreciation of the many ways in which people practice social justice work. We have also had the opportunity to learn from social work students as they apply the Just Practice Framework as a guide to their thinking and action. We hope the example will encourage readers to reflect on the ways in which they might engage in social justice work and imagine new practice possibilities.

The Story of Working for Equality and Economic Liberation (WEEL)

WEEL is an education, advocacy, and action organization dedicated to promoting welfare rights in Montana. The organization is grounded in principles of popular education and concerns about the intersections of sexism, racism, and classism. WEEL's mission statement reflects these principles: "WEEL is a grassroots organization committed to securing justice for people living in poverty. We envision a world with equal access to quality shelter, food, health care, education, and economic opportunity. We are dedicated to changing the beliefs and policy systems that keep people oppressed. Through action and education, we are working on a future of equality and economic liberation for all."

Launched in 1996 in Missoula, Montana, WEEL is currently located in Helena, Montana, the state capital. WEEL has more than 1,000 members and supporters statewide and an active core membership of 40. WEEL organizers write, "By educating, organizing, speaking out, rallying, and testifying on many of the issues concerning low-income Montanans, WEEL plays an integral part in Montana's welfare rights battle." WEEL has also gained national attention for its advocacy work on behalf of people living in poverty. By 2001, 5 years after President Clinton's authorization of the Personal Responsibility and Work Opportunity Act, WEEL members had built a credible organization and claimed a place at the table in negotiating the future direction of welfare and its reform.

This bold organization had modest beginnings in the conversations between two women employed in a Montana welfare-to-work program. In the antiwelfare climate of the 1990s, the state of Montana followed the national trend and introduced "Families Achieving Independence in Montana" (FAIM), a time-limited, welfare-to-work program. FAIM sought to replace "welfare dependency" with "self-sufficiency" through mandatory work requirements and strict time limits. Welfare workers were encouraged to "divert" their clients from benefits and programs. Further, the policy specifically discouraged out-of-wedlock births and promoted marriage as a "better choice" than welfare.

The two women felt the contradictory effects of this policy in the *context* of their everyday work and lives. Their program was committed to the education and empowerment of poor women. But these new policies undermined that commitment. At the same time, program funding was contingent upon implementation of state policy. The women and their clients were caught in a no-win situation. The women began to question the *meaning* of "self-sufficiency" and "dependency" and the *power* of the state to impose particular moral codes and sanctions on its more vulnerable citizens. They began to question the *power* of gendered images and discourses in shaping the life chances of poor women. They began meeting after work each day to share their frustrations and analyze what they were experiencing.

The two invited other women to come together to reflect on their experiences and talk about the *possibilities* for action. At first, seven or eight women came together to share their stories, reflect on their own *histories* and experiences, and learn through dialogue. They began to ask questions of *history* as a guide for future action: How did "ending welfare as we know it" rather than "ending poverty as we know it" become an issue of national priority? How have others challenged the limits of public policy and won?

Drawing on their many community ties, this core group formed an advisory board of low-income women who had an interest in welfare activism. They began to build a grassroots organization run by and for people living in poverty. They took a two-pronged approach: (1) focus on mitigating the *immediate* harm to low-income people as a result of the punitive welfare policies and (2) collective action to challenge and change the punitive direction of "welfare reform." The fledgling group did not "go it alone." They turned to other women activists and community organizations to learn lessons of *history* and *possibility* from their experiences.

WEEL's founding board of directors was made up of nine low-income women, all single mothers. Some were working in low-paying jobs, some were trying to complete their college education, and others had found themselves unemployed or homeless after a family or health crisis. Members crafted spaces of support for women to come together, validate their experiences, and build the personal and collective capacities for action. They recognized that a *context* of affection and mutual support was key to their activism, and they made caring relations the foundation for their collective action. Being together and caring for one another is not separate from activism, but central to its success. As one WEEL member describes:

My WEEL sisters have always accepted me for just who I am. They never tried to change me or alter the way I think or feel, and I have always loved and accepted them just the way they are. I don't know where I would be, or who, if they had not come into my life... There is no way I could ever put into words the love and acceptance I have felt and feel for these brave and incredible women.

WEEL members advocate for and with people on welfare and educate the community regarding welfare reform. Members know and use the *power* of communication for popular education. From its inception, WEEL has combined organization building with direct action. Members have used the *possibilities* at hand—popular theater, community forums, newsletters, radio shows, letter-writing campaigns, and encampments at the State Capitol—to communicate their messages. WEEL's annual "Momma Jam" is a celebration of children and motherhood and a reminder of the hard work that parenting entails. WEEL has received national recognition for its advocacy work, and members are now mentoring other budding activists and organizations in order to share the *meaning* of their work and keep the *history* and *possibilities* of activism alive. WEEL works in collaboration with other progressive groups to build coalitions for social justice throughout the western United States. WEEL has also joined with other welfare rights groups across the country in National Days of Action. WEEL connects local and global concerns by engaging in International Human Rights Day actions that address economic and social well-being as fundamental human rights.

WEEL members have become effective advocates and lobbyists. They have taken leadership in campaigns for children's health insurance, and they have lobbied hard for the rights of people on welfare to pursue a college education. They have claimed a voice and demanded a place at the welfare reform policy table. One of WEEL's early activists, Kate Kahan, was appointed in January of 2004 by Montana Senator Max Baucus to fill the position of lead welfare reform staff member on the Senate Finance Committee. Kate received the Center for Policy Alternatives' Emerging Leader Award in 2002 for her work on poverty issues. In 2004 she received the Ms. Foundation Gloria Award for challenging Montana legislators to accept parenting as work with the introduction of the At-Home Infant Care Program and for increasing voter turnout among low-income and minority groups.

WEEL has demonstrated its capacity to blend nurture and activism, use the media and create media events, and renew itself with expanding membership, changing leadership, and ongoing reflection on its action. WEEL has met with some resistance from those who did not appreciate their feminist-informed approach and has weathered some internal struggles as well. Through these struggles WEEL members have come to clarify and value their positions as women and organizers. Reflecting collectively on their experiences, members offered these lessons for success that may benefit other women's efforts: (1) Value relationships; (2) Keep the process heart-centered because the head is going to fail sometimes; (3) Don't be afraid to think that your intuition matters; (4) Take time to reflect and question; (5) Think and act holistically; (6) Recognize and respect your limits; (7) Collaborate with others and help build bridges; (8) Keep your creative spark; (9) Take pride in and celebrate your accomplishments; (10) Have fun together. WEEL members speak a language of love and justice and recognize the inseparability of the two. "WEEL moves ahead by remaining respectful of the partiality of its knowledge, hopeful of the possibilities for social transformation, and ever mindful of the delicate interplay of head, heart, and hand" (Finn et al., 2000, p. 308). What aspects of the Just Practice Framework play out here? What principles of Just Practice does WEEL draw on in its work? Where do you see similar efforts underway in your community?

Questions for Discussion

1. What additional issues do you believe will have an important effect on the practice of social work in years to come? Why?

2. What principles of social justice work might you add to our list? Are there any that you would eliminate and why?

3. What is your vision of a just world? What steps might you take locally to begin to realize that vision?

4. If you were to give a guest lecture on social justice work to a class of Social Work 100 students how would you proceed? What would be the key components of your presentation? How might you involve the students in the learning process?

5. If you were to write a letter to the editor of your local newspaper with a number of concrete suggestions for promoting social justice in your community, what would you include?

Suggested Readings

Abramovitz, M. (1993). Should all social workers be educated for social change? Pro. *Journal of Social Work Education, 29,* 6-11.

Adams, R., Dominelli, L., & Payne, M. (2005). *Social work futures: Crossing boundaries, transforming practice.* New York: Palgrave Macmillan.

Allan, J., Pease, B., & Briskman, L. (2003). *Critical social work: An introduction to theories and practices.* Crows Nest, Australia: Allen & Unwin.

Ferguson, I., Lavalette, M., & Whitmore, E. (Eds.). (2005). *Globalisation, global justice and social work.* New York: Routledge.

Harvey, D. (2000). *Spaces of hope.* Berkeley: University of California Press.

Hick, S., Fook, J., & Pozzuto, R. (2005). *Social work: A critical turn.* Toronto: Thompson Educational Publishing, Inc.

Ramanathan, C. & Link, R. (Eds.). (1999). *All our futures: Social work practice in a global era.* Belmont, CA: Wadsworth.

End Notes

[1] From Paulo Freire (1999), *Pedagogy of hope: Reliving pedagogy of the oppressed.* New York: Continuum Press, p. 9.

[2] From David Harvey (2000). *Spaces of hope.* Berkeley: University of California Press, p. 281. Permission to quote courtesy of Board of Regents of the University of California.

Universal Declaration of Human Rights

Preamble

Whereas recognition of the inherent dignity and of the equal and inalienable rights of all members of the human family is the foundation of freedom, justice and peace in the world,

Whereas disregard and contempt for human rights have resulted in barbarous acts which have outraged the conscience of mankind, and the advent of a world in which human beings shall enjoy freedom of speech and belief and freedom from fear and want has been proclaimed as the highest aspiration of the common people,

Whereas it is essential, if a man is not to be compelled to have recourse, as a last resort, to rebellion against tyranny and oppression, that human rights should be protected by the rule of the law,

Whereas it is essential to promote the development of friendly relations between nations,

Whereas the peoples of the United Nations have in the Charter reaffirmed their faith in fundamental human rights, in the dignity and worth of the human person and in the equal rights of men and women and have determined to promote social progress and better standards of life in larger freedom,

Whereas Member States have pledged themselves to achieve, in co-operation with the United Nations, the promotion of universal respect for and observance of human rights and fundamental freedoms,

Whereas a common understanding of these rights and freedoms is of the greatest importance for the full realization of this pledge,

Now Therefore,
The General Assembly
proclaims
This Universal Declaration of Human Rights

as a common standard of achievement for all peoples and all nations, to the end that every individual and every organ of society, keeping this Declaration constantly in mind, shall strive by teaching and education to promote respect for these rights and freedoms and by progressive measures, national and international, to secure their universal and effective recognition and observance, both among the people of Member States themselves and among peoples of territories under their jurisdiction.

Article 1
All human beings are born free and equal in dignity and rights. They are endowed with reason and conscience and should act toward one another in a spirit of brotherhood.

Article 2
Everyone is entitled to all the rights and freedoms set forth in this Declaration, without distinction of any kind, such as race, color, sex, language, religion, political or other opinion, national or social origin, property, birth or other status.

Furthermore, no distinction shall be made on the basis of the political, jurisdictional or international status of the country or territory to which a person belongs, whether it be independent, trust, non-self governing or under any other limitation of sovereignty.

Article 3
Everyone has the right to life, liberty and security of person.

Article 4
No one shall be held in slavery or servitude; slavery and the slave trade shall be prohibited in all their forms.

Article 5
No one shall be subjected to torture or to cruel, inhuman or degrading treatment or punishment.

Article 6
Everyone has the right to recognition everywhere as a person before the law.

Article 7
All are equal before the law and are entitled without any discrimination to

equal protection of the law. All are entitled to equal protection against any discrimination in violation of this Declaration and against any incitement to such discrimination.

Article 8
Everyone has the right to an effective remedy by the competent national tribunals for acts violating the fundamental rights granted him by the constitution or by law.

Article 9
No one shall be subjected to arbitrary arrest, detention or exile.

Article 10
Everyone is entitled in full equality to a fair and public hearing by an independent and impartial tribunal, in the determination of his rights and obligations and of any criminal change against him.

Article 11
(1) Everyone charged with a penal offence has the right to be presumed innocent until proved guilty according to law in a public trail at which he has had all the guarantees necessary for his defense.

(2) No one shall be held guilty of any penal offence on account of any act or omission which did not constitute a penal offence, under national or international law, at the time when it was committed. Nor shall a heavier penalty be imposed than the one that was applicable at the time the penal offence was committed.

Article 12
No one shall be subjected to arbitrary interference with his privacy, family, home or correspondence, nor to attacks upon his honor and reputation. Everyone has the right to the protection of the law against such interference or attacks.

Article 13
(1) Everyone has the right to freedom of movement and residence within the borders of each State.

(2) Everyone has the right to leave any country, including his own, and to return to his country.

Article 14
(1) Everyone has the right to seek and to enjoy in other countries asylum from persecution.

(2) This right may not be invoked in the case of prosecutions genuinely arising from non-political crimes or from acts contrary to the purposes and principles of the United Nations.

Article 15

(1) Everyone has the right to a nationality.

(2) No one shall be arbitrarily deprived of his nationality nor denied the right to change his nationality.

Article 16

(1) Men and women of full age, without any limitation due to race, nationality or religion, have the right to marry and found a family. They are entitled to equal rights as to marriage, during marriage and at its dissolution.

(2) Marriage shall be entered into only with the free and full consent of the intending spouses.

(3) The family is the natural and fundamental group unit of society and is entitled to protection by society and the State.

Article 17

(1) Everyone has the right to own property alone as well as in association with others.

(2) No one shall be arbitrarily deprived of his property.

Article 18

Everyone has the right to freedom of thought, conscience and religion; this right includes freedom to change his religion or belief, and freedom, either alone or in community with others and in public and private, to manifest his religion or belief in teaching, practice, worship and observance.

Article 19

Everyone has the right to freedom of opinion and expression; this right includes freedom to hold opinions without interference and to seek, receive and impart information and ideas through any media and regardless of frontiers.

Article 20

(1) Everyone has the right to freedom of peaceful assembly and association.

(2) No one may be compelled to belong to an association.

Article 21

(1) Everyone has the right to take part in the government of his country, directly or through freely chosen representatives.

(2) Everyone has the right of equal access to public service in his country.

(3) The will of the people shall be the basis of the authority of government; this will shall be expressed in periodic and genuine elections which shall be by universal and equal suffrage and shall be held by secret vote or by equivalent free voting procedures.

Article 22

Everyone, as a member of society, has the right to social security and is entitled to realization, through national effort and international cooperation and in accordance with the organization and resources of each State, of the economic, social and cultural rights indispensable for his dignity and the free development of his personality.

Article 23

(1) Everyone has the right to work, to free choice of employment, to just and favorable conditions of work and to protection against unemployment.

(2) Everyone, without any discrimination, has the right to equal pay for equal work.

(3) Everyone who works has the right to just and favorable remuneration ensuring for himself and his family an existence worthy of human dignity, and supplemented, if necessary, by other means of social protection.

(4) Everyone has the right to form and to join trade unions for the protection of his interests.

Article 24

Everyone has the right to rest and leisure, including reasonable limitations of working hours and periodic holidays with pay.

Article 25

(1) Everyone has the right to a standard of living adequate for the health and well-being of himself and of his family, including food, clothing, housing and medical care and necessary social services, and the right to security in the event of unemployment, sickness, disability, widowhood, old age or other lack of livelihood in circumstances beyond his control.

(2) Motherhood and childhood are entitled to special care and assistance. All children, whether born in or out of wedlock, shall enjoy the same social protection.

Article 26

(1) Everyone has the right to education. Education shall be free, at least in the elementary and fundamental stages. Elementary education shall be compulsory. Technical and professional education shall be made generally available and higher education shall be equally accessible to all on his basis of merit.

(2) Education shall be directed to the full development of the human personality and to the strengthening of respect for human rights and fundamental freedoms. It shall promote understanding, tolerance and friendship among all nations, racial or religious groups, and shall further the activities of the United Nations for the maintenance of peace.

(3) Parents have a prior right to choose the kind of education that shall be given to their children.

Article 27

(1) Everyone has the right freely to participate in the cultural life of the

community, to enjoy the arts and to share in scientific advancement and its benefits.

(2) Everyone has the right to the protection of the moral and material interests resulting from any scientific, literary or artistic production of which he is the author.

Article 28

Everyone is entitled to a social and international order in which the rights and freedoms set for them in this Declaration can be fully realized.

Article 29

(1) Everyone has duties to the community in which alone the free and full development of his personality is possible.

(2) In the exercise of his rights and freedoms, everyone shall be subject only to such limitations as are determined by law solely for the purpose of securing due recognition and respect for the rights and freedoms of others and of meeting the just requirements of morality, public order and the general welfare in a democratic society.

(3) These rights and freedoms may in no case be exercised contrary to the purposes and principles of the United Nations.

Article 30

Nothing in this Declaration may be interpreted as implying for any State, group or person any right to engage in any activity or to perform any act aimed at the destruction of any of the rights and freedoms set forth herein.[1]

---

[1] For a summary history of the United Nations Declaration of Human Rights see www.un.org/Depts/dhl/resguide/hrdec.htm. For further information regarding and links to The United Nations Committee on Human Rights, Committee against Torture, Committee on Economic, Social and Cultural Rights, Committee on Elimination of Discrimination against Women; Committee on Elimination of Racial Discrimination, and Committee on the Rights of the Child see www.un.org/Depts/dhl/resguide/spechr.htm. For materials relating to the Universal Declaration of Human Rights and a small pocket size pamphlet of the Declaration we distribute in our classes, contact: Human Rights USA Resource Center, 229-19th Avenue South, Room 439, Minneapolis, MN 55455, Phone: 612-626-0041 or the toll free number: 1-888-HREDUC8. Web Site: www.hrusa.org or email: hrusa@tc.umn.edu

Just Practice
Film Suggestions

We have suggested the possibility of organizing a showing and discussion of a film or presentation of a film series that speaks to social justice issues as one form of teaching-learning. Films can be excellent media for provoking critical dialogue and consciousness. We have included the following list of films as a starting point to get you thinking about the possibilities. We invite readers to expand the list, recommend favorite films, and share ideas with one another.

Trading Democracy (Film by Bill Moyers, 2002, 58 minutes, Films for the Sciences and Humanities). Moyers examines Chapter 11 of the North American Free Trade Agreement (NAFTA), which is being used by corporations to undermine the basic workings of democracy by overturning local government decisions, suing local governments, and hearing cases in closed trade tribunals rather than open court processes.

What Free Trade Looks Like (Film by Jay Finneburgh and Activist Media Project, 2004, 60 minutes). Made by Mexican activists, the film provides a bottom-up view of how free trade operates and its consequences for those at the bottom. Shot in Cancún in 2003 at the time of the 5th World Trade Organization meeting, the film addresses the failures of free trade in reducing poverty and the detrimental impacts on farmers, workers, immigrants, and youth.

Life and Debt (Film by Stephanie Black and Tuff Gong productions, 2003, 86 minutes, New Yorker Videos) Film examines the impact of the World Bank, International Monetary Fund, Inter-American Development Bank, and current globalization policies on developing countries, using Jamaica as an example. It documents the stories of everyday Jamaicans in their struggle for survival in the face of foreign economic agendas and their consequences.

T-Shirt Travels (Film by Shanta Bloeman, 2001, 57 minutes). Explore the global second-hand clothes market and its troubling role in the economies of poor countries. The film uses the journey of the T-Shirt as an opening to explore growing global inequalities, the connections to historic practices of slavery, colonialism, and resource exploitation, and the current impacts of structural adjustment policies.

Thirst (Film by Shantha Bloemen, 2004, 62 minutes. Filmmakers Library). Examines the corporate battles to control the most precious resource of the 21st century - water. Using examples from Indian, Bolivia, and Stockton, California, the film shows how water has become the focal point of growing local and international conflicts, and the life-and-death issues at stake in these battles.

Global Banquet: Politics of Food (Film by Ann Macksoud and John Ankele, 2001, 50 minutes. Old Dog Documentaries). Examines how several large multinational corporations have come to control the business of food production globally, driving small-scale producers both in U.S. and internationally out of the market. The film looks at the role of global corporate food production in exacerbating poverty, hunger, and inequality.

Price of Aid (Film by Jihan El Tahri, 2004, 55 minutes. First Run/Icarus Films). Film examines the "hunger business" and the bureaucratic workings of U.S. aid agencies charged with the work of hunger relief to famine victims. Using Zambia as an example, the film questions how America's well-intentioned foreign aid program spawned a self-serving relationship between humanitarian aid and U.S. business and politics.

Everyone Their Grain of Sand (Film by Beth Bird, 2005, 87 minutes, Women Make Movies). Presents a three-year account of the struggles and determination of the residents of Maclovio Rojas, a Tijuana, Mexico *población*. Their collective resistance to corporate attempts to evict them, and the resourcefulness and organization in securing basic services.

Los Sin Tierra (The Landless) (Film by Miguel Barros and Pedro Almodovar, 2004, 77 minutes, El Deseo). Traces the rise and struggles of Brazil's Landless Movement over the past 20 years. This remarkable people's movement demonstrates the capacity of collective organizing as people peacefully occupy unproductive land, redistribute it among occupying families, and build community against the odds.

Last Chance for Eden (Film by Lee Mun Wah, 2002, Stir Fry Seminars and Consulting, 90 minutes). Documents a discussion among eight men and women about racism and sexism in the workplace. Participants address the power of stereotypes and their impact within and beyond the workplace, and they explore the relationship between sexism and racism.

The Color of Fear (Film by Lee Mun Wah, 1994, Stir Fry Seminars and Consulting, 90 minutes). Powerful examination of racism and race relations in the U.S. as seen and experienced by a group of eight North American men of African, Asian, European, and Latino descent. Film draws from an emotional and at times confrontational group process in which the men speak to the realities of racism in their lives.

Stolen Ground (Film by Lee Mun Wah, 2003, Stir Fry Seminars and Consulting, 40 minutes). Explores the experiences of six Asian American men, their struggles against racism, the trauma of "assimilation," and the pressures of expectations to be a "model minority."

Invisible People (Film by Jason Massie, 2006, Mediarights, 86 minutes). Filmmaker "goes undercover" to live on the street and attempt to understand the experience of homelessness. He documents his own struggle to feed himself by panhandling and eating from garbage cans, find a safe place to sleep, and maintain hygiene, all while being virtually invisible to the society around him.

Waging a Living: Opportunities for Action (Film by Roger Weisberg, 2006, 26 minutes, Mediarights, Filmmakers Library). Film examines the idea and experience of the "working poor" in the U.S. chronicling the everyday struggles for survival of four wage earners trying to move their families out of poverty.

Voices of Dissent (Film by Karil Daniels, 2004, 42 minutes, Points of View Productions). A documentary that addresses the need to defend First Amendment rights and civil liberties in the U.S. against government attempts to undermine democracy and repress our freedom to dissent.

February One (Film by Steven Channing and Rebecca Cerise, 2003, 60 minutes California Newsreel.). This film explores the historic day in 1960 when four African American college freshmen began a sit-in at a lunch counter in Greensboro, North Carolina. The act revitalized the Civil Rights Movement and exemplified the power and possibility of student action. This film shows how a small committed group can galvanize a mass movement for social justice.

After Innocence (Film by Jessica Sanders, 2005, 95 minutes. American Film Foundation). Explores the experiences of eight men who were exonerated thanks to DNA evidence after spending more than 100 collective years in prison on wrongful convictions. The film shows the failure of the justice system and the appalling treatment of these same men following exoneration.

Deadline (Film by Katy Chevigny, Kirsten Johnson, and Dallas Brennan, 2004, Big Mouth Productions). An account of former Illinois Governor George Ryan decision to commute the death sentences of 167 prisoners on death row once he had become convinced that the justice system was seriously flawed. Ryan, a Republican and former proponent of the death penalty, took this bold action in the last days of his term in 2003 when faced with evidence of the possible innocence of some death row inmates in his state.

Inside Outside: Building a Meaningful Life After the Hospital (Film by Pat Deegan and Terry Strecker, (n.d.), 49 minutes, Pat Deegan & Associates.). The film-makers, both former patients, document the stories of eight people with significant histories of institutionalization in the mental health system and their transition to recovery and community living. This hopeful film documents the possibilities of recovery and community inclusion for people with psychiatric disabilities.

The Politics of Memory (Film by Pat Deegan, 55 minutes (n.d.), Pat Deegan & Associates). Film challenges the top-down expert approach that has characterized the history of intervention in mental health services and celebrates the experiences, voices, and views of those diagnosed with mental illness. Deegan takes a historical perspective, documenting the ways in which people confined to institutions and treatment facilities have struggled through the centuries to make their voices heard.

Bloodletting: Life, Death, and Health Care (Film by Lorna Greene, 2004, 67 minutes). Tells the story of health care systems and services in the U.S. and Cuba. Green provides a richly contexualized account of health care in Cuba and contrasts that with U.S. realities where so many, including Greene's own family, are without a health safety net.

Coming to Say Goodbye: Stories of AIDS in Africa (Film by Ann Macksoud and John Ankele, 2002, 30 minutes, Old Dog Documentaries). Documents the force of the AIDs pandemic as it has been experienced in East Africa. Through the stories of those suffering from the disease and their caregivers, this film presents a poignant and provocative insight into the pandemic and the realities of poverty and inequality that shape its context.

World Stopped Watching (Film by Peter Rayment and Harold Crooks, 2003, 52 minutes, White Pine Pictures). This sequel to the filmmakers' previous documentary of the U.S.-financed Contra war against Nicaragua's revolutionary government explore Nicaraguan reality 14 years later, revisiting mothers, children, taxi drivers, and politicians. They find more strip malls, fast-food franchises, and development NGOs alongside decreased literacy and increased infant mortality.

The Barbarian Invasions (Film by Denys Arcand, Canada, 2003, 99 minutes, Miramax). Film tells the story of a man dying of cancer and struggling to come to terms with the reality of death and with his own past. With the help of his estranged son, he opens himself to reconnection with his ex-wife, old friends, and former lovers who join him to share his end-of-life journey.

Ma Vie en Rose (My Life in Pink) (Film by Alain Berliner, 1997, 88 minutes, Sony Pictures). This evocative film tells the story of Ludovic, a little girl born and trapped in the body of a boy. Ludovic struggles valiantly to be a girl, first to the amusement and later to the outrage of family, friends, and neighbors. This is a touching story of gender, fear, confusion, love, and, finally, acceptance.

Ponette (Film by Jacques Doillon, 1996, 97 minutes). A powerful film about children's experience of loss and grief. Ponette is a little girl who loses her mother suddenly in an accident. The adults in her world exclude her from the grieving process and fail to recognize a child's need to grieve. Ponette finds her own ways to both mourn and claim her mother.

Two Towns of Jasper (ABC News, Films for the Humanities, 2003, 87 minutes, POV/American Documentary/ABC news). In 1998 three white men chained James Byrd Jr., a Black man, to a pickup truck and dragged him to his death. To create this film two film crews, one black, one white, set out to record the aftermath and repercussions of this modern-day lynching.

Carved from the Heart (Film by Ellen Frankenstein and Louise Brady, 2000, 45 minutes, New Day Films). This film tells the story of loss, grieving, and community healing in Craig, Alaska. After Stan Marsden, a Tsimpsean tribal member, loses his son to a cocaine overdose, he begins a journey of mourning and healing. Stan decides to create a totem pole in honor of his son and invites the participation of whole community. The film weaves together personal accounts of participants' own experiences with loss and the process of carving and erecting the Healing Heart totem.

In Whose Honor? (Film by Jay Rosenstein, 1997, 46 minutes, New Day Films, 46). This film documents the experiences of University of Illinois student Charlene Teters, a Native American woman who became active in protests against the use of Chief Illiniwek as a school mascot. The film examines the power of stereotypes and racism at work in these practices and the possibilities for change.

Tough Guise (Film by Jonathan Katz, and Sut Jhally, 2002, 105 minutes, Media Education Foundation) This film, geared for student audiences, explores social constructions of masculinity across a broad range of popular culture and considers the consequences in the lives of men and boys. Informed by feminist theory, the film engages in a critical examination of gender and the gendered experiences of men and boys.

Killing Us Softly III (Film by Jean Kilbourne and Sut Jhally, 34 minutes, 2004, Media Education Foundation) Continued documentation of the work of media critic Jean Kilbourne's important exploration of the devastating power of advertising on the self-image of women. Since 1979 Kilbourne has brought a feminist critique of advertising to bear and has sought to educate women about the insidious power of media images. This film brings her work to a new generation of viewers.

Rabbit-proof Fence (Film by Phillip Noyce, 2002, 93 minutes, Miramax) Tell the story of Molly Craig, a young black Australian girl who leads her younger sister and cousin in an escape from an official government "school" set up to train them as domestic workers for Australian white society. Molly leads the girls on a 1,500 mile journey through Australia's outback in search of the rabbit-proof fence that bisects the country and will lead them to home. Based on a true story.

Ladybird, Ladybird (Film by Ken Loach and Sally Hibben, 1994, 102 minutes, Evergreen Entertainment) Inspired by real events, this powerful film tells the story of Maggie, mother of four, who becomes trapped in the contradictions of social service systems and is deemed "unfit." The film raises important ethical questions about helping systems and the power of bureaucracy.

Bibliography

Abrams, F, Slosar, J. & Walls, R. (2005). Reverse mission: A model for international social work education and transformative intra-national practice. *International Social Work, 48*(2), 161-176.

Abramovitz, M. (1993). Should all social workers be educated for social change? *Journal of Social Work Education, 29*, 6-11.

Abramovitz, M. (1996). *Regulating the lives of women: Social welfare policy from colonial times to the present*. Boston: South End Press.

Abramovitz, M. (1998). Social work and social reform: an arena of struggle. *Social Work, 43*(6), 512-526.

Abramovitz, M. (2000). *Under attack, fighting back: Women and welfare in the United States*. New York: Monthly Review Press.

Abramsky, S. (2004, July 19/26). Incarceration, Inc. *The Nation*, 22-25.

Abramson, J. & Bronstein, L. (2004). Group process dynamics and skills in interdisciplinary teamwork. In C. Garvin, L. Gutiérrez, & M. Galinsky, (Eds.), *Handbook of social work with groups* (pp. 384-399). New York: Guilford Press.

Abramson, M. (1996). Reflections on knowing oneself ethically: Toward a working framework for social work practice. *Families in Society, 77*(4), 195-201.

Adam, N., Zosky, D., & Unrau, Y. (2004). Improving the research climate in social work curricula: Clarifying learning expectations across BSW and MSW research courses. *Journal of Teaching in Social Work, 24*(3/4), 1-18.

Adams, M., Blumenfeld, W., Castañeda, R., Hackman, H., Peters, M., & Zuñiga, X. (2000). *Readings for diversity and social justice*. New York: Routledge.

Adams, R., Domenelli, L., & Payne, M. (Eds.). (2002). *Social work: Themes, issues and critical debates* (2nd ed.). New York: MacMillan.

Adams, R., Domenelli, L., & Payne, M. (Eds.) (2005). *Social work futures: Crossing boundaries and transforming practice*. New York: Palgrave/MacMillan.

Addams, J. (1902). *Democracy and social ethics*. New York: Macmillan.

Addams, J. (1910). *Twenty years at Hull House*. New York: Crowell/Macmillan.

Addams, J. (1922). *Peace and bread in time of war*. New York: Macmillian.

Addams, J. (1960). *A centennial reader*. New York: Macmillan.

Agger, B. (1998). *Critical social theories: An introduction.* Boulder: Westview Press.

Albee, G. (1986). Toward a just society: Lessons on observation of primary prevention of psychopathology. *American Psychologist, 41*(8), 891-898.

Albelda, R. & Withorn, A. (Eds.). (2002). *Lost ground: Welfare reform, poverty, and beyond.* Boston: South End Press.

Allan, J. (2003a). Practising critical social work. In J. Allan, B. Pease, & L. Briskman (Eds.), *Critical social work: An introduction to theories and practices* (pp. 52-71). Crows Nest NSW, Australia: Allen & Unwin.

Allan, J. (2003b). Theorizing critical social work. In J. Allan, B. Pease, & L. Briskman (Eds.), *Critical social work: An introduction to theories and practices* (pp. 32-51). Crows Nest NSW, Australia: Allen & Unwin.

Allan, J., Pease, B., & Briskman, L. (Eds.). (2003). *Critical social work: An introduction to theories and practices.* Crows Nest NSW, Australia: Allen & Unwin.

Allen, F. (1957). *Only yesterday.* New York: Harper.

Altepeter, M., Schopler, J., Galinsky, M., & Pennell, J. (1999). Participatory research as social work practice: When is it viable? *Journal of Progressive Human Services, 10*(2), 31-53.

Alvarez, S., Dagnino, E., & Escobar, A. (Eds.). (1998). *Cultures of politics and politics of cultures: Revisioning Latin American social movements.* Boulder: Westview Press.

American Anthropological Association Executive Board. (1998). *Statement on race.* Alexandria, VA: American Anthropological Association.

American Heritage Dictionary of the English Language (4th ed). (2000). New York: Houghton Mifflin.

Amsden, J. & VanWynsberghe, R. (2005). Community mapping as a research tool with youth. *Action Research, 3*(4), 357-381.

Anderson, C. & Jack, D. (1991). Learning to listen: Interview techniques and analyses. In S. Gluck & D. Patai (Eds.), *Women's words: The feminist practice of our history* (pp. 11-26). New York: Routledge.

Anderson, J. & Carter, R. (2003). *Diversity perspectives for social work practice.* Boston: Allyn & Bacon.

Anderson, M. & Hill Collins, P. (1995). *Race, class, and gender: An anthology.* Belmont, CA: Wadsworth.

Anderson, R. & Carter, I. (1990). *Human behavior in the social environment: A social systems approach* (4th ed.). New York: Aldine de Gruyter.

Anderson, R.E., Carter, I., & Lowe, G. (1999). *Human behavior in the social environment: A social systems approach* (5th ed.). New York: Aldine De Gruyter.

Anderson, S. (2002). Engaging students in community-based research: A model for teaching social work research. *Journal of Community Practice, 10*(2), 71-87.

Andrews, J. & Reisch, M. (1997). Social work and anti-communism: A historical analysis of the McCarthy era. *Journal of Progressive Human Services, 8*(2), 29-49.

Anner, J. (1996). (Ed.) *Beyond identity politics: Emerging social justice movements in communities of color.* Boston: South End Press.

Anzaldúa, G. (2000). Allies. In M. Adams, W. Blumfeld, R. Castañeda, H. Hackman, M. Peters, & X. Zuñiga (Eds.), *Readings for diversity and social justice* (pp. 475-477). New York: Routledge. (Reprinted from Sinister Wisdom, *52*, Spring/Summer, 1994, pp. 47-52.)

Aotearoa New Zealand Association of Social Workers. (2006). *Professional standards for social workers.* Retrieved July 19, 2006, from http://www.anzasw.org.nz/profstandards.htm

Apple, M. (1982). *Education and power.* London: Routledge and Kegan Paul.

Apple, M. (2003). *The state and politics of education.* New York: Routledge.

Apple, M. (2004). *Ideology and curriculum* (3rd ed.). New York: Routledge.

Arendt, H. (1973). *The origins of totalitarianism.* New York: Harcourt, Brace, Jovanovich.

Argyris, C. (1970). *Intervention theory and method.* Reading, PA: Addison-Wesley.

Armstrong, L. (1995). *Of 'sluts' and 'bastards:' A feminist decodes the child welfare debate.* Monroe, ME: Common Courage Press.

Aronowitz, S. & Giroux, H. (1985). *Education under siege: The conservative, liberal and radical debate over schooling.* South Hadley, MA: Bergin & Garvey.

Ascione, W. & Dixson, J. (2002). Children and their incarcerated mothers. In J. Figueira-McDonough, & R. Sarri (Eds.), *Women at the margins: Neglect, punishment, and resistance* (pp. 271-294). New York: Haworth Press.

Ashley, F. & Gaventa, J. (1997). Researching for democracy and democratizing research. *Change, 29*(10), 46-54.

Atkinson, D. R., Morten, G., & Sue, D. W. (1989). *Counseling American minorities: A cross-cultural perspective* (3rd ed.). Dubuque, IA: William C. Brown, Publishers.

Aull Davies, C. (1999). *Reflexive ethnography: A guide to researching selves and others.* London: Routledge.

Baber, K. & Allen, K. (1992). *Women and families: Feminist reconstructions.* New York: Guilford.

Baca Zinn, M. (1990). Family, feminism, and race in America. *Gender and Society, 4*, 68-82.

Bailey, R. & Brake, M. (1976). *Radical social work.* New York: Random House.

Bandura, A. (2006). Toward a psychology of human agency. *Perspectives on Psychological Science, 1*(2), 164-180.

Baptist, W. & Bricker-Jenkins, M. (2002). A view from the bottom: Poor people and their allies respond to welfare reform. In R. Albeda & A. Withorn (Eds.), *Lost ground: Welfare reform, poverty, and beyond* (pp. 195-210). Cambridge, MA: South End Press.

Baptist, W., Bricker-Jenkins, M., Gentry, S., Johnson, M., & Novak, C. (2006). "The history becomes you": Narratives and today's movement to end poverty. In D. Saleebey (Ed.), *The strengths perspective in social work practice* (4th ed, pp. 221-240). Boston: Pearson Education, Inc.

Barber, J. G. (1995). Politically progressive casework. *Families in Society: The Journal of Contemporary Human Services, 76*(1), 30-37.

Barbuto, D. (1999). *American settlement houses and progressive social reform: An encyclopedia of the American Settlement Movement.* Phoenix, AZ: Oryx Press.

Barker, R. (2003). (Ed.) The social work dictionary (5th ed.). Washington, D.C.: NASW Press.

Bartlett, H. (1970). *The common base of social work practice.* New York: NASW.

Bates, R. (1996). Popular theatre: A useful process for adult educators. *Adult Education Quarterly, 46*(4), 224-236.

Baum, G. (1971). *Man becoming.* New York: Herder and Herder.

Bazemore, G. & Schiff, M. (2001). *Restorative community justice: Repairing harm and transforming communities.* Cincinnati, OH: Anderson.

Beck, A., Karlberg, J., & Harrison, P. (2002). *Prison and jail inmates at midyear 2001.* Washington, DC: Bureau of Justice Statistics.

Bell, B. (2001) *Walking on fire: Haitian women's stories of survival and resistance.* Ithaca: Cornell University Press.

Benard, B. (2006). Using strengths-based practice to tap the resilience of families. In D. Saleebey (Ed.), *The strengths perspective in social work practice* (4th ed., pp. 197-215). Boston: Pearson Education, Inc.

Bennett, J. & O'Brien, M. (1994). The building blocks of the learning organization. *Training, 31*(6), 41-49.

Berger, P. & Luckman, T. (1966). *The social construction of knowledge: A treatise in the sociology of knowledge.* New York: Anchor Books.

Biestek, F. (1957). *The casework relationship.* Chicago: Loyola University Press.

Bigelow, B. & Peterson, B. (2002). *Rethinking globalization: Teaching for justice in an unjust world.* Milwaukee: Rethinking Schools Press.

Blackburn, S. (2001). *Being good: A short introduction to ethics.* Oxford: Oxford University Press.

Blundo, R. (2006). Shifting our habits of mind: Learning to practice from a strengths perspective. In D. Saleebey (Ed.), *The strengths perspective in social work practice* (4th ed., pp. 25-45). Boston: Pearson Education, Inc.

Boal, A. (1985). *Theatre of the oppressed.* New York: Routledge. (Originally published in 1979).

Boal, A. (1998). *Legislative theatre.* New York: Routledge.

Bock, S. (1980). Conscientization: Paulo Freire and class-based practice. *Catalyst 2*, 5-25.

Bojer, M., Knuth, M. & Magner, C. (2006). *Mapping dialogue.* Retrieved June 16, 2006, from http://www.pioneersofchange.net

Boris, E. (1995). The radicalized gender state: Constructions of citizenship in the United States. *Social Politics, 2*(2), 160-180.

Boshara, R. (2003). The $6,000 solution. *Atlantic Monthly, 291*(1), 91-94.

Bourdieu, P. (1977). *Outline of a theory of practice* (Trans. R. Nice). Cambridge: Cambridge University Press.

Bourdieu, P. (1984). *Distinction: A social critique of the judgment of taste* (Trans. R. Nice). Cambridge: Harvard University Press. (Original work published in 1979)

Boyd, A. (1999). *The activist cookbook: Creative actions for a fair economy.* Boston, MA: United for a Fair Economy.

Boyle, S., Hull, G., Mather, J., Smith, L., & Farley, O. W. (2006). *Direct practice in social work.* Boston: Pearson Education, Inc.

Brace, C. L. (1872). *The dangerous classes of New York and my twenty years' work among them.* New York: Wynkoop & Hallenbeck.

Brahsears, F. (1995). Supervision as social work practice. *Social Work, 40*, 692-699.

Brave Heart-Jordan, M. & DeBruyn, L. (1995). So she may walk in balance: Integrating the impact of historical trauma in the treatment of American Indian women. In J. Adelman & G. Enguidanos (Eds.), *Racism in the lives of women: Testimony, theory, and guides to antiracist practice* (pp. 345-368). Binghamton, NY: Haworth Press.

Briar-Lawson, K. (2001). Promoting new alliances among families, family advocates, and helping professionals. In K. Briar-Lawson, H. Lawson, C. Hennon, & A. Jones (Eds.), *Family-centered policies and practices: International implications* (pp. 275-292). New York: Columbia University Press.

Briggs, J. (1970). *Never in anger: Portrait of an Eskimo family*. Cambridge, MA: Harvard University Press.

Brill, N. & Levine, J. (2002). *Working with people: The helping process* (7th ed.). Boston: Allyn and Bacon.

Briskman, L. (2005). Pushing ethical boundaries for children and families: Confidentiality, transparency and transformation. In R. Adams, L. Dominelli, & M. Payne (Eds.), *Social work futures: Crossing boundaries, transforming practice* (pp. 208-220). New York: Palgrave/MacMillan.

Broussard, J. (2002). Mary Church Terrell: A Black woman journalist seeks to elevate her race. *American Journalism, 19*(4), 13-25.

Brown C. & Mazza, G. (1997*). Healing into action: A leadership guide for creating diverse communities*. Washington, DC: National Coalition Building Institute.

Brown, L.D. & Tandon, R. (1978). Interviews as catalysts. *Journal of Applied Psychology, 63*(2), 197-205.

Brown, L. (1985). People centered development and participatory research. *Harvard Educational Review, 55,* 69-75.

Brun, M. (1972). Animation and social work. *Proceedings of the XVI International Congress of Schools of Social Work* (pp. 60-71), The Hague, Netherlands. New York: International Association of Schools of Social Work.

Bryan, M. & Davis, A. (1990). *One hundred years at Hull-House*. Bloomington, IN: Indiana University Press.

Bubeck, D. (1995). *Care, gender, and justice*. Oxford: Claredon.

Bulhan, H. (1985). *Frantz Fanon and the psychology of oppression*. New York: Plenum Press.

Bureau of the Census (1999). *World population at a glance: 1998 and beyond*. Washington, DC: U.S. Department of Commerce.

Burkett, I. & McDonald, C. (2005). Working in a different space: Linking social work and social development. In I. Ferguson, M. Lavalette, & E. Whitmore (Eds.), *Globalisation, global justice and social work* (pp. 173-188). New York: Routledge.

Cable, J. (2005, February 8). Grand jury indictment: W. R. Grace lied about dangers of asbestos exposure. *Occupational Hazards,* Retrieved June 1, 2006, from http://www.occupationalhazards.com/articles/12965

Canadian Association of Social Work. (1994). Code of ethics. Ottawa, Canada: Author.

Carniol, B. (1990). *Case critical: Challenging social work in Canada* (2nd ed.). Toronto: Between the Lines.

Carr, E. (1961). *What is history?* New York: St. Martin's Press.

Carr-Hill, R. (1984). Radicalizing survey methodology. *Quality and Quantity, 18,* 275-292.

Carroll, R. (2005, November 3). Number of U.S. adults in prison rise. *The Boston Globe*. Retrieved June 12, 2006, from http://www.boston.com/mews/nation/washington/articles

Carter, P. (1986/1987). *Parts work: Seminars on trance work and mind/body healing*. Nelson, British Columbia, 1986; Edmonton, Alberta, 1987.

Caufield, C. (1996). *Masters of illusion: The World Bank and poverty nations.* New York: Henry Holt.

Center for Conflict Resolution. (n.d.). *Group process: A manual for group facilitators*. Madison, WI: Center for Conflict Resolution. (Reprinted in *A very popular economic education sampler,* Highlander Research and Education Center, New Market, TN.)

Chambers, C. (1963). *Seedtime of reform: American social service and social action - 1918-1933*. Minneapolis, MN: University of Minnesota.

Chambers, R. (1997). *Whose reality counts? Putting the first last.* London: Intermediate Technology Publications.

Chambron, A. (1999). Foucault's approach: Making the familiar visible. In A. Chambron, A. Irving, & L. Epstein (Eds.), *Reading Foucault for social work* (pp. 51-82). New York: Columbia University Press.

Chandler, S. (2005). Addie Hunton and the construction of an African American female peace perspective. *Affilia: Journal of Women and Social Work, 20*(3), 270-283.

Chapin, R. (1995). Social policy development: The strengths perspective. *Social Work, 40*(4), 506-514.

Checkoway, B. (1990). *Six strategies of community change*. Arnulf Pins Memorial Lecture, Hebrew University, Jerusalem.

Cherin, D. & Meezan, W. (1998). Evaluation as a means of organizational learning. *Administration in Social Work, 22*(2), 1-21.

Child Friendly Cities (2006). Homepage, Project of UNICEF, Retrieved March 15, 2006, from http://www.childfriendlycities.org

Chin, E. (2003). Children out of bounds in globalising times. *Postcolonial Studies, 6*(3), 309-317.

Cho, E., Paz y Puente, F. Louie, M., & Khokha, S. (2004). *Bridges: Building a race and immigration dialogue in a global economy*. Oakland, CA: National Network for Immigrant and Refugee Rights.

Cholewa K. & Smith, J. (1999). *Montana welfare reform today: Shifting alliances, dropping caseloads, and lost opportunity.* Coping with Block Grants Project, Missoula, MT: Women's Opportunity and Resource Development.

Christopher, S. (2005). Recommendations for conducting successful research with Native Americans. *Journal of Cancer Education, 20,* 47-51.

Chung, I. (2003). Creative use of focus groups: Providing healing and support to NYC Chinatown residents after the 9/11 attacks. *Social Work with Groups, 26*(4), 3-19.

Claassen, R. (1996). *Restorative justice I: Fundamental principles.* Center for Peacemaking and Conflict Studies, Fresno, CA: Fresno Pacific University. Retrieved April 10, 2006, from http://www.fresno.edu/pacs/docs/restj1.html

Claiborne, N. & Lawson, H. (2005). An intervention framework for collaboration. *Families in Society, 86*(1), 93-103.

Clark, R. (1988). Social justice and issues of human rights in the international context. In D. Sanders & J. Fisher (Eds.), *Vision for the future: Social work and the Pacific-Asian perspective* (pp. 3-10). Honolulu: University of Hawaii Press.

Clarke, J., Gewirtz, S., & McLaughlin, E. (2000). *New managerialism, new welfare?* London: Sage.

Clifford, J. (1986). Introduction: Partial truths. In J. Clifford & G. Marcus (Eds.), *Writing culture: The poetics and politics of ethnography* (pp. 1-26). Berkeley: University of California Press.

Clinton, B. (2006, May 15). My quest to improve care. *Newsweek, 147*(20), 50-52.

Coates, J. (1992). Ideology and education for social work practice. *Journal of Progressive Human Services, 3*(2), 15-30.

Coates, J. & McKay, M. (1995). Toward a new pedagogy for social transformation. *Journal of Progressive Human Services, 6*(1), 27-43.

Confer, C. (1997). *Managing anger: Yours and mine.* King George, Virginia: American Foster Care Resources, Inc.

Congress, E. (1994). The use of culturagrams to assess and empower culturally diverse families. *Families in Society: The Journal of Contemporary Human Services, 75*(9), 531-539.

Council on Social Work Education (2004). *Educational policy and accreditation standards.* Alexandria, VA: Author.

Cournoyer, B. (2004). *The evidence-based social work skills book.* Boston: MA: Allyn & Bacon.

Coute, D. (1973). *The fellow travelers: A post-script to the Enlightenment.* New York: Macmillian.

Cowger, C. (1994). Assessing client strengths: Clinical assessment for client empowerment. *Social Work, 39*(2), 262-268.

Cowling, W. R. (2001). Unitary appreciative inquiry. *Advances in Nursing Science, 23*(4), 32-48.

Cree, V. & Wallace, S. (2005). Risk and protection. In R. Adams, L. Dominelli, & M. Payne (Eds.), *Social work futures: Crossing boundaries, transforming practice* (pp. 115-127). New York: Palgrave/MacMillan.

Critical Resistance. (2001). Mission Statement. Critical Resistance Website: Oakland, CA: Authors. Retrieved April 26, 2006, from http://www.criticalresistance.org/mission

Cross, T. (1986). Drawing on cultural tradition in Indian child welfare practice. *Social Casework, 67,* 283-289.

Danaher, K. (Ed.). (1994). *Fifty years is enough: The case against the World Bank and the International Monetary Fund.* Boston: South End Press.

Davis, A. (1967). *Spearheads for reform: The social settlements and the progressive movement 1890-1914.* New York: Columbia University Press.

Davis, A. (2001). Writing on the wall: Prisoners on punishment. *Punishment and Society, 3*(3), 427-432.

Davis, L. & Srinivasan, M. (1995). Listening to the voices of battered women: What helps them escape violence. *Affilia: Journal of Women and Social Work, 10*(1), 49-69.

Day, P. (2003). *A new history of social welfare* (4th ed.). Boston, MA: Allyn and Bacon.

Dean, R. (2001). The myth of cross-cultural competence. *Families in Society, 82*(6), 623- 630.

Deegan, P. (1990). Spiritbreaking: When the helping professions hurt. *The Humanistic Psychologist, 18*(3), 301-313.

Deegan, P. (1996). *Recovery and the Conspiracy of Hope.* Presentation at the 6th Annual Mental Health Services Conference of Australia and New Zealand, Brisbane, Australia.

Delgado, R. & Stefanic, J. (2001). *Critical race theory: An introduction.* New York: New York University Press.

Deloria, V. (2004). *Red earth, white lies: Native Americans and the myth of scientific fact.* Golden, CO: Fulkrum Publishing.

Denzin, N. & Lincoln, Y. (Eds.). (1994). *Handbook of qualitative research.* Thousand Oaks, CA: Sage Publications.

Derrida, J. (1976). *Of grammatology* (G. Spivak, Trans.). Baltimore: John Hopkins. (Originally published in 1967)

Desai, A. (1987). Development of social work education. In *Encyclopedia of social work of India.* New Delhi: Government of India, Ministry of Social Welfare.

DeSchweinitz, K. (1955). Correspondence to Fedele Fauri, 8 September, Council of Social Work Education Manuscripts, Box 7, Folder, 24, Social Welfare History Archives, University of Minnesota, Minneapolis, MN.

Devore, W. & Schlesinger, E. (1981). *Ethnic-sensitive social work practice.* Boston: Allyn & Bacon.

Dewees, M. (2006). *Contemporary social work practice.* Boston: McGraw Hill.

Dewey, J. (1910). *How we think.* Boston: D.C. Heath & Co.

Dewey, J. (1933). *How we think: A restatement of the relations of reflective thinking to the educative process.* Boston: D. C. Heath & Co.

Díaz, C. (1995). *El Diagnóstico para la participación.* San Jose, Costa Rica: Alforja.

Díaz, C. (1997). *Planificación participativa.* San Jose, Costa Rica: Alforja.

DiLeonardo, M. (1984). *The varieties of ethnic experience: Kinship, class and gender among California Italian-Americans.* Ithaca, NY: Cornell University Press.

DiLeonardo, M. (1987). The female world of cards and holidays: Women, families and the work of kinship. *Signs, 12,* 440-453.

Dirks, N., Eley, G., & Ortner, S. (1994). Introduction. In N. Dirks, G. Eley, & S. Ortner (Eds.), *Culture/power/history: A reader in contemporary social theory* (pp. 3-45). Princeton: Princeton University Press.

Dobelstein, A. (1999). *Moral authority, ideology and the future of American social welfare.* Boulder: Westview Press.

Dominelli, L. (1996). Deprofessionalizing social work: Anti-oppressive practice, competencies and post-modernism. *British Journal of Social Work, 26,* 153-157.

Dominelli, L (1998). Anti-oppressive practice in context. In R. Adams, L. Dominelli, & M. Payne (Eds.), *Social work: Themes, issues and critical debates.* London: Macmillian.

Dominelli, L. (1999). Neo-liberalism, social exclusion and welfare clients in a global economy. *International Journal of Social Welfare, 8,* 14-22.

Dominelli, L. (2002). *Anti-oppressive social work theory and practice.* London: Macmillan.

Dominelli, L, & McLeod, E. (1989). *Feminist social work.* London: MacMillan.

Donaldson, T. (1996). Values in tension: Ethics away from home. *Harvard Busines Review, 74*(5), 48-62.

Dubois, B. & Miley, K. (2005). *Social work: An empowering profession* (5th ed.). Needham Heights, MA: Allyn & Bacon.

DuBois, W.E.B. (Apthekeer, Ed.). (1968). *The autobiography of W. E. B. DuBois: A soliloquy on viewing my life from the last decade of its first century.* New York: International Publishers.

DuBois, W.E.B. (1968). *The autobiography of W. E. Burghardt DuBois: A soliloquy on viewing my life from the last decade of its first century.* New York: International Publishers.

DuBois, W.E.B. (1989). *The souls of black folk.* New York: Bantam. (Originally published in 1903)

Dujon, D. & Withorn, A. (Eds.). (1996). *For crying out loud: Women's poverty in the United States.* Boston: South End Press.

Duster, A. (Ed.). (1970). *Crusade for justice: The autobiography of Ida B. Wells.* Chicago, IL: University of Chicago Press.

Dworkin, J. (2005). *Advanced social work practice: An integrative, multilevel approach.* Boston: Allyn & Bacon.

Ecumenical Coalition for Economic Justice. (2001). Structural adjustment programs. Toronto: Canada: Authors. Ecumenical Coalition for Economic Justice website: http://www.ecej.org

Edelman, P. (1997). The worst thing the Bill Clinton has done. *Atlantic Monthly, 279*(3), 43-58.

Edmunds, D. (Ed.). (2001). *The new warriors: Native American leaders since 1900.* Lincoln, NB: University of Nebraska Press.

Ehrenreich, J. H. (1985). *The altruistic imagination: A history of social work and social policy in the United States.* Ithaca, NY: Cornell University Press.

Encyclopedia of Social Welfare History in North America. (2006). Thousdand Oaks, CA: Sage. Retrieved June 20, 2006, from http://www.referenceworld.com/sage

Epstein, I. (1987). Pedagogy of the perturbed: Teaching research to the reluctants. *Journal of Teaching in Social Work, 1*(1), 71-89.

Epstein, L. (1999). The culture of social work. In A. Chambon, A. Irving, & L. Epstein (Eds.), *Reading Foucault for social work* (pp. 3-26). New York: Columbia.

Erikson, E. (1963). *Childhood and society.* New York: Norton. (Originally published in 1950)

Escuela de Trabajo Social (ETS). (1984). *Modelo del professional del trabajo social.* Managua, Nicaragua: Universidad Centroamericana Escuela de Trabajo Social.

Essential Action (2001). How structural adjustment worsens poverty. Retrieved Aug 1, 2006, from http://www.essentialaction.org

Fadiman, A. (1997). *The spirit catches you and you fall down.* New York: Farrar, Strauss, Giroux.

Farmer, P. (2003). *Pathologies of power: Health, human rights, and the new war on the poor.* Berkeley: University of California Press.

Faver, C. (2004) Relational spirituality and social caregiving. *Social Work, 49*(2), 241-249.

Ferguson, I., Lavalette, M., & Whitmore, E. (2005). *Globalisation, global justice, and social work.* New York: Routledge.

Fernandes, W. (1989). Participatory research and action in India today. *Social Action, 39,* 1-21.

Ferré, F. (2001). *Living and value: Toward a constructive postmodern ethics.* Albany: State University of New York Press.

Ferree, M. (1990). Beyond separate spheres: Feminism and family research. *Journal of Marriage and the Family, 52,* 866-884.

Figueira-McDonough, J. (1993). Policy practice: The neglected side of social work intervention. *Social Work, 38*(2), 179-188.

Figueira-McDonough, J., Netting, F. E., & Nichols-Casebolt, A. (Eds.). (1998). *The role of gender in practice knowledge: Claiming half the human experience.* New York: Garland.

Figueira-McDonough, J. & Sarri, R. (Eds.). (2002). *Women at the margins: Neglect, punishment, and resistance.* New York: Haworth Press.

Fine, M., Weis, L., Powell, L., & Wong, L.M., (Eds.). (1997). *Off white: Readings on race, power and society.* New York: Routledge.

Finn, J. (1994a). The promise of participatory research. *Journal of Progressive Human Services. 5,* 25-42.

Finn, J. (1994b). Contested caring: Women's roles in foster family care. *Affilia: Journal of Women and Social Work, 9,* 382-400.

Finn, J. (1998a). *Tracing the veins: Of copper, culture, and community from Butte to Chuquicamata.* Berkeley: University of California Press.

Finn, J. (1998b). Gender and families. In J. Figuiera-McDonough, F. Netting, & A. Nichols-Casebolt (Eds.), *The role of gender in practice knowledge* (pp. 205-239). New York: Garland.

Finn, J. (2001a). Text and turbulence: Representing adolescence as pathology in the human services. *Childhood, 8*(2), 167-191.

Finn, J. (2001b).The women of Villa Paula Jaraquemada: Building community in Chile's transition to democracy. *Community Development Journal, 36*(3), 183-197.

Finn, J. (2005). La Victoria comprometida: Reflections on neoliberalism from a Santiago *población*. In N. Dannhauser & C. Werner (Eds.), *Research in Economic Anthropology Volume 24, Markets and Market Liberalization: Ethnographic Reflections* (pp. 207-240). Oxford, UK: Eslevier Publishing.

Finn, J., Castellanos, R., McOmber, T., & Kahan, K. (2000). Working for equality and economic liberation: Advocacy and education for welfare reform. *Affilia: Journal of Women and Social Work, 15*(2), 294-310.

Finn, J. & Checkoway, B. (1998). Young people as competent community builders: A challenge to social work. *Social Work, 43*(4), 335-345.

Finn, J., Jacobson, M., & Dean Campana, J. (2004). Participatory research, popular education, and popular theatre. In C. Garvin, L. Gutiérrez, & M. Galinsky, (Eds.), *Handbook of social work with groups* (pp. 326-343). New York: Guilford Press.

Finn, J., Rodriguez, & G. Nuñez, N. (2000). *La Victoria: Rescatando la historia.* Community History Project Document. La Victoria, Santiago, Chile.

Finn, J. & Underwood, L. (2000). The state the clock and the struggle: An inquiry into the discipline for welfare reform in Montana. *Social Text 62, 18*(1), 109-134.

Firestone, W. (1986). Meaning in method: The rhetoric of quantitative and qualitative research. *Educational Researcher, 16*(7), 16-21.

Fisher, D. & Chamberlin, J. (2004) Consumer-driven transformation to a recovery-based mental health system. Executive Summary. National Empowerment Center, Inc.

Fisher, J. (1990). The rank and file movement - 1930-1936. *Journal of Progressive Human Services, 1*(1), 95-99. (Originally published in 1936)

Fisher, R. (1995). Political social work. *Journal of Social Work Education, 31*(2), 194-203.

Fisher, R. (1999). Speaking for the contribution of history: Context and the origins of the Social Welfare History Group. *Social Service Review, 73*(2), 191-217.

Flowers, N., Bernbaum, M., Rudelius-Palmer, K., & Tolman, J. (2000). *The human rights education handbook: Effective practices for learning, action, and change.* Minneapolis, MN: Human Rights Resource Center, University of Minnesota.

Fook, J. (2000). Critical perspectives on social work practice. In E. O'Connor, P. Smyth, & J. Warburton (Eds.), *Contemporary perspectives on social work and the human services: Challenges and change.* Sydney: Pearson Education Australia.

Forgacs, D. (Ed.). (1988). *An Antonio Gramsci reader: Selected writings, 1919-1935.* New York: Schocken Books.

Foucault, M. (1977). *Discipline and punish.* London: Allen Lane.

Foucault, M. (1978). *The history of sexuality: An introduction, Vol. 1* (R. Hurley, Trans.). New York: Random House. (Originally published in English in 1976).

Foucault, M. (1979). Truth and power. In M. Morris & P. Patton (Eds.), *Michel Foucault: Power, truth, and strategy* (pp. 29-48). Sydney: Feral Publications.

Foucault, M. (1980). *Power/knowledge: Selected interviews and others writings, 1972-77* (C. Gordon, Ed., Trans.). New York: Pantheon.

Franklin, C. (2000). Predicting the future of school social work practice in the new millennium. *Journal of Social Work Education.* 22(1), 3-5.

Fraser, N. & Gordon, L. (1994). A genealogy of dependency: Tracing a keyword of the U.S. welfare state. *Signs, 19*(2), 309-336.

Freire, P. (1973). *Pedagogy of the oppressed.* New York: Seabury.

Freire, P. (1974). *Pedagogy of the oppressed.* New York: Seabury/Continuum. (Originally published in English in 1970)

Freire, P. (1990). A critical understanding of social work. *Journal of Progressive Human Services, 1*(1), 3-9.

Freire, P. (1999). *Pedagogy of hope: Reliving pedagogy of the oppressed.* New York: Continuum.

Frick, W. (1995). Sweden. In T. Watts, D. Elliot, & N. Mayadas (Eds.), *International handbook on social work education* (p. 149-160). Westport, CT: Greenwood Publishing Co.

Galper, J. (1975). *The politics of social services.* Englewood Cliffs, NJ: Prentice-Hall.

Gallagher, C. (2004). 'Our town': Children as advocates for change in the city. *Childhood, 11*(2), 251-262.

Garcia, A. M. (1982). *La operación* (Film). New York: Cinema Guild.

Garretón, M. (1996). Human rights in democratization processes. In E. Jelin & E. Hershberg (Eds.), *Constructing democracy: Human rights, citizenship and society in Latin America* (pp. 39-56). Boulder: Westview Press.

Garvin, C. (1985). Work with disadvantaged and oppressed groups. In M. Sundel, P. Glasser, R. Sarri, & R. Vinter (Eds.), *Individual change through small groups* (2nd ed., pp. 461-472). New York: Free Press.

Garvin, C., Gutiérrez, L. & Galinsky, M. (2004). (Eds.). *Handbook of social work with groups.* New York: Guilford Press.

Garvin, C. & Reed, B. (1995). Sources and visions for feminist group work: Reflective processes, social justice, diversity, and connection. In N. Van Den Bergh (Ed.), *Feminist social work practice in the 21ˢᵗ century.* Washington, DC: NASW.

Garvin, C. & Seabury, B. (1997). *Interpersonal practice in social work: Promoting competence and social justice* (2ⁿᵈ ed.). Boston: Allyn and Bacon.

Gates, H. L. & West, C. (1996). *The future of the race.* New York: Knopf.

Gaventa, J. (1988). Participatory research in North America. *Convergence, 21*(1), 19-29.

George, J. (1997). Global graying: What role for social work? In M. Hokenstad & J. Midgley (Eds.), *Issues in international social work: Global challenges for a new century.* Washington, D.C: NASW Press.

George, J. (1999). Conceptual muddle, practical dilemma: Human rights, social development, and social work education. *International Social Work, 42*(1), 15-26.

Gergen, K. (1999). *An invitation to social construction.* London: Sage Publications.

Germain, C. (1979). Ecology and social work. In C. B. Germain (Ed.), *Social work practice: People and environments* (pp. 1-22). New York: Columbia University Press.

Germain, C. (1983). Using social and physical environments. In A. Rosenblatt & D. Waldfogel (Eds.), *Handbook of clinical social work* (pp. 110-133). San Francisco: Jossey Bass.

Germain, C. (1994a) Human behavior in the social environment. In F. Reamer (Ed.), *The foundations of social work knowledge* (pp. 88-121). New York: Columbia University Press.

Germain, C. (1994b). Emerging conceptions of family development over the life course. *Families in Society, 75*(5), 259-268.

Germain, C. & Gitterman, A. (1980). *The life model of social work practice.* New York: Columbia University Press.

Germain, C. (1995). Ecological perspective. In R. L. Edwards (Ed.), *Encyclopedia of social work, Vol. I* (19ᵗʰ ed., pp. 816-824). Washington, DC: NASW Press.

Gettleman, M. (1975). Philanthropy as social control in late nineteenth-century America: Some hypotheses and data on the rise of social work. *Societas, 5*(1), 49-59.

Giddens, A. (1979). *Central problems in social theory: Action, structure and contradiction in social analysis.* Berkeley: University of California Press.

Giddens, A. (1991). *The consequences of modernity.* Cambridge: Polity Press.

Gil, D. (1994). Confronting injustice and oppression. In F. Reamer (Ed.), *The foundations of social work knowledge.* New York: Columbia University Press.

Gil, D. (1998). *Confronting injustice and oppression: Concepts and strategies for social workers.* New York: Columbia University Press.

Gilens, M. (1999). *Why Americans hate welfare: Race, media, and the politics of antipoverty policy.* Chicago: University of Chicago Press.

Gilligan, C. (1982). *In a different voice: Psychological theory and women's development.* Cambridge: Harvard University Press.

Gilman, S. (1985). *Difference and pathology: Stereotypes of sexuality, race and madness.* Ithaca, NY: Cornell University Press.

Gilson, S., Bricou, J., & Baskind. F. (1998). Listening to the voices of individuals with disabilities. *Families in Society: The Journal of Contemporary Human Services, 79*(2), 188-196.

Ginsberg, F. & Tsing, A. (Eds.). (1990). *Uncertain terms: Negotiating gender in American culture.* Boston: Beacon.

Glasser, I. (1978). Welfare and liberty: Prisoners of benevolence. *The Nation, 226,* 370-372.

Gold, N. (1998). Using participatory research to help promote the physical and mental health of female social workers in child welfare. *Child Welfare, 77*(6), 701-724.

Gonzalez, J. (2006, March 28). "Latino giant" awakens: Demonstrations gaining strength. Retrieved March 28, 2006, from http://www.commondreams.org/views06/0328-20.htm

Goodman, D. (2004). Class dismissed. *Mother Jones, 29*(3), 43.

Gordon, L. (1988). *Heroes of their own lives: The politics and history of family violence.* New York: Viking Penguin, Inc.

Gordon, L. (Ed.). (1990). *Women, the state and welfare.* Madison: University of Wisconsin Press.

Gordon, L. (1994) *Pitied but not entitled: Single mothers and the history of welfare.* New York: Free Press.

Goroff, N. (1983.) *A pedagogy for radical social work practice.* Unpublished manuscript, West Hartford, CT: University of Connecticut.

Gould, E. (2003, March 16). Recent developments in the GATS negiotiations: The good and the bad news for local governments. The Council of Canadians report. Retrieved August 17, 2006, from http://www.canadians.org

Gould, S. (1981). *The mismeasure of man.* New York: W.W. Norton and Co.

Gramsci, A. (1987). *The modern prince and other stories.* New York: International Publishers. (Originally published in 1957)

Green, D. (1995). *Silent revolution: The rise of market economics in Latin America.* London: Cassell/Latin American Bureau.

Greenfield, L. & Snell, T. (2000). *Women offenders.* Washington, DC: Bureau of Justice Statistics.

Greenwood, E. (1957). Attributes of a profession. *Social Work, 2*(3), 45-55.

Grinnell, R. & Unrau, Y. (2005). *Social work research and evaluation: Quantitative and qualitative approaches.* New York: Oxford University Press.

Gutiérrez, L. (1990). Working with women of color: An empowerment perspective. *Social Work, 35*(2), 149-153.

Gutiérrez, L. & Lewis, E. (1999). *Empowering women of color.* New York: Columbia University Press.

Guzman Bouvard, M. (1994). *Revolutionizing motherhood: The mothers of the Plaza de Mayo.* Wilmington, DE: Scholarly Resources, Inc.

Hall, B. (1975). Participatory research: An approach for change. *Convergence, 8*(2), 24-32.

Hall, B. (1981). Participatory research, popular knowledge, and power. A personal reflection. *Convergence, 14*(3), 6-19.

Hall, B. (1993). Introduction. In P. Park, M. Brydon-Miller, B. Hall, & T. Jackson (Eds.), *Voices of change: Participatory research in the United States and Canada* (pp. xiii-xxii). Westport, CN: Bergin & Garvey.

Halperin, R. (1998). *Practicing community: Class, culture, and power in an urban neighborhood.* Austin: University of Texas Press.

Hamilton, G. (1940). *The theory and practice of social casework.* New York: Columbia University Press.

Hanmer, J. & Statham, D. (1989). *Women and social work: Towards a woman-centered practice.* Chicago: Lyceum.

Harding, S. (2004). A socially relevant philosophy of science? Resources for standpoint theory's controversality. *Hypatia, 19*(1), 25-47.

Harris, J. (2005). Globalisation, neo-liberal managerialism and UK social work. In I. Ferguson, M. Lavalette, & E. Whitmore (Eds.), *Globalisation, global justice and social work,* (pp. 81-93). New York: Routledge.

Hartman, A. (1978). Diagrammatic assessment of family relationships. *Social Casework, 59*(8). 465-476.

Hartman, A. & Laird, J. (1983). *Family-centered social work practice.* New York: Free Press.

Hartmann, H. (1981). The family as locus of gender, class and political struggle: The example of housework. *Signs, 6*, 366-394.

Harvey, D. (1989). *The condition of postmodernity: An enquiry into the origins of cultural change.* Oxford, UK: Basil Blackwell, Ltd.

Harvey, D. (2000). *Spaces of hope.* Berkeley: University of California Press.

Hatcher, G. (2000). Finding the private self: James' story of joining. *Families in Society, 81*(3), 333-338.

Hatton, N. & Smith, D. (1995). Reflection in teacher education: Towards definition and implementation. *Teaching and Teacher Education, 11*(1), 33-39.

Healy, K. (2002) Managing human services in a market environment: What role for social workers? *British Journal of Social Work, 32,* 527-540.

Healy, K. (2005). Under reconstruction: Renewing critical social work practices. In S. Hick, J. Fook, & R. Pozzuto (Eds.), *Social work: A critical turn* (pp. 219-229). Toronto: Thompson Educational Publishing, Inc.

Healy, L. (2001). *International social work: Professional action in an interdependent world.* New York: Oxford University Press.

Held, V. (2006). *Ethics of care: Personal, political, and global.* New York: Oxford University press.

Henderson, P. & Thomas, D. (1987). *Skills in neighbourhood work.* London: George Allen and Unwin.

Hepworth, D. & Larsen, J. (1982). *Direct social work practice.* Homewood, IL: Dorsey Press.

Hick, S., Fook, J., & Pozzuto, R. (2005). *Social work: A critical turn.* Toronto: Thompson Educational Publishing, Inc.

Hill Collins, P. (1990). *Black feminist thought: Knowledge, consciousness, and the politics of empowerment.* New York: Unwin Hyman.

Hill Collins, P. (1991). Learning from the outsider within: The sociological significance of black feminist thought. In M. Fonow & J. Cook (Eds.), *Beyond methodology: Feminist scholarship as lived research* (pp. 35-59). Bloomington, IN: Indiana University Press.

Hill, J. (1998). Toward louder voices: ActionAid Nepal's experience of working with children. In V. Johnson, E. Ivan-Smith, G. Gordon, P. Pridmore, & P. Scott (Eds.), *Stepping forward: Children and young people's participation in the development process* (pp. 92-95). London: Intermediate Technology Publications.

Hochman, S. (1997). School-community collaboratives: The missing links. In M. Reisch & E. Gambrill (Eds.), *Social work in the 21st century* (pp. 260-270). Thousand Oaks, CA: Pine Forge Press.

Hodges, D. (2005). Developing a spiritual assessment toolbox: A discussion of the strengths and limitations of five different assessment methods. *Health and Social Work, 30*(4), 314-323.

Hof, L. & Berman, E. (1986). The sexual genogram. *Journal of Marital and Family Therapy, 12*, 39-47.

Hoff-Wilson, J. (n.d.). *The Jeannette Rankin Commemorative Booklet.* Bloomington, IN: Organization of American Historians. (www.oag.org)

Hokenstad, M. & Midgley, J. (Eds.). (1997). *Issues in international social work: Global challenges for a new century.* Washington, D.C.: NASW Press.

Holt, J. (2004, August 15). Decarcerate? *New York Times Magazine.* Retrieved April 24, 2006, from the Critical Resistance website: http://www.criticalresistance.org

Homan, M. (2004) *Promoting community change: Making it happen in the real world* (3rd ed.). Pacific Grove, CA: Brooks/Cole.

hooks, b. (1984). *Feminist theory from margin to center.* Boston: South End Press.

hooks, b. (1994). *Teaching to transgress.* New York: Routledge.

hooks, b. (1995). *Killing rage: Ending racism.* New York: Henry Holt.

Hope, A. & Timmel, S. (1999). *Training for transformation: A handbook for community workers - Books 1-4.* London, UK: Intermediate Technology Publications. (Originally published in 1984).

Hopmeyer, E., Kimberly, M. & Hawkins, F. (1995). Canada. In T. Watts, D. Elliott, & N. Mayadas (Eds.), *Instructional handbook of social work education* (pp. 23-29). Westport, CT: Greenwood Publishing Co.

Horejsi, C. (1999). Social and economic justice: Concepts and principles for social work practice. Unpublished manuscript, University of Montana, School of Social Work.

Horton, M. (with Judith Kohl and Herbert Kohl). (1998). *The long haul: An autobiography.* New York: Teachers College Press.

Howe, D. (1994). Modernity, postmodernity, and social work. *British Journal of Social Work, 24*, 513-532.

Houston, S., Magill, T., McCollum, M., & Spratt, T. (2001). Developing creative solutions to the problems of children and their families: Communicative reason and the use of forum theatre. *Child and Family Social Work, 6*, 285-293.

Huff, D. (2006). *Social work history station.* Retrieved June 1, 2006, from http://www.idbsu.edu/socwork/dhuff/history

Hull-House Residents. (1895). *Hull-House maps and papers.* New York: Thomas Y. Crowell & Co.

Hull-House Residents. (1916). *Hull house yearbook.* Chicago, IL: University of Illinois at Chicago, Richard J. Daley Library, Special Collections - Hull House Collection, Box 44, Folder, 437.

Human Rights Watch (2006). Essential background: Overview of human rights issues in United States. Retrieved March 14, 2006, from http://hrw.org/english/docs

Hunter, F. (1953). *Community power structure*. Chapel Hill: University of North Carolina Press.

Husock, H. (1993). Bringing back the settlement house. *Public Welfare, 51*(4), 16-25.

Hutchinson, E. & Charlesworth, L. (1998). Human behavior in the social environment: The role of gender in the expansion of practice knowledge. In J. Figuiera-McDonough, F. Netting & A. Nichols-Casebolt (Eds.), *The role of gender in practice knowledge: Claiming half the human experience* (pp. 41-92). New York: Garland.

Ife, J. (1997). *Rethinking social work: Towards critical practice.* Melbourne: Longman.

Ife, J. (2000). Localized needs and a globalized economy: Bridging the gap with social work practice. *Canadian Social Work (Social Work and Globalization: Special Issues), 2*(1), 50-64.

Ife, J. (2001). *Human rights and social work: Towards rights-based practice.* Cambridge, UK: Cambridge University Press.

International Federation of Social Workers. (1997). *Policy Paper: Human Rights.* Oslo: Author.

International Federation of Social Workers. (2001). *IFSW General Information.* IFSW website: http://www.ifsw.org

International Federation of Social Workers. (2004). *Statement of ethical principles.* Bern, Switzerland: International Federation of Social Workers. Retrieved January 7, 2006, from http://www.ifsw.org/en/p38000324.html

Institute for Women's Policy Research. (2005). *The gender wage ratio: Women's and men's earnings.* Washington, DC: Author.

Irwin, K. (1992). Towards theories of Maori feminisms. In R. du Plessis (Ed.), *Feminist voices: Womens' studies texts for Aotearoal New Zealand* (p. 5). Auckland, New Zealand: Oxford University Press.

Iverson, R., Gergen, K., & Fairbanks II, R. (2005). Assessment and social construction: Conflict or co-creation? *British Journal of Social Work, 35*, 689-708.

Jacobson, M. (1997). *Child sexual abuse and the multidisciplinary teach approach in Montana: A mixed methods, participatory study.* Unpublished doctoral dissertation, University of Utah, Salt Lake City.

Jacobson, M. (2001). Child sexual abuse and the multidisciplinary teach approach: Contradictions in practice. *Childhood, 8*(2), 231-250.

Jacobson, M. (in press). Food matters: Community food assessments as a tool for change. *Journal of Community Practice. 15*(3).

Jacobson, M. & Goheen, A. (2006). Engaging students in research: A participatory BSW program evaluation. *Journal of Baccalaureate Social Work, 12*(1), 87-104

Jacobson, M. & Hassanein, N. (2004). *Food matters: Farm viability and food consumption in Missoula County*. The University of Montana, Missoula, MT.

Jacobson, M. & Rugeley, C. (in press). Community-based participatory research: Group work for social justice and community change. *Social Work with Groups, 30*(4).

Jaggar, A. (1983). *Feminist politics and human nature*. Totowa, NJ: Rowman & Littlefield Publishers, Inc.

Jalonick, M. (2005, September 28). Baucus bill would force W. R. Grace to provide health care for Libby residents. *Billings Gazette*. Retrieved May 23, 2006, from http://www.billingsgazette.com

Jansson, B. (1999). *Becoming an effective policy advocate: From policy practice to social justice*. Pacific Grove, CA: Brooks/Cole Publishing Co.

Jara, O. (1998). *Para sistematizar experiencias*. San Jose, Costa Rica: Alforja.

Jelin, E. (1996). Citizenship revisited: Solidarity, responsibility, and rights. In E. Jelin & E. Hershberg (Eds.), *Constructing democracy: Human rights, citizenship and society in Latin America* (pp. 101-120). Boulder: Westview Press.

Jenkins, K. (1995). *On 'What is history?' From Carr and Elton to Rorty and White*. London: Routledge.

Jicks, T. (1979). Mixing qualitative and quantitative methods: Triangulation in action. *Administrative Science Quarterly, 24*, 602-611.

Jimenez, M. & Aylwin, N. (1992). Social work in Chile: Support for the struggle for justice in Latin America. In M. C. Hokenstad, S. K. Khinduka, & J. Midgley (Eds.), *Profiles in International Social Work*. Washington, DC: NASW.

Johnson, K. (2002). In old mining town, new charges over asbestos. *The New York Times*, April 22, Section A. Col. 3, National, p. 1.

Johnson, L. & Yanca, S. (2007). *Social work practice: A generalist approach* (9ᵗʰ ed.). Boston: Allyn & Bacon.

Jones, C. (2005). The neo-liberal assault: Voices from the front line of British state social work. In I. Ferguson, M. Lavalette, & E. Whitmore (Eds.), *Globalisation, global justice and social work* (pp. 97-109). New York: Routledge.

Jones, J. (1984). *Labor of love, labor of sorrow: Black women, work and family from slavery to the present*. New York: Basic Books.

Jones, M. & Kerr, C. (1996). *The autobiography of Mother Jones*. Chicago: Charles H. Kerr Publishing Co.

Kaner, S. (with Lind, J., Toldi, C., Fisk, S., & Berger, D.). (2007). *Facilitator's guide to participatory decision-making* (2nd ed). San Francisco: John Wiley & Sons/Jossey-Bass.

Kanter, R. M. (1977). *Men and women of the corporation*. New York: Basic Books.

Kanter, R. M. (1979) Power failure in management circuits. *Harvard Business Review 57*, 65-75.

Karger, H. (1987). Minneapolis settlement houses in the 'not so roaring 20s': Americanization, morality, and the revolt against popular culture. *Journal of Sociology and Social Welfare, 14*(2), 89-110.

Karger, H. J. & Hernández, M. T. (2004). The decline of the public intellectual in social work. *Journal of Sociology and Social Welfare, 31*(3), 51-68.

Karger, H. & Stoesz, D. (1998). *American social welfare policy: A pluralist approach*. White Plains, NY: Longman.

Karston-Larson, J. (1977, January 26). And then there were none: IHA sterilization practice. *Christian Century, 94*, 61-63.

Kates, E. (1996). Colleges can help women in poverty. In D. Dujon & A. Withorn (Eds.), *For crying out loud: Women's poverty in the United States* (pp. 341-348). Boston: South End Press.

Keefe, T. (1980). Empathy and critical consciousness. *Social Casework, 61*, 387-393.

Keigher, S. & Lowry, K. (1998). The sickening implications of globalization. *Health and Social Work, 23*(2), 153-160.

Kellogg, P. (1914). Field work of the Pittsburgh survey. In Russell Sage Foundation, *The Pittsburgh district civic frontage* (pp. 492-515). New York: Survey Associates.

Kelly, A. & Sewell, S. (1988). *With head, heart, and hand: Dimensions of community building* (4th ed.). Brisbane, Qld: Boolarong Press.

Kennedy, A. (1953). *The settlement heritage*. Presentation at the National Conference of Social Work. Retrieved January 26, 2006, from http://www.ifsnetwork.org/uploads/THESETTLEMENTHERITAGE.pdf

Kensington Welfare Rights Union (2006). Mission statement. KWRU Home Page: Retrieved July 12, 2006, from http://www.kwru.org

Kirst-Ashman, K. & Hull, G. (2001). *Generalist practice with organizations and communities*. (2nd ed.) Belmont, Ca: Wadsworth.

Kirst-Ashman, K. & Hull, G. (2006). *Understanding generalist practice* (4th ed.). Belmont, CA: Thomson Higher Education.

Kivnick, H. & Murray, S. (2001). Life strengths interview guide: Assessing elder clients' strengths. *Journal of Gerontological Social Work, 34*(4), 7-32.

Kleinman, A. (1980). *Patients and healers in the context of culture: An exploration of the borderland between anthropology, medicine, and psychiatry.* Berkeley: University of California Press.

Korten, D. (2001). *When corporations rule the world* (2nd ed.). West Hartford, CN: Kumarian Press.

Kotlowitz, A. (1991). *There are no children here.* New York: Doubleday.

Kozol, J. (1991). *Savage inequalities: Children in America's schools.* New York: Crown.

Kreuger, L. (1997). The end of social work. *Journal of Social Work Education, 33*(1), 19-27.

Krueger, R. (1994). *Focus groups: A practical guide for applied research.* Thousand Oaks, CA: Sage Publications.

Krueger, R. & King, J. (1998). *Involving community members in focus groups.* Thousand Oaks, CA: Sage Publications.

Kübler-Ross, E. (1970). *On death and dying.* New York: MacMillan.

Kuruvilla, S. (2005). Social Work and development in India. In I. Ferguson, M. Lavalette, & E. Whitmore (Eds.), *Globalisation, global justice and social work* (pp. 41-54). New York: Routledge.

Laird, J. (Ed.). (1993a). *Revisioning social work education: A social constructivist approach.* New York: Haworth.

Laird, J. (1993b). Theorizing culture: Narrative ideas and practice principles. In M. McGoldrick (Ed.), *Revisioning family therapy* (2nd ed.). New York: Guilford.

Landon, P. (1999). *Generalist social work practice.* Dubuque: Eddie Bowers Publishing.

Lappe, F.M. & DuBois, P.M. (1994). *The quickening of America: Rebuilding our nation, remaking our lives.* San Francisco, CA: Jossey-Bass, Inc. Publishers.

Lather, P. (1986). Research as praxis. *Harvard Educational Review, 56*(3), 257-277.

Lather, P. (1991). *Getting smart: Feminist research and pedagogy with/in the postmodern.* New York: Routledge.

Lawrence, J. (2000). The Indian Health Service and the sterilization of Native American women. *The American Indian Quarterly, 24*(3), 400-419.

Ledwith, M. & Asgill, P. (2000). Critical alliance: Black and white women working together for social justice. *Community Development Journal, 35*(3), 290-299.

Lee, J. (1992). Jane Addams in Boston: Intersecting time and space. *Social Work with Groups*, 15 (2/3), 7-21.

Lee, P. (1930). Cause and function. In *Proceedings of the National Conference of Social Work 1929* (pp. 3 -20). Chicago: University of Chicago Press.

Lemert, C. (2004). *Social theory: Multicultural and classical readings.* Boulder: Westview Press.

Lengermann, P. & Niebrugge-Brantly, J. (1998). *The women founders: Sociology and social theory, 1830-1930.* Boston: McGraw-Hill.

Leonard, P. (1997). *Postmodern welfare: Reconstructing an emancipatory project.* London: Sage.

Levi-Strauss, C. (1966). *The savage mind* (2nd ed.). Chicago: University of Chicago Press.

Levy, C. S. (1973). The value base of social work. *Journal of Education for Social Work, 9*(1), 34-42.

Levy, C. S. (1976). *Social work ethics.* New York: Human Sciences Press.

Lieberman, A. & Lester, C. (Eds.). (2004). *Social work practice with a difference.* Boston: McGraw-Hill.

Lightfoot, E., Pappas, V., & Chait, J. (2003). Using Open Space Technology to enable citizens to set the agenda for state disabilities planning. *Journal of Disability Policy Studies, 14*(1), 7-16.

Limbert, W. & Bullock, H. (2005). 'Play the fool': US welfare policy from a critical race perspective. *Feminism and Psychology, 15*(3), 253-274.

Lincoln, Y. & Guba, E. (1985). *Naturalistic inquiry.* Newbury Park, CA: Sage Publications.

Lindsey, D. & Kirk, S. (1992). The role of social work journals in the development of a knowledge base for the profession. *Social Service Review, 66*(2), 295-310.

Link, B. G. & Phelan, J. C. (2001). On the nature and consequences of stigma. *Annual Review of Sociology, 27*, 363-385.

Link, R. (1999). Infusing global perspectives into social work values and ethics. In C. Ramanathan & R. Link (Eds.), *All our futures: Social work practice in a global era* (pp. 69-93). Belmont, CA: Wadsworth.

Link, R. Ramanathan, C., & Asamoah, Y. (1999). Understanding the human condition and human behavior in a global era. In C. Ramanathan & R. Link (Eds.), *All our futures: Social work practice in a global era* (pp. 30-51). Belmont: CA: Wadsworth Publishing.

Lister, R. (2004). *Poverty.* Cambridge, UK.: Polity Press.

Locke, B., Garrison, R., & Winship, J. (1998). *Generalist social work practice: Context, story, and partnerships*. Pacific Grove, CA: Brooks/Cole.

Loewenberg, F. & Dolgoff, R. (1996). *Ethical decisions for social work practice* (5th ed.). Itasca, IL: F. E. Peacock.

Loewenberg, F., Dolgoff, R., & Harrington, D. (2000). *Ethical decisions for social work practice* (6th ed.). Itasca, IL: F. E. Peacock.

Longres, J. & McLeod, E. (1980). Consciousness raising and social work practice. *Social Casework, 61*, 267-277.

Lott. B. (2002). Cognitive and behavioral distancing from the poor. *American Psychologist, 57*(2), 100-110.

Lowe, L. & Lloyd, D. (1997). *The politics of culture in the shadow of capital*. Durham, NC: Duke University Press.

Lum, D. (1992). *Social work with people of color: A process stage approach* (2nd ed.). Pacific Grove, CA: Brooks Cole.

Lum, D. (1999) *Culturally competent practice: A framework for growth and action*. New York: Wadsworth.

Lyons, K. (1999). *International social work: Themes and perspectives*. Brookfield, VT: Ashgate Publishing.

Mackelprang, R. & Salsgiver, R. (1996). People with disabilities and social work: Historical and contemporary issues. *Social Work, 41*(1), 7-14.

Macklin, A. (2003). Dancing across borders: 'Exotics dancers,' trafficking, and Canadian immigration policy. *International Migration Review, 37*(2), 464-500.

Maguire, P. (1987). *Doing participatory research: A feminist approach*. Amherst, MA: The Center for International Education, University of Massachusetts.

Magnuson, S. & Shaw, H. (2003). Adaptations of the multifaceted genogram in counseling, training and supervision. *The Family Journal: Counseling and Therapy for Couples and Families, 11*(1), 45-54.

Marable, M. (1997). *Speaking truth to power: Essays on race, resistance and radicalism*. Boulder: Westview Press.

Marable, M. (1999). *How capitalism underdeveloped Black America*. Boston: South End Press.

Margolin, L. (1997). *Under the cover of kindness: The invention of social work*. Richmond: University of Virginia Press.

Marion, M. (1996). Living in an era of multiple loss and trauma: Understanding global loss in the gay community. In C. Alexander (Ed.), *Gay and lesbian mental health: A sourcebook for practitioners* (pp. 61-94). Binghamton, NY: Harrington Park Press.

Marlow, C. (2005). *Research methods for generalist social work* (4th ed.). Belmont, CA: Brooks/Cole.

Matson, F. & Montagu, A. (1967). *The human dialogue: Perspectives on communication.* New York: Free Press.

Matsubara, N. (1992). Social work in Japan: Responding to demographic dilemmas. In M. C. Hokenstad, S. K. Khinduka, & J. Midgley (Eds.), *Profiles in international social work* (pp. 85-90). Washington, DC: NASW Press.

Mayadas, N. & Elliott, D. (1992). Integration and xenophobia: An inherent conflict in international migration. *Journal of Multicultural Social Work, 2*(1), 47-62.

Mayer, S. (1996). Building community capacity with evaluation activities that empower. In D. M. Fetterman, S. J. Faftarian, & A. Wandersman (Eds.), *Empowerment evaluation: Knowledge and tools for self-assessment and accountability* (pp. 332-375). Thousand Oaks, CA: Sage Publications.

Mayo, G. (1933). *The human problems of an industrial civilization.* Boston: Harvard Business School, Division of Research.

McFadden, R. (2006, April 10). Across the U.S.: Growing rallies for immigration. New York Times. Retrieved June 8, 2006, from http://www.commondreams.org

McIntosh, P. (1995). White privilege and male privilege: A personal account of coming to see correspondences through work in women's studies. In M. Anderson & P. Hill Collins, *Race, class, and gender: An anthology* (2nd ed., pp. 76-87). Belmont, CA: Wadsworth Publishing.

McKnight, J. & Kretzmann, J. (1990). Mapping community capacity. Report of the Neighborhood Innovations Network. Evanston, Ill.: Northwestern University Institute for Policy Research.

McLaren, P. & Farahmandpur, R. (2006). The pedagogy of oppression: A brief look at 'No Child Left Behind.' *Monthly Review, 58*(3), 94-99.

Medoza Rangel, M. (2005). Social work in Mexico: Towards a different practice. In I. Ferguson, M. Lavalette, & E. Whitmore (Eds.), *Globalisation, global justice, and social work* (pp. 11-22). New York: Routledge.

Mendoza Strobel, L. (2003). The maid of the world. *The Other Side, 39*(5), 46-51.

Merriam-Webster. (2005). *Merriam Webster collegiate dictionary.* Springfield, MA: Author.

Merriam-Webster Online. (2006). Retrieved July 25, 2006, from http://www.m-w.com/dictionary/theory

Mesothelioma Research Foundation of America. (2006). *Patient stories: Libby, Montana: A town rife with asbestos disease.* Retrieved July 12, 2006, from http://www.mesorfa.org

Mezirow, J. (1998). On critical reflection. *Adult Education Quarterly, 48*(3), 185-198.

Michael, S. (2005). The promise of Appreciative Inquiry as an interview tool for field research. *Development in Practice, 15*(2), 222-230.

Midgley, J. (1997). Social work in international context: Challenges and opportunities for the 21ˢᵗ century. In M. Reisch & E. Gambrill (Eds.), *Social work in the 21ˢᵗ century* (pp. 59-67). Thousand Oaks, CA.: Pine Forge Press.

Miley, K., O'Melia, M., & DuBois, B. (2007). *Generalist social work practice: An empowering perspective* (5ᵗʰ ed.).Boston: Allyn and Bacon.

Miller, D. (1976). *Social justice.* Oxford: Clarendon Press.

Miller, P. (1998). *Hunger, welfare reform, and non-profits: Food banks and churches.* Missoula, Department of Sociology, University of Montana.

Mohanty, C. (1991). Under western eyes: Feminist scholarship and colonial discourses. In C. Mohanty, A. Russo, & L. Torres (Eds.), *Third world women and the politics of feminism* (pp. 1-47). Bloomington, IN: University of Indiana Press.

Mohanty, C. (2003). *Feminism without borders: Decolonizing theory, practicing solidarity.* Durham, London: Duke University Press.

Mohanty, C., Russo, A., & Torres, L. (Eds.). (1991). *Third world women and the politics of feminism.* Bloomington, IN: University of Indiana Press.

Moore, M. (1996). *Downsize this.* New York: Crown Publishers.

Moraga, C. & Anzaldúa, G. (Eds.). (1983). *This bridge called my back. Writings by radical women of color.* New York: Kitchen Table/Women of Color Press.

Moreau, M. (1977). A structural approach to social work. Unpublished manuscript, School of Social Work, Carleton University, Ottowa.

Moreau, M. (1979). A structural approach to social work practice. *Canadian Journal of Social Work Education, 5*(1), 78-94.

Morgan, D. L. (1988). *Focus groups as qualitative research.* Newbury Park, CA: Sage Publications.

Morgan, J. T. (1889). Annual report of the Commissioner of Indian Affairs. In W. Washburn (Ed.) (1973). *The American Indian and the United States: A documentary history, V. 1* (pp. 434+). New York: Random House.

Morgan, J. T. (1890). Annual report of the Commissioner of Indian Affairs. In W. Washburn (Ed.), *The American Indian and the United States: A documentary history, V. 2* (pp. 44+). New York: Random House.

Mullaly, R. (1997). *Structural social work: Ideology, theory and practice* (2ⁿᵈ ed.). Oxford: Oxford University Press.

Murphy, B. & Dillon, C. (1998). *Interviewing in action: Process and practice.* Pacific Grove, CA: Brooks/Cole.

Nagenast, C. & Turner, T. (1997). Introduction: Universal human rights versus cultural relativity. *Journal of Anthropological Research, 53*(3), 269-272.

Nakanishi, M. & Ritter, B. (1992). The inclusionary cultural model. *Journal of Social Work Education, 28*(1), 27-35.

Naples, N. (1998). *Grassroots warriors: Activist mothering, community work, and the war on poverty.* New York: Routledge.

Nasuti, J., York, R., & Henley, H. (2003). Teaching social work research: Does andragogy work best? *Journal of Baccalaureate Social Work, 9*(1), 149-173.

National Association of Black Social Workers. (1971). *Code of Ethics of the National Association of Black Social Workers.* Detroit, MI: Author.

National Association of Social Workers. (1977). *Encyclopedia of social work.* New York: Author.

National Association of Social Workers. (1979). *Code of Ethics of the National Association of Social Workers.* Washington, DC: Author.

National Association of Social Workers. (1999). *Code of Ethics of the National Association of Social Workers.* Washington, DC: Author.

National Association of Social Workers. (2003). *Social work dictionary.* Washington, DC: Author.

Nearing, S. (1916). *Poverty and riches: A study of the industrial regime.* Philadelphia, PA: The John C. Winston Company.

Nelson, S. & Baldwin, N. (2004). The Craigmillar Project: Neighbourhood mapping to improve children's safety from sexual crime. *Child Abuse Review, 13,* 415-425.

Nelson, C. Treichler, P., & Grossberg, L. (1992). Cultural studies. In L. Grossberg, C. Nelson, & P. Treichler (Eds.), *Cultural studies* (pp. 1-16). New York: Routledge.

Nerney, T. (2004). The promise of freedom for persons with psychiatric disabilities. In J. Jonikas & J. Cook (Eds.), *UIC NRIC's national self-determination and psychiatric disability invitational conference papers* (p. 129+). Chicago: University of Illinois.

Netting, F. E., Kettner, P. M., & McMurtry, S. (1998). *Social work macro practice.* (2nd ed.) New York: Longman.

Netting, F.E. & O'Connor, K. (2003). *Organization practice: A social worker's guide to understanding human services.* Boston: Allyn and Bacon.

Neuman, W. & Kreuger, L. (2003). *Social research methods: Qualitative and quantitative approaches.* Needham Heights, MA: Allyn and Bacon.

Nicholson, L. (1986). *Gender and history: The limits of social theory in the age of the family*. New York: Columbia University Press.

Nordstrom, C. (1999). Visible wars and invisible girls, shadow industries, and the politics of not-knowing. *International Feminist Journal of Politics, 1*(1), 14-33.

O'Brien, M. (1995*). Jeannette Rankin, 1880-1973: Bright star in the big sky*. Helena, Montana: Falcon Press.

O'Connor, A. (2001*). Poverty knowledge: Social science, social policy, and the poor in twentieth-century U.S. history*. New Jersey: Princeton University Press.

O'Connor, D. & O'Neill, B. (2004). Toward social justice: Teaching qualitative research. *Journal of Teaching in Social Work, 24*(3/4), 19-33.

Okamoto, T. and Kuroki, Y. (1997). Japan. In N. Mayadas, T. Watts, & D. Elliott (Eds.), *International handbook on social work theory and practice* (pp. 263-281). Westport, CT: Greenwood Press.

Ong, A. (1987). *Spirits of resistance and capitalist discipline: Factory women in Malaysia*. Albany: SUNY Press.

Ortner, S. (1984). Theory in anthropology since the sixties. *Comparative Studies in Society and History. 26*(19), 126-66.

Ortner, S. (1989) *High religion*. Princeton: Princeton University Press.

Ortner, S. (1994). Theory in anthropology since the sixties. In N. Dirks, G. Eley, & S. Ortner (Eds.), *A reader in contemporary social theory*. Princeton, NJ: Princeton University Press.

Ortner, S. (1996). *Making gender: The politics and erotics of culture*. Boston: Beacon Press.

Ortner, S. & Whitehead, H. (Eds.). (1981). *Sexual meanings*. Cambridge: Cambridge University Press.

Owen, H. (1997a). *Expanding our now: The story of open space technology*. San Francisco: Berrett-Koehler.

Owen, H. (1997b). *Open space technology: A user's guide*. San Francisco: Berrett-Koehler.

Ozawa, M. (1997). Demographic changes and their implications. In M. Reisch & E. Gambrill (Eds.), *Social work in the 21st century* (pp. 8-27). Thousand Oaks, CA: Pine Forge Press.

Park, P. (1993). What is participatory research: A theoretical and methodological perspective. In P. Park, M. Brydon-Miller, B. Hall, & T. Jackson (Eds.), *Voices of change: Participatory research in the United States and Canada* (pp. 1-19). Westport, CT: Bergin & Garvey.

Park, P. (1997). Participatory research, democracy and community. *Practicing Anthropology, 19*(3). 8-13.

Parsons, R. (1991). Empowerment: Purpose and practice principle in social work. *Social Work with Groups, 14*, 7-21.

Parton, N. (Ed.). (1996). *Social theory, social change, and social work.* London: Routledge.

Patton, M. (1975). *Alternative evaluation research paradigm.* Grand Forks, ND: University of North Dakota.

Payne, M. (2005). *Modern social work theory.* Chicago: Lyceum Books.

Pease, B. & Fook, J. (Eds.). (1999). *Transforming social work practice: Postmodern critical perspectives.* New York: Routledge.

Peebles-Wilkins, W. & Francis, E. (1990). Two outstanding black women in social welfare history: Mary Church Terrell and Ida B. Wells-Barnett. *Affilia: Journal of Women and Social Work, 5*(4), 87-100.

Perlman, Helen Harris. (1957). *Social casework: A problem solving process.* Chicago: University of Chicago Press.

Perlman, Helen Harris. (1979). *Relationship: The heart of helping people.* Chicago: University of Chicago Press.

Pernell, R. (1985). Empowerment and social group work. In M. Parenes (Ed.), *Innovations in social group work: Feedback from practice to theory* (pp. 107-117). New York: Hawthorn.

Perry, J. (Ed.). (2002). *Restorative justice: Repairing communities through restorative justice.* Lanham, MD: American Correctional Association.

Peterfreund, D. (1992). *Great traditions in ethics* (7th ed.). Belmont, CA: Wadsworth Publishing.

Pfohl, S. (1977). The discovery of child abuse. *Social Problems, 24*, 310-323.

Phadke, R. (2005). People's science in action: The politics of protest and knowledge brokering in India. *Society and Natural Resources, 18*, 363-375.

Picht, W. (1916). *Toynbee Hall and the Settlement Movement.* London: G. Bell and Sons, Ltd.

Pimlott, S. & Sarri, R. (2002). The forgotten group: Women in prisons and jails. In Figueira-McDonough, J. & Sarri, R. (Eds.), *Women at the margins: Neglect, punishment, and resistance* (pp. 55-84). New York: Haworth Press.

Pincus, F. (2000). Discrimination comes in many forms: Individual, instituional, and structural. In M. Adams, W. J. Blumenfeld, R. Castenada, H. W. Hackman, M. L. Peters, & X. Zuniga (Eds.), *Readings for diversity and social justice* (31-34). New York: Routledge.

Pincus, A. & Minahan, A. (1973). *Social work practice: Model and method.* Itasca, IL: F.E. Peacock Publishers.

Pincus, A. & Minahan, A. (1977). A conceptual framework for social work practice. *Social Work, 22*(5). 347-352.

Piven, F. F. & Cloward, R. (1997). *The breaking of the American social compact.* New York: Free Press.

Plastas, M. A. (2001). *"A band of noble women": The WILPF and the politics and consciousness of race in the women's peace movement, 1915 - 1945.* Unpublished doctoral dissertation, State University of New York, Buffalo.

Polack, R. (2004). Social justice and the global economy: New challenges for social work in the 21st century. *Social Work, 49*(2), 281-290.

Pothukuchi, K., Joseph, H., Fisher, A., & Burton, H. (2002). *What's cooking in your food system? A guide to community food assessment.* Venice, CA: Community Food Security Coalition.

Private prisons see rising profits. (2005, February 15). *Alcoholism and Drug Abuse Weekly, 17*(7), 7.

Prison: The clang of the gate. (2006, June 24). *Economist, 379*(8483), 64.

Ramanathan, C. & Link, R. (Eds.). (1999). *All our futures: Principles and resources for social work practice in a global era.* Belmont: CA: Wadsworth.

Rangel, M. & del Carmen, M. (2005). Social work in Mexico: Towards a different practice (Mike Gonzalez, Trans., University of Glasgow). In I. Ferguson, M. Lavalette, & E. Whitmore (Eds.), *Globalisation, global justice and social work* (pp. 81-93). New York: Routledge.

Rao, A. (1995). The politics of gender and culture in international human rights discourse. In J. Peters & A. Wolper (Eds.), *Women's rights, human rights: International feminist perspectives* (pp. 176-188). New York: Routledge.

Rappaport, J., Davidson, W., Wilson, M., & Mitchell, A. (1975). Alternatives to blaming the victim or the environment: Our places to stand have not moved the earth. *American Psychologist, 30*, 525-528.

Rawls, J. (1995). *A theory of justice.* (2nd ed.). Cambridge, MA: Harvard University Press. (Originally published in 1971)

Reamer, F. (1994). Social work values and ethics. In F. Reamer (Ed.), *The foundations of social work knowledge* (pp. 195-230). New York: Columbia University Press.

Reamer, F. (1995). *Social work values and ethics.* New York: Columbia University.

Reamer, F. (1998). *Ethical standards in social work: A critical review of the NASW code of ethics.* Washington, DC: National Association of Social Workers.

Reason, P. & Rowan, J. (Eds). (1981). *Human inquiry: A sourcebook of new paradigm research.* New York: John Wiley and Sons.

Reed, B. G., Newman, P., Suarez, Z., & Lewis, E. (1997). Interpersonal practice beyond diversity and toward social justice: The importance of critical consciousness. In C. Garvin & B. Seabury (Eds.), *Interpersonal practice in social work: Promoting competence and social justice* (2nd ed., pp. 44-78). Boston: Allyn and Bacon.

Reese, W. (1980). *Dictionary of philosophy and religion.* Atlantic Highlands, NJ: Humanities Press.

Reese, D. (2004). Risk of domestic violence after natural disaster: Teaching research and statistics through the use of a participatory action research model. *Journal of Teaching in Social Work, 24*(3/4), 79-94.

Reichert, E. (2003). *Social work and human rights: A foundation for policy and practice.* New York: Columbia University Press.

Reichert, K. (1965). Introductory remarks. *Social Work, 10*(Suppl. 4), 140-141.

Reinhartz, S. (1992). *Feminist methods in social research.* New York: Oxford University Press.

Reisch, M. (1988). The uses of history in teaching social work. *Journal of Teaching in Social Work, 2*(1), 3-16.

Reisch, M. (1993). Lessons from the history of social work for our time. *The Jewish Social Work Forum, 29,* 3-27.

Reisch, M. (1997). The political context of social work. In M. Reisch & E. Gambrill (Eds.), *Social work in the 21st century* (pp. 80-92). Thousand Oaks, CA: Pine Forge Press.

Reisch, M. (1998a). Economic globalization and the future of the welfare state. Welfare Reform and Social Justice Visiting Scholars Program. Ann Arbor: The University of Michigan School of Social Work.

Reisch, M. (1998b). The sociopolitical context and social work method, 1890-1950. *Social Service Review, 72*(2), 163-181.

Reisch, M. (2005). American exceptionalism and critical social work: A retrospective and prospective analysis. In I. Ferguson, M. Lavalette & E. Whitmore (Eds), *Globalisation, global justice, and social work* (pp. 157-172). New York: Routledge.

Reisch, M. & Andrews, J. (2001). *The road not taken: a history of radical social work in the United States.* New York: Brunner/Routledge.

Reisch, M. & Wenocur, S. (1986). The future of community organization in social work: Social activism and the politics of profession building. *Social Service Review, 60*(1), 70-91.

Reisch, M., Wenocur, S., & Sherman, W. (1981). Empowerment, conscientization, and animation as core social work skills. *Social Development Issues, 5*(2/3), 108-120.

Reynolds, B. C. (1934). Between client and community. *Smith College Studies in Social Work, 5*(1).

Reynolds, B. C. (1942). *Learning and teaching in the practice of social work.* New York: Farrar & Rinehart, Inc.

Reynolds, B. C. (1963). *An uncharted journey.* Washington, DC: NASW Press.

Reynolds, B. C. (1987). *Social work and social living.* Silver Spring, MD: NASW Press. (Originally published in 1951)

Reynolds, B. C. (1992). Rethinking social case work. *Journal of Progressive Human Services, 3*(1), 73-84. (Originally published in 1932)

Rhodes, M. (1986). *Ethical dilemmas in social work practice.* Boston: Routledge and Kegan Paul.

Richmond, M. (1917). *Social diagnosis.* New York: Russell Sage Foundation.

Richmond, M. (1922). *What is social case work? An introductory description.* New York: Russell Sage Foundation.

Richmond, M. (1930). *The long view.* New York: Russell Sage Foundation.

Riding In, J. (1996). Reservations. In F. E. Hoxie (Ed.), *Encyclopedia of North American Indians.* New York. Houghon Mifflin. Retrieved July 20, 2006, from http://college.hmco.com/history/readerscomp

Rief, M. (2004). Thinking locally, acting globally: The international agenda of African American Clubwomen, 1880-1940. *The Journal of African American History, 89*(3), 203-222.

Riis, J. (1890). *How the other half lives.* New York: Charles Scribner and Sons.

Robbins, S. P., Chatterjee, P., & Canda, E. R. (1999). Ideology, scientific theory, and social work practice. *Families in Society, 80*(4), 374-384.

Robbins, S. P., Chatterjee, P., & Canda, E. R. (2006). *Contemporary human behavior theory: A critical perspective for social work* (2nd ed.). Needham Heights, MA: Allyn & Bacon.

Roby, P. (1998). Creating a just world: Leadership for the twenty-first century. *Social Problems, 45*(1), 1-20.

Rogers, C.(1951). *Client-centered therapy: Its current practice implications and theory.* Boston: Houghton Mifflin.

Rogers, C. Gendlin, E. Kiesler, D., & Truax, C. (1967). *The therapeutic relationship and its impact: A study of psychotherapy with schizophrenics.* Madison: University of Wisconsin Press.

Rosaldo, M. & Lamphere, L. (Eds). (1974). *Women, culture, and society.* Stanford: Stanford University Press.

Rosaldo, R. (1989). *Culture and truth: The remaking of social analysis.* Boston: Beacon Press.

Rose, N. (1997). The future economic landscape: Implications for social work practice and education. In M. Reisch & E. Gambrill (Eds.), *Social work in the 21st century* (pp. 28-38). Thousand Oaks, CA: Pine Forge Press.

Rose, S. (2000). Reflections on empowerment based practice. *Social Work, 45*(5), 403-412.

Rossi, P. & Freeman, H. (1993). *Evaluation: A systematic approach.* Newbury Park, CA: Sage Publications.

Rossiter, A. (1996). A perspective on critical social work. *Journal of Progressive Human Services, 7*(2), 23-441.

Rossiter, A. (2005). Where in the world are we? Notes on the need for a social work response to global power. In S. Hick, J. Fook, & R. Pozzuto (Eds.), *Social work: A critical turn* (pp. 189-202). Toronto: Thompson Educational Publishing, Inc.

Rossiter, A., de Boer, C., Narayan, J., Razack, N., Scollay, V., & Gillette, C. (1998). Toward an alternative account of feminist practice ethics in mental health. *Affilia: Journal of Women and Social Work, 13*(1), 9-22.

Rouse, R. (1995). Thinking through transnationalism: Notes on the cultural politics of class relations in the contemporary United States. *Public Culture, 7,* 353-402.

Royse, D. (1999). *Research methods in social work.* Chicago: Nelson-Hall.

Rubin, A. & Babbie, E. (2005). *Research methods for social work* (5th ed.). Belmont, CA: Wadsworth/Thompson Learning.

Sakamoto, I. & Pitner, R. (2005). Use of critical consciousness in anti-oppressive social work practice: Disentangling power dynamics at personal and structural levels. *British Journal of Social Work, 35,* 435-452.

Sahlins, M. (1981). *Historical metaphors and mythical realities: Structure in the early history of the Sandwich Island Kingdom.* Ann Arbor: University of Michigan Press.

Saleebey, D. (1990). Philosophical disputes in social work: Social justice denied. *Journal of Sociology and Social Welfare, 17*(2), 29-40.

Saleebey, D. (1993). Theory and the generation and subversion of knowledge. *Journal of Sociology and Social Welfare, 20*(1), 5-25.

Saleebey, D. (1994). Culture, theory, and narrative: the intersection of meanings in practice. *Social Work, 39*(4), 351-359.

Saleebey, D. (2001). The diagnostic strengths manual? *Social Work, 46*(2), 183-187.

Saleebey, D. (Ed.). (2006). *The strengths perspective in social work practice* (4th ed.). Boston: Pearson Education, Inc.

Sapey, B. (2003). [Review of the book *Anti-oppressive social work theory and practice*]. *Disability and Society, 18*(3), 381-388.

Sarr, F. (2005). Changes in social policy and the social services of Senegal (Andrew Stafford, Trans., University of Leeds). In I. Ferguson, M. Lavalette, & E. Whitmore (Eds), *Globalisation, global justice, and social work* (pp. 55-65). New York: Routledge.

Sarri, R. (1988). The impact of federal policy change on the well-being of poor women and children. In P. Voydanoff & L. Majka (Eds.), *Families and economic distress* (pp. 209-232). Newbury Park, CA: Sage Publication.

Sarri, R. (1997). International social work at the millennium. In M. Reisch & E. Gambrill (Eds.), *Social work in the 21st century* (pp. 387-395). Thousand Oaks, CA: Pine Forge Press.

Sayce, L. (2005). Risk, rights and anti-discrimination work in mental health: Avoiding the risks in considering risk. In R. Adams, L. Dominelli, & M. Payne (Eds.), *Social work futures: Crossing boundaries, transforming practices* (pp. 167-181). New York: Palgrave/MacMillan.

Schein, E. (1969). *Process consultation*. Reading, MA: Addison Wesley.

Schein, E. (1992). *Organizational culture and leadership* (2nd ed.) San Francisco: Jossey-Bass.

Schlosser, E. (1998, December). The prison industrial complex. *Atlantic Monthly*, 51-77.

Schnieider, R. & Netting, E. (1999). Influencing social policy in a time of devolution: Upholding social work's great tradition. *Social Work, 44*(4), 349-357.

Schorr, L. (1997). *Common purpose: Strengthening families and neighborhoods to rebuild America*. New York: Anchor Books.

Schreiber, M. (1995). Labeling a social worker a national security risk: A memoir. *Social Work, 40*(5), 656-660.

Schriver, J. (2004). *Human behavior in the social environment* (4th ed.). Needham Heights, MA: Allyn & Bacon.

Schwartz, W. (1971). Social group work: The interactional approach. *Encyclopedia of Social Work*, V. II (p. 1255). New York: NASW.

Schwartz, W. (1986). The group work tradition and social work practice. *Social Work with Groups, 8*(4), 7-27. (Originally published in 1961)

Scott, D. (2002). Adding meaning to measurement: The value of qualitative methods in practice research. *British Journal of Social Work, 32*, 923-930.

Scott, J. (1985). *Weapons of the weak: Everyday forms of resistance.* New Haven: Yale University Press.

Segura, D. & Pearce, J. (1993). Chicano/a family structure and gender personality: Chodorow, familism, and psychoanalytic sociology revisited. *Signs, 19*, 62-91.

Seldes, G. (Ed.). (1985). *The great thoughts.* New York: Balantine Books.

Selmi, P. & Hunter, R. (2001). *Beyond the rank and file movement: Mary van Kleeck and social work radicalism in the Great Depression, 1931-1942.* Journal of Sociology and Social Welfare, *28*(2), 75-100.

Sen, R. (1994). Building community involvement in health care. *Social Policy, 24*(3), 32-43.

Sen, R. (2003). *Stir it up: Lessons in community organizing and advocacy.* San Francisco: John Wiley & Sons.

Sewell, W. (1992). A theory of structure: Duality, agency, and transformation. *American Journal of Sociology, 98*(1), 1-29.

Sheafor, B., Horejsi, C., & Horejsi, G. (2006). *Techniques and guidelines for social work practice* (7th ed.). Boston: Allyn and Bacon.

Sherman, R. (1993). The intimacy genogram. *The Family Journal, 1*, 91-93.

Shor, I. (1980). *Critical teaching and everyday life.* Boston: South End Press.

Schriver, J (2004). *Human behavior and the social environment: Shifting paradigms in essential knowledge for social work practice* (4th ed.). Boston: Pearson/Allyn and Bacon.

Shulman, L. (1986). The dynamics of mutual aid. In A. Gitterman & L. Shulman (Eds.), *The legacy of William Schwartz* (pp. 51-60). Binghamton, NY; Haworth.

Shulman, L. (1992). *The skills of helping individuals, families and groups* (3rd ed.). Itasca, IL: F. E. Peacock Publishers.

Simon, B. (1994). *The empowerment tradition in American social work: A history.* New York: Columbia University Press.

Simon, B. (2002). Women of conscience: Jeannette Rankin and Barbara Lee. *Affilia: Journal of Women and Social Work, 17*(3), 384-388.

Skegg, A. (2005). Human rights and social work: Western imposition or empowerment to the people? *International Social Work, 48*(5), 667-672.

Smith, B. (1985). Business, politics, and Indian land settlement in Montana, 1881-1904, *Canadian Journal of History, 20*(1), 45-64.

Smith, D. (1987). *The everyday world as problematic: A feminist sociology.* Toronto: University of Toronto Press.

Smith, D. (1990). *The conceptual practices of power: A feminist sociology of knowledge.* Boston: Northeastern University Press.

Smith, L. Tuhiwai. (1999). *Decolonizing methodologies: Research and indigenous people.* London: Zed.

Solomon, B. (1976). *Black empowerment.* New York: Columbia University Press.

Specht, H. & Courtney. M. (1994). *Unfaithful angels: How social work has abandoned its mission.* New York: Free Press.

Spratt, T., Houston, S., & Magill, T. (2000). Imaging the future: Theatre and change within the child protection system. *Child and Family Social Work, 5,* 117-127.

Srikandath, S. (1991, May). *Social change via people's theatre.* Paper presented at the 41st Annual Convention of the International Communications Association, Chicago, IL.

Stack, C. (1974). *All our kin: Strategies for survival in a black community.* New York: Harper and Row.

Stack, C. (1990). Different visions: Gender, culture, and moral reasoning. In F. Ginsberg & A. Lowenhaupt Tsing (Eds.), *Uncertain terms: Negotiating gender in American culture.* Boston: Beacon, 19-27.

Stack, C. & Burton, L. (1993). Kinscripts. *Journal of Comparative Family Studies, 24,* 157-170.

Stake, R.E. (1995). *The art of case study research.* Thousand Oaks, CA: Sage Publications. *standards.* Berne: Switzerland.

Steng, J., Rhodes, S., Ayala, G., Eng, E., Arceo, R., & Phipps, S. (2004). *Realidad Latina*: Latino adolescents, their school, and a university use photovoice to examine and address the influences of immigration. *Journal of Interprofessional Care, 18*(4), 403-415.

Stern, M. (1997). Poverty and postmodernity. In M. Reisch & E. Gambrill (Eds.), *Social work in the 21st century* (pp. 48-58). Thousand Oaks, CA: Pine Forge Press.

Sternbach, J. (2000). Lessons learned abut working with men: A prison memoir. *Social Work 45*(5), 413-423.

Strom-Gottfried, K. (1999). *Social work practice: Cases, activities, and exercises.* Thousand Oaks, CA: Pine Forge Press.

Sue, D. W. (1981). *Counseling the culturally different: Theory and practice.* New York: John Wiley & Sons.

Sullivan, M. (1993). Social work's legacy of peace: Echoes from the early 20th century. *Social Work, 38*(5), 513-520.

Swigonski, M. (1994). The logic of feminist standpoint theory for social work research. *Social Work, 39*(4). 387-393.

Takaki, R. (1979). *Iron cages: race and culture in nineteenth century America.* New York: Knopf.

Takaki, R. (1993). *A different mirror: A history of multicultural America.* Boston: Little, Brown.

Talley, B., Rushing, A., & Gee, R.M. (2005). Community assessment using Cowling's Unitary Appreciative Inquiry: A beginning exploration. *Journal of Rogerian Nursing, 13*(1), 27-40.

Taylor, F. (1947). *Scientific Management.* New York: Harper and Row. (Originally published in 1911)

Tew, J. (2006). Understanding power and powerlessness. *Journal of Social Work, 6*(1), 33-51.

Thompson, E. P. (1966). *The making of the English working class.* New York: Vintage.

Thompson, L. (1992). Feminist methodology for family studies. *Journal of Marriage and the Family, 54*, 3-18.

Thorne, B. & Yalom, M. (1982). *Rethinking the family: Some feminist questions.* New York: Longman.

Tice, K. (1998). *Tales of wayward girls and immoral women.* Chicago: University of Illinois Press.

Todd, A. J. (1920). *The scientific spirit and social work.* NY: Macmillan.

Tonn, M. (1996). Militant motherhood: Labor's Mary Harris "Mother" Jones. *Quarterly Journal of Free Speech, 82*(10), 1-21.

Tonnies, F. (1957). *Community and society* (C. Loomis, Trans. and Ed.). New York: Harper & Row.

Towle, C. (1945). A social work approach to course in growth and behavior. *Social Service Review, 34*, 402-414.

Townsend, J., Zapata, E., Rowlands, J., Alberti, P. & Mercado, M. (1999). *Women and power: Fighting patriarchies and poverty.* London: Zed Books.

Tropman, J. (1984). *Policy management in the human services.* New York: Columbia University Press.

Turner, T. (1997). Human rights, human difference: Anthropology's contribution to an emancipatory cultural politics. *Journal of Anthropological Research, 53*(3), 273-291.

UNAIDS. (1999). HIV/AIDS in Africa: A socioeconomic response. Geneva, New York: Joint UN Programme on HIV/AIDS.

United Nations Children's Fund. (2005). The state of the world's children 2006: Excluded and invisible. New York: Author.

United Nations Development Programme. (2005). Human development report 2005: International cooperation at a crossroads. New York: Author.

United States Catholic Bishops. (1986). Economic justice for all: Pastoral letter on Catholic social teaching and the U.S. economy. Washington, DC: National Conference of Catholic Bishops.

U.S. Census. (2004). Poverty 2004 highlights. Retrieved August 6, 2006, from http://www.census.gov/hhes/www/poverty/poverty04/pov04hi.html

U.S. Department of Justice. (2005, February, 7). *W. R. Grace and executives charged with fraud, obstruction of justice, and endangering Libby, Montana community.* Press release: Retrieved July 1, 2006, from www.usdoj.gov

Urban Institute. (2006). *A decade of welfare reform: Facts and figures.* Retrieved July 27, 2006, from http://www.urban.org/UploadedPDF/900980_welfarefeform.pdf

Uribe, V. & Harbeck, K. (1991). Addressing the needs of lesbian, gay, and bisexual youth: The origin of PROJECT 10 and school-based intervention. *Journal of Homosexuality, 22*(3/4), 9-28.

Valenstein, E. (1986). *Great and desperate cures: The rise and decline of psychosurgery and other radical treatments for mental illness.* New York: Basic Books, Inc.

Van Kleeck, M. (1913). *Artificial flower makers.* New York: Russell Sage Foundation.

Van Kleeck, M. (1917). *A seasonal industry: A study of the millinery trade in New York.* New York: Russell Sage Foundation.

Van Kleeck, M. (1991). Our illusions regarding government. Reprinted in *Journal of Progressive Human Services, 2*(1), 75-86. (Originally published in 1934)

Van Soest, D. & Garcia, B. (2003). *Diversity education for social justice: Mastering teaching skills.* Alexandria, VA: Council on Social Work Education.

van Wormer, K. (2001). *Counseling female offenders and victims: A strengths-restorative approach.* New York: Springer Publishing.

van Wormer, K. (2004). *Confronting oppression, restoring justice: From policy analysis to social action.* Alexandria, VA: Council on Social Work Education.

van Wormer, K. (2005). Concepts for contemporary social work: Globalization, oppression, social exclusions, human rights, etc. *Social Work and Society, 3*(1), 1-9.

van Wormer, K. (2006). *Introduction to social welfare and social work: The U.S. in global perspective.* Belmont, CA: Thomson/Brooks/Cole.

van Wormer, K. & McKinney, R. (2003). What schools can do to help gay/lesbian/

bisexual youth: A harm reduction approach. *Adolescence 38*(151), 409-420.

Velasquez, C., Andre, T., Shanks, T., Moberg, D., McClean, M., DeCosse, D., Hanson, K., & Meyer, M. (2004). *A framework for ethical decision-making.* Santa Clara, CA: Markkula Center for Applied Ethics, Santa Clara University. Retrieved October 2, 2005, from http://www.scu.edu/ethics/practicing/decision/framework.html

VeneKlasen, L. & Miller, V. (2002). *A new weave of power, people, and politics.* Oklahoma City, PK: World Neighbors.

Vidika-Sheman, L. & Vigginai, P. (1996). The impacts of federal policy change on children: Research needs for the future. *Social Work, 41*(6), 594-600.

Vollers, M. & Barnett, A. (2000, May/June). Libby's deadly Grace. *Mother Jones,* 53-59, 87.

Vosler, N. (1990). Assessing family access to basic resources: An essential component of social work practice. *Social Work, 35*(5), 434-441.

Vosler, N. (1996). *New approaches to family practice: Confronting economic stress.* Thousand Oaks, CA: Sage Publications.

Wade, C. & Travis, C. (1999). *Invitation to psychology.* New York: Longman.

Wagner, D. (2000). *What's love got to do with it? A critical look at American charity.* New York: The New Press.

Wainstock, S. (1994). Swimming against the current: Teaching research methodology to reluctant social work students. *Journal of Teaching in Social Work, 9*(1/2), 3-16.

Wakefield, J. (1988a). Psychotherapy, distributive justice and social work: Part I - Distributive justice as a conceptual framework for social work. *Social Service Review, 62*(2), 187-210.

Wakefield, J. (1988b). Psychotherapy, distributive justice, and social work: Part II - Psychotherapy and the pursuit of justice. *Social Service Review, 62*(3), 353-382.

Waldegrave, C. (2000). Just therapy with families and communities. In G. Burford & J. Hudson (Eds.), *Family group conferencing: New directions in community-centered child and family practice* (pp. 153-163). New York: Aldine de Gruyter.

Walden, J. & Mountfield, H. (1999). *Blackstone's guide to the human rights act.* London: Blackstones.

Waller, M. (2006).Strengths of indigenous people. In Dennis Saleebey (Ed.), *The strengths perspective in social work practice* (4th ed., pp. 46-60). Boston: Allyn & Bacon.

Waller, M., Risley-Curtiss, S., Murphy, S., Medill, A., & Moore, G. (1998). Harnessing the positive power of language. American Indian women, a case example. *Journal of Poverty, 2*(4), 63-81.

Wang, C. & Burris, M. (1997). Photovoice: Concept, methodology, and use for participatory needs assessment. *Health Education & Behavior, 24*(3), 369-387.

Wang, C., Cash, J., & Powers, L. (2000). Who knows the streets as well as the homeless? Promoting personal and community action through photovoice. *Health Promotion Practice, 1*(1), 81-89.

Warner, R. (2000). *The environment of schizophrenia: Innovations in practice, policy, and communications.* London: Brunner-Routledge.

Warren, R. (1963). *The community in America.* Chicago: Rand McNally.

Washburn, W. (Ed.). (1973). *The American Indian and the United States: A documentary history, V. I and II.* New York: Random House.

Weaver, H. (1998). Indigenous people in a multicultural society: Unique issues for human services. *Social Work, 43*(3), 203 - 211.

Weaver, H. (2005). Reexamining what we think we know: A lesson learned from Tamil Refugees. *Affilia: Journal of Women and Social Work, 20*(2), 238-245.

Weber, M. (1922). Bureaucracy. In H. Gerth & W. Mills (Eds.), *Max Weber: Essays on sociology.* Oxford: Oxford University Press.

Webster's New Universal Unabridged Dictionary (2nd ed.). (1983). New York: New World Dictionaries/Simon and Schuster.

Weedon, C. (1987). *Feminist practice and poststructuralist theory.* Oxford: Basil Blackwell.

Weick, K. (1995). *Sensemaking in organizations.* Thousand Oaks, Ca: Sage Publications.

Weiler, K. (1988). *Women teaching for change: Gender, class and power.* New York: Bergin & Garvey.

Weingarten, K. (1995). Radical listening: Challenging cultural beliefs for and about mothers. In K. Weingarten (Ed.), *Cultural resistance: Challenging beliefs about men, women, and therapy* (pp. 7-22). New York: Harrington Park Press.

Wells, H. G. (1911). *The country of the blind and other stories.* New York: T. Nelson and Sons.

Wenocur, S. & Reisch, M. (1989). *From charity to enterprise: The development of American social work in a market economy.* Chicago: University of Illinois Press.

Werner, D. (1977). *Where there is no doctor: A village health care handbook.* Palo Alto, CA: The Hesperian Foundation.

West, C. (1993). *Race matters.* New York: Vintage.

Whitakker, J. Schinke, S., & Gilchrist, L. (1986). The ecological paradigm in child, youth, and family services: Implications for policy and practice. *Social Service Review, 60*, 483-503.

White, M.B., & Tyson-Rawson, K.J. (1995). Assessing the dynamics of gender in couples and families: The gendergram. *Family Relations, 44*, 253-260

Whitmore, E. & Wilson, M. (1997). Accompanying the process: Social work and international development practice. *International Social Work, 40*(1), 57-74.

Whitmore, E. & Wilson, M. (2005). Popular resistance to global corporate rule: The role of social work (with a little help from Gramsci and Freire). In I. Ferguson, M. Lavalette & E. Whitmore (Eds), *Globalisation, global justice and social work* (pp. 189-206). New York: Routledge.

Williams, Jr., R. (1979). Change and stability in values and value systems: A sociological perspective. In M. Rokeach (Ed.), *Understanding human values: Individual and societal* (pp. 15-46). New York: Free Press.

Williams, R. (1977). *Marxism and literature.* Oxford: Oxford University Press.

Williams, R. (1980). *Problems in Marxism and culture.* Oxford: Oxford University Press.

Willis, P. (1981). *Learning to labor: How working class kids get working class jobs.* New York: Columbia. (Originally published in 1977).

Wilson, A. & Beresford, P. (2000). 'Anti-oppressive practice': Emancipation or appropriation? *British Journal of Social Work, 30*, 553-573.

Wilson, M. & Whitmore, E. (1995). Accompanying the process: Social work and international development practice. *Canadian Journal of Development Studies, 1*, 57-74.

Winkelman, M. (1999). *Ethnic sensitivity in social work.* Dubuque, IA: Eddie Bowers Publishing, Inc.

Withorn, A. (1984). *Serving the people: Social services and social change.* New York: Columbia University Press.

Withorn, A. (1998). No win... facing the ethical perils of welfare reform. *Families in Society, 79*, 277-287.

Witkin, S. (1998). Human rights and social work. *Social Work, 43*(3), 197-201.

Wolfelt, A. (2004). *The understanding your grief support group guide.* Ft Collins, CO: Companion Press.

Women's Intellectual Contributions to the Study of Mind and Society. (n.d.). Retrieved July 31, 2006, from http://www.webster.edu/~woolflm/gilligan.html

World Bank. (2004). *2004 World development indicators.* Washington, DC: Author.

Wrong, D. (1995). *Power: Its forms, bases and uses.* New Brunswick, NJ: Transaction.

Wylie, M. (n.d.). The untold story: Carol Gilligan on recapturing the lost voice of pleasure. Psychotherapy Networker. Retrieved July 31, 2006, from http://www.psychotherapynetworker.org/interviews.htm

Yan, M.C. (2004). Bridging the fragmented community: Revitalizing settlement houses in the global era. *Journal of Community Practice, 12*(1/2), 51-69.

Yin, R. (1994). *Case study research: Design and methods.* Thousand Oaks, CA: Sage Publications.

Yoder, G. (2005). *Companioning the dying. A soulful guide for caregivers.* Ft. Collins, CO: Companion Press.

Young, I. M. (1990). *Justice and the politics of difference.* Princeton: Princeton University Press.

Zavella, P. (1987). *Women's work and Chicano families.* Ithaca: Cornell University Press.

Zayas, L. (2001). Incorporating struggles with racism and ethnic identity in therapy with adolescents. *Clinical Social Work Journal, 29*(4), 361 - 373.

Zimbalist, S. (1977). *Historic themes and landmarks in social welfare research.* New York: Harper & Row.

Zinn, H. (1970). *The politics of history.* Boston: Beacon Press.

Zinn, H. (1990). *Declarations of independence - Chapter Four: The uses and abuses of history.* New York: Harper Collins.

Zinn, H. (1997). *The Zinn reader: Writings on disobedience and democracy.* New York: Seven Stories Press.

Zinn, H. (2003). *A people's history of the United States - 1492 to present.* New York: Harper/Collins.

Permissions and Credits

Permission to describe and discuss the Social Work History Station website courtesy of Professor Dan Huff, School of Social Work, Boise State University.

Permission to print summary of D. Van Soest and B. Garcia's (c. 2003) discussion of Five Perspectives on Social Justice and excerpt on oppression, drawn from *Diversity education for social justice: Mastering teaching skills*, Alexandria, VA: Council on Social Work Education, courtesy of the publisher.

Permission to print summary discussion of social justice from D. Salleebey (c.1990), Philosophical disputes in social work: Social justice denied, *Journal of Sociology and Social Welfare, 17*(6), 29-40, courtesy of *Journal of Sociology and Social Welfare.*

Permission to print American Anthropological Association Statement on Race (c. 1998), courtesy of the American Anthropological Association, Arlington, VA.

Permission to reprint an excerpt from B.C. Reynolds (c. 1963), *An uncharted journey: Fifty years in social work by one of its great teachers*, pp. 173-174, courtesy of the publisher, National Association of Social Workers, Washington, D.C.

Original essay/assignment by Carol Hand reproduced here with permission of the author.

Permission to print a brief discussion and excerpt from B. Link and J. Phelan (c. 2001) On the nature and consequences of stigma, *Annual Review of Sociology, 27*, 363-385, courtesy of *Annual Review of Sociology.*

Permission to print a brief summary of Iris Marion Young (c. 1990), Five faces of oppression, in *Justice and the politics of difference,* Princeton: Princeton University Press, courtesy of the publisher.

Original essay by Annie Kaylor reproduced here with permission of the author.

Permission to print the essay, Red clay, blue hills: In honor of my ancestors, courtesy of the author, John Brown Childs.

Permission to quote H. Zinn (1990), *Declarations of independence - Chapter four: The uses and abuses of history.* New York: Harper Collins courtesy of the Publisher.

Permission to print quotation from Myles Horton (c. 1998), *The long haul*, New York: Teachers College Press, Columbia University, p. 51, courtesy of the publisher.

Permission to print quotation from B. C. Reynolds (C. 1987), *Social work and social living,* Silver Spring, MD: National Association of Social Workers, courtesy of the publisher.

Permission to print quotation from I. Glasser (c. 1978), Welfare & liberty: Prisoners of benevolence, *The Nation*, 226, April 1, 1978, courtesy of *The Nation*.

Permission to print the Social Class Questionnaire, (c. 1995) courtesy of *Radical Teacher*.

Permission to print a discussion from the article, A framework for thinking ethically, accessed at www.scu.edu/ethics/framework (c. 2006), courtesy of the Markkula Center for Applied Ethics, Santa Clara University.

Permission to print the interview, Exiles from a city and from a nation, *Observer/ UK*, Sunday, September 11, 2005, of Cornel West by Joanna Walters, courtesy of Guardian Newspapers-UK.

Permission to print the National Association of Black Social Workers Code of Ethics courtesy of the National Association of Black Social Workers, Detroit, MI.

Permission to print The International Federation of Social Workers Declaration of Ethical Principles (c. 2004) courtesy of the International Federation of Social Workers, Berne Switzerland.

Permission to print summary discussion and adaptation of M. Abramson (c. 1996), Reflections on knowing oneself ethically: Toward a working framework for social work practice, *Families in Society*, *77*(4), 195-201, courtesy of the Alliance for Families and Children.

Permission to print a summary discussion of R. Link (c. 1999), Infusing global perspectives into social work values and ethics. In C. Ramanathan & R. Link (Eds), *All our futures: Social work practice in a global era* (pp. 69-93). Belmont, CA: Thomson Wadsworth, courtesy of the publisher.

Original essay by Eric Diamond printed here with permission of the author.

Permission to reproduce quotation from b. hooks (c. 1994), *Teaching to transgress*. New York: Routledge, courtesy of Routledge/Taylor & Francis Group, LLC.

Permission to print excerpt from E. Valenstein (c. 1986), *Great and desperate cures: The rise and fall of psychosurgery and other radical treatments for mental illness*, New York: Basic Books, courtesy of the author.

Permission to print summary discussion and excerpt from L. VeneKlasen and V. Miller, (c. 2003), *A new weave of power, people & politics*, courtesy of Just Associates, Washington, D.C.

Permission to print summary discussion and excerpt from C. Germain (1994), Emerging conceptions of family development over the life course. *Families in Society*, *75* (5), 259-268, courtesy of the Alliance for Families and Children.

Permission to print excerpt and discussion from A. Bandura (c. 2006), Toward a psychology of human agency, *Perspectives on Psychological Science*, *1*(2), 164-180, courtesy of Blackwell Publishing, Oxford, UK.

Permission to print excerpt from S. Rose (c. 2000), Reflections on empowerment based practice, *Social Work*, *45* (5), 403-412, courtesy of the National Association of Social Workers, Washington, DC.

Permission to print two excerpts from P. Deegan (c.1990), Spiritbreaking: When the helping professions hurt," *The Humanistic Psychologist*, 18 (3), pp. 301-313, and (c.1996) Recovery and the conspiracy of hope, Presentation at the 6th annual Mental Health Services Conference of Australia and New Zealand, Brisbane, Australia, courtesy of the author.

Original essay by Cindy Hunter, MSW, James Madison University, printed here with permission of the author.

Permission to print summary discussion and excerpt from G. Hatcher (c. 2000), Finding the private self: James' story of joining, *Families in Society 81*(3), 333-338, courtesy of the Alliance for Families and Children.

Permission to print excerpts and a summary discussion of segments including, "Our names, our stories," "Popular education," "Human rights," and "Conflict transformation" from *Bridge - Building a race and immigration dialogue in the global economy - A popular education resource for immigrant and refugee community organizers,* National Network for Immigrant and Refugee Rights (NNIRR) BRIDGE project, Berkeley, CA, courtesy of NNIRR.

Original essay by Deborah Bey printed here with permission of the author.

Original essay by Rosemary Barbera printed here with permission of the author.

Original essay by Chuck Wayland printed here with permission of the author.

Permission to print summary of "Participatory Planning" based on C. Diaz (c. 1997) and *"Planificación Participativa,"* and "Diagnosis for Participation" based on C. Diaz (c. 1995) "El Diagnóstico para la Participación" courtesy of Central de Estudios y Publicaciones ALFORJA, San Jose, Costa Rica.

Permission to print summary discussion of H. Weaver (c. 2005), Reexamining what we think we know: A lesson from Tamil refugees, *Affilia: Journal of Women in Social Work 20*(2), 238-245, courtesy of Sage Publications.

Permission to print an excerpt and summary discussion of L. Shulman, D. Krause, M. Cameron (c. 2006), *The skills of helping individuals, families, groups, and communities,* Belmont, CA: Thomson- Brooks/Cole, courtesy of the publisher.

Permission to print a summary discussion and accompanying diagram from A. Hartman, (c. 1978). Diagrammatic assessment of family relationships. *Social Casework, 59*(8), 465-476, courtesy of the Alliance for Families and Children.

Permission to print a summary discussion and accompanying diagram of the ecomap courtesy of Joan Laird.

Permission to print summary discussion of I. Chung (c. 2003), Creative use of focus groups: Providing healing and support to NYC Chinatown residents after the 9/11 attacks, *Social Work with Groups, 26*(4), 3-19, courtesy of the Haworth Press.

Permission to print excerpt from E. Lightfoot, V.C. Pappas and J. Chait (c. 2003), Starting off right: Using open space technology to enable citizens to set the agenda for state disability planning, *Journal of Disability Policy Studies, 14*, 7-16, courtesy of PRO-ED, Inc., Austin, Texas.

Permission to print summary discussion and excerpts from R. Sen (c. 1994), Building community involvement in health care, *Social Policy, 24*(3), 32-43, courtesy of the American Institute for Social Justice.

Permission to print summary discussion and excerpts from H. Kivnick and S. Murray (c. 2001), Life strengths interview guide: Assessing elder clients' strengths, *Journal of Gerontological Social Work, 34*(4), 7-32, courtesy of Haworth Press, Binghamton, NY.

Permission to print summary discussion of D. Saleebey (c. 2001), Diagnostic strengths manual, *Social Work, 46*(4), 183-187, courtesy of the National Association of Social Workers, Washington, D.C.

Permission to reprint a summary discussion of N. Vosler (c. 1990), Assessing family access to basic resources: An essential component of social work practice. *Social Work, 35*(5), 434-441, courtesy of the National Association of Social Workers, Washington, D.C.

Original essay by Scott Nicholson printed here with permission of the author.

Original essay by Nancy McCourt printed here with permission of the author.

Permission to print story and photo of the Michigan Battered Women's Clemency Project courtesy of Carol Jacobsen, The University of Michigan, Ann Arbor, MI.

Permission to print excerpts from C. Brown and G. Mazza (c. 1997), *Healing into action: A leadership guide for creating diverse communities*, courtesy of National Coalition Building Institute (NCBI), Inc., Washington, D.C.

Permission to print summary discussion of "Defusing skills" from Charles E. Confer (c. 1997), *Managing anger: yours and mine*, courtesy of American Foster Care Resources, Inc, King George, VA.

Permission to print summary discussion of J. Anner (c. 1996), Having tools at hand: Building successful multicultural social justice organizations, In J. Anner (Ed), *Beyond identity politics.* Boston: South End Press, courtesy of the publisher.

Permission to print summary discussion of policy practice based on J. Figueira-McDonough (c. 1993), Policy practice: The neglected side of social work intervention," *Social Work*, *38*(2), 179-188, courtesy of the National Association of Social Workers, Washington, D.C.

Permission to print Summary of Skills for Family-centered Policy Practice from Katherine Briar-Lawson (c. 2001), Promoting new alliances among families, family advocates, and helping professionals, In K. Briar-Lawson, H. Lawson, C. Hennon, & A. Jones (Eds.) *Family-centered policies and practices: International implications,* New York: Columbia University Press, courtesy of the publisher.

Permission to print excerpts from the case study of Fuerza Unida by J. Finn (c. 2002), originally published in *Affilia: Journal of Women in Social Work*, *17*(4), 2002, 497-500, courtesy of Sage Publications and Fuerza Unida.

Permission to print Fuerza Unida mission statement and accompanying photos courtesy of Fuerza Unida.

Permission to print summary discussion and excerpts from S. Christopher (c. 2005), Recommendations for conducting successful research with Native Americans, *Journal of Cancer Education*, *20*, 47-51, courtesy of Lawrence Erlbaum Associates.

Permission to reprint excerpts from F. Lappe and P. Dubois (c. 1994), *The quickening of America: Rebuilding our nation, remaking our lives*, Newark: John Wiley & Sons courtesy of the publishers.

Permission to reprint a summary discussion and excerpt from R. Chapin (c. 1995), Social policy development: The strengths perspective. *Social Work*, *40*(4), 506-514, courtesy of the National Association of Social Workers, Washington, D.C.

Original essay by Bonnie Buckingham reprinted here with permission of the author.

Permission to print an excerpt from D. Harvey (c. 2000), *Spaces of hope*. University of California Press, courtesy of the publisher.

Permission to print summary discussion from S. Mayer (1996), Building community capacity with evaluation activities that empower. In D.M. Fetterman, S. J. Faftarian, & A. Wandersman (Eds.), *Empowerment evaluation: Knowledge and tools for self-assessment and accountability* (pp. 332-375). Thousand Oaks, CA: Sage Publications courtesy of the Publisher.

Index

A